Lecture Notes in Computer Science

Lecture Notes in Artificial Intelligence   **14019**

Founding Editor

Jörg Siekmann

Series Editors

Randy Goebel, *University of Alberta, Edmonton, Canada*
Wolfgang Wahlster, *DFKI, Berlin, Germany*
Zhi-Hua Zhou, *Nanjing University, Nanjing, China*

The series Lecture Notes in Artificial Intelligence (LNAI) was established in 1988 as a topical subseries of LNCS devoted to artificial intelligence.

The series publishes state-of-the-art research results at a high level. As with the LNCS mother series, the mission of the series is to serve the international R & D community by providing an invaluable service, mainly focused on the publication of conference and workshop proceedings and postproceedings.

Dylan D. Schmorrow · Cali M. Fidopiastis
Editors

Augmented Cognition

17th International Conference, AC 2023
Held as Part of the 25th HCI International Conference, HCII 2023
Copenhagen, Denmark, July 23–28, 2023
Proceedings

 Springer

Editors
Dylan D. Schmorrow
Soar Technology Inc.
Orlando, FL, USA

Cali M. Fidopiastis
Katmai Government Services
Orlando, FL, USA

ISSN 0302-9743   ISSN 1611-3349 (electronic)
Lecture Notes in Artificial Intelligence
ISBN 978-3-031-35016-0   ISBN 978-3-031-35017-7 (eBook)
https://doi.org/10.1007/978-3-031-35017-7

LNCS Sublibrary: SL7 – Artificial Intelligence

This Springer imprint is published by the registered company Springer Nature Switzerland AG
The registered company address is: Gewerbestrasse 11, 6330 Cham, Switzerland

Foreword

Human-computer interaction (HCI) is acquiring an ever-increasing scientific and industrial importance, as well as having more impact on people's everyday lives, as an ever-growing number of human activities are progressively moving from the physical to the digital world. This process, which has been ongoing for some time now, was further accelerated during the acute period of the COVID-19 pandemic. The HCI International (HCII) conference series, held annually, aims to respond to the compelling need to advance the exchange of knowledge and research and development efforts on the human aspects of design and use of computing systems.

The 25th International Conference on Human-Computer Interaction, HCI International 2023 (HCII 2023), was held in the emerging post-pandemic era as a 'hybrid' event at the AC Bella Sky Hotel and Bella Center, Copenhagen, Denmark, during July 23–28, 2023. It incorporated the 21 thematic areas and affiliated conferences listed below.

A total of 7472 individuals from academia, research institutes, industry, and government agencies from 85 countries submitted contributions, and 1578 papers and 396 posters were included in the volumes of the proceedings that were published just before the start of the conference, these are listed below. The contributions thoroughly cover the entire field of human-computer interaction, addressing major advances in knowledge and effective use of computers in a variety of application areas. These papers provide academics, researchers, engineers, scientists, practitioners and students with state-of-the-art information on the most recent advances in HCI.

The HCI International (HCII) conference also offers the option of presenting 'Late Breaking Work', and this applies both for papers and posters, with corresponding volumes of proceedings that will be published after the conference. Full papers will be included in the 'HCII 2023 - Late Breaking Work - Papers' volumes of the proceedings to be published in the Springer LNCS series, while 'Poster Extended Abstracts' will be included as short research papers in the 'HCII 2023 - Late Breaking Work - Posters' volumes to be published in the Springer CCIS series.

I would like to thank the Program Board Chairs and the members of the Program Boards of all thematic areas and affiliated conferences for their contribution towards the high scientific quality and overall success of the HCI International 2023 conference. Their manifold support in terms of paper reviewing (single-blind review process, with a minimum of two reviews per submission), session organization and their willingness to act as goodwill ambassadors for the conference is most highly appreciated.

This conference would not have been possible without the continuous and unwavering support and advice of Gavriel Salvendy, founder, General Chair Emeritus, and Scientific Advisor. For his outstanding efforts, I would like to express my sincere appreciation to Abbas Moallem, Communications Chair and Editor of HCI International News.

July 2023   Constantine Stephanidis

HCI International 2023 Thematic Areas and Affiliated Conferences

Thematic Areas

- HCI: Human-Computer Interaction
- HIMI: Human Interface and the Management of Information

Affiliated Conferences

- EPCE: 20th International Conference on Engineering Psychology and Cognitive Ergonomics
- AC: 17th International Conference on Augmented Cognition
- UAHCI: 17th International Conference on Universal Access in Human-Computer Interaction
- CCD: 15th International Conference on Cross-Cultural Design
- SCSM: 15th International Conference on Social Computing and Social Media
- VAMR: 15th International Conference on Virtual, Augmented and Mixed Reality
- DHM: 14th International Conference on Digital Human Modeling and Applications in Health, Safety, Ergonomics and Risk Management
- DUXU: 12th International Conference on Design, User Experience and Usability
- C&C: 11th International Conference on Culture and Computing
- DAPI: 11th International Conference on Distributed, Ambient and Pervasive Interactions
- HCIBGO: 10th International Conference on HCI in Business, Government and Organizations
- LCT: 10th International Conference on Learning and Collaboration Technologies
- ITAP: 9th International Conference on Human Aspects of IT for the Aged Population
- AIS: 5th International Conference on Adaptive Instructional Systems
- HCI-CPT: 5th International Conference on HCI for Cybersecurity, Privacy and Trust
- HCI-Games: 5th International Conference on HCI in Games
- MobiTAS: 5th International Conference on HCI in Mobility, Transport and Automotive Systems
- AI-HCI: 4th International Conference on Artificial Intelligence in HCI
- MOBILE: 4th International Conference on Design, Operation and Evaluation of Mobile Communications

List of Conference Proceedings Volumes Appearing Before the Conference

1. LNCS 14011, Human-Computer Interaction: Part I, edited by Masaaki Kurosu and Ayako Hashizume
2. LNCS 14012, Human-Computer Interaction: Part II, edited by Masaaki Kurosu and Ayako Hashizume
3. LNCS 14013, Human-Computer Interaction: Part III, edited by Masaaki Kurosu and Ayako Hashizume
4. LNCS 14014, Human-Computer Interaction: Part IV, edited by Masaaki Kurosu and Ayako Hashizume
5. LNCS 14015, Human Interface and the Management of Information: Part I, edited by Hirohiko Mori and Yumi Asahi
6. LNCS 14016, Human Interface and the Management of Information: Part II, edited by Hirohiko Mori and Yumi Asahi
7. LNAI 14017, Engineering Psychology and Cognitive Ergonomics: Part I, edited by Don Harris and Wen-Chin Li
8. LNAI 14018, Engineering Psychology and Cognitive Ergonomics: Part II, edited by Don Harris and Wen-Chin Li
9. LNAI 14019, Augmented Cognition, edited by Dylan D. Schmorrow and Cali M. Fidopiastis
10. LNCS 14020, Universal Access in Human-Computer Interaction: Part I, edited by Margherita Antona and Constantine Stephanidis
11. LNCS 14021, Universal Access in Human-Computer Interaction: Part II, edited by Margherita Antona and Constantine Stephanidis
12. LNCS 14022, Cross-Cultural Design: Part I, edited by Pei-Luen Patrick Rau
13. LNCS 14023, Cross-Cultural Design: Part II, edited by Pei-Luen Patrick Rau
14. LNCS 14024, Cross-Cultural Design: Part III, edited by Pei-Luen Patrick Rau
15. LNCS 14025, Social Computing and Social Media: Part I, edited by Adela Coman and Simona Vasilache
16. LNCS 14026, Social Computing and Social Media: Part II, edited by Adela Coman and Simona Vasilache
17. LNCS 14027, Virtual, Augmented and Mixed Reality, edited by Jessie Y. C. Chen and Gino Fragomeni
18. LNCS 14028, Digital Human Modeling and Applications in Health, Safety, Ergonomics and Risk Management: Part I, edited by Vincent G. Duffy
19. LNCS 14029, Digital Human Modeling and Applications in Health, Safety, Ergonomics and Risk Management: Part II, edited by Vincent G. Duffy
20. LNCS 14030, Design, User Experience, and Usability: Part I, edited by Aaron Marcus, Elizabeth Rosenzweig and Marcelo Soares
21. LNCS 14031, Design, User Experience, and Usability: Part II, edited by Aaron Marcus, Elizabeth Rosenzweig and Marcelo Soares

47. CCIS 1836, HCI International 2023 Posters - Part V, edited by Constantine Stephanidis, Margherita Antona, Stavroula Ntoa and Gavriel Salvendy

https://2023.hci.international/proceedings

Preface

Augmented Cognition research innovates computing technologies for next-generation adaptive systems that are capable of improving and extending human information management capacity. Advancing real-time assessment of a user's cognitive status for novel human-system integration requires methods and tools for studying elusive brain constructs such as cognitive bottlenecks (e.g., limitations in attention, memory, learning, comprehension, visualization abilities, and decision making). The augmented cognition research approach significantly contributes to a better understanding of the human brain and behavior, optimized reaction time, and improved learning, memory retention, and decision-making in real-world contexts.

The International Conference on Augmented Cognition (AC), an affiliated conference of the HCI International (HCII) conference, arrived at its 17th edition and encouraged papers from academics, researchers, industry, and professionals, on a broad range of theoretical and applied issues related to augmented cognition and its applications.

The papers accepted for publication this year reflect emerging trends across various thematic areas of the field. Advancements in brain-computer interfaces and neurotechnology were employed to gain a better understanding of the human brain and behavior, analyze visual patterns, discover mental strategies, and optimize reaction time. A considerable number of the papers delved into the intersection between technology and human cognition, focusing on physiological measurements and neuroergonomics to assess user engagement, human spatial ability, perceptual load, and human factors aspects that can impact technology design. Practical and theoretical perspectives on augmented cognition were also explored, including a taxonomy of cognitive augmentations, a study on the effect of information type on cognitive augmentations, as well as research on cognitive augmentation in education, health and well-being, and social engineering. Furthermore, several articles focused on how Virtual and Augmented Reality can be used to improve learning, memory retention, and decision-making in various contexts. Finally, the topic of cybersecurity was explored, providing insights into the challenges and opportunities in the field and exploring them through the lens of human cognition.

This volume of the HCII 2023 proceedings is dedicated to this year's edition of the AC conference and focuses on topics related to brain-computer interfaces and neurotechnology; neuroergonomics, physiological measurements, and human performance; evolving theory and practice of AC; Augmented and Virtual Reality for AC; as well as understanding human cognition and performance in IT security.

Papers accepted for publication in this volume received a minimum of two single –blind reviews from the members of the AC Program Board or, in some cases, from members of the Program Boards of other affiliated conferences. We would like to extend a heartfelt thankyou to all the members of the AC Program Board and other affiliated conference program boards for their invaluable contributions and support. The ground-breaking work presented in this volume would not have been possible without their tireless efforts.

July 2023

Dylan D. Schmorrow
Cali M. Fidopiastis

17th International Conference on Augmented Cognition (AC 2023)

Program Board Chairs: **Dylan D. Schmorrow**, *Soar Tech, USA* and **Cali M. Fidopiastis**, *Nitere, USA*

Program Board:

- Nitesh Bhatia, *Imperial College London, UK*
- Martha Crosby, *University of Hawai'i at Mānoa, USA*
- Fausto De Carvalho, *Altice Labs, Portugal*
- Daniel Dolgin, *Hellcat Hangar Studio, USA*
- Rodolphe Gentili, *University of Maryland - College Park, USA*
- Monte Hancock, *4Digital, Inc, USA*
- Kurtulus Izzetoglu, *Drexel University, USA*
- Ion Juvina, *Wright State University, USA*
- Benjamin J. Knox, *Norwegian Armed Forces Cyber Defence, Norway*
- Ricardo G. Lugo, *Norwegian University of Science and Technology, Norway*
- Arne Norlander, *NORSECON, Sweden*
- Stefan Sütterlin, *Albstadt-Sigmaringen University, Germany*
- Suraj Sood, *Autism Behavior Consultants, USA*
- Ana Rita Teixeira, *University of Aveiro, Portugal*
- Martin Westhoven, *German Federal Institute for Occupational Safety and Health, Germany;*
- Ren Xu, *g.tec medical engineering GmbH, Austria*

The full list with the Program Board Chairs and the members of the Program Boards of all thematic areas and affiliated conferences of HCII2023 is available online at:

http://www.hci.international/board-members-2023.php

HCI International 2024 Conference

The 26th International Conference on Human-Computer Interaction, HCI International 2024, will be held jointly with the affiliated conferences at the Washington Hilton Hotel, Washington, DC, USA, June 29 – July 4, 2024. It will cover a broad spectrum of themes related to Human-Computer Interaction, including theoretical issues, methods, tools, processes, and case studies in HCI design, as well as novel interaction techniques, interfaces, and applications. The proceedings will be published by Springer. More information will be made available on the conference website: http://2024.hci.international/.

General Chair
Prof. Constantine Stephanidis
University of Crete and ICS-FORTH
Heraklion, Crete, Greece
Email: general_chair@hcii2024.org

https://2024.hci.international/

Contents

Augmented Cognition: Evolving Theory and Practice

Brain-Computer Interfaces
and Neurotechnolgy

Brain State-Triggered Stimulus Delivery Helps to Optimize Reaction Time

Vladislav Aksiotis$^{(\boxtimes)}$ (ID), Alexey Tumyalis (ID), and Alexey Ossadtchi (ID)

Center for Bioelectric Interfaces, HSE University, Moscow, Russia
va.aksiotis@hse.ru

Abstract. In the present study, a fast and adaptive technique for the presentation of stimuli based on ongoing brain rhythm is described. Sensorimotor cortical mu rhythm (divided by two components: alpha (mu) and beta) was used as target for assessment of prestimulus rhythm's power influence on the consequent reaction time. The final sample consisted of 15 participants who was instructed to response immediately after change of stimuli color. As a result of the method application, a longer reaction time in the case of highly synchronized beta oscillations compared to desynchronization was achieved in the simple reaction time task. It indicates, firstly, a crucial role of baseline, prestimulus beta in motor action initiation and, secondly, the possibility to change reaction using adaptive processing and timing of presentation in real-time.

Keywords: brain state-dependent presentation · EEG · mu-rhythm · motor response · brain-computer interface · augmented intelligence

1 Introduction

The advancement in computational technology has made it possible to quickly process biological signals and has led to the growth of research in the field of brain-computer interfaces (BCI). One of the most promising areas of BCI is the use of adaptive algorithms that are based on brain signals. With increasing interest in the topic (Jensen et al. 2011), there has been a surge of research in brain-state dependent transcranial-magnetic-stimulation (TMS), prestimulus neuronal activity, and brain-triggered stimuli presentation.

The ability to stimulate or present stimuli based on the state of the brain has only become feasible recently. Brain responses to stimuli occur rapidly, on a timescale of milliseconds, typically around 100–400 ms (Luck 2005). To adaptively time the presentation of stimuli, fast computational processing is required, which only became available in recent decades with the increase in computational power. For both theoretical and practical reasons, this study will focus on exploring the performance of human subjects in an adaptive task where the timing of stimuli presentation is based on brain states. The main question is whether we can influence motor responses by delivering stimuli at different states of brain rhythms that can be detected using electroencephalography (EEG).

D. D. Schmorrow and C. M. Fidopiastis (Eds.): HCII 2023, LNAI 14019, pp. 3–15, 2023.
https://doi.org/10.1007/978-3-031-35017-7_1

1.1 Brain State-Dependence

The investigation of prestimulus neuronal activity has gained significant attention in recent years, with researchers focusing mostly on perception (Iemi et al. 2017; Boncompte et al. 2016; Mathewson et al. 2009). In particular, L. Iemi and colleagues (Iemi et al. 2019) aimed to shed light on how baseline rhythmic oscillations of neural activity can influence the perception of visual stimuli. To test their hypothesis, they recorded EEG data from human subjects as they were presented with uniform visual stimuli. The ERP (event-related potential) induced by the pictures was analyzed as the target effect.

By using an offline processing pipeline, the researchers aimed to understand how prestimulus neural oscillations influence various stages of the brain's sensory response by examining different components of the ERP. They found that prestimulus alpha- and beta-band power significantly impacted the suppression of early ERP components (before 0.2 s) and the amplification of late ERP components (after 0.4 s). This study provides further evidence of the importance of prestimulus neuronal activity in shaping perception.

Recent research has demonstrated the potential to predict the onset of event-related potentials (ERP) by analyzing fluctuations before a stimulus presentation. In a study conducted by L. Zhang and colleagues (Zhang et al. 2012), it was shown that the amplitude of the P300 ERP component induced by a visual stimulus varied along with the phase of spontaneous oscillations in the alpha frequency band just prior to the stimulus. This variation suggests that perceptual and cognitive systems influence the P300 component periodically. This can be leveraged to increase the P300 response by presenting a stimulus during an optimal state for visual processing.

While these results provide insights into the significance of spontaneous oscillations, it has limitations in its application. Traditional research methods use a predetermined timeline to present stimuli, with data analyzed offline after the conclusion of the experiment. However, this approach may not effectively capture rare states of the brain that are not aligned with the sensory presentation, as noted by M. Andermann and colleagues (Andermann et al. 2012). In their study, they computed an instantaneous bias towards processing sounds from the left or right ear and successfully utilized this information to help subjects detect a target stimulus.

Online signal processing has the potential to augment or enhance a person's perception or action, particularly in high uncertainty or memory training scenarios. For example, a study by Yoo and colleagues (Yoo et al. 2012) used functional magnetic resonance imaging (fMRI) to evaluate the brain's readiness to learn and showed a significant advantage in subsequent scene recognition when presented during a "good" pattern. Although fMRI can provide valuable information about deep brain structures, it is not suitable for fast events and processing due to the 3–5 s latency associated with BOLD signal.

The field of physiological computing is focused on creating a supportive human-computer system to enhance the user experience (Fairclough 2009; Mühl et al. 2015; Ewing et al. 2016). However, many approaches fail to achieve this due to the complex and rapidly changing connections between emotional and physiological states. Instead, researchers are turning towards focusing on specific brain events that have a strong connection to behavioral outcomes.

1.2 Mu-Rhythm and Motor Cortex

The mu-rhythm, first studied in the 1950s (Gastaut et al. 1954), has been widely investigated in various scenarios, including motor action, observing others' movements, and motor imagery (Pineda 2005). The clear pattern of desynchronization in the mu-rhythm indicates its close connection to motor planning and execution (Llanos et al. 2013; Aleksandrov et al. 2012). A meta-analysis (Fox et al. 2016) has shown a significant effect size for mu during both execution and observation of action, further validating it as an indicator of mirror neurons' firing. Typically, two main frequencies are distinguished: 7–13 Hz (similar to alpha) and 14–25 Hz (similar to beta). Riitta Hari (Hari 2006) emphasizes that the 20-Hz activity, associated with the subject's immobility, is likely related to cortical inhibition. In this scenario, a high level of the mu-rhythm is associated with the stabilization of the motor system.

In addition to the well-known desynchronization in the sensori-motor rhythm, there is growing research on so-called "transient" beta. According to studies with humans, monkeys, and mice (Shin et al. 2017; Sherman et al. 2016), such transient beta over the central and frontal regions can appear as an event lasting around 150 ms. This beta event, in addition to inhibiting the motor system, can impair perception by predicting the failure to effectively transmit information through specific neocortical representations. However, most of the results in these human studies were obtained using magnetoencephalography (MEG), which provides better spatial resolution and less noisy signals, making it less likely to detect such a wave with EEG recording.

Overall, the mu-rhythm in the motor cortex presents a strong relationship with motor planning and execution, making it a prime target for brain-state dependent stimulation. Following the literature, we distinguish two frequencies and implement them separately to prove their validity for effective response induction.

1.3 Computational Side

In order to enhance the efficiency of physiological computing in human-computer systems, several computational methods and software have been developed to process information rapidly and precisely. One example is the study by Rutishauser et al. (2013), which showed that fast-timed visual stimuli could be presented to awake animals based on the features of their ongoing brain state, with a delay of only 48 ms. However, this method was developed for animal research and may not be easily applicable to human EEG processing.

An alternative approach for studying adaptive presentation is neurofeedback, where stimuli are changed according to brain activity to train the subject to manipulate their own brain activity. Belinskaya et al. (2020) showed that latency from signal processing is a crucial factor in neurofeedback performance, with lower latency leading to better performance and a steeper learning curve. To address this, a fast signal filter has been developed by Smetanin et al. (2020) specifically for EEG signals, providing a universal pipeline for data processing that our study can take advantage of.

1.4 Hypothesis

In the current study we aimed to causally and in real-time interact with the sensorimotor system based on the rhythmic activity of the motor cortex. Specifically, we focused on the impact on a simple reaction time task of the instantaneous power of the two components of the sensorimotor rhythm (SMR): slow (alpha) and fast (beta) mu-rhythm components oscillating at 7–12 Hz and 14–25 Hz correspondingly.

The idea is to control during the experiment the time moment when the "Go" signal is presented based on monitoring of the instantaneous power of the rhythmic components. The hypothesis is that the reaction time will be greater when the "Go" signal occurs within the SMR bursts as compared to the trials when we presented the "Go" signal outside of the burst.

While the study does not delve into the underlying mathematical methods for low latency extraction of rhythmic components, it focuses on the psychological and behavioral outcomes of the described brain-state dependent interaction with the human's motor system.

2 Methods

2.1 Participants and Experimental Setup

The final sample consisted of 15 right-handed subjects (7 males and 8 females; aged 20.3 ± 0.8 years, mean ± SD). The procedure was conducted under the ethical standards of the Declaration of Helsinki (1964). All participants gave their informed consent prior to the experiment.

The instruction to the participants focused on pressing the spacebar on the keyboard whenever they saw a green circle is presented. Closing the eyes and volitional shift of attention from the monitor were prohibited. Additionally, participants were instructed not to move and speak during the experiment but were allowed to do so during the breaks.

Subjects were seated in a comfortable chair facing a computer screen at a distance of ~ 1 m. The LCD monitor had a 24 cm diagonal and a 60 Hz refresh rate.

Throughout the experiment, EEG was recorded with a 5-electrode AgCl cap positioned according to the 10–20 system, referenced to the digital common ear from the electrodes placed on both ears. EEG was recorded from the following 5 electrodes: Fz, Cz, C3, C4, Pz. Additionally, 2 bipolar surface electromyographic (sEMG) electrodes, Ag-AgCl, were attached. Each subject was first asked to perform index finger flexion and extension movements to find the target muscle location. Following the surface EMG for non-invasive assessment of muscles (SENIAM) guidelines (Stegeman et al. 2007), bipolar sEMG electrodes were placed along and above the flexor digitorum superficialis.

Each EEG and EMG channel was sampled at 10 kHz using an NVX-136 amplifier (Medical Computer Systems Ltd). EEG was bandpass-filtered in the 0.1–100 Hz band, while EMG was filtered in the 1–1000 Hz band. A notch filter at 50 ± 5 Hz was applied to every channel. The impedance for each electrode was kept below 10 kOhm. This processing was done with NeoRec software, which includes a built-in protocol for data transfer via the Lab Stream Layer (LSL) stream. The LSL pipeline was set to "very fast" mode to ensure fast chunk streaming and the 10 kHz sampling rate was employed to speed up data transfer from NeoRec to our custom program implementing the real-time processing pipeline.

2.2 Experimental Design

The experiment is designed to interactively study the causal effect of motor cortex oscillations on a subject's reaction time in an adaptive motor task. The process starts with the recording of two resting state blocks. The first one, lasting 1 min, is used to create a spatial filter through independent component analysis (ICA), to be subsequently applied in real-time to suppress eye-movement artifacts. The second resting state block, also lasting 1 min, is used to evaluate the thresholds that will be applied in the online procedure. These thresholds are computed based on the 25th and 75th percentiles of the minimum and maximum values of the envelopes for each rhythm (mu and beta) at the C3 electrode.

The main task involves the subject's responding to a green circle displayed on the screen by pressing the spacebar. A red circle is initially presented for a random interval between 2–3 s. Then, its color changes to green when an event (high or low amplitude) is detected, and the subject must respond as fast as one can and before the trial repeats.

A sequence of target conditions that get realized based on the rhythmic activity monitoring is generated before the experiment, consisting of 100 trials for each condition (low beta, high beta, low mu, high mu), for a total of 400 trials. The conditions to be implemented are shuffled before the start of the procedure, and there is a pause after every 100 trials, lasting at least 1 min, to prevent fatigue. The entire procedure takes approximately 45 min, see Fig. 1(A), per subject.

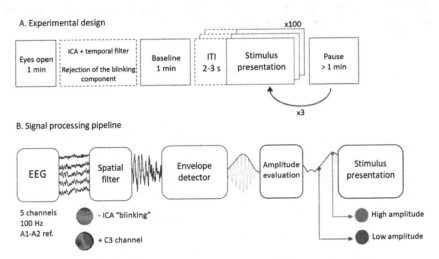

Fig. 1. Schematics of the experiment and the signal processing pipeline.

2.3 Real-Time Data Acquisition and Analysis

The implemented online signal processing is depicted in Fig. 1(B). The target signals were collected from the C3 channel over the left central region, which corresponds to the sensorimotor area of the right hand. The instantaneous mu and beta power were derived using 7–12 Hz and 14–25 Hz bandpass cFIR filters (Smetanin et al. 2020), respectively. This filter outputs complex valued analytic signal which can be instantaneously turned into the envelope, eliminating the need for additional filters which would lead to additional phase lags. The same method for obtaining the alpha envelope was used in a previous study evaluating the effects of neurofeedback latency (Belinskaya et al. 2020), ensuring minimal delay in the target stimulus presentation.

The raw signals were then sent to the NFB lab software (Smetanin et al. 2018) for spatial and temporal filtering and envelope detection. The resulting envelope was again sent via the LSL protocol and intercepted by a custom python script (Python version 3.10), which visualized the circles on the subject's monitor and recorded their responses, along with EEG, EMG, and event markers. The event markers were detected by a photosensor at the right corner of the subject's screen and were sent to the software.

The presentation of stimuli was based on the threshold crossing by rhythm's envelope. As outlined above, the thresholds for each condition were computed from the resting-state data, as the 25th and 75th percentiles of the minimum and maximum values.

2.4 Closed Loop Delay Estimation.

The study's focus on real-time stimuli presentation based on EEG signals made the timing of utmost importance. In order to measure the delay between the raw data and screen response, a photosensor was used to detect screen brightness, which corresponded to the amplitude of the input data. The results, shown in Fig. 2, indicate an overall delay

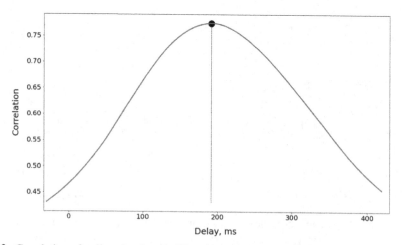

Fig. 2. Correlation of online signal and offline (zero-phase) processed (filtered) raw data as a function of the delay. The peak's argument is informative of the total delay incurred by the corresponding processing scheme.

of approximately 190 ms, which is not considered inconvenient compared to previous research on prestimulus effects (Iemi et al. 2017).

2.5 Behavioral Data Processing

Responses from two main conditions (beta and mu) were analyzed separately. Firstly, we turn RTs into standardized values by applying z-score computing to the data from one participant. Then, we dropped outliers inside subconditions (low/high amplitude) using Tukey's fences after computing the interquartile range with $k = 1.5$. About 4 responses for every person were removed. Finally, mean RT was added to the sequence for comparison.

Sequences with means were tested for normality by the Shapiro-Wilk test and compared by the Student's t-test if the hypothesis about normality was not rejected.

2.6 Offline EEG and EMG Processing

The electrophysiological data was processed using the open-source package MNE-python, version 1.0 (Gramfort et al. 2013). The focus was on the C3 electrode and the data was down-sampled to 1000 Hz, and then divided into epochs. To ensure the correct functioning of the experimental procedure, epochs with the rhythm's envelope were extracted from 500 ms before to 500 ms after the stimulus onset and corrected for baseline drift across the 500–300 ms prestimulus interval. The envelopes were calculated by applying the FFT based implementation of Hilbert transform to the zero phase FIR bandpass filtered data for mu (7–12 Hz) and beta (14–25 Hz) conditions.

The time-frequency representation (TFR) was calculated using Morlet wavelets on prefiltered data (1 and 30 Hz) in the epochs between 500 ms before the stimulus and 200 ms after it. Major artifacts, such as eye blinks and noisy data segments, were manually screened using the Fz channel response. If a blink or muscle noise occurred within 500 ms before a stimulus, the entire trial was discarded to ensure that the participant's eyes were open at stimulus onset and the presentation trigger was not affected by artifacts. On average, 6 trials (6%) from each condition were removed.

For the EMG data, a filter between 10 and 350 Hz was applied, and the envelope was calculated using the Hilbert transform. The epochs were extracted between 500 and 200 ms before the button press.

3 Results

To evaluate the validity of the procedure, we compared the magnitudes of the rhythms around the "Go" signals in the low and high rhythm conditions. Since according to Fig. 1 the overall incurred latency of our processing was about 190 ms which corresponded to the time between the actual neuronal event and presentation of the corresponding stimulus, we evaluated the increase in power in the averaged epochs, see Fig. 3, at this latency. Both series had a normal distribution (W = 0.926, p = 0.27 for low beta; W = 0.927, p = 0.28 for high beta). The paired t-test for beta component indicated a significant difference (t = -3.765 (14), p < 0.001) between low and high conditions. The amplitudes of alpha components are normally distributed (W = 0.926, p = 0.3 and W = 0.936, p = 0.41 for low and high mu), a paired *t*-test shows a significant difference (t = -2.515, p = 0.027).

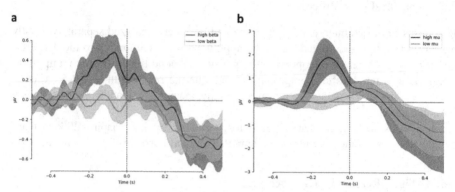

Fig. 3. Grand average of beta (a) and mu (b) envelopes between 500 ms before and 500 ms after a stimulus presentation. The transparent area indicates the 95% confidence interval.

Time-frequency analysis was done to investigate the contribution of other frequencies. Below, in Fig. 4, three subjects' averaged spectrograms are presented, computed as a difference between high and low conditions.

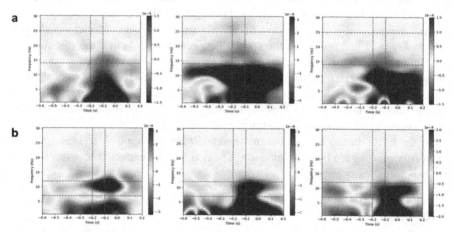

Fig. 4. Averaged spectrograms of the difference between high and low states for 3 subjects for beta (a) and mu (b) conditions. The blue rectangle in the middle indicates the region where we expected the increased power.

As illustrated in Fig. 4, the increase in beta power is accompanied by the increase in alpha power. It is expected since alpha and beta rhythms have similar functional roles in the motor cortex. Relatively small amplitude values here are not so important because we used individual setup to choose thresholds for stimulus presentation.

Behavioral datasets were also tested for normality. In both cases, RT results appeared to be normally distributed (high beta: W = 0.972, p = 0.89; low beta: W = 0.975, p = 0.925). Since we are interested in obtaining the within-subject effects, a paired t-test was applied to compare the conditions. The test shows a significant difference between conditions where high-beta presentation resulted in slower RT (t = -2.275 (14), p = 0.039). Figure 5 (a, b) visualizes this distinction.

For the alpha component-based events, the averaged behavioral responses are also normally distributed (W = 0.94, p = 0.425; W = 0.931, p = 0.31, low mu and high mu). The paired t-test did not show a significant difference (t = -0.98 (14), p = 0.34) between the reaction times observed for the events generated based on tracking the alpha band component of the mu-rhythm.

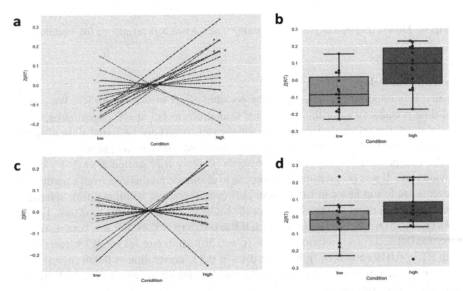

Fig. 5. Pattern of relationships between RTs observed for the "low" and "high" events generated online from the SMR's alpha and beta components. Dots show the averaged and standardized reaction time of every participant. Lines indicate the connection between a person's performance in both conditions. The green lines (a) focus on subjects that were influenced by the procedure in a negative way; that is, their RT was shorter in the high-rhythm condition. Boxplots (b, d) of averaged standardized reaction time grouped by the experimental condition, low and high prestimulus synchronization in bands.

As evident from Fig. 5a, not every person was affected by the procedure as hypothesized, but the overall trend is visible – trials with high prestimulus beta resulted in longer responses in the majority of our subjects. Figure 5c shows a variation around the mean score for alpha based conditions, in this case we don't see the expected relationship.

Muscle response was analyzed by comparison of peak amplitudes. They are normally Distributed (W = 0.85, p = 0.1; W = 0.91, p = 0.153; W = 0.928, p = 0.327; W = 0.912, p = 0.2, for low beta and mu and high beta and mu conditions correspondingly).

The paired t-test did not indicate a significant difference (t = -0.959 (14), p = 0.35 for beta; t = 0.841 (14), p = 0.416 for mu) (Fig. 6).

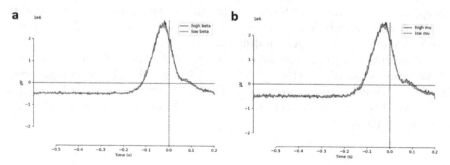

Fig. 6. Muscle response aligned with pressing time for two beta (a) and mu (b) conditions.

Presentation Delay

Finally, it is important to investigate the possible effect of waiting on RT. We used a real-time processing algorithm that added limitations to our study. In particular, high-power states are relatively rare and, in some cases, could not be found right after the trial's start, especially if synchronization is associated with a resting state.

As was pointed out above (see "Methods"), every trial started after 2–3 s of the previous one. It was programmed on purpose to eliminate predictions from a participant if events are found faster in succession. However, there was additional time related to searching for an event by the system. For the high beta condition, this time took 1.7 s ± 0.9 s (mean; SD), with a correlation with RT = 0.028 (p = 0.4). For low beta searching time was 0.8 ± 0.6 s, correlation = -0.08 (p = 0.56). High mu: 1.2 s ± 0.7 s, correlation with RT = 0.049 (p = 0.162); low mu: 0.4 s ± 0.3 s, correlation = 0.038 (p = 0.204). Therefore, the observed correlations between the condition search time with the RT appear to be not significant.

4 Discussion

Our investigation into the influence of central rhythms on the motor response utilized a brain-state dependent visual stimulation procedure. Our results indicated a successful differentiation between high and low states based on ongoing brain activity and its use to interactively generate the corresponding "Go" signals. Additionally, the behavioral results showed a significant change in reaction time (RT) when stimuli were presented immediately following synchronization in the beta components of the SMR. This aligns with previous research that has established the central beta-rhythm as a predictor of motor planning and execution, and it suggests that this information can be used in an adaptive system to optimize RT (Shin et al. 2017; Hari 2006). The findings also showed an event-related desynchronization (ERD) in both frequencies.

Our results showed that the condition with lower component of mu-rhythm (7–12 Hz) did not exhibit any significant changes in behavioral reaction. This could be due to the contamination of the central alpha oscillations by the occipital alpha rhythm, which has the same frequency, large amplitude, and the ability to propagate easily to the central area. However, the occipital alpha rhythm has a different functional role (Klimesch 1999), and if the presentation was triggered by it, there would be no advantage to the motor response. On the other hand, beta-oscillations outside the motor area are not as strong, and they provide an opportunity to effectively use them to optimize action. Further research, such as the method presented by Z. Garakh and colleagues (2020), which uses a baseline procedure and principal component analysis (PCA) to extract the central mu-component while suppressing the occipital alpha, may provide more insight into the effects of lower mu-band.

Our time-frequency analysis revealed a mixing of the alpha frequency with beta oscillations in the prestimulus activity. Although the lower band oscillations did not seem to harm the procedure, the results suggest that only lower-band oscillations without suppression of occipital activity are not enough for significant change. Another unexpected finding from the EMG recordings was that the baseline modulation seemed to affect only the initiation of the movement and not its strength. Participants also reported automatic reactions a few minutes after starting, which suggests they became habituated to the same reaction.

A major drawback of the real-time adaptive procedure was the lack of time-locked stimuli presentation. Although the waiting time in both mu and beta conditions had only a small correlation with RT and no effect on responses, it is still a factor that should be considered in future studies.

5   Conclusion

The present study explores the use of a fast and adaptive technique for presenting stimuli based on ongoing brain rhythms. The focus is on the impact of prestimulus power on the reaction time, with sensorimotor cortical beta and mu rhythms being used as target states. The results showed a significant increase in rhythm power, leading to longer reaction times in the case of highly synchronized beta oscillations. This highlights the importance of baseline beta rhythms in motor action initiation and the possibility of changing reaction time through adaptive processing. The study also found no significant difference in reaction time when using the lower mu-frequency band.

Some limitations should be described. Firstly, it is the presence of a lower alpha frequency during the heightening of beta power. With the similar function and nature (synchronization at the rest, desynchronization during any kind of motor system processing) of the rhythms, it is possible that the result was achieved by means of increased amplitude of both rhythms. Additionally, the time of the stimuli presentation could not be the same for the entire procedure due to online processing of the data. A relatively small difference (1–2 s) was found between low and high state conditions in terms of time before an event happens, with an insignificant correlation between reaction time and time for searching. However, future work could be improved by considering ways to implement a real-time presentation in the gaming environment, for example, where a subject will not be waiting purposely for the stimulus to appear.

In conclusion, the study's results correspond to previous findings on beta rhythm's functional role and suggest the possibility of influencing simple and fast motor reactions.

However, further research is needed to explore the prospects of modulation in other cognitive processes, such as perception and memory.

Funding. This work is an output of a research project implemented as part of the Basic Research Program at the National Research University Higher School of Economics (HSE University)

References

Aleksandrov, A., Tugin, S.: Changes in the mu rhythm in different types of motor activity and on observation of movements. Neurosci. Behav. Physiol. **42**, 302–307 (2012). https://doi.org/10.1007/s11055-012-9566-2

Andermann, M.L., et al.: Brain state-triggered stimulus delivery: an efficient tool for probing ongoing brain activity. Open J. Neurosci. **2**, 5 (2012)

Belinskaya, A., Smetanin, N., Lebedev, M.A., Ossadtchi, A.: Short-delay neurofeedback facilitates training of the parietal alpha rhythm. J. Neural Eng. **17**, 066012 (2020). https://doi.org/10.1088/1741-2552/abc8d7

Boncompte, G., Villena-González, M., Cosmelli, D., López, V.: Spontaneous alpha power lateralization predicts detection performance in an un-cued signal detection task. PLoS ONE **11**(8), e0160347 (2016)

Ewing, K.C., Fairclough, S.H., Gilleade, K.: Evaluation of an adaptive game that uses EEG measures validated during the design process as inputs to a biocybernetic loop. Front. Hum. Neurosci. **10**, 223 (2016)

Fairclough, S.H.: Fundamentals of physiological computing. Interact. Comput. **21**, 133–145 (2009)

Fox, N.A., et al.: Assessing human mirror activity with EEG mu rhythm: a meta-analysis. Psychol. Bull. **142**(3), 291–313 (2016)

Garakh, Z., Novototsky-Vlasov, V., Larionova, E., Zaytseva, Y.: Mu rhythm separation from the mix with alpha rhythm: principal component analyses and factor topography. J. Neurosci. Methods **346**, 108892 (2020)

Gastaut, H.J., Bert, J.: EEG changes during cinematographic presentation; moving picture activation of the EEG. Electroencephalogr. Clin. Neurophysiol. **6**(3), 433–444 (1954)

Gramfort, A., et al.: MEG and EEG data analysis with MNE-Python. Front. Neurosci. **7**, 267 (2013)

Hari, R.: Action-perception connection and the cortical mu rhythm. Prog. Brain Res. **159**, 253–260 (2006)

Iemi, L., Chaumon, M., Crouzet, S.M., Busch, N.A.: Spontaneous neural oscillations bias perception by modulating baseline excitability. J. Neurosci. Offi. J. Soc. Neurosci. **37**(4), 807–819 (2017)

Iemi, L., et al.: Multiple mechanisms link prestimulus neural oscillations to sensory responses. elife **8**, e43620 (2019)

Jensen, O., et al.: Using brain-computer interfaces and brain-state dependent stimulation as tools in cognitive neuroscience. Front. Psychol. **2**, 100 (2011)

Klimesch, W.: EEG alpha and theta oscillations reflect cognitive and memory performance: a review and analysis. Brain Res. Brain Res. Rev. **29**(2–3), 169–195 (1999)

Llanos, C., Rodriguez, M., Rodriguez-Sabate, C., Morales, I., Sabate, M.: Mu-rhythm changes during the planning of motor and motor imagery actions. Neuropsychologia **51**(6), 1019–1026 (2013)

Luck, S.J.: An Introduction to the Event-Related Potential Technique. MIT Press, Cambridge (2005)

Mathewson, K.E., Gratton, G., Fabiani, M., Beck, D.M., Ro, T.: To see or not to see: prestimulus alpha phase predicts visual awareness. J. Neurosci. Off. J. Soc. Neurosci. **29**(9), 2725–2732 (2009)

Mühl, C., Heylen, D., Nijholt, A.: Affective Brain-Computer Interfaces: Neuroscientific Approaches to Affect Detection. Oxford University Press, Oxford (2015)

Pineda, J.A.: The functional significance of mu rhythms: translating "seeing" and "hearing" into "doing." Brain Res. Brain Res. Rev. **50**(1), 57–68 (2005)

Rutishauser, U., Kotowicz, A., Laurent, G.: A method for closed-loop presentation of sensory stimuli conditional on the internal brain-state of awake animals. J. Neurosci. Methods **215**(1), 139–155 (2013)

Sherman, M.A., et al.: Neural mechanisms of transient neocortical beta rhythms: converging evidence from humans, computational modeling, monkeys, and mice. Proc. Natl. Acad. Sci. U.S.A. **113**(33), E4885–E4894 (2016)

Shin, H., Law, R., Tsutsui, S., Moore, C.I., Jones, S.R.: The rate of transient beta frequency events predicts behavior across tasks and species. eLife **6**, e29086 (2017)

Smetanin, N., Belinskaya, A., Lebedev, M., Ossadtchi, A.: Digital filters for low-latency quantification of brain rhythms in real time. J. Neural Eng. **17**(4), 046022 (2020)

Smetanin, N., Volkova, K., Zabodaev, S., Lebedev, M.A., Ossadtchi, A.: NFBLab-A versatile software for neurofeedback and brain-computer interface research. Front. Neuroinform. **12**, 100 (2018)

Stegeman, D., Hermens, H.: Standards for surface electromyography: the european project surface EMG for non-invasive assessment of muscles (SENIAM). Roessingh Res. Dev. Enschede, The Netherlands **10**, 8–12 (2007)

Yoo, J.J., et al.: When the brain is prepared to learn: enhancing human learning using real-time fMRI. Neuroimage **59**(1), 846–852 (2012)

Zhang, L., Zhang, J., Yao, L.: Correlation analysis between momentary phases of ongoing EEG oscillations and ERP amplitudes to identify the optimal brain state for stimulus presentation. In: ICME International Conference on Complex Medical Engineering (CME), pp. 101–106 (2012)

Discovering Mental Strategies for Voluntary Control Over Brain-Computer Interfaces

Eddy J. Davelaar[✉] [iD]

Birkbeck, University of London, London WC1E 7HX, UK
e.davelaar@bbk.ac.uk

Abstract. When novices engage with a brain-computer interface, the first challenge is to discover what mental strategy allows some rudimentary control over the system. In some instances, the strategy is clear and provided by the trainer. In most cases, the strategy is not always known. In neurofeedback training, the goal is to increase or decrease a particular brain signature, whilst participants discover which mental strategies are helpful. The question is how? The starting point is the assumption that reinforcement learning underlies the neurofeedback learning and is involved in evaluating the utility of a candidate strategy. Candidate strategies are proposed via activation of neural representations of task goals that are part of a neural network that includes the target brain region. Early in the learning stage, positive feedback allows the accumulation of activation in this neural network until the task goal representation (i.e., the mental strategy) becomes fully activated. Low levels of reward prediction error lead to the candidate strategy to remain activated. High levels of reward prediction error lead to a specific deselection of the candidate strategy and allows selection of a new candidate. The process of selection and deselection within this mental space demonstrates area-restricted search, which is an optimal search strategy in situations where rewards are heterogeneously distributed, typically clustered, over a certain area. Further investigation into strategy discovery is needed to advance our current understanding of neurofeedback learning, its relation to reinforcement learning, and the role of conscious awareness.

Keywords: Neurofeedback · Mental Strategy · Brain-Computer Interface

1 Introduction

Neurofeedback is a neuroscientific paradigm in which brain activity is recorded from individuals who are tasked with the goal of influencing this brain activity. Although electroencephalography (EEG) is the most common neural modality, recent years have seen an increase in the use of real-time functional magnetic resonance imaging (rt-fMRI) [1, 2], functional near-infrared spectroscopy (fNIRS) [3, 4] and magnetoencephalography (MEG) [5, 6].

The history of neurofeedback research dates back to the early 1900s and was a logical extension of the behaviorist research agenda [for a brief overview see 7]. The

© The Author(s), under exclusive license to Springer Nature Switzerland AG 2023
D. D. Schmorrow and C. M. Fidopiastis (Eds.): HCII 2023, LNAI 14019, pp. 16–25, 2023.
https://doi.org/10.1007/978-3-031-35017-7_2

focus was on whether a reflex called alpha blocking – the decrease in occipital alpha wave power when opening the eyes – could be conditioned. Jasper and Shagass [8, 9] demonstrated this using classical conditioning and voluntarily through subvocalisation. Later, Wyrwicka and Sterman [10] showed that brain oscillations themselves could also be influenced through operant conditioning. This led to a large literature investigating how to train people to willfully modulate their brain dynamics, mostly for a clinical purpose.

Of considerable interest is the observation that participants report phenomenological experiences specific to the brain oscillation being trained [11, 12]. This association between neural brain activation patterns and phenomenology is the focus of the field called neurophenomenology [13]. Bagdasaryan and Le Van Quyen [14] argued that neurofeedback is well-suited to investigate mind-brain associations and several studies have used the neurofeedback paradigm to do exactly that [15–17]. Davelaar et al. [15] made a distinction between subjective experiences and mental strategies. In particular, mental strategies are cognitive actions, such as mental arithmetic or memory retrieval, whereas subjective experiences are much broader. A subjective experience could be the experience associated with mental arithmetic, but also include sensations that are not related to any cognitive action. In their study on frontal alpha upregulation (increasing the power in the alpha frequency band over frontal EEG electrodes), they observed that learners – those who were able to upregulate alpha – were reporting "feeling relaxed", whereas non-learners were "trying to relax". The cognitive action of "trying" was hampering reaching the desired brain state. Many studies that investigate phenomenology during neurofeedback training focus on the narrow experience of strategies [12, 18–20].

Within the discussions on mental strategies and neurofeedback, there is a parallel discussion on implicit or covert versus explicit or overt neurofeedback [21, 22]. The difference between these two types of neurofeedback is that in the overt condition the participants are explicitly told that they are in a closed-loop training situation, whereas in the covert condition no reference is made to training. Typically, people in the covert condition are doing a training-unrelated task. For example, in an rt-fMRI study by Ramot et al. [23], participants were told to press one button for positive and another for negative feedback stimuli. In order to create the valence, positive and negative stimuli would increase or decrease monetary compensation. In addition, to maintain attention to the stimuli, incorrect button presses were penalized by decreasing the monetary compensation. Results showed that 10 out of 16 participants showed a learning effect and participants were not aware that there was a brain-feedback contingency. This is of considerable importance, as it suggests that the brain naturally organizes itself in the presence of appetitive stimuli. However, the study does not demonstrate that neurofeedback learning occurs in the absence of consciousness.

2 Theories of Neurofeedback Learning

During a neurofeedback training session there are many changes in neural activity and structural connectivity. The temporal sequence of the veridical feedback is unique to the particular training session and so are the experiences and neural dynamics of the participant. This makes it very difficult to address all components in a comprehensive theory. As a consequence, theories have been developed that either discuss neurofeed-back learning in terms of abstract principles or omit various complexities [24–26]. These high-level theories are well-suited in identifying computational targets. For example, a common phrase is that neurofeedback is "normalizing the brain". This implies that there is a neural profile of spontaneous activity that is considered normative which may be due to a homeostatic system. In clinical cases where the spontaneous activity is not within the normative range, the training procedure moves the clinical homeostatic set point towards that found in the normative range. High-level theories will necessarily lack the mechanistic detail to explore or investigate specific predictions.

With the increased interest in neurofeedback research, more sophisticated theories are being developed based on established knowledge in computational neuroscience. One such theory is the multi-stage theory of neurofeedback learning [7, 27], which consists of three temporally overlapping stages. These stages were identified to have different neural substrates and timecourses, which account for learning curves within sessions, between sessions, and post-training maintenance. The model was developed to address EEG neurofeedback, but the framework also extends to hemodynamic brain signals. The first stage involves associating a task goal representation (i.e., "get as many points as possible") to a configuration of striatal neurons (see Fig. 1) that via the thalamus alter the EEG power spectrum. The process by which this striatal learning occurs is reinforcement learning. When a striatal pattern leads to the desired outcome, the feedback signal leads to an increase in the connectivity between the goal and striatal representations.

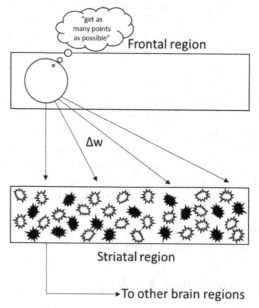

Fig. 1. Depiction of the striatal learning stage. In the frontal region, the task goal is active for the duration of the training period. Striatal neurons create random activation patterns that affect the brain activity in other brain areas. Those that lead to positive feedback get reinforced by updating the frontal-striatal connections.

The second stage involves structural changes to the striatal-thalamic and thalamic-cortical pathways. Whereas the learning in the first stage still allows going back and forth between multiple set points, the thalamic consolidation leads to a change in the set point. Therefore, changes in spontaneous brain activity as a function of neurofeedback training are considered to be due to structural changes involving stage 2 learning. The third stage involves a phenomenological dimension in that internal brain states might be correlated with subjective sensations. The sensations that coincide with target brain states will therefore become associated with positive feedback and in turn become secondary reinforcers. It should be noted that these subjective sensations are not mental strategies, as these are not actions.

The multistage theory undergoes continual development and there are a few insights obtained from this development. First, the theory does not implement a negative feedback loop that controls the brain state to be around a certain set point. The key reason for this is that learning and therefore the asymptotic level is conditional on the goal representation. That is, the set point around which the brain pattern fluctuates can be adjusted (voluntarily) by consciously retrieving the task goal. In effect, the striatal learning is enhancing the representational space of stable set points. This makes the overall system more adaptive. It also means that this theory does not subscribe to the idea of brain normalization in its strictest sense. Second, during striatal learning, the system conducts a search through a high-dimensional neural space. The search behavior can be optimized by dynamically modifying the learning rate as a function of effort, motivation, and saliency among others. This is yet an unexplored area of research within this framework.

Recently, another theory was developed that also harnesses reinforcement learning theory and focuses on rt-fMRI and the various experimental paradigms within that literature [21]. In particular, Lubianiker and colleagues address both intermittent and continuous neurofeedback. The framework's implementation of learning in an explicit training protocol is similar to the striatal learning stage, with the difference that the system is provided with a set of mental strategies. First one strategy is randomly chosen and its impact on reward evaluated. Through standard reinforcement learning, the strategy that best predict the reward gets chosen more often. The provision of a set of mental strategies to choose from is not a typical scenario in neurofeedback studies. However, Lubianiker et al. argue that without the addition of a "choice block" with options, participants may select an arbitrary strategy at any time during the training period. This leads to an increase in variability within and across participants, with suboptimal selection of strategies, potentially leading to inability to learn to influence the brain dynamics. This recommendation comes from the specific consideration of the computational details involved in neurofeedback learning.

The fact that the same reinforcement learning principles have been proposed in two computationally detailed theories of neurofeedback learning demonstrates a progression towards greater understanding. With this consensus, knowledge gaps become apparent and one such gap is addressed here.

In Davelaar's computational work there is no explicit strategy that is chosen and instead a random configuration of striatal neurons that increases the likelihood of the target brain activation becomes reinforced. The theory is missing a representation for a conscious mental strategy. In fact, the only conscious components are the goal representation (i.e., "get as many points as possible") and the awareness of a subjective sensation that coincides with a positive feedback stimulus. In Lubianiker et al.'s work, the strategies are given to the model from which it selects the strategy that leads to the target brain activation. This theory is missing a process by which the strategies enter the set of possible options. In other words, both theories are silent to how mental strategies are discovered.

3 Discovery of Mental Strategies

Here, a theory of strategy discovery is proposed in the context of neurofeedback learning. The field of cognitive neuroscience has revealed that overlapping brain regions and networks are activated in a task-specific manner. For example, when doing motor imagery, the motor cortex become activated. If the goal of a neurofeedback session is to activate the motor cortex, a useful strategy would be to imagine playing tennis. The experimenter could instruct the participant to engage in this imagery. However, how could the participant discover this for themselves?

The starting point is a mapping between all possible cognitive actions and brain regions that become activated (or deactivated) when the action is performed. There will be clusters of strategies that activate a very similar network of regions. In a multidimensional space this would be depicted as a scattering of points, which each point representing a strategy. The distance between pairs of strategies reflect the dissimilarity in profile between the strategy-supporting neural networks.

We begin with a situation in which the person has no mental strategy. The random configuration of striatal neurons meanders without any learning ensuing. By chance, a configuration occurs that activates the target brain region, which triggers the receipt of positive feedback. Through reinforcement learning this leads to an increase in occurrence of this striatal configuration. As the target brain region gets activated more often and more strongly, the network that includes this brain region becomes more activated as well. This network includes brain regions related to perception or memory and also a variety of task goals (see Fig. 2). For example, the activation of the motor cortex might trigger a memory of jogging or swimming. There could be a large number of possible motor representations becoming activated, but do not yet reach consciousness.

Figure 3 shows a neural network structure that is capable of selecting and deselecting specific representations while being given a general prediction error signal. This is not to say that this is the actual structure used. Instead, this network illustrates that strategy discovery is possible with limited computational complexity. In Fig. 3, the situation is where several task goal representations are receiving input from the target brain region. They all compete with each other through a winner-take-all lateral inhibition. When a prediction error is detected, all representations increase in activation, until one wins the competition and is therefore selected. The selected task goal representation is in conscious awareness and is the mental strategy which the participant will execute (Fig. 3).

On execution of the strategy one of two things can happen. First, the strategy is successful in activating the target brain region. This prevents another prediction error and no changes occur other than associating the neurofeedback task goal with the mental

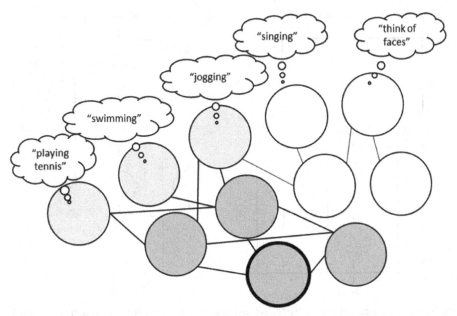

Fig. 2. The activation of the target brain region (shown as the circle with thick border) spreads through a neural network that encompasses task goals associated with moving arms and legs. These task goals will form the set of candidate mental strategies.

strategy (using the feedback as a learning signal). Second, the strategy might not be appropriate or may still produce a strong enough prediction error (Fig. 4). When this happens, the currently active task goal becomes deactivated while the other possible strategies compete for selection. In addition, a negative association is learned between the neurofeedback task goal and the unsuccessful strategy, preventing it from being re-selected later during strategy search.

Going back to the multidimensional space of strategies, the selection and deselection of strategies will result in a trajectory within this map. Successive strategies are likely to be similar to preceding ones. In the literature on cognitive search this is referred to area-restrictive search [28]. This type of search is an optimal strategy in situations where rewards are heterogeneously distributed, typically clustered, over the search space. However, at a certain point in time it is clear that further searching for candidate strategies that relate to a particular content (e.g., strategies related to numerical processing) is futile. The literature on cognitive search allows an explicit formulation of when a person (or any agent) decides to stop searching in a particular within the multidimensional search space. This type of analysis is yet to be undertaken in human neurofeedback studies and the current hypothesis is that the decision to stop searching for a new candidate strategy might relate to an internal decision to not engage with the study any further.

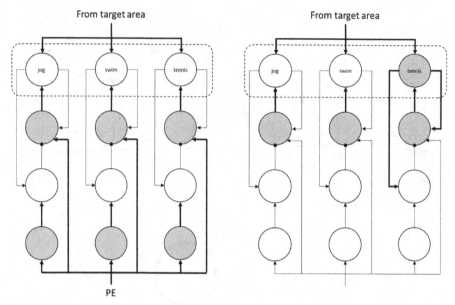

Fig. 3. Network architecture that can select and deselect specific representations. The task goal representations (shown in the dashed box) compete with each other via lateral inhibition. A prediction error, PE, activates all possible candidates (left). Through the winner-takes-all competitive process, a single representation remains active and sustains its activation via a positive feedback loop (right). In the absence of further PE signals, the task goal (e.g., imagining playing tennis) remains the mental strategy chosen by the participant.

4 Discussion

In this paper, I have described a new proposal for strategy discovery within the context of neurofeedback learning. The assumption is that early on in learning, the positive feedback in response to the desired brain activation triggers awareness of cognitive actions that are supported by a neural network that involves the target brain region. These cognitive actions – mental strategies – are performed and subjected to reinforcement learning. The reason why the neurocognitive system spends much neural energy on discovering strategies could be that it dramatically increases the effective learning rate and drives down the frequency of prediction errors.

The proposal explains why when a study designed as an implicit neurofeedback study transforms into an explicit neurofeedback study. Ramot and Martin [22] describe a study in which participants were not told about the feedback contingency and where participants produced idiosyncratic strategies. The proposal advanced here explains the genesis of these idiosyncratic strategies and in doing so questions the validity of some study designs as demonstrating implicit neurofeedback.

The proposal of strategy discovery also argues in favor of conducting post-training interviews to understand the strategies that participants have been using. In Davelaar, et al. [15], the focus was on general experiences or sensations. However, during the interviews cognitive actions were also reported. In other studies, we expanded this work and

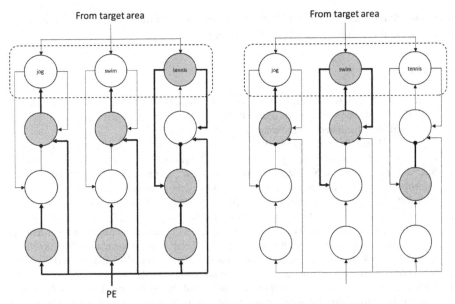

Fig. 4. Process of deselecting an inadequate mental strategy. When a PE signal arrives at a time when a mental strategy is active, the combined input from the task goal and the PE activates the feedforward inhibitory pathway (left). This breaks the positive feedback loop and allows another candidate strategy to win the winner-takes-all competition (right).

observed various idiosyncratic strategies. The neural mechanism of strategy discovery allows the emergence of strategies that are uncommon. Yet, for that participant it sufficiently activates the target brain region to trigger a high frequency of positive feedback signals. The scheme is also sensitive to "rider strategies", which are strategies that have no impact on the target brain activation, but are correlated with a chosen successful strategy. An example would be imagining the voice of a famous person counting numbers. The auditory imagery will not activate the target brain area for numerical processing. In this instance, auditory imagery is riding on top of a counting strategy. Teasing apart collections of strategies will require participants to write down exactly what they were doing, but better still would be to have an interviewer extract the information with higher precision.

The proposal comes with some limitations. First and foremost, there is quite a bit of machinery needed for the system to activate and select a candidate strategy and deselect unsuccessful strategies. There are currently no neuroscientific studies available against which to test this proposal. In addition, different neural network configurations are possible that can all activate, select, and deselect specific strategies, which complicates comparing different configurations, even when data is available.

Despite these challenges, the proposal fills an important gap in our knowledge and directs our attention to a more fundamental question of how an autonomic system interacts with the external and internal environment. Outside the domain of neurofeedback, this question could apply to any situation in which an agent receives reinforcement based on behavior and has to find that type of behavior in their memory of behavioral repertoires that maximizes the amount of reward.

References

1. Emmert, K., Kopel, R., Sulzer, J., Bruhl, A.B., Berman, B.D., Linden, D.E.J., et al.: Me-ta-analysis of real-time fMRI neurofeedback studies using individual participant data: how is brain regulation mediated? Neuroimage **124**, 806–812 (2016)
2. Sulzer, J., Haller, S., Scharnowski, F., Weiskopf, N., Birbaumer, N., Blefari, M.L., et al.: Real-time fMRI neurofeedback: progress and challenges. Neuroimage **76**, 386–399 (2013)
3. Sakatani, K., Takemoto, N., Tsujii, T., Yanagisawa, K., Tsunashima, H.: NIRS-based neurofeedback learning systems for controlling activity of the prefrontal cortex. Adv. Exp. Med. Biol. **789**, 449–454 (2013). https://doi.org/10.1007/978-1-4614-7411-1_60
4. Marx, A.-M., Ehlis, A.-C., Furdea, A., Holtmann, M., Banaschewski, T., Brandeis, D., et al.: Near-infrared spectroscopy (NIRS) neurofeedback as a treatment for children with at-tention deficit hyperactivity disorder (ADHD) - a pilot study. Front. Human Neuro-Sci. **8**, 1038 (2015)
5. Florin, E., Bock, E., Baillet, S.: Targeted reinforcement of neural oscillatory activity with real-time neuroimaging feedback. Neuroimage **88**, 54–60 (2014)
6. Okazaki, Y.O., Horschig, J.M., Luther, L., Oostenveld, R., Murakami, I., Jensen, O.: Real-time MEG neurofeedback training of posterior alpha activity modulates subsequent visual detection performance. Neuroimage **107**, 323–332 (2015)
7. Davelaar, E.J.: A multi-stage theory of neurofeedback learning. In: Schmorrow, D.D., Fidopiastis, C.M. (eds.) HCII 2020. LNCS (LNAI), vol. 12196, pp. 118–128. Springer, Cham (2020). https://doi.org/10.1007/978-3-030-50353-6_9
8. Jasper, H., Shagass, C.: Conditioning the occipital alpha rhythm in man. J. Exp. Psychol. **28**(5), 373–388 (1941)
9. Jasper, H., Shagass, C.: Conscious time judgments related to conditioned time intervals and voluntary control of the alpha rhythm. J. Exp. Psychol. **28**(6), 503–508 (1941)
10. Wyrwicka, W., Sterman, M.B.: Instrumental conditioning of sensorimotor cortex EEG spindles in the waking cat. Physiol. Behav. **3**(5), 703–707 (1968)
11. Ancoli, S., Green, K.F.: Authoritarianism, introspection, and alpha wave biofeedback training. Psychophysiology **14**(1), 40–44 (1977)
12. Nowlis, D.P., Kamiya, J.: The control of electroencephalographic alpha rhythms through auditory feedback and the associated mental activity. Psychophysiology **6**, 476–483 (1970)
13. Varela, F.: Neurophenomenology: a methodological remedy to the hard problem. J. Conscious. Stud. **3**, 330–350 (1996)
14. Bagdasaryan, J., Le Van Quyen, M.: Experiencing your brain: neurofeedback as a new bridge between neuroscience and phenomenology. Front. Human Neurosci. **7**, 680 (2013)
15. Davelaar, E.J., Barnby, J.M., Almasi, S., Eatough, V.: Differential subjective experiences in learners and non-learners in frontal alpha neurofeedback: piloting a mixed-method approach. Front. Hum. Neurosci. **12**, 402 (2018)
16. Edge, J., Lancaster, L.: Phenomenological analysis of superior musical performance facilitated by neurofeedback: enhancing musical performance through neurofeedback: playing the tune of life. Transpers. Psychol Rev **8**, 23–35 (2004)
17. Garrison, K.A., Santoyo, J.F., Davis, J.H., Thornhill, T.A., Kerr, C.E., Brewer, J.A.: Effortless awareness: using real time neurofeedback to investigate correlates of posterior cingulate cortex activity in meditators' self-report. Front. Hum. Neurosci. **7**, 440 (2013)
18. Kober, S.E., Witte, M., Ninaus, M., Neuper, C., Wood, G.: Learning to modulate one's own brain activity: the effect of spontaneous mental strategies. Frontiers Human Neuroscience **7**, 695 (2013)

19. Nan, W., Rodrigues, J.P., Ma, J., Qu, X., Wan, F., Mak, P., et al.: Individual alpha neurofeedback training effect on short term memory. Int. J. Psychophysiol. **86**, 83–87 (2012)
20. Hinterberger, T., Veit, R., Wilhelm, B., Weiskopf, N., Vatine, J.-J., Birbaumer, N.: Neuronal mechanisms underlying control of a brain computer interface. Eur. J. Neurosci. **21**, 3169–3181 (2005)
21. Lubianiker, N., Paret, C., Dayan, P., Hendler, T.: Neurofeedback through the lens of reinforcement learning. Trends Neurosci. **45**(8), 579–593 (2022)
22. Ramot, M., Martin, A.: Close-loop neuromodulation for studying spontaneous activity and causality. Trends Cogn. Sci. **26**(4), 290–299 (2022)
23. Ramot, M., Grossman, S., Friedman, D., Malach, R.: Covert neurofeedback without awareness shapes cortical network spontaneous connectivity. In: Proceedings of the National Academy of Sciences (2016)
24. Birbaumer, N., Ruiz, S., Sitaram, R.: Learned regulation of brain metabolism. Trends Cogn. Sci. **17**, 295–302 (2013)
25. Niv, S.: Clinical efficacy and potential mechanisms of neurofeedback. Pers. Ind. Diff. **54**, 676–686 (2013)
26. Ros, T., Baars, B.J., Lanius, R.A., Vuilleumier, P.: Tuning pathological brain oscillations with neurofeedback: a systems neuroscience framework. Front. Hum. Neurosci. **8**, 1008 (2014)
27. Davelaar, E.J.: Mechanisms of neurofeedback: a computation-theoretic approach. Neuroscience **378**, 175–188 (2018)
28. Todd, P.M., Hills, T.T., Robbins, T.W.: Cognitive Search: Evolution, Algorithms, and The Brain. MIT Press, Cambridge (2012)

Mental Face Image Retrieval Based on a Closed-Loop Brain-Computer Interface

Nona Rajabi[1]([✉]), Charles Chernik[2], Alfredo Reichlin[1], Farzaneh Taleb[1], Miguel Vasco[3], Ali Ghadirzadeh[1,4], Mårten Björkman[1], and Danica Kragic[1]

[1] KTH Royal Institute of Technology, Stockholm, Sweden
nonar@kth.se
[2] Karolinska Institute, Stockholm, Sweden
[3] INESC-ID & Instituto Superior Técnico, University of Lisbon, Lisbon, Portugal
[4] Stanford University, Stanford, CA, USA

Abstract. Retrieval of mental images from measured brain activity may facilitate communication, especially when verbal or muscular communication is impossible or inefficient. The existing work focuses mostly on retrieving the observed visual stimulus while our interest is on retrieving the imagined mental image. We present a closed-loop BCI framework to retrieve mental images of human faces. We utilize EEG signals as binary feedback to determine the relevance of an image to the target mental image. We employ the feedback to traverse the latent space of a generative model to propose new images closer to the actual target image. We evaluate the proposed framework on 13 volunteers. Unlike previous studies, we do not restrict the possible attributes of the resulting images to predefined semantic classes. Subjective and objective tests validate the ability of our model to retrieve face images similar to the actual target mental images.

Keywords: EEG · Brain-Computer Interface · Mental Image Retrieval · Generative Models

1 Introduction

Humans are experts at processing and creating representations of visual images in their minds, even in the absence of visual stimuli. Representations of sensory information without a direct external stimulus are referred to as *mental images* [1–3]. Although mental imagery can cover different sensory modalities such as auditory, tactile, and olfactory, research about the phenomena has been mostly centered around visual mental imagery[1] [1–3]. Mental images can depict any objects, events, or scenes, such as a human face, a car accident, or the city view from the top of a tower. Alongside language impairment caused by severe brain injuries, limited expressivity of verbal language can result in incomplete and

---

[1] Throughout this paper we designate visual mental images as "mental images".

inaccurate communication of one's intentions and messages to others. Retrieving mental images from brain activity facilitates interaction with the environment especially when verbal communication is impossible or ineffective.

Prior works have investigated retrieving observed visual stimuli directly from brain activity. The approach usually involves implementing an encoder-decoder framework, in which the visual stimuli are reconstructed from a compact latent representation encoded from brain activity. Recently, Bayesian inference and conditional generative networks were employed to reconstruct simple geometrical shapes from either functional magnetic resonance imaging (fMRI) or electroencephalogram (EEG) data [4,5]. Other studies attempted to reconstruct more complex natural images by adding prior information about them to the image generators [6–10]. However, while reconstructing images directly from brain data is possible for simple geometrical shapes, applying it to retrieve more complex images results in coarse or inaccurate approximations of the actual target image [6–10]. The challenge of this task mainly lies in the low signal-to-noise ratio of measured brain responses and the high dimensionality of both brain data and output images. To avoid the complexity of decoding images directly from brain signals, some works employ an iterative search method. They utilize brain signals, usually EEG, as binary feedback to determine the relevance of proposed images to the target mental image. The search can be performed in an existing image database to rank the images based on their similarity to the subject's mental image [11–14]. However, due to the finite number of images in an existing database, there is no guarantee that the model can find an exact match of the mental image. A better approach is to leverage generative models to generate proposed images instead of finding them in a database and update the model's estimation based on user's feedback [15–17]. However, selecting an appropriate input to the generative model to make it generate an image that resembles the true mental image is still a challenging problem. In fact, existing approaches limit the search space to only specific semantic classes such as gender, hair color, and attractiveness [16,17].

In this paper, we address the question of *how we can utilize binary EEG feedback to retrieve mental images of previously observed stimuli without predefining any semantic classes for the target image.* Our focus is on the task of face image retrieval. We propose a closed-loop framework that retrieves mental face images by iteratively searching the latent space of a generative model, guided by binary feedback from EEG signals. Unlike prior works, we exploit the information gained about target-relevant regions of the latent space to sample new images for the next iterations. Candidate images are proposed by the generative model where the selected latent variable is iteratively regulated through a novel search algorithm within its latent space. The search is mediated by the EEG signals feedback until converging to the target mental image.

The main contributions of our work are: **(i)** A framework for image retrieval based on a closed-loop search that repeatedly generates images, provides these as rapid serial visual presentation (RSVP) stimuli, and decodes the brain response as feedback to guide the search. **(ii)** We instantiate our framework in the context of human face images and present an optimization and a sampling approach that effectively use human feedback to search for and improve the estimation of the target mental image, without restricting the result to pre-defined semantic classes. **(iii)** We present a user study with 13 participants to evaluate the proposed approach. Qualitative and quantitative assessment show that our approach retrieves face images that closely resemble the target mental face image.

2 Background

2.1 EEG Correlates of Face Recognition

EEG-based BCI systems utilize neurophysiological signals present in EEG to control and communicate commands and intentions to a computer. A category of these control signals is Event-Related Potentials (ERP) which are voltage changes in response to sensory, motor, or cognitive events or stimuli [18]. ERPs have been used extensively to study the processes involved in recognition memory, i.e., the judgment that a stimulus has been previously experienced [19].

Neuroscientific studies show signs of specific oscillations in brain signals while encountering familiar objects compared with unfamiliar ones [19–21]. Particularly in face images, several stages are involved in face processing, recognition, and identification which are manifested in specific temporal patterns in brain responses [22–25]. The N250r component is an ERP modulation that occurs for immediate face repetition. The corresponding negativity peaks around 230 to 300 ms over inferior temporal regions and has a larger amplitude for repeated faces compared with unfamiliar unrepeated ones [26,27]. It has been suggested that the N250r is associated with face recognition, i.e., a successful match between a perceptual face representation and an episodic memory trace of a previously seen face [23,28]. However, the difference in EEG signals associated with familiar and unfamiliar faces is not limited to face repetition paradigms. In two separate studies, an enhanced negativity was observed for familiar faces compared with unfamiliar faces between 300 to 500 ms after stimulus onset at centrofrontal and centroparietal electrodes [29,30]. The component is called N400f and is followed by an enhanced positivity, larger for familiar faces, between 400 to 700 ms and broadly distributed over the brain called P600f [23,30].

Our visual task includes finding relevant images to the target mental image among irrelevant ones. As such, it can also be considered a target or relevance detection task, which also elicits another ERP, the P300 signal. The P300 is a parietal positive waveform with a peak around 300 to 500 ms after stimulus onset. The amplitude of the peak is enhanced when target stimuli are delivered to the subject infrequently and unpredictably (*the oddball paradigm*) [31]. We consider this constraint in our design to maximize the probability of eliciting P300 with the observation of target stimuli.

2.2 Generative Models

Generative models are statistical models learning representations of data distribution to generate novel samples. Formally, the assumption is that data samples are generated according to an unknown distribution $p(x)$ and our goal is to get a model P such that P is as similar as possible to $p(x)$ [32]. In this paper, we use variational autoencoders (VAEs) and generative adversarial networks (GANs).

VAEs are a group of generative models called latent variable models. The idea behind latent variable models is that data samples are generated from unobserved variables z (latent variables) existing in a latent space Z, usually of lower dimensionality than the actual data space. The generative process contains two steps: (1) a value $z^{(i)}$ is generated from a prior distribution $p(z)$; (2) a data sample $x^{(i)}$ is generated from the conditional distribution $p(x|z)$. Equation 1 relates the data distribution $p(x)$ to the generative process,

$$p(x) = \int p(x|z)p(z)dz. \tag{1}$$

However, integrating over all possible z values to calculate $p(x)$ is intractable. A practical way used by VAEs [32,33] is to instead find a tractable distribution $q_\phi(z|x)$, parameterized by ϕ, over z values that are likely to produce real data samples x from $p_\theta(x|z)$, an approximation of $p(x|z)$ parameterized by θ. These two steps can be taken by approximating two-stage encoder-decoder functions: (1) encode real data x to get latent variables z ($q_\phi(z|x)$); (2) reconstruct data samples x from latent variables z ($p_\theta(x|z)$). Since neural networks are function approximators, they have been widely used in these encoder-decoder frameworks where the parameters θ and ϕ are given by their weights (Fig. 1a).

Although VAEs can learn very expressive latent distributions, the quality of generated data, particularly images, is poor. GANs are also a type of generative models [34], successful in generating realistic high-resolution images. GANs consist of two networks: (1) a generator and (2) a discriminator (Fig. 1b). The networks are trained in an adversarial scheme: the generator generates better fake data that cannot be distinguished from the real ones by the discriminator, and the discriminator gets better at discriminating between fake and real data. After training, the generator can generate novel realistic data samples from input noise vectors.

Despite the generative capabilities of GANs, their latent space is not easily interpretable. The reason is that no likelihood-related constraints are placed on the latent space of GANs during training. On the other hand, latent variable models learn a more structured latent space. In this work, we leverage both models in our generative module: we use the latent space of a VAE for optimizing and sampling new latent vectors and generate high-resolution images from those vectors using a GAN.

3   Related Work

Several works attempt to reconstruct the mental image directly from brain signals, recorded while observing a visual stimulus. A common approach is to consider a two-stage encoder-decoder framework where brain activity is embedded into a latent space. Mental images are then reconstructed from these embeddings using a generative model. Du et al. [4] employed Bayesian deep learning to

(a)   (b)

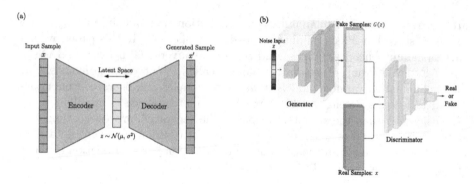

Fig. 1. **(a)** A simple variational autoencoder (VAE) diagram with a Normal prior distribution on the latent space. **(b)** A diagram of a generative adversarial network (GAN).

reconstruct images of simple geometrical shapes from fMRI activity. Zhang et al. [5] employed a deep convolutional neural network (CNN) to encode EEG signals and used this encoding to condition a conditional GAN [35]. To reconstruct more complex images, such as natural images, some works included natural image priors in their models and retrieved a more diverse set of images from fMRI activity [6–8,10]. Instead of using fMRI, other studies employed EEG signals which are less expensive, portable, and require less training compared to fMRI [10,36,37]. Although the retrieved images in some of these works are almost photo-realistic, they are unable to retrieve the exact target image. Furthermore, the methods have only been tested for retrieving the observed visual stimuli from brain responses recorded during exposure to the target visual stimulus, and their effectiveness for imagined mental images is yet to be explored.

Due to the low signal-to-noise ratio of non-invasive brain recordings, especially EEG signals, and also, due to the high-dimensional space of images, it is very challenging to directly reconstruct the exact mental image from available information in brain signals. On the other hand, numerous studies have demonstrated high accuracy in classifying EEG signals, especially when using deep neural networks as the classifier [38]. Some studies leverage this fact and classify target and non-target trials based on the difference in brain activity while obtained as binary relevance feedback, i.e., a signal that determines whether the stimulus is related to a previously shown target image. In that line of research, a combined BCI and computer vision (CV) module was proposed in [13,14]. At each iteration, EEG interest scores were obtained for a subset of images presented to the subject, and all the other images were re-ranked by the CV module based on their similarity to the interesting images. Although this method can find images similar to the target mental image in a database, there is no guarantee that the exact mental image can be found in the limited database. A solution to this limitation is to utilize generative models to generate images, instead of retrieving them from the database [15]. The work of [16] and [17] proposed an interactive search system using GANs to retrieve mental face images, where the human feedback came from EEG signals. [16] employed the system to find which of the eight categories of human faces the subjects have in their mind, and [17] aimed to discover personally attractive images to the subjects. Although employing generative models is an innovative solution to overcome the problem of limited-size databases, none of the above studies have explored their full potential: they generate a set of images at the beginning of the interaction and choose images to display only from that fixed set afterward. The only benefit they get from using generative models is that they keep latent vectors corresponding to target-relevant images (based on the subject's feedback) and average them at the end of the experiment. The final estimated image would then be the image that is generated from this averaged latent vector. Although averaging seems a simple practical method, since the latent space of GANs is not linear, one cannot guarantee that the averaged latent vector result in attributes of the image averaged. Moreover, the focus of these works is on identifying the general category of the mental image and not the exact target, e.g., a specific person in human faces.

In this work, we propose a closed-loop EEG-based BCI framework for mental face image retrieval. We do not limit the search results to pre-defined semantic classes, as we leverage generative models to produce any face image the users have in mind. Unlike prior works [15–17], we generate the batch of images presented to the user at each iteration based on the user's feedback in the previous iteration. This corresponds to having the continuous latent space of the generative model as our image database, thus overcoming the problem of limited-size databases. Furthermore, we do not rely on the complex nonlinear latent space of the GANs and do not average the target-relevant latent vectors to get the final estimated mental image. Instead, our optimization algorithm leverages the available local information in the latent space together with user feedback through their EEG signals to find the target mental image.

4   Generative Face Image Retrieval

In this work, we propose a closed-loop BCI system that aims at reconstructing a user's mental face image in an iterative process by considering a feedback signal provided by the EEG data of the user. As shown in Fig. 2a, the system consists of four main components: a generative model, an EEG signal classifier, an optimizer, and a display model. The process starts with showing a batch of random images to the subject sampled from the generative model. We record the EEG signals of the user when subjected to the visual stimuli which are passed to the EEG classifier. The classifier is trained separately for each subject prior to the retrieval experiment and determines the relevance of presented face images to the target mental face image. Subsequently, the optimizer receives the EEG classification result. The optimizer is responsible for finding the latent variable which results in a face image most resembling the target mental face image and checking the convergence status of the system. Finally, the display model samples new points from the generative model's latent space. Unlike prior works, in our model user feedback informs the sampling process, which closes the interaction loop with the computer system. The sampled points are fed to the generative

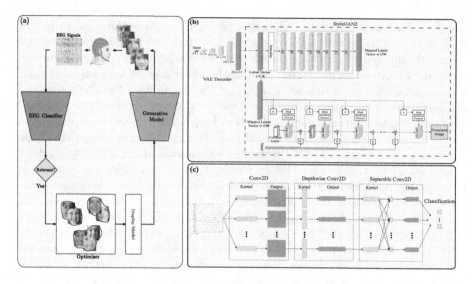

Fig. 2. (a) The proposed framework. (b) Our generative module composed of a VAE followed by a StyleGAN [39,40]. (c) The EEGNet architecture [41].

model to produce a new batch of images for the next iteration. This process is repeated until the system meets the convergence criterion. In the rest of this section, we formally define each component of our framework in detail.

4.1 Generative Model

We employ a generative model to create photo-realistic images of human faces and perform the search for the user's mental face image in its continuous latent space. The latent space is an n-dimensional space $Z \subseteq \mathbb{R}^n$, where n is a hyper-parameter. This space should ideally be built such that each point z in it maps to a realistic face image (*non-sparsity*) and if two points z_1 and z_2 are close enough in the latent space (in the Euclidean sense), the generated images from them have similar semantics (*smoothness*) [15]. If $\{G(z)|z \in Z\}$ is the image generated by the generative model when z is given as input, the goal is to find a $\hat{z} \in Z$ such that $G(\hat{z})$ closely resembles the mental face image imagined by the subject. Our generative module is depicted in Fig. 2b. We use a StyleGan2 architecture pretrained on the Flickr-Faces-HQ (FFHQ) dataset [39,40], due to its ability to generate high-quality face images. The network takes 512-d vectors as input and generates (1024, 1024) RGB images. The output images are then cropped to remove irrelevant background and resized to (400, 400). To reduce the complexity of the latent space, we trained a VAE to generate 512-d vectors from a lower dimensional space (here, 8-d). The smoothness and non-sparsity properties are also preserved in the VAE latent space where optimization and sampling procedures are performed in its lower dimensional space.

4.2   EEG Classifier

The EEG classifier is employed to perform binary classification on the EEG signals collected during the presentation of each face image to the user to distinguish the images that attracted their attention. The classifier is trained for each subject separately using their EEG data collected while performing a target face detection task (Sect. 5.2). We expect this classification to reveal images relevant to the target face from the subjects' point of view. More specifically, relevant images refer to the images that resemble the subject's target mental image, although the similarity metric is defined by the subjects individually. We use EEGNet [41] (Fig. 2c), a deep convolutional neural network, as the classifier, as it performs well on many BCI tasks. We collected EEG data from 4000 trials for each subject out of which 200 were target trials (the initially presented target face image) and labeled as 1. All the other trials (arbitrary face images) were labeled as 0. We trained the classifier on 80% of the data and kept the remaining 20% for validation. Due to the importance of detecting target samples, we used true positive rate, balanced accuracy, and area under the ROC curve as evaluation metrics for the classifier. In the closed-loop task, in each iteration, the output Sigmoid scores from the classifier for each EEG segment was calculated and the trial with the maximum score was labeled as target.

4.3   Optimizer

Each of the face images presented to the user maps to a point in the latent space of the generative model. The optimizer's task is to define the regions in the latent space that contain information about the target mental image and find the latent variable z which results in a face image equivalent to the target mental face. The pseudo-code of our optimization algorithm is shown in Algorithm 1. We implemented an extended K-means clustering algorithm for this module. Due to the smoothness property of the latent space, we can assume that points close enough to each other result in similar faces that can belong to a single person. Therefore, all of these points can be assigned to a cluster with its centroid considered as a prototypical representation of that person's face. Assume that $\{z_1, z_2, ..., z_m\} \in Z$ is the set of points corresponding to the face labeled as relevant by the classifier from the first to the mth iteration and z_{m+1} is obtained from the $(m + 1)^{th}$ iteration. The optimizer first adds z_{m+1} to the existing set of relevant points and runs the K-means clustering algorithm for them with a specific K (lines 5–6). After clustering, there will be K clusters in which points in the same cluster are closer to each other than the other clusters' points. Due to the smoothness property, the assumption is that reasonably close points result in similar faces. In order to quantify this distance, we define a neighborhood constraint. More formally, for each point z in a cluster, we have:

$$d(z, z^*) < \varepsilon \tag{2}$$

where z^* is the centroid of the cluster and $d(.)$ is the Euclidean distance function and we set ε to 0.5. Based on this constraint, we check the resulting clusters

Algorithm 1. Optimizer Algorithm to Cluster Relevant Points

```
1:  K ← 1
2:  converged ← False
3:  while i < max_iter & not converged do
4:      neighbourhood = True
5:      Z.append(z_i)
6:      C ← KMeans(Z, K)
7:      for each {z ∈ c| c ∈ C} do
8:          if d(z, centroid(c)) > ε then
9:              neighbourhood = False
10:             K + +
11:             C ← KMeans(Z, K)
12:             break
13:         end if
14:     end for
15:     if not neighbourhood then
16:         for each {z ∈ c| c ∈ C} do
17:             if d(z, centroid(c)) > ε then
18:                 dissociate(z, c)
19:             end if
20:         end for
21:     end if
22:     for each c ∈ C do
23:         if n(c) > Δ then
24:             converged = True
25:         end if
26:     end for
27:     i + +
28: end while
```

from the K-means algorithm, and if at least one of the points does not satisfy it, K will be incremented, and K-means will be rerun (lines 7–14). After this rerun, we check the constraint again, and if any of the clusters' members do not satisfy it, we dissociate them from their clusters and reserve them for processing in the next steps (lines 15–21). Finally, after each iteration, there will be K clusters, each representative of a person's face. We define the cluster *score* as the number of points assigned to that cluster. At the end of each iteration, the optimizer checks if any clusters have a score exceeding a specified threshold or if a maximum number of iterations have been reached (lines 22–26 and 3). If any of these conditions are met, the system is considered converged.

4.4　Display Model

At the beginning of each iteration, the generative model generates a batch of images to be presented to the subject and the display module is responsible for this task. The batch should include images generated from both explored and unexplored regions in the latent space. The selection of a face image by the classifier signifies that the image has attracted the subject's attention more than the other images. This attention is ideally aligned with the task's goal, i.e., the image resembles the target mental image from the subject's point of view. However, it is always possible that some characteristics of a specific face result in unintended attention to it, e.g., similarity to a person that the subject knows. Moreover, there is always the possibility of classification error in distinguishing target images from non-targets. By scoring the existing clusters in the optimizer module, we aim to gather evidence for each face to validate the target relevance of the selected images in the previous iterations.

To score the clusters marked as target-relevant, in each iteration, our display model considers samples from the neighborhood of those clusters (in terms of Euclidean distance). Therefore, the images generated from these samples can be further evaluated by the human in the following iteration. Sampling this neighborhood also helps the system to move gently toward the target face in the latent space of the generative model. On the other hand, we should always explore the latent space to check if other faces are more relevant to the target mental face image. In other words, we keep a balance between exploring the latent space and exploiting the acquired knowledge. Furthermore, the proportion of points from existing clusters to those from non-target regions should satisfy the oddball paradigm's criteria to maximize the probability of eliciting P300 ERP [31].

Having the mentioned conditions, our display model samples new points at the beginning of each iteration as follows: At each iteration, based on the number of formed clusters, at most, m clusters are selected with a probability proportional to their score, where m is set to 5 in our model. Afterward, one point is sampled from each of these clusters according to a normal distribution. These points constitute target-like samples. All the remaining points (batch size minus m) will be sampled uniformly from the latent space to ensure exploring the unexplored regions.

5 Experiments

5.1 Data Collection and Preprocessing

We invited 17 subjects to participate in our study, of which 9 were male, and the rest were female. Their ages ranged from 18 to 36 years, with a mean age of 26.3 years. Data from the first 4 subjects were used to calibrate the hyper-parameters, and the model was evaluated on the other 13. EEG signals were recorded using 32 Ag/AgCl BrainProducts active electrodes, positioned at equidistant locations of the 10–20 system. The sampling frequency was set to 1000 Hz; however, the data were decimated afterward by a factor of 4 to speed up the process of classifier training. A high-pass FIR filter at 0.05 Hz was applied to the signal to remove the DC offset. Next, the data were time-locked to the stimulus onset and segmented into 1 s segments containing 800 ms post and 200 ms pre-stimulus signal, used as the baseline. Finally, the signals were z-score normalized to keep a mean of zero and their amplitude between zero and one.

5.2   Experimental Setup

To evaluate our framework, we designed a two-phase experiment: first, we train the EEG classifier for each subject (*the classifier task*) and subsequently we evaluate the performance of our closed-loop system in a mental face image retrieval task (*the closed-loop task*). Both tasks follow an *RSVP* paradigm in which images are shown sequentially at the same spatial location and high presentation rate. To maximize the probability of eliciting P300 by seeing faces that resemble the target mental face image, we keep the ratio of target images to the rest of images low. In the classifier task, the target image is the exact face image that is presented to the subject at the beginning of the task, while in the closed-loop task, it is defined as images that elicit target-dependent ERPs in the subject's EEG responses.

The Classifier Task. At the beginning of the first task, a target face image is presented to the subjects for 10 s. Afterward, they are shown a sequence of 10 RSVP blocks; each contains 100 images, from which 5 are exactly the same as the initial face image. Other images are arbitrary face images (different from the target face). All the images are cropped to remove the irrelevant background. The participants are asked to look for the target image and silently count its occurrences. The duration for presenting each image is 300 ms, and there is a 10 s rest between every two blocks. This process is repeated 4 times for 4 different target images to collect a total of 4000 EEG segments to train the classifier.

The Closed-Loop Task. The second task is designed to evaluate the closed-loop system. At the beginning of this section, a face image is presented to the subjects. However, unlike the first task, the model is not initially aware of this target face and it is not necessarily included in the images presented to the participants afterward. As the participants remember the initially presented face, they create a mental image of it which will be the target mental face image that the model should retrieve. The participants are asked to look for similar[2] (and not the same) faces to the target face. Presentation of the target face is followed by a sequence of at most 30 RSVP blocks. Each block contains 40 images generated by the generative module. During each RSVP block, the model evaluates the subjects' interest in each of the presented images. Based on that evaluation, the target-relevant faces are selected and clustered as described in Sect. 4.3. Each cluster's score is defined by its number of members and if a pre-defined score is reached for one of the clusters, the model stops and announces the result as the face image generated from the centroid of that cluster. If the model is not confident enough for any of the clusters, it breaks the loop after 30 iterations and returns the face corresponding to the centroid of the cluster with the highest score as the final result.

---

[2] Similarity here is subjective and the subjects decide by themselves whether a face is similar to the target face or not.

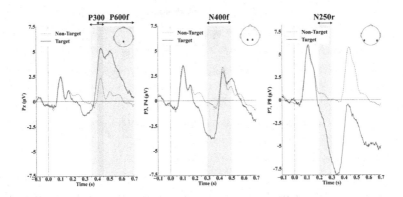

Fig. 3. An averaged ERP taken from **(a)** Pz electrode with P300 (green) and P600f (yellow) windows, **(b)** P3 and P4 electrodes with N400f window, and **(c)** P7 and P8 electrodes with N250r window, showing evoked responses to target faces (solid lines) and non-target faces (dashed lines). (Color figure online)

6   Results

6.1   Event-Related Potential Analysis

ERP analysis was conducted to verify that target-relevant features modulate EEG signals differently compared to non-targets. For this evaluation, we only considered the data collected for the *classifier* task, as it explicitly includes target trials. ERPs recorded from the Pz, P3-P4, and P7-P8 electrodes to images labeled as target and non-target were averaged separately for each participant (all trials shown in Fig. 3). The electrodes were chosen based on where the P600f, N400f, and N250r ERPs can be detected respectively (more details on Sect. 2.1). We perform a series of paired-sample t-tests to assess the statistical significance of variations between target and non-target EEG responses. The results demonstrate a significant increase in the amplitude of the recorded signal related to target images, as compared to non-target images, at the Pz electrode within the time frames of 350–450 ms (P300 window) and 400–700 ms (P600f window) after stimulus onset (Fig. 3a (green); $t(24) = 1.81$, p-value $= 0.04$ and Fig. 3a (yellow); $t(24) = 2.24$, p-value $= 0.02$). The results of additional tests on the average amplitude between 300–500 ms and 200–300 ms for channels P3–P4, and P7–P8, indicate a significant decrease in the amplitude of the recorded signals for target trials in comparison to non-target trials (Fig. 3b; $t(24) = -2.31$, p-value $= 0.02$ and Fig. 3c; $t(24) = -6.9$, p-values < 0.001), confirming the presence of N400f and N250r, respectively.

6.2   EEG Classifier Performance

To validate that the classifier distinguishes between target and non-target EEG responses, we calculated the area under its ROC curve (AUC) when trained on

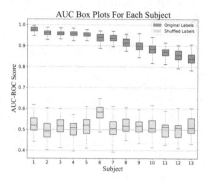

Fig. 4. Boxplot of AUC scores for each participant with scores for random baselines computed using label permutation.

the data collected during the *classifier* task. We then performed a permutation test to examine whether AUC scores are significantly higher than chance. To get the random baselines, the classifier was trained with 50 different random permutations of the labels and the AUC scores were calculated. The performance of the classifier was assessed on true labels over 50 different train-test splits of the data (Fig. 4), confirming that the classifier performed significantly better than random baselines for all the subjects (p-value < 0.001). All classifiers had an average AUC of more than 0.84 and 8 out of 13 had an average AUC of more than 0.9, suggesting that the classifier can distinguish between the signals corresponding to relevant and irrelevant images to the target mental image.

6.3   Closed-Loop System Results

Finally, we evaluate the performance of our system for accurate mental face image retrieval. Figure 5a shows some examples of the final images obtained by our system in comparison with the target images. Comparing the images shows that many attributes such as age, gender, and skin tone are retrieved, resulting in similar images to the target ones. As the measure of similarity throughout the experiment is subjective, the model finds the face image that resembles the target face from the subject's point of view. Moreover, since the target image is only shown at the beginning of the experiment and not afterward during the experiment, forgetting the exact target face is possible. Therefore, evaluating whether the final image looks like the target face remains a challenging problem.

To qualitatively evaluate the results, we conducted an online survey similar to Spape et al. [17] with two tasks: a *free selection* task and an *explicit evaluation* task[3]. In the free selection task, for each target face presented in the experiments, all the estimated mental images by the model were placed among randomly generated faces to create a batch of 14 face images (each batch contained around

---

[3] 19 people participated in the survey from the autonomous systems division at KTH. Participants were not aware of the details of the study, particularly the results.

3–4 estimated mental images on average). For each target face image, the participants were asked to select all the face images that they thought resembled that target face. The results show that for each target a significant portion of total votes belongs to the estimated images by the model which means they were actually selected as similar to the target image (Fig. 5b). In the explicit evaluation task, for each pair of target and estimated face images, the participants were asked to score from 1 (not similar) to 7 (very similar) on how similar they think the two images are. As depicted in Fig. 5b, the average score is around 4.3 indicating a significant distance from random irrelevant images (score 1).

Quantitatively comparing the target and the estimated image by the model is challenging due to the subjective similarity metric (Sect. 7.2 for more details). We compared the model's estimated images and the target faces using two different methods: structural similarity index (SSIM) [42] and comparing Facenet [43] embedding vectors. The first method is based on the structural similarity index introduced by Wang et al. [42]. SSIM is a value between 0 and 1, measured between two images. The closer the value is to 1, the more similar the two images are. In the second method, face images are encoded in the embedding space of Facenet, a Googlenet architecture [44] pre-trained on VGGFace2 [45] and CASIA-WebFace [46] datasets. Then, Euclidean distance is measured between the two embedding vectors to determine their similarity. Smaller Euclidean distance indicates more similar face images. For both methods, 1000 random face images were generated using our generative model. Indices are then calculated for the model outcomes or the randomly generated images and the corresponding target face image. The results for both methods are illustrated in Fig. 5c. SSIM compares the luminance, contrast, and structure in two images and it mainly determines whether the query image is the same as the reference image with some deviations due to artifacts. Therefore, although the two faces might look similar, the SSIM value can be small if they are not the exact same images. Our results (Fig. 5c, left figure) show that out of 25 estimated images by the model, 20 have an SSIM value more than the median of randomly generated images. For the second approach, we used a Facenet architecture pre-trained on specific face image datasets. Therefore, the model has only learned to distinguish between different facial attributes based on their availability in those datasets. Since it is not guaranteed that facial attributes are uniformly distributed in the datasets used, the trained network is biased toward specific attributes. As a result, the distance between the final embedding vectors is based on the attributes that the network has learned better, regardless of their importance with respect to the concept of facial similarity. Nevertheless, 17 out of 25 of the Facenet embedding vectors of our model's estimated mental images have an L2 distance smaller than the median of randomly generated images to the corresponding target image. These results show that despite the fact that the employed network for evaluation has not been trained on our data, our proposed framework is able to generate face images that resemble the actual mental face image.

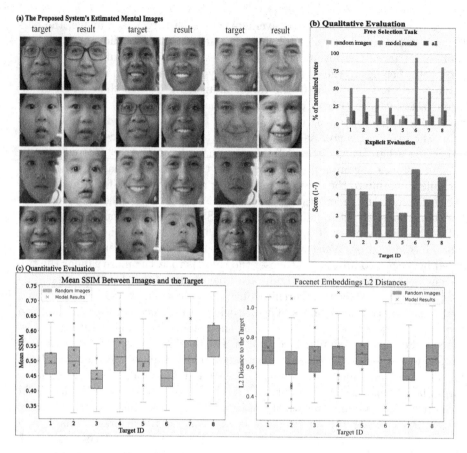

Fig. 5. (a) Retrieved mental images and their corresponding target faces; (b) Results of qualitative evaluations: the free selection task (top) and the explicit evaluation (bottom); (c) Results of quantitative evaluation: the structural similarity index (left) and comparison of Facenet embeddings (right).

7   Discussion and Future Work

We proposed a closed-loop BCI framework that employs EEG signals as relevance feedback to retrieve the most likely mental face image in a person's mind. To validate our model, we collected EEG responses to artificial face images generated by a GAN from 13 participants. Using an EEG classifier, we classified EEG signals and found relevant images to the target mental image. These relevant images were then clustered to locate the neighborhoods in the generative model's latent space containing relevant information about the target mental image. In each iteration, the participant unconsciously voted –with their EEG signals– on these neighborhoods to choose the one that resulted in images closer to the target mental image. The final mental image was produced by the centroid of the cluster with a number of votes above a pre-defined threshold or with the highest number of votes when the maximum number of iterations was reached.

7.1   Summary of Contributions

This work proposes a closed-loop framework to condition a generative model with brain activity and retrieve mental face images. The generative model allows the system to produce novel images that closely resemble the actual mental image. Previous works only use a fixed set of previously randomly generated images, averaging the latent vectors corresponding to attended images in order to estimate the mental image [16,17]. In contrast, we close the interaction loop by using attended images to sample new images for the next iteration. This informed sampling method helps the convergence and overall accuracy of the system. Our framework creates images that closely resemble the actual target image, retrieving its semantic properties (e.g., skin tone, gender, age). We reconstruct the mental image as accurately as possible and we optimize this iterative process by using an informed sampling method that exploits information about the target gained, while exploring unvisited regions of the latent space.

7.2   Implications and Limitations

Although we are not limiting the attributes of the retrieved mental face image, e.g., skin tone and hair color, we do not claim that our model retrieves the exact same face image the user imagines. Since the user defines the similarity metric, the final estimated image depends on the attributes they considered for defining the similarity. To confirm this assumption, after each experiment, we asked the subjects how they considered a presented face image similar to the target face. We observed that the result indeed had the mentioned attributes in common with the target image. Additionally, we noticed that non-face features like face angle and smile affected the final result. However, the effect is unavoidable if attending to an image is the only condition for selecting it as relevant to the target image.

The subjectiveness of the similarity metric also affects the optimization algorithm since it is unclear how the semantic similarity translates to the Euclidean distance between latent vectors. This is why we only consider the very close neighborhood of each latent variable (in terms of the Euclidean distance) to have information about the target mental image. Furthermore, the subjective nature of the similarity metric makes the evaluation of similarity between the final result and the target image also subjective. A considerable variance was also observed in the survey responses to explicit evaluation task for each pair of estimated and target face images, suggesting that people's opinions on how similar two faces are may differ quite significantly.

As previously mentioned, generative models like GANs turn the discrete search space of image databases into the continuous space of latent variables and mitigate the problem of finite alternatives in image databases. However, they are still limited by the distribution of images on which they had been trained. This limitation means that if the target mental image does not fall in the learned distribution, its retrieval is not straightforward[4]. The structure of

---

[4] We acknowledge recent work on GAN inversion for out-of-distribution images [47].

the latent space also affects the search algorithm. Precisely, the Euclidean distance between latent vectors does not necessarily determine the similarity of resulting images. Therefore, the search in the latent space for relevant latent vectors can only take place locally. As a result of this local search, we do not claim that our optimizer finds the global optimal latent variable, which results in the exact target mental image of the subject. Instead, we leverage the available local information and assess it by getting EEG feedback from the user.

A further factor that might affect the final result is the visual task design. As described in Sect. 5.2, our visual task follows an RSVP paradigm, and the target face image is only shown to the subject at the beginning of the experiment and is not available during the task. The reason for not showing the target face throughout the task is to retrieve the imagined mental image only existing in the subject's mind. However, this choice can result in the user forgetting the exact target face and instead having some self-made image of it in mind. Therefore, the final result would be similar to the subject's own mental image and not the presented target image. Moreover, since face images are both randomly generated and presented sequentially, it is possible that the subject attends to an image only because they have seen them previously in the sequence or the presented face resembles a familiar face to the subject irrelevant to the task. By scoring the relevant clusters throughout several iterations, we hoped to minimize the effect of this problem on the final result, although it cannot be totally omitted.

7.3   Future Work

Our approach searches the latent space for the imagined mental face image, using a binary feedback signal from EEG data. Previous works have focused on retrieving the visual stimulus directly from brain activity by finding and using discriminative encodings with generative decoders. They show that there is information about the features of the visual stimulus encoded in the brain activity, which can provide the search in the latent space with additional information in order to achieve improved mental image estimation and convergence time.

The communication between the human subject and the computer in BCI is traditionally built by classifying the user's brain activity into a (predefined) discrete set of instructions and commands. While some tasks can be accomplished through discrete instructions (e.g., spelling [48–50], moving cursors or robotic arm with specific directions), others are intrinsically continuous (e.g., movement trajectory prediction, user attention control in neurofeedback applications, retrieving mental images from the user's memory). Face image retrieval is an example of the former class of tasks, due to the continuous nature of different characteristics of individual faces (e.g., skin tone, eye color, the shape of eyes). Our proposed method can possibly be extended for solving other continuous tasks using BCI systems. The general problem can be formulated as interpreting the latent space of a generative model as the space of all possible user intents [15]. Since this space is continuous, it is theoretically possible to generate any command which falls within this space, using an appropriate optimization algorithm. This opens for building better interaction systems, such as predicting human movement or intention in human-robot interaction tasks [51–53].

References

1. Pearson, J., Naselaris, T., Holmes, E.A., Kosslyn, S.M.: Mental imagery: functional mechanisms and clinical applications. Trends Cogn. Sci. **19**(10), 590–602 (2015)
2. Ganis, G.: Mental imagery. In: Ramachandran, V. (ed.) Encyclopedia of Human Behavior, 2nd edn., pp. 601–607. Academic Press, San Diego (2012)
3. Pearson, J.: The human imagination: the cognitive neuroscience of visual mental imagery. Nat. Rev. Neurosci. **20**(10), 624–634 (2019)
4. Du, C., Du, C., He, H.: Sharing deep generative representation for perceived image reconstruction from human brain activity. In: 2017 International Joint Conference on Neural Networks (IJCNN), pp. 1049–1056. IEEE (2017)
5. Zhang, X., Chen, X., Dong, M., Liu, H., Ge, C., Yao, L.: Multi-task generative adversarial learning on geometrical shape reconstruction from EEG brain signals. arXiv preprint arXiv:1907.13351 (2019)
6. Nishimoto, S., Vu, A.T., Naselaris, T., Benjamini, Y., Yu, B., Gallant, J.L.: Reconstructing visual experiences from brain activity evoked by natural movies. Curr. Biol. **21**(19), 1641–1646 (2011)
7. Shen, G., Horikawa, T., Majima, K., Kamitani, Y.: Deep image reconstruction from human brain activity. PLoS Comput. Biol. **15**(1), e1006633 (2019)
8. Gaziv, G., et al.: Self-supervised natural image reconstruction and large-scale semantic classification from brain activity. Neuroimage **254**, 119121 (2022)
9. Naselaris, T., Prenger, R.J., Kay, K.N., Oliver, M., Gallant, J.L.: Bayesian reconstruction of natural images from human brain activity. Neuron **63**(6), 902–915 (2009)
10. Kavasidis, I., Palazzo, S., Spampinato, C., Giordano, D., Shah, M.: Brain2image: converting brain signals into images. In: Proceedings of the 25th ACM International Conference on Multimedia, pp. 1809–1817 (2017)
11. Fang, Y., Geman, D.: Experiments in mental face retrieval. In: Kanade, T., Jain, A., Ratha, N.K. (eds.) AVBPA 2005. LNCS, vol. 3546, pp. 637–646. Springer, Heidelberg (2005). https://doi.org/10.1007/11527923_66
12. Ferecatu, M., Geman, D.: A statistical framework for image category search from a mental picture. IEEE Trans. Pattern Anal. Mach. Intell. **31**(6), 1087–1101 (2008)
13. Pohlmeyer, E.A., Wang, J., Jangraw, D.C., Lou, B., Chang, S.F., Sajda, P.: Closing the loop in cortically-coupled computer vision: a brain-computer interface for searching image databases. J. Neural Eng. **8**(3), 036025 (2011)
14. Uśćumlić, M., Chavarriaga, R., Millán, J.D.R.: An iterative framework for EEG-based image search: robust retrieval with weak classifiers. PloS One **8**(8), e72018 (2013)
15. Ukkonen, A., Joona, P., Ruotsalo, T.: Generating images instead of retrieving them: Relevance feedback on generative adversarial networks. In: Proceedings of the 43rd International ACM SIGIR Conference on Research and Development in Information Retrieval, pp. 1329–1338 (2020)
16. Kangassalo, L., Spapé, M., Ruotsalo, T.: Neuroadaptive modelling for generating images matching perceptual categories. Sci. Rep. **10**(1), 1–10 (2020)
17. Spape, M., Davis, K., Kangassalo, L., Ravaja, N., Sovijarvi-Spape, Z., Ruotsalo, T.: Brain-computer interface for generating personally attractive images. IEEE Trans. Affect. Comput. **1**(1) (2021)

18. Luck, S.J.: Event-related potentials (2012)
19. Rugg, M.D., Curran, T.: Event-related potentials and recognition memory. Trends Cogn. Sci. **11**(6), 251–257 (2007)
20. Smith, M.E.: Neurophysiological manifestations of recollective experience during recognition memory judgments. J. Cogn. Neurosci. **5**(1), 1–13 (1993)
21. Johnson, J.S., Olshausen, B.A.: The earliest EEG signatures of object recognition in a cued-target task are postsensory. J. Vis. **5**(4), 2–2 (2005)
22. Bruce, V., Young, A.: Understanding face recognition. Br. J. Psychol. **77**(3), 305–327 (1986)
23. Gosling, A., Eimer, M.: An event-related brain potential study of explicit face recognition. Neuropsychologia **49**(9), 2736–2745 (2011)
24. Touryan, J., Gibson, L., Horne, J.H., Weber, P.: Real-time measurement of face recognition in rapid serial visual presentation. Front. Psychol. **2**, 42 (2011)
25. Caharel, S., Poiroux, S., Bernard, C., Thibaut, F., Lalonde, R., Rebai, M.: ERPS associated with familiarity and degree of familiarity during face recognition. Int. J. Neurosci. **112**(12), 1499–1512 (2002)
26. Schweinberger, S.R., Pfütze, E.M., Sommer, W.: Repetition priming and associative priming of face recognition: evidence from event-related potentials. J. Exp. Psychol. Learn. Mem. Cogn. **21**(3), 722 (1995)
27. Schweinberger, S.R., Huddy, V., Burton, A.M.: N250r: a face-selective brain response to stimulus repetitions. NeuroReport **15**(9), 1501–1505 (2004)
28. Schweinberger, S.R., Burton, A.M.: Covert recognition and the neural system for face processing. Cortex **39**(1), 9–30 (2003)
29. Bentin, S., Deouell, L.Y.: Structural encoding and identification in face processing: ERP evidence for separate mechanisms. Cogn. Neuropsychol. **17**(1–3), 35–55 (2000)
30. Eimer, M.: The face-specific N170 component reflects late stages in the structural encoding of faces. NeuroReport **11**(10), 2319–2324 (2000)
31. Courchesne, E., Hillyard, S.A., Galambos, R.: Stimulus novelty, task relevance and the visual evoked potential in man. Electroencephalogr. Clin. Neurophysiol. **39**(2), 131–143 (1975)
32. Doersch, C.: Tutorial on variational autoencoders. arXiv preprint arXiv:1606.05908 (2016)
33. Kingma, D.P., Welling, M.: Auto-encoding variational bayes. arXiv preprint arXiv:1312.6114 (2013)
34. Goodfellow, I.J., et al.: Generative adversarial nets. In: NIPS (2014)
35. Mirza, M., Osindero, S.: Conditional generative adversarial nets. arXiv preprint arXiv:1411.1784 (2014)
36. Tirupattur, P., Rawat, Y.S., Spampinato, C., Shah, M.: ThoughtViz: visualizing human thoughts using generative adversarial network. In: Proceedings of the 26th ACM International Conference on Multimedia, pp. 950–958 (2018)
37. Khare, S., Choubey, R.N., Amar, L., Udutalapalli, V.: NeuroVision: perceived image regeneration using cProGAN. Neural Comput. Appl. **34**(8), 5979–5991 (2022)
38. Craik, A., He, Y., Contreras-Vidal, J.L.: Deep learning for electroencephalogram (EEG) classification tasks: a review. J. Neural Eng. **16**(3), 031001 (2019)
39. Karras, T., Laine, S., Aila, T.: A style-based generator architecture for generative adversarial networks. In: Proceedings of the IEEE/CVF Conference on Computer Vision and Pattern Recognition, pp. 4401–4410 (2019)

40. Karras, T., Laine, S., Aittala, M., Hellsten, J., Lehtinen, J., Aila, T.: Analyzing and improving the image quality of StyleGAN. In: Proceedings of the IEEE/CVF Conference on Computer Vision and Pattern Recognition, pp. 8110–8119 (2020)

41. Lawhern, V.J., Solon, A.J., Waytowich, N.R., Gordon, S.M., Hung, C.P., Lance, B.J.: EEGNet: a compact convolutional neural network for eeg-based brain-computer interfaces. J. Neural Eng. **15**(5), 056013 (2018)

42. Wang, Z., Bovik, A.C., Sheikh, H.R., Simoncelli, E.P.: Image quality assessment: from error visibility to structural similarity. IEEE Trans. Image Process. **13**(4), 600–612 (2004)

43. Schroff, F., Kalenichenko, D., Philbin, J.: FaceNet: a unified embedding for face recognition and clustering. In: Proceedings of the IEEE Conference on Computer Vision and Pattern Recognition, pp. 815–823 (2015)

44. Szegedy, C., et al.: Going deeper with convolutions. In: Proceedings of the IEEE Conference on Computer Vision and Pattern Recognition, pp. 1–9 (2015)

45. Cao, Q., Shen, L., Xie, W., Parkhi, O.M., Zisserman, A.: VGGFace2: a dataset for recognising faces across pose and age. In: 2018 13th IEEE International Conference on Automatic Face & Gesture Recognition (FG 2018), pp. 67–74. IEEE (2018)

46. Yi, D., Lei, Z., Liao, S., Li, S.Z.: Learning face representation from scratch. arXiv preprint arXiv:1411.7923 (2014)

47. Xia, W., Zhang, Y., Yang, Y., Xue, J.H., Zhou, B., Yang, M.H.: GAN inversion: a survey. IEEE Trans. Pattern Anal. Mach. Intell. (2022)

48. Chen, X., Wang, Y., Nakanishi, M., Gao, X., Jung, T.P., Gao, S.: High-speed spelling with a noninvasive brain-computer interface. Proc. Natl. Acad. Sci. **112**(44), E6058–E6067 (2015)

49. Furdea, A., et al.: An auditory oddball (P300) spelling system for brain-computer interfaces. Psychophysiology **46**(3), 617–625 (2009)

50. Kübler, A., Furdea, A., Halder, S., Hammer, E.M., Nijboer, F., Kotchoubey, B.: A brain-computer interface controlled auditory event-related potential (P300) spelling system for locked-in patients. Ann. N. Y. Acad. Sci. **1157**(1), 90–100 (2009)

51. Song, D., et al.: Predicting human intention in visual observations of hand/object interactions. In: 2013 IEEE International Conference on Robotics and Automation, pp. 1608–1615. IEEE (2013)

52. Butepage, J., Black, M.J., Kragic, D., Kjellstrom, H.: Deep representation learning for human motion prediction and classification. In: Proceedings of the IEEE Conference on Computer Vision and Pattern Recognition, pp. 6158–6166 (2017)

53. Bütepage, J., Kjellström, H., Kragic, D.: Anticipating many futures: online human motion prediction and generation for human-robot interaction. In: 2018 IEEE International Conference on Robotics and Automation (ICRA), pp. 4563–4570. IEEE (2018)

Analysis of Visual Patterns Through the EEG Signal: Color Study

Ana Rita Teixeira[1,2]([✉]) [iD] and Anabela Gomes[3,4] [iD]

[1] Polytechnic Institute of Coimbra- ESEC, UNICID, Coimbra, Portugal
ateixeira@ua.pt
[2] Institute of Electronics and Informatics Engineering of Aveiro, University of Aveiro, Aveiro, Portugal
[3] Polytechnic Institute of Coimbra- ISEC, Coimbra, Portugal
[4] CISUC—Department of Informatics Engineering, University of Coimbra, Coimbra, Portugal

Abstract. This study quantifies the amplitude and latency variability of the visual pattern evoked potential (P100) using the MUSE device and compares this variability between two populations: color blind versus normal eyes.

The main objective of this work is to identify the impact of color on brain waves in color-blind and non-color-blind individuals. Thus, P100 wave was used and the amplitude and latency generated by each visual stimulus was analyzed. The results show that different colors present different amplitudes and latencies in the two samples and between colors. The Wilcoxon test was used to compare the samples. In both samples, blue and red color with 100% saturation present higher amplitudes. Blue amplitudes value is statistically different considering the two samples. The blue amplitude is higher in color-blind individuals, meaning that it causes greater stimulation in brain activity. On the other hand, although the amplitude of the red color is high, it is similar in both samples. Yellow, Blue, Yellow and Saturated Green present discrepant values of P100 wave amplitude in both samples. Amplitudes are much higher in non-color-blind individuals than in color-blind individuals. According to this study, different colors can cause different amplitudes and latency in P100 waves, considering color blind and non-color-blind people. In addition, our findings also confirm previous studies that indicate that energy in theta and alpha bands can be used to discriminate some colors. In summary, this study is useful to find metrics to classify colors helping in marketing strategies and design typography. The P100 wave used in this kind of strategies is a novelty in the literature and can be considered for future studies.

1 Introduction

Nowadays, with the accelerated development of technology and the long exposure of the population to the screens, color and its use has begun to play a significant role. Color perception is one of the most important cognitive features of human brain. Different colors lead to different cognitive activities and different mental arousal levels as revealed by power spectral density obtained from EEG signals [1]. There are several studies in the literature regarding color in different research areas, such as psychology [2, 3], neuromarketing [1, 3–6] and design [7, 8]. Color has aesthetic value, and it also

D. D. Schmorrow and C. M. Fidopiastis (Eds.): HCII 2023, LNAI 14019, pp. 46–53, 2023.
https://doi.org/10.1007/978-3-031-35017-7_4

influences cognition, emotion, and behavior. Cool colors (green, blue, and violet) are associated with being comfortable, relaxing, peaceful, and calming, thus reducing stress and anxiety levels. On the other hand, warm colors (red, yellow, and orange) are more arousing, which can stimulate human feelings and activate people. Neutral colors have less emotional content and, thus, lesser psychological impact [2]. Studies have revealed that colored multimedia learning materials have a positive effect on learner's emotion and learning where it was assessed by subjective/objective measurements [3]. Color has an important role in object recognition and visual memory [9]. Decoding color in the human brain is helpful to understand the mechanism of visual cognitive process and evaluate memory ability as well as to understand the impact that each color has in the human brain. Colors define our emotions and many times target our impulses and decisions. Therefore, picking the right colors will have a dramatic effect on the engagement results. Human feelings and moods are changeable overtime thus, every marketing manager should know the importance of colors and make their products or packaging accordingly [4]. The color is important in marketing and packaging industry, so, neuro-marketing research, based on color stimuli is considered to be an important tool for market research. Brain-Computer Interaction (BCI) technology can be used in several areas and has recently gained increased interest with diverse applications in the area of Human Computer Interaction (HCI). The color is one of the central elements in perceiving information that, when properly used, can provide better readability and understanding of the information to be communicated. In this sense, this multidisciplinary work (Theory of Visual Perception, HCI and cognitive neuroscience) examines how the brain processes color information using EEG technology. So, BCI technology is used in neuromarketing to study the brain's responses to marketing stimuli [10].

This paper is organized as follows: First, the introduction of the problem is done; second, the methodology (samples, protocol and devices) is presented, after which we have the results, and finally we present the discussions and some conclusions.

2 Methodology

2.1 Sample

The current study included 25 people, aged between 18 and 60 years, 12 women and 13 men. Of the 25 participants, 5 are people who have some type of color blindness (2 have high-grade deuteranopia color blindness, 1 has color blindness of the same type at a moderate degree, and 2 have tritanopia-type color blindness in a moderate degree) and the remaining 20 do not have any degree of deficiency in color distinction.

2.2 Protocol

The experimental protocol based on [12], consisted of viewing 10 distinct colors on the screen of a PC interspersed with the gray color. Initially, the colors of the RGB model with 100% saturation (S.) were presented. Subsequently, the same shades of color were presented, with 50% saturation. The duration time was 2 s in gray and only 1 s in the remaining colors, making a total of 21 colors and 32 s of viewing. The protocol starts with grey color, then the other colors and between them the grey color is shown for 2 s and the protocol finishes with the grey color. In the following table 1 it is possible to check the order of the colors used between grey color:

Table 1. Designation Color, where S. means Saturated

# Color	RGB	Name	# Color	RGB	Name
2	(0; 0; 255)	S. Blue	12	(62; 62; 194)	Blue
4	(255; 255; 0)	S.Yellow	14	(193; 194; 62)	Yellow
6	(255; 0; 255)	S.Violet	16	(218; 150; 218)	Violet
8	(255; 0; 0)	S. Red	18	(194; 62; 62)	Red
10	(0; 255; 0)	S.Green	20	(62; 194; 62)	Green

2.3 Device

To carry out this project the BCI device used is an EEG acquisition equipment, in the form of a headband, called InteraXon's MUSE 2 (InteraXon, 2018) designed to be placed on the front of the head, being very practical, lightweight and adjustable [11]. With a sampling of 256 Hz, the EGG system consists of 5 dry sensors: 2 on the forehead (F7 and AF8), 2 behind the ears (TP9 And TP10) and a reference sensor for calibration that is in the center of the forehead (FPZ) (Muse), Fig. 1.

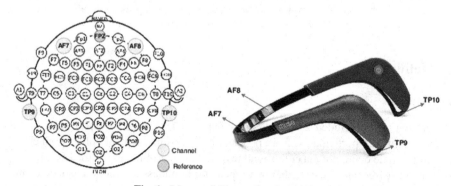

Fig. 1. Muse and Electrodes placement

3 Results

The main goal of this work is to identify the impact of color on brain waves in colorblind and non-color-blind individuals. Thus, the data examined in this study refers to acquisitions of the P100 wave (Fig. 2), namely, amplitude and latency, generated by each visual stimulus.

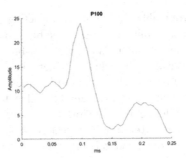

Fig. 2. P100 wave

Aspect of selective attention such as task difficulty will affect the latency and amplitude of the P100. For example, if a task is more difficult, it will take longer for the P100 to occur and the amplitude will be higher. On the other hand, if the task is easier, it will take less time for the P100 to occur and the amplitude will be lower. Stimulus encoding also affects latency and amplitude of the P100. If the stimulus is more novel or requires more effort to encode, it will take longer for the P100 to occur and the amplitude will be higher. If the stimulus is more familiar or requires less effort to encode, it will take less time for the P100 to occur and the amplitude will be lower. This effort can be seen in the P100 wave, which is a component of the ERP (event-related potential) that is generated in response to a stimulus. This wave is typically seen in the range of 80–120 ms and is thought to represent the selection and allocation of attentional resources. Therefore, increased task difficulty may lead to increased latency and amplitude of the P100 wave.

3.1 Amplitude

In Fig. 3, the P100 wave amplitudes are represented considering the color-blind individuals and non-color-blind individuals.

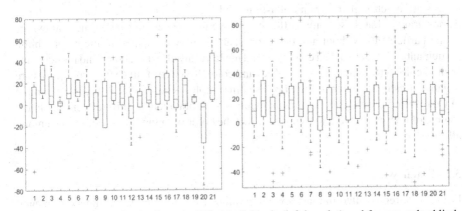

Fig. 3. P100 wave amplitudes for color-blind individuals (left boxplot) and for non-color-blind individuals (right boxplot) considering each color.

In both samples it is irrefutable that the most impacting color visually and which promotes significantly higher amplitude values is the blue color, with 100% saturation (Table 2). This amplitude value is slightly higher in color-blind individuals than in non-colored-blind individuals, meaning this causes greater stimulation in brain waves and can influence any decision-making. Then, in both samples the color 18 (Red) is the color with the highest impact on brain waves, and this value does not differ much in the two Samples. Color 6 (S. Violet), color 16 (Violet) and color 10 (S. Green) resulted in intermediate values, i. e., not in P100 wave high peaks, but were still indifferent, giving rise to values identical to each other and in both samples, as can be seen in the Table 2.

Table 2. Average values of the P100 wave amplitude along the color segment in the two Samples.

#	Color-Blind	Non-Color-Blind
2	23,49	18,03
4	1,98	10,11
5	11,86	11,08
8	−1,31	4,74
10	10,8	12,18
12	−1,4	13,47
14	3,96	15,17
16	11,29	12,19
18	17,63	16,05
20	−2,87	14,5

On the other hand, color 4 (S. Yellow), color 12 (Blue), color 14 (Yellow) and color 20 (Green), resulted in discrepant amplitude values of P100 wave in both samples. These figures are much higher in non-color-blind individuals than in color-blind individuals, demonstrating that these colors, effectively have the greatest impact on the brainwaves of the participants without any type of visual anomaly compared to the color - blind participants. There are in fact colors that did not have any effect in color blind participants, such as color 8 (S. Red), color 12 (Blue) and color 20 (Green), since the wave values are negative. Lastly the color which impacts both samples is color 8 (S. Red). In the sample of Color-blind Individuals, as already mentioned, it obtained negative effects and in the sample of non-color-blind individuals it was the color with the lowest amplitude among all.

3.2 Latency

In Fig. 4 is represented the latency color values for all colors along the experimental protocol.

Since latency is directly related to the response generated by the stimulus, the higher the latency value, the more amplitude occurs in the process of responding to the stimulus.

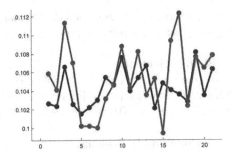

Fig. 4. Latency comparison between color-blind (grey) and non-color-blind (black) participants, considering the protocol colors (1–21)

In this sense, comparing the P100 wave latencies originated by each visual stimulus in the two samples, it can be concluded that there are no significant differences. It is, however, possible to highlight in non-color-blind individuals color 6 (S. Violet) with higher latency value compared to color-blind participants. On the other hand, color-blind participants obtained higher latency values in color 16 (Violet) and in color 20 (Green), these being the colors with the longest response time compared to the other sample.

3.3 Statistical Analysis

The Mann-Whitney U-test was used to compare the latency and amplitude between colors in the two groups of data, and the results showed that there was a statistically significant difference between some colors. This test is suitable for comparing two independent populations when the data is not normally distributed or when the variances of the two groups are not equal.

In this statistical analysis this test was chosen since only a small sample is available and the variable does not present a normal variation. In this sense, the hypotheses for the nonparametric test are presented as follows:

H0: No differences between colors
H1: Differences between colors

If the p-value obtained is lower than the alpha level of 0.05, which indicates that we can reject the null hypothesis (H0) and conclude that there are statistically significant differences between the two groups.

Color Amplitude in Color-Blind Individuals

In order to statistically analyze the amplitude of colors in the sample of color-blind individuals, it is immediately perceived, by the analysis of Fig. 1, that color 2 (S. Blue) is the one that has a more accentuated difference ($p < 0.05$) in relation to the others. Displays statistical differences with the remaining colors, except with color 16 (Violet) ($p = 0.076$). In addition, color 12 (Blue) is also incompatible with several colors, specifically, color 2 (S. Blue) ($p = 0.0006$), color 6 (S. Violet) ($p = 0.0294$) and color 18 (Red) ($p = 0.0154$). Color 6 (S. Violet) is statistically different with color 8 (S. Red) ($p = 0.033$), color 12 (Blue) ($p = 0.0294$) and color 20 (Green) ($p = 0.0083$). On the other hand, there are statistically compatible colors, such as color 4 (S. Yellow), color 10 (S. Green) and color 16 (Violet), meaning that no difference is present.

Color Latency in Color-Blind Individuals
The statistical differences in the sample of color-blind individuals regarding latency is not so evident, highlighting color 16 (Violet) that differs statistically from color 10 (S. Green) (p = 0.0024), color 12 (Blue) (p = 0.0032) and color 18 (Red) (p = 0.0012).

Color Amplitude in Non-Color-Blind Individuals
Statistically, the differences between colors in amplitude between non-color-blind individuals are not accentuated, and the greatest differences are in saturated colors. Color 4 (S. Yellow) differs with more colors such as: color 14 (Yellow) (p = 0.0147), color 16 (Violet) (p = 0.00226), color 18 (Red) (p = 0.0027) and color 20 (Green) (p = 0.0055).

In addition, color 2 (S. Blue) differs with color 4 (S. Yellow) (0.0017) and color 12 (Blue) (p = 0.041), as well as color 18 (Red) differs from color 6 (S. Violet) (p = 0.041) and color 12 (Blue) (p = 0.038). It should be noted that colors such as color 8 (S. Red) and color 10 (S. Green) are statistically compatible with all color tones.

Color Latency in Non-Color-Blind Individuals
In the statistical study of latency between colors, in non-color-blind individuals, it is evident that only color 10 (S. Green) is statistically incompatible with: color 2 (S. Blue) (p = 0.049), color 4 (S. Yellow) (p = 0.007), color 6 (S. Violet) (p = 0.0016), color 14 (Yellow) (p = 0.0068), color 18 (Red) (p = 0.00032) and color 20 (Green) (p = 0.0042).

4   Discussion and Conclusions

The main objective of this work is to identify the impact of color on brain waves in color-blind and non-color-blind individuals.

Blue amplitudes value is statistically different considering the two samples. The blue amplitude is higher in color-blind individuals, meaning that it causes greater stimulation in brain activity. On the other hand, although the amplitude of the red color is high, it is similar in both samples. Yellow, Blue, and Saturated Green present discrepant values of P100 wave amplitude in both samples. Amplitudes are much higher in non-color-blind individuals than in color-blind individuals. According to this study, different colors can cause different amplitudes and latency in P100 waves, considering color-blind and non-color-blind people. In summary, this study is useful to find metrics to classify colors helping in marketing strategies and design typography. The P100 wave used in this kind of strategies is a novelty in the literature and can be considered for future studies.

The results also suggest that there are differences in the brain responses to other colors. For example, S. Red, Blue, Yellow, S. Yellow and Green amplitudes are higher in non-color-blind individuals, while S. Blue amplitude is higher in color-blind individuals.

To further analyze this difference, the study should be conducted in a larger sample size, and a t-test should be applied to compare the amplitude of colors between color-blind and non-color-blind individuals. This test would enable us to determine whether the difference between the amplitude of colors is significant or not. Additionally, a multiple linear regression analysis could be applied in order to evaluate the effect of different factors (such as age, gender, etc.) on the amplitude of colors.

Overall, the results of this study suggest that color has a significant impact on brain activity and suggest that color-blind individuals have different responses to color than non-color-blind individuals. This has implications for the design of visual stimuli and may be used to tailor visual stimulation to better meet the needs of specific individuals.

References

1. Rakshit, A., Lahiri, R.: Discriminating different color from EEG signals using interval-type 2 fuzzy space classifier (a neuro-marketing study on the effect of color to cognitive state). In: 1st IEEE International Conference on Power Electronics, Intelligent Control and Energy Systems, ICPEICES 2016, February 201. https://doi.org/10.1109/ICPEICES.2016.7853388

2. Clarke, T., Costall, A.: The emotional connotations of color: a qualitative investigation. Color Res. Appl. **33**(5), 406–410 (2008). https://doi.org/10.1002/COL.20435

3. Chai, M.T., et al.: Exploring EEG effective connectivity network in estimating influence of color on emotion and memory. Front. Neuroinform. **13**, 66 (2019). https://doi.org/10.3389/FNINF.2019.00066/BIBTEX

4. Haider Ali, S.R.K., Khan, Y., Shah, M.: Color psychology in marketing. J. Bus. Tour.**4**(1), 183–190 (2021). https://doi.org/10.34260/JBT.V4I1.99

5. Yoto, A., Katsuura, T., Iwanaga, K., Shimomura, Y.: Effects of object color stimuli on human brain activities in perception and attention referred to EEG alpha band response. J. Physiol. Anthropol. **26**(3), 373–379 (2007). https://doi.org/10.2114/JPA2.26.373

6. Wilms, L., Oberfeld, D.: Color and emotion: effects of hue, saturation, and brightness. Psychol. Res. **82**(5), 896–914 (2017). https://doi.org/10.1007/s00426-017-0880-8

7. Ko, Y.H., Shen, I.H., Lee, D.S.: Color combinations of visual display terminal (VDT) icon on user preferences and EEG response. Percept. Mot .Skills **110**(2), 411–428 (2010). https://doi.org/10.2466/PMS.110.2.411-428

8. Wang, Y., Wang, S., Xu, M.: The function of color and structure based on EEG features in landscape recognition. Int. J. Environ. Res. Public Health **18**(9), 4866 (2021). https://doi.org/10.3390/IJERPH18094866

9. Che, X., Zheng, Y., Chen, X., Song, S., Li, S.: Decoding color visual working memory from EEG signals using graph convolutional neural networks. Int. J. Neural Syst. **32**(2), 2250003 (2022). https://doi.org/10.1142/S0129065722500034.

10. Al-Nafjan, A.: Feature selection of EEG signals in neuromarketing. PeerJ Comput. Sci. **8**, e944 (2022). https://doi.org/10.7717/PEERJ-CS.944

11. Krigolson, O.E., Williams, C.C., Norton, A., Hassall, C.D., Colino, F.L.: Choosing MUSE: validation of a low-cost, portable EEG system for ERP research. Front. Neurosci. **11**(Mar), 109 (2017). https://doi.org/10.3389/FNINS.2017.00109/BIBTEX

12. D'Andrade, R.G., Romney, A.K.: A quantitative model for transforming reflectance spectra into the Munsell color space using cone sensitivity functions and opponent process weights. Proc. Natl. Acad. Sci. U S A **100**(10), 6281–6286 (2003). https://doi.org/10.1073/PNAS.103 1827100/ASSET/19338334-3275-4800-A5F5-BC9D084FB470/ASSETS/GRAPHIC/PQ1 031827006.JPEG

Neuroergonomics, Physiological Measurement, and Human Performance

Using Eye Tracking to Measure User Engagement with a Decision Aid

Doaa Alrefaei[1]([✉]), Lidan Zhang[1], Gaayathri Sankar[1], Soussan Djamasbi[1],
Bengisu Tulu[1], Carlie Flanagan[1], Adam Kalayjian[1], Connie Ge[2], Camarlin Franco[2],
Shazeb Meraj[2], and Susanne Muehlschlegel[3]

[1] Worcester Polytechnic Institute, Worcester, MA 01609, USA
{Dalrefaei,lzhang11,gsankar,djamasbi,bengisu,ceflanagan,
ankalayjian}@wpi.edu
[2] Department of Neurology, University of Massachusetts Chan Medical School, Worcester,
MA 01655, USA
{Geconnie.ge,camarlin.franco,shazeb.meraj}@umassmed.edu
[3] Departments of Neurology, Anesthesiology/Critical Care and Surgery, University of
Massachusetts Chan Medical School, Worcester, MA 01655, USA
Susanne.Muehlschlegel@umassmemorial.org

Abstract. Eye tracking has become the gold standard in measuring human attention and information-processing behavior. As such, eye tracking in mixed-methods user experience (UX) research serves as an invaluable tool to learn about user needs and to create actionable insights for improving product and service design during the development cycle. Here, we discuss the iterative process that we used to improve the design of a decision aid (DA) developed to facilitate shared decision making. We explain the use of eye tracking during this process to examine how users processed the information provided by the DA. We also explain how we used eye tracking in a retrospective "think-aloud" protocol to gain insight about users' needs. Our results show that user reactions captured by eye tracking can not only be used to optimize design decisions but also to gather user feedback about their information processing needs.

Keywords: User-centered design · iterative formative studies · retrospective "think-aloud" · area of investigation (AOI) maps · user experience design and evaluation · shared decision-making tool

1 Introduction

Decision aids (DAs) refer to digital or paper-based tools designed to facilitate shared decision-making between patients or their surrogate decision-makers and clinicians (Barry & Edgman-Levitan, 2012). DAs provide information about a specific medical condition, possible treatment paths, as well as pros and cons of different treatment options clinicians (Barry & Edgman-Levitan, 2012). DAs typically support non-recurring context-specific health decisions to help select treatment options that are best aligned with patients' values and preferences. Therefore, the engagement design goal for DAs should focus on helping users to thoroughly process the provided information.

© The Author(s), under exclusive license to Springer Nature Switzerland AG 2023
D. D. Schmorrow and C. M. Fidopiastis (Eds.): HCII 2023, LNAI 14019, pp. 57–70, 2023.
https://doi.org/10.1007/978-3-031-35017-7_5

Designing successful user-centric systems requires a series of iterative formative user experience (UX) studies, each with the objective to discover insights for improving the design in the next development cycle. Because the most dominant sense for sighted people is vision, eye tracking offers an effective methodology for measuring how people process visual information provided in a DA. Eye-tracking devices provide a continuous and unobtrusive stream of moment-to-moment objective gaze data about a person's focus of attention on various parts of a visual display without placing an additional burden on users. Consequently, eye tracking has become the gold standard for investigations that rely heavily on measuring visual attention (Djamasbi, 2014; Gaffiero et al., 2019).

In this paper, we present how we evaluate and improve user engagement with a digital DA using a series of iterative formative studies. The main goal of the DA we examined, is to help surrogate decision makers of incapacitated neurocritically ill patients (with severe traumatic brain injury, hemorrhagic, or large ischemic strokes) to prepare for clinician-family meetings. During this meeting, surrogate decision makers are asked to make a goals-of-care decision. That is, surrogates must choose a treatment pathway between two options: survival or comfort. Choosing survival means that the patient will continue receiving invasive medical therapies. Choosing comfort care means that the patient will have life-sustaining measures withdrawn while the patient is provided with medications for comfort; the patient is allowed to pass away with as little suffering as possible (Barry & Edgman-Levitan, 2012; Goostrey et al., 2021; Muehlschlegel et al., 2020).

2   Improving the DA with Iterative Formative Studies

The information provided by the pilot digital DA in our study was originally displayed on 18 pages with a left navigation bar (Norouzi Nia et al., 2021). The DA explained the available treatment pathways, visualized an estimated prognosis for the patient via an icon array with data derived from validated disease-specific prediction models, summarized the information important for decision-making in a table to compare treatment options, and provided a worksheet to be completed by the surrogate as a value-clarification exercise. The DA also provided two real patient/family examples.

To improve the design of our DA, grounded in a user-centered approach to product development, we conducted a series of iterative formative UX studies (Djamasbi & Strong, 2019). In two of our four formative studies, we used eye tracking to understand how people process the DA's information. We also used eye tracking to conduct a retrospective "think-aloud" protocol after participants completed reviewing the DA at their own pace. Retrospective "think-aloud" protocol is particularly helpful in the assessment of complex systems because it allows participants to complete the task without interruption (Eger et al., 2007; Schiessl et al., 2003). Similar to generative UX research that uses stimuli such as mockups and/or storyboards to gain a deeper understanding of user needs, retrospective "think-aloud" protocols serve as an ideal tool to engage users in a conversation about their thoughts and feelings.

To facilitate an efficient and effective development process, as customary in formative UX studies after collecting data from a few participants, the research team convened regularly to decide whether the collected data provided enough information to adjust the

DA. This process resulted in four iterative formative studies, through which we collected information to adjust the DA and evaluated the impact of the adjustments we made on users' engagement with the DA.

2.1 Iteration 1: Collecting Information for Revising the Original Pilot DA

The objective of the first iteration was to gather feedback about the pilot DA's content and organization from the clinicians' and surrogates' perspectives. Feedback from clinicians was important to improve the accuracy and flow of information based on clinicians' experience providing this information to their patients and their families. Feedback from the surrogates was important to improve the engagement design with the DA.

We performed remote (Zoom) interviews with seven multidisciplinary clinicians such as neurosurgeons, stroke doctors, and palliative care providers. We also conducted interviews with five surrogate decision makers of prior neurocritical ill patients with the diseases of interest. Participants were provided with a link to the DA via the chat function in Zoom and were asked to share their screens. Using the "think-aloud" protocol each participant reviewed all 18 pages of the DA. Participants were encouraged to provide suggestions for improvements as they reviewed the DA. We also asked them to give us overall feedback at the end of the interview.

The feedback from participants provided strong support and encouragement for the development of the tool. In particular, the availability of accurate and reliable information (e.g., estimated prognosis visualized via the icon array and information about possible treatment pathways and their pros and cons) was considered highly valuable. The feedback also indicated that the DA would benefit from reorganizing some of its content. For example, clinicians suggested changing the order of some of the provided information. They also made suggestions about formatting the textual content in a way that the most important information is moved to the top of the page and emphasized with boldface. Including more images to accompany the text and short video clips that provided the same textual information in a non-textual format was recommended to improve engagement with content by all participants, i.e., both clinicians and surrogates with lived experience. Similarly, it was suggested to provide users with the option to review or skip patient examples.

2.2 Iteration 2: Revising the DA and Evaluating the Changes Made

Based on the feedback gathered in the first iteration, we reorganized some of the DA's content: 1) we reduced the number of DA pages from 18 to 14; 2) we provided users with the option to review or skip patient examples before completing their worksheet; 3) we simplified the language in certain paragraphs; 4) we moved text that was identified by clinicians as important information to top locations on pages and used formatting (e.g., bold text) to draw attention to important information; 5) we added more images with special emphasis on inclusion (i.e., images depicting people of color) to accompany the text; and 6) created six new videos with a physician explaining the content in plain language and embedded these videos in six different pages of the DA.

After implementing these changes, we conducted another remote round of interviews. We recruited one clinician and two surrogates with lived experience who participated in the first iteration of our user study to examine whether they preferred the revised DA over the original one. Again, participants were asked to share their screens while reviewing the DA and providing feedback.

All participants in this second round found that the revised DA, compared to its original version, made it much easier to process the provided information. Participants indicated that they preferred the way information was organized and presented to users in the new version of the DA. They found that the newly added images and videos made the revised DA notably easier to understand than its original version.

Summary of the Result of Iterations 1 and 2

The design objective of the first two iterations of our study was to see whether we can improve the organization of the provided information to enhance user engagement with the DA. To do so we collected feedback from seven multidisciplinary clinicians (e.g., neurosurgeons, stroke doctors, and palliative care providers) who help surrogates with decision-making in the neuro intensive care unit (neuro ICU) to improve the flow of DA's content. We also gathered feedback from five surrogates with lived experience to see how we can improve user engagement with the DA. The feedback from clinicians and surrogates helped us to make major revisions in content organization and presentation to users. The revised DA was ready for a more in-depth evaluation of user engagement with a new set of surrogates which will be discussed in the following sections.

2.3 Iteration 3: Assessing User Engagement with Eye Tracking

The data for this iteration was collected at a university-based hospital in New England. Participants were recruited from the neuro ICU waiting room among individuals whose family member was admitted to the neuro ICU as a patient. We used eye tracking to capture how people read the DA's content. We also used the gaze data from three specific pages deemed to be the most important aspects of the DA by our physician author (i.e., the prognosis page that contained the icon array, the page comparing treatment options, and the worksheet) to conduct a retrospective "think-aloud" session. The retrospective "think-aloud" process allowed both the collection of evaluative user feedback that was cued by their gaze data (Elling et al., 2012) and facilitated engaging users in a conversation that helped us gain a deeper understanding of their thoughts, feelings, and needs.

We invited participants (two men and one woman, mean age = 62.33, SD = 5.13) to a room adjacent to the neuro ICU where we had set up a laptop with a Tobii X-60 eye tracker attached to the laptop screen. The laptop used Tobii Pro Lab software (version 1.18) to calibrate the eye tracker for each participant. This setup allowed us to capture participants' gaze data as they reviewed the web-based DA. Participants were randomly assigned to review one of the three available DAs (i.e., traumatic brain injury, large acute ischemic stroke, and hemorrhagic stroke). Once participants finished reviewing the DA, we showed them their gaze replay for the three aforementioned pages. We ask them to recall their thought processes as they reviewed their gaze videos. Finally, we asked participants to tell us about their overall impression and experience with the DA.

All three participants reported an overall positive experience with the DA. The feedback gathered through the retrospective "think-aloud" for three specific pages, indicated that we could further improve the user experience of DA by adjusting the content of the table that compared treatment options. Participants indicated that they were partially confused by the information presented in the table. For example, user feedback during the retrospective "think-aloud" and exit interviews included statements such as: "I am not sure what to do with the table" and "The table is confusing". This table was displayed twice in the DA, first on page 9 and then in the worksheet which was provided as the last page of the DA.

The collected eye-tracking data was analyzed by focusing on fixation, saccade, and visit metrics. Fixations refer to slow eye movements that we use to process visual information. Saccades refer to fast eye movements that we use to change our focus of attention. Visits refer to a sequence of fixation and saccades that we use to view an area of investigation (AOI), i.e., a specific area on a visual display (Djamasbi, 2014).

Figure 1.a shows the fixation duration heatmap for page 9 where the comparison table for goals of care is shown for the first time. This color heatmap displays participants' cognitive effort by visualizing their fixation duration intensity from highest (red) to medium (yellow) to lowest (green). The heatmap in Fig. 1.a reveals a scattered viewing pattern. This heatmap also shows that the bottom cells in the table, which explain reasons for avoiding survival and comfort, received more intensive fixations as indicated by more and larger red color clusters in these areas. Similarly, the heatmap indicates more intense fixation on the column heading "survival" compared to the column heading "comfort."

Figure 1.b displays the order by which various sections of the table were reviewed by the three participants. The map in Fig. 1b. was developed by calculating the average time to first fixation for each AOI (Djamasbi, 2014). The AOIs in Fig. 1.b are displayed as dark gray boxes. The AOI gaze order map shows that participants reviewed the cells related to survival before looking at the cells that provided information for comfort. They also show that users did not read the page title ("Comparing and summarizing different goals of care") and table titles ("Survival" and "Comfort") before reading the content of the table. This viewing behavior is important because designing the page in a way to encourage users to read the titles before looking at the content makes it easier for them to understand the provided information (Djamasbi et al., 2012).

The fixation order as well as the scattered viewing pattern in the heatmap in Fig. 1 indicates that participants were looking around for information. This interpretation is supported by the results of the retrospective "think-aloud" which indicated that users were not quite sure how to process the content of the table.

1.a. Fixation duration heatmap   1.b. AOI map

Fig. 1. Iteration 3: Fixation duration heatmap and AOI map for page 9

The heatmaps in Fig. 2 display the distribution of attention on the table on page 9 and the same table on the last page of the DA (page 14, the worksheet page). Figure 2 also displays three quantitative eye-tracking metrics that capture cognitive effort for reviewing the tables on page 9 and the worksheet page: average visit duration, saccade-to-fixation frequency, and fixation-visit-duration. Average visit duration captures the average amount of time for every single visit (every single time that the table area was visited). Higher average visit durations indicate more effort expended to view the table. Saccade-to-fixation frequency (i.e., total number of saccades/total number of fixations) reveals changes in focus. Higher values of saccade-to-fixation frequency indicate more changes in focus when viewing the table (e.g., more intense search behavior) (Wu et al., 2015). Fixation-to-visit duration (total fixation duration/total visit duration) reveals the effort expended to read the content of the table. The larger the value of fixation-to-visit duration, the more effort is expended to read the content (Pool & Ball 2005).

Because the table is presented to users twice, we expected to observe differences in viewing patterns and behavior when the table was viewed for the first time on page 9, compared to the second time that it was viewed on the last page of the DA (the worksheet page). Due to familiarity with the table, it is reasonable to expect that participants would exhibit less cognitive effort (i.e., less intense viewing behavior) when they view the table on the worksheet page. The data displayed in Fig. 2, however, does not support this expectation. As shown in Fig. 2, participants' fixations on both tables had a similar scattered pattern. Additionally, quantitative eye-tracking metrics did not show a decreasing trend in cognitive effort. For example, the results showed that on average people exhibited more cognitive effort when viewing the table on the worksheet page (56,576 ms) compared to when they viewed it for the first time on page 9 (46,213 ms). While saccade-to-fixation frequency values indicated slightly fewer changes of focus on the worksheet table compared to the table on page 9 (51% vs. 57%), fixation-to-visit duration ratios indicated that participants expended slightly more effort reading the table in the worksheet (67%) compared to the effort they expended to read the table on page 9 (64%). The information summarized in Fig. 2 indicates that participants did not exhibit an overall decrease in cognitive effort when they reviewed the table for the second time on the worksheet page. These eye-tracking results suggest that participants may have not fully understood what the table intended to communicate. Participants' feedback, which indicated confusion about the table, supported the interpretation of the eye-tracking results.

Visual Engagement with the Icon Array
We also investigated how participants visually processed the icon array. An Icon array is a graphical depiction of probabilities and proportions, which uses a matrix of icons. (e.g., probability of dying from an injury and/or surviving it with serious disabilities, etc.) (Scalia et al., 2021).This information is essential for surrogates to understand the probability of a predicted outcome to help them select a treatment pathway that most likely matches the values and preferences of the patient. Hence, the icon array in our DA is presented to users before the table that compares treatment options on page 9.

Figure 3 displays the heatmap for the icon array used in the DA to visualize the probability of death, survival with severe disability, and survival with minimal or no disability, all derived from disease-specific, validated prediction models. As shown in

Saccade-to-fixation frequency=57%
Fixation-to-visit duration=64%

Saccade-to-fixation frequency=51%
Fixation-to-visit duration=67%

Fig. 2. Iteration 3: Attention, search, and reading behavior

Fig. 3, the aggregated gaze patterns cover mostly the right side of the icon array indicating that participants mostly focused on the icon array legend. This viewing behavior can be explained by the fact that the only information conveyed by the graph on the icon array is the visual representation of the proportion of three possible outcomes (death, survival with severe disability, and survival with no or minimal disability). The explanations for these outcomes are provided by text in the legend of the icon array.

People's fixation intensity tends to decrease from top to bottom when they read textual information that is presented in a list format (such as the textual information in the icon array). As shown in Fig. 3, the explanation for the legend (the paragraph above the legend) received relatively less intense attention compared to the two first two items of the three-item legend. The color clusters on the legend indicate that participants read the first two items of the legend with relatively similar intensity. They also indicate that the first two items of the legend were viewed more intensely than the last item of the legend.

The eye-tracking results and feedback from participants indicated that we did not need to make any changes to the icon array.

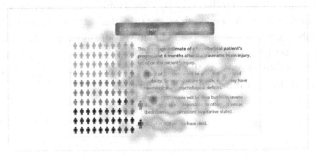

Fig. 3. Iteration 3: Fixation duration heatmap for Icon array

2.4 Iteration 4: Assessing User Engagement with Eye Tracking After 3rd DA Revision

The results of the user study in iteration 3 provided a number of actionable insights for revising the table that compared the survival and comfort treatment options. To make the table easier to process, we simplified its content in several ways. For example, to make it clearer that the treatment goal must be considered from the patient's point of view we changed the subtitles in the table from "Reasons for choosing <treatment goal>" to "The patient may choose <treatment goal> because:"). We also simplified the language in bulleted points (e.g., changed "The patient has said in the past that they don't wish to be dependent on others to live" to "The patient does not wish to be dependent on others to live"), and balanced the number of bulleted points for each section in the table (i.e., three bulleted points in each cell). Additionally, we simplified the title of page 9, where this table is shown for the first time, to create an easier-to-read summary of the entire page. The title of page 9 was changed from "Comparing and summarizing different goals of care" to "Comparing different goals of care". The table in the worksheet was the exact copy of the table on page 9 with one exception; The table was simplified on the worksheet by removing the column titles Survival and Comfort. Because patients were already familiar with the table, we did not expect any problem removing the table titles on the worksheet. Removing the table titles helped simplify the content-heavy worksheet page.

After making these adjustments, we resumed eye-tracking data collection in the same hospital, using the same room and setup. We again recruited individuals whose family member was admitted as a patient to the neuro ICU. Four new participants (three men and one woman, mean age = 44.25, SD = 20.04) were recruited. Again, participants reported a positive overall experience with the DA. The feedback from the retrospective "think-aloud" indicated that the adjustments made to the table improved engagement with its content because participants no longer reported any confusion about the table.

Figure 4.a displays the heatmap and Fig. 4.b displays the AOI map for the revised page. The heatmap in Fig. 4.a shows that participants had more intense fixations (red and yellow color clusters) on the survival column than on the comfort column. Figure 4.b shows the AOI map representing the order by which table content was viewed. As shown in Fig. 4.b, participants first looked at the page title, then at the titles of the table before looking at the table content. The observed viewing order suggests that the changes made to the page had a positive impact on how people reviewed it. As mentioned before, because titles and subtitles provide the summary of the content, they are important in effective communication of information (Djamasbi et al., 2012).

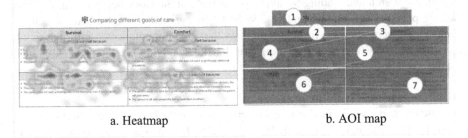

a. Heatmap   b. AOI map

Fig. 4. Iteration 4: Fixation duration heatmap and AOI maps for page 9

Figure 5 displays heatmaps for the table when it was viewed by participants for the first time (Fig. 5.a) and for a second time on the worksheet (Fig. 5.b). Because the table titles were not included in the worksheet, qualitative metrics were measured for the area of the table that was common on both pages (i.e., the table AOI in Fig. 5 does not include table titles). The heatmaps show that in this iteration participants read the column that explained the survival goal of care more carefully on both tables as evidenced by the spread and intensity of the color clusters in the tables.

As mentioned in iteration 3, because of familiarity with the table (i.e., participants already reviewed the table on page 9), we expected them to read the content of the table on the worksheet with less intense viewing patterns or cognitive effort. The eye-tracking results summarized in Fig. 5 support our expectation. For example, the heatmaps show less intense color clusters covering fewer areas on the worksheet table compared to the table on page 9.

The quantitative measures of average visit duration, saccade-to-fixation frequency, and fixation-to-visit duration also supported our expectation that the table in the worksheet, compared to the table on page 9, would be reviewed with less cognitive effort. As shown in Fig. 5, the average visit duration was notably shorter for the table on the worksheet (16,403 ms) than the average visit duration for the table on page 9 (50,956 ms). Similarly, saccade-to-fixation frequency and fixation-to-visit duration ratios indicated

Average visit duration = 50,956 ms
Saccade-to-fixation frequency= 48%
Fixation-to-visit duration=54 %

5.a. Page 9

Average visit duration = 16,403 ms
Saccade-to-fixation frequency= 41%
Fixation-to-visit duration=48%

5.b. Last page (worksheet)

Fig. 5. Iteration 4: heatmaps, attention, search, and reading behavior

less intense search and reading behavior for the table in the worksheet compared to the table on page 9 (41% vs 48% and 48% vs 54%). These results suggest that the adjustments made were effective in improving how the table communicated information to users. Participants' feedback indicating that they knew how to use the table supported the interpretation of these eye-tracking results.

Visual Engagement with the Icon Array

Because no changes were made to the icon array in iteration 4 (i.e., the results of iteration 3 indicated no adjustment was needed), the icon array heatmap in iteration 4 was created with the eye movement data for all seven participants in iterations 3 and 4 (Fig. 6).

The heatmap for the icon array in iteration 4 shows that the aggregated viewing pattern of all participants is similar to the viewing patterns of the first 3 participants in iteration 3 (Fig. 3). The gaze patterns in Fig. 6 cover mostly the textual information with participants' most intense fixation covering the first two items of the three-item legend. There are intense fixations (red clusters) on the textual information that reveals percentages (39 and 28 out of hundred) on the survival items (first two items of the legend) but no red cluster on the percentage for those who die from their injury (last item of the legend). Within the first two items of the legend, the larger number of red and yellow clusters on the first item of the legend indicates that the explanation for survival with no or mild disabilities was viewed more attentively than the explanation for survival with severe disabilities. The observed viewing pattern for the legend items could be due to their presentation order (i.e., attention decreases from top to bottom on lists). It could also be due to their content indicating that participants attended the information on survival outcomes more intensely than information on death due to injuries. The eye-tracking data in iteration 4 shows that attention to information about survival (compared to attention to information about comfort) was more intense on the tables on pages 9 and 14. While these results suggest that surrogates may exhibit attentional bias toward information about survival, future research is needed to examine such a possibility more directly.

Fig. 6. Fixation duration heatmap for Icon array

Summary of the Result of Iterations 3 and 4

The objective of iterations 3 and 4 was to examine user engagement with the DA at a deeper cognitive level. The average time to review the DA for all seven participants in iterations 3 and 4 was 27.71 min. The analysis of eye movements showed that participants reviewed the DA without skipping any textual or image-based communication.

Because the comparison table appears twice (on pages 9 and 14) in the DA, we expected participants to exhibit less intense cognitive effort the second time they review the table. In iteration 3, participants' viewing patterns and behavior did not support our expectation; participants' fixation patterns and viewing behavior did not show an overall decreased trend in cognitive effort. In iteration 4, however, after we revised the DA, the eye-tracking results suggested that participants reviewed the table on page 14 with less cognitive effort. The differences in cognitive effort between reviewing the table on page 9 and page 14 suggest that the changes made to pages 9 and 14 were effective in helping users process the provided information more easily. User feedback supported the above interpretation derived from these eye-tracking results.

The heatmaps for the icon array in iterations 3 and 4 showed similar viewing patterns indicating that the information provided in this graph was thoroughly reviewed. The heat maps (Figs. 3 and 6) also showed more intense attention to the legend that described the possibility of survival with mild or no disability. Attention to survival was also observed in heatmaps in Fig. 5. After revising the table to make it easier to process, the column in the table that described survival was covered with more fixations on page 9 (Fig. 5.a) and more intense fixations on page 14 (Fig. 5.b).

The similarity of viewing patterns in Fig. 3 (the icon array heatmap generated for the first three participants) and Fig. 5 (the icon array heatmap generated for all seven participants) shows that we were able to capture the overall viewing behavior for the icon array with only three participants. Similarly, we were able to use the eye movement data of a small number of participants (i.e., the first 3 participants) to test the DA and generate actionable insight for revising it. The ability to generate actionable insight for design and the ability to evaluate the impact of revisions on cognitive effort with only a small number of participants (in our case 3 to 4 participants), highlights the value of eye tracking in iterative formative studies which by mere nature have small sample sizes.

3 Discussion

Here we showed four iterative formative user studies to gather actionable insight for improving the engagement design with the DA and evaluating the changes made. The DA in our study was designed to help surrogate decision makers of patients with severe brain injuries to make a goals-of-care decision. We used the "think-aloud" protocols in the first two rounds and eye tracking in the last two. During the eye-tracking recordings, we did not use the "think-aloud" protocol to avoid interruption of participants' interaction with the DA. On average, participants required 27.71 min to review the DA without interruption. Eye-tracking results showed that no textual or image-based communication was skipped by users. This is notable because research shows that textual information is rarely reviewed thoroughly (Djamasbi et al., 2016).

Our mixed methods analysis showed that our iterative revisions effectively improved participants' engagement with the DA. The results showed that users looked at the survival table column more intensely than the comfort treatment column. A similar attention pattern was observed for the icon array: the survival outcome received more attention than death. The observed viewing patterns may indicate surrogate decision makers' attentional bias toward survival-related information. They may also reflect the tendency to view information from top-to-bottom (e.g., legends in the icon array) or left-to-right (e.g., table content). Future research is needed to examine these possibilities.

Our study results highlight the value of eye tracking in evaluating engagement design. For example, similar gaze patterns captured by heatmaps in Figs. 3 and 5, suggest that stable viewing patterns can be captured with a small number of participants (e.g., n = 3 in our case). Similarly, our results show that capturing visual information processing behavior (e.g., via heatmaps, eye tracking metrics, and retrospective "think-aloud") even from a small number of participants can generate valuable insight for revising the DA and/or testing the effectiveness of its revisions.

A recent industry report points out the need for more user experience research that can generate actionable insight for improving products during the development cycle (User Zoom, 2022). The iterative "design, test, and revise" process in our study shows how to take advantage of various techniques (e.g., "think-aloud" protocol, eye tracking, retrospective "think-aloud") to gain insights for improving the engagement design of a DA. The "think-aloud" protocol in the first two iterations allowed us to gather feedback and suggestions for improvement from participants as they were viewing each page of the DA. This process allowed us to learn about reorganization and simplification of the DA's content. The eye-tracking protocol allowed us to investigate engagement with the revised DA without interrupting participants. This process allowed us to capture how the provided information was processed in the moment. Finally, the retrospective "think-aloud" helped us collect participants' feedback on specific pages by cueing them with their own gaze data.

4   Strengths and Limitations

Our study has important strengths. The mixed methods approach used in our study facilitated the evaluation of the engagement with the DA at a cognitive level not possible with the more traditional UX methods. It also facilitated a deeper and more nuanced understanding of user information processing needs. Our small sample size in each iteration could be viewed as a limitation; as such, the result should be considered with caution. However, the objective of iterative studies in our project was not to find statistically significant differences in the results, rather we intended to provide actionable insights for the development team in a timely manner. Conducting multiple studies with small sample sizes to provide timely and cost-effective insight for the development team is grounded in user-centered approach to product development (Albert & Tullis 2013; Djamasbi & Strong 2019). Additional limitations include that we did not collect user feedback for every single page of the DA, but limited our retrospective "think-aloud" investigations to the three most important pages of the DA.

5 Conclusion

Because our DA provides crucial information about the continuation or withdrawal of life-sustaining measures for a neurocritically ill patient, it is critical to effectively present the information needed for decision-making. The DA's content must be presented in a way that can be easily processed by surrogate decision makers. The results of our study show that including eye tracking in iterative formative studies can serve as a valuable and feasible methodology for assessing how provided content is reviewed by users. The results also show that the retrospective "think-aloud" protocol provides an important tool for gaining insights about users' needs and preferences.

Acknowledgement. . Research reported in this publication was supported by the National Institute of Nursing Research of the National Institutes of Health under Award Number R21NR020231. The content is solely the responsibility of the authors and does not necessarily represent the official views of the National Institutes of Health.

References

Albert, B., Tullis, T.: Measuring the user experience: collecting, analyzing, and presenting usability metrics. Newnes (2013)

Barry, M.J., Edgman-Levitan, S.: Shared decision making — the pinnacle of patient-centered care. N. Engl. J. Med. **366**(9), 780–781 (2012). https://doi.org/10.1056/NEJMp1109283

Djamasbi, S.: Eye tracking and web experience AIS. Trans. Hum.-Comput. Interact. **6**(2), 37–54 (2014)

Djamasbi, S., Chen, P., Shojaeizadeh, M., Rochford, J.: Text simplification and generation Y: an eye tracking study. In: SIGHCI 2016 Proceedings, p. 12 (2016)

Djamasbi, S., Siegel, M., Tullis, T.S.: Faces and viewing behavior: an exploratory investigation. AIS Trans. Hum. Comput. Interact. **4**(3), 190–211 (2012)

Djamasbi, S., Strong, D.: User experience-driven innovation in smart and connected worlds. AIS Trans. Hum. Comput. Interact. **11**(4), 215–231 (2019)

Eger, N., Ball, L.J., Stevens, R., Dodd, J.: Cueing retrospective verbal reports in usability testing through eye-movement replay. In: Proceedings of HCI 2007 The 21st British HCI Group Annual Conference University of Lancaster, UK 21, pp. 1–9, September 2007

Elling, S., Lentz, L., de Jong, M.: Combining concurrent think-aloud protocols and eye-tracking observations: an analysis of verbalizations and silences. IEEE Trans. Prof. Commun. **55**(3), 206–220 (2012). https://doi.org/10.1109/TPC.2012.2206190

Gaffiero, D., Elander, J., Maratos, F.: Do individuals with chronic pain show attentional bias to pain-related information? An early stage systematic review of the eye-tracking evidence. Cogn. Psychol. Bull **4**, 37–45 (2019)

Goostrey, K.J., et al.: Adapting a traumatic brain injury goals-of-care decision aid for critically ill patients to intracerebral hemorrhage and hemispheric acute ischemic stroke. Crit. Care Explor. **3**(3), e0357 (2021). https://doi.org/10.1097/cce.0000000000000357

Muehlschlegel, S., et al.: Goals-of-care decision aid for critically ill patients with TBI. Neurology **95**(2), e179 (2020). https://doi.org/10.1212/WNL.0000000000009770

Norouzi Nia, J., Varzgani, F., Djamasbi, S., Tulu, B., Lee, C., Muehlschlegel, S.: Visual hierarchy and communication effectiveness in medical decision tools for surrogate-decision-makers of critically Ill traumatic brain injury patients. In: Schmorrow, D.D., Fidopiastis, C.M. (eds.) HCII 2021. LNCS (LNAI), vol. 12776, pp. 210–220. Springer, Cham (2021). https://doi.org/10.1007/978-3-030-78114-9_15

Poole, A., Ball, L.J.: Eye tracking in human-computer interaction and usability research: current status and future prospects. Encyclopedia Hum.-Comput. Interact. 211–219 (2005)

Scalia, P., et al.: Comparing the impact of an icon array versus a bar graph on preference and understanding of risk information: results from an online, randomized study. PLoS ONE **16**(July) (2021). https://doi.org/10.1371/journal.pone.0253644

Schiessl, M., Duda, S., Thölke, A., Fischer, R.: Eye tracking and its application in usability and media research. MMI-interaktiv J. **6**(2003), 41–50 (2003)

UserZoom. (2022). State of UX report: Bridging the gap between UX insights and business impact (2022). https://info.userzoom.com/rs/293-RDJ-600/images/UserZoom_State_of_UX_22.pdf

Wu, X., Xue, C., Zhou, F.: An experimental study on visual search factors of information features in a task monitoring interface. In: Kurosu, M. (ed.) HCI 2015. LNCS, vol. 9171, pp. 525–536. Springer, Cham (2015). https://doi.org/10.1007/978-3-319-21006-3_50

Technical Function Evaluation of Two Smart Wearables and Data Analysis Methods for Step Counts

Katrina K. Boles[1]([⊠]) [iD], Malaika R. Gallimore[2] [iD], Chelsea Howland[2,3] [iD],
Chuka Emezue[2,4] [iD], and Blaine Reeder[1,2] [iD]

[1] MU Institute for Data Science and Informatics, University of Missouri, Columbia, MO, USA
{boleskk,blaine.reeder}@missouri.edu
[2] Sinclair School of Nursing, University of Missouri, Columbia, MO, USA
{malaika.gallimore,chelsea-howland}@missouri.edu,
chuka_n_emezue@rush.edu
[3] College of Nursing, University of Iowa, Iowa City, IA, USA
[4] College of Nursing, Rush University, Chicago, IL, USA

Abstract. Smart wearable devices that capture physical activity data are increasingly used for health research and show potential for augmented cognition. These devices must be tested to understand their function before use in research and everyday life. However, there are few standards for the evaluation of step count comparisons between devices. We completed a technical function evaluation of two consumer-grade devices – Fitbit Versa 3 and generation 2 Oura Ring – against research-grade gold standard ActiGraph devices – wGT3X-BT and GT9X-Link. We compared data analysis methods to evaluate smart wearable physical activity data to inform development of standards and guidance for data analysis. Based on this effort, we suggest the use of Median Absolute Percent Difference along with Spearman's Rho as a correlation measure and Bland-Altman plots to visualize the agreement. This combination of measures provides a multi-perspective view of step counts and can assist researchers in determining limitations and best uses for smart wearable devices.

Keywords: Smart watch · fitness tracker · digital health · usability · evaluation

1 Introduction

Smart wearable technology (SWT) devices are increasingly available as consumer products to support awareness and improvement of health and wellness [1, 2]. These technologies include but are not limited to wearable devices with onboard sensors such as smartwatches that can track activity levels, heart rate, temperature, sleep patterns, and other physiologic states. SWT devices provide unique opportunities for supporting augmented cognition (AugCog) in health and wellness by aiding wearers and care teams in understanding behavior patterns and physiologic states [3]. Wearable technologies from prominent companies such as Fitbit [4–7] Garmin [8, 9], Apple [10–12], and Samsung

© The Author(s), under exclusive license to Springer Nature Switzerland AG 2023
D. D. Schmorrow and C. M. Fidopiastis (Eds.): HCII 2023, LNAI 14019, pp. 71–88, 2023.
https://doi.org/10.1007/978-3-031-35017-7_6

[13, 14], and smaller start-up companies like WHOOP [15], PINE64 [16] and Oura [17] show great promise for use in research that can be quickly and widely translated to health interventions and wellness programs in everyday life [18–21].

One estimate is that the SWT market will grow to 93.7 million users by the year 2025 [22]. With the rapid growth in the SWT market, opportunities for behavior change that are supported through AugCog approaches are many. As one example, a person might wear a SWT device for step tracking that identifies personal activity patterns, use that information to set a targeted goal, and subsequently adjust behavior to meet that goal through real-time prompts from the device. As another example, a health care team could use remotely captured data through continual heart rate monitoring capability on a SWT device to identify sudden or unexpected changes in wearer heart rate. Expert advice combined with device alerts could form the basis of a human-in-the-loop AugCog system that supports the wearer. These are two simple examples of low-level computerized assistance [23]. However, there are uncounted ways SWT and their data could be leveraged in more complex ways and included with other data to identify wearer state and develop mitigation strategies for behavior change for health.

Much of the research using SWT necessarily has focused on proof-of-concept studies that seek to understand the reliability and accuracy of SWT [2, 18]. However, given the early stage of research with these devices, methods to analyze and compare the data they generate vary widely [10, 24]. A major focus of the Precision Smart Technologies and Applications for Rapid Translation (Precision START) laboratory at the University of Missouri Sinclair School of Nursing is to formalize methods for rapid and longitudinal evaluation of new technologies and position them for inclusion in larger studies. As part of the Precision START stepwise evaluation methodology, evaluators complete a technical function test which includes scripted activities over a prescribed period of time [25]. The aim of this paper is to review data analysis methods in prior studies of SWT and report results of the sensor data analysis from the technical function test of two SWT (Fitbit Versa 3 [7] and generation 2 Oura Smart Ring [17]).

Step counts are one metric for exploring the measurement of daily physical activity and are common in wearable fitness devices [4, 11, 21, 26–28]. Device manufacturers commonly calculate steps using a proprietary algorithm to convert accelerometry data that is often hidden from researchers. Unfortunately, consumer-grade device manufacturers typically do not test the function of their productions in relationship to a gold standard. With no way to see the raw data collected by the accelerometers from consumer-grade devices, independent researchers are left to evaluate step counts generated by these devices by comparing their output to a de facto research-grade device whose function is well-understood, such as the Actigraph [29–31].

As indicated in systematic reviews of the commercial SWT field, there is no apparent standard methodology for evaluating the validity of fitness tracking devices [10, 24]. Studies have used a variety of methods for assessing the validity of devices, including Mean or Median Absolute Percentage Error (MAPE) [21, 28, 32], Group Mean Percentage Difference [5], Spearman's Rho [33], Pearson's R [6, 26], Intraclass Correlation Coefficient (ICC) [6, 21, 28, 32], Wilcoxon signed-rank tests [21] and Bland-Altman limits of agreement plots [21, 26, 28]. In their systematic review, Gorzelitz et al. found Bland-Altman plots to be the most frequently used assessment, followed closely by

Pearson or Spearman correlation [24]. Similarly, Johnston et al. reviewed methods for evaluating wearables and proposed a standardization procedure and analysis [34]. Below we review methods, present the results of our data analysis and describe future steps for research.

2 Materials and Methods

This study uses data collected during proof-of-concept tests to assess usability and functionality of the Fitbit Versa 3 smart watch [7] and the Oura generation 2 smart ring [17]. As part of the Precision START stepwise evaluation methodology [25], five evaluators tested two consumer devices—the Fitbit Versa 3 and Oura Ring (generation 2)—against two control devices ActiGraph wGT3X-BT and ActiGraph GT9X-Link for a prescribed seven-day period.

The Fitbit Versa 3 (Versa) is a commercial smart watch that tracks activity: steps, distance, calories burned, sleep, oxygen saturation and heart rate using a triaxial accelerometer, GPS, optical heart rate sensor and red/infrared sensors. The Versa is designed to be worn on the wrist and has an "always-on" display and free mobile app [7]. The generation 2 Oura Smart Ring (Oura) is a device that is worn on the finger, and collects metric data for sleep tracking and step counting. The Oura has no display and all interactions are through its free mobile app [17, 35]. The ActiGraph wGT3X-BT (GT3X) is a research-grade medical device that measures physical activity using a triaxial accelerometer and includes an ambient light sensor. It can be worn on the wrist, waist, ankle, or thigh, but most commonly on the waist. It does not have an LCD screen and its corresponding ActiLife software is used to convert the raw acceleration data to steps or other activity measures [36]. The ActiGraph GT9X-Link (Link) is a newer research-grade medical device worn on the wrist but can alternately be worn on the waist; it has an LCD display that can provide real-time feedback. Like the GT3X, raw acceleration, gyroscope and magnetometer data can be downloaded and converted to activity measures on its accompanying ActiLife software [36].

Researchers often test consumer-grade devices against a "gold-standard" device such as the ActiGraph devices. We did not assume the data from both ActiGraph devices would be comparable as control measurements, rather we sought to evaluate both. Our team did not alter factory settings for the devices. Evaluators wore the GT3X on their dominant hip, and Link and Versa on their non-dominant wrist. Two evaluators wore the Ring on the ring finger of their dominant hand and the other three on the ring finger of their non-dominant hand.

After completing the seven-day testing period, evaluators assessed usability by completing an Everyday Use Checklist, Mobile Application Rating Scale (MARS) [37] from the Queensland University of Technology, and a System Usability Scale (SUS) [38]. To assess device functionality, evaluators downloaded all their Fitbit and Oura data from the developer websites. Both Fitbit and Oura data downloads only include daily summary information and are not granular enough for our comparative evaluation. For the GT3X and Link devices, evaluators used the ActiLife Lite software to download Actigraph AGD files. Using the full ActiLife software, we converted these files into 60-s epoch CSV data tables, from which we kept date, time, and steps.

2.1 Device Functionality Data Methodology

Using Python in a Jupyter notebook environment, we calculated daily step counts for the GT3X and Link devices from the 60-s epoch data to compare with daily step counts from Fitbit and Oura CSV downloads. Since our start and end times for the study were mid-day, we removed the first and last days' data for each evaluator to preclude partial data comparisons with full day aggregates. The daily total steps table includes the ability to subset by evaluator, day, and device (Table 1).

Table 1. Total daily step counts acquired by each device for each evaluator.

Evaluator	Date	GT3X	Link	Versa	Ring
E01	2/2/21	5663	13266	9478	10342
	2/3/21	6326	15068	13132	12798
	2/4/21	8327	15510	14975	15197
	2/5/21	5908	12928	9917	9859
	2/6/21	8382	16905	15259	15133
	2/7/21	8133	18116	16594	15066
E02	2/2/21	2478	7480	3398	8909
	2/3/21	3548	13362	6887	12353
	2/4/21	2924	12037	6572	6754
	2/5/21	2304	6145	2804	4041
	2/6/21	4119	8109	4192	5870
	2/7/21	3959	14267	9409	12896
E03	2/2/21	10185	13201	10866	10480
	2/3/21	11174	12850	11941	10788
	2/4/21	11953	12858	14116	13363
	2/5/21	10730	11392	11142	9846
	2/6/21	9909	11675	10607	11107
	2/7/21	11786	11953	11370	11809
E04	2/2/21	2594	10717	3369	5826
	2/3/21	1950	9645	5185	5709
	2/4/21	3840	10827	5597	7854
	2/5/21	2572	9459	3043	5911
	2/6/21	3411	10032	4402	5664
	2/7/21	3371	9563	2241	4093
E05	2/2/21	3803	8358	6034	6291
	2/3/21	2290	8333	3399	2767

(*continued*)

Table 1. (*continued*)

Evaluator	Date	GT3X	Link	Versa	Ring
	2/4/21	3045	8248	4500	3741
	2/5/21	1474	7500	1581	999
	2/6/21	2945	8057	3480	2807
	2/7/21	3302	9366	5270	4604

Data Analysis of Daily Total Step Activity. After exploring several methods used for data analysis and validation of consumer devices, we sought to evaluate correlation and agreement between pairs of devices. We disregarded techniques like Group Mean Percentage Difference and Intraclass Correlation Coefficient that might overlook variations between daily activities by using the data in groups rather than pairs (ICC) [4, 5, 26]. For example, group mean percentage difference would take a mean of all steps, in our case ranging from 1,474 to 11,174 for one device. Such an approach could disregard the variability of the level of activity.

We also considered the distribution of our data and rejected the inference that the pairs must be linearly correlated, so we chose to use Spearman's Rho to measure the strength of the association between pairs (Table 2). This measurement requires neither the normal distribution of data nor a linear association.

Table 2. Spearman's Rho and p-value for daily total comparisons.

	rho	p-value
Versa:GT3X	0.86	1.15E-09
Versa:Link	0.85	3.36E-09
Versa:Ring	0.88	2.12E-10
Ring:GT3X	0.78	4.64E-07
Ring:Link	0.87	2.81E-10
GT3X:Link	0.68	3.33E-05

While correlation can be valuable depending on the goals of the study, it is not sufficient for estimating agreement; our goal in comparing devices is to identify how closely they agree so we can use them interchangeably [37–39]. The degree of agreement needed varies based on use.

The Bland-Altman plot was developed for visualizing limits of agreement between measurements in medicine [37, 40]. Figure 1 shows example comparisons between Versa and GT3X daily total values three ways. The first is a scatter plot comparison of totals with one device in the x-axis and another in the y-axis, which appears to indicate that the Versa often counts more steps than the GT3X, with a perfect agreement as the diagonal

line. The second scatter plot shows the average of an individuals' Versa daily value and
GT3X daily value against the difference between those two values. And the third plot
is a Bland-Altman plot, which also shows the difference and the means/average in the
axes, adding the mean and standard deviation. Altman and Bland argue for this method
of displaying comparison study results [40].

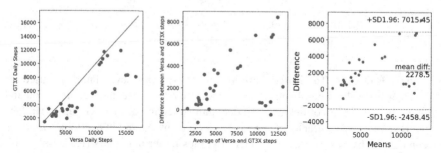

Fig. 1. This example displays comparisons between Versa and GT3X daily total values three
ways.

While these visualizations are valuable, they do not provide a value to the difference or error between devices. For that, we looked at percentage error and difference
calculations. At each data point (by day and evaluator), we calculated the absolute percentage error (APE), which assumes one value is the accepted or control value. For these
comparisons, we calculated APE using the Versa and Ring as the test device and the
ActiGraph devices as control devices. In addition, we calculated APE using the Link as
the test device and the GT3X as the control device.

$$absolute\ percent\ error = \frac{|control\ device\ steps - test\ device\ steps|}{control\ device\ steps} \times 100\%$$

To compare the Versa and Ring, since neither is a control device, we calculated
a percent difference. Though it is not standard in the literature to calculate percent
difference when using a control device such as the GT3X, we opted to calculate the
percent difference between devices since we did not have another exacting measure for
the control. We are accepting the GT3X or the Link as the control device without an
exact step count or other measurement for the sake of comparison.

$$percent\ difference = \frac{|first\ device\ steps - second\ device\ steps|}{(first\ device\ steps + second\ device\ steps)/2} \times 100\%$$

With APE and percent difference calculated between each pair of devices, next we
took the mean and the median of each pairing (Table 3 and Fig. 2). While often used
for evaluating forecasting models, Mean Absolute Percentage Error (MAPE) is also a
commonly-used validation metric for evaluating device error [4, 26, 30, 33]. With a large
dataset, we would accept the median values because they are more resistant to outliers.
While our data skew favors the left in the percent difference values (except between the
Ring and Link), it is more split between right and left skew for APE values. With either

of these calculations, there can be more than a one-hundred percent error or difference. Our data show the largest difference in daily step counts are between the two research devices, the GT3X and the Link. These values suggest there is a considerable difference between the devices, perhaps partially associated with the difference in wear locations (wrist vs. waist).

Table 3. Mean and median percentage errors (MAPE and MdAPE), mean and median percentage differences between devices' daily aggregate step counts.

	Versa: GT3X	Versa: Link	Ring: GT3X	Ring: Link	Link: GT3X
Median % error	41.44	44.57	66.46	24.23	168.79
Mean % error	51.14	36.59	78.19	29.78	164.98
Median % diff	37.9	57.35	49.89	27.58	91.53
Mean % diff	36.75	49.99	48.15	39.17	79.38

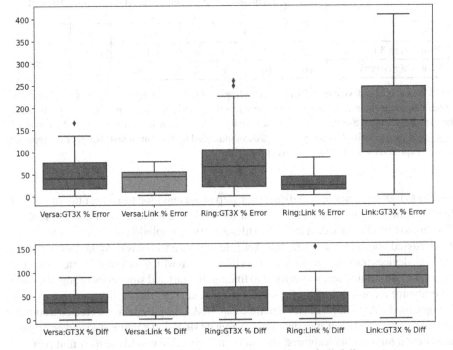

Fig. 2. Box and whisker plots indicating quartiles and outliers of all daily step count percent errors (top) and percent differences (bottom).

Data Analysis of Scripted Activities. The comparative viability of devices is not complete using only daily step totals; this method hides the variability of how effectively devices count steps based on activity. Per the stepwise methodology, our evaluators followed protocol for scripted tasks on day four of testing [25]. All five evaluators completed walking tests, capturing steps for very light walking, light walking, and moderately hard walking. Three of the five evaluators also completed a stair climbing test, ascending and descending a set of stairs three times. Evaluators manually logged their start time and step counts at the beginning of each activity and took a two-minute rest time between each activity. During this two-minute rest time, they logged the step count displayed on their devices (Fig. 3). Due to latency between device and phone, evaluators visually verified that step counts stopped updating before copying totals into their log.

	Start	After "Very Light" Walking	After "Light" Walking	After "Moderately Hard" Walking
Time	18:08			
Fitbit Versa 3 (steps)	3157	3560	4258	5092
Oura Ring (steps)	5668	5855	6355	7110

	Start	Ascend 1	Descend 1	Ascend 2	Descend 2	Ascend 3	Descend 3
Time	18:39						
Fitbit Versa 3 (steps)	5102	5111	5119	5128	5142	5150	5159
Oura Ring (steps)	7116	7116	7230	7230	7230	7230	7230

Fig. 3. Evaluator 4 device log of step activity (top) and stair climbing activity (bottom) with step values manually entered at start, during 2-min rest times and end. Start time only needed because the protocol dictates 8-min for each walk activity with 2-min rests and varies based on number of stairs in the stair climb activity and is always indicated by the 2-min rest. Number of steps per activity captured by subtracting the previous value.

The GT3X does not have a display for step counts and we turned off the step count display option to preserve battery life on the Link. Each evaluator used the ActiLife software to export device data into AGD files after the completion of all activity tracking. As discussed above, we used the full ActiLife software to convert AGD files of GT3X and Link devices into 60-s epoch CSV data tables, from which we utilized date, time, and steps. The two-minute rest was critical to finding the start and stop times of activity since the evaluator recorded time as displayed on a timekeeping device that may not exactly line up with the ActiGraph device datetime captured. Using Python, we created a custom function to accept a target start datetime, aggregate steps and capture start and end times, breaking on minutes that captured zero steps. In future, we would use the Fitbit API and Oura API to get 60-s epoch tables, target the activities, and use the function to aggregate steps for each activity. We merged all device data for each evaluator to create a data table with total steps for each walk or stair climbing activity and device comparisons. We removed date and time information, keeping activity and evaluator labels as well as total steps for each device. We also calculated means and medians of APE and percent difference (Tables 4, 5 and 6).

Table 4. Walk activity step counts aggregated, and percent errors and percent differences calculated.

Activity	Device	E01	E02	E03	E04	E05
Very Light Walk	Versa	451	175	638	403	703
	Ring	304	420	467	187	560
	GT3X	460	221	76	211	316
	Link	231	233	270	309	360
	Versa:GT3X % Error	2	20.8	739.5	91	122.5
	Versa:Link % Error	95.2	24.9	136.3	30.4	95.3
	Ring:GT3X % Error	33.9	90	514.5	11.4	77.2
	Ring:Link % Error	31.6	80.3	73	39.5	55.6
	Versa:Ring % Difference	38.9	82.4	31	73.2	22.6
	Link:GT3X % Difference	66.3	5.3	112.1	37.7	13
Light Walk	Versa	910	713	640	698	760
	Ring	464	801	570	500	761
	GT3X	591	626	374	371	360
	Link	388	338	347	412	390
	Versa:GT3X % Error	54	13.9	71.1	88.1	111.1
	Versa:Link % Error	134.5	110.9	84.4	69.4	94.9
	Ring:GT3X % Error	21.5	28	52.4	34.8	111.4
	Ring:Link % Error	19.6	137	64.3	21.4	95.1
	Versa:Ring % Difference	64.9	11.6	11.6	33.1	0.1
	Link:GT3X % Difference	41.5	59.8	7.5	10.5	8
Moderate Walk	Versa	832	841	769	834	792
	Ring	963	886	750	755	854
	GT3X	716	813	807	630	390
	Link	429	338	417	436	394
	Versa:GT3X % Error	16.2	3.4	4.7	32.4	103.1
	Versa:Link % Error	93.9	148.8	84.4	91.3	101
	Ring:GT3X % Error	34.5	9	7.1	19.8	119
	Ring:Link % Error	124.5	162.1	79.9	73.2	116.8
	Versa:Ring % Difference	14.6	5.2	2.5	9.9	7.5
	Link:GT3X % Difference	50.1	82.5	63.7	36.4	1

One challenge of the percent error calculations is the lack of upper limit. A device that does not measure any values could have a lower percent error than a device that measures more than double what the control device measures. For example, evaluator

Table 5. Stair activity step counts aggregated, and percent errors and percent differences calculated.

Activity	Device	E01			E02			E04		
Stair Ascend	Versa	14	14	20	14	17	27	9	9	8
	Ring	0	0	0	0	0	0	0	0	0
	GT3X	14	15	18	18	15	18	6	6	9
	Link	10	20	12	24	26	24	8	7	8
	Versa:GT3X % Error	0	6.7	11.1	22.2	13.3	50	50	50	11.1
	Versa:Link % Error	40	30	66.7	41.7	34.6	12.5	12.5	28.6	0
	Ring:GT3X % Error	100	100	100	100	100	100	100	100	100
	Ring:Link % Error	100	100	100	100	100	100	100	100	100
	Versa:Ring % Difference	200	200	200	200	200	200	200	200	200
	Link:GT3X % Difference	33.3	28.6	40	28.6	53.7	28.6	28.6	15.4	11.8
Stair Descend	Versa	30	19	19	35	20	14	8	14	9
	Ring	0	0	0	21	0	15	114	0	0
	GT3X	14	16	16	10	14	14	7	7	19
	Link	11	12	12	4	4	20	7	9	23
	Versa:GT3X % Error	114	18.8	18.8	250	42.9	0	14.3	100	52.6
	Versa:Link % Error	173	58.3	58.3	775	400	30	14.3	55.6	60.9
	Ring:GT3X % Error	100	100	100	110	100	7.1	1529	100	100
	Ring:Link % Error	100	100	100	425	100	25	1529	100	100
	Versa:Ring % Difference	200	200	200	50	200	6.9	174	200	200
	Link:GT3X % Difference	24	28.6	28.6	85.7	111	35.3	0	25	19

two's second stair descent has 20 steps from the Versa, 0 from the Ring, 14 from the GT3X, and 4 from the Link. The Versa (20) to Link (4) percent error is 400. The Ring (0) to GT3X (14) or Link (4) percent error is 100. Should the lack of agreement between Versa and Link be considered higher than the Ring-Link or Ring-GT3X? The percent

Table 6. Device comparisons of Mean Absolute Percent Error (MAPE), Median Absolute Percent Error (MdAPE), Mean Absolute Percent Difference (MAPD), Median Absolute Percent Difference (MdAPD), Spearman's Rho, and p-value for Spearman's Rho for each activity.

Devices	Activity	MAPE	MdAPE	MAPD	MdAPD	Rho	Rho p-value
Versa: GT3X	Very Light	195.14	91.00	64.23	62.54	0.1	0.873
	Light Walk	67.65	71.12	48.11	52.47	0.1	0.873
	Moderate Walk	31.96	16.20	23.82	14.99	0.3	0.624
	Stair Ascend	23.83	13.33	20.74	12.5	0.83	0.006
	Stair Descend	67.95	42.86	44.98	35.29	0.03	0.939
Versa: Link	Very Light	76.43	95.24	52.99	64.52	0.5	0.391
	Light Walk	98.84	94.87	65.41	64.35	0.1	0.873
	Moderate Walk	103.89	93.94	67.68	63.92	-0.1	0.873
	Stair Ascend	29.61	30	29.07	33.33	0.76	0.018
	Stair Descend	180.57	58.33	72.77	45.16	-0.45	0.225
Ring: GT3X	Very Light	145.40	77.22	62.94	55.71	0	1
	Light Walk	49.60	34.77	38.26	29.62	0.1	0.873
	Moderate Walk	37.87	19.84	27.60	18.05	0.1	0.873
	Stair Ascend	100	100	200	200	N/A	N/A
	Stair Descend	249.52	100	161.64	200	-0.57	0.106
Ring: Link	Very Light	55.97	55.56	46.14	49.19	0.4	0.505
	Light Walk	67.46	64.27	46.31	48.64	-0.5	0.391
	Moderate Walk	111.28	116.75	70.12	73.72	-0.2	0.747
	Stair Ascend	100	100	200	200	N/A	N/A
	Stair Descend	286.51	100	171.27	200	-0.33	0.394
Versa: Ring	Very Light	56.87	48.36	49.62	38.94	0.7	0.188
	Light Walk	31.82	12.28	24.26	11.63	-0.2	0.747
	Moderate Walk	7.79	7.26	7.96	7.53	0.5	0.391
	Stair Ascend	inf	inf	200	200	N/A	N/A
	Stair Descend	inf	inf	158.96	200	-0.185	0.634
Ring: Versa	Very Light	54.67	32.59	49.62	38.94	0.7	0.188
	Light Walk	20.16	12.34	24.26	11.63	-0.2	0.747
	Moderate Walk	8.17	7.83	7.96	7.53	0.5	0.391
	Stair Ascend	100	100	200	200	N/A	N/A
	Stair Descend	219.13	100	158.96	200	-0.19	0.634

(continued)

Table 6. (*continued*)

Devices	Activity	MAPE	MdAPE	MAPD	MdAPD	Rho	Rho p-value
GT3X: Link	Very Light	44.02	31.72	46.88	37.69	-0.3	0.624
	Light Walk	32.59	9.95	25.44	10.47	-0.8	0.104
	Moderate Walk	69.29	66.9	46.76	50.13	-0.4	0.505
	Stair Ascend	28.79	25	29.83	28.57	0.80	0.01
	Stair Descend	62.62	30	39.70	28.57	0.71	0.033
	High	286.51	116.75	200	200	0.83	1
	Median	67.46	55.56	48.11	48.64	0.1	0.505
	Mean	85.32	56.35	73.84	74.16	0.09	0.509
	Low	7.79	7.26	7.96	7.53	-0.8	0.006

difference metric has an upper limit of 200, and a measurement of zero for one device will produce a percent difference of 200, as seen with all comparisons where the Ring had a measurement of zero. When working with a large dataset, this upper bound could be very significant. Consider the many evaluations of the same dataset when capturing the mean or median of all errors or differences, as well as the correlation presented as Spearman's Rho (Table 6).

3   Results

3.1   Usability Results

Fitbit Versa 3 Usability Results. The Versa device was favorably accepted by evaluators for activity tracking. One evaluator mentioned they "liked the device so much, they purchased one for personal use at the end of the study." However, there was a considerable difference between evaluators regarding the wristband provided by the manufacturer. One evaluator mentioned needing to purchase a separate band for the study, another thought the band was comfortable. The device had an excellent average SUS score of 86.5% (80, 90, 82.5, 100, 80). Similarly, using the Everyday Use Checklist, the average user experience score was 91.2% (see Table 7 for a breakdown).

The Fitbit mobile app – an accompaniment of the Versa device – was also acceptable. The MARS app quality average score was 82.2% (4, 4.1, 3.9, 4.2, 4.3 out of 5) and the subjective quality average score was 64% (2.5, 3.5, 3.3, 4.8, 2 out of 5), primarily skewed due to most evaluators' noting an unwillingness to pay for the app. The app also had an excellent average SUS score of 92.5% (87.5, 92.5, 90, 97.5, 95). The app user experience scores from the Everyday Use Checklist had an average score of 85% (see Table 7 for a breakdown).

Oura Ring Usability Results. The Oura Ring device resulted in more diversity of opinion among evaluators. Evaluators noted that the Ring was "bulky" and "masculine-looking" and was "less appealing for those with smaller hands or fingers, though it fit well." For use in participant studies, researchers should consider whether the extra requirement of acquiring a participant's ring size, ordering, and distributing correct sizes constitutes undue burden. We could not evaluate SUS due to a lack of display or physical controls on the device. Using the Everyday Use Checklist, we could only score two of the five categories for this same reason. The Ring had an average score of 86% (see Table 7 for a breakdown).

Without a display and physical controls, the mobile app becomes the primary means of interacting with the device and user experience of the app holds considerable significance. The MARS app quality average score was 72% (3.5, 3.5, 3.4, 4.3, 3.9 out of 5) and the subjective quality average score was 74.4% (4.5, 4, 2.8, 3.8, 3 out of 5). The device had a good average SUS score of 84% (90, 90, 70, 92.5, 77.5). The app user experience scores from the Everyday Use Checklist had an average score of 88% (see Table 7 for a breakdown).

Table 7. Results of Everyday Use Checklist.

Device					
	Ease of Physical Controls	Wearability	Aesthetics	Display Viewability	Display Interpret-ability
Versa	3.8/5	4.6/5	4.8/5	5/5	4.6/5
Oura Ring	N/A	4.4/5	4.2/5	N/A	N/A
Mobile App					
	Ease of Setup	Syncing	Mobile Battery	Mobile App Ease of Use	
Fitbit app	4.6/5	3.6/5	4/5	4.8/5	
Oura app	4.6/5	4.6/5	4.8/5	3.6/5	

3.2 Device Functionality Results

Walk tests indicated that the two consumer devices, Ring and Versa, counted more steps than the research-grade devices, GT3X and Link. The consumer device values were more similar to the GT3X in the moderate walk cycles than the two lighter walk activities, perhaps indicating the Ring and Versa calculate more movement as steps than the GT3X (Fig. 4).

Stair tests revealed the Ring's inability to calculate steps while ascending and erroneously calculating steps while descending, making it the least useful device for stair activity from this study. The stair test was also slightly different in that we know the actual number of stairs each evaluator used for evaluation, as indicated by the grey line in the box plots (Fig. 4). All devices had more difficulty accurately counting descending stair steps.

While the dataset is limited due to the nature of the proof-of-concept for evaluation, the preliminary data from this study suggest the Versa is the better of these devices to be used interchangeably with the GT3X due to the closeness in daily steps (Fig. 2), moderate walk tests, and stair-climbing tests (Fig. 5). While we created Bland-Altman plots of activities between the Versa and GT3X, with our limited dataset, these plots may be of limited value (Fig. 6).

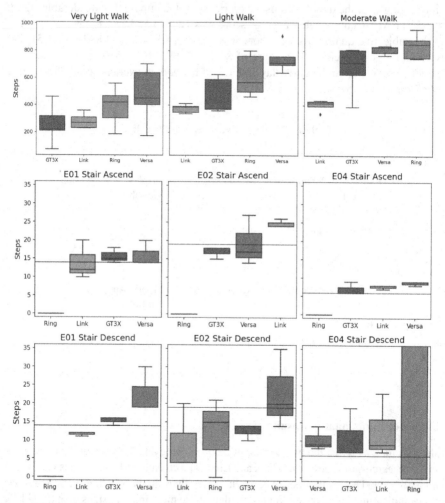

Fig. 4. First row: box plots of actual values from all evaluators and devices in very light, light, and moderate walk cycles. Second and third rows: stair ascensions and descensions by evaluator with a line indicating number of actual stairs. X-axis ordered by mean values.

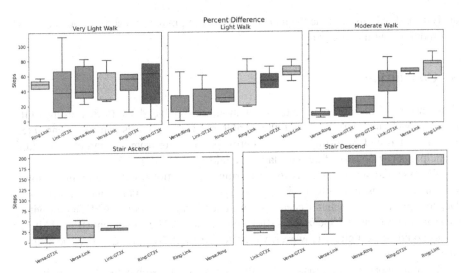

Fig. 5. Box plots of percent difference for all device comparisons and activities

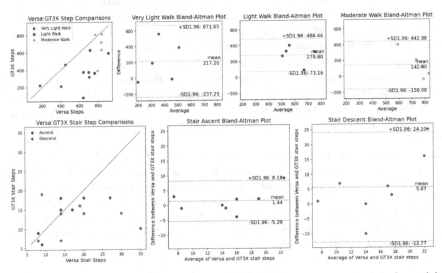

Fig. 6. Versa and GT3X step comparisons and Bland-Altman agreement plots for activity evaluations.

4   Discussion

Our study observed an issue already noted by other researchers wherein the GT3X fails to pick up steps during very light activity [39, 40]. Surprisingly, the wrist-worn devices, Link and Versa, were not considerably closer in value for any of the activities. We also observed that the Link may not be suited for interchangement with the GT3X from our analysis and will discontinue the inclusion of the Link in the next steps of our step-wise methodology with participants.

5 Conclusion

From this proof-of-concept team test evaluation, we concluded that further testing of the Fitbit Versa 3 and Oura Ring with the ActiGraph wGT3X-BT as control is warranted. In our next round of testing, we will enroll participants from our target older adult participants (>65 years of age) for lab- and field-based testing [25].

We assessed several options for analyzing the functional data, including absolute percent error, absolute percent difference, Spearman's Rho, and Bland-Altman plots. Depending on a researcher's need, use of either mean or median APE, along with a measure of correlation (Spearman's Rho) and visualizing the agreement (Bland-Altman plots) could be sufficient. However, we preferred MdAPE to APE, since the scale of those results are finite.

In future work, we anticipate adding the evaluation of documented daily activities on an average weekday and weekend day during the 7-day field testing. This documentation includes start and stop times, a description of the activity performed (ex. Cooking, doing laundry, cleaning house, walking the dog), and a potential additional impact rating (ex. Scale of 1–5 with 5 as highest exertion or impact). We will use the API for the devices to access 60-s epoch step counts for assessing the devices' ability to capture activities of daily living. This work will require continued application and evaluation of data analysis methods to identify and recommend standards for wearable devices. Development and adoption of data standards would increase rigor of SWT research, enable comparison of results between devices and across studies, and facilitate the use augmented cognition approaches in applications for health behavior change.

Acknowledgements and Declarations. The Precision START lab is supported in part by internal funding from the University of Missouri Sinclair School of Nursing and MU Institute for Data Science and Informatics. The authors thank Drs. Jo-Ana D. Chase and Knoo Lee for their guidance. Malaika R. Gallimore (MRG) and Chelsea Howland received funding as pre-doctoral fellows from the National Institutes of Health (NIH) T32 Health Behavior Science Research training grant 5T32NR015426 and the Sinclair PhD Student Fellowship at the MU Sinclair School of Nursing. MRG is supported by NIH F31 training grant NR019923.

References

1. Henriksen, A., et al.: Using fitness trackers and smartwatches to measure physical activity in research: analysis of consumer wrist-worn wearables. J. Med. Internet Res. **20**, e9157 (2018). https://doi.org/10.2196/jmir.9157
2. Puterman, E., Pauly, T., Ruissen, G., Nelson, B., Faulkner, G.: Move more, move better: a narrative review of wearable technologies and their application to precision health. Health Psychol. **40**, 803–810 (2021). https://doi.org/10.1037/hea0001125

3. Reeder, B., Cook, P.F., Meek, P.M., Ozkaynak, M.: Smart watch potential to support augmented cognition for health-related decision making. In: Schmorrow, D.D., Fidopiastis, C.M. (eds.) AC 2017. LNCS (LNAI), vol. 10284, pp. 372–382. Springer, Cham (2017). https://doi.org/10.1007/978-3-319-58628-1_29

4. Chu, A.H.Y., et al.: Comparison of wrist-worn Fitbit Flex and waist-worn ActiGraph for measuring steps in free-living adults. PLoS ONE 12, e0172535 (2017). https://doi.org/10.1371/journal.pone.0172535

5. Feehan, L.M., et al.: Accuracy of Fitbit devices: systematic review and narrative syntheses of quantitative data. JMIR Mhealth Uhealth 6, e10527 (2018). https://doi.org/10.2196/10527

6. Evenson, K.R., Goto, M.M., Furberg, R.D.: Systematic review of the validity and reliability of consumer-wearable activity trackers. Int. J. Behav. Nutr. Phys. Act. 12, 159 (2015). https://doi.org/10.1186/s12966-015-0314-1

7. Fitbit Official Site for Activity Trackers and More. https://www.fitbit.com/global/us/home

8. Evenson, K.R., Spade, C.L.: Review of validity and reliability of Garmin activity trackers. J. Measur. Phys. Behav. 3, 170–185 (2020)

9. Garmin International | Home. https://www.garmin.com/en-US/

10. Bunn, J.A., Navalta, J.W., Fountaine, C.J., Reece, J.D.: Current state of commercial wearable technology in physical activity monitoring 2015–2017. Int. J. Exerc. Sci. 11, 503–515 (2018)

11. Bai, Y., Tompkins, C., Gell, N., Dione, D., Zhang, T., Byun, W.: Comprehensive comparison of Apple watch and Fitbit monitors in a free-living setting. PLoS ONE 16, e0251975 (2021). https://doi.org/10.1371/journal.pone.0251975

12. Apple. https://www.apple.com/

13. Nair, S., et al.: ROAMM: a software infrastructure for real-time monitoring of personal health (2016)

14. Mobile | TV | Home Electronics | Home Appliances. https://www.samsung.com/us/

15. Labs, D.I.: WHOOP | Your Personal Digital Fitness and Health Coach. https://www.whoop.com/

16. Open. Friendly. Community Driven. https://www.pine64.org/

17. Oura Ring: Accurate Health Information Accessible to Everyone. https://ouraring.com

18. Shin, G., et al.: Wearable activity trackers, accuracy, adoption, acceptance and health impact: a systematic literature review. J. Biomed. Inform. 93, 103153 (2019). https://doi.org/10.1016/j.jbi.2019.103153

19. Connelly, K., et al.: Evaluation framework for selecting wearable activity monitors for research. mHealth 7 (2021). https://doi.org/10.21037/mhealth-19-253

20. Reeder, B., David, A.: Health at hand: a systematic review of smart watch uses for health and wellness. J. Biomed. Inform. 63, 269–276 (2016). https://doi.org/10.1016/j.jbi.2016.09.001

21. Fokkema, T., Kooiman, T.J.M., Krijnen, W.P., Van Der Schans, C.P., De Groot, M.: Reliability and validity of ten consumer activity trackers depend on walking speed. Med. Sci. Sports Exerc. 49, 793–800 (2017). https://doi.org/10.1249/MSS.0000000000001146

22. Intelligence, I.: US smart wearables users (2021–2025). https://www.insiderintelligence.com/charts/smart-wearables-users/

23. Glenn, L.M., Boyce, J.A.S.: At the Nexus: augmented cognition, health care, and the law. J. Cogn. Eng. Decis. Mak. 1, 363–373 (2007). https://doi.org/10.1518/155534307X255663

24. Gorzelitz, J., Farber, C., Gangnon, R., Cadmus-Bertram, L.: Accuracy of wearable trackers for measuring moderate- to vigorous-intensity physical activity: a systematic review and meta-analysis. J. Measur. Phys. Behav. 3, 346–357 (2020)

25. Reeder, B., et al.: Stepwise evaluation methodology for smart watch sensor function and usability. In: Schmorrow, D.D., Fidopiastis, C.M. (eds.) HCII 2021. LNCS (LNAI), vol. 12776, pp. 221–233. Springer, Cham (2021). https://doi.org/10.1007/978-3-030-78114-9_16

26. Ferguson, T., Rowlands, A.V., Olds, T., Maher, C.: The validity of consumer-level, activity monitors in healthy adults worn in free-living conditions: a cross-sectional study. Int. J. Behav. Nutr. Phys. Act. **12**, 42 (2015). https://doi.org/10.1186/s12966-015-0201-9

27. Gaz, D.V., et al.: Determining the validity and accuracy of multiple activity-tracking devices in controlled and free-walking conditions. Am. J. Health Promot. **32**, 1671–1678 (2018). https://doi.org/10.1177/0890117118763273

28. Kooiman, T.J.M., Dontje, M.L., Sprenger, S.R., Krijnen, W.P., van der Schans, C.P., de Groot, M.: Reliability and validity of ten consumer activity trackers. BMC Sports Sci. Med. Rehabil. **7**, 24 (2015). https://doi.org/10.1186/s13102-015-0018-5

29. Hedayatrad, L., Stewart, T., Duncan, S.: Concurrent validity of ActiGraph GT3X+ and Axivity AX3 accelerometers for estimating physical activity and sedentary behavior. J. Measur. Phys. Behav. **4**, 1–8 (2021)

30. Karaca, A., Demirci, N., Yılmaz, V., Hazır Aytar, S., Can, S., Ünver, E.: Validation of the ActiGraph wGT3X-BT accelerometer for step counts at five different body locations in laboratory settings. Meas. Phys. Educ. Exerc. Sci. **26**, 63–72 (2022). https://doi.org/10.1080/1091367X.2021.1948414

31. O'Brien, C.M., Duda, J.L., Kitas, G.D., Veldhuijzen van Zanten, J.J.C.S., Metsios, G.S., Fenton, S.A.M.: Measurement of sedentary time and physical activity in rheumatoid arthritis: an ActiGraph and activPAL™ validation study. Rheumatol. Int. **40**(9), 1509–1518 (2020). https://doi.org/10.1007/s00296-020-04608-2

32. O'Brien, M.W., Wojcik, W.R., Fowles, J.R.: Validity and interinstrument reliability of a medical grade physical activity monitor in older adults. J. Measur. Phys. Behav. **4**, 31–38 (2021)

33. Jimenez-Moreno, A.C., et al.: Analyzing walking speeds with ankle and wrist worn accelerometers in a cohort with myotonic dystrophy. Disabil. Rehabil. **41**, 2972–2978 (2019). https://doi.org/10.1080/09638288.2018.1482376

34. Johnston, W., et al.: Recommendations for determining the validity of consumer wearable and smartphone step count: expert statement and checklist of the INTERLIVE network. Br. J. Sports Med. **55**, 780–793 (2021). https://doi.org/10.1136/bjsports-2020-103147

35. Ellis, C.: Oura (Generation 2) review. https://www.techradar.com/reviews/oura

36. ActiGraph. https://actigraphcorp.com/

37. Stoyanov, S.R., Hides, L., Kavanagh, D.J., Zelenko, O., Tjondronegoro, D., Mani, M.: Mobile app rating scale: a new tool for assessing the quality of health mobile apps. JMIR mHealth uHealth **3**, e3422 (2015). https://doi.org/10.2196/mhealth.3422

38. Sauro, J.: A Practical Guide to the System Usability Scale: Background, Benchmarks & Best Practices. Measuring Usability LLC, Denver, CO (2011)

39. Feng, Y., Wong, C.K., Janeja, V., Kuber, R., Mentis, H.M.: Comparison of tri-axial accelerometers step-count accuracy in slow walking conditions. Gait Posture **53**, 11–16 (2017). https://doi.org/10.1016/j.gaitpost.2016.12.014

40. Storti, K.L., Pettee, K.K., Brach, J.S., Talkowski, J.B., Richardson, C.R., Kriska, A.M.: Gait speed and step-count monitor accuracy in community-dwelling older adults. Med. Sci. Sports Exerc. **40**, 59–64 (2008). https://doi.org/10.1249/mss.0b013e318158b504

Studying Human Factors Aspects of Text Classification Task Using Eye Tracking

Jeevithashree Divya Venkatesh[1], Aparajita Jaiswal[2], Meet Tusharbhai Suthar[1],
Romila Pradhan[3], and Gaurav Nanda[1]([✉])

[1] School of Engineering Technology, Purdue University, West Lafayette, IN 47907, USA
gnanda@purdue.edu
[2] Center for Intercultural Learning, Mentorship, Assessment and Research (CILMAR), Purdue
University, West Lafayette, IN 47907, USA
[3] Department of Computer and Information Technology, Purdue University, West Lafayette,
IN 47907, USA

Abstract. Text classification has a wide range of applications in today's world
including filtering spam emails, identifying health conditions, categorizing news
articles, business intelligence, and finding relevant legal documents. This has
become scalable due to the use of supervised machine learning models which
are usually trained on manually labelled text data and their performance is heavily
dependent on the quality of training data. Manual text classification tasks involve
a person reading the text and assigning the most appropriate category, which can
incur a significant amount of cognitive load. Therefore, an in-depth understanding of human factors aspects of the text classification task is important, and it
can help in determining the expected level of accuracy of human-labelled text as
well as identifying the challenging aspects of the task. To the best of our knowledge, previous studies have not studied the text classification task from a human
computer interaction (HCI) and human factors perspective. Our study is an early
effort towards studying text classification task using eye-tracking information captured during the manual labelling process. We aim to analyze ocular parameters
to understand the manual text classification process from an HCI perspective. We
designed an eye-tracking study that involved 30 human subjects reading narratives of injury-related texts and selecting the best-suited category for the cause of
injury events. Ocular parameters such as fixation count, average fixation duration,
and pupil dilation values were recorded for each participant. Preliminary results
from our study indicate that (a) reasonable level of average classification accuracy (75%) was observed for study participants, (b) a positive correlation between
fixation count and fixation duration, and fixation count and pupil diameter was
observed, and (c) we did not observe a consistent pattern between ocular parameters representative of cognitive load, the time taken to complete the task, and the
classification accuracy, maybe due to underlying variations among humans and
interpretability of textual narratives.

Keywords: Text Classification · Eye Tracking · Ocular Parameters · Cognitive
Load · Natural Language Processing

© The Author(s), under exclusive license to Springer Nature Switzerland AG 2023
D. D. Schmorrow and C. M. Fidopiastis (Eds.): HCII 2023, LNAI 14019, pp. 89–107, 2023.
https://doi.org/10.1007/978-3-031-35017-7_7

1   Introduction

The problem of text classification has witnessed a significant surge of interest in recent years because of the huge volume of natural language and text data available on the Internet. Text classification seeks to label natural language texts with categories from a predefined set [1] and has applications in wide range of domains [2] such as identifying spam emails [3], organizing and retrieving business and legal documents [4], filtering and organizing news articles [5] predicting health conditions [6] and causes from electronic health records [7] and so on. In these domains, machine learning models are being used to perform automated text classification for various practical applications as they can classify a large number of records in few minutes.

The classification performance of supervised machine learning models in general is heavily dependent on the correctness and quality of the labeled training data [8, 9]. In the context of text classification, training labels are typically assigned manually by human coders (domain experts or crowd workers) after reading the text and following a rulebook containing definitions and labelling criteria of each class label. Assigning training data labels is both time-consuming and cumbersome, and, therefore, is an active area of recent research [10, 11].

Several aspects of human factors stand out in the manual assignment of training data labels. From a cognitive load standpoint, the human coder is required to perform multiple steps to label each record in the dataset: (a) processing the text they are reading, (b) remembering the labeling criteria for different class labels, and (c) selecting the most appropriate class label for that textual record. The outcome of manual labelling task is further dependent on the *expertise* and *training* of the human coders. When performed by individuals with different levels of experience and training on the same dataset, training data labels may vary substantially because the coders' interpretation of text and memory recall of the labelling criteria can influence their judgement about the most applicable class label [12]. Manual labelling performed by multiple human coders has been observed to result in inconsistent labels [13] due to several factors such as the multi-category nature of text, subjective interpretation by different individuals, and overlapping nature of classification categories.

Obtaining an in-depth understanding of human factors aspects of the text classification task is important as it can help in determining the expected level of accuracy of human-labelled text as well as identifying different types of cases in the dataset such as easy-to-classify, confusing, and non-classifiable. Another important aspect related to studying the human text classification process is understanding the human reasoning behind their selection of classification categories. Some of the previous studies [14, 15] have tried to study the human reasoning aspect of text classification process but to the best of our knowledge, no previous study has studied the human factors aspects of text classification task using eye tracking. To fill this gap in literature, this study aims to conduct an in-depth analysis of the manual text classification process from a human-computer interaction perspective through eye-tracking. Specifically, we seek to answer the following research questions:

1. Can eye-tracking data capture the cognitive load and challenges faced by human coders?

2. Can ocular parameters recorded by eye tracker during manual text classification be indicative of task performance, i.e., time taken and expected coding accuracy?

A manual text classification user study was designed where 30 participants were asked to perform text classification tasks and their eye-tracking data were recorded. The eye-tracking data was then analyzed to understand the attention level, engagement level, and cognitive load during the text classification task. The text dataset used for classification consisted of injury narratives collected at hospitals which were to be classified into cause-of-injury categories. This dataset involved several of the above-mentioned challenges of manual text classification and is also of practical significance in the areas of injury surveillance, public health, and workplace safety. A schematic diagram summarizing the study design is shown in Fig. 1.

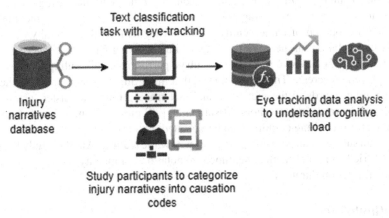

Fig. 1. Schematic experimental flow diagram.

The rest of the paper is organized as follows. The next section, Background presents a brief overview of related previous studies on eye tracking and its applications for analyzing human text reading. It is followed by Sect. 3 explaining the Methodology of this study and Sect. 4 discussing the results and findings. The last Sect. 5 summarizes the conclusions from this study, realizes the limitations, and lists some possible directions for future research.

2   Background

Eye tracking is an experimental method to record eye motion and gaze location relative to the head, across time and task. An eye tracker is a device for measuring eye positions and eye movement [16]. Eye gaze plays an important role in nonverbal communication as well as Human-Computer Interaction (HCI) [17]. Eye tracking can be used as an analytical tool to make interaction between human and computer more simple, natural, and efficient. Ocular parameters obtained from eye tracking system can be used in visual assessment [18], estimating cognitive workload [19], analyze visual behavior [20], identify emotional state and mental occupancy [21], diagnose learning disabilities [22,

23] and other user behaviors [24] while performing a particular task. Zagermann [25] and colleagues presented a refined model to investigate users' cognitive load while interacting with a system using eye tracking. Results from the model showed high correlation between major eye movements and cognitive load thus concluding that eye tracking can be a valuable instrument to measure and analyze cognitive load in the context of HCI and visual computing. Kruger et al. [26] studied the impact of subtitles in video recordings of a first-year Psychology class. The authors measured cognitive load by means of eye tracking, electroencephalography (EEG), and comprehension test. Results found that same-language subtitles in an educational context reduced cognitive load facilitating students' processing and understanding of the stimulus presented to them.

Measuring eye movements while reading is one of the most accurate methods for measuring moment-wise processing demands during text comprehension [27]. They provide the advantage of measuring reading behavior relative to measuring the reading times for an entire sentence or paragraph. Tomanek et al. [28] analyzed eye tracking data during their annotation of named entity in texts. They defined the difficulty of named entity instances based on the cognitive load estimated using gaze data. Another study by Raney et al. [27] used eye tracking to evaluate performance of reading when stimuli were displayed on screen. The study showed that more time was spent reading the last word than other words in the metaphor, and that reading time was faster for familiar than unfamiliar words in metaphors. Mishra et al. [29] proposed and evaluated various approaches for modelling cognitive load associated with text comprehension using eye tracking data such as scan path complexity of gaze while reading. Another study by Joshi et al. [30] tried to model manual sentiment annotation complexity using eye tracking data such as fixation duration.

3 Methodology

The user study participants were asked to classify injury related narrative texts into specific injury event cause groups. Ocular parameters were recorded from the eye tracker while performing the text classification task. Their eye tracking data was analyzed to understand the cognitive load involved in manual text classification process. The participants were asked to complete a survey post completion of task based on NASA TLX [31] and SUS (System Usability Scale) survey instruments. The survey scores and eye-tracking data were analyzed to evaluate performance of task, estimate cognitive workload and determine expected coding accuracy while performing the study. The details of the experiment are described in this section as follows.

3.1 Participants

We collected data from 30 participants including 18 male and 12 female. All participants were either native or non-native English speakers and aged between 23 to 30 years.

3.2 Materials

All participants were initially briefed about the task and asked to sit in a comfortable posture facing a 22″ LED Display with 1920 × 1080 UHD panel monitor, which was used to display the injury classification software (see Fig. 2). The dataset used in the study was generously provided by the Queensland Injury Surveillance Unit (QISU), Australia. The dataset contained anonymized injury records collected from emergency department of various hospitals in Australia. For each record in the dataset, one external-cause-of-injury code (E-code) out of 30 unique E-codes, was assigned by human coders based on the injury narratives describing how the accident happened [32]. For this study, six E-codes were used, as described later in the paper. The study participants had to read the injury narrative and then select the most appropriate cause of injury code using the injury classification software. For interaction with the software, a standard computer mouse was used. We used the Tobii Pro Fusion Eye Tracker with 250 Hz sampling frequency to capture gaze data and Tobii Pro Lab software to record ocular parameters for each participant. The Tobii Pro Lab uses the Velocity-Threshold Identification (IV-T) Fixation Filter algorithm [33] to calculate angular velocity for each data point and depending on threshold values, the data points are classified as a fixation or a saccade [34]. A EVIDA digital voice recorder was used to record participants responses during the think-aloud in course of the study.

Fig. 2. Experiment setup.

3.3 Design

The study was approved by the Institutional Review Board (IRB) at Purdue University. Taking part in the study was voluntary, in the sense that each participant was given a consent form which was required to be read and signed before starting the study if they wished to participate. Participants were allowed to choose to quit the study at any point in time. Additionally, participants were compensated with cash for their time and effort upon completing the study. The consent form included details like key information, purpose of the study, duration, compensation details, and potential risk of taking the study. Each participant was then briefed about the task and asked to sit in a comfortable posture facing the monitor. The eye tracker was placed along the lower edge of the monitor that displayed the injury classification software (see Figs. 2 and 3). The software consisted of the instructions page (see Fig. 3(a)) and 12 prompts. Each prompt displayed one injury narrative text and 6 cause of injury code groups (see Fig. 3(b)) from which the participant had to select one. The 6 groups included 'Fall', 'Struck', 'Cut', 'Burn', 'Motor Vehicle' and 'Other' (explained in Table 1 later). The 12 prompts consisted of a set of two unique narratives texts belonging to each injury event cause group. The 'NEXT' and 'UNDO' buttons on each prompt were used to navigate to next prompt and clear selection of injury event cause group to reselect the appropriate group respectively. Participants could read the prompt and use the mouse to select the desired injury event cause group. We created 17 unique sets of the 12 prompts and used them for 30 participants.

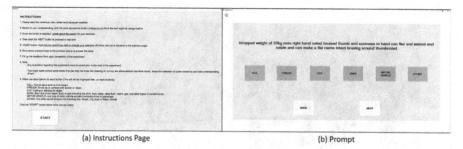

(a) Instructions Page   (b) Prompt

Fig. 3. Injury classification software.

3.4 Procedure

The study was carried out in a well-lit indoor room. Each participant was called individually to the room and asked to position themselves comfortably towards the screen in a way they could read content on screen and access the mouse. They were asked to read and sign the consent form to confirm their willingness to participate in the study and record their voice and ocular parameters. Participants were then briefed about the process of the study and a trial session was given for them to be familiarized with the injury classification software. Then, the eye tracker was calibrated using the Tobii nine-point calibration routine. After the eye tracker was successfully calibrated, the injury classification software was displayed on screen. Throughout the study, participants did not have any restriction about head movement and study completion time.

Then, the participant executed the study in below sequential flow:

- An instruction page (see Fig. 3(a)) was displayed at the start of study which included meanings to each injury event cause group (Table 1). Participants were asked to read the instructions carefully and select the 'START' button when ready.

- Participant read the injury narrative text displayed on screen and selected one of the 6 injury event cause groups that they felt was most appropriate.
- Once the group was selected, a prompt was displayed which required the participant to think-aloud the reason for selecting the group before proceeding to the next prompt.
- Participant could use the 'UNDO' button to clear existing group selection and reselect appropriate group if needed.
- The 'NEXT' button was used to navigate to the next prompt to continue with the study.
- Each participant was required to complete 12 such prompts. Once the study was completed, participants were asked to take a survey that included biographical information like gender, language, major, ethnicity, and NASA Task Load Index (TLX) and System Usability Scale (SUS) questionnaire.

Table 1. Description for injury event cause groups.

Injury event cause group	Description
Fall	Fall on some level or height
Struck	Struck by or collision with person or object
Cut	Cutting or piercing by object
Burn	Burn due to hot object, fluid, or gas including hot drink, food, water, other fluid, steam, gas, and other types of contact burns
Motor Vehicle	Any type of motor vehicle accident involving driver or passenger
Other	Any other cause of injury not including Fall, Struck, cut, Burn or Motor Vehicle

4 Results and Discussion

We used eye tracking to record ocular parameters including fixation count, average fixation duration, average and standard deviation of pupil diameter for left and right eyes respectively. The injury classification software recorded total time taken to complete the task involving 12 prompts, average time taken to read injury narrative text and select appropriate injury event cause group, and selected injury event cause group. The voice recorder was used to capture participant's response during the think-aloud. It may be noted that analysis for think-aloud is not in the scope of this paper and will be explored in subsequent studies. Further, mental workload and system usability were measured using the NASA TLX and SUS questionnaire for each of the 30 participants.

All participants completed all 12 prompts. In total we recorded 360 selections of injury event cause groups which included 60 selections for each of the 6 groups. Two participants used the 'UNDO' button to reselect the desired injury event cause group.

4.1 Time and Accuracy

The task completion time is the time taken by a participant to read injury narrative text and select appropriate injury event cause group for all 12 prompts. The task completion time taken for the 30 participants is presented in Fig. 4. The response time is the time taken by participant for reading narrative text and selecting appropriate injury event cause group. The response time for the 30 participants is shown in Fig. 5.

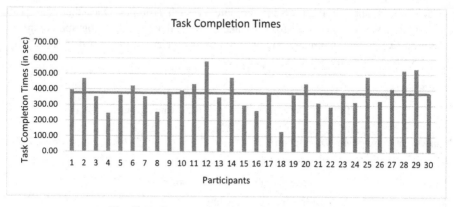

Fig. 4. Task completion times for all participants.

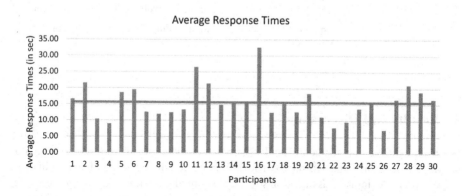

Fig. 5. Average response times for all participants.

As shown in Fig. 4, the average task completion time for all participants was 376.25 s. The average response time for reading the narrative text and selecting appropriate injury event cause group in each prompt was 15.66 s (see Fig. 5). From Figs. 4 and 5, we may note that 16 of 30 participants showed less than average task completion and 15 of 30 participants showed less than average response times. 12 out of 30 participants showed less than average task completion and response times when compared to the other participants.

The injury event cause group selected by the participants were compared against the original E-code assigned in the QISU dataset to check if the participant's selected agreed with the original code or not. Figure 6 presents the coding accuracy with response time for all 30 participants, and Fig. 7 shows the coding accuracy in percentage for all participants.

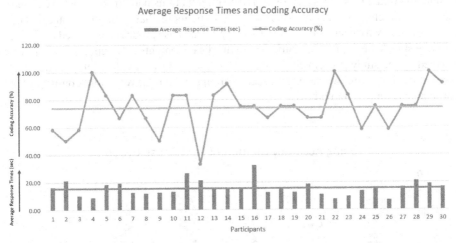

Fig. 6. Participant-wise average response times and coding accuracy.

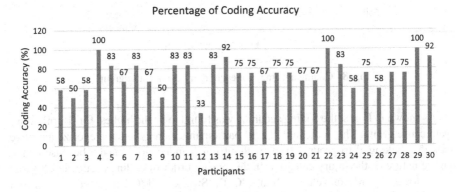

Fig. 7. Participant-wise percentage of coding accuracy.

As shown in Fig. 6, the average number of correct selections of injury event cause group, i.e., where the participant selection agreed with the E-code in QISU dataset, was 9 out of total 12 prompts across all participants, hereafter referred as coding accuracy (75% = 9/12). This relatively high level of coding accuracy indicates that the narrative text comprehension and the task of selecting the most appropriate cause of injury group was not very confusing for participants. 18 out of 30 participants showed higher than average coding accuracy, out of which 8 participants had less than average response times (see Fig. 6). Figure 7 demonstrates participant-wise breakdown for percentage of coding accuracy. From the bar plot we can note that 3 out of 30 participants (participants 4, 22, and 29) showed 100% coding accuracy, indicating that these participants selected the correct injury event cause groups for all 12 prompts. Among the participants, participant 12 demonstrated the least coding accuracy of 33% (see Fig. 7) with a relatively high task completion time of 580.25 s (see Fig. 4) indicating that this participant may have found the text comprehension and classification task to be more challenging than others. The coding accuracy for each of the different injury event cause groups is presented in Fig. 8. Figure 9 shows the confusion matrix where the disagreements between the cause group selected by the study participants and the original E-code assigned by QISU coders are highlighted indicating which pairs of cause groups were relatively more confusing for participants compared to others.

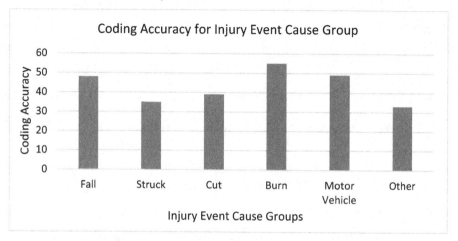

Fig. 8. Coding accuracy for each injury event cause group.

As shown in Fig. 8, the coding accuracy was found to be the highest for 'Burn' injury event cause group. This indicated that all participants were able to categorize narrative texts that belonged to group 'Burn' without much indecision, maybe because of the unique nature of the injury category. In decreasing order of coding accuracies, "Burn" was followed by 'Motor Vehicle', 'Fall', 'Cut', 'Struck' and 'Other' respectively. From the confusion matrix in Fig. 9 showing the selected and correct injury event cause groups, it can be observed that many participants had difficulty in correctly categorizing narrative texts into 'Other' and 'Struck' injury event cause groups. "Other" was often incorrectly categorized into 'Fall', 'Struck', Cut' injury groups and "Struck" was miscategorized into 'Fall', Cut', and 'Other' injury event cause groups by participants. One of the possible explanations for this behavior may be that based on their definitions, "Burn" and "Motor Vehicle" injury groups are relatively unique in nature, while the injury groups "Fall", "Struck", and "Other" are not as distinctive and may be more confusing for participants while making a selection about the most applicable category. It is also to be noted that

Correct Injury Event Cause Group

Selected Injury Event Cause Group	Fall	Struck	Cut	Burn	Motor Vehicle	Other
Fall	47	6	9	1	1	13
Struck	8	35	6	0	5	5
Cut	2	7	41	0	0	4
Burn	0	0	0	58	3	2
Motor Vehicle	0	4	0	0	50	2
Other	2	8	3	1	1	35

Fig. 9. Confusion matrix for selected vs correct injury event cause group.

the narratives also had varying levels of complexity which would have influenced the coding accuracy of participants. The impact of narrative complexity is not in the scope of this paper and will be examined in a future study.

4.2 Ocular Parameters

Analysis of participants' ocular parameters recorded from the eye-tracker provided insights about their cognitive load during the task. These are presented in Figs. 10 and 11. Figure 10 shows the values of Fixation Count (Y-axis) and Fixation Duration (X-axis) for each participant and Fig. 11 shows the Average Pupil Diameter of left and right eye for each participant.

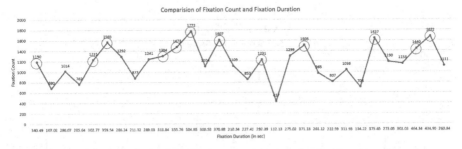

Fig. 10. Comparison of fixation count and average fixation duration values.

The average number of fixations across all participants was 1175 and the average fixation duration was 291.90 s. As shown in Fig. 10 with red circles, 12 out of 30 participants reported relatively higher (values greater than the average) number of fixations and average fixation duration values indicating that these participants spent more time to read the narrative text and select appropriate injury event cause group. From Fig. 11, it can

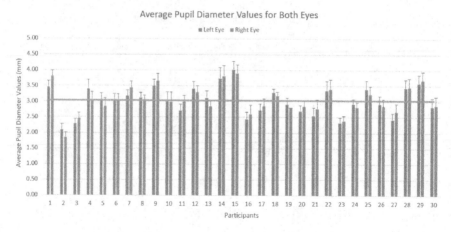

Fig. 11. Average pupil diameter values for left and right eyes.

be noted that the average pupil diameter values for both left and right eyes was observed to be 3.03 and 3.05 respectively for all participants. 14 out of 30 participants showed to have higher (values greater than the average) pupil diameter values (see Fig. 11). Further, 6 out of these 14 participants showed higher (values greater than the average) fixation count and fixation duration values (see Fig. 10 and Fig. 11) leading to higher cognitive load estimation when compared to other participants.

4.3 Surveys

We calculated performance and mental workload scores of participants by interpreting results from SUS and NASA TLX survey, these are presented in Fig. 12.

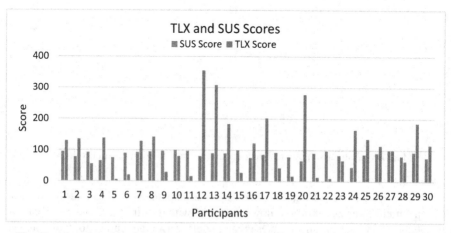

Fig. 12. Mental workload (TLX score) and performance (SUS score) for each participant.

The average performance (SUS score) and mental workload (TLX score) for all participants was found to be 85.67 and 112.67 with standard deviation of 12.52 and 90.25 respectively (see Fig. 12). Based on general guidelines on interpreting SUS score [35] as shown in Table 2, the Performance scores were interpreted. These performance scores for each participant are shown in Fig. 13.

Table 2. SUS score interpretation.

SUS Score	Grade	Adjective rating
>80.3	A	Excellent
68–80.3	B	Good
68	C	Okay
51–68	D	Poor
<51	F	Awful

From Fig. 13, it can be observed that 27 participants showed Excellent/Good performance and reported the system to be easy to use while 3 participants found the system to be difficult to use showing low performance scores (Poor/Awful). The distribution of TLX scores across various TLX dimensions for all participants is presented in Fig. 14.

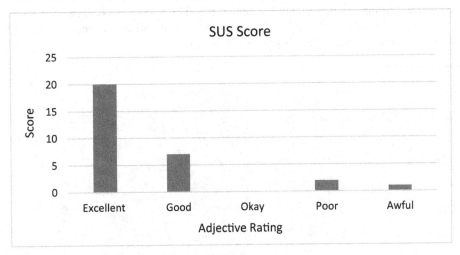

Fig. 13. Performance scores.

From Fig. 14, we can observe that all participants rated relatively high on the dimensions of mental demand, effort, and performance indicating that they required considerable time and effort to think and decide on selecting appropriate injury event cause group, and that they were successful in completing the study. Then, we assigned the mental workload scores based on the interpretation illustrated in Chen et al. [36]. The

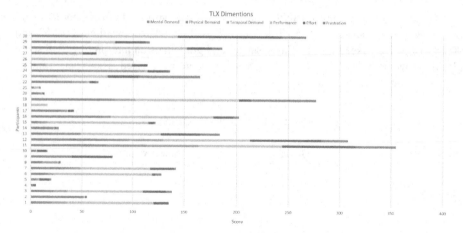

Fig. 14. TLX dimensions scores for all participants.

authors noted that a mental workload score measured by NASA TLX exceeding 69 points is considered a high mental workload, score between 54 to 68 is considered a medium workload, and a score below 53 is considered a low mental workload. Based on these thresholds, we found that 18 participants showed high mental workload, 9 participants showed low mental workload and 3 participants had medium mental workload (see Fig. 14). Additionally, 3 out of these 18 participants reported the system to be difficult to use showing low performance as demonstrated by SUS scores (indicated as Poor and Awful in Fig. 12). An overall holistic view of the distribution of different variables associated with each participant is provided in Fig. 15.

Participants	Fixation Count	Fixation Duration	Coding Accuracy	AveragePupil DiaRight	TLX Grade	SUS Grade
1	1190	340.486	53	3.63	High	A
2	850	167.023	50	3.97	High	B
3	3014	260.068	58	2.37	Medium	A
4	762	205.643	100	3.23	High	D
5	1231	302.773	63	2.93	Low	B
6	1365	359.538	67	3.03	Low	A
7	1292	295.743	83	3.30	High	A
8	877	211.321	87	3.07	High	A
9	1241	230.027	50	3.58	Low	A
10	1304	313.835	83	2.99	High	A
11	3473	956.764	62	2.86	Low	A
12	2772	504.451	23	3.35	High	B
13	1104	306.527	83	2.98	High	A
14	1607	370.33	92	3.77	High	A
15	1109	216.337	75	3.96	Low	A
16	653	227.412	75	2.52	High	B
17	1231	292.385	67	2.79	High	A
18	427	112.126	75	3.24	Low	A
19	1299	275.033	75	2.86	Low	B
20	1568	371.178	67	2.78	High	D
21	965	261.121	67	2.67	Low	A
22	892	222.586	100	3.37	Medium	A
23	1096	311.912	83	2.36	Low	A
24	704	134.222	58	2.88	High	F
25	1633	325.551	75	3.21	High	A
26	1100	273.048	58	2.80	High	A
27	1159	340.975	75	2.55	High	A
28	1440	464.543	75	3.44	Medium	B
29	2672	434.893	100	3.63	High	A
30	1132	260.843	92	2.85	High	B

Fig. 15. Comparison of all variables for all participants.

4.4 Statistical Analysis

A non-parametric test was used to measure association between ocular parameters and coding accuracy. We used the Spearman's Rho correlation test as the data was not normally distributed, consisted of ordinal data, and had a few outliers. The test results shown in Fig. 16 below indicated (a) a strong positive correlation between fixation count and fixation duration, [r (29) $= .74$, $p < 0.01$], (b) a weak positive correlation between fixation count and pupil diameter values, [r (29) $= .26$, $p < 0.05$], (c) no correlation between coding accuracy and ocular parameters (fixation count, fixation duration, and pupil diameter), and (d) negative correlation between the coding accuracy and TLX score.

Correlations

			FixationCount	FixationDuration	CodingAccuracy	PupilDiameter	TLXScore
Spearman's rho	FixationCount	Correlation Coefficient	1.000	.889**	.063	.371*	-.070
		Sig. (2-tailed)	.	.000	.740	.044	.712
		N	30	30	30	30	30
	FixationDuration	Correlation Coefficient	.889**	1.000	.074	.263	-.057
		Sig. (2-tailed)	.000	.	.696	.160	.765
		N	30	30	30	30	30
	CodingAccuracy	Correlation Coefficient	.063	.074	1.000	.194	-.064
		Sig. (2-tailed)	.740	.696	.	.304	.736
		N	30	30	30	30	30
	PupilDiameter	Correlation Coefficient	.371*	.263	.194	1.000	-.229
		Sig. (2-tailed)	.044	.160	.304	.	.223
		N	30	30	30	30	30
	TLXScore	Correlation Coefficient	-.070	-.057	-.064	-.229	1.000
		Sig. (2-tailed)	.712	.765	.736	.223	.
		N	30	30	30	30	30

**. Correlation is significant at the 0.01 level (2-tailed).

*. Correlation is significant at the 0.05 level (2-tailed).

Fig. 16. Results from Spearman's Rho correlation test.

We also performed a detailed participant wise analysis for all variables including ocular parameters, coding accuracy, mental workload, and performance scores as shown in Fig. 15 to identify any prominent patterns. Some of the groups identified are described here. Participants 1, 12, 14, 25, 28 and 29 had higher than average values of task completion and response times, fixation count, fixation duration, pupil diameter and mental workload, thereby indicating to have higher cognitive load when compared to other participants. Among these, except for participant 1 and 12, participants 14, 25, 28, 29 had relatively higher (values greater than the average) coding accuracy. All of these 6 participants were able to categories narrative texts that belonged to group 'Burn' without any indecision followed by 'Fall', 'Cut', 'Motor Vehicle', 'Struck' and 'Other' injury event cause groups respectively.

Another group of participants, 2, 3, 16, 21, 24 and 30, had lower than the average values of fixation count, fixation duration and average pupil diameter values. Of these, except for participant 16, participants 2, 3, 21, 24 and 30 showed below average coding accuracy. These 5 participants were also able to categories narrative texts that belonged to the group 'Burn' without any indecision, followed by 'Fall', 'Motor Vehicle', 'Other',

'Cut' and 'Struck' injury event cause groups in decreasing order of coding accuracy respectively. Participants 4, 22, and 29 had 100% coding accuracy with participants 4 and 22 showing relatively lower (values less than the average) values of fixation count, fixation duration, and pupil diameter, and participant 29 showing higher than average values of fixation count, fixation duration and average pupil diameter values.

Then, participants 5, 6, 10, 11, 17 and 20 recorded higher than average values of fixation count, fixation duration and lower than average of pupil diameter values. All 6 participants were able to categories narrative texts that belonged to the group 'Burn' without any indecision followed by 'Motor Vehicle', 'Fall', 'Cut', 'Other', and 'Struck' injury event cause groups in decreasing order of coding accuracy. Participants 8, 15 and 18 showed lower than average values of fixation count and fixation duration with above average values of pupil diameter. Except for participant 8, participant 15 and 18 showed higher (values greater than the average) coding accuracy. All 3 participants were able to categories narrative texts that belonged to the group 'Burn' without any indecision followed by 'Motor Vehicle', 'Fall', 'Cut', 'Other', and 'Struck' injury event cause groups respectively. Finally, participants 7, 13, 19, 23 and 27 showed higher than average coding accuracy and participants 9 and 26 showed lower than average coding accuracy. All 7 participants were able to categories narrative texts that belonged to group 'Burn' without any indecision followed by 'Fall', 'Cut', 'Motor Vehicle', 'Struck' and 'Other' event cause groups respectively.

Overall, we did not observe any generalizable patterns between ocular parameters indicative of cognitive load, time taken to complete the task, and the accuracy of text classification. There may be various underlying reasons for this, such as, variation in English proficiency and cautious behavior among participants, and variation in complexity and interpretability of injury narratives. The negative correlation between the TLX score and coding accuracy may be indicative that people who found the text classification to be challenging were not sure about which injury code group was most applicable and may have been a function of text complexity or their proficiency with English language or any other factors. The various groups of participants indicated these variations. For example, some participants (4 and 22) were able to achieve high accuracy with relatively less time and low cognitive load indicating the task was straightforward for them, while others (29 and 30) were able to attain good accuracy with more time and cognitive load, indicating they carefully processed the text and made the selection.

5 Conclusion

This pilot study aimed to analyze ocular parameters recorded using eye tracking to understand the cognitive load during manual text classification process and how it can be indicative of the task performance in terms of time taken and classification/coding accuracy. With regards to the first research question, *Can eye-tracking data capture the cognitive load and challenges faced by human coders?*, the results indicated that the ocular parameters recorded by the eye tracker were able to identify the level of cognitive load experienced by the human participant. The ocular parameters also indicated consistency through positive correlation among them, such as, fixation count and fixation duration, and fixation count and pupil diameter. Regarding the second research question, *Can ocular parameters recorded by eye tracker during manual text classification be indicative of task performance, i.e., time taken and expected coding accuracy?*, the results did not indicate any consistent pattern between the ocular parameters indicative of cognitive load and the task performance in terms of the time taken or coding accuracy. There were different groups of participants who exhibited different patterns, such as, high coding accuracy with low time and low cognitive load, high coding accuracy with high cognitive load and more time, and low coding accuracy with more time taken and high cognitive load, and others. These findings indicate that there might be various underlying factors such as the proficiency level in English, behavioral aspects of participants, and complexity of narratives, which can lead to such variations in task performance and associated cognitive load level.

This study was an initial effort in the direction of studying the HCI aspects of manual text classification process using eye tracking and had several limitations, such as, the number of participants was limited to 30, the text classification task was from a specific domain of injury narrative classification which may not be generalizable to other types of text classification tasks such as classifying sentiments or type of news article, and in-depth analysis of underlying factors of variations among human participants and text complexity has not been completed yet. Future studies should address these limitations and investigate the above-mentioned underlying factors in detail with possibly larger number of participants and by collecting open-ended feedback from participants about their task experience. Future studies can analyze the linkage between the participant background (e.g., English proficiency) with their task performance and cognitive load, study the reasoning behind participant's selection of injury code groups, and examine the linkage between task performance, cognitive load, and narrative complexity.

References

1. Sebastiani, F.: Machine learning in automated text categorization. ACM Comput. Surv. **34**(1), 1–47 (2002)
2. Li, Q., et al.: A survey on text classification: from traditional to deep learning. ACM Trans. Intell. Syst. Technol. **13**(2), 1–41 (2022)
3. Karim, A., Azam, S., Shanmugam, B., Kannoorpatti, K., Alazab, M.: A comprehensive survey for intelligent spam email detection. IEEE Access **7**, 168261–168295 (2019)
4. Castano, S., Falduti, M., Ferrara, A., Montanelli, S.: A knowledge-centered framework for exploration and retrieval of legal documents. Inf. Syst. **106**, 101842 (2022)
5. Barberá, P., Boydstun, A.E., Linn, S., McMahon, R., Nagler, J.: Automated text classification of news articles: a practical guide. Polit. Anal. **29**(1), 19–42 (2021)
6. Hughes, M., Li, I., Kotoulas, S., Suzumura, T.: Medical text classification using convolutional neural networks. In: Informatics for Health: Connected Citizen-Led Wellness and Population Health, pp. 246–250. IOS Press (2017)
7. Nanda, G., Vallmuur, K., Lehto, M.: Semi-automated text mining strategies for identifying rare causes of injuries from emergency room triage data. IISE Trans. Healthc. Syst. Eng. **9**(2), 157–171 (2019)
8. Jain, A., et al.: Overview and importance of data quality for machine learning tasks. In: Proceedings of the 26th ACM SIGKDD International Conference on Knowledge Discovery Data Mining, pp. 3561–3562 (2020)
9. Gupta, N., et al.: Data quality for machine learning tasks. In: Proceedings of the 27th ACM SIGKDD Conference on Knowledge Discovery Data Mining, pp. 4040–4041 (2021)

10. Sheng, V.S., Provost, F., Ipeirotis, P.G.: Get another label? Improving data quality and data mining using multiple, noisy labelers. In: Proceedings of the 14th ACM SIGKDD International Conference on Knowledge Discovery and Data Mining, pp. 614–622 (2008)
11. Paun, S., Artstein, R., Poesio, M.: Statistical methods for annotation analysis. Synth. Lect. Hum. Lang. Technol. **15**(1), 1–217 (2022)
12. Nanda, G.: Improving the autocoding of injury narratives using a combination of machine learning methods and natural language processing techniques. Doctoral dissertation, Purdue University (2017)
13. Nanda, G., Vallmuur, K., Lehto, M.: Improving autocoding performance of rare categories in injury classification: is more training data or filtering the solution? Accid. Anal. Prev. **110**, 115–127 (2018)
14. Sen, C., Hartvigsen, T., Yin, B., Kong, X., Rundensteiner, E.: Human attention maps for text classification: do humans and neural networks focus on the same words? In: Proceedings of the 58th Annual Meeting of the Association for Computational Linguistics, pp. 4596–4608 (2020)
15. Nguyen, D.: Comparing automatic and human evaluation of local explanations for text classification. In: Proceedings of the 2018 Conference of the North American Chapter of the Association for Computational Linguistics: Human Language Technologies, vol. 1 (Long Papers), pp. 1069–1078 (2018)
16. Wikimedia Foundation: Eye tracking. https://en.wikipedia.org/wiki/Eye_tracking
17. Jiang, J., Zhou, X., Chan, S., Chen, S.: Appearance-based gaze tracking: a brief review. In: Yu, H., Liu, J., Liu, L., Ju, Z., Liu, Y., Zhou, D. (eds.) ICIRA 2019. LNCS (LNAI), vol. 11745, pp. 629–640. Springer, Cham (2019). https://doi.org/10.1007/978-3-030-27529-7_53
18. Kooiker, M.J., Pel, J.J., van der Steen-Kant, S.P., van der Steen, J.: A method to quantify visual information processing in children using eye tracking. J. Vis. Exp. **113**, e54031 (2016)
19. Babu, M.D., JeevithaShree, D.V., Prabhakar, G., Saluja, K.P.S., Pashilkar, A., Biswas, P.: Estimating pilots' cognitive load from ocular parameters through simulation and in-flight studies. J. Eye Mov. Res. **12**(3) (2019)
20. King, A.J., Bol, N., Cummins, R.G., John, K.K.: Improving visual behavior research in communication science: an overview, review, and reporting recommendations for using eye-tracking methods. Commun. Methods Meas. **13**(3), 149–177 (2019)
21. Li, J., et al.: Identification and classification of construction equipment operators' mental fatigue using wearable eye-tracking technology. Autom. Constr. **109**, 103000 (2020)
22. Rello, L., Ballesteros, M.: Detecting readers with dyslexia using machine learning with eye tracking measures. In: Proceedings of the 12th International Web for All Conference, pp. 1–8 (2015)
23. Saluja, K.S., Dv, J., Arjun, S., Biswas, P., Paul, T.: Analyzing eye gaze of users with learning disability. In: Proceedings of the 3rd International Conference on Graphics and Signal Processing, pp. 95–99 (2019)
24. Tzafilkou, K., Protogeros, N.: Diagnosing user perception and acceptance using eye tracking in web-based end-user development. Comput. Hum. Behav. **72**, 23–37 (2017)
25. Zagermann, J., Pfeil, U., Reiterer, H.: Measuring cognitive load using eye tracking technology in visual computing. In: Proceedings of the Sixth Workshop on Beyond Time and Errors on Novel Evaluation Methods for Visualization, pp. 78–85 (2016)
26. Kruger, J.L., Hefer, E., Matthew, G.: Measuring the impact of subtitles on cognitive load: eye tracking and dynamic audiovisual texts. In: Proceedings of the 2013 Conference on Eye Tracking South Africa, pp. 62–66 (2013)
27. Raney, G.E., Campbell, S.J., Bovee, J.C.: Using eye movements to evaluate the cognitive processes involved in text comprehension. J. Vis. Exp. **83**, e50780 (2014)

28. Tomanek, K., Hahn, U., Lohmann, S., Ziegler, J.: A cognitive cost model of annotations based on eye-tracking data. In Proceedings of the 48th Annual Meeting of the Association for Computational Linguistics, pp. 1158–1167 (2010)

29. Mishra, A., Bhattacharyya, P.: Scanpath complexity: modeling reading/annotation effort using gaze information. In: Cognitively Inspired Natural Language Processing. CIR, pp. 77–98. Springer, Singapore (2018). https://doi.org/10.1007/978-981-13-1516-9_4

30. Joshi, A., Mishra, A., Senthamilselvan, N., Bhattacharyya, P.: Measuring sentiment annotation complexity of text. In: Proceedings of the 52nd Annual Meeting of the Association for Computational Linguistics, vol. 2 (Short Papers), pp. 36–41 (2014)

31. Hart, S.G.: NASA-task load index (NASA-TLX); 20 years later. In: Proceedings of the Human Factors and Ergonomics Society Annual Meeting, vol. 50, no. 9, pp. 904–908. Sage Publications, Los Angeles, CA (2006)

32. Catchpoole, J., Nanda, G., Vallmuur, K., Nand, G., Lehto, M.: Application of a machine learning–based decision support tool to improve an injury surveillance system workflow. Appl. Clin. Inform. 13(03), 700–710 (2022)

33. Salvucci, D.D., Goldberg, J.H.: Identifying fixations and saccades in eye-tracking protocols. In: Proceedings of the 2000 Symposium on Eye Tracking Research Applications, pp. 71–78 (2000)

34. Olsen, A.: The Tobii I-VT fixation filter. Tobii Technol. 21, 4–19 (2012)

35. Will, T.: Measuring and interpreting system usability scale (SUS) (2021). https://uiuxtrend.com/measuring-system-usability-scale-sus/

36. Chen, W., Sawaragi, T., Hiraoka, T.: Comparing eye-tracking metrics of mental workload caused by NDRTs in semi-autonomous driving. Transp. Res. F Traffic Psychol. Behav. 89, 109–128 (2022)

Physiological and Psychological Effects of Light Illumination on Hygiene Regions of Space Stations in Short-Term Simulations of Gravity and Noise

Junbo Dong[1], Ao Jiang[2,3]($\boxtimes$), and Yuqing Liu[1]

[1] Xiangtan University, Xiangtan 411100, Hunan, China
[2] Imperial College London, London, UK
aojohn928@gmail.com
[3] EuroMoonMars ILEWG at ESA, Amsterdam, The Netherlands

Abstract. Astronauts are forced to deal with stress from microgravity, claustrophobic environments and loud noise during missions on the space station, which can have a variety of negative psychological and physiological effects on astronauts. The use of appropriate lighting in the hygiene areas of the ISS can help provide a comfortable experience for the astronauts and thereby reduce their stress. The aim of this study was to investigate the effects of light illumination on near-infrared brain images, the emotions and satisfaction level of astronauts during the disposal of metabolic waste in the hygiene area of the space station. Participants were tested using head-mounted headphones in a $-12°$ head-down (HD) bed rest simulating microgravity, where the headphones play 60 dBA noise to simulate space station background noise. The results showed significant variation in cortical activity and emotions among participants at different light illumination levels. Comparing these results with the participants' resting-state NIR brain imaging data, we found that 300 lx light illumination had a negative effect on the participants, who showed a significant increase in cortical metabolic activity. The 500 lx light illumination resulted in optimal emotion states and lower cortical metabolic activity, which provides a valuable reference for future improvements to the illumination of the hygiene areas of the space station.

Keywords: Illuminance · FNIRS · Space station hygiene area · Psychological and physiological effects

1 Introduction

Astronauts have to face stresses such as microgravity, claustrophobic environments and noise when performing tasks on the space station, and these stressors can cause various psychological and physiological effects on the astronauts1. It is essential to understand the challenges faced by astronauts living and working in the space environment and to know how to address them for the development and mapping of future human space missions [5]. When in orbit, the spacecraft and everything inside goes into microgravity.

D. D. Schmorrow and C. M. Fidopiastis (Eds.): HCII 2023, LNAI 14019, pp. 108–121, 2023.
https://doi.org/10.1007/978-3-031-35017-7_8

The microgravity environment makes traditional excretory devices such as flush toilets inoperable and makes normal excretion a difficult task. There is also noise on the space station, with spacecraft systems and experimental equipment including fans, pumps and motors generating continuous noise. Most locations on the ISS have acoustic levels close to 60dBA, yet certain areas of the station are particularly noisy and are a potential source of hearing loss for astronauts [24, 25]. With advances in technology, the development of new technologies will send astronauts further into space and stay there for longer periods of time [2], making it necessary for astronauts to adapt to using the toilet in space. Therefore, how to improve the comfort of the hygienic area and thus enhance the astronaut's defecation experience became an inevitable problem.

With the advent of manned spaceflight in the early 1960s, head-down bed rest (HDBR) has been widely used to simulate certain physiological responses of the human body in the microgravity environment in space [26, 27]. With the significant impact of microgravity and noise on astronauts on the space station, this study uses head-down recumbency and headphones playing space station noise to simulate the microgravity and noise environment of the space station for a short period of time respectively. Light profoundly influences human consciousness by producing stimuli to the visual system [6]. And light can also influence emotions through directly modulating the availability of neurotransmitters such as serotonin that are directly involved in mood regulation [17]. Studies have shown that long-term light exposure has an antidepressant effect [19]. Meanwhile different light levels under short artificial light exposure also affected participants' emotions [18, 20]: for example, after 30 min of artificial light exposure, the positive effects of the two illumination levels (1000 lx versus 200 lx) were significantly different for participants, with higher positive effects reported in the 1000 lx condition [18]. As a result, many countries have established standards for indoor lighting illumination. However, there are few standards for lighting on space stations. In the meantime, previous ground-based studies have pointed out the importance of solid-state lighting for space stations is to balance the application of lighting countermeasures with the need for good visual stimulation [7]. In order to ensure a good workplace during space flight, illumination not only needs to provide good visibility for astronaut operations, but also needs to make the astronauts feel relaxed and comfortable while completing the relevant operational tasks [8, 9]. For spacecraft designers, the lighting and layout of the environment in the space station have an essential influence on the level of habitability, and the design of the space station indirectly affects the working performance and efficiency of the astronauts. It has been shown that lighting intensity levels can have an effect on people's visual fatigue [3], and also that lighting can have a significant effect on people's visual acuity [4]. Therefore, illumination levels can play an important role in emotional regulation and the comfort of astronauts at work, and may also influence the level of habitability of the space station.

Some studies have shown that the illumination level in the ground environment affects people's comfort when using bathrooms or toilets, for example people prefer brighter environments when using bathrooms [21]. However, the characteristics of the space station environment are very different from those of the ground environment, where the main objective is to ensure the safety and operational reliability of the crew in a confined and microgravity environment [1]. As one of the essential functional areas in the space station, the hygiene area plays a vital role in collecting and disposing human metabolic waste and in supporting human life in space [10]. Recent reports from astronauts on the International Space Station (ISS) and the Chinese Space Station have shown that the enclosed environment of the hygiene area and the factors of microgravity have a negative impact on the astronauts' ability to manoeuvre and defecate [1]. Hence, improving the lighting environment in hygiene areas may affect their physical needs as well as their emotional experience [11, 12]. Currently, the effect of colour temperature on the lighting environment in hygiene areas has been investigated [1], yet the effect of illuminance on the lighting environment in hygiene areas has not been studied. The aim of this study was to explore the effect of different illumination levels on participants' emotions when using the urine/stool collector in a simulated space station hygiene area.

Near Infrared Spectroscopy (NIRS) was used in this study to measure the level of activation of the cortical brain during the participants' activities in the hygiene area of the space station. NIRS provides a technique for continuous, non-invasive, bedside monitoring of brain metabolism. These instruments use the principles of light transmission and absorption to measure oxyhaemoglobin (oxy Hb) and deoxyhaemoglobin (deoxy Hb) concentrations in tissue (most commonly brain tissue) in a non-invasive manner [14]. Some studies have demonstrated that neuroimaging data reveal different responses of the cerebral cortex to the same stimuli, which suggests that they can be perceived or processed by the brain in different ways [15]. In addition, it has been shown that fNIRS provides a reliable measure of brain function and dynamic changes in local brain regions in functional brain imaging [16]. This is why it is logical for us to use NIR brain imaging to examine the brain load of astronauts during hygiene area activities in space. In addition, due to the complexity of the equipment in the hygiene area environment, crews need to follow strict equipment guidelines when defecating, which means that the basic defecation and flushing process often takes longer to complete than it would on the ground. Therefore, the illuminated environment in hygiene areas is likely to affect physiological needs, information access and judgment, and emotional experience [1, 11, 12, 22, 23]. Accordingly, differences in cortical activation at different illumination levels can provide valuable information on how to design ISS hygiene areas in the future.

2   Method

2.1   Participants

Thirty-five healthy Chinese participants (mean age = 36.33 years, SD = 2.62 years, 13 females) were recruited based on the age group that the majority of current reserve active duty astronauts and crew members belong to. All participants are physically healthy without mental impairment. Their visual acuity or corrected visual acuity was better than 0.6 (1/min view) [28, 29]. They had been trained in a urine/stool collection simulator before the experiment began. Throughout the experiment, participants were asked to maintain a normal routine (sleep at 10pm and wake up at 6am) and diet, avoiding the intake of caffeine and alcohol. All participants signed a written informed consent prior to the experimental study and received a participation fee of RMB 100. The study was approved by the Ethics Committee of Xiangtan University.

2.2 Experimental Setup and Scenarios

Participants wore a headset model SONY WH-1000X M5 and began the experiment by wearing the headset and playing audio at 1000 Hz with a sound pressure level of 60 dBA. The audio was generated from various equipment on the space station, such as environmental control equipment, thermal control equipment, attitude control equipment, etc.

Experimental scenario using a simulated lighting system (LED, supplied by Touslite Lighting System, TLS Lighting, Badersfield, UK) for the hygiene area. All equipment is installed one month before the official experiment. According to previous studies, the colour temperature for this experiment was 5000 K, as this was the more satisfactory colour temperature for the participants [30]. Table 1 shows the illuminance and colour temperature for the five lighting conditions selected for this experiment. The principle of illuminance selection is based on the minimum illuminance levels for indoor lighting recommended by British Standards. Illuminance was measured at eye level using a calibrated spectroradiometer (JETI Specbos 1201, JETI Technische Instrumente GmbH, Jena, Germany) and the lamps were switched on thirty minutes in advance of each experiment to stabilise the illuminance. The walls and ceiling of the laboratory are off-white and reflect 72% and 67% respectively. The reflectivity of the light grey floor is 31% and the reflectivity of the off-white operating panel is 66%. The lighting system is mounted on the ceiling and is clearly visible to participants, although their main view is the operating panel in front of them.

Table 1. Illuminance measured at desk level after the lighting animations had been set up.

	Illuminance (Lux)	Nomial CCT(K)
1	300	5000
2	400	5000
3	500	5000
4	600	5000
5	700	5000

2.3 Experimental Setup and Scenarios

The day before the experiment, participants were familiarised with the operation of the urine/stool collector and the surroundings of the operation to avoid the emotional impact of the unfamiliar environment on them.

The study consisted of five sets of experiments, each separated by at least 72 h to eliminate residual effects from the previous one. Participants entered the laboratory in the afternoon (15:00–17:30), connected the FNIRS unit and then took a 5-min break in the laboratory, which simulates the external environment of a hygiene area, to adjust to the environment and ease their minds. After acclimatisation, changes in oxyhaemoglobin (oxy Hb) and deoxyhaemoglobin (deoxy Hb) levels were recorded from 35 participants at five light levels. The CCT of the illuminated environment remained constant at 5000 K. The participants were required to participate in the experiment in a −12° head-down position and the recording process took approximately 15 min, which is the time it would normally take for an astronaut to perform a hygiene area operation. During the experiment, participants used the urine/stool collector strictly as prescribed. After the task was completed, participants took a 10-min break in the laboratory and completed the PANAS questionnaire. To avoid the possible effects of differing illuminance, the order of magnitude of light illumination was randomised for each participant.

The CCT of the illuminated environment remains constant at 5000 K. The participants were required to participate in the experiment in a −12° head-down position and the recording process took approximately 15 min, which is the time it would normally take for an astronaut to perform a hygiene area operation. During the experiment, participants used the urine/stool collector strictly as prescribed. After the task was completed, participants took a 10-min break in the laboratory and completed the PANAS questionnaire. To avoid possible effects of order, the order of light illumination was randomised for each participant. At the end of the break, participants exited the laboratory.

2.4 Experimental Setup and Scenarios

This study was performed in parallel with fNIRS recording. The fNIRS system (OT-R40; two wavelengths: 695 and 830 nm; Hitachi Medical Corporation, Japan) measurements were performed using a 20-channel optical morphology system with a sampling rate of 10 Hz used to acquire imaging data in the frontal lobe region, with the emitters and detectors distributed as in Fig. 1. The data from fNIRS is independently analysed and filtered to obtain the required output signal.

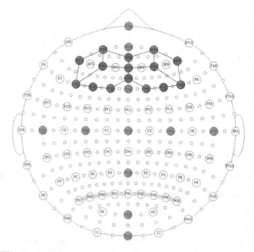

Fig. 1. NIRS Distribution of transmitters and receivers

To investigate the fNIRS data, a Butterworth fifth-order band-pass filter of 0.02 to 0.5 Hz was used in this study to eliminate low-frequency oscillations and heartbeat effects. A baseline correction was applied to each block by subtracting the mean of 20 s rest from each data point of the task, and then all blocks were combined to obtain a block representing the average haemodynamic response, see Fig. 1.

The PANAS questionnaire has good validity and reliability in measuring subjective emotions [31]. The measure consists of two dimensions which are positive and negative emotions, each measured by nine emotional adjectives. The internal consistency coefficients for PANAS in this study were $\alpha(PA) = 0.90$ and $\alpha(NA) = 0.92$ respectively. At the end of each experiment, participants were asked to assess their emotional state on a 5-point response scale varying from 1 = not at all to 5 = very much.

The Relevant Illumination Satisfaction Vote (RISV) uses a five-point scale including very satisfied (+2), satisfied (+1), neutral (0), dissatisfied (−1) and very dissatisfied (−2). The internal consistency of the scale was set at $\alpha = 0.91$.

Before the experiment, the experimenter gave a comprehensive introduction to each questionnaire and the participants filled in the questionnaires based on their true feelings.

2.5 Statistical Analysis

The study began by testing all data for normality using the Shapiro-Wilk test. For the processing of physiological signals, the fNIRS signal, which may contain instrumental noise and experimental errors unrelated to brain activity, was removed in this study [32] before converting the raw optical density signal to changes in the levels of oxy Hb and deoxy Hb using a modified Beer-Lambert law, which also enabled the use of band-pass filters to remove physiological noise [33]. Statistical analysis was performed using a paired t-test MATLAB function ($p < 0.05$ indicates significance level) together with Bonferroni correction and Cohen effect size to examine the effect of different illumination levels on the fNIRS data. For the questionnaire data, a one-way ANOVA was performed on the experimental data to check whether there were significant differences in emotions and satisfaction across illumination levels and to determine their statistical significance (if any); $\alpha < 0.05$ was considered to be statistically significant. Tukey HSD post-tests were carried out for pairwise comparisons and corrected using Bonferroni.nirsLAB_v201904_64bit, SPSS (version 26; IBM Corporation; Armonk, NY, USA) was used for all analyses in this study.

3 Result

3.1 Brain Activation at Different Illumination Levels

As there were 6 sets of data with large errors, the available data was 29 sets, so only the results of the 29 valid sets of data were analysed in this study.

As shown in Fig. 2, from left to right, the mean values characterize the trend of cortical activation in brain regions in response to illumination. Compared to the resting state, participants in the five different light conditions showed different levels of activation in the prefrontalcortex (PFC) region during the execution of the urine/stool collector task.

With changes in illumination levels, significant activation occurs in the Ventromedial prefrontal cortex (vmPFC) region where oxygen molecules and energy supply are concentrated at 300 lx, 600 lx and 700 lx. The graph shows that the PFC activation is greatest at 300 lx illumination. In contrast, PFC activation is minimal at 500 lx illumination.

Resting state   300lx   400lx   500lx   600lx   700lx

Fig. 2. Brain activation

The p-values for the five groups of NIRS brain activation level data were 0.461, 0.108, 0.206, 0.351 and 0.263 according to the S-W (Shapiro-Wilk) test, which were all greater than 0.05; therefore, the data is considered to be normally distributed. A one-way ANOVA revealed significant differences in brain activation when operating the urine/stool collector under five different light illumination conditions ($F(4,140) = 3.766$, $p < 0.001$, $\eta_p^2 = 0.051$). The lowest mean values of oxy Hb and deoxy Hb for participants in the five experimental groups are shown in Fig. 2. The lowest mean values of oxyHb in the 500 lx illumination condition also indicated the least brain activation ($M = 0.001181$, $= 0.000000076135$), while the highest mean values of oxyHb in the 300 lx illumination condition indicated the greatest brain activation ($M = 0.001526965$, $= 0.000000165397$). The analysis revealed a significant difference in the effect of the level of illumination on the participants' cortical activation ($F(4, 140) = 2.064$, $p = 0.042$, $\eta_p^2 = 0.088$). After post-hoc testing, we learned that there was a significant difference in cortical activation between participants performing the task at 300 lx illumination and 500 lx illumination ($p = 0.022 < 0.05$), as well as between participants performing the task at 300 lx illumination and 600 lx illumination ($p = 0.042 < 0.05$).

The lowest mean values of oxyHb in the 500 lx illumination condition also indicated the lowest activation of the brain ($M = 0.001181$, $= 0.000000076135$), while the highest mean values of oxyHb in the 300 lx illumination condition indicated the highest activation of the brain ($M = 0.001526965$, $= 0.000000165397$). The analysis revealed a significant difference in the level of illumination on the participants' cortical activation ($F(4, 140) = 2.064$, $p = 0.042$, $= 0.088$). After post-hoc testing we learned that there was a significant difference in cortical activation between participants performing the task at 300 lx illumination and 500 lx illumination ($p = 0.022 < 0.05$), as well as between participants performing the task at 300 lx illumination and 600 lx illumination ($p = 0.042 < 0.05$) (Fig. 3).

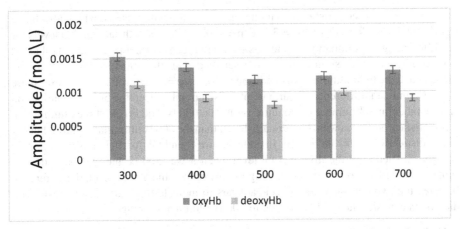

Fig. 3. Average values of oxyHb and deoxyHb for participants at five illumination levels (the error bars show the standard error of the means.)

3.2 Subjective Questionnaire Results

The results of the PANAS questionnaire showed a significant effect of illumination level on participants' emotions ($F(4,170) = 12.703$, $p = 0.046 < 0.05$). The data are shown in Fig. 4 and the positive impact was significantly higher at 500 lx compared to the other four light illumination conditions ($p = 0.048 < 0.05$). There was a significant difference between illumination levels of 500 lx and 300 lx ($p = 0.023 < 0.05$) and no significant difference between 500 lx and the other three illumination conditions (400 lx, 600 lx, 700 lx). In addition, we found that the main effect of light illumination on negative mood was not significant ($F(4,170) = 6.549$, $p = 0.065 > 0.05$).

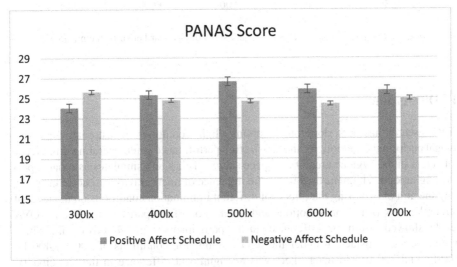

Fig. 4. PANAS questionnaire scores (the error bars show the standard error of the means.)

Next, we analysed satisfaction among the five illumination levels, which also had a significant main effect (F(4,170) = 3.646, p = 0.037 < 0.05), with satisfaction levels for the different light illumination conditions shown in Fig. 5. Further post-hoc tests showed that participants were significantly more satisfied with the 500 lx light illumination compared to the light illumination condition of 300 lx (p = 0.036 < 0.05). However there was no significant difference in participant satisfaction between the 500 lx illumination and the other three Illumination conditions (400 lx, 600 lx, 700 lx); all three illumination level satisfaction scores were numerically lower than the 500 lx illumination level, but not to a statistically significant degree. In addition, we found that participants were almost equally satisfied with the illumination level when it was 500 lx and 600 lx. Although satisfaction with the 600 lx level was slightly lower than the 500 lx level, the difference between the two was very small. This appears to indicate that participant satisfaction did not change significantly in the 500 to 600 lx illumination range.

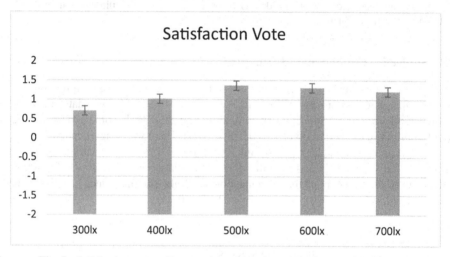

Fig. 5. Satisfaction scores (the error bars show the standard error of the means.)

4   Discussion

Little research has been done on the optimal light conditions for astronauts' physiological performance, emotions and satisfaction performance when operating urine/feces collectors in the hygiene area of the space station. This study simulates astronauts performing tasks in a hygiene area under the influence of microgravity and noise in space, with the aim of exploring the effects of different illumination conditions on the level of cerebral cortex activation, emotions and satisfaction of the participants. The ANOVA results showed significant differences in the participants' cortical activation, positive emotions, and satisfaction under the light illumination conditions of 300 lx, 400 lx, 600 lx, and 700 lx. However, there was no significant difference in the participants' performance when the light illumination level was 500 lx and 600 lx. It can be seen from the data that the participants' physiological and psychological performance was similar when the light illumination level was 500 lx or 600 lx.

Illumination conditions are highly influential on the degree of NIR brain activation. Compared to other luminance conditions, brain activation is lowest at 500 lx with minimal brain load for the same task. This finding is similar to previous studies, where 500 lx is exactly the level of illumination that a comfortable office should also have [35]. In the meantime the brain activation is highest at 300 lx. This is similar to most previous studies: higher illumination levels at higher colour temperatures reduce brain load during task performance more than lower illumination levels (300 lx) [34], and higher brain activation levels are associated with lower illumination levels [43]. Many previous studies have shown that stronger light or light illumination may have a positive effect on a person's spirit and energy [18, 39]. However, most of the previously available articles have studied large gaps between illuminance levels, tested fewer luminance values and may not capture the relationship between illuminance and brain load in more detail.

In addition to physiological effects, we also studied the effect of light illumination on emotions and satisfaction. Participants had the lowest positive emotions and satisfaction when operating in the simulated hygiene area of the space station at an illumination level of 300 lx. As the illumination level increased, both positive emotions and satisfaction increased, reaching a maximum at 500 lx. After that, positive emotions and satisfaction slowly decreased as the illumination level increased, but the decrease was not significant, and both positive emotions and satisfaction were greater than at 300 lx. This is similar to previous studies: at high CCT, low illumination is unpleasant [40]. And it has been reported that at lower levels of light illumination (300 lx) participants had higher drowsiness, lower vigour and lower levels of positive affect compared to brighter light illumination [18, 39]. Humans abhor dark environments [36, 37]. However, too much light may increase the burden on the optic nerve, which can lead to premature visual fatigue [46]. There are also some studies with results that differ from the present study, with one showing that the change in illumination level from 300 lx to 500 lx was not a significant increase in subjective comfort [45]. This may be explained by the longer duration of exposure or the different age range of the participants in this study. Furthermore, the results show that the trend of the effect of light illumination on physiological signals is similar to the effect of emotions and satisfaction, which may also indicate from another perspective that there is a positive effect of 500 lx light illumination on the participants, while 300 lx has a negative effect on the participants' physiological and psychological signals. Although the positive impact of 600 lx–700 lx light illumination conditions is lower than that of 500 lx, it is still higher than that of 300 lx. Between 600 lx and 700 lx of light illumination, there is only a slow downward trend of positive effects.

5 Limitations and Future Research

The degree of simulation of the space station hygiene area in this study is limited and still remains somewhat different from the space station hygiene area in real conditions, for example the microgravity conditions in a real space station cannot be simulated on the ground. In microgravity conditions, it is often more difficult for the crew to operate in hygiene areas. The main shortcomings of this experiment are: gender differences in light illumination studies were not considered [38], and participants were not potential astronauts. The crews are often well-trained personnel who meet strict psychological and physical requirements. And the average person is physically and mentally removed from a real crew member. In future experiments, participants should be selected from special groups, such as astronauts, pilots and other highly trained groups.

Many studies have also shown that light levels have different psychological effects on humans at different times of the day: in the morning or in the evening. Further exploration can be done in the future with regard to the effect of different time periods on light illumination effects [41].

The method of lighting also has an impact on the effect of light illumination, with some studies showing that direct versus indirect lighting affects the effect of light illumination [42]. This is also a potential direction for future research.

The effect of light illumination is also highly dependent on CCT conditions, with the most comfortable light illumination levels varying between CCT conditions [47]. It needs to be further explored whether illumination under low CCT conditions has a more significant effect on the level of brain activation, positive mood and satisfaction. At the same time, the range of light illumination in studies and the duration of exposure should be further extended in the future.

6 Conclusions

The results of this study contribute to the optimization of environmental lighting of the hygiene area of the space station in several ways. First, we simulated the environment of microgravity and noise in space and demonstrated that different illumination levels had significantly different effects on the participants' brain activation, emotions, and satisfaction level while performing activities in the hygiene area. Secondly, this study found that when participants used the Hygiene Area Simulator under the five illumination conditions tested, they had the lowest levels of cortical activation and the highest levels of positive emotion and satisfaction in a 500 lx illumination environment. We also found that the participants' physiological and psychological performance was similar at light levels of 500 lx and 600 lx, which may indicate that the optimal illumination level for the hygiene area of the space station is 500 lx–600 lx. The above results provide a valuable reference for future improvements in the lighting of the hygiene areas of the space station.

References

1. Jiang, A., Yao, X., Westland, S., Hemingray, C., Foing, B., Lin, J.: The effect of correlated colour temperature on physiological, emotional and subjective satisfaction in the hygiene area of a space station. Int. J. Environ. Res. Public Health **19**(15), 9090. MDPI AG (2022)
2. Thirsk, R., Kuipers, A., Mukai, C., Williams, D.: CMAJ **180**(12), 1216–1220 (2009). https://doi.org/10.1503/cmaj.081125
3. Jiang, A., Yao, X., Schlacht, I.L., Musso, G., Tang, T., Westland, S.: Habitability study on space station colour design. In: Stanton, N. (ed.) AHFE 2020. AISC, vol. 1212, pp. 507–514. Springer, Cham (2020). https://doi.org/10.1007/978-3-030-50943-9_64

4. Lu, S., et al.: Effects and challenges of operational lighting illuminance in spacecraft on human visual acuity. In: Stanton, N. (ed.) AHFE 2021. LNNS, vol. 270, pp. 582–588. Springer, Cham (2021). https://doi.org/10.1007/978-3-030-80012-3_67

5. Gong, Y., et al.: Effects of intensity of short-wavelength light on the EEG and performance of astronauts during target tracking. In: Harris, D., Li, W.C. (eds.) HCII 2022. LNCS, vol. 13307, pp. 279–289. Springer, Cham (2022). https://doi.org/10.1007/978-3-031-06086-1_21

6. Brainard, G.C., Hanifin, J.P.: Photons, clocks, and consciousness. J. Biol. Rhythms 20(4), 314–325 (2005). https://doi.org/10.1177/0748730405278951

7. Jiang, A., Foing, B.H., Schlacht, I.L., Yao, X., Cheung, V., Rhodes, P.A.: Colour schemes to reduce stress response in the hygiene area of a space station: a Delphi study. Appl. Ergon. 98, 103573 (2022)

8. Connors, M.M., Harrison, A.A., Akins, F.R.: Psychology and the resurgent space program. Am. Psychol. 41(8), 906 (1986)

9. Zimmenman, W.F.: Space station man-machine trade-off analysis. NASA-CR-176046 2, 6–18 (1985)

10. Link, D.E., Jr., Broyan, J.L., Jr., Philistine, C., Balistreri, S.F., Jr.: International space station USOS waste and hygiene compartment development. SAE Trans. 119–124 (2007). https://doi.org/10.4271/2007-01-310

11. Fleri, E.L., Jr., Galliano, P.A., Harrison, M.E., Johnson, W.B., Meyer, G.J.: Proposal for a Zero-Gravity Toilet Facility for the Space Station. NASA, Washington, DC, USA (1989)

12. Kitmacher, G.H.: Reference Guide to the International Space Station. NASA, Washington, DC, USA (2006)

13. Kai, A.: Recent patents on space toilet. Recent Patents Space Technol. 1, 1–5 (2009)

14. Wahr, J.A., Tremper, K.K., Samra, S., Delpy, D.T.: Near-infrared spectroscopy: theory and applications. J. Cardiothorac. Vasc. Anesth. 10(3), 406–418 (1996)

15. Wilcox, T., Biondi, M.: fNIRS in the developmental sciences. Wiley Interdisc. Rev. Cogn. Sci. 6(3), 263–283 (2015)

16. Perrey, S.: Non-invasive NIR spectroscopy of human brain function during exercise. Methods 45(4), 289–299 (2008)

17. Blume, C., Garbazza, C., Spitschan, M.: Effects of light on human circadian rhythms, sleep and mood. Somnologie 23(3), 147–156 (2019). https://doi.org/10.1007/s11818-019-00215-x

18. Smolders, K.C.H.J., de Kort, Y.A.W.: Bright light and mental fatigue: effects on alertness, vitality, performance and physiological arousal. J. Environ. Psychol. 39, 77–91 (2014). https://doi.org/10.1016/j.jenvp.2013.12.010

19. Yu, K., Jiang, A., Wang, J., Zeng, Xi., Yao, X., Chen, Y.: Construction of crew visual behaviour mechanism in ship centralized control cabin. In: Stanton, N. (ed.) AHFE 2021. LNNS, vol. 270, pp. 503–510. Springer, Cham (2021). https://doi.org/10.1007/978-3-030-80012-3_58

20. Knez, I.: Effects of indoor lighting on mood and cognition. J. Environ. Psychol. 15(1), 39–51 (1995)

21. Fernandez, P., Giboreau, A., Fontoynont, M.: Relation between preferences of luminous environments and situations experienced by users. A hotel case study. In: Proceedings of the 3rd International Conference on Appearance, Edinburgh, UK, 17–19 April 2012, pp. 177–180 (2012)

22. Akbay, S., Avci, A.N.: Evaluation of color perception in different correlated color temperature of LED lighting. GRID Arch. Plan. Des. J. 1, 139–162 (2018)

23. Connolly, J.H., Arch, M.: NASA standard 3000, human systems integration standards (HSIS) update. In: Proceedings of the Human Factors and Ergonomics Society Annual Meeting, vol. 49, pp. 2018–2022 (2005)

24. Thirsk, R., Kuipers, A., Mukai, C., Williams, D.: The space-flight environment: the International Space Station and beyond. CMAJ 180(12), 1216–1220 (2009)

25. Goodman, J.R.: International Space Station acoustics. J. Acoust. Soc. Am. **108**, 2475 (2000)
26. Fortney, S.M., Schneider, V.S., Greenleaf, J.E.: The physiology of bed rest. In: Fregly, M.J., Blatteis, C.M. (eds.) Handbook of Physiology: Environmental Physiology, Section 4, Part 39, pp. 889–939. Oxford University Press, New York (1996)
27. Hirayanagi, K., et al.: Changes in prevalence of subjective fatigue during 14-day 6 head-down bed rest. Acta Astronaut. **64**(11–12), 1298–1303 (2009)
28. Jiang, A., et al.: Space habitat astronautics: multicolour lighting psychology in a 7-day simulated habitat. Space Sci. Technol (2022)
29. Jiang, A., et al.: Short-term virtual reality simulation of the effects of space station colour and microgravity and lunar gravity on cognitive task performance and emotion. Build. Environ. **227**, 109789 (2023)
30. Cantin, F., Dubois, M.C.: Daylighting metrics based on illuminance, distribution, glare and directivity. Light. Res. Technol. **43**(3), 291–307 (2011)
31. Jiang, A.O.: Effects of colour environment on spaceflight cognitive abilities during short-term simulations of three gravity states (Doctoral dissertation, University of Leeds) (2022)
32. Huppert, T.J., Diamond, S.G., Fransceshini, M.A., Boas, D.A.: HomER: a review of time-series analysis methods for near-infrared spectroscopy of the brain. Appl. Opt. **48**, D280–D298 (2009). https://doi.org/10.1364/AO.48.00D280
33. Naseer, N., Hong, K.S.: fNIRS-based brain-computer interfaces: a review. Front. Hum. Neurosci. **9**, 3 (2015)
34. Park, J.I.N.Y., Min, B.K., Jung, Y.C., et al.: Illumination influences working memory: an EEG study. Neuroscience **247**, 386–394 (2013)
35. Jiang, A., Zhu, Y., Yao, X., Foing, B.H., Westland, S., Hemingray, C.: The effect of three body positions on colour preference: an exploration of microgravity and lunar gravity simulations. Acta Astronaut. **204**, 1–10 (2023)
36. Veenstra, L., Koole, S.L.: Disarming darkness: effects of ambient lighting on approach motivation and state anger among people with varying trait anger. J. Environ. Psychol. **60**, 34–40 (2018)
37. Bailey, R.L., Wang, G.T., Liu, J.: Ambient lighting alters motivational responses to advertisements for foods of different energetic value. Motiv. Emot. **45**(5), 574–584 (2021)
38. Knez, I., Kers, C.: Effects of indoor lighting, gender, and age on mood and cognitive performance. Environ. Behav. **32**(6), 817–831 (2000)
39. Smolders, K.C.H.J., De Kort, Y.A.W., Cluitmans, P.J.M.: A higher illuminance induces alertness even during office hours: findings on subjective measures, task performance and heart rate measures. Physiol. Behav. **107**(1), 7–16 (2012)
40. Huang, Z., Wang, S., Jiang, A., Hemingray, C., Westland, S.: Gender preference differences in color temperature associated with LED light sources in the autopilot cabin. In: Krömker, H. (ed.) HCII 2022, pp. 151–166. Springer, Cham (2022). https://doi.org/10.1007/978-3-031-04987-3_10
41. Xiao, H., Cai, H., Li, X.: Non-visual effects of indoor light environment on humans: a review✰. Physiol. Behav. **228**, 113195 (2021)
42. Shin, Y.B., Woo, S.H., Kim, D.H., et al.: The effect on emotions and brain activity by the direct/indirect lighting in the residential environment. Neurosci. Lett. **584**, 28–32 (2015)
43. Castilla, N., Higuera-Trujillo, J.L., Llinares, C.: The effects of illuminance on students' memory. A neuroarchitecture study. Build. Environ. **228**, 109833 (2023). https://doi.org/10.1016/j.buildenv.2022.109833
44. Partonen, T., Lönnqvist, J.: Bright light improves vitality and alleviates distress in healthy people. J. Affect. Disord. **57**(1–3), 55–61 (2000)
45. Jiang, A., Yao, X., Foing, B., Westland, S., Hemingray, C., Mu, S.: Integrating human factors into the colour design of human-machine interfaces for spatial habitat. In: EGU General Assembly Conference Abstracts, pp. EGU22-622 (2022)

46. Lan, L.: Mechanism and Evaluation of the Effects of Indor Environmental Quality of Human Productivity. Shanghai Jiaotong University, Shanghai (2010)
47. Bao, J., Song, X., Li, Y., et al.: Effect of lighting illuminance and colour temperature on mental workload in an office setting. Sci. Rep. **11**(1), 15284 (2021)

The Effect of Perceptual Load
on Performance Within IDE in People
with ADHD Symptoms

Vseslav Kasatskii[1], Agnia Sergeyuk[2(✉)], Anastasiia Serova[3], Sergey Titov[4],
and Timofey Bryksin[4]

[1] Neapolis University Pafos, Paphos, Cyprus
v.kasatskii@nup.ac.cy
[2] JetBrains Research, Belgrade, Serbia
agnia.sergeyuk@jetbrains.com
[3] JetBrains Limited, Paphos, Cyprus
anastasiia.serova@jetbrains.com
[4] JetBrains Research, Paphos, Cyprus
{sergey.titov,timofey.bryksin}@jetbrains.com

Abstract. In this paper, we describe the research on how perceptual load can affect programming performance in people with symptoms of Attention Deficit/Hyperactivity Disorder (ADHD). We asked developers to complete the Barkley Deficits in Executive Functioning Scale, which indicates the presence and severity levels of ADHD symptoms. After that, participants solved mentally active programming tasks (coding) and monotonous ones (debugging) in the integrated development environment in high perceptual load modes (visually noisy) and low perceptual load modes (visually clear). The development environment was augmented with the plugin we wrote to track efficiency metrics, *i.e.* time, speed, and activity. We found that the perceptual load does affect programmers' efficiency. For mentally active tasks, the time of inserting the first character was shorter and the overall speed was higher in the low perceptual load mode. For monotonous tasks, the total time for the solution was less for the low perceptual load mode. Also, we found that the effect of perceptual load on programmers' efficiency differs between those with and without ADHD symptoms. This effect has a specificity: depending on efficiency measures and ADHD symptoms, one or another level of perceptual load might be beneficial. Our findings support the idea of behavioral assessment of users for providing appropriate accommodation for the workforce with special needs.

Keywords: Cognitive Load and Performance · Interactive technologies for population with special needs · ADHD · Accessibility · Cognitive psychology · Perceptual load · Coding efficacy

1 Introduction

The diversity of employees in the rapidly changing and demanding field of software engineering is high. Partially, this diversity is dictated by the cognitive

D. D. Schmorrow and C. M. Fidopiastis (Eds.): HCII 2023, LNAI 14019, pp. 122–141, 2023.
https://doi.org/10.1007/978-3-031-35017-7_9

abilities and mental states of the workers. Due to the efforts of IT companies to be more inclusive, the neurodiversity of employees has become a focus of stakeholders and researchers in recent years [8,21,32,37,43,46].

Neurodiversity is the variability of mental functioning caused by neurodevelopmental disorders that cannot be cured but should be considered [21]. This means that people with such conditions can be socialized but need some accommodations at school and work. This paradigm was first applied to people with Autistic Spectrum Disorder [17], but now it also accounts for people with Attention-Deficit/Hyperactivity Disorder (ADHD), Dyslexia, etc.

The majority of existing research regarding accommodation for the differently abled workforce is focused on flexibility of work-related circumstances, social support, and coaching [40,50]. However, the field lacks thorough experimental works [23,47]. To broaden the field of experimental research on workstation adjustments, we investigate whether and how integrated development environments (IDEs) can assist neurodiverse developers.

There are studies that show that the task performance of neurodiverse people could be affected by the amount of information involved in the processing of the task [18,25,39], *i.e.* by the perceptual load of the environment and task. This is especially true for people with ADHD, who struggle with self-directed activities related to time management, Self-organization and problem-solving, Self-restraint, Self-motivation, and Self-regulation of emotions [9,13,14]. People with a higher frequency and severity of ADHD symptoms were found to have a better ability to inhibit unwanted processes, distract less, and therefore perform effectively when the perceptual load of the task was high [18,25].

We wanted to test this effect in the field of programming, using an IDE as a medium. We conducted an experiment in which developers fill out the Barkley Deficits in Executive Functioning Scale (BDEFS-SF) to measure the existence and severity of ADHD symptoms in them. Then, they solved two types of programming tasks — mentally active (coding) and monotonous (debugging). Each type of tasks was presented twice — in the low and high perceptually loaded modes of IDE. In our research, the low perceptual load mode (Low PLM) has two interactable panels, while the high perceptual load mode (High PLM) has seven. To manipulate the user interface and present tasks, we created a plugin, which also registered all indicators of solution efficiency.

We found that the mode of IDE and one's attentional difficulties affect the efficiency of programming. For mentally active tasks, the time of inserting the first character was significantly shorter and the solution speed was significantly higher in Low PLM compared to High PLM (p = .005 for both metrics). For monotonous tasks, the total time for the solution and the time when the first bug was fixed were also significantly less in Low PLM than in High PLM (p = .035 and p = .042, respectively). The effect of perceptual load differed across people with and without ADHD symptoms in our research. We found that the efficiency measure in question and the specificity of the symptoms might dictate the type of preferable accommodation. Namely, if the user has difficulties in self-organization, self-restraint, and self-regulation of emotions, and their effectiveness is measured as the activeness of the user, they may benefit from the Low PLM environment (p = .036, p = .022, p = .01, respectively). People with time-management impairment speed-wise benefit from Low PLM (p = .048). If one struggles with self-regulation of emotions and the measure of efficiency is time, one might benefit from High PLM (p = .03).

The results show that visual representation is an important aspect of IDE accessibility. A well-designed environment helps boost user productivity. Developing just-in-time work-station adjustments for neurodiverse people working in the programming field may support the efficiency of their performance.

2 Background

Research on the neurodiverse workforce in the field of software engineering highlights some challenges and counterbalancing advantages of such people. A literature review conducted by E. Costello and colleagues [19] points out interpersonal and work-station usability challenges. From the interviews and survey conducted by Microsoft Research [43] it can be concluded that neurodiverse people who are involved in the field of programming usually struggle with focusing on tasks that are not interesting for them, with reviewing other peoples' code, with self-organization and self-motivation. Case studies, interviews, and blog posts of neurominorities show that in the field of software engineering, they are struggling with communication, self-organization, self-motivation, and focus on monotonous tasks [19,30,43]. This is usually dictated by the structure of the IT companies and the specificity of job tasks. Working with code in a noisy environment where there are social rules and various distractors may be not easy for anyone, but especially challenging for neurodiverse people.

However, neurodiverse people also have strengths and unique traits that make them good candidates for positions in the field of software engineering. The advantages that a neurodiverse workforce inherits, such as the ability to notice patterns, creativity, hyperfocus, and adhering to rules, bring about a rise in team productivity and product quality along with other benefits for companies and employees [37,43]. These advantages might be less visible because of the difficulties people encounter. Therefore, to highlight their advantages and support their performance at work, neurodiverse people should be aided with different kinds of accommodations [22,44].

According to the review by N. Doyle [23], there are several categories of possible workplace adjustments for neurominorities: work environment flexibility; schedule flexibility; supervisor or co-worker support; support from different stakeholders; executive functions coaching; literacy coaching; training; assistive technologies and tools; work-station adjustments.

To provide appropriate tools to them, detailed research must be carried out; however, the field lacks thorough experimental works [23,47]. The majority of existing research regarding accommodation for the differently abled workforce is focused on the flexibility of work-related circumstances, social support, and coaching [40,50]. In our work, our aim was to broaden the field of experimental research on work-station adjustments, investigating how an IDE might help neurodiverse developers cope with programming tasks.

In this paper, we focus on people with ADHD. ADHD is the diagnostic label for those who demonstrate significant problems with attention and/or impulsiveness and hyperactivity [7]. According to the ADHD Institute [1], the worldwide prevalence of ADHD in adults (18 to 44 years) has been estimated at 2.8% overall (ranging from 0.6 to 7.3% depending on the study) [24]. In fact, the prevalence may be higher due to the underdiagnosis of this disorder [26]. The percentage of adults who have the disorder can be shadowed by (a) lack of proper diagnostic tools, (b) lifetime adaptation to the symptoms. It is also known that people with neurodiversity are not always willing to disclose themselves at work [23,43,49]. For this reason, in the present work we are more oriented not on the diagnosis of ADHD itself in the sample, but on the specific results of the scale, measuring the severity of related symptoms.

The scale we use in the present research is an empirically supported [15], valid [31] scale that was developed to assess the difficulties people with ADHD encounter. The scale in question is the Barkley Deficits in Executive Functioning Scale (BDEFS) and is based on the theory of ADHD [9], which was developed by Barkley [10]. This is the author whose work had an impact on the formation of diagnostic criteria for ADHD in the fifth edition of the Diagnostic and Statistical Manual of Mental Disorders (DSM-V) [5,11,16].

The theory states that ADHD symptoms arise from biologically based difficulties that underpin the impairment of self-regulation of executive functions [13]. In this context, executive functions are self-regulation abilities to internalize and use self-directed actions to choose goals and select, implement, and sustain actions toward those goals [6]. In other words, executive functions help people set goals and achieve them through self-regulation. Five self-regulatory self-directed activities accounted for in the Barkley's theory are [9]:

- Self-inhibition — the ability to stop one's reactions and behaviors, the capacity to prevent disruption of one's goal-oriented activity;
- Self-directed sensory-motor action — polymodal nonverbal reexperiencing of past events, *i.e.*, nonverbal working memory;
- Self-directed private speech — internalized speech, verbal working memory;
- Self-directed emotion/motivation — regulation of one's emotions and motivation using the first three executive functions;
- Self-directed play — problem-solving with the help of analysis and synthesis.

Therefore, if one has persistent self-regulation difficulties that affect their adaptation to everyday life, we might suspect the disorder, which might be labeled as ADHD and that might imply the presence of neurodevelopmental differences.

According to diagnostic criteria and based on the theory described above, people with ADHD symptoms might struggle the most with monotonous tasks [5]. This is especially true for people with the inattention prevalence, which is known to persist in adults more than hyperactivity [5]. Monotonous tasks generally require self-regulation, concentration, and maintaining attention, *e.g.*, lengthy reading, thoroughly instructed activities. Software engineering might be considered such a task due to the repetitive, mentally demanding, and heavily regulated nature [20,29]. This idea is also supported by the feedback of the work-force themselves [19,30,43]. This raises the question of how we can aid developers with ADHD symptoms in performing monotonous tasks during their work.

Previous research shows that one's ability to concentrate and self-regulate their attention can be affected by the perceptual load of the environment [34]. The perceptual load is a limited amount of information that must be processed while performing a task [39]. According to the integrated theory of structural and capacity approaches to attention [36], if the perceptual load is high, distractors are not perceived, since most or all of the available capacity is exhausted. This might make it easier to concentrate on the task.

It was noted in neuroimaging probes that patients with attention-related brain liaisons showed a reduction in the capacity of attention and even a small increase in the perceptual load stopped them from being distracted [35]. The same effect could be expected in neurodiverse people, since their brain is developmentally affected. Indeed, people with a higher frequency and severity of ADHD symptoms were found to have a better ability to inhibit unwanted processes and distract less when the perceptual load of the task was high [18,25].

To test whether the perceptual load of the IDE affects developers with ADHD symptoms in terms of the efficiency of solving programming tasks, we carried out an experiment, in which participants were asked to perform the most common programming tasks — coding and debugging — each in both low and high perceptually loaded IDE modes. With this experiment, our aim was to show if there is a possible way to compensate for attentional impairment with the help of software design tools.

3   Methodology

Based on the theory and related work described in the previous section, we formulated the following research questions for programming tasks of different levels of attention activeness:

RQ 1. Does the perceptual load of the programming environment affect the efficiency of task solving?

RQ 2. Does the effect of perceptual load differ between people with and without impaired executive functions?

To find answers to these questions, we conducted experimental research, which is described in detail further in this section. All code for experiment replication and data analysis can be found in a public repository.[1]

3.1   Sample

The sample for our research consisted of adult developers — students and practitioners — who are familiar with the Python language. The participants were invited via e-mail and personal invitations across colleagues and acquaintances, using snowball sampling. We managed to gather 36 respondents.

---

[1] Data: https://github.com/JetBrains-Research/adhd-study.

3.2   Materials

Barkley Deficits in Executive Functioning Scale

We used BDEFS-SF [12,48] as a valid self-assessment tool to measure the number and severity of difficulties with executive function in the sample. This multifactor scale allowed us to find specifically which executive functions might be deficient in participants.

BDEFS was first developed as a tool to perform a theory-based assessment of deficits in executive functioning in a clinical setting. Its early self-report version included five subscales labeled as five core dimensions of executive functions [14]:

- Self-Management to Time — a sense of time, time-scheduling;
- Self-Organization/Problem-Solving — arrangement of one's activities, coming up with ideas and solutions to encountered problems;
- Self-Discipline (Restraint or Inhibition) — the ability to inhibit one's reactions, consider consequences, self-awareness;
- Self-Motivation — the ability to cope with indolence and boredom, fulfilling duties without external motivators;
- Self-Activation/Concentration — sustaining attention and keeping up at work and in boring, uninteresting activities.

This scale was tested in several studies in adults with ADHD and proved to be effective in distinguishing nonclinical and clinic-referred participants [15]. Further work with the obtained data enabled Barkley and colleagues to notice and fix the underrepresentation of Self-regulation of the emotion domain in the scale. This resulted in the scale that tests one's executive functions related to Time management, Self-organization and problem-solving, Self-restraint, Self-motivation, and Self-regulation of emotions. This scale is now widely used in research such as ours, as well as in clinical settings.

While filling out the scale, people were asked to indicate from 1 (never or rarely) to 4 (very often) how often they encounter one or another problem in their day-to-day life.

The scale enabled us to not fixate on labels and diagnoses, which represent sensitive data and gather those who were not necessarily diagnosed with ADHD but may have still attentional difficulties [12].

Tasks. To emulate the programming activity, we used two types of tasks: (a) to write a programming function that performs the calculation in accordance with a given math formula and (b) to debug a code snippet that contains typos and syntactic errors. The tasks were chosen to be solvable by developers on any level of experience with the Python programming language. To test whether perceptual load affects the efficiency of the solution, we made two comparable tasks of every type to present them in High PLM and Low PLM. Thus, we came up with 4 tasks of the same level of complexity — two for coding and two for debugging (for full texts, see replication package [4]).

In our research, the coding task was used to trigger a more mentally active state, while debugging was considered monotonous. To amplify those traits, we

Fig. 1. The coding task in high perceptual load mode.

Fig. 2. The debugging task in low perceptual load mode.

made the coding task relatively short and active — the task triggered a problem-solving process and the solution was expected to be less than 10 lines long.

Snippets for debugging on the other hand were long and focus-demanding — they consisted of 186 and 196 lines of code with 32 typos to be fixed in each. This division of tasks on the basis of mental activeness allowed us to test if the experimental intervention has specificity for the efficiency of the solution of a monotonous programming task.

IDE Plugin. The described tasks were presented with the help of a plugin for the IntelliJ Platform [33], which we created to manipulate the interface and collect data. To fit the means and goals of our research, we adapted the TaskTracker plugin [38]. This plugin was developed by E. Lyulina and colleagues to be used in IntelliJ-based IDEs. To display the user interface, it used JavaFX [3] technology, which is deprecated since IntelliJ Platform 2020.2. The original TaskTracker supported logging the progress of solving problems, but did not support changing the configuration of the IDE and was not compatible with the latest versions of the IDE. Therefore, the plugin required significant improvement to suit our research.

Our version of the extension was developed in Kotlin. The overall implementation is a combination of a server and a plugin for the IntelliJ platform. The server part was built on Node.js. For the UI, instead of JavaFX, we used the

Java Chromium Embedded Framework [2], which is a built-in browser with all features that are usual for browsers.

The architecture of our approach consists of several components: **virtual server** — sends tasks and configurations, receives and stores data; **server** — transmits tasks and configurations to the controller and passes on logs to the virtual server; **controller** — implements configurations, initiates data logging; **user interface** — developing environment; **logger** — tracks activity and all symbol-by-symbol changes in the solution; **IntelliJ Platform SDK** — software development kit to support customization of the IDE needed for our experiment.

This architecture allowed us to perform the following tasks: (a) embed research-related UI into the IDE, (b) log the progress of problem solving, and (c) change the configuration (perceptual load) of the development environment.

In our study, we operationalize perceptual load as the number of interactable panels in the IDE. As can be seen in Fig. 2, the IDE in Low PLM has two visible panels (*i.e.*, a logically and visually united block of buttons and clickable elements), while High PLM has seven of them (see Fig. 1).

Research-related UI consisted of pages with the informed consent form, BDEFS-SF, and feedback form. Each user was randomly assigned to the group after completing the consent form. Depending on the group, the user's IDE configuration was initially set to low or high perceptual load mode. The group also affected the sequence of task types in each mode — whether coding or debugging would be the first. After the first pair of coding and debugging tasks, the perceptual load switched to the opposite one where again the sequence of task's type was counterbalanced between the sample. That resulted in eight possible configurations of the tasks' sequence.

After the completion of the study, all data on the user's solutions, as well as the data received from the activity tracker was sent to the server.

To test real-world effects, we set up our experiment settings to be as close as possible to habitual ones — using a production-grade IDE on a personal computer with real-world tasks helped us to do so. Low PLM is represented by a built-in "Zen" mode of the IntelliJ-based IDE PyCharm, this feature turns off the unneeded warnings and windows. High PLM is IDE's default visual representation. Thus, we maintained ecological validity, *i.e.*, the potential to make "a generalization of the experimental findings to the real world outside the laboratory" [45]. The plugin only implemented several changes to the habitual IDE functioning to build a more formal experimental environment. Such functions as auto-completion, error inspections and highlighting of code duplicates were turned off to test the mental activity of the participants themselves and to maintain the monotony when needed.

Metrics. The plugin collected and recorded time, as well as all actions and every symbol change made by a user, *i.e.*, indicators of solution efficiency. From this, we build two sets of metrics — for coding and debugging, respectfully.

For the coding task, the measures were as follows: **Total time taken to solve the task** (sec) — time delta between the appearance of the task on the screen and the "Next" button press; **Time of input of the first character** (sec) — time delta between the appearance of the task on the screen and the first keystroke; **Average time for one line of code** (sec) — time delta between the first and last keystroke divided by the number of lines in the task's solution; **Speed** (diff/sec) — the number of changed characters in the solution (*i.e.*, insertion of letters, deletions, newlines, tabs) divided by the total time spent on the solution; **Number of deletions** — the number of times when the symbol was deleted in the solution; **Number of actions** — the number of times special keys and shortcuts were used (*i.e.*, Enter, Shift, Backspace, arrows, Ctrl+A, etc.); **Number of lines in the solution**;

For the debugging task, the following indicators were tracked: **Total time taken to solve the task** (sec) — time delta between the appearance of the task on the screen and the "Next" button press; **Time of the first bug fix** (sec) — time delta between the appearance of the task on the screen and the first bug fix; **Number of changes in the snippet** — the number of changed characters in the initial snippet (*i.e.*, insertion of letters, deletions, newlines, tabs) compared to the final snippet; **Number of actions** — the amount of usage of special keys and shortcuts; **Number of fixed bugs**.

3.3   Data Collection

The experiment consisted of three steps, where participants:

1. installed the pre-configured plugin and completed the built-in BDEFS-SF questionnaire. There, they indicated how frequently they encounter difficulties in self-directed actions, *i.e.*, executive functions.
2. were presented with two pairs of tasks in the IDE. Each pair consisted of one coding task and one debugging task. To counterbalance possible learning and fatigue effects, half of the sample was presented with the first pair of tasks in Low PLM, and the other half — in High PLM. After the second task, perceptual load of the environment changed to the opposite one, and a new pair of tasks was presented. In each mode, the sequence of appearance of coding and debugging tasks was counterbalanced between groups.
3. received BDEFS-SF feedback and were asked to name the techniques (if any) they use to cope with self-regulation problems in their daily lives. Finally, they received questions about their months of experience with the Python language and familiarity with the "Zen" mode.

All experimental sessions were administered online via video conference with screen sharing from the participant's side. This helped us (a) to notice and control environmental variables such as level of noise, participant's posture, etc.; (b) to make sure everybody in the sample understand the flow and tasks of the experiment comparatively at the same level; (c) to troubleshoot immediately if needed; (d) to ensure that participants completed the tasks bonafide.

3.4   Data Analysis

All data obtained was analyzed in Python. Statistical analysis was performed with Scipy [52], NumPy [28], Pandas [41], and Pingouin [51]. In our research, the dependent variables are the solution's efficiency measures. The independent variables were represented by: (a) impairment of executive functions (presence or absence of the symptom) and (b) IDE's perceptual load (high and low).

The decision on the presence or absence of the symptom was made on the grounds of the overall factor's score — if a participant had a score greater than 8 on the BDEFS-SF factor under investigation, they were considered as having that ADHD symptom.

The results of the survey did not appear to be significantly correlated with the efficiency measures of the tasks according to performed Spearman's pairwise correlation with Bonferroni corrections.

The statistical hypotheses of our research to answer the research questions for coding and debugging programming tasks are presented further.

Hypothesis 1.1 (RQ1) There is a difference in efficiency measures depending on the perceptual load of the IDE.

To test whether perceptual load of the programming environment affects the efficiency of task solving, we used the paired-samples T test [53] to assess the difference in efficiency metrics between tasks solved in high and low perceptual load for all participants without dividing them into groups.

Hypothesis 2.1 (RQ2) Perceptual load mode and impairment of executive functions together affect the efficiency of the task's solution.

When the effect of perceptual load was confirmed, to investigate the effect of perceptual load across people with and without impaired executive functions, we performed a series of two-way repeated measures analysis of variance (ANOVA) [27]. We tested whether the interaction of (a) IDE's perceptual load and (b) impairment of executive functions affects the efficiency metrics.

Hypothesis 2.2 (RQ2) There is a difference in the ratio of efficiency for people with and without ADHD symptoms.

After the interaction of factors was confirmed, we used the Mann-Whitney U test [42] to see how exactly the perceptual load effect differs for people with and without ADHD symptoms. For that, we calculated *the ratio of efficiency*, which is an indicator of the perceptual load effect normalized to the one's results.

The ratio of efficiency is calculated as the proportion of the efficiency measures in High PLM to those in Low PLM. Let us provide an example of its calculation. For instance, if the efficiency measure in question is the number of actions in debugging task, *the ratio of efficiency* would be calculated for two groups — with and without an ADHD symptom (*e.g.*, with difficulties in Self-restraint). The ratio would be equal to the proportion of the number of actions in High PLM to those in Low PLM. That might result in $300 \div 400 = 0.75$ for those without the symptom and $963 \div 321 = 3$ for those with the symptom. If the ratio is greater than 1, the measure was greater in High PLM. Accordingly, if the ratio is less than 1, the measure was greater in Low PLM. This makes this measure an indicator of the perceptual load effect. The ratio of efficiency allows us to consistently compare the obtained data and to draw conclusions about the effects of perceptual load on the efficiency of programmers with different symptoms of ADHD.

For all statistical tests, we used an alpha level of .05.

Testing the stated hypotheses provided insights into the usefulness of the change of IDE's perceptual load for neurodiverse people in software engineering for mentally active and monotonous programming tasks.

Table 1. Descriptive statistics for Coding efficiency measures

	PL*	mean	std	min	25%	50%	75%	max
Total time (sec)	High	226.39	107.08	87.14	158.06	201.39	264.05	583.89
	Low	208.74	128.09	89.08	121.44	170.31	247.13	634.65
Number of actions	High	68.56	40.45	26	43	59.5	75.25	189
	Low	77.44	60.22	2	41.25	66.5	86	326
Time of input of the first character (sec)	High	34.68	26.3	2.36	10.88	31.2	50.27	112.01
	Low	22.53	13.47	4.61	12.29	19.26	27.17	63.21
Average time for one line of code (sec)	High	54.77	28.86	16.55	32.6	46.19	78.22	115.95
	Low	50.38	42.49	12.9	23.85	33.06	62.55	206.07
Number of deletions	High	21.69	19.89	1	9	15	26.5	92
	Low	23.61	17.13	5	12.75	18	29.75	8
Number of lines in the solution	High	4.75	1.93	2	3	5	6	9
	Low	5.25	2.37	1	4	5	7	12
Speed (diff/sec)	High	0.77	0.35	0.27	0.5	0.72	0.95	1.77
	Low	0.99	0.49	0.24	0.67	0.93	1.28	2.65

*PL — perceptual load

Table 2. Descriptive statistics for Debugging efficiency measures

	PL*	mean	std	min	25%	50%	75%	max
Total time (sec)	High	885.29	400.95	301.24	544.51	846.4	1027.87	1753.38
	Low	780.34	324.2	245.56	573.55	770.31	1059.25	1497.81
Number of changes in the snippet	High	41.64	17.25	13	32.75	4	52.25	10
	Low	40.94	18.08	8	27.75	38	46.75	97
Number of fixed bugs	High	21.92	6.09	6	19	23	27	3
	Low	21	6.2	2	18	21.5	26	3
Number of actions	High	373.08	602.5	26	63.75	131	358.75	3101
	Low	447.03	657.65	2	73.25	141.5	699	3085
Time of the first bug fix (sec)	High	62.86	42.52	12.82	32.97	55.22	77.59	189.9
	Low	45.41	36.48	11.42	18.91	35.78	55.91	181.26

*PL — perceptual load

Table 3. Descriptive statistics for the BDEFS-SF results

	symptom*	mean	std	min	25%	50%	75%	max
Time management	21	10.06	3.24	5	8	10.5	12	16
Self-organization	14	7.67	2.15	4	6	7	1	12
Self-restraint	8	7.44	2.79	4	5	7	8	14
Self-motivation	3	11.17	3.04	7	9	1	12.25	19
Self-regulation of emotions	4	6.42	2.29	3	5	6	8	12

*Symptom — number of people who have such a symptom

4   Results

We hypothesize that for active programming tasks (coding) and monotonous ones (debugging), the perceptual load of the IDE might affect the time spent on the task and the number of user actions. Also, this effect might be different across people with different levels of executive function impairment. In this section, we provide the results of testing these hypotheses on data from 36 Python developers of various levels of experience (min = 6 months, max = 10 years, Median ≈ 3.5 years), who mostly never use the Low PLM of the IDE, the Zen mode, while working (35 out of 36 people did not use this mode, 10 out of 36 have known about the option).

Descriptive statistics for coding and debugging efficiency measures, as well as for BDEFS-SF, are presented in Tables 1 to 3.

RQ1. Does perceptual load of the programming environment affect the efficiency of task solving?

Hypothesis 1.1 *There is a difference in the efficiency measures depending on the perceptual load of the IDE.*

The difference in efficiency metrics between tasks solved in high and low perceptual load was assessed using the paired-samples T test [53].

For the coding task: We found a significant difference in the time of inserting the first character. In Low PLM(M = 22.53, SD = 13.47) it was less than in High PLM(M = 34.68, SD = 26.3), t(35) = -2.743, p = .005; d = .582.

We found that the coding speed in Low PLM(M = 0.99, SD = 0.49) was significantly higher then in High PLM(M = 0.77, SD = 0.35), t(35) = 2.717, p = .005; d = .532).

For debugging tasks: The overall debugging time was significantly different between modes — less in Low PLM(M = 780.34, SD = 324.2) than in High PLM(M = 885.29, SD = 400.95), t(35) = -1.866, p = .035; d = .288.

Time when the first bug was fixed significantly less in Low PLM(M = 45.41, SD = 36.48) than in High PLM(M = 62.96, SD = 42.52), t(35) = -1.778, p = .042; d = 0.44.

Other efficiency measures did not show any statistical significance in the difference between modes.

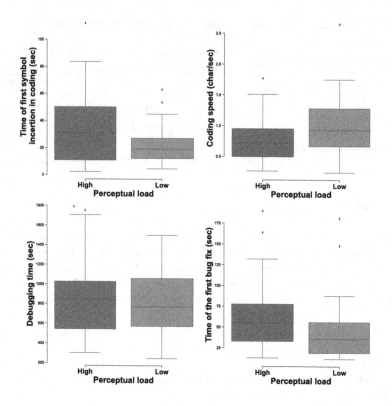

Fig. 3. Box plots of the effect of the perceptual load on the efficiency measures.

In our research, the perceptual load did affect some of the solution efficiency measures (see Fig. 3). For coding, people tend to start solving the task earlier, and the speed of writing the code was higher in Low PLM, compared to High PLM. For debugging, the overall time taken and the time when the first bug was fixed were less in Low PLM, compared to High PLM. When the effect of perceptual load was confirmed, we investigated to see if it differs between people with and without ADHD symptoms.

RQ2. Does the effect of perceptual load differ between people with and without impaired executive functions?

Hypothesis 2.1 *Perceptual load mode and the impairment of executive functions together affect the efficiency of the tasks' solution.*

To test whether the factors of the IDE's perceptual load and ADHD symptoms together affect the efficiency measures of task solving, we performed a series of two-way repeated measures analysis of variance (ANOVA) [27].

In coding: The timing of the input of the first character was influenced by the combination of perceptual load and self-restraint impairment $F(1, 34) = 5.869$, $p = .021$, $\eta^2 p = .147$.

The number of lines in the solution appeared to depend on difficulties with Self-motivation combined with the perceptual load as factors $F(1, 34) = 5.656$, $p = .023$, $\eta^2 p = .143$.

In Debugging: The time when the first bug was fixed was affected by the interaction of perceptual load and the presence of Time management executive function impairment ($F(1, 34) = 7.441$, $p = .01$, $\eta^2 p = .18$).

The time of the first bugfix was also affected by the interaction of perceptual load with difficulties in Self-motivation ($F(1, 34) = 5.726$, $p = .022$, $\eta^2 p = .144$).

Visualization of the effect of perceptual load and impairment of executive functions on efficiency metrics can be found in Fig. 4.

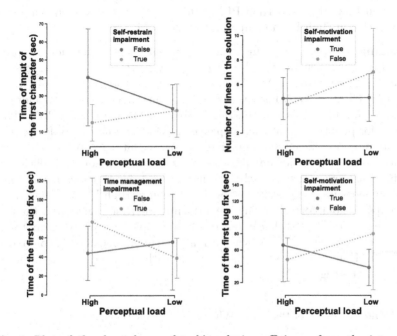

Fig. 4. Plot of the dependence of task's solution efficiency from the interaction of ADHD symptom and the Perceptual load

> *In our research, people with and without executive function impairments are affected differently by the perceptual load.*
> *We were able to register a statistically significant effect of the interaction of perceptual load and ADHD symptoms on efficiency measures. However, to see the specificity of that effect, further tests were needed.*

Hypothesis 2.2. *There is a difference in the ratio of efficiency for people with and without ADHD symptoms.*

To see how the perceptual load effect, expressed in the ratio of efficiency, differs for people with and without ADHD symptoms, we used the Mann-Whitney U test [42]. To represent *the ratio of efficiency*, the proportions of efficiency measures on High PLM to those on Low PLM were calculated. If the ratio is greater than 1, the measure was greater in High PLM. Accordingly, if the ratio is less than 1, the measure was greater in Low PLM.

In Coding: The efficiency ratio of time when the first symbol was entered was significantly less for the group of those who have difficulties with Self-restraint ($M = 0.9$, $SD = 0.62$), than for the group without that executive function impairment ($M = 2.07$, $SD = 1.64$), $U = 57$, $p = .02$, $CLES = .746$. This could be interpreted as the fact that people with Self-restraint difficulties were almost equally fast in Low PLM and High PLM, while people without such symptom were more active in High PLM compared to Low PLM.

In Debugging: Only for the group with time-management difficulties, the proportion of the time when the first bug was fixed was greater ($M = 2.62$, $SD = 2.12$) than for those with no ADHD symptoms ($M = 1.41$, $SD = 1.14$), $U = 210$, $p = .048$, $CLES = .667$. For the people with time-management difficulties, it took longer to find and fix the first bug in High PLM than in Low PLM. The same is true for people without such impairment. On the other hand, for people with symptoms, that efficiency proportion was significantly greater.

For the groups with other impairments of executive function, the efficiency ratio of the measurements was mostly less than 1 (see Table 4), which means that the efficiency measure was greater in Low PLM than in High PLM. In contrast, for the groups without corresponding impairments, the ratio was greater than 1. This might be interpreted as that in our research, people with ADHD symptoms were more active on the Low PLM when solving the monotonous task, compared with High PLM, and at the same time, people without those symptoms were more active in the High PLM.

Table 4. Results of the Mann-Whitney U test for Debugging task

ADHD symptom	Efficiency Measure	Efficiency ratio for group		U	p	CLES
		with S*	without S*			
Time management	Time of first bug fix (sec)	2.62 ± 2.11	1.41 ± 1.14	210	.048	.667
Self-restraint	Number of actions	0.61 ± 0.44	1.31 ± 0.93	59	.022	.737
Self-organization	Number of changes in the snippet	0.97 ± 0.35	1.2 ± 0.45	98	.036	.682
Self-regulation of emotions	Total time (sec)	0.84 ± 0.15	1.25 ± 0.44	26	.03	.797
	Number of changes in the snippet	0.7 ± 0.2	1.16 ± 0.42	19	.01	.852

*S — the symptom
U — Mann-Whitney test statistic, reflecting the difference between groups
p — probability value, describing how likely it is that the results would have occurred by random chance
CLES — Common Language Effect Size, the effect size of the difference between groups

> *Our results support the idea that people with and without executive function impairments are affected differently by the perceptual load.*
>
> *For coding and debugging, the mean efficiency ratio was mostly not greater than 1 for those who have symptoms of ADHD, which means that the efficiency measure was greater in the Low PLM.*

5 Threats to Validity

In our research, we found statistically significant changes in the measures of the efficiency of solving tasks, related to the perceptual load of the IDE. This change was different for mentally active programming tasks (coding) and monotonous ones (debugging), and it also differs across people with different levels of impairment of executive functions.

Several limitations of the study are important to note. In our research, we study people with self-reported symptoms of ADHD. To determine the presence and the severity level of ADHD symptoms, we used a questionnaire, which is not enough to make any medical conclusions. This might cast a question of the generalizability of our results to those who have the diagnosis and specific neurodevelopmental issues. In future work, it is important to work with ADHD-diagnosed people. However, finding a large enough sample of diagnosed people who are also proficient in coding could be a challenging task.

In the sample we managed to obtain, there is a variation in symptom-group sizes, some of them are relatively small. While that has no effect on the statistical analysis we perform due to the absence of relevant assumptions for the tests, the larger sample would possibly make effect sizes more notable.

Another limitation of the generalization of results is due to the changes we made to the IDE functionality for this study. To make the tasks independent of the participants' experience of using IDE and to make them challenging, we turned off some features that people use in IDE on a regular basis: autocompletion, error inspections, and highlighting of code duplicates. Enabling such features would make tasks as those presented in the study too easy. However, our goal was to test the effect of the perceptual load not on simple or difficult tasks, but on mentally active and passive ones. Thus, disabling hints helped us do this on smaller tasks. For this reason, we believe that the results of the study can still generalize to more complex tasks with the enabled features of the IDE if they are still mentally active or monotonous for developers.

The same argumentation is also applied to the design of the tasks — suggested tasks significantly differ from the ones that professional developers meet in their day-to-day practice. However, we chose to present simpler cases of programming and debugging for the sake of independence from the participants' skill levels. As well as for the IDE changes, we believe that tasks used in our research could accurately represent more complex, real-life cases. These limitations could be solved by balancing the experimental sample by skill level and experience working in the IDE. However, finding such a sample is not trivial and is left for future work.

6   Discussion

Acknowledging the limitations listed above, we conclude that the perceptual load does affect the solution efficiency of programming tasks and that this effect differs across people with and without ADHD symptoms.

In our research, Low PLM proved to be beneficial in terms of the speed of task completion in both mentally active and monotonous tasks.

We found that programmers' efficiency might be affected by the interaction of the perceptual load and executive functions' impairment. This means that the effect of these factors together differs between people with various levels of severity and types of ADHD symptoms.

Our data shows that, while solving a monotonous programming task: (a) people with difficulties in Self-organization, Self-restraint, and Self-regulation of emotions might be more active in the Low PLM environment; (b) people who struggle with Self-regulation of emotions might get time-wise benefits from High PLM; (c) people with difficulties in time management benefit from Low PLM if the measure of efficiency is speed.

This makes our findings somewhat controversial. However, the important note here is the division of ADHD symptoms into clusters of impairments of executive functions in our work. The results of our experiments might be interpreted as confirming that people with some symptoms or with the overall severity of ADHD will indeed benefit from the high perceptual load as shown in previous work. At the same time, in some cases, where the severity of ADHD symptoms is dictated by a specific executive function impairment, for instance, time management, as in our research, people may still benefit from the low perceptual mode for monotonous tasks. This supports Barkley's idea of domains of ADHD symptoms, which might cause their specificity and therefore emphasize the need for different accommodations.

7   Conclusion

There is a trend in the IT field to hire more neurodiverse people due to their special advantages and unique traits, which are beneficial in terms of innovation and profit. This presents a problem of accommodating such a workforce and helping them to cope with their day-to-day work life. One possible workplace adjustment is changing the work-station, which in software engineering might be presented by an IDE. Considering related work, we conducted research on how the perceptual load of the software interface might support developers with ADHD symptoms being efficient in their job. In our experimental research, 36 developers filled out the scale of ADHD symptoms and solved mentally active and monotonous programming tasks on high and low perceptual load modes of the IDE. Overall, our findings support the idea of perceptual load effect on the programmers' productivity. The results also show that people with ADHD symptoms might benefit from the low or high perceptual load of the environment, depending on the core specificity of the symptom. Therefore, we think that it would be useful to develop the IDE with built-in appearance adjustment tools to support the professional performance of neurodiverse people.

References

1. Adhd institute. https://adhd-institute.com/burden-of-adhd/epidemiology/
2. Java chromium embedded framework. https://github.com/chromiumembedded/java-cef
3. Javafx, client application platform. https://openjfx.io/
4. Replication package. https://github.com/JetBrains-Research/adhd-study
5. American Psychiatric Association, D., Association, A.P., et al.: Diagnostic and statistical manual of mental disorders: DSM-5, vol. 5. American psychiatric association Washington, DC (2013)
6. Antshel, K.M., Hier, B.O., Barkley, R.A.: Executive functioning theory and ADHD. In: Handbook of Executive Functioning, pp. 107–120. Springer, New York (2014)
7. Antshel, K.M., Joseph, G.R.: Maternal stress in nonverbal learning disorder: a comparison with reading disorder. J. Learn. Disabil. **39**(3), 194–205 (2006)
8. Austin, R.D., Pisano, G.P.: Neurodiversity as a competitive advantage. Harv. Bus. Rev. **95**(3), 96–103 (2017)
9. Barkley, R.: Deficits of Executive Functioning Scale (BDEFS for adults). Guilford Press, New York (2013)
10. Barkley, R.A.: Behavioral inhibition, sustained attention, and executive functions: constructing a unifying theory of ADHD. Psychol. Bull. **121**(1), 65 (1997)
11. Barkley, R.A.: What may be in store for DSM-v. ADHD Rep. **15**(4), 1–7 (2007)
12. Barkley, R.A.: Barkley Deficits in Executive Functioning Scale (BDEFS). Guilford Press, New York (2011)
13. Barkley, R.A.: History of ADHD. The Guilford Press, New York (2015)
14. Barkley, R.A., Murphy, K.R.: The nature of executive function (EF) deficits in daily life activities in adults with ADHD and their relationship to performance on EF tests. J. Psychopathol. Behav. Assess. **33**(2), 137–158 (2011)
15. Barkley, R.A., Murphy, K.R., Fischer, M.: ADHD in Adults: What the Science Says. Guilford press, New York (2010)
16. Bell, A.S.: A critical review of ADHD diagnostic criteria: What to address in the DSM-v. J. Atten. Disord. **15**(1), 3–10 (2011)
17. Blume, H.: Neurodiversity: on the neurological underpinnings of geekdom. The Atlantic 30 (1998)
18. Carreiro, L., Machado-Pinheiro, W., Junior, A.A.: Adults with ADHD symptoms express a better inhibitory capacity when the perceptual load is higher. Eur. Psychiatry **64**(1), S613–S613 (2021)
19. Costello, E., Kilbride, S., Milne, Z., Clarke, P., Yilmaz, M., MacMahon, S.T.: A professional career with autism: findings from a literature review in the software engineering domain. In: Yilmaz, M., Clarke, P., Messnarz, R., Reiner, M. (eds.) EuroSPI 2021. CCIS, vol. 1442, pp. 349–360. Springer, Cham (2021). https://doi.org/10.1007/978-3-030-85521-5_23
20. Couceiro, R., et al.: Pupillography as indicator of programmers' mental effort and cognitive overload. In: 2019 49th Annual IEEE/IFIP International Conference on Dependable Systems and Networks (DSN), pp. 638–644. IEEE (2019)
21. Dalton, N.S.: Neurodiversity & hci. In: CHI'13 Extended Abstracts on Human Factors in Computing Systems, pp. 2295–2304 (2013)

22. Dong, S., Guerette, A.R.: Workplace accommodations, job performance and job satisfaction among individuals with sensory disabilities. Aust. J. Rehabil. Counselling **19**(1), 1–20 (2013)
23. Doyle, N.: Neurodiversity at work: a biopsychosocial model and the impact on working adults. Br. Med. Bull. **135**(1), 108 (2020)
24. Fayyad, J., et al.: The descriptive epidemiology of DSM-iv adult ADHD in the world health organization world mental health surveys. ADHD Attention Deficit Hyperactivity Disord. **9**(1), 47–65 (2017)
25. Forster, S., Robertson, D.J., Jennings, A., Asherson, P., Lavie, N.: Plugging the attention deficit: perceptual load counters increased distraction in ADHD. Neuropsychology **28**(1), 91 (2014)
26. Ginsberg, Y., Quintero, J., Anand, E., Casillas, M., Upadhyaya, H.P.: Underdiagnosis of attention-deficit/hyperactivity disorder in adult patients: a review of the literature. Primary Care Companion CNS Disord. **16**(3), 23591 (2014)
27. Girden, E.R.: ANOVA: Repeated Measures. Sage, Newbury Park (1992)
28. Harris, C.R., et al.: Array programming with NumPy. Nature **585**(7825), 357–362 (2020). https://doi.org/10.1038/s41586-020-2649-2
29. Hindle, A., Barr, E.T., Gabel, M., Su, Z., Devanbu, P.: On the naturalness of software. Commun. ACM **59**(5), 122–131 (2016)
30. Ikävalko, J.: Dear future colleague, i learned to embrace my neurodiversity as a developer. and so can you., https://www.reaktor.com/blog/dear-future-colleague-i-learned-to-embrace-my-neurodiversity-as-a-developer-and-so-can-you/
31. Kamradt, J.M., et al.: Barkley deficits in executive functioning scale (BDEFS): validation in a large multisite college sample. Assessment **28**(3), 964–976 (2021)
32. Krzeminska, A., Austin, R.D., Bruyère, S.M., Hedley, D.: The advantages and challenges of neurodiversity employment in organizations. J. Manag. Organ. **25**(4), 453–463 (2019). https://doi.org/10.1017/jmo.2019.58
33. Kurbatova, Z., Golubev, Y., Kovalenko, V., Bryksin, T.: The intellij platform: a framework for building plugins and mining software data. In: 2021 36th IEEE/ACM International Conference on Automated Software Engineering Workshops (ASEW), pp. 14–17. IEEE (2021)
34. Lavie, N.: Distracted and confused?: selective attention under load. Trends Cogn. Sci. **9**(2), 75–82 (2005)
35. Lavie, N., Robertson, I.H.: The role of perceptual load in neglect: rejection of ipsilesional distractors is facilitated with higher central load. J. Cogn. Neurosci. **13**(7), 867–876 (2001)
36. Lavie, N., Tsal, Y.: Perceptual load as a major determinant of the locus of selection in visual attention. Percept. Psychophysics **56**(2), 183–197 (1994)
37. Loiacono, E.T., Ren, H.: Building a neurodiverse high-tech workforce. MIS Quarterly Executive 17(4) (2018)
38. Lyulina, E., Birillo, A., Kovalenko, V., Bryksin, T.: Tasktracker-tool: a toolkit for tracking of code snapshots and activity data during solution of programming tasks. In: Proceedings of the 52nd ACM Technical Symposium on Computer Science Education, pp. 495–501 (2021)
39. Macdonald, J.S., Lavie, N.: Visual perceptual load induces inattentional deafness. Attention Percept. Psychophysics **73**, 1780–1789 (2011)
40. McGonagle, A.K., Beatty, J.E., Joffe, R.: Coaching for workers with chronic illness: evaluating an intervention. J. Occup. Health Psychol. **19**(3), 385 (2014)
41. Wes McKinney: Data structures for statistical computing in Python. In: Stéfan van der Walt, Jarrod Millman (eds.) Proceedings of the 9th Python in Science Conference, pp. 56–61 (2010). https://doi.org/10.25080/Majora-92bf1922-00a

42. McKnight, P.E., Najab, J.: Mann-whitney u test. The Corsini encyclopedia of psychology,p. 1 (2010)
43. Morris, M.R., Begel, A., Wiedermann, B.: Understanding the challenges faced by neurodiverse software engineering employees: towards a more inclusive and productive technical workforce. In: Proceedings of the 17th International ACM SIGACCESS Conference on Computers & Accessibility, pp. 173–184. ASSETS '15, Association for Computing Machinery, New York, NY, USA (2015). https://doi.org/10.1145/2700648.2809841
44. Motti, V.G.: Designing emerging technologies for and with neurodiverse users. In: Proceedings of the 37th ACM International Conference on the Design of Communication, pp. 1–10 (2019)
45. Orne, M.T., Holland, C.H.: On the ecological validity of laboratory deceptions. Int. J. Psychiatry $6(4)$, 282–293 (1968)
46. Pisano, G.P.: Neurodiversity as a Competitive Advantage. Harvard Business Review, pp. 1–9 (2017)
47. Reiss, M., Brooks, G.: Developmental dyslexia in adults: a research review. National Research and Development Centre for Adult Literacy and Numeracy (2004)
48. Sheble, B.: Validation of the barkley deficits of executive functioning-short form. Ph.D. thesis, University of Missouri-Saint Louis (2019)
49. Sumner, K.E., Brown, T.J.: Neurodiversity and human resource management: employer challenges for applicants and employees with learning disabilities. Psychol. Manager J. $18(2)$, 77 (2015)
50. Telwatte, A., Anglim, J., Wynton, S.K., Moulding, R.: Workplace accommodations for employees with disabilities: a multilevel model of employer decision-making. Rehabil. Psychol. $62(1)$, 7 (2017)
51. Vallat, R.: Pingouin: statistics in python. J. Open Source Softw. $3(31)$, 1026 (2018)
52. Virtanen, P., et al.: Scipy 1.0: fundamental algorithms for scientific computing in python. Nature Methods 17(3), 261–272 (2020)
53. Zimmerman, D.W.: Teacher's corner: a note on interpretation of the paired-samples t test. J. Educ. Behav. Stat. $22(3)$, 349–360 (1997)

Classification of Error-Related Potentials Evoked During Observation of Human Motion Sequences

Su Kyoung Kim[1]([⊠]) [iD], Julian Liersch[2] [iD], and Elsa Andrea Kirchner[1,3] [iD]

[1] Robotics Innovation Center,
German Research Center for Artificial Intelligence (DFKI), Bremen, Germany
su-kyoung.kim@dfki.de
[2] Robotics Lab, Faculty of Mathematics and Computer Science,
University of Bremen, Bremen, Germany
jliersch@uni-bremen.de
[3] Institute of Medical Technology Systems, University of Duisburg-Essen,
Duisburg, Germany
elsa.kirchner@uni-due.de

Abstract. In recent studies, electroencephalogram (EEG)-based interfaces that enable to infer human intentions and to detect implicit human evaluation contributed to the development of effective adaptive human-machine interfaces. In this paper, we propose an approach to allow systems to adapt based on implicit human evaluation which can be extracted by using EEGs. In our study, human motion segments are evaluated according to an EEG-based interface. The goal of the presented study is to recognize incorrect motion segments before the motion sequence is completed. This is relevant for early system adaptation or correction. To this end, we recorded EEG data of 10 subjects while they observed human motion sequences. Error-related potentials (ErrPs) are used to recognize observed erroneous human motion. We trained an EEG classifier (i.e., ErrP decoder) that detects erroneous motion segments as part of motion sequences. We achieved a high classification performance, i.e., a mean balanced accuracy of 91% across all subjects. The results show that it is feasible to distinguish between correct and incorrect human motion sequences based on the current intentions of an observer. Further, it is feasible to detect incorrect motion segments in human motion sequences by using ErrPs (i.e., implicit human evaluations) before a motion sequence is completed. This is possible in real time and especially before human motion sequences are completed. Therefore, our results are relevant for human-robot interaction tasks, e.g., in which model adaptation of motion prediction is necessary before the motion sequence is completed.

Keywords: error-related potentials (ErrPs) · brain-computer interfaces (BCIs) · human motion sequences · human-machine interaction

Supported by the Federal Ministry for Economic Affairs and Climate Action (BMWK) FKZ: 50RA2023 and 50RA2024 and Federal Ministry for Education and Research (BMBF) FKZ: 01IW21002.

D. D. Schmorrow and C. M. Fidopiastis (Eds.): HCII 2023, LNAI 14019, pp. 142–152, 2023.
https://doi.org/10.1007/978-3-031-35017-7_10

1   Introduction

Inference of future human behavior and intentions is essential for an effective adaptive human-machine interaction. In particular, electroencephalogram (EEG)-based interfaces, e.g., brain-computer interfaces, enable systems to perform such inference and thus to flexibly adapt to human intentions, expectations, motion planning, or implicit evaluations of behavior [5,11,14–16,18–20]. In recent years, it could be shown that EEG-based interfaces enable continuous adaptive learning of systems (e.g., robots). For example, a robot learns and updates a policy based on human intrinsic evaluation (e.g., EEG-based feedback). The robot chooses a correct action that corresponds to the current context (human gesture) according to the EEG-based feedback, where the current context is unknown to the robot (i.e., the meaning of the human gestures is unknown and may change depending on the current human intention) [16,18]. Such applications are mostly shown in robot learning, e.g., adaptation of learning algorithms. Therefore, EEG-based interfaces are a good choice for human-in-the-loop approaches such as human-robot interaction, especially when continuous access to human intrinsic feedback is required.

Human intention can be inferred in various ways, e.g., by analyzing human motion sequences, human gestures, human EEGs as well as other biosignals such as electromyogram (EMG), etc. That means, human intention can be inferred by accessing both explicit (e.g., human motion, gesture) and implicit data (e.g., ErrP in the EEG). We propose an approach to allow systems (e.g., robots) to adapt based on human intention. In our application, we extracted human intentions by analyzing human motion and inferring implicit human evaluations by EEG analysis. For motion analysis, we trained a motion analyzer that segments trajectories, classifies segmented trajectories, and predicts the next motion segments in motion sequences (Fig. 1, blue boxes and lines). For EEG analysis, we trained an EEG classifier to detect/recognize erroneous motions segments while observing human motion sequences. Specifically, we used EEG to detect motion segments (as part of motion sequences) that have been defined as "incorrect" in the current situation (context). To enable this detection, we used error-related potentials (ErrPs), which are elicited in the human brain, for example, when observing erroneous behavior. In this paper, we focus on EEG analysis.

The ErrP is a well established event-related potential (ERP) component, which has been applied in several research and application areas (see, review, [5]). Like other ERP components (P300, MRCP, etc., details, see [13]), ErrPs have been applied in brain-computer interfaces (BCIs), human-machine interactions (HMIs), and human-robot interactions (HRIs). In many cases, ErrPs have been investigated in observation tasks, e.g., observations of motions of an abstract entity [12,14,24,26] or observations of motion of robots on a monitor [9,23], or observations of motion of real robots [8,10,16,17,23,29]. Further, ErrPs have been used not only to correct erroneous actions of the robot [29], but also to learn or adjust the behavioral strategy of robots [11,16,18]. In recent studies, ErrPs have been applied in HRIs, i.e., a robot learns a behavior strategy through interactions with humans. Here, the robot learns a behavior strategy not

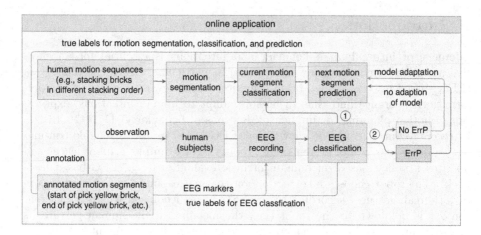

Fig. 1. Concept of our approach (Color figure online)

only by updating the strategy based on implicit human evaluation (i.e., the correctness of robot's behavior) via BCIs, but also by interpreting human intentions e.g., from human gestures [16,18]. To our knowledge, there are no publications that investigate the use of ErrPs when observing *real human movements* or *real human motion sequences*. However, there is one study in which ErrPs were elicited when observing simulated human hand movements [27]. In [27], subjects' grasping movements were simulated in a virtual reality (VR) environment, and subjects observed their own hand movements simulated in a VR environment in which hand movements were simplified.

In our approach, EEG analysis can be applied in two ways (Fig. 1, green boxes and lines). First, EEG classifications (e.g., the presence of ErrP) can be used to correct erroneous results of the motion analyzer (e.g., misclassification of motion segments). Second, EEG classification can be used to control a potential model adaptation (e.g., retraining) of the motion analyzer. That means, we can use EEG analysis both for direct correction of erroneous outputs of the motion analyzer as well as for model adaptation of the motion analyzer.

As mentioned above, in this paper, we focus on EEG analysis and evaluation of EEG classifiers. For training an EEG classifier, a reasonable amount of training instances is required to avoid overfitting. Thus, we recorded videos of human motion sequences to be used as EEG stimuli in various context, i.e., various stacking orders in our scenario (Fig. 2). In our scenario, a motion sequence of the stacking process consists of eight motion segments, which can be arranged into different sequences depending on human intention (Fig. 2). The goal of our study is to detect erroneous motion segments before the motion sequences are completed in order to adjust the systems according to the EEG classification even before the motion is completed. To this end, we recorded EEGs while observing human motion sequences and trained subject-specific EEG classifiers (i.e., ErrP decoders) that detect erroneous motion segments as part of motion sequences, i.e., before the entire motion sequence is completed.

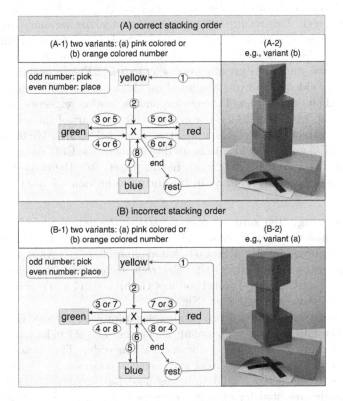

Fig. 2. Concept of motion sequences for correct and incorrect stacking orders (A, B). We have two variants each to stack in correct and incorrect order (A-1, B-1). For each condition, an example of the correct and incorrect stacking order is shown (A-2, B-2). (Color figure online)

2   Methods

Experimental Setup. We designed an experiment, in which ten subjects observed video recordings of human motions on a monitor. To this end, we recorded videos, in which a person stacks four colored bricks (yellow, green, red, and blue) in different orders (see Fig. 2). The motion sequences of the stacking process consist of eight motion segments ("pick yellow", "place yellow", "pick red", "place red", "pick green", "place green", "pick blue", and "place blue"), which can be arranged into different sequences (Fig. 3) depending on human intention.

We defined two conditions for training an EEG classifier (Fig. 2 A, B). First, we defined the stacking order as correct, if the blue brick was on top and the yellow brick was at the bottom of the resulting stack (e.g., Fig. 2A-2). This results in two correct stacking variants (Fig. 2A-1). Second, if the blue brick was placed as the third brick instead of on the top (e.g., Fig. 2B-2), we defined the stacking order as incorrect. This resulted in two incorrect stacking variants (Fig. 2B-1).

We annotated the motion segments (e.g., "pick blue" for reaching for and picking up the blue brick) in the videos. Based on the annotation, markers at the start of the motion segments were sent to the EEG recording, when the corresponding video frame was displayed on the monitor. These markers were labeled based on the position of the corresponding motion segments in the stacking orders (Fig. 2A-1, Fig. 2B-1). For example for the start of the segment "pick blue" in the correct condition the marker S7 is used (Fig. 3A). We defined these markers as EEG markers, which were used to segment the EEG data stream into epochs for training a classifier (Fig. 4). In this paper, only the markers S5 in the incorrect condition and S6 and S7 in the correct condition are used (Fig. 3).

Data Recording. Ten subjects participated in the experiment. We recorded EEG data while the subjects observed the videos of human motion sequences. EEGs were recorded 500 Hz with a 64-channel amplifier (LiveAmp, Brain Products GmbH) using an extended 10–20 electrode system with the reference electrode at FCz (actiCapSlim, Brain Products GmbH). EEG markers were sent to the EEG data stream in real time (Fig. 4).

Ten datasets were recorded in a single session for each subject. Each dataset contained the EEG data for observing 25 videos, i.e., 20 videos with correct stacking order and 5 videos with incorrect stacking order. That means, the class ratio was 1:4 with respect to incorrect and correct stacking order. Due to the class imbalance a stratified cross validation was used for evaluation and the classes were differently weighted for classifier training (details, see Sect. 2. Evaluation and Sect. 2. EEG processing respectively).

EEG Processing. The EEG processing pipeline consists of three steps: preprocessing, feature extraction and classification. For EEG processing, we used pySPACE [21], in which relevant methods are implemented (e.g., xDAWN [28]) or external packages (e.g., libSVM [4], pyriemman [1]) are integrated.

The EEG data stream was segmented into epochs from 0s to 1s and labeled as "correct" or "incorrect" based on EEG markers (Sect. 2. Experimental setup and Fig. 3). All epochs were band pass filtered using Fast Fourier Transform (FFT) with a pass band from 0.1 to 12 Hz[1], decimated to 50 Hz, and normalized to have zero mean for each channel.

For feature extraction, we combined xDAWN and a Riemmanian manifold approach [6,30]. Using xDAWN, we reduced the 64 physical channels to 5 pseudo channels, in which the signal-to-noise ratio for the "incorrect" class is maximized. All epochs were projected into the pseudo channels that consist of 50

---

[1] Potential artifacts due to the Gibbs phenomenon can be neglected here, as only the classification of the signals and not their shape is of interest.

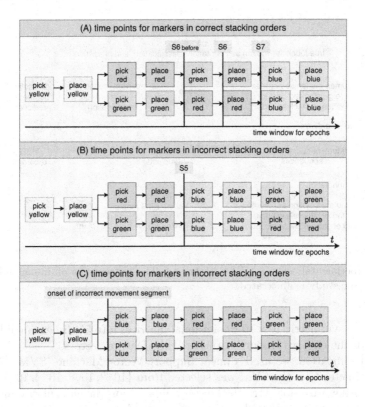

Fig. 3. Concepts of EEG markers in both correct and incorrect condition (A, B). The time points at which markers are sent to the EEG recordings are visualized with vertical lines with the names for the corresponding markers above. The subfigures A and B are analogous to Fig. 2. The time point used for classifier transfer (details, see Sect. 4. Discussion) is depicted in C. EEGs are segmented according to EEG markers (details, see Sect. 2. EEG processing). (Color figure online)

data points, i.e., we obtained 250 data points (5 channels × 50 data points) after applying xDAWN. After applying xDAWN, we used a Riemmanian manifold approach [6, 30]. To this end, we generated *extended epochs* (cf. [2]) so that we obtained 10 pseudo channels ($5 \cdot 2 = 10$ channels). A 10×10-dimensional covariance matrix was estimated across the 50 data points for each of the extended epochs using the shrinkage regularized estimator of Ledoit-Wolf [22], which ensures that the estimated covariance matrices are positively defined. After the estimation of the covariance matrices, we approximated their Riemannian center of mass[2] [3], which is used as reference point to append a tangent space. All training and testing data (i.e., each epoch) were projected into this tangent space and vectorized using Mandel notation [25]. Using Mandel notation, we

---

[2] The Riemannian center of mass is also called geometric mean in the field of BCI or Fréchet mean in general.

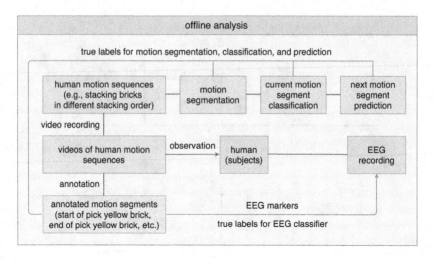

Fig. 4. Experimental setup for EEG recording. The concept the offline analysis performed in the study is illustrated.

reduced the symmetric 10×10-dimensional matrices into 55-dimensional feature vectors. In the end, we Z-score normalized the feature vectors.

For classification, we used a linear Support Vector Machine (SVM) [7]. The hyperparameter C of the SVM was selected from $\{10^{-6}, 10^{-5}, 10^{-4}, 10^{-3}, 10^{-2}, 10^{-1}, 1\}$ using a five-fold stratified cross validation on the current training data and the classes were weighted as $2{:}1 \sim$ "incorrect":"correct" in the formulation of the optimization problem.

Evaluation. For evaluation, we used three EEG markers (i.e., three labels, see Fig. 3). The evaluations were performed for each of the ten subjects individually. Either S6 or S7 was used as the marker for the correct class (Fig. 3A). In both cases, S5 was used for the incorrect class (Fig. 3B). As mentioned in Sect. 2. Data recording, we recorded 10 datasets for each subject. First, we concatenated the epochs of the 10 datasets, resulting in 200 correct and 50 incorrect epochs. A 5×5 stratified cross validation was applied on the concatenated datasets. By averaging across the folds and repetitions, we obtained classification performances for each of the 10 subjects. For performance metric, we used a balanced accuracy, i.e.,the arithmetic mean of true positive rate (TRP) and true negative rate (TNR). Note that the positive class stands for incorrect stacking order and negative class stands for correct stacking order.

3   Results

Table 1 shows the classification performance for each subject in both label combinations (label S6 vs. label S5; label S7 vs. label S5). In addition, we reported the means and standard errors as well as the medians across all subjects. In

Table 1. EEG classification performance: mean balanced accuracies (bACC=(TPR+TNR)/2) of 5 × 5 stratified cross validation for each subject. Two labels (label S6 and label S7) for correct class were used for comparison. For incorrect class, only one label (label S5) was used for evaluation. The mean and standard error of the mean (SEM) are given. In addition, the median is reported.

subject	label S6 vs. label S5			label S7 vs. label S5		
	TPR (%)	TNR (%)	bACC (%)	TPR (%)	TNR (%)	bACC (%)
1	96.0	99.5	97.8	76.8	89.8	83.3
2	82.0	94.8	88.4	62.8	89.6	76.2
3	84.4	97.1	90.8	74.4	90.3	82.4
4	81.2	96.2	88.7	69.2	89.0	79.1
5	89.6	94.5	92.1	71.6	91.1	81.4
6	97.2	99.5	98.4	74.0	89.8	81.9
7	90.4	97.3	93.9	79.6	96.6	88.1
8	90.4	97.2	93.8	68.4	90.3	79.4
9	55.6	89.6	72.6	42.4	84.6	63.5
10	86.0	97.7	91.9	68.4	89.9	79.2
mean±SEM	85.3±3.7	96.3±0.9	90.8±2.3	68.8±3.3	90.1±0.9	79.4±2.0
median	87.8	97.2	92.0	70.4	89.9	80.4

average, we achieved 91% and 79% for label S6 vs. label S5 and label S7 vs. label S5 respectively. However, one subject (subject 9) was found to have lower performance compared to the other subjects. This subject reported after the experiment that he had difficulty concentrating on watching the videos. Further, the use of S6 yielded a better classification performance than the use of S7 for the correct class. This result pattern, i.e., the superior performance by using S6 compared to the use of S7, was observed for all subjects.

4   Discussion

In this paper, we evaluated EEG data segmented based on the labels S6 and S7 for the correct class (Fig. 2A-1, Fig. 3A) and the label S5 for the incorrect class (Fig. 2B-1, Fig. 3B). The classification performance was higher when using the label S6 than when using the label S7 for the correct class (Table 1). This indicates that, as expected, subjects already recognized the correct stacking orders when they observed the placement of the red or green brick as the third brick (Fig. 2B-1, Fig. 3B), i.e., before the blue brick was picked (label S7). If our assumption is correct, the use of the label $S6_{before}$ for the correct class (Fig. 3B) could also improve the classification performance compared to use of the label S7. This should be investigated in the future work. Further, the decreased classification performance when using label S7 compared to label S6 may be caused by subjects paying less attention to the videos after S6. This reduced attention might have resulted in less relevant features for distinction between the correct and incorrect class.

In this study, we used only the videos showing that the blue brick was placed as the third brick for the incorrect stacking order (Fig. 2B-1, B-2). That means, the stacking orders are different between two variants of incorrect condition, but the position of the blue bricks (incorrect motion segments) in the stacking order was the same (Fig. 3B). However, it should in principle be feasible to detect ErrPs in any other position in the stacking sequence as well (e.g., Fig. 3B vs. C). Thus, we tested our approach in case of context change, i.e., the position of incorrect motion segments as part of motion sequences is changed. That means, we also detected incorrect motion segments, in which the blue brick is placed as the second brick for the incorrect condition (Fig. 3C). Here, we achieved a bACC of 98.4%. This classification performance was comparable with the case of Fig. 3B (Fig. 3B vs. Fig. 3C: 98.4% vs. 97.8% for label S6 vs. label S5). Further, we tested a classifier transfer approach on one subject, i.e., the classifier trained on incorrect motion segments in Fig. 3B was applied to the test data containing incorrect motion segments in Fig. 3C. Our preliminary results suggest that it is even feasible to transfer an ErrP classifier trained to detect an incorrect placement of the blue brick as the third (Fig. 3B) to detect motion segments, in which the blue brick was placed as the second brick for the incorrect condition (Fig. 3B). Here, we obtained a bACC of 88.7%. In a preliminary study, we evaluated the classifier transfer on one subject (Subject 1). Future work should systematically investigate the classifier transfer approach with an appropriate sample size.

For sending markers at the start of the motion segments, we used manual annotations of the motion segments in the observed videos. This is infeasible in real-time applications of ErrP detection when observing human motion. Instead, the time points of the start of the motion segments could be estimated by an online motion analysis. Thus, in future work, we will send markers directly from the motion analyzer online to the EEG recordings instead of from video annotations.

Our results show that it is feasible to distinguish between correct and incorrect human motion sequences based on the current intentions of an observer. This is possible in real time and especially before human motion sequences are completed. Therefore, our results are relevant to human-robot interaction tasks, since robots can adapt their behavioral strategy or interaction strategy ,,on the fly". On the one hand, we can use our approach described in Fig. 1, in which a motion classifier or a motion predictor can be adapted or not according to ErrP-based human evaluations. On the other hand, our approach can be applied to adapt robot behavior. If we detect ErrP-based evaluations of erroneous robot motion segments before the robot motion trajectories are completed, we can directly adjust the model underlying the control of the robot trajectories.

References

1. Barachant, A., et al.: pyriemann/pyriemann: v0.3 (2022). https://doi.org/10.5281/zenodo.7547583
2. Barachant, A., Congedo, M.: A plug&play P300 BCI using information geometry. https://doi.org/10.48550/arXiv.1409.0107
3. Cartan, E.J.: Groupes simples clos et ouverts et géométrie riemannienne. J. Math. Pures Appl. **8**, 1–34 (1929)
4. Chang, C.C., Lin, C.J.: LIBSVM: a library for support vector machines. ACM Trans. Intell. Syst. Technol. (TIST) **2**(3), 1–27 (2011). https://doi.org/10.1145/1961189.1961199
5. Chavarriaga, R., Sobolewski, A., Millán, J.D.R.: Errare machinale est: the use of error-related potentials in brain-machine interfaces. Front. Neurosci. **8**, 208 (2014). https://doi.org/10.3389/fnins.2014.00208
6. Congedo, M., Barachant, A., Bhatia, R.: Riemannian geometry for EEG-based brain-computer interfaces; a primer and a review. Brain-Comput. Interfaces **4**(3), 155–174 (2017). https://doi.org/10.1080/2326263X.2017.1297192
7. Cortes, C., Vapnik, V.: Support-vector networks. Mach. Learn. **20**(3), 273–297 (1995). https://doi.org/10.1007/BF00994018
8. Ehrlich, S., Cheng, G.: A neuro-based method for detecting context-dependent erroneous robot action. In: 2016 IEEE-RAS 16th International Conference on Humanoid Robots (Humanoids), pp. 477–482 (2016). https://doi.org/10.1109/HUMANOIDS.2016.7803318
9. Iturrate, I., Montesano, L., Minguez, J.: Robot reinforcement learning using EEG-based reward signals. In: 2010 IEEE International Conference on Robotics and Automation, pp. 4822–4829. IEEE (2010). https://doi.org/10.1109/ROBOT.2010.5509734
10. Iturrate, I., Montesano, L., Minguez, J.: Single trial recognition of error-related potentials during observation of robot operation. In: 2010 Annual International Conference of the IEEE Engineering in Medicine and Biology, pp. 4181–4184. IEEE (2010). https://doi.org/10.1109/IEMBS.2010.5627380
11. Iturrate, I., Chavarriaga, R., Montesano, L., Minguez, J., Millán, J.D.R.: Teaching brain-machine interfaces as an alternative paradigm to neuroprosthetics control. Sci. Rep. **5**, 13893 (2015). https://doi.org/10.1038/srep13893
12. Iturrate, I., Grizou, J., Omedes, J., Oudeyer, P.Y., Lopes, M., Montesano, L.: Exploiting task constraints for self-calibrated brain-machine interface control using error-related potentials. PLoS ONE **10**(7), e0131491 (2015). https://doi.org/10.1371/journal.pone.0131491
13. Kappenman, E.S., Luck, S.J.: The Oxford Handbook of Event-Related Potential Components. Oxford University Press, Oxford (2011). https://doi.org/10.1093/oxfordhb/9780195374148.001.0001
14. Kim, S.K., Kirchner, E.A.: Classifier transferability in the detection of error related potentials from observation to interaction. In: 2013 IEEE International Conference on Systems, Man, and Cybernetics, pp. 3360–3365 (2013). https://doi.org/10.1109/SMC.2013.573
15. Kim, S.K., Kirchner, E.A.: Handling few training data: classifier transfer between different types of error-related potentials. IEEE Trans. Neural Syst. Rehabil. Eng. **24**(3), 320–332 (2016). https://doi.org/10.1109/TNSRE.2015.2507868
16. Kim, S.K., Kirchner, E.A., Kirchner, F.: Flexible online adaptation of learning strategy using EEG-based reinforcement signals in real-world robotic applications.

In: 2020 IEEE International Conference on Robotics and Automation (ICRA), pp. 4885–4891 (2020). https://doi.org/10.1109/ICRA40945.2020.9197538

17. Kim, S.K., Kirchner, E.A., Schloßmüller, L., Kirchner, F.: Errors in human-robot interactions and their effects on robot learning. Front. Robot. AI **7**, 558531 (2020). https://doi.org/10.3389/frobt.2020.558531

18. Kim, S.K., Kirchner, E.A., Stefes, A., Kirchner, F.: Intrinsic interactive reinforcement learning - using error-related potentials for real world human-robot interaction. Sci. Rep. **7**, 1–16 (2017). https://doi.org/10.1038/s41598-017-17682-7

19. Kirchner, E.A., Fairclough, S.H., Kirchner, F.: Embedded multimodal interfaces in robotics: applications, future trends, and societal implications. In: Monash University, Oviatt, S., Schuller, B., University of Augsburg and Imperial College London, Cohen, P.R., Monash University, Sonntag, D., German Research Center for Artificial Intelligence (DFKI), Potamianos, G., University of Thessaly, Krüger, A., Saarland University and German Research Center for Artificial Intelligence (DFKI) (eds.) The Handbook of Multimodal-Multisensor Interfaces: Language Processing, Software, Commercialization, and Emerging Directions - Volume 3. Association for Computing Machinery (2019). https://doi.org/10.1145/3233795.3233810

20. Kirchner, E.A., et al.: On the applicability of brain reading for predictive human-machine interfaces in robotics. PLoS ONE **8**(12), e81732 (2013). https://doi.org/10.1371/journal.pone.0081732

21. Krell, M., et al.: pySPACE-a signal processing and classification environment in Python. Front. Neuroinform. **7**, 40 (2013). https://doi.org/10.3389/fninf.2013.00040

22. Ledoit, O., Wolf, M.: A well-conditioned estimator for large-dimensional covariance matrices. J. Multivar. Anal. **88**(2), 365–411 (2004). https://doi.org/10.1016/S0047-259X(03)00096-4

23. Lopes-Dias, C., et al.: Online asynchronous detection of error-related potentials in participants with a spinal cord injury using a generic classifier. J. Neural Eng. **18**(4), 046022 (2021). https://doi.org/10.1088/1741-2552/abd1eb

24. Lopes-Dias, C., Sburlea, A.I., Müller-Putz, G.: Masked and unmasked error-related potentials during continuous control and feedback. J. Neural Eng. **15**, 036031 (2018). https://doi.org/10.1088/1741-2552/aab806

25. Mandel, J.: Generalisation de la theorie de plasticite de WT Koiter. Int. J. Solids Struct. **1**(3), 273–295 (1965). https://doi.org/10.1016/0020-7683(65)90034-X

26. Omedes, J., Iturrate, I., Minguez, J., Montesano, L.: Analysis and asynchronous detection of gradually unfolding errors during monitoring tasks. J. Neural Eng. **12**, 056001 (2015). https://doi.org/10.1088/1741-2560/12/5/056001

27. Pavone, E.F., Tieri, G., Rizza, G., Tidoni, E., Grisoni, L., Aglioti, S.M.: Embodying others in immersive virtual reality: electro-cortical signatures of monitoring the errors in the actions of an avatar seen from a first-person perspective. J. Neurosci. **36**(2), 268–279 (2016). https://doi.org/10.1523/JNEUROSCI.0494-15.2016

28. Rivet, B., Souloumiac, A., Attina, V., Gibert, G.: xDAWN algorithm to enhance evoked potentials: application to brain-computer interface. IEEE Trans. Biomed. Eng. **56**(8), 2035–2043 (2009). https://doi.org/10.1109/TBME.2009.2012869

29. Salazar-Gomez, A.F., DelPreto, J., Gil, S., Guenther, F.H., Rus, D.: Correcting robot mistakes in real time using EEG signals. In: 2017 IEEE International Conference on Robotics and Automation (ICRA), pp. 6570–6577 (2017). https://doi.org/10.1109/ICRA.2017.7989777

30. Yger, F., Berar, M., Lotte, F.: Riemannian approaches in brain-computer interfaces: a review. IEEE Trans. Neural Syst. Rehabil. Eng. **25**(10), 1753–1762 (2017). https://doi.org/10.1109/TNSRE.2016.2627016

How Do Programming Students Read and Act upon Compiler Error Messages?

Maria Mercedes T. Rodrigo[1][(✉)] [iD] and Christine Lourrine S. Tablatin[1,2] [iD]

[1] Ateneo de Manila University, Quezon City, Metro Manila, Philippines
mrodrigo@ateneo.edu
[2] Pangasinan State University, Urdaneta City, Pangasinan, Philippines

Abstract. The research on understanding how programmers read and comprehend error messages is still limited. Through an eye-tracking study, we hope to add to what is known about how student programmers read and act upon error messages. In this paper, we elaborate on the methodology that we plan to use in the hopes of eliciting feedback from the research community that can help us improve upon our research design. We propose the study to enable us to collect data about whether student programmers read error messages, how they parse the code to find the source of the error, and how students with different ability and confidence levels vary in the way they process the errors. We will be examining where the participants fixate and how they read through the code to find the error. We are also interested in comparing the scan patterns of students who are proficient versus less proficient as well as those with high and low self-efficacy. We hope that the findings will contribute to the discourse about how student programmers read and parse code for errors, as well as to the discourse about the design of better error messages.

Keywords: eye-tracking · compiler error messages · scan patterns

1 Introduction

In 1984, Du Boulay and Matthew [7] observed that computer programming students are unable to relate compiler error messages to the actual error in the code. Why this occurs can be traced to two possible causes: First is the students' lack of programming knowledge, and second is that the messages themselves do not point to the actual source of the problem. The literature sometimes refers to the latter as "non-literal errors" [8] or the mismatch between the error message reported by the compiler and the actual error that occurs in the code. To student programmers, compiler error messages are pedagogically important because they provide students with feedback about what has gone wrong [2]. However, the difficulties that novices have with interpreting and acting upon compiler error messages continue to exist today, so much so that computer programming as a subject contributes to low student motivation and high student attrition [3].

In response to this problem, some computer science education researchers have suggested that compilers are the wrong tools to deliver error messages to novices and that

D. D. Schmorrow and C. M. Fidopiastis (Eds.): HCII 2023, LNAI 14019, pp. 153–168, 2023.
https://doi.org/10.1007/978-3-031-35017-7_11

another layer of software should be responsible for reporting errors to students in a meaningful way [7, 14]. Researchers have therefore invested efforts in creating systems that provide students with enhanced, i.e. more informative error messages [8, 15, 18]. Some found that adding subheadings, color codes, or using a progressive disclosure approach made error messages easier to parse and enabled programmers to find errors more easily [6]. Other studies were not as positive. Early work by Nienaltowski and colleagues [17] found that providing more information regarding an error did not necessarily result in greater debugging accuracy.

The investments in these systems give rise to the issues of cost vs. benefit: Do student programmers read error messages [15] (whether enhanced or not), and how do student programmers act upon the information that they receive [1].

The research on understanding how programmers read and comprehend error messages is still limited [1]. Through an eye-tracking study, we hope to add to what is known about how student programmers read and act upon error messages. Our research questions include:

1. To what extent do student programmers read compiler error messages?
2. How do student programmers parse the code to find the source of the error?
3. How do students with differing programming and self-efficacy levels vary in the way they process compiler error messages?

2   Eye Tracking and Program Comprehension

A growing number of researchers have made and are making use of eye-tracking to study programmer error comprehension. Barik and colleagues [1] used eye tracking to determine how software developers made use of error messages. In a study of 56 graduate and undergraduate students, they found that study participants indeed read error messages. Similarly, the group of Prather [18] conducted a study to determine if students found enhanced compiler error messages more helpful than standard compiler error messages. They found that students did indeed read the enhanced messages and found them more helpful than standard messages.

Other researchers have used eye-tracking to measure the difficulty that student programmers had in understanding or interpreting the errors that they read. They found that understanding error messages was similar in difficulty to reading source code [1]. Part of the challenge comes from a lack of familiarity with error message vocabulary [16]. Another part of the challenge comes from programmers' need to switch between the error message and the source code in order to understand the full context of the problem.

Finally, researchers have examined the reading patterns that students employ to parse through code to find an error, and how these patterns differed depending on ability level. Sharif, Falcone, and Maletic [20] found that programmers with higher levels of expertise took less time to scan the code. Experts also tended to focus on lines of code that are likely to contain problems. Peitek, Siegmund, and Apel (2020) examined how the linear structure of code influences the reading order. They found that programmers do not read code as linearly as they read natural text and that there were no significant differences in the linearity of reading patterns between novices and experts. The study of Tablatin and Rodrigo [21] corroborated the former finding. Their analysis showed that programmers regardless of expertise read code non-linearly. Their data did show some differences in the reading patterns of high- and low-performing students, though: High-performing students employed a greater variety of code reading patterns including pattern matching, flicking, and jump control. Lower performers tended to limit themselves to scanning and thrashing.

3 Prior Eye Tracking and Program Comprehension in the Philippines

The work of [21] and [23] relied on data collected from 128 college-level participants from five universities in the Philippines. We asked the participants to read 12 short Java programs (15 to 35 lines long; each program could fit on one screen) with known errors. In terms of complexity, these programs approximated what novice programmers would usually be asked to write, e.g. reverse a string, check if a string is a palindrome, create a program that plays "rock, paper, scissors", and so on. Nine of the 12 programs had three errors each while 3 programs just had one error each. Each participant's task was to encircle the error or errors. There is no need for the participants to correct them. A few of these errors took a minimal number of scans to detect, some took more time and involved the participant's analytical skills and prior knowledge in programming.

The experimental setup consisted of a laptop, a 17-inch monitor, a mouse, a keyboard, and a Gazepoint GP3 table-mounted eye tracker with a sampling rate of 60 Hz and a 0.5–1 degree of accuracy. The laptop's display was extended to the monitor. The eye tracker was placed in front of the monitor to allow the participant to view the codes while the eye tracker records the eye movements. The participant sat in front of the monitor, keyboard, and mouse. Figure 1 shows the standard setup of the eye-tracking experiment.

After calibrating the eye tracker, the research team activated a custom-built slide viewer loaded with the Java programs. The slide viewer shown in Fig. 2 enabled the participant to navigate through the programs using Previous and Next buttons. It also enabled the participant to mark error locations with a red ellipse. A Reset button cleared marked errors on a given page and a Finish button saved the participant's answers and ended the session.

The studies that emerged from the data contributed to the discourse about novice programming comprehension. However, our experience in analyzing the dataset and subsequent discussions in Dagstuhl Seminar 22402 on Foundations for a New Perspective of Understanding Programming [4] enabled us to identify many shortcomings in our study design that may threaten the validity of our prior analyses: There was no uniformity in the type of errors inserted in the code. They could be syntactic or semantic. The number of errors per program varied. Some programs had one error while others had three. Although each program did not exceed one screen length, the font size could be small. If areas of interest are too small, this may lead to ambiguity when interpreting fixation locations. The programs were shown in a uniform sequence, so familiarization may have had an effect towards the last programs. These and other shortcomings made it clear that our methods of data collection had to be improved.

Fig. 1. Standard Set-up of the Eye Tracking Experiment

```
1    import java.util.*;
2    import java.lang.*;
3    import java.io.*;
4
5    class p01{
6        public static void main (String[] args) throws
7            java.lang.Exception{
8
9            Scanner input = new Scanner(System.in);
10           int x, y, z
11
12           x = input.nextInt();
13           y = input.nextInt();
14           z = input.nextInt();
15
16           if ( y - x == z - y )
17               System.out.println(z + y - x);
18           else
19               System.out.println(z / (x / y));
20       }
21   }
```

Fig. 2. Screenshot of the Slide Viewer Program

4 Methodological Considerations

The critical decisions that we need to make regarding experiment design are summarized in [12] and Wyrich and colleagues' [24] presented in Table 1.

Table 1. Summary of Experimental Design

Attribute	Description
Study design [24]	The ways in which the subjects will be grouped relative to the tasks; includes factor design, allocation design, and randomization and counterbalancing
Participant selection [12, 24]	The number of participants and their composition. Participants have to be characterized according to knowledge, skills, and motivation as these will have an impact on their performance as well as their levels of engagement with the task
Experiment location [24]	Where the experiment takes place, i.e. laboratory or in vivo
Code scope [12]	The programming knowledge, i.e. vocabulary, principles, and constructs, represented in the code. The code can be a snippet that is a few lines long, a complete class, a package, or a whole system. A more limited scope enables the researchers to focus on a specific skill or knowledge fragment, but if the goal of the study is to assess understanding, then a larger volume of code should be used
Code difficulty [12]	The complexity of the code's logic. Assessing whether code is simple or complex depends on the participants and their level of expertise
Code pool size [24]	The number of possible code fragments available for the tasks
Number of code samples per participant [24]	The number of code fragments assigned to each participant
Code source [12, 24]	The origins of the code. Code samples may be self-made or may be drawn from external sources, e.g. open source, textbooks, industry, or contests
Code criteria [24]	Basis for choosing the code, e.g. balance between simplicity and complexity, novice-friendliness, taken from prior studies, self-contained functionality, no special domain knowledge, no unnecessary cognitive load, written in a familiar language, small enough to avoid excessive scrolling, no extensive use of rare APIs, and so on

(continued)

Table 1. (*continued*)

Attribute	Description
Comprehension task [12, 24]	The participant's goal. Task types can include explaining the code, giving personal opinion about code readability, debugging the code, using or extending the code, and others
Comprehension measures [12, 24]	Methods used to measure participant performance. These include correctness, time, subjectivity ratings, physiological methods, and others

We add the following dimensions based on our own experience of experiment design and based on the discussions following Dagstuhl Seminar 22402:

- Stimulus mode (static or dynamic) - Static or non-editable stimuli will confine the task to reading, tracing, and identifying errors on a single stimulus. Dynamic or editable code will require the use of an integrated development environment. The data captured will include a dynamic stimulus, one that changes with each edit and compilation.
- Pretests to determine participants' level of programming ability and self-efficacy - When analyzing the data, it may be necessary to segment the population according to their levels of expertise or confidence.
- Analysis methods - These vary depending on the granularity of the data. First order data are the raw readings from the eye tracker. These usually have to be aggregated to be interpretable. Second order data refers to fixations and saccades. Third order aggregates fixation information into counts, durations, and percentages. Finally, fourth order data represents scan paths in forms that allow comparison or matching with other scan [19].

In this paper, we elaborate on the methodology that we plan to use in the hopes of eliciting feedback from the research community that can help us improve upon our research design.

5 Proposed Data Collection Methods

The goal of the study is to determine how student programmers read and act upon error messages. Based on the research questions enumerated in Sect. 1, we propose the study below to enable us to collect data about whether student programmers read error messages, how they parse the code to find the source of the error, and how students with different ability and confidence levels vary in the way they process the errors.

Following the data collection methods for the dataset used by [21] and [23], participants will be shown brief programs with deliberately-inserted syntax errors.

5.1 Study Design

We will be using a within- and between-subject design where each participant will be shown all programs. The program sequence will be randomized to combat familiarization effects.

5.2 Participant Selection

Participants will be limited to undergraduate students taking their first collegiate programming course. These students will be selected from two universities in the Philippines. We plan to collect data from the students of Ateneo de Manila University (AdMU) and Pangasinan State University (PSU).

5.3 Experiment Location

Because the experiment will require the use of the eye tracker, the study will be conducted in a laboratory setting. The hardware will be set up following the configuration illustrated in Fig. 1.

5.4 Code Scope

The programs shown to the participants will be brief (15 to 35 lines) and will represent Java or C + + constructs discussed during the first 6 to 8 weeks of a first collegiate programming course. These include data types, variables, operations, conditionals, and loops. Table 2 shows the characteristics of the programs and the errors injected in the stimuli.

Table 2. Characteristics of the Programs and Errors Injected

Program	Description	Lines of Code	Line with Error	Error Description	Error Type
P01	The program asks the user to input 3 values and then displays the next number from the series of values entered by the user	17	9	';' expected	Literal

(continued)

Table 2. (*continued*)

Program	Description	Lines of Code	Line with Error	Error Description	Error Type
P02	The program must read a line of positive integers separated by spaces where the first integer corresponds to the number of elements in the set followed by unique numbers. Then the Q Prime numbers in the set will be identified. A Q Prime is a number in a given set where there are no other divisors in the set which are divisors of Q other than itself	26	21	Cannot find symbol	Literal
P03	The program determines if the input string is a palindrome or not. A palindrome is a string that reads the same backward as forward	19	5	'{' expected	Non-literal
P04	The program performs arithmetic operation based on user input. The user will enter two integer values that corresponds to the operands and a character value that corresponds to the arithmetic operator	28	10	Incompatible types	Non-literal

(*continued*)

Table 2. (*continued*)

Program	Description	Lines of Code	Line with Error	Error Description	Error Type
P05	The program determines the winner of the tournament of Rock, Paper, and Scissor game. The program has four sub-goals: input and assignment of number of data pairs, input and assignment of the data of the 2 players, determine the winner in each game, and determine the winner of the tournament	34	28	Illegal start of expression	Non-literal

Figure 3 presents a screenshot of the first stimuli that will be used in the experiment. The program's main objective is to display the next number in the given series. It was injected with a missing semicolon syntax error located in line 9.

5.5 Code Difficulty

It will be assumed that the participants would not have taken any prior programming courses. The level of difficulty of the code will be limited to the types of exercises given to students who are being introduced to the constructs listed under Sect. 5.4. We will only limit the error types to syntax errors that are usually encountered by students who are trying to complete these programming exercises. Only 1 syntax error will be injected in each program. No semantic errors will be included. We will choose 5 syntax errors from the syntax errors identified in the study of [5, 8] to be injected in the programs. Note that, despite this limitation, some of the errors may be non-literal. That is, they may not accurately reflect the error or its location. Figure 4 shows a sample program injected with a non-literal error "{ expected" since the class header has extra "()" after Palindrome located in line 5.

```
1          import java.util.*;
2          import java.lang.*;
3          import java.io.*;
4
5          public class NextNumber {
6                  public static void main(String[] args) throws
7                          java.lang.Exception{
8                          Scanner input = new Scanner (System.in);
9                          int x, y, z
10
11                         x = input.nextInt();
12                         y = input.nextInt();
13                         z = input.nextInt();
14
15                         if (y - x == z - y)
16                                 System.out.print(z + y - x);
17                         else
18                                 System.out.print(z / (x / y));
19                 }
20         }
   Compiler Error Message
   NextNumber.java:9: error: ';' expected
```

Fig. 3. Program P01 with a "missing semicolon" error in line 9

5.6   Code Pool Size

The code pool size will be limited to at most 5 unique programs with different syntax errors.

5.7   Number of Code Samples Per Participant

Each participant will be shown all of the 5 programs, in random order.

5.8   Code Source

The program code will be taken from open-source references or will be self-made.

```
1          import java.util.*;
2          import java.lang.*;
3          import java.io.*;
4
5          public class Palindrome () {
6               public static void main(String[] args) throws
7                    java.lang.Exception{
8                    Scanner input = new Scanner (System.in);
9                    int j=0,k;
10                   String S;
11
12                   S = input.nextLine();
13
14                   for (k=S.length()-1; j<S.length()/2; j++, k--){
15
16                        if (S.charAt(j) != S.charAt(k) ) {
17                             System.out.println("NO");
18                             return;
19                        }
20                   }
21                   System.out.println ("YES");
22              }
23         }
Compiler Error Message
Palindrome.java:5: error: '{' expected
```

Fig. 4. Program P03 showing a non-literal error "{ expected" for having "()" after Palindrome

5.9 Code Criteria

The programs that will be used must be novice-friendly, must be self-contained, must not require any special domain knowledge, must be written in the language that is familiar to the students, must be brief enough to fit on a single screen, and must not use unfamiliar APIs.

5.10 Comprehension Task

The participants will be shown the program code and the error message and will be asked to locate the exact error.

5.11 Comprehension Measures

Participant performance will be measured based on correctness and time. Eye tracking metrics will also be collected (to be discussed under Sect. 5.14).

5.12 Stimulus Mode

The stimuli will be static. Participants will only have to point to the location of the error. They will not need to correct it.

5.13 Pretests

The participants will be given two types of pre-tests: a knowledge pre-test and a self-efficacy test. The knowledge pre-test will be analogous to the experiment: It will be composed of five simple programs with syntax errors and the error message. The participants will be asked to mark the error and suggest a correction. The self-efficacy questionnaire shown in Table 3 will be taken from [22].

Table 3. Computer Programming Self-Efficacy Scale [22]

Subscale	Question
Logical Thinking	1. I can understand the basic logical structure of a program 2. I can understand a conditional expression such as "if… Else…" 3. I can predict the final result of a program with logical conditions 4. I can predict the result of a program when given its input values
Cooperation	1. I know programming work can be divided into sub-tasks for people 2. I can work with others while writing a program 3. I can make use of divisions to enhance programming efficiency
Algorithm	1. I can figure out program procedures without a sample 2. I don't need others' help to construct a program 3. I can make use of programming to solve a problem
Control	1. I can open and save a program in a program editor 2. I can edit and revise a program in a program editor 3. I can run and test a program in a program editor
Debug	1. I can find the origin of an error while testing a program 2. I can fix an error while testing a program 3. I can learn more about programming via the debugging process

5.14 Analysis Methods

We are interested in analyzing third and fourth order data. We will be examining where the participants fixate and how they read through the code to find the error. We are interested in comparing the scan patterns of students who are proficient versus less proficient as well as those with high and low self-efficacy.

The eye-tracking data that will be collected will be saved in an individual Comma-Separated Values (CSV) file. The timestamp, fixation location, and fixation duration can be extracted from the individual CSV file to construct the individual scanpaths. The fixation count and fixation duration metrics can be used to determine the visual effort of the students. The sequence of consecutive fixations and saccades, commonly referred to as scanpaths, can be used to determine the scan patterns of the students while reading through the code to find the error.

Scanpaths have been analyzed using different techniques for different purposes or goals. To compare the scan patterns of the students, we will bring the individual scanpaths together to generate a common scanpath for the group of students. Some of the common scanpath identification algorithms used by previous studies were the Dotplots algorithm [13], eMINE algorithm [9], Scanpath Trend Analysis (STA) algorithm [10], and STA with a tolerance [11, 21].

The Dotplots algorithm was proposed to address the difficulty of aggregating multiple scanpaths to understand and represent common scanning strategies. This algorithm can be used to detect patterns among scanpaths by listing one series of scanpaths on the horizontal axis based on their AOI labels and one sequence on the vertical axis of a matrix. Matching AOIs are indicated by a dot located in the intersecting cells. The common scanpath can be generated by finding the longest straight line connected by the dots. Hierarchical clustering is applied by selecting the two most similar scanpaths from the list of scanpaths and are then concatenated. The concatenated scanpath is then added to the list of scanpaths while removing the two selected scanpaths from the list. This process is repeated until only one scanpath remains in the list, representing the common scanpath. This algorithm chooses an aggregate strategy that is entirely dependent on the sequential matches found between the pair of scanpaths. Thus, the result can be uncertain if there are only a few matches found in the scanpaths [13].

The eMINE algorithm was developed to address the limitations of the Dotplots algorithm. This algorithm uses the String-edit algorithm to choose the two most similar scanpaths from the list of individual scanpaths. It then employs the Longest Common Subsequence (LCS) algorithm to the two most similar scanpaths to find their common scanpath. This procedure is continued until only one scanpath remains. The common scanpath is the last item on the list. However, because this approach employs hierarchical clustering, certain visual elements may be lost at intermediate stages. This technique is likely to generate short common scanpaths that are not useful for defining scanning or reading patterns [8].

To build a common scanpath, the STA algorithm [9] employs a multi-pass technique comprised of three main stages: (1) Preliminary Stage, (2) First Pass, and (3) Second Pass. The preliminary stage maps fixations with the visual elements or the specified Areas of Interest (AOIs). As a result, the individual scanpaths are generated and represented in terms of the AOIs. The next stage was responsible for analyzing the individual scanpaths to identify the trending AOIs by considering the total number of fixations and the total duration of fixations on the AOIs. Trending AOIs refer to AOIs shared by all participants. When the trending AOIs are identified, other instances of the AOIs that were not identified as trending AOI instances are removed from the individual scanpaths. The last stage in the algorithm is the second pass wherein the common scanpath is constructed. The common scanpath was based on the minimum total number of fixations and minimum total durations, and their positions in the individual scanpaths. STA has been evaluated and based on the result, the generated trending scanpath is more similar to individual scanpaths compared to Dotplots and eMINE.

The algorithms described above include all scanpaths in identifying a common scanpath. However, the variance between individual scanpaths can negatively affect the identification of a common scanpath. A tolerance level parameter was introduced to STA to account for the variances between individual scanpaths. This parameter was employed in the STA algorithm's first pass stage, which allowed researchers to alter the tolerance level in the stage of identifying trending AOIs. The tolerance level parameter can be set from 0 to 1. By default, the parameter is set to 1, which means that all individual scanpaths are considered in identifying a trending scanpath. Setting the parameter value to 0.95 makes the algorithm more tolerant of variances between scanpaths since it would only include AOI instances shared by 95% of individual scanpaths [10]. Therefore, STA with a tolerance can be used to identify a common scanpath that tolerates variances between scanpaths of a group. The work of [21] used STA with a tolerance to determine the common code reading patterns and strategies of high and low performing students engaged in a debugging task.

These are some of the possible algorithms that we can use to generate common scanpaths that describe scan patterns of students. At this point, we have not decided which algorithm to use. Once we have the data, we will determine which of these algorithms is best suited for the task and will consider other approaches if necessary.

6 Hypothesis

We hypothesize that we will find differences between more/less proficient and more/less self-efficacious students in the ways they read compiler error messages and parse code:

- To what extent do student programmers read compiler error messages?

We hypothesize that more proficient and more self-efficacious student programmers read error messages but limit their reading to the line number and not to the actual content of the error message while less proficient or self-efficacious students may read the entire error message.

- How do student programmers parse the code to find the source of the error?

We hypothesize that more proficient or self-efficacious student programmers will parse the lines of code surrounding the line with the error message while less proficient or self-efficacious student programmers will spend more time reading the line where the error is indicated.

We hope that the findings will contribute to the discourse about how student programmers read and parse code for errors, as well as to the discourse about the design of better error messages.

Acknowledgment. The authors would like to acknowledge the following Dagstuhl Workshops:
• The Human Factors Impact of Programming Error Messages (22052)
• Foundations for a New Perspective of Understanding Programming (22402).

References

1. Barik, T., et al.: Do developers read compiler error messages?. In: 2017 IEEE/ACM 39th International Conference on Software Engineering (ICSE), pp. 575–585. IEEE (2017)
2. Becker, B.A., et al.: Compiler error messages considered unhelpful: the landscape of text-based programming error message research. In: Proceedings of the Working Group Reports on Innovation and Technology in Computer Science Education, pp. 177–210 (2019)
3. Becker, B.A., Murray, C., Tao, T., Song, C., McCartney, R., Sanders, K.: Fix the first, ignore the rest: dealing with multiple compiler error messages. In: Proceedings of the 49th ACM Technical Symposium on Computer Science Education, pp. 634–639 (2018)
4. Brechmann, A., Sharif, B., Siegmund, J., Weimer, W., Endres, M.: Foundations for a New Perspective on Programming. Report from Dagstuhl Seminar 22402 (to appear)
5. Denny, P., Luxton-Reilly, A., Carpenter, D.: Enhancing syntax error messages appears ineffectual. In: Proceedings of the ITiCSE '14: Proceedings of the 2014 Conference on Innovation & Technology in Computer Science Education, pp. 273–278 (2014)
6. Dong, T., Khandwala, K.: The IMPACT of "Cosmetic" changes on the usability of error messages. In: Extended Abstracts of the 2019 Chi Conference on Human Factors in Computing Systems, pp. 1–6 (2019)
7. Du Boulay, B., Matthew, I.: Fatal error in pass zero: how not to confuse novices. Behav. Inf. Technol. 3(2), 109–118 (1984)
8. Dy, T., Rodrigo, M.M.: A detector for non-literal Java errors. In: Proceedings of the 10th Koli Calling International Conference on Computing Education Research, pp. 118–122 (2010)
9. Eraslan, S., Yesilada, Y., Harper, S.: Identifying patterns in eyetracking scanpaths in terms of visual elements of web pages. In: Casteleyn, S., Rossi, G., Winckler, M. (eds.) ICWE 2014. LNCS, vol. 8541, pp. 163–180. Springer, Cham (2014). https://doi.org/10.1007/978-3-319-08245-5_10
10. Eraslan, S., Yesilada, Y., Harper, S.: Scanpath Trend Analysis on Web Pages: Clustering Eye Tracking Scanpaths. ACM Trans. Web 10(4), 35 (2016). Article 20. https://doi.org/10.1145/2970818
11. Eraslan, S., Yesilada, Y., Harper, S.: Engineering web- based interactive systems: trend analysis in eye tracking scanpaths with a tolerance. In: Proceedings of the ACM SIGCHI Symposium on Engineering Interactive Computing Systems, pp. 3–8 (2017)
12. Feitelson, D.G.: Considerations and pitfalls in controlled experiments on code comprehension. In: 2021 IEEE/ACM 29th International Conference on Program Comprehension (ICPC), pp. 106–117. IEEE (2021)
13. Goldberg, J.H., Helfman, J.I.: Scanpath clustering and aggregation. In: Proceedings of the 2010 Symposium on Eye Tracking Research and Applications, pp. 18–27 (2010)
14. Kohn, T.: The error behind the message: finding the cause of error messages in python. In: Proceedings of the 50th ACM Technical Symposium on Computer Science Education, pp. 524–530 (2019)
15. Marceau, G., Fisler, K., Krishnamurthi, S.: Measuring the effectiveness of error messages designed for novice programmers. In: Proceedings of the 42nd ACM Technical Symposium on Computer science Education, pp. 499–504 (2011)

16. Marceau, G., Fisler, K., Krishnamurthi, S.: Mind your language: on novices' interactions with error messages. In: Proceedings of the 10th SIGPLAN Symposium on New Ideas, New Paradigms, and Reflections on Programming and Software, pp. 3–18 (2011)
17. Nienaltowski, M.H., Pedroni, M., Meyer, B.: Compiler error messages: what can help novices?. In: Proceedings of the 39th SIGCSE Technical Symposium on Computer Science Education, pp. 168–172 (2008)
18. Prather, J., et al.: On novices' interaction with compiler error messages: a human factors approach. In: Proceedings of the 2017 ACM Conference on International Computing Education Research, pp. 74–82 (2017)
19. Sharafi, Z., Sharif, B., Guéhéneuc, Y.-G., Begel, A., Bednarik, R., Crosby, M.: A practical guide on conducting eye tracking studies in software engineering. Empir. Softw. Eng. 25(5), 3128–3174 (2020). https://doi.org/10.1007/s10664-020-09829-4
20. Sharif, B., Falcone, M., Maletic, J.I.: An eye-tracking study on the role of scan time in finding source code defects. In: Proceedings of the Symposium on Eye Tracking Research and Applications, pp. 381–384 (2012)
21. Tablatin, C.L.S., Rodrigo, M.M.T.: Identifying code reading strategies in debugging using STA with a tolerance algorithm. APSIPA Trans. Sig. Inf. Process. 11(1) (2022)
22. Tsai, M.-J., Wang, C.-Y., Hsu, P.-F.: Developing the computer programming self-efficacy scale for computer literacy education. J. Educ. Comput. Res. 56(8), 1345–1360 (2019)
23. Villamor, M.M., Rodrigo, M.M.T.: Predicting pair success in a pair programming eye tracking experiment using cross-recurrence quantification analysis. APSIPA Trans. Sig. Inf. Process. 11(1) (2022)
24. Wyrich, M., Bogner, J., Wagner, S.: 40 years of designing code comprehension experiments: a systematic mapping study. arXiv preprint arXiv:2206.11102 (2022)

How Human Spatial Ability is Affected by the Misalignment of Idiotropic and Visual Axes

Faezeh Salehi[(✉)], Fatemeh Pariafsai, and Manish K. Dixit

Texas A&M University, College Station, TX 77843, USA
{faezehsalehi,pariafsai,mdixit}@tamu.edu

Abstract. This paper presents the results of a study investigating the impact of misaligned idiotropic and visual axes on spatial ability in a simulated microgravity environment in virtual reality. The study involved 99 participants who completed two spatial tests, the Purdue Spatial Visualization Test: Rotations and the Perspective Taking Ability test, in three different scenarios: control (axes aligned), static misalignment, and dynamic misalignment. The results showed that dynamic misalignment significantly impacted mental rotation and spatial visualization performance, but not spatial orientation ability. Additionally, the gaming experience did not moderate mental rotation outcomes but did enhance spatial orientation ability. These findings provide insight into how altered visuospatial conditions may affect human spatial cognition and can inform the development of simulation-based training tools to help people adapt to such environments more effectively. Furthermore, the study highlights the potential of using games as a learning tool to improve productivity and safety in extreme or altered work environments.

Keywords: Spatial Ability · Spatial Cognition · Virtual Reality

1 Introduction

Emerging technologies are transforming the future of work and transforming working conditions [1]. As part of the exploration process, deep space, low Earth orbit (LEO), deep oceans, and polar regions with different climates will need to be explored [2]. Human cognitive abilities, particularly spatial cognitive abilities, must be examined and enhanced to ensure enhanced safety and productivity in such conditions [3]. Spatial abilities are important to students' success in STEM education and careers [4] as well as people's complete and accurate perception of spatial environments [4]. An individual's spatial ability is their ability to acquire imagery, store it, retrieve it, and transform it in order to build a mental representation of the spatial setting that is complete and accurate [5]. Consequently, we are able to locate objects in space, perceive objects visually, and understand their spatial relationship in two and three dimensions [6]. Orientation, spatial relations, and spatial visualization are three key abilities that determine human spatial ability. Information about space can be mentally gathered, manipulated, and visualized through spatial visualization. One of the spatial visualization tasks is mental

© The Author(s), under exclusive license to Springer Nature Switzerland AG 2023
D. D. Schmorrow and C. M. Fidopiastis (Eds.): HCII 2023, LNAI 14019, pp. 169–186, 2023.
https://doi.org/10.1007/978-3-031-35017-7_12

rotation, which is the ability to mentally rotate an object in 2D or 3D space. Routine tasks such as, applying makeup in the mirror or combing one's hair and organizing items into a suitcase utilize mental rotation and visualization abilities [7, 8]. Work related tasks such as driving, operating a piece of equipment, or packaging also use spatial visualization abilities. Spatial relations represent the ability to relate 2-dimensional (2D) projections of a 3-dimensional (3D) shape to form a mental representation of the object. For instance, understanding construction or engineering drawings to create a mental image of a building or object involves spatial relations ability. Spatial orientation ability denotes the ability to imagine positioning at a point and visualizing a particular spatial environment. For instance, mentally aligning a north-up map to egocentric orientation may involve spatial orientation ability. These three abilities are applied in different combinations by individuals to perform day-to-day personal and professional tasks safely and efficiently.

Our workplaces or daily lives may require us to utilize each of these abilities in a variety of ways [9]. In order to do this, one must be able to perceive and visually understand the features, properties, measurements, shapes, positions, and movements of external objects [10]. People's ability to represent and transform visuospatial information impacts everyday activities such as driving, walking, and climbing stairs. Significant research has been done on spatial ability in many fields such as STEM education [1, 11–16], science [1, 12–16], mathematics [17–21], psychology [5, 22–24], and medicine [22–26]. Some studies have examined spatial ability and adjusting to work conditions in difficult-to-reach locations without adequate visuospatial support [27–30]. Most experiments on spatial abilities are conducted on Earth in a familiar environment and in the presence of both gravitational and visual cues. Research into human spatial abilities in microgravity environments still needs to be conducted [31]. A number of altered static or dynamic conditions exist in workplaces like space and deep ocean due to a lack of gravity, misalignment of body and visual axes, and the absence of visual cues or frames of reference [4, 32, 33]. A workplace in such an environment may be unsafe, uncomfortable, and less productive for workers not accustomed to such environments [34].

The purpose of this study is to explore the effects of altered conditions of misaligned idiotropic and visual axes on human spatial abilities when engaged in these environments using Virtual Reality (VR). This knowledge is essential to designing tools to train future workers in such settings. Future workers will potentially benefit from such tools by increasing their efficiency, reducing errors and adapting quickly and easily to these situations, which will potentially lead to a safer and more productive workplace.

1.1 Background

Emerging technologies have brought about significant changes to the world we live in today. The advancements in technology have transformed the way we communicate, work, and interact with each other. From phone calls to business operations, technology has made a significant impact. With the rapid pace of technological progress, it is highly likely that the working environment will undergo further transformation in the near future. This means that the way we work, the skills required for various jobs, and the workplace itself are likely to change in the coming decades, making it important for individuals and organizations to be adaptable and ready for these changes.

Emerging technologies are having a significant impact on the future of work places, particularly in the construction industry. As construction projects are managed and executed, remote construction technologies are becoming more prevalent, allowing for greater flexibility and efficiency. Humans have not previously been able to explore the deep oceans, deep space, or polar regions because of technological advancements [35]. In such work environments, however, conditions may exist that alter spatial cognitive processing. As a result of such environments, people's visuospatial processing can be adversely affected and they can eventually lose the ability to work efficiently and safely [36].

1.2 Spatial Ability

Our understanding of spatial environments is governed by spatial cognitive processing, an integral part of human cognition. In spatial cognition, spatial ability is one of many facets that have been defined in various ways. It is the skill of generating, storing, retrieving, and transforming well-structured visual images, according to Lohman (1979) [5]. The process of representing, transforming, generating, and extracting symbols and non-verbal information is defined by Linn and Petersen's framework [7]. According to them, spatial ability is composed of three components: visual perception, mental rotation, and spatial imagination. In addition to comprehending three-dimensional objects, spatial ability also involves the ability to manipulate objects according to Garg (1999) [37]. Basically, spatial ability refers to the ability to produce, visualize, memorize, remember, and transform any visual information, including images, maps, and 3D models. Spatial ability is defined differently by researchers, but all agree that it is a natural ability that assists individuals in solving tasks involving visual perception and spatial judgment [38]. According to Liao (2017) [39], it is not a single ability but a result of several spatial ability components combining into an overall ability that controls spatial cognition. Several studies examined the components and subfactors of spatial ability. Among the subfactors of spatial ability, McCgee classified spatial perception and spatial orientation [40]. A similar classification was made by Lohman (2014) [41] between spatial visualization, spatial orientation, and speeded rotation. As Carroll (1993) [9] observed, the perception of speed is composed of five elements: visualization, spatial relations, closure speed, closure flexibility, and perceptual speed. A recent study by Harris and colleagues (Harris et al., 2021) [42] examined spatial reasoning under mental rotation, spatial visualization, and spatial orientation functions. However, several studies [9, 38, 43–52] agreed that there are three key dimensions of spatial ability, spatial visualization, spatial orientation, and spatial relations, which may help understand how people perceive and mentally manipulate objects.

1.3 Dimensions of Spatial Ability: Spatial Visualization, Relations, and Orientation

A sense of spatial ability is manifested both directly and indirectly in the way words, numbers, and letter-like forms are arranged on a page. Spatial visualization, spatial orientation, and spatial relations have been discussed in literature as three key dimensions of spatial ability. Object rotation, turning, and twisting ability is measured by the ability to visualize an object rotating, turning, or twisting in a specified sequence [4, 31, 32]. In order to test spatial ability in this dimension, participants must mentally manipulate (rotate, turn, or twist) an object following explicit instructions on its nature and sequence of manipulation and identify the object's new appearance, location, or position based on given options. A number of tests are available that assess spatial visualization of rotation, including the Purdue Spatial Visualizations Test: Visualization of Rotations (PSVT: R), the Shepard-Metzler Mental Rotation Test (MRT), and the Vandenberg and Kuse Mental Rotations Test, a modified version of MRT [53–55]. The Lowrie et al. (2019) [56] study defines spatial visualization as the ability to "manipulate spatial properties of an object mentally". The Form Board Test and the Paper Folding Test are described as instruments to measure spatial visualization. A participant's ability to mentally rotate a 2D figure in one step is attributed to spatial relations ability [57]. The ability to perceive spatial relations can also be measured with tests such as the Cards Rotation Test and Cube Comparison Test [57–59]. Additionally, a mental rotation may be required to relate a 2D object to its orthographic projections [45, 46]. Orientation to spatial settings is measured by participants' ability to imagine and visualize them from different perspectives [4, 32]. Tests to measure this ability include the Perspective Taking Ability (PTA) and the Guilford-Zimmerman Spatial Orientation Test [43, 57].

1.4 Virtual Reality (VR) in Spatial Cognition Research

The concept of Virtual Reality (VR) combines computer graphics with a wide range of sensory inputs in real-time to create a more intuitive and naturalistic experience so that the user is immersed in a simulated physical environment and can interact more intuitively and naturally with it [60]. Researchers have used VR technology to evaluate spatial cognition and simulate physical conditions [35, 61, 62]. A virtual reality spatial test was administered to a group of students by Guzsvinecz et al. in 2021, to analyze their interaction time. Guzsvinecz et al. (2022) [63] revealed that males with Gear VR experienced significant increases in interaction time during those Mental Rotation Tests, compared to males with desktop displays who experienced a significant decrease. When it comes to simulating an environment that is difficult to experience in person, VR has proven particularly effective and useful. A multimodule space station was simulated by Shebilske et al. [64] and Guo et al. [65] and spatial tests were used to predict work and navigation performance. A VR simulation of scuba diving was developed by Jain et al. [27], which found that a variety of underwater sensations could be produced. For a training game aimed at teaching important scuba procedures, Schaller [66] created VR mockups to outline design principles. Some studies [27, 29, 64] have demonstrated that VR can be used to simulate extreme environments and provide similar physiological responses to microgravity. Virtual reality simulations have been recommended as a safer and more cost-effective alternative to parabolic flights for testing and training astronauts [29, 67]. Spacecraft crews can improve spatial orientation and navigation, minimize motion sickness, and avoid disorientation by using VR-based training [30, 60, 64]. Teaching-learning processes have been long supported by VR in various educational environments at all educational levels. The use of virtual reality (VR) can be a powerful tool for creating learning environments. A review of over 50 papers was conducted by Mikropoulos and Natsis [68], concerning the use of VR in the creation of educational virtual environments (EVE).

2 Materials and Methods

2.1 Research Goal and Objectives

This study aims to investigate how altered visuospatial conditions of misaligned idiotropic and visual axes found in extreme microgravity environments can affect human spatial ability indicated by spatial visualization and orientation dimensions. The following research objectives are pursued to reach this goal:

- Create in VR settings the control group condition of aligned body and visual axes and experiment group conditions of statically and dynamically misaligned body and visual axes;
- Measure the spatial visualization and orientation abilities of the participants by imbedding in VR the PSVT: R and PTA test stimuli;
- Compare the scores the control and experiment groups to examine the extent to which altered condition of misaligned idiotropic and visual axes impact spatial visualization and orientation abilities.

2.2 Participants

Although this study focuses on people who work in extreme conditions such as, astronauts, divers, and polar researchers, to avoid bias in spatial testing, they were excluded because they have already undergone rigorous training or have extensive experience in altered conditions [69, 70]. The study included 99 participants (including 27 females), all with normal or corrected-to-normal vision. Participants were recruited from Texas A&M University student population through email announcements sent through the university's email system. The participants' age ranged from 18 to 52 years with an average age of 24.45 years and a standard deviation of 6.188. The Institutional Review Board (IRB) of the university approved the study and all subjects provided written consent before the study began.

Table 1. Participants Information

Age	min:18/max:52	mean: 24.45
Major	Engineer	Non-engineer
Gender	Female: 27	male: 72
Video game	Gamers: 44	Non-gamers: 55

2.3 Instruments

In order to assess spatial orientation ability, the perspective-taking ability (PTA) test was used, whereas PSVTR (Revised Purdue Spatial Visualization Test) was utilized to measure spatial visualization ability.

The Purdue Spatial Visualization Test: Visualization of Rotation (PSVT: R) assesses an individual's capacity for mental three-dimensional rotation. It comprises of 30 items, consisting of 13 symmetrical and 17 nonsymmetrical 3D figures. Participants are shown an example object and its rotated view and must select the matching rotation from five options. PSVT: R is part of the larger Purdue Spatial Visualization Test, developed by Guay in 1976, which is composed of 12 items divided into three sections: "Developments", "Rotations", and "Views". Figure 1 shows an example item from PSVT: R.

Perspective Taking Ability (PTA). As a measure of participants' ability to imagine a view from another viewpoint, we used PTA [71]. There were 6–7 routine objects that were positioned on a surface in an immersive VR environment. In this exercise, participants are asked to imagine themselves standing at the point where one of the objects faces another. Following that, they will be asked to point towards a third object. An individual's score is determined by how far he or she deviates from the correct answer. This means that a lower score value means less deviation and a higher score on the PTA task. Being able to understand how an environment looks from different perspectives requires different skills than being able to transform individual objects spatially.

2.4 Study Environment

VR environments with spatial test stimuli were created using Unity 3D game engine [26] to simulate three conditions. The first condition, the control group condition, had participants' bodies aligned with their visual frame of reference and vertically aligned with their idiotropic axis. The remaining two conditions represented two experiment group conditions. In the second condition, participants' idiotropic axis was statically misaligned at a random angle in either the X, Y, or Z directions. However, this misalignment was dynamic in the third experiment condition with the spatial environment rotating randomly around X, Y, or Z axes; In other words, the misalignment kept changing with time throughout the study session.

The control group (CG) is comprised of participants tested under the first condition, while the experiment group EG 1 and experiment group EG2 are composed of participants tested under the second and third conditions. A visual and idiotropic axis alignment distinguished the control group from the two experimental groups. In Figs. 1 through 3, you can see screenshots of the three VR settings with test stimuli. VR sessions are conducted with participants sitting upright on a swivel chair, while stimuli and the spatial environment rotate statically or dynamically. Control group CG had aligned axes, but experiment group EG did not. Table 1 shows the number and types of spatial tasks performed in each experiment and control group. EG1 represents a static absence of alignment, while EG2 represents a dynamic misalignment. There were three groups of participants, as shown in Table 2 (e.g., N1, N2, and N3). In order to prevent participants from working on the same spatial task repetitively, each control and experimental group was randomly assigned a group. No participant repeated a test under any of the three conditions.

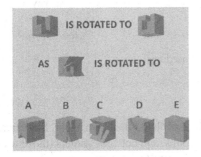 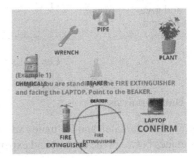

Fig. 1. Experiment Tests: A) PSVT-R Test, C) PTA Test

Table 2. Spatial tasks for different experiments

	CG1	EG1	EG2
PSVT: R	N1	N2	N3
PTA	N3	N1	N2

2.5 Procedures and Data Collection

As shown in Fig. 2, the experiment procedures are schematically outlined. Prior to the test, an introductory session was conducted to familiarize participants with the tests, apparatus, and experiment instructions. They were given two surveys after consenting to participate. On the first questionnaire, they were asked about their demographics and majors and hobbies. A second survey asked them to describe what they expected to feel during the test, such as headaches or fatigue. For each question, they could give a score between 0 and 5. Experimental conditions were set at a set temperature and humidity in a room with white walls. With HTC VIVE Pro Eye Head-Mounted Displays (HMDs), participants sat upright in swivel chairs and completed the three tests in VR wearing Virtual Environments (VE) created in Unity 3D.

Test participants were required to select from a set of options and record their choices using a handheld controller. Each test was carried out by graduate students who were trained to collect data. Test results were compiled automatically in a spreadsheet by using a programming script that collected correct/incorrect answers. In addition, a spreadsheet was used to collect the participants' responses to the two surveys. During study sessions, graduate students made sure both hardware and software worked properly. At the end of the test, the survey was administered again to participants to compare their responses prior to and after the Intervention. Cleanup was performed by team members by removing headsets and caps from participants and giving them napkins and wipes. Paper towels, hand sanitizers, and soaps were provided as cleaning supplies.

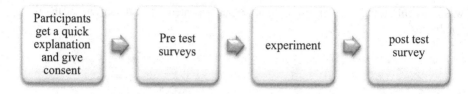

Fig. 2. Experiment Procedures

2.6 Data Analysis

A total of 27 females and 72 males successfully completed the experiment. Statistical differences between the control and experiment groups, and between gamers (those who play video games on a regular basis) and non-gamers (those who do not play video games on a regular basis) are examined. The difference in accuracy score of the tests between control and experiment groups was determined with a Kruskal-Wallis H Test and Dunn's post hoc test when there was a statistically significant difference in accuracy score of the tests. The difference in accuracy score of the tests between gamers and non-gamers was revealed with a Mann-Whitney U test. On the PSVTR test, there were 25 tasks with options. Participants received 1 for each correct answer and a 0 for each incorrect answer. Each PTA test consisted of 36 tasks, and the angular distance from the correct answer was calculated for each response. The mean of the 36 angular distances calculated as a factor reflecting the participant's performance on the test. The lower the mean, the more accurate performance.

3 Results

The collected data was first analyzed to see whether there is a significant difference in the response accuracy of the control group (CG), experiment group EG1, and experiment group EG2 in PSVTR and PTA tests. The one-way analysis of variance (ANOVA) could be used to determine whether there are any statistically significant differences between the means of the three independent groups in each test when the required assumption of the test is met. As Fig. 3 shows, no outliers exist in any independent variable group in the PSVTR test. However, the Shapiro-Wilk Test results indicate that the data significantly deviate from a normal distribution since two p-values are below 0.05. It means all required assumptions of one-way ANOVA are not met. As a result, the required assumption for Kruskal-Wallis H Test was checked. Levene's test results show that the assumption of the equality of variances is met since the p-value is greater than 0.05. The Kruskal-Wallis H test indicated that there was a statistically significant difference in accuracy score of the PSVT: R test between the three groups ($\chi 2(2) = 12.267, p = 0.002$) with a mean rank accuracy score of 49.83 for the control, 62.44 for the experiment group EG1 (static misalignment), and 37.73 for the experiment group EG2 (dynamic misalignment) (Table 3). This means that the condition of static misalignment of idiotropic and visual axes helped participants in rotation task performance. Furthermore, the dynamic misalignment condition may worsen the mental rotation performance. The Dunn's post hoc test results indicate only a statistically significant difference between the accuracy mean rank of experiment group EG1 and II: the corresponding p-value is below 0.05 (Table 4). Surprisingly, there was no statistically significant difference found in the pairwise comparison of control group with both experiment groups. The pairwise comparison, however, shows that the experiment group EG1 answered the questions more accurately than the experiment group EG2 (Fig. 4).

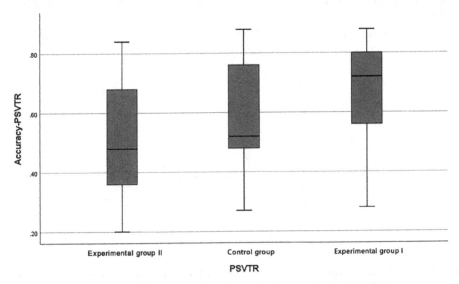

Fig. 3. Boxplots for each independent variable group in the PSVTR test.

Table 3. Kruskal-Wallis H test results for accuracy in the PSVTR test

PSVTR	N	Mean Rank
Control group	33	49.83
Experiment group EG1	33	62.44
Experiment group EG2	33	37.73
Total	99	

Table 4. Dunn's post hoc test results for accuracy in the PSVTR test

Sample 1-Sample 2	Test Statistic	Std. Error	Std. Test Statistic	p-value
Experiment group EG2- Control group	−12.106	7.056	−1.716	.086
Experiment group EG2- Experiment group EG1	−24.712	7.056	−3.502	.000
Control group - Experiment group EG1	−12.606	7.056	−1.787	.074

Fig. 4. Pairwise comparisons of accuracy in the PSVTR test: 1, 2, and 0 stand for the mean rank of Control group, Experiment group EG1, and Experiment group EG2

Figure 5 shows the existence of outliers in the control group in the PTA test, which means all required assumptions of one-way ANOVA are not met. As a result, the required assumption for Kruskal-Wallis H Test was checked. Levene's test results show that the assumption of the equality of variances is met since the p-value is greater than 0.05. The Kruskal-Wallis H test showed no statistically significant difference in accuracy score between the groups in the PTA test ($\chi 2(2) = 5.911$, p $= 0.052$).

In addition, the second research question asks whether the gaming experience of participants moderates their spatial visualization and orientation performance. A point-biserial correlation could be used to answer this question. When the assumptions for point-biserial correlation are not met, the independent-samples t-test or the Mann-Whitney U test could be used to compare differences between gamers and non-gamers.

As Fig. 6 shows, no outliers exist in any independent variable group in the PSVTR test. However, the Shapiro-Wilk Test results indicate that the data significantly deviate from a normal distribution since one of the p-values is below 0.05. Since all the required assumptions of Point-biserial correlation are not met, either the independent-samples t-test or the Mann-Whitney U test should be used to compare differences between genders. However, the normal distribution of the dependent variable for each independent variable group is one of the required assumptions of the independent-samples t-test, which is not

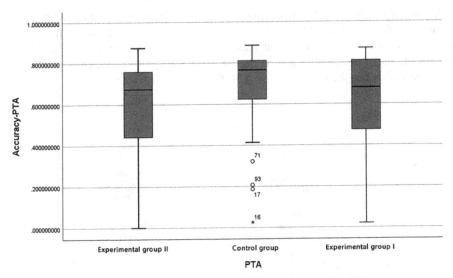

Fig. 5. Boxplots for each independent variable group in the PTA test.

met. As a result, the required assumption for the Mann-Whitney U test was checked. Levene's test results show that the assumption of the equality of variances is met since the p-value is greater than 0.05. The Mann-Whitney U test showed no statistically significant difference in accuracy between gamers and non-gamers in the PSVTR test, p = .078.

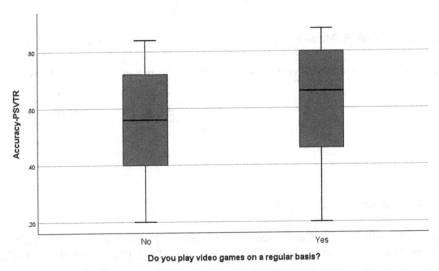

Fig. 6. Boxplots for each category of the dichotomous variable in the PSVTR test.

As Fig. 7 shows, there are outliers in the group who play video games on a regular basis in the PTA test. It means neither for the point-biserial correlation nor for the independent-samples t-test, the required assumptions are met. However, the required assumption for the Mann-Whitney U test is met. In other words, Levene's test results show the equality of variances is met since the p-value is greater than 0.05. The Mann-Whitney U test results indicate gamers' performance was statistically significantly better than non-gamers' in the PTA test (U = 874.000, p = .018) (Table 5).

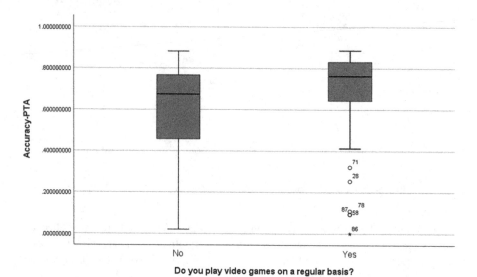

Fig. 7. Boxplots for each category of the dichotomous variable in the PTA test.

Table 5. Mann-Whitney U test results for accuracy in the PTA test

Do you play video games on a regular basis?	N	Mean Rank	Sum of Ranks
No	55	43.89	2414.00
Yes	44	57.64	2536.00
Total	99		

4 Discussion

The results of the PSVT: R test reveal that participants' performance was significantly different between the two experiment groups, EG1 and EG2. Comparing EG1 to EG2, it was evident that EG1 participants excel at PSVT: R tasks. Surprisingly, the scores of the control group and the two experiment groups did not differ statistically from one another. This indicates that the performance of the participants' mental rotation and spatial visualization may be impacted by dynamically misaligned body and visual axes. Regarding the PTA test, there was no statistically significant difference in accuracy scores between the control and the two experiment groups, demonstrating that static and dynamic misalignment of idiotropic and visual axes may not influence spatial orientation ability. It is noteworthy to understand these results in the context of the nature of these tests. In contrast to the PTA test, which use an egocentric frame of reference, the PSVT: R test uses an object-based frame of reference (FOR) [72, 73]. In mental rotation tasks like those in the PSVT: R tests, the relationship between objects and space (or visual FOR) may alter as a result of the transformation of the visual FOR. Consequently, participants with static misaligned FOR performed better than those with dynamic misaligned FOR, whose object-for relationship is constantly changing. It might also contribute to the explanation of why the performance of the experimental group EG1 and control group CG, both of which have a fixed stimulus-FOR relationship, is not statistically different.

In PTA tasks, gamers outperformed non-gamers, while in PSVT: R, no differences were found between gamers and non-gamers. This may indicate that gaming experience may not moderate mental rotation outcomes. However, it might help enhance spatial orientation ability. A study by Martin et al. (2009) [74] concluded that playing video games improves spatial abilities. In 2012, a study by Adams et al. [75] found a significant correlation between dynamic and static spatial skills and video game performance. In 2019, Ogunkola et al. [76] examined the effects of video games on participants' spatial visualization and orientation. Similar to the findings of our study, their examination indicated that video games significantly affected spatial orientation but not spatial visualization. However, older studies concluded that computer games could improve mental rotation performance. For instance, a study conducted by Pepin et al. in 1986 [77] indicated video game playing could improve spatial visualization test scores. In addition, a study by Cherney in 2008 [78] concluded computer game practice may improve mental rotation performance even very minimally. In 2010, Spence et al. [79] reported that playing action video games improves performance on more complex spatial tasks such as mental rotation. Again in 2010, Lisi et al. [80] found that students' mental rotation abilities can be enhanced through computer-based instructional activities in schools. However, it is important to note that older games may differ significantly from the current games in their nature and design as well as delivery, which may impact cognitive learning and outcomes. Further research is required to reveal if the gaming experience helps enhance mental rotation outcomes in addition to spatial orientation ability.

The spatial visualization ability of the dynamically misaligned group (EG2) was significantly lower than that of the static misaligned group (EG1). According to Dye et al. (2009) [81] it was found that perceptual vertical changed when visual backgrounds were oriented differently under altered gravitational conditions. Microgravity conditions had a lesser effect on perceptual upright than normal conditions on visual background orientations. The control group and experiment groups EG1 and EG2 showed no significant differences in the PSVT: R, a small scale spatial exam. The perceptual upright under static and dynamic visual cues in microgravity, hypogravity, and hypergravity environments were compared in a study by Jenkins et al. (2011) [82]. Dynamic cues were provided using video clips, and static orientation cues were given by static frames taken from a video clip. Their research found no relationship between gravity circumstances and the visual effect. It has been demonstrated that dynamic visual cues outperform static visual cues in recognizing the perceptual vertical. They explained not only why dynamic cues might improve visual cues more than static ones, but also why static cues would not. Visual efficiency may be enhanced by the enhanced depth information provided by dynamic conditions. The only difference between EG1 and EG2 is how the visual frame moves. The PTA test results did not differ between experiment groups, which requires explanation. It might be that both experiment groups had misaligned visual and idiotropic axes, and since motion may improve visual effectiveness, it may have compensated for the challenges associated with dynamically misaligned visual and idiotropic axes. Even while there was no statistically significant difference between the control and experimental settings in some aspects of spatial ability, there may be more mental allocation required in some situations, which has to be examined in future research. By analyzing and comprehending the spatial strategies utilized by participants on the three tests in the three situations, the eye-tracking approach can also offer insightful information about why participants' performance is more impacted by rotation of the visual FOR.

5 Conclusions

The findings of this study demonstrate that spatial orientation performance in terms of accuracy measured through PTA test may not be impacted by either a static or dynamic misalignment of the visual and body axes. However, this dynamic misalignment of these axes may influence the human spatial visualization performance in terms of accuracy. The key difference here is the random movement of the visual FOR, which may moderate spatial cognitive processing. No difference between gamers and non-gamers was found in the accuracy of participants on the PSVT:R test. This was not the case in the PTA test results of which showed gamers performing better than non-gamers. The findings of this study are significant to understand how spatial ability is affected in altered visuospatial conditions and how simulation- or game-based training tools can be developed to train people and help them better adapt to such conditions. According to this research, using games as a learning tools can aid people in adapting to extreme or altered work environments and working more productively and safely.

Acknowledgements. This work is supported by the U.S. National Science Foundation (NSF) through grant CNS 1928695. Any opinions, findings, conclusions, and recommendations expressed in this paper are those of the authors and do not necessarily represent those of the NSF.

References

1. He, X., Li, T., Turel, O., Kuang, Y., Zhao, H., He, Q.: The impact of stem education on mathematical development in children aged 5–6 years. Int. J. Educ. Res. **109**, 101795 (2021)
2. Stapleton, T., et al.: Environmental control and life support for deep space travel. In: 46th International Conference on Environmental Systems (2016)
3. Kanas, N.: Psychology in deep space. https://www.bps.org.uk/psychologist/psychology-deep-space
4. Marin, F., Beluffi, C.: Computing the minimal crew for a multi-generational space travel towards Proxima Centauri b (2018)

5. Lohman, D.F.: Spatial ability: a review and reanalysis of the correlational literature (1979)
6. de Bruin Nutley, N., Bryant, D.C., MacLean, J.N., Gonzalez, C.L.: Assessing visuospatial abilities in healthy aging: a novel visuometor task (2016)
7. Linn, M.C., Petersen, A.C.: Emergence and characterization of sex differences in spatial ability: a meta-analysis. Child Dev. 1479–1498 (1985)
8. Quasha, W.H., Likert, R.: The revised Minnesota paper form board test. J. Educ. Psychol. 28(3), 197 (1937)
9. Carroll, J.B.: Human Cognitive Abilities: A survey of Factor-Analytic Studies, no. 1. Cambridge University Press (1993)
10. Ekstrom, R.B., French, J.W., Harmon, H.H.: Manual for kit of factor-referenced cognitive tests (1976)
11. Buckley, J., Seery, N., Canty, D.: A heuristic framework of spatial ability: a review and synthesis of spatial factor literature to support its translation into STEM education. Educ. Psychol. Rev. 30(3), 947–972 (2018)
12. Ha, O., Fang, N.: Development of interactive 3D tangible models as teaching aids to improve students' spatial ability in STEM education. In: 2013 IEEE Frontiers in Education Conference (FIE), pp. 1302–1304. IEEE (2013)
13. Harle, M., Towns, M.: A review of spatial ability literature, its connection to chemistry, and implications for instruction. J. Chem. Educ. 88(3), 351–360 (2011)
14. Khine, M.S.: Spatial cognition: key to STEM success. In: Khine, M. (ed.) Visual-Spatial Ability in STEM Education: Springer, pp. 3–8. Springer, Cham (2017). https://doi.org/10.1007/978-3-319-44385-0_1
15. Li, X., Wang, W.: Exploring spatial cognitive process among STEM Students and its role in STEM education. Sci. Educ. 30(1), 121–145 (2021)
16. Tracy, D.M.: Toys, spatial ability, and science and mathematics achievement: Are they related? Sex Roles 17(3), 115–138 (1987)
17. Casey, M.B., Nuttall, R., Pezaris, E., Benbow, C.P.: The influence of spatial ability on gender differences in mathematics college entrance test scores across diverse samples. Dev. Psychol. 31(4), 697 (1995)
18. Dowker, A.: How important is spatial ability to mathematics? Behav. Brain Sci. 19(2), 251 (1996)
19. Fennema, E.: Mathematics, Spatial Ability and the Sexes (1974)
20. Kyttälä, M., Björn, P.M.: The role of literacy skills in adolescents' mathematics word problem performance: controlling for visuo-spatial ability and mathematics anxiety. Learn. Individ. Differ. 29, 59–66 (2014)
21. Xie, F., Zhang, L., Chen, X., Xin, Z.: Is spatial ability related to mathematical ability: a meta-analysis. Educ. Psychol. Rev. 32(1), 113–155 (2020)
22. Annett, M.: Spatial ability in subgroups of left-and right-handers. Br. J. Psychol. 83(4), 493–515 (1992)
23. Heo, M., Toomey, N.: Learning with multimedia: the effects of gender, type of multimedia learning resources, and spatial ability. Comput. Educ. 146, 103747 (2020)
24. Höffler, T.N.: Spatial ability: Its influence on learning with visualizations—a meta-analytic review. Educ. Psychol. Rev. 22(3), 245–269 (2010)
25. Hegarty, M., Keehner, M., Cohen, C., Montello, D.R., Lippa, Y.: The role of spatial cognition in medicine: applications for selecting and training professionals. In: Applied Spatial Cognition, pp. 285–316. Psychology Press (2020)
26. Hier, D.B., Crowley, W.F., Jr.: Spatial ability in androgen-deficient men. N. Engl. J. Med. 306(20), 1202–1205 (1982)
27. Jain, D., et al.: Immersive terrestrial scuba diving using virtual reality. In: Proceedings of the 2016 CHI Conference Extended Abstracts on Human Factors in Computing Systems, pp. 1563–1569 (2016)

28. Meirhaeghe, N., Bayet, V., Paubel, P.-V., Mélan, C.: Selective facilitation of egocentric mental transformations under short-term microgravity. Acta Astronaut. **170**, 375–385 (2020)
29. Miiro, S.: The issues and complexities surrounding the future of long duration spaceflight (2017)
30. Oman, C.: Spatial orientation and navigation in microgravity. In: Mast, F., Jäncke, L. (eds.) Spatial Processing in Navigation, Imagery and Perception, pp. 209–247. Springer, Boston (2007). https://doi.org/10.1007/978-0-387-71978-8_13
31. Park, H., Dixit, M., Faghihi, N., McNamara, A., Vaid, J.: Understanding spatial abilities and spatial strategy under extreme visual and gravitational environments. In: 17th Biennial International Conference on Engineering, Science, Construction, and Operations in Challenging Environments (2021)
32. Alberty, M.: How to train your astronauts. https://www.nasa.gov/mission_pages/station/research/news/astronaut_trainingaccessed
33. Jenkin, M., Zacher, J., Dyde, R., Harris, L., Jenkin, H.: Perceptual upright: the relative effectiveness of dynamic and static images under different gravity states (2011)
34. Gholami, S., et al.: Hybrid microwave sintering of a lunar soil simulant: effects of processing parameters on microstructure characteristics and mechanical properties. Mater. Des. **220**, 110878 (2022)
35. Clement, G., et al.: Long-duration spaceflight increases depth ambiguity of reversible perspective figures. PLoS One **10**(7), e0132317 (2015)
36. Kincl, L., Bhattacharya, A., Succop, P., Bagchee, A.: The effect of workload, work experience and inclined standing surface on visual spatial perception: fall potential/prevention implications. Occup. Ergon. **3**(4), 251–259 (2003)
37. Garg, A., Norman, G.R., Spero, L., Maheshwari, P.: Do virtual computer models hinder anatomy learning? Acad. Med. (1999)
38. Lin, Y., Suh, A.: The role of spatial ability in learning with virtual reality: a literature review. In: 54th Hawaii International Conference on System Sciences (HICSS 2021), pp. 94–103 (2021)
39. Liao, H., Dong, W.: An exploratory study investigating gender effects on using 3D maps for spatial orientation in wayfinding. ISPRS Int. J. Geo Inf. **6**(3), 60 (2017)
40. McGee, M.G.: Human spatial abilities: psychometric studies and environmental, genetic, hormonal, and neurological influences. Psychol. Bull. **86**(5), 889 (1979)
41. Lohman, D.F.: Spatial abilities as traits, processes, and knowledge. In: Advances in the Psychology of Human Intelligence, pp. 181–248. Psychology Press (2014)
42. Lowrie, T., Harris, D., Logan, T., Hegarty, M.: The impact of a spatial intervention program on students' spatial reasoning and mathematics performance. J. Exp. Educ. **89**(2), 259–277 (2021)
43. Contero, M., Naya, F., Company, P., Saorín, J.L., Conesa, J.: Improving visualization skills in engineering education. IEEE Comput. Graphics Appl. **25**(5), 24–31 (2005)
44. Fatemah, A., Rasool, S., Habib, U.: Interactive 3D visualization of chemical structure diagrams embedded in text to aid spatial learning process of students. J. Chem. Educ. **97**(4), 992–1000 (2020)
45. Katsioloudis, P.J., Jovanovic, V.: Spatial visualization ability and impact of drafting models: a quasi experimental study. Eng. Design Graphics J. **78**(2) (2014)
46. Liao, K., Xiao, R., Gonzalez, J., Ding, L.: Decoding individual finger movements from one hand using human EEG signals. PLoS One **9**(1), e85192 (2014)
47. Maeda, Y., Yoon, S.Y.: Scaling the revised PSVT-R: characteristics of the first-year engineering students' spatial ability. In: 2011 ASEE Annual Conference & Exposition, pp. 22.1273.1–22.1273. 19 (2011)

48. Miyake, A., Friedman, N.P., Rettinger, D.A., Shah, P., Hegarty, M.: How are visuospatial working memory, executive functioning, and spatial abilities related? A latent-variable analysis. J. Exp. Psychol. Gen. **130**(4), 621 (2001)
49. Park, Y., Brösamle, M., Hölscher, C.: The function of gesture in architectural-design-related spatial ability. In: Šķilters, J., Newcombe, N.S., Uttal, D. (eds.) Spatial Cognition 2020. LNCS (LNAI), vol. 12162, pp. 309–321. Springer, Cham (2020). https://doi.org/10.1007/978-3-030-57983-8_24
50. Pittalis, M., Christou, C.: Types of reasoning in 3D geometry thinking and their relation with spatial ability. Educ. Stud. Math. **75**(2), 191–212 (2010)
51. Rahmawati, L., Wulandari, Y.: Visual-spatial ability in solving geometry problems viewed from gender using the flipped classroom model. In: International Seminar Proceeding, no. 2 (2021)
52. Wulandari, N., Ekowati, D., Novitasari, D., Hamdani, D., Gunawan, G.: Spatial reasoning profile of the students with good number sense ability. In: Journal of Physics: Conference Series, vol. 1933, no. 1, p. 012077. IOP Publishing (2021)
53. Ernst, J.V., Williams, T.O., Clark, A.C., Kelly, D.P.: Factors of spatial visualization: an analysis of the PSVT: R. Eng. Design Graphics J. **81**(1) (2017)
54. Maeda, Y., Yoon, S.Y.: A meta-analysis on gender differences in mental rotation ability measured by the Purdue spatial visualization tests: visualization of rotations (PSVT: R). Educ. Psychol. Rev. **25**(1), 69–94 (2013)
55. Samsudin, K., Rafi, A., Hanif, A.S.: Training in mental rotation and spatial visualization and its impact on orthographic drawing performance. J. Educ. Technol. Soc. **14**(1), 179–186 (2011)
56. Lowrie, T., Logan, T., Hegarty, M.: The influence of spatial visualization training on students' spatial reasoning and mathematics performance. J. Cogn. Dev. **20**(5), 729–751 (2019)
57. Kozhevnikov, M., Hegarty, M.: A dissociation between object manipulation spatial ability and spatial orientation ability. Mem. Cognit. **29**(5), 745–756 (2001)
58. Fehringer, B.C.: Supplementary materials to: R-Cube-SR test: a new test for spatial relations distinguishable from visualization (2021)
59. Long, L.O., Gomer, J.A., Wong, J.T., Pagano, C.C.: Visual spatial abilities in uninhabited ground vehicle task performance during teleoperation and direct line of sight. Presence Teleoper. Virtual Environ. **20**(5), 466–479 (2011)
60. Schlack, A., Sterbing-D'Angelo, S.J., Hartung, K., Hoffmann, K.-P., Bremmer, F.: Multisensory space representations in the macaque ventral intraparietal area. J. Neurosci. **25**(18), 4616–4625 (2005)
61. Harris, S.E., Deary, I.J.: The genetics of cognitive ability and cognitive ageing in healthy older people. Trends Cogn. Sci. **15**(9), 388–394 (2011)
62. Li, D., Shao, Z., Zhang, R.: Advances of geo-spatial intelligence at LIESMARS. Geo-Spat. Inf. Sci. **23**(1), 40–51 (2020)
63. Guzsvinecz, T., Orbán-Mihálykó, É., Sik-Lányi, C., Perge, E.: Investigation of spatial ability test completion times in virtual reality using a desktop display and the Gear VR. Virtual Reality 1–14 (2022)
64. Shebilske, W.L., Tubré, T., Tubré, A.H., Oman, C.M., Richards, J.T.: Three-dimensional spatial skill training in a simulated space station: random vs. blocked designs. Aviat. Space Environ. Med. **77**(4), 404–409 (2006)
65. Guo, J., Jiang, G., Liu, Y., An, M.: Predicting navigation performance in a multi-module space station through spatial abilities. In: Long, S., Dhillon, B. (eds.) Man-Machine-Environment System Engineering. MMESE 2016. Lecture Notes in Electrical Engineering, vol. 406, pp. 39–46. Springer, Singapore (2016). https://doi.org/10.1007/978-981-10-2323-1_5
66. Schaller, S., Yucel, I., Kahn, R.: Applying game learning principles to analyze and identify improvements for scuba training simulations (2018)

67. Kanas, N., Manzey, D.: Space Psychology and Psychiatry. Springer, Heidelberg (2008). https://doi.org/10.1007/978-1-4020-6770-9
68. Mikropoulos, T.A., Natsis, A.: Educational virtual environments: a ten-year review of empirical research (1999–2009). Comput. Educ. **56**(3), 769–780 (2011)
69. Sandor, A., Moses, H., Sprufera, J., Begault, D.R.: Memo on speech alarms: Replication and validation of results (2016)
70. Strauss, S.: Extravehicular mobility unit training suit symptom study report (2004)
71. Hegarty, M., Waller, D.: A dissociation between mental rotation and perspective-taking spatial abilities. Intelligence **32**(2), 175–191 (2004)
72. Ramful, A., Lowrie, T., Logan, T.: Measurement of spatial ability: construction and validation of the spatial reasoning instrument for middle school students. J. Psychoeduc. Assess. **35**(7), 709–727 (2017)
73. Tito, J., Basso, T., Moraes, R.: Digital measurement of spatial ability using a virtual reality environment. In: 2021 International Conference on Computational Science and Computational Intelligence (CSCI), pp. 1103–1107. IEEE (2021)
74. Martin, J., Saorín, J.L., Martín, N., Contero, M.: Do video games improve spatial abilities of engineering students? Int. J. Eng. Educ. **25**(6), 1194–1204 (2009)
75. Adams, D., Mayer, R.: Examining the connection between dynamic and static spatial skills and video game performance. In: Proceedings of the Annual Meeting of the Cognitive Science Society, vol. 34, no. 34 (2012)
76. Ogunkola, B., Knight, C.: Technical drawing course, video games, gender, and type of school on spatial ability. J. Educ. Res. **112**(5), 575–589 (2019)
77. Pepin, M., Dorval, M.: Effect of playing a video game on adults' and adolescents' spatial visualization. Educ. Technol. **26**(10), 48–52 (1986)
78. Cherney, I.D., Brabec, C.M., Runco, D.V.: Mapping out spatial ability: sex differences in way-finding navigation. Percept. Mot. Skills **107**(3), 747–760 (2008)
79. Spence, I., Feng, J.: Video games and spatial cognition. Rev. Gen. Psychol. **14**(2), 92–104 (2010)
80. De Lisi, R., Wolford, J.L.: Improving children's mental rotation accuracy with computer game playing. J. Genet. Psychol. **163**(3), 272–282 (2002)
81. Dye, M.W., Green, C.S., Bavelier, D.: The development of attention skills in action video game players. Neuropsychologia **47**(8–9), 1780–1789 (2009)
82. Jenkin, M., Zacher, J., Dyde, R., Harris, L., Jenkin, H.: Perceptual upright: the relative effectiveness of dynamic and static images under different gravity states. Seeing Perceiving **24**(1), 53–64 (2011)

Augmented Cognition: Evolving Theory and Practice

Augmented Cognition Compass: A Taxonomy of Cognitive Augmentations

Nicola Felicini$^{(\boxtimes)}$ ⓘ and Letizia Mortara ⓘ

Institute for Manufacturing (IfM), University of Cambridge, Cambridge, UK
{nf382,lm367}@cam.ac.uk

Abstract. Despite long-standing practices in human augmentation, the field of Augmented Cognition still lacks a generalized 'theory of augmentation' which guides the selection of such augmentations. We do not yet have a taxonomy that could help understand which augmentation to use to address which type of cognitive problem. By reviewing past applications of cognitive augmentation, this paper provides a framework that helps navigating the growing knowledge and guides the selection of cognitive-enhancing augmentations. Like a compass, the proposed taxonomy can be used to map previous steps in the field, to navigate the current state of the art, and to orient future research directions.

Keywords: Augmented Cognition · Human Augmentation · Taxonomy

1 Introduction

1.1 Background

Attempts to augment human abilities can be traced back through much of human history, when they included functional extensions of the human body through a physical medium [1]. Contemporary technological innovations allow more forms of Human Augmentation (HA), such as the extension of our senses via sensory technologies (e.g., night vision goggles), the improvement of physical abilities by hardware means (e.g., exoskeletons) or the enhancement of cognitive capabilities through a human-computer 'closed-loop', which characterize the field of Augmented Cognition (AC) [2].

Despite long-standing practices in HA, the field still lacks a generalized 'theory of augmentation' which guides the selection of such augmentations with respect to the types of tasks humans need to perform. In other words, we do not yet have a taxonomy which could help us understand which augmentation to use to resolve which type of cognitive problem. This lack of structure affects the access to existing knowledge and the integration of new contributions. The gap is more critical now that digital tools are becoming prevalent means of delivering augmentations [3], multiplying the augmentation possibilities. This paper focuses on the field of AC. It aims to provide a solid framework that helps to navigate the growing knowledge and guides the selection of cognitive-enhancing augmentations to address cognitive problems.

© The Author(s) 2023

D. D. Schmorrow and C. M. Fidopiastis (Eds.): HCII 2023, LNAI 14019, pp. 189–205, 2023.
https://doi.org/10.1007/978-3-031-35017-7_13

1.2 Previous Works

The recent classification of De Boeck, et al. [4] (see Table 1) summarizes several recent contributions that have attempted a categorization for the broad field of HA [5–9]. Their work identifies (a) four categories of augmentations (the type of aid: sensory, physical, cognitive, and social) and (b) three dimensions of augmentation (the 'amount' of aid relative to the human innate capabilities: replicating or replacing, supplementing, and exceeding).

The taxonomy introduced by de Boeck et al. has been useful for the development of the field, the four categories proposed are broad enough to cover previous HA applications. However, they are weak in describing the specificities of each case. The diagram helps to position a single HA within the dimensions, but it does not explain how an HA application could be generalized and linked to other cases. The absence of any correlation between augmentations restricts its potential to generate insights and to guide designers in their choices.

Table 1. HA domain adapted from De Boeck, et al. [4] with examples of HA applications. Highlighted is the domain of the taxonomy.

<table>
<tr><th colspan="2" rowspan="2"></th><th colspan="3">DIMENSIONS</th></tr>
<tr><th>Replicating human abilities</th><th>Supplementing human abilities</th><th>Exceeding human abilities</th></tr>
<tr><td rowspan="4">CATEGORIES</td><td>Social augmentation</td><td>*Electrolarynx*</td><td>*Real time translator*</td><td>*Hologram telecommunication*</td></tr>
<tr><td>Cognitive augmentation</td><td>*Dementia clocks*</td><td>*Memory reminders*</td><td>*GPS navigation system*</td></tr>
<tr><td>Physical augmentation</td><td>*Prosthesis*</td><td>*Exoskeleton for weightlifting*</td><td>*Wingsuit*</td></tr>
<tr><td>Sensory augmentation</td><td>*Eyeglasses*</td><td>*Telescope*</td><td>*Infrared camera*</td></tr>
</table>

1.3 Objective

Given the mentioned gaps, this work aims to answer the following questions:

- For each type of cognitive problem, what type of AC has been tested?
- How was each cognitive augmentation applied?
- What other forms of AC have been tested for that problem?

This paper answers the questions by proposing a taxonomy for AC which has four dimensions:

i. Field of Application (e.g., medical, military, education)
ii. Limitation (the human condition which justifies an augmentation of capabilities, e.g., incorrect focus, memory fault)

iii. Augmentation (the aid provided to the user, e.g., knowledge provision, task load reduction)

iv. Implementation (the form through which the augmentation is delivered e.g., instructions, visual cues, alerts).

These dimensions are combined in linking grids and can be used to map previous steps in the field, to navigate the current state of the art, and to orient future research directions, like a compass. The user of the compass can start from any of the four dimensions and explore the others following the prompts shown in the compass dial (Fig. 1).

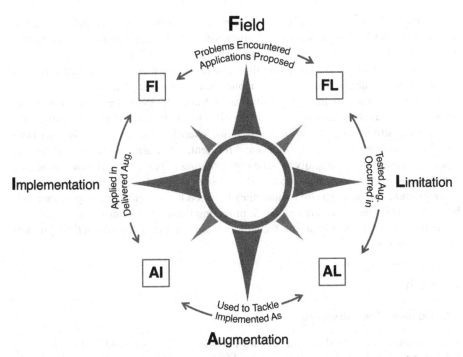

Fig. 1. The AC compass: the cardinal directions correspond to the four dimensions of the taxonomy. Each quadrant of the compass (FL, AL, AI, FI) is a linking grid that intersects two dimensions and provides insights about the AC field (see Tables 4, 5, 6 and 7 in the appendix).

As in *Fuchs et al.* [10], the taxonomy separates the cognitive augmentations from the implementation strategies. In fact, the same augmentation can be implemented in multiple ways (e.g., knowledge provision via instructions or analytics). Likewise, the same implementation method can be used to provide different augmentations (e.g., visual cues for action correction or attentional deployment).

In this paper the compass is applied in the field of AC, however its dimensions are applicable to any type of augmentation, making it a robust tool to classify the whole HA field.

1.4 Definition of Augmentation

Several definitions of augmentation have been proposed in recent years [5, 6, 9, 11–16]. This paper adopts the robust definition by *Moore* [14] who defines human augmentation as:

> "[…] *any attempt to temporarily or permanently overcome the current limitations of the human body through natural or artificial means. It is the use of technological means to select or alter human characteristics and capacities, whether or not the alteration results in characteristics and capacities that lie beyond the existing human range.*"

In this work, *'technological means'* doesn't necessarily indicate digital equipment, but any *"artifact* […] *to extend human capabilities"* [17]. That is to say: augmentation as an extension of our faculties and capabilities, regardless of the tool.

This is rather important given that the same technology used in different ways can provide different augmentations (e.g., haptic technology can be used for controllers' feedback or as vibration alert for smartphones). Similarly, the same augmentation can be provided using different tools (e.g., wayfinding through signposting or by using GPS navigation instructions). Moreover, a taxonomy where the augmentations are independent from the tools will be more robust and resilient, especially in a fast-paced context where new technologies rapidly replace obsolete ones. Consider for instance sundials, mechanical watches, digital watches and now smartwatches. They are all tools made from different technologies. Over time, they replaced the functions of the previous one, but they all offer the same augmentation: providing the user with information.

In light of these considerations, technologies are not used as criteria in the definition of the taxonomy.

2 Method

2.1 Domain of the Taxonomy

The taxonomy is obtained from a review of articles in the area of AC, which is a sub-field of HA that seeks to extend cognitive abilities by addressing the humans' intrinsic limitations in attention, memory, learning, comprehension, visualization abilities, and decision-making [18]. As per *de Boeck and Vaes'* classification, case studies of cognitive augmentation that supplement or exceed human abilities have been categorized. The domain of the taxonomy is highlighted in Table 1.

2.2 Search Design

The selection of eligible articles for the taxonomy was based on the following criteria:

1. Search for published journal articles, conference papers and reviews only, written in English language, in Scopus (Elsevier) and Web of Science (Clarivate) databases. No timespan was considered, and the latest articles analyzed were published by December 2022.

2. Identify relevant articles by looking for one of the following terms in title, abstract or paper keywords: *"augmented cognition"*, *"augcog"*, *"human augment*"*, *"human enanc*"*, *"cognitive augment*"*.
3. Filter by subject areas and paper keywords related to AC.
4. Ensure relevance of the articles by reading all titles and abstracts, excluding duplicates, and checking that they fall within the domain of the taxonomy
5. The remaining articles have to be read completely to make sure that the discussion is related to AC and that all the four types of attributes of the compass (field of application, limitation, augmentation, implementation) are explicitly stated.

Description of tools, lists of hypothetical applications, references to other papers proposed as generic augmentations and papers without the explicit four attributes have not been considered. The final sample consisted of 77 articles. Table 2 gives an overview of the search process.

Table 2. Database search results.

	Scopus (Elsevier)	Web of Science (Clarivate)	Total
After keyword search	663	478	1141
After filtering by subject and paper keywords	483	395	878
After deleting duplicates	483	53	536
After reading title and abstract			233
After reading the entire article			77

2.3 Categorization of the Dimensions

From each of the shortlisted articles, four attributes corresponding to each of the taxonomy's dimensions (field of application, limitation, augmentation, implementation) were identified and listed as in the original text. If a case study presented more than an augmentation for the same situation or context, they were listed as separate entries (e.g., Dorneich, et al. [19] in Table 3). A total of 137 quartets of attributes were extracted from the 77 articles.

Each attribute was categorized through an inductive process [20], where categories are tentatively assigned. While progressing with the categorization, those categories are revised, eventually reduced to main categories and checked in respect to their reliability. The categories were finally aggregated in super-categories to build a hierarchical structure of the taxonomy. Three examples of categorization of augmentation attributes in quartets are shown in Table 3.

Table 3. Examples of attributes categorization.

Paper	Attributes			
	Field	Limitation	Augmentation	Implementation
Dorneich, et al. [19]	*"[...] system to support [...] dismounted soldiers."* **(Military)**	*"This was to avoid disorientation and lack of context [...]."* **(Incorrect focus)**	*"[...]drawing attention to higher priority items [...]."* **(Attentional deployment)**	*"[...]with the additional alerting tones [...]."* **(Audio cues)**
Dorneich, et al. [19]	*"[...] system to support [...] dismounted soldiers."* **(Military)**	*"[...] performance on these tasks deteriorates considerably over time"* **(Variable performance)**	*"[...] target identification agent provides assistance in locating potential targets [...]."* **(Task load distribution)**	*"Automated systems trained to detect target [...]."* **(Automation)**
Vadiraja, et al. [21]	*"[...] a technique to assist a reader."* **(Reading)**	*"[...] if the reader is under-confident in some topics [...]."* **(Low engagement)**	*"[...] providing summaries about unclear descriptions [...]."* **(Knowledge provision)**	*"[...]text summary augmentation system [...]."* **(Analytics)**

2.4 Validation of the Taxonomy

The taxonomy's adequacy was evaluated through its content validity [22–24]. Two independent judges re-coded 'limitation', 'augmentation', and 'implementation' attributes from a random sample of 50 quartets (out of 137). The 'field' attributes were omitted as the less equivocal of the attribute types.

The content validity of the taxonomy was inferred by the level of agreement between coders (calculated using a coefficient kappa method [25] as suggested by Boateng, et al. [26]) and by the number of new categories generated. The higher the agreement, the more the categories represent the attributes. Conversely, the fewer new categories that were generated, the more the taxonomy reflects the domain of AC.

The validation process showed an agreement level which is deemed substantial given the obtained kappa values: 0.572 for limitations attributes, 0.650 for augmentations attributes and 0.696 for implementations ones. Finally, only in three cases new categories were proposed by the judges, which suggests a good coverage of the AC domain given the 40 initial categories.

3 Results and Discussion

The aim of this study was to provide a taxonomy of cognitive augmentations useful to navigate the growing field of AC and to guide the choice of augmentations.

The taxonomy's framework is made of four dimensions intersected in four linking grids which constitutes the quadrants of the compass (Tables 4, 5, 6 and 7 in the appendix). The grids offer a quick overview of the AC field, while the categories and their mutual relationships give insights in specific areas. The individuated categories are described in Table 8.

Several fields of application were found in the AC literature (Table 4). Military, medical, educational, and driving fields presented the largest variety of activities and addressed limitations. The military sector experimented with the most implementations (Table 7). The vast majority of the encountered tasks are operational tasks.

In terms of limitations, not all those faced in the studies are related to cognitive bottlenecks, such as problems of information processing and storage, or an incorrect mental state of the operator. They are also due to physical limitations, like the hypothetical cost/risk of a situation and the unpredictability of human error (variable performance), or by the lack of some sort of knowledge (Table 4).

The augmentations proposed by the AC field to face those problems can be grouped in few categories (Table 5). Aid consisted in managing the task load or by giving assistance during the task. But also through modifying the flow of information during the task, the mental state of the user, or by giving the possibility to simulate scenarios (simulativity).

Finally, augmentations have been implemented using three main strategies of addition, subtraction, or modification (Table 6). Addition of prompts, analysis, cues or experiences during the task, subtraction by reduction or delegation, or modification of the information flow, of some elements of the task or of the task itself.

3.1 Limitations

There are limitations in the construction of the taxonomy. First, the article sampling is far from perfect. Despite the high number of searched papers, the sample was obtained from few keywords and some relevant studies could have been missed. The fact that no articles were dated before 2003, suggests that similar studies could have used different terms before that date (e.g., intelligence amplification).

Second, to maximize objectivity in the coding, only papers which clearly indicated the four types of attributes were categorized. Again, possible relevant studies could have been excluded because not explicit enough to comply with the protocol.

Similarly, the rejection of other types of augmentations apart from the cognitive ones could have excluded some hybrid cases (e.g., a cognitive augmentation for a physical limitation, like in Futami, et al. [27]).

Another limitation comes from the abstraction of the categories which is an inevitably subjective process. This work followed a thorough validation process, with good agreement outcomes, that however involved a small number of independent judges.

Finally, the taxonomy has breadth to cover the whole field but shallow depth of analysis. The intersection of two categories in a linking grid indicates that they have been combined in at least one of the examined papers. However, it doesn't indicate any evaluation, frequency, or recommendation of that combination.

3.2 Future Directions

The taxonomy gives an overview of what has been done so far in the field of AC. Evident future directions are individuated by the white spaces in the quadrants of the compass. Those graphical gaps indicate unexplored possible applications of augmentations for problems that have been addressed in other methods, perhaps in improvable ways.

Another clear future development is the extension of the taxonomy to the whole field of HA, including social, physical, and sensory augmentations. In this paper the compass is applied in the field of AC, however its dimensions are stable enough to be applicable to any type of augmentation.

To address the limited depth of analysis, in a more extended publication the taxonomy could keep track of the evaluated cases and provide more information to the user. For instance, an example application for each combination in the linking grids and the number of encountered application which fall in that combination.

Looking at the whole field of AC, almost all the analyzed studies involved operational tasks. AC is practically unexplored for applications in tactical and strategic tasks. Fields like management and strategic cognition would benefit from tools that augment cognitive capabilities of decision-making.

AC has already been described as a young research field with no commonly agreed-upon definitions on what it includes or what constitutes an augmentation [4, 6]. Unsurprisingly, form the analysis of the literature emerged a significant heterogeneity in the type of studies, methodologies, language, definitions. A joint effort from scholars in AC for the definition of solid and recognized foundations in the field is deemed necessary. The taxonomy introduced in this paper, like the one from De Boeck, et al. [4], is an attempt in that direction.

Another relevant gap is the absence of an evaluation framework to assess the effectiveness of an augmentation. In fact, only few of the analyzed articles presented an evaluation of the proposed augmentation, some of which proved to be counterproductive [28, 29]. Objective and recognized metrics of cognitive augmentations, similar to the concept proposed by Fulbright [30, 31], would allow a comparison between cases, steering the field of AC towards the most promising applications.

Acknowledgements. This project has received funding from the European Union's Horizon 2020 research and innovation programme under the Marie Skłodowska-Curie grant agreement No 956745.

For the purpose of open access, the authors have applied a Creative Commons Attribution (CC BY) licence to any Author Accepted Manuscript version arising.

Appendix

Table 4. Quadrant FL of the compass: it links the fields of application with the limitations.

FIELD	LIMITATION	Physical limits		Info processing			Info storage		Mental state		Missing knowledge	
		Costly Simulation	Variable Performance	Working Memory	Psychomotor Bottleneck	Perceptual Bottleneck	Memory Fault	Memory Capacity	Low Engagement	Incorrect Focus	Lack of Expertise	Lack of Information
Art	Drawing										•	
Aviation	Flight operations			•								•
	Training		•									
Cooking	Assembly											•
Cyber security	Memorizing						•					
	Monitoring			•	•							•
IT	Design			•	•						•	•
Driving	Social network					•						
	Navigation			•	•	•				•		
	Training	•										
	Safety									•		
Education	Learning		•						•	•	•	
	Monitoring											•
	Planning										•	
Environment	Persuasion								•			
Firefight	Testing	•										
Justice	Investigation				•							
Management	Decision making				•							
Medical	Detection	•			•							
	Diagnosis	•				•						
	Monitoring				•							
	Persuasion	•							•			
	Surgery			•								
	Communication			•						•		
	Detection	•		•		•				•		
Military	Flight operations			•	•	•				•		•
	Monitoring	•			•							
	Navigation			•								
	Orientation			•								
	Training			•	•	•						•

(*continued*)

Table 4. (*continued*)

Space	Wellbeing								•		
	Gym									•	
Sport	Ping-pong										•
	Pool									•	
	Assembly										•
	Collaboration	•									
	Detection		•								
	Generic task	•						•	•		
	Identification	•				•					•
	Jumping	•									
Generic	Learning							•			
	Memorization					•	•				
	Monitoring		•		•				•		
	Persuasion	•			•						
	Reading							•			
	Self-control	•									
	Training								•		
	Assembly	•									•
Workforce	Sorting	•									
	Training	•							•		

Table 5. Quadrant AL of the compass: it links the limitations with the augmentations.

AUGMENTATION \ LIMITATION		Physical limits		Cognitive bottlenecks — Info processing			Info storage		Mental state		Missing knowledge	
		Costly simulation	Variable performance	Working memory	Psychomotor bottleneck	Perceptual bottleneck	Memory fault	Memory capacity	Low engagement	Incorrect focus	Lack of Expertise	Lack of information
Task assistance	Action correction	•			•						•	
	Action suggestion	•	•	•	•					•		•
Task load management	Task load distribution	•	•	•	•							
	Task load reduction	•	•	•	•	•					•	•
Mental state modification	Attentional Deployment		•							•		
	Cognitive Change	•			•				•	•		
	Stimuli Reduction		•							•		
Info flow modification	Knowledge Provision	•	•	•	•	•			•		•	•
	Memory Expansion							•				
Simulativity			•						•			

Table 6. Quadrant AI of the compass: it links the augmentations with implementation strategies.

AUGMENTATION / IMPLEMENTATION		Instructions	Motivational	Suggestions	Analytics	Evaluation	Audio Cues	Visual Cues	Life Logging	Virtual simulation	Decluttering	Deferring	Automation	Repartition	Adaptivity	Gamification	Data Ergonomics	Multimodality	Diversification	Role Change
		Prompts		Analysis			Cues		Experiences		Reduction		Delegation		Task elements		Info provision		Task executed	
		Addition of									Subtraction by				Modification of					
Task assistance	Action correction	•		•		•		•												
	Action suggestion	•		•				•												
Task load management	Task load distribution											•	•	•	•					
	Task load reduction			•	•								•		•		•	•		
Mental state modification	Attentional Deployment						•	•									•	•	•	
	Cognitive Change		•													•			•	•
Info flow modification	Stimuli Reduction				•						•									
	Knowledge Provision	•		•	•		•	•	•						•		•			
	Memory Expansion									•										
Simulativity											•									

Table 7. Quadrant FI of the compass: it links the fields of application with implementation strategies.

Column groups — **Addition of**: Prompts (Instructions, Motivational, Suggestions), Analysis (Analytics, Evaluation), Cues (Audio Cues, Visual Cues), Experiences (Life Logging, Virtual simulation); **Subtraction by**: Reduction (Decluttering), Delegation (Deferring, Automation, Repartition); **Modification of**: Task elements (Adaptivity, Gamification), Info provision (Data Ergonomics, Multimodality), Task executed (Diversification, Role Change).

Field	Subfield	Instructions	Motivational	Suggestions	Analytics	Evaluation	Audio Cues	Visual Cues	Life Logging	Virtual simulation	Decluttering	Deferring	Automation	Repartition	Adaptivity	Gamification	Data Ergonomics	Multimodality	Diversification	Role Change
Art	Drawing							•												
Aviation	Flight operations							•					•							
Aviation	Training	•																		
Cooking	Assembly	•																		
Cyber-security	Memorizing																	•		
Cyber-security	Monitoring				•															
IT	Design				•	•	•						•							
IT	Social network				•															
Driving	Navigation				•								•				•	•		
Driving	Training									•										
Driving	Safety																	•		
Education	Learning														•	•	•		•	•
Education	Monitoring				•															
Education	Planning	•			•															
Environment	Persuasion																•			
Firefight	Testing									•										
Justice	Investigation				•															
Management	Decision making				•															
Medical	Detection				•								•							
Medical	Diagnosis			•	•															
Medical	Monitoring				•															
Medical	Persuasion				•						•						•			
Medical	Surgery											•		•			•			
Military	Communication						•	•			•	•						•		
Military	Detection					•	•	•			•	•	•					•		
Military	Flight operations	•		•			•	•			•	•	•				•	•		
Military	Monitoring			•								•	•							
Military	Navigation				•															
Military	Orientation	•		•																
Military	Training				•				•		•							•		

(continued)

Table 7. (*continued*)

	IMPLEMENTATION	Addition of									Subtraction by				Modification of					
FIELD		Prompts		Analysis			Cues		Experiences		Reduction	Delegation			Task elements	Info provision			Task executed	
		Instructions	Motivational	Suggestions	Analytics	Evaluation	Audio Cues	Visual Cues	Life Logging	Virtual simulation	Decluttering	Deferring	Automation	Repartition	Adaptivity	Gamification	Data Ergonomics	Multimodality	Diversification	Role Change
Space — Wellbeing																•				
Gym						•														
Sport — Ping-pong		•																		
Pool		•																		
Generic — Assembly		•																		
Collaboration															•					
Detection											•									
Generic task		•	•					•								•				
Identification				•									•							
Jumping										•										
Learning		•																		
Memorization								•										•		
Monitoring		•											•							•
Persuasion		•	•																	
Reading					•															
Self-control				•																
Training				•																
Workforce — Assembly		•						•												
Sorting								•												
Training				•						•										

Table 8. The categories of the taxonomy and their description.

LIMITATIONS	
Costly simulation	A simulation of an event, experience, object, etc. (e.g., for training) that would be complex, impossible, risky, or expensive to run
Incorrect focus	The user's attention is directed to a low-relevance aspect given the task at hand

(*continued*)

Table 8. (*continued*)

LIMITATIONS	
Lack of expertise	Lack of skills or wisdom required to optimally perform the task
Lack of information	Missing information or knowledge from the user
Low engagement	Low motivation from the user towards the task at hand
Memory capacity	Limited amount of information which can be stored by the human memory
Memory fault	Failure to retrieve previously memorized information
Perceptual bottleneck	Limited stimuli that can be perceived by the attentional resources, at the same time or in a prolonged period. [32]
Psychomotor bottleneck	Limit of the stimuli that can be processed at the same time (e.g., "[…] *The user knows what to do but is incapable of keeping up with the task load*" [10])
Variable performance	Quality and quantity of performance variates in time or between individuals (e.g., human error)
Working memory bottleneck	Limit of the information the brain can temporarily store and manipulate for executive functions [33]
AUGMENTATIONS	
Action correction	Evaluation of a performed action and/or recommendation of the optimal way of execution (i.e., how to do it)
Action suggestion	Recommendation of the action to be taken (i.e., what to do)
Attentional deployment	Call the attention of the operator and/or direct it towards the most relevant aspects in the given situation
Cognitive change	Induced change of the state of mind, mood, perspective, attitudes of the user
Knowledge provision	Provision of previously unknown information
Memory expansion	Increased amount of information that can be stored and retrieved
Simulativity	Artificial simulation of events, situations, experiences, objects, roles, spaces, etc.
Stimuli reduction	Decrease in the amount of stimuli, through any of the human senses, to which the operator is subject to
Task load distribution	Distribution of the user's effort over time (e.g., scheduling, delaying tasks) or between operators (e.g., collaboration). The overall effort doesn't vary
Task load reduction	Reduction of the user's effort to complete a task

(*continued*)

Table 8. (*continued*)

IMPLEMENTATION STRATEGIES

Adaptivity	Adjustment of a task or some of its aspects (e.g., difficulty, content) according to the situation
Alerts/audio cues	Audio signals, tones, messages
Analytics	Automatic elaboration, sorting, summarization, extraction of patterns, and insights from data
Automation	Delegation to a machine of a task of part of a task
Data ergonomics	Visualization, positioning, expression of information in ways/locations that makes data more understandable, manageable, memorable
Decluttering	Reduction of the amount of information that is visualized or transmitted
Deferring	Postponing of communications, inputs, and tasks to a later time
Diversification	Change of user activity
Evaluation	Assessment of a performed activity/outcome
Gamification	Insertion of game/interactive elements in the activity
Instructions	Prescriptive information to guide actions
Life logging	Capture/recording and retrieval of events/information
Motivational	Encouragement to take or keep performing an action. Incentive towards a specific attitude or mental state
Multimodality	Advantage deriving from the provision of information using multiple senses (visual, audio, tactile, etc.)
Repartition	Distribution of the task effort between multiple operators
Role change	Taking over the role of someone else
Suggestions	Provision of information in a non-prescriptive way
Virtual simulation	Artificial simulation of events, situations, experiences, objects, roles, spaces, in a virtual environment
Visual cues	Graphic symbols, lights, indicators, pointers

References

1. Alicea, B.: An integrative introduction to human augmentation science. arXiv preprint arXiv: 1804.10521 (2018)
2. Kruse, A.A., Schmorrow, D.D.: Session overview: foundations of augmented cognition. Found. Augmented Cogn. 441–445 (2005)
3. Guerrero, G., da Silva, F.J.M., Fernandez-Caballero, A., Pereira, A.: Augmented humanity: a systematic mapping review. Sensors (Basel) **22**, 514 (2022)
4. De Boeck, M., Vaes, K.: Structuring human augmentation within product design. Proc. Des. Soc. **1**, 2731–2740 (2021)
5. Pirmagomedov, R., Koucheryavy, Y.: IoT technologies for augmented human: a survey. Internet Things **14**, 100120 (2021)
6. Raisamo, R., Rakkolainen, I., Majaranta, P., Salminen, K., Rantala, J., Farooq, A.: Human augmentation: past, present and future. Int. J. Hum. Comput. Stud. **131**, 131–143 (2019)
7. Lee, J., Kim, E., Yu, J., Kim, J., Woo, W.: Holistic quantified self framework for augmented human. In: Streitz, N., Konomi, S. (eds.) DAPI 2018. LNCS, vol. 10922, pp. 188–201. Springer, Cham (2018). https://doi.org/10.1007/978-3-319-91131-1_15
8. Huber, J., Shilkrot, R., Maes, P., Nanayakkara, S.: Assistive Augmentation. Springer, Berlin
9. Daily, M., Oulasvirta, A., Rekimoto, J.: Technology for human augmentation. Comput. Graph. **50**, 12–15 (2017)
10. Fuchs, S., Hochgeschurz, S., Schmitz-Hübsch, A., Thiele, L.: Adapting interaction to address critical user states of high workload and incorrect attentional focus – an evaluation of five adaptation strategies. In: Schmorrow, D.D., Fidopiastis, C.M. (eds.) HCII 2020. LNCS (LNAI), vol. 12197, pp. 335–352. Springer, Cham (2020). https://doi.org/10.1007/978-3-030-50439-7_23
11. Cabrera, L.Y.: Reframing human enhancement: a population health perspective. Front. Sociol. **2**, 4 (2017)
12. Oertelt, N., et al.: Human by design: an ethical framework for human augmentation. IEEE Technol. Soc. Mag. **36**, 32–36 (2017)
13. Bostrom, N., Roache, R.: Ethical issues in human enhancement. New Waves Appl. Ethics, 120–152 (2008)
14. Moore, P.: Enhancing Me: The Hope and the Hype of Human Enhancement. Wiley, Hoboken (2008)
15. Suzuki, K.: Augmented human technology. In: Sankai, Y., Suzuki, K., Hasegawa, Y. (eds.) Cybernics, pp. 111–131. Springer, Tokyo (2014). https://doi.org/10.1007/978-4-431-541 59-2_7
16. Matarić, M.J.: Socially assistive robotics: human augmentation versus automation. Sci. Robot. **2**, eaam5410 (2017)
17. Steinert, S.: Taking stock of extension theory of technology. Philos. Technol. **29**(1), 61–78 (2015). https://doi.org/10.1007/s13347-014-0186-3
18. Schmorrow, D.D., Kruse, A.A.: Augmented cognition. Berkshire Encycl. Hum.-Comput. Interact. **1**, 54–59 (2004)
19. Dorneich, M.C., Ververs, P.M., Mathan, S., Whitlow, S.D.: A joint human-automation cognitive system to support rapid decision-making in hostile environments.pdf. In: 2005 IEEE International Conference on Systems, Man and Cybernetics, pp. 2390–2395 (Year)
20. Mayring, P.: Qualitative content analysis. Forum: Qual. Soc. Res. **1**, 159–176 (2000)
21. Vadiraja, P., Dengel, A., Ishimaru, S.: Text summary augmentation for intelligent reading assistant. In: 2021 Augmented Humans Conference (2021)
22. DeVillis, R.F.: Scale Development: Theory and Applications (1991)

23. Ghiselli, E.E., Campbell, J.P., Zedeck, S.: Validity of measurment. Measurement Theory for the Behavioral Sciences. WH Freeman, San Francisco (1981)
24. Kerr, M., et al.: Taxonomic validation: an overview. Nurs. Diagn. **4**, 6–14 (1993)
25. Fleiss, J.L.: Measuring nominal scale agreement among many raters. Psychol. Bull. **76**, 378–382 (1971)
26. Boateng, G.O., Neilands, T.B., Frongillo, E.A., Melgar-Quinonez, H.R., Young, S.L.: Best practices for developing and validating scales for health, social, and behavioral research: a primer. Front. Public Health **6**, 149 (2018)
27. Futami, K., Seki, T., Murao, K.: Unconscious load changer: designing method to subtly influence load perception by simply presenting modified myoelectricity sensor information. Front. Comput. Sci. **4** (2022)
28. Boyce, M.W., et al.: Enhancing military training using extended reality: a study of military tactics comprehension. Front. Virtual Reality **3** (2022)
29. Lee, W., Winchester III, W.W., Smith-Jackson, T.L.: WARD an exploratory study of an affective sociotechnical framework for addressing medical errors. In: Proceedings of the 44th Annual Southeast Regional Conference, pp. 377–382. (Year)
30. Fulbright, R.: Cognitive augmentation metrics using representational information theory. In: Schmorrow, D.D., Fidopiastis, C.M. (eds.) AC 2017. LNCS (LNAI), vol. 10285, pp. 36–55. Springer, Cham (2017). https://doi.org/10.1007/978-3-319-58625-0_3
31. Fulbright, R.: Calculating cognitive augmentation – a case study. In: Schmorrow, D.D., Fidopiastis, C.M. (eds.) HCII 2019. LNCS (LNAI), vol. 11580, pp. 533–545. Springer, Cham (2019). https://doi.org/10.1007/978-3-030-22419-6_38
32. Tombu, M.N., Asplund, C.L., Dux, P.E., Godwin, D., Martin, J.W., Marois, R.: A Unified attentional bottleneck in the human brain. Proc. Natl. Acad. Sci. U S A **108**, 13426–13431 (2011)
33. Baddeley, A.: Working memory. Science **255**, 556–559 (1992)

The Effect of Information Type on Human Cognitive Augmentation

Ron Fulbright and Samuel McGaha[✉]

University of South Carolina Upstate, 800 University Way, Spartanburg, SC 29303, USA
fulbrigh@uscupstate.edu, 2sm30@email.uscupstate.edu

Abstract. When performing a task alone, humans achieve a certain level of perfor-mance. When humans are assisted by a tool or automation to perform the same task, performance is enhanced—augmented. Recently developed cognitive systems are able to perform cognitive processing at or above the level of a human in some domains. When humans work collaboratively with such "cogs" in a human/cog ensemble, we expect augmentation of cognitive processing to be evident and mea-surable. This paper shows the degree of cognitive augmentation depends on the nature of the information the cog contributes to the ensemble. Results of an exper-iment are reported showing conceptual information is the most effective type of information resulting in increases in cognitive accuracy, cognitive precision, and cognitive power.

Keywords: human cognitive augmentation · cognitive systems · human/cog ensembles

1 Introduction

Recent developments, most notably in the fields of unsupervised deep learning, have produced systems capable of outperforming human experts in many domains. Comput-ers have outplayed human experts in various games such as card games, Checkers, and Chess for several years and within the last decade have conquered human champions in Jeopardy! and Go [1–3]. Going far beyond gameplaying, systems now diagnose can-cer, childhood depression, dementia, heart attacks, achieve reading comprehension, and discover new patterns in mathematics better than human experts [4–7]. These systems are not artificially intelligent, yet they mimic, perform, or replace parts of human-level thinking. Systems like this are called cognitive systems, or "cogs" for short [8–10].

Cogs like these are assistive tools used by humans in a collaborative engagement called a *huma/cog ensemble*. Aggregate cognitive processing of a human/cog ensemble is therefore a mixture of artificial and biological thinking and exceeds the cognitive pro-cessing of a human acting alone. Using cogs, augmented humans outperform unassisted humans therefore we say the human is cognitively augmented. If cognitive performance is enhanced, we should be able to measure it. To do so requires us to measure either the information itself, the cognition, or the results of the cognition. Neither of these is an easy task yet. However, theoretical and practical work is progressing.

D. D. Schmorrow and C. M. Fidopiastis (Eds.): HCII 2023, LNAI 14019, pp. 206–220, 2023.
https://doi.org/10.1007/978-3-031-35017-7_14

This paper presents the results of an experiment designed to investigate hypothesis H1, shown below, that the degree of cognitive augmentation achieved in a human/cog ensemble is dependent on the nature of information supplied to the human by the cog.

H1: The degree of cognitive augmentation achieved by humans working together on a task in collaboration with cognitive systems is dependent on the nature of information contributed by the cognitive system.

To investigate the hypothesis, we performed an experiment asking humans to solve several non-trivial puzzles. To simulate different contributions of a cognitive system, some humans were given no assistive information whereas others were given assistive information of two different types: *conceptual* and *policy/principle*. Results showed both types of assistive information improved performance, but conceptual information had greater impact on cognitive performance than policy/principle information. Furthermore, we were able to calculate cognitive augmentation by calculating increases in cognitive accuracy and cognitive precision.

2   Literature and Previous Work

2.1   Measuring Cognitive Augmentation

We can view data, information, knowledge, and wisdom (DIKW) as a hierarchy based on value as shown in Fig. 1. [11]. Data is obtained by sensing disturbances in the environment, information is processed data, knowledge is processed information, and wisdom is processed knowledge. Each level is of a higher value than the level below it because of the processing involved and the utility of information stock at that level.

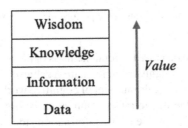

Fig. 1. The DIKW Hierarchy.

Processing at each of the level in the DIKW can be modeled as a cognitive process transforming data, information, or knowledge, generically referred to as information stock, to a higher-valued form as depicted in Fig. 2 where the transformation of the information stock is accomplished by the expenditure of a certain amount of cognitive work (W) [12].

To illustrate how cognitive processing increases the value of information stock, consider a temperature sensor. The electrical conductivity of two different metals in a thermocouple is affected by the temperature of the environment in which the thermo-couple is placed causing a detectable voltage potential. Detecting the voltage represents

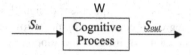

Fig. 2. A cognitive process as a transformation of information stock.

data—a direct sensing of a physical disturbance. To convert this reading to temperature a calculation must be performed. The calculation is a cognitive process combining the data sensed from the environment with information obtained from an engineering units reference table, and the knowledge of how to calculate the formula. The result of this cognitive process is *degrees* and represents new information of a higher value than the data input into the cognitive process. Similarly, information is processed into knowledge and knowledge is processed into wisdom by additional cognitive processing.

In a human/cog ensemble (a collaborative team), cognitive processing of the entire ensemble is a mixture of human cognitive processing and artificial cognitive processing (W* = WH + WC) as depicted in Fig. 3 [12–14].

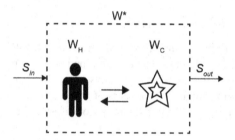

Fig. 3. A Human/Cog ensemble performing a cognitive process.

In earlier work, we have proposed several methods of measuring and calculating cognitive work and the degree of cognitive augmentation achieved in a human/cog ensemble [12, 15–17]. A way of measuring the amount of cognitive work done by a cognitive process is to compare the value of the information stock before and after the processing as shown in Eq. (1) where the value of the information stock is evaluated by the value function, ψ.

$$W = |\psi(S_{out}) - \psi(S_{in})| \tag{1}$$

Equation (1) therefore, focuses on the transformation effected by the cognitive process. One way to measure cognitive augmentation is to calculate a quantity called *cognitive power* as shown in Eq. (2) where W represents an amount of cognitive work performed by one or more cognitive processes and t is the time required to perform W.

$$P = \frac{W}{t} \tag{2}$$

In general, cognitive power increases as the amount of cognitive work increases or the amount of time decreases. In a human/cog ensemble, contributions by either the human or the cog can result in either.

Another way to measure cognitive augmentation is to measure the increase in cognitive accuracy and/or cognitive precision of an augmented human. Cognitive accuracy is a measure of the ability to produce the correct, or preferred, output. Cognitive precision is a measure of the ability to produce only the correct or preferred output as depicted in Fig. 4 where the oval represents the correct or preferred output.

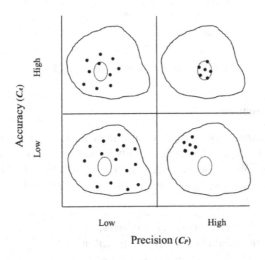

Fig. 4. Cognitive Accuracy and Cognitive Precision.

The goal, of course, is to achieve high accuracy and high precision (upper right quadrant of Fig. 4). Using a chosen accuracy and precision performance metric (x and y), comparing the performance of a human working alone (x) to a human working in partnership with a cog in a human/cog ensemble (x′) will calculate any change in cognitive accuracy and cognitive precision as shown in Eq. (3).

$$\Delta C_A = \frac{x - x'}{x} \qquad \Delta C_P = \frac{y - y'}{y} \tag{3}$$

For example, a human working alone might produce the correct result 4 times out of 10. If the same human, working in partnership with a cog, produces the correct result 8 times out of 10, then the cognitive accuracy has increased by two-fold, a 100% increase.

Human performance is *augmented* by partnering with cogs and is superior to humans acting alone. However, not all human/cog ensembles result in the same level of cognitive augmentation. Different Levels of Cognitive Augmentation have been defined ranging from no augmentation at all (all human thinking) to fully artificial intelligence (no human thinking) as shown in Fig. 5 [12–14].

Level 0: No Augmentation
human performs all cogntiive processing

Level 1: Assistive Tools
abacus, calculators, software, etc.

Level 2: Low-Level Cognition
pattern recognition, classification, speech
human makes all high-level decisions

Level 3: High-Level Cognition
concept understanding, critique,
conversational natural language

Level 4: Creative Autonomy
human-inspired, unsupervised synthesis

Level 5: Artificial Intelligence
no human cognitive processing

Fig. 5. Levels of Cognitive Augmentation.

2.2 Types of Information

Earlier, we characterized various types of information (data, information, knowledge, and wisdom) based on processing and the utility value of the information at the various levels. However, DIKW is not the only way to characterize information. Hertz and Rubenstein identified six types of information as shown in Fig. 6 [18–20].

- **Conceptual** ideas, theories, hypotheses, etc.
- **Procedural** method of how to do something
- **Policy** laws, rules, guidelines, theorem, etc.
- **Stimulatory** information causing activity
- **Empirical** information through sensing, observation, experiment, etc.
- **Directive** information provided to achieve a particular outcome
- **Fact** a statement of data asserted with certainty

Fig. 6. Hertz and Rubenstein's Six Types of Information.

Robert Horn, the developer of Information Mapping™, identified seven types of information as shown in Fig. 7 [21–23].

- **Procedure** a set of specific steps and decisions to be made
- **Process** a series of events or phases taking place over time
- **Concept** a group or class of objects, conditions, events, ideas etc.
- **Structure** physical structure divided into parts by boundaries
- **Classification** division of items into categories using one or more factors
- **Principle** rule, policy, guideline, theorem, axiom, postulate, etc.
- **Fact** a statement of data asserted with certainty

Fig. 7. Horne's Seven Types of Information.

Even though these two sources use different names and words, the categories of information types defined are very similar. In our experiment, we chose to use *conceptual* and *policy* (also called *principle*) information. Examples of conceptual information include definitions, examples, and counter examples. Examples of principle information include guidelines, rules, goals, and objectives [24].

3 The Experiment

Participants were asked to solve four different puzzles listed below and shown in Fig. 8.

- **Task 1:** "Square"   (3-row math puzzle)
- **Task 2:** "X puzzle"   (diagonal math puzzle)
- **Task 3:** "4 X 4"   (4-row sequence puzzle)
- **Task 4:** "Message"   (6-word decryption puzzle)

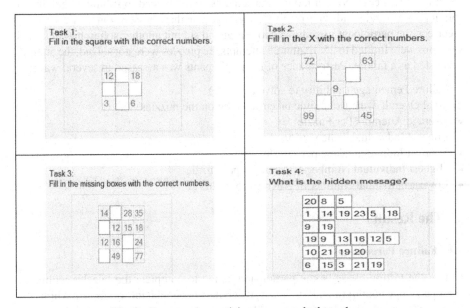

Fig. 8. Four puzzles participants were asked to solve.

The puzzles were presented to the participants one at a time with the participant allowed to continue to the next puzzle only upon successful completion of the current puzzle. Two of the four puzzles involved basic mathematical functions (addition, subtraction, multiplication). One puzzle involved recognizing a pattern in a sequence of numbers. One puzzle involved solving decoding a simple substitution cyber. Each puzzle involved non-trivial kinds of cognition but was simple enough to be solved by anyone with grade-school education and knowledge.

To investigate the effect of different types of information, some participants were presented with a hint along with the puzzle. Approximately 1/3 of the participants were given no hint (the "normal" group) and served as the control group. Approximately 1/3 of the participants were given a hint in the form of conceptual information (the "concept" group). The conceptual hint was an example of a completed puzzle shown to the participants. The remaining 1/3 of the participants were given a hint in the form of principle/policy information (the "policy" group). The policy/principle hint for each puzzle involved a guideline or rule as shown below:

- **Square** "Each row is a different mathematical operation".
- **X puzzle** "The middle box and the empty box combine to equal the third box".
- **4×4** "Each row is based on a specific number. One row is a combination of the other three rows".
- **Message** "Each number is tied to a specific letter in the English alphabet".

To take part in the experiment, participants downloaded a computer program presenting each of the four puzzles and the assistive information (if any). Participants were given up to one hour to complete the puzzles. If, after an hour, all puzzles were not solved the attempt was counted as a failure. Participants were allowed to submit an attempted solution to a puzzle and then receive a message whether the solution was correct. If incorrect, the participant was allowed to repeat and submit another solution. Attempted solutions were limited to 25. If after 25 attempts the puzzles were not solved, the attempt was listed as a failure. Performance of the participants was assessed in several ways:

- Failure Percentage (inability to solve a puzzle)
- Total Overall Time (total time taken working on the puzzles)
- Average Attempts Per Puzzle
- Longest Individual Time per Puzzle
- Shortest Individual Time per Puzzle
- Highest Individual Number of Attempts per Puzzle
- Lowest Individual Number of Attempts per Puzzle

4 The Results

4.1 Failure Percentage

During the testing phase, some participants failed to complete the puzzles within 25 attempts or one hour of time. Participants receiving conceptual information as a hint (the "concept" group) had the least number of failures whereas those receiving no information at all (the "normal" group) had the most failures as seen in Fig. 9. Success of the "concept" group was three times better than the "normal group."

Failure percentage (F) is a measure of *accuracy*. A failure percentage of 100% would mean a complete lack of accuracy and a failure percentage of 0% would mean perfect accuracy. Using, Eq. (3), the decrease in failure percentage for each type of information can be calculated showing conceptual information has the greatest impact on failure percentage:

$$\Delta F_{Policy} = \frac{75\% - 37\%}{75\%} = 51\% \tag{4}$$

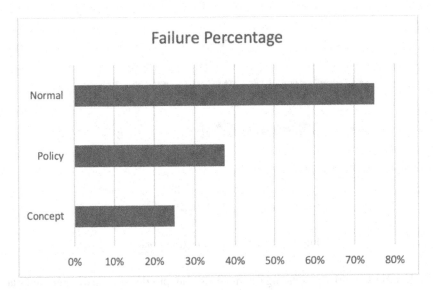

Fig. 9. Failure Percentage for Different Types of Information.

$$\Delta F_{Conceptual} = \frac{75\% - 25\%}{75\%} = 67\% \tag{5}$$

The inverse of failure percentage is also a measure of cognitive accuracy. Participants receiving conceptual information as a hint were successful 75% of the time. Participants receiving policy/principle information were successful 63% of the time. Participants receiving no assistive information were successful only 25% of the time. Therefore, when compared to no information, policy/principle information increased cognitive accuracy by 60% ($\Delta C_A = 60\%$), a 1.7 fold increase, and conceptual information increased cognitive accuracy by 200% ($\Delta C_A = 200\%$), a three-fold increase.

4.2 Total Overall Time

The total overall time for a group of participants is the sum of all times spent by participants in the group, measured in seconds. Participants receiving conceptual information as a hint had the shortest overall time (the "concept" group) whereas those receiving no information at all (the "normal" group) had the longest overall time as seen in Fig. 10. The "concept" group spent less than half the amount of time the "normal" group did.

By calculating the reduction in time, we see conceptual information had the greatest impact on time spent on the puzzles.

$$\Delta T_{Policy} = \frac{90,000 - 55,000}{90,000} = 39\% \tag{6}$$

$$\Delta T_{Conceptual} = \frac{90,000 - 35,000}{90,000} = 61\% \tag{7}$$

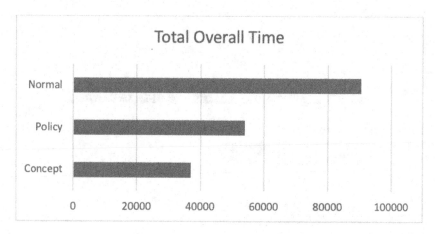

Fig. 10. Total Overall Time (*in seconds*).

Before any cognitive processing was done, the four puzzles were in the unsolved state with a certain amount of value associated. After successfully solving the four puzzles, they were in the solved state at an increased value. Therefore, according to Eq. (1), a nonzero amount of cognitive work was performed by the participants (W > 0). Therefore, using Eq. (2), cognitive power can be calculated for each type of information as shown in Eq. (8).

$$P_{Normal} = \frac{W}{90,000} < P_{Policy} = \frac{W}{55,000} < P_{Conceptual} = \frac{W}{35,000} \tag{8}$$

Cognitive augmentation by virtue of conceptual information yielded a cognitive power more than 2.5 times greater than no information (no augmentation) and more than 1.5 times that of policy/principle information.

4.3 Average Attempts Per Puzzle

Participants were allowed to attempt each puzzle multiple times (up to 25 times). The number of attempts for each group is the average of the number of attempts for each participant in a group for each puzzle. Participants receiving conceptual information as a hint (the "concept" group) had the fewest number of attempts for each puzzle whereas those receiving no information at all (the "normal" group) had the greatest number of attempts for each puzzle as seen in Fig. 11. The "normal" group had three times the number of attempts over the "concept" group.

The number of attempts per puzzle is a measure of *precision*. Correct solution of a puzzle on the first try would represent maximal cognitive precision with cognitive precision decreasing as the number of incorrect attempts increases. For each puzzle, comparing the impact of policy/principle information and conceptual information against no information yields:

Message Puzzle:

$$\Delta C_P(policy) = \frac{19 - 11}{19} = 42\% \quad \Delta C_P(Conceptual) = \frac{19 - 7}{19} = 63\%$$

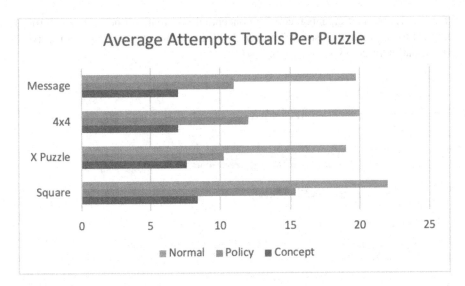

Fig. 11. Average Attempts Per Puzzle.

4×4 Puzzle:

$$\Delta C_P(policy) = \frac{20 - 12}{20} = 40\% \quad \Delta C_P(Conceptual) = \frac{20 - 7}{20} = 65\%$$

X Puzzle:

$$\Delta C_P(policy) = \frac{20 - 12}{20} = 40\% \quad \Delta C_P(Conceptual) = \frac{20 - 7}{20} = 65\%$$

Square Puzzle:

$$\Delta C_P(policy) = \frac{22 - 16}{22} = 27\% \quad \Delta C_P(Conceptual) = \frac{22 - 8}{22} = 64\%$$

Cognitive augmentation by virtue of conceptual information increased cognitive precision by 63%–65%.

4.4   Longest and Shortest Individual Time Per Puzzle

Participants were allowed to spend as much time as they wished on each puzzle. Since each puzzle required different types and kinds of cognitive effort to complete, time (measured in seconds) spent on each puzzle varied:

Message 160 s–1000 s.
4×4 100 s–1800 s.
X 25 s–800 s.
Square 60 s–2600 s.

Here, we considered only the times resulting in a completed puzzle. As seen in Fig. 12, the type of information did not significantly affect the shortest times on three out of four of the puzzles but participants receiving conceptual information (the "concept" group) were able to complete the "square" puzzle 3–4 times faster than participants receiving no information or policy information.

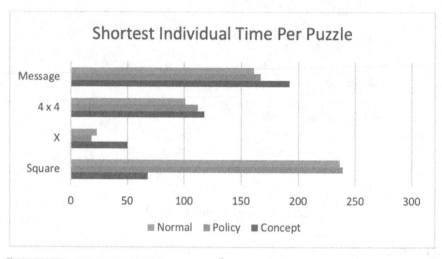

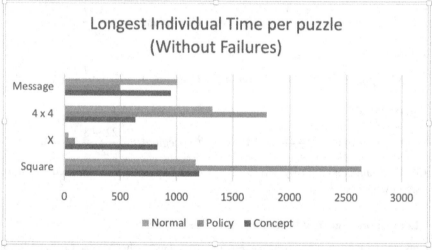

Fig. 12. Shortest and Longest Time Per Puzzle.

4.5 Lowest and Highest Individual Number of Attempts Per Puzzle

Participants were allowed to attempt a puzzle multiple times. The number of attempts before achieving a successful completion varied with the "4×4" and the "square" puzzle being the most difficult to solve.

Message 1–6 attempts.
4×4 1–14 attempts.
X 1–6 attempts.
Square 1–19 attempts.

As seen in Fig. 13, all four puzzles were able to be solved in one or two attempts regardless of the type of information received as a hint. The exception is the "square" puzzle. Without any hint at all (the "normal" group) participants required at least seven attempts to achieve success. However, with some information (the "policy" and "conceptual" groups), participants were able to solve the "square" puzzle in only one or two

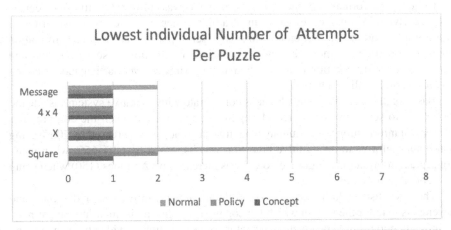

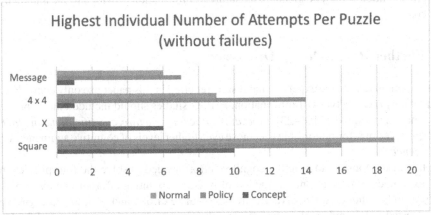

Fig. 13. Lowest and Highest Individual Number of Attempts Per Puzzle.

attempts. The effect of type of information on "square" puzzle performance is also seen when considering the highest number of attempts per puzzle as seen in Fig. 13. Participants receiving no information (the "normal" group) required as many as 19 attempts to complete whereas participants receiving policy information (the "policy" group) required fewer attempts and participants receiving conceptual information (the "concept" group) required far fewer attempts. The "concept" group required almost one-half the number of attempts as the "normal" group.

5 Conclusion

We have confirmed the hypothesis described earlier:

H1: The degree of cognitive augmentation achieved by humans working together on a task in collaboration with cognitive systems is dependent of the nature of information contributed by the cognitive system.

Cognitive performance of the human participants was enhanced to differing degrees when receiving information in the form of a hint. When presented with two different types of information as a hint on how to solve a set of puzzles, *conceptual* information improved performance more than *policy/principle* information. Also, *conceptual* and *policy/principle* information improved human performance over participants receiving no information at all as a hint.

Based on these results, when humans collaborate with cognitive systems as a team, we expect to see a greater degree of cognitive augmentation when the cog provides conceptual information to the human. Cognitive accuracy was increased by 200% using conceptual information. Cognitive precision was increased by 63%-65% when using conceptual information. Cognitive power was increased by 2.5 times (150) when using conceptual information.

These results should be taken into consideration by cognitive system designers and developers to tailor the way in which the cognitive systems assist their human partners. Careful attention should be given to the nature of information provided to the human by the cog.

6 Further Research and Discussion

It is important to note the experimental results reported in this paper use only *conceptual* and *policy/principle* types of information. Further studies should include other types of information identified by [21–23]: *procedure, process, structure, classification, and fact.* Is there a type of information able to achieve even higher levels of cognitive augmentation than *conceptual*?

It is also important to note the cognitive effort needed to solve the four puzzles in our experiment represent only a fraction of possible cognitive efforts to be examined. Future studies should utilize a vast array of cognitive efforts and seek to use cognitive effort tested and scored in other studies. Has "the type of information leading to different levels of cognitive augmentation" phenomenon been observed in other studies already?

When running similar experiments in the future it would be of value to capture age, gender, and other identifying information. This could lead to discovering if the effects of certain types of information differ for different age groups, gender groups, etc.

We realize the wording and presentation of the information given as hints could have an effect. Future studies could present the same type of information in multiple ways to discover if the way information is presented affects cognitive augmentation.

References

1. Ferrucci, D.A.: Introduction to "This is Watson", IBM J. Res. Dev. **56**(3/4) (2012). https://ieeexplore.ieee.org/document/6177724. Accessed Feb 2023
2. Silver, D., et al.: Mastering the game of Go with deep neural networks and tree search, *Nature*, 529. (2016). https://www.nature.com/articles/nature16961. Accessed Feb 2023
3. [DeepMind] AlphaGo Zero: learning from scratch, *DeepMind* (2018). https://deepmind.com/blog/alphago-zero-learning-scratch/. Accessed Feb 2023
4. Wehner, M.: AI is now better at predicting mortality than human doctors, *New York Post,* published 14 May (2019). https://nypost.com/2019/05/14/ai-is-now-better-at-predicting-mortality-than-human-doctors/?utm_campaign=partnerfeed&utm_medium=syndicated&utm_source=flipboard. Accessed Feb 2023
5. Lavars, N.: Machine learning algorithm detects signals of child depression through speech, *New Atlas,* published 7 May (2019). https://newatlas.com/machine-learning-algorithm-depression/59573/. Accessed Feb 2023
6. Towers-Clark, C.: The Cutting-Edge of AI Cancer Detection, *Forbes,* published 30 April (2019). https://www.forbes.com/sites/charlestowersclark/2019/04/30/the-cutting-edge-of-ai-cancer-detection/#45235ee77336. Accessed Feb 2023
7. Gregory, M.: AI Trained on Old Scientific Papers Makes Discoveries Humans Missed, Vice (2019). https://www.vice.com/en_in/article/neagpb/ai-trained-on-old. Accessed Feb 2023
8. Wladawsky-Berger, I.: The Era of Augmented Cognition, The Wall Street Journal: CIO Report (2015). http://blogs.wsj.com/cio/2013/06/28/the-era-of-augmented-cognition/. Accessed Feb 2023
9. Gil, D.: Cognitive systems and the future of expertise, YouTube video (2019). https://www.youtube.com/watch?v=0heqP8d6vtQ. Accessed Feb 2023
10. Kelly, J.E., Hamm, S.: Smart Machines: IBMs Watson and the Era of Cognitive Computing. Columbia Business School Publishing, Columbia University Press, New York, NY (2013)
11. Ackoff, R.: From data to wisdom. J. Applied Syst. Anal. **16** (1989). https://faculty.ung.edu/kmelton/Documents/DataWisdom.pdf. Accessed Feb 2023
12. Fulbright, R.: Democratization of Expertise: How Cognitive Systems Will Revolutionize Your Life. CRC Press, Boca Raton, Fl (2020)
13. Fulbright, R., Walters, G.: Synthetic expertise. In: Schmorrow, D.D., Fidopiastis, C.M. (eds.) HCII 2020. LNCS (LNAI), vol. 12197, pp. 27–48. Springer, Cham (2020). https://doi.org/10.1007/978-3-030-50439-7_3
14. Fulbright, R.: The expertise level. In: Schmorrow, D.D., Fidopiastis, C.M. (eds.) HCII 2020. LNCS (LNAI), vol. 12197, pp. 49–68. Springer, Cham (2020). https://doi.org/10.1007/978-3-030-50439-7_4
15. Fulbright, R.: Cognitive augmentation metrics using representational information theory, In: Schmorrow D., Fidopiastis C. (eds.) Augmented Cognition. Enhancing Cognition and Behavior in Complex Human Environments, AC 2017, Lecture Notes in Computer Science, vol. 10285, pp. 36–55. Springer, Cham (2017). https://doi.org/10.1007/978-3-319-58625-0_3. Accessed 2023

16. Fulbright, R.: On measuring cognition and cognitive augmentation. In: Yamamoto, S., Mori, H. (eds.) Human Interface and the Management of Information. Information in Applications and Services HIMI 2018 20th International Conference, HIMI 2018, Held as Part of HCI International 2018, Las Vegas, NV, USA, July 15–20, 2018, Proceedings, Part II Las Vegas, NV USA 2018 07 15 2018 07 20 Lecture Notes in Computer Science LNCS, Vol. 10905, pp. 494–507. Springer, Cham (2018).https://doi.org/10.1007/978-3-319-92046-7_41. Accessed Feb 2023

17. Fulbright, R.: Calculating cognitive augmentation -a case study, In: Schmorrow, D., Fidopiastis, C. (eds.) Augmented Cognition, AC 2019, Lecture Notes in Computer Science, vol. 11580, 533–545. Springer, Cham (2019). https://doi.org/10.1007/978-3-030-22419-6_38. Accessed Feb 2023

18. Hertz, D.B., Rubenstein, A.H.: Team Research. Columbia University Department of Industrial Engineering, New York (1953)

19. [LISBON] Definition and Types of Information, *LIS Education Network* (2014). https://www.lisedunetwork.com/definition-and-types-of-information/. Accessed Jan 2023. (Updated 2022)

20. [Indeed] 6 Types of Information (with examples), *Indeed.com* (2021). https://www.indeed.com/career-advice/career-development/types-of-information. Accessed Jan 2022

21. Horn, R.E.: A terminal behavior locater system. *Programmed Learning*, No. 1(Feb) (1966)

22. Horn, R.E.: Mapping hypertext: analysis, linkage, and display of knowledge for the next generation of on-line text and graphics. Lexington, MA: The Lexington Institute (available from Information Mapping, Inc. 303 Wyman St. Waltham, MA. 02154) (1989). https://archive.org/details/mappinghypertext0000horn/page/110/mode/2up?ref=ol&view=theater. Accessed Jan 2023

23. Horn, R.E.: Structured Writing at Twenty-Five, *Performance and Instruction*, 32, (Feb) (1993). https://citeseerx.ist.psu.edu/viewdoc/download?doi=10.1.1.175.3630&rep=rep1&type=pdf. Accessed Jan 2023

24. Thomas, K.: Information Design, *Rocky Mountain Alchemy* (2004). http://www.rockymountainalchemy.com/whitePapers/rma-wp-information-design.pdf. Accessed Jan 2023

Personality Traits as Predictors for Social Engineering Vulnerability

Jake Imanaka, Michael-Brian Ogawa[✉], and Martha E. Crosby

University of Hawai'i at Mānoa, Honolulu, HI 96822, USA
{jimanaka,ogawam,crosby}@hawaii.edu

Abstract. As security measures to protect against cyberattacks increase, hackers have begun to target the weakest link in the cybersecurity chain–people. Such attacks are categorized as Social Engineering and rely on the manipulation and deception of people rather than technical security flaws [4]. This study attempts to examine the relationship between people and their vulnerability to Social Engineering attacks by posing the following questions: (1) what relationship, if any, exists between personality traits and Social Engineering vulnerability, and (2) what relationship, if any, exists between personality traits and the speed at which an individual makes cybersecurity-related decisions. To answer these questions, 79 undergraduate students at the University of Hawaii were surveyed to measure their personality traits and cybersecurity awareness. The survey results indicated that there was no significant correlation between the measured personality traits and measured vulnerability. The relationship between different personality traits and the elapsed time to complete the survey was slightly more significant; however, it was still statistically insignificant overall.

Keywords: Social engineering · personality traits · computer security

1 Introduction

Now, more than ever, information systems are at risk of being breached due to the weakest link in cybersecurity–people [1]. Hackers equip themselves not only with advanced technologies to exploit our information systems but also with techniques to coerce individuals into willingly giving up their sensitive information–Social Engineering (SE). Social Engineering attacks bypass most security features implemented in information systems by targeting humans who own and use the systems directly. Once a Social Engineering attack is successful, and depending on the privilege level of the victim, a hacker can access sensitive information without throwing exploits, bypassing firewalls, or cracking a password [14]. Social Engineering's effectiveness and the relative ease at which it can be performed make it one of the most efficient and effective access vectors for a hacker.

D. D. Schmorrow and C. M. Fidopiastis (Eds.): HCII 2023, LNAI 14019, pp. 221–231, 2023.
https://doi.org/10.1007/978-3-031-35017-7_15

1.1 Social Engineering Techniques

Social engineering techniques may use physical, social, technical, or socio-technical aspects to deceive their victim into divulging sensitive information [10]. Examples of classical SE techniques as described by Krombholz et al. [10] are as follows:

- **Phishing:** An attack which can be performed over any electronic communication channel in which the attacker masquerades as a trusted individual. Phishing attacks can target large groups of people at the same time making them cost and time efficient. Sub-techniques include **spear-phishing**—where attackers target specific individuals rather than everyone, or **whaling**—where attackers target high-profile targets.
- **Shoulder surfing:** Technique where an attacker directly observes a victim to gain sensitive information. This could be performed by looking at a victim's screen or keyboard while they input their password.
- **Reverse social engineering**: Technique where an attacker establishes themselves as someone who can solve the victim's problems. The attacker will then create a situation where the victim may feel compelled to reach out to the attacker to ask for help.
- **Baiting**: An attacker leaves malware-infected storage mediums around so that potential victim's may pick them up, insert them into their computers, and infect themselves. These may take the form of USB sticks left in libraries or in classrooms.

1.2 Measuring Social Engineering Vulnerability

Prior studies have resulted in three main approaches in measuring Social Engineering vulnerability: Surveys, imitation studies, and lab experiments [11]. Each approach has inherent weaknesses and strengths. Surveys are simple to create and easy to distribute, but answers are self-reported by the subject and are thus vulnerable to the subject's biases. Individuals may feel embarrassed to admit they have fallen for a SE technique or fail to comprehend the severity of a situation due to the low-risk environment leading to inaccurate results. Imitation studies provide real-world situations where subjects can fully immerse themselves in the situations; however, they are difficult to proctor and time-consuming to create. Furthermore, the ethical dilemma of deceiving and testing subjects without their knowledge is also an issue. Lastly, lab experiments offer a controlled environment with well-defined boundaries, but subjects may become hyper-aware of the fact they are participating in a study which may also introduce bias.

1.3 Social Engineering and Personality

Personality traits and Social Engineering have been thought to be related due to how our personality may influence our susceptibility to persuasion and manipulation [14]. Existing studies suggest that individual personality traits may indicate higher susceptibility to SE and email phishing [2, 7–9]. However, results from these studies show conflicting conclusions as to which personality traits correspond with higher levels of SE vulnerability. For example, Cusak and Adedokun [9] found that agreeableness and extraversion were indicators SE vulnerability, Halevi et al. [7] concluded that individuals with high levels of neuroticism were more susceptible to phishing, and Alseadoon et al. [8] concluded that individuals with higher levels of openness, extraversion, and agreeableness were more susceptible to phishing. One study also suggests a "Social Engineering Personality Framework" based upon the Big Five personality traits [13].

1.4 Big Five Personality Traits

The Big Fiver Personality Traits are a taxonomy of personality traits distributed amongst 5 categories: extraversion, agreeableness, openness, conscientiousness, and neuroticism [6]. Characteristics of each trait are as follows:

- Extraversion: positive emotions, activity, sociability, assertiveness [6, 14].
- Agreeableness: trust, compliance, modesty, and kindness [6, 14].
- Openness: creativity, fantasy, and openness to different experiences [6, 14].
- Conscientiousness: self-discipline, order, goal-directed behavior, and impulse control [6, 14].
- Neuroticism: anxiety, self-consciousness, depression, and vulnerability [6, 14].

1.5 Goals and Research Questions

The first step to combat and decrease the effectiveness of Social Engineering is to understand why people are vulnerable to it. As Social Engineering seeks to manipulate and deceive individuals, it is logical to ask questions of whether our personality and augmented cognition plays a role in our vulnerability to it. Therefore, the goal of this study is to better understand the relationship between our augmented cognition and our vulnerability to Social Engineering cyber attacks. Results and deliverables from this study may benefit future Social Engineering researchers and our overall security posture against Social Engineering attacks. To achieve these goals, this study aims to answer the following research questions (RQs):

1. What relationship, if any, exists between personality traits and Social Engineering vulnerability?
2. What relationship, if any, exists between personality traits and the speed at which an individual makes cybersecurity-related decisions?

2 Methods

To achieve the goals described by RQ1 and RQ2, a survey was designed and administered online through Google Forms to undergraduate students in low-level Computer Science classes at the University of Hawaii at Manoa. The survey consisted of two parts: a security survey and a personality survey. The survey results were then statistically analyzed to produce quantitative results about the relationship between personality traits and Social Engineering vulnerability and the time it takes to make cybersecurity decisions.

2.1 Security Survey Design

The security survey consisted of 22 scored questions designed to measure an individual's susceptibility and vulnerability to Social Engineering. This section of the survey consisted of 3 types of questions. The first question type was related to "situational awareness" and Social Engineering techniques. These questions began by presenting a cybersecurity situation and subjects would answer questions regarding how they felt about the situation and what they would do. Figure 1 depicts an example of a fake email presented in the security survey–a phishing email.

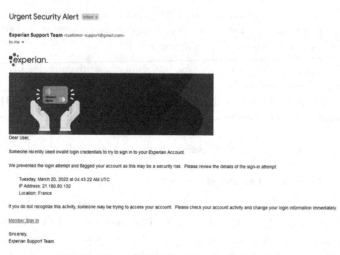

Fig. 1. Example Security Situational Question

The subject line, name of the sender, and the body of the email seem to be a normal security email; however, the sender's email address is "customer-support@gmail.com" which would not be the case if this email was truly from Experian. The subject would then be presented with statements such as "I would click the link" where they respond on a Likert scale. During this section of the survey, subjects were also asked to input their start time at before reviewing the question and their end time after completing each question. Time measurements were self-reported via a stopwatch application, www.timertab.com. In total, the survey consisted of 4 "fake" situations and 2 controls. The second type of security question was the "general security" questions. These were simple questions about the subject's general security practices. An example general security question was "When downloading files, I make sure to verify the download source and file content before opening it" where they would again respond to a Likert-scale question. The third type of security question was the "short answer" questions. Short answer questions asked the subject for further explanations of their reasonings and thoughts on the situational and general security questions. These questions were intended to be used as additional qualitative data or for future research.

2.2 Personality Survey Design

The personality section of the survey used the publicly available Big-Five Personality Inventory [6]. The Big-Five Personality Test is a 44-item survey that asks subjects to respond to questions about their personality and behavior on a Likert scale between 1 and 5. An example question from the Big-Five Personality Inventory is "[I am] full of energy".

The total score of a given survey was calculated by adding the numerical values of each answer. For the security survey, the answer "strongly disagree" corresponded to 1, "disagree" corresponded to 2, "neutral" corresponded to 3, "agree" corresponded to 4, and "strongly agree" corresponded to 5. For both the security and personality surveys, certain questions were marked for inverse scoring. For any inverse score question, the inverse of the subject's answer would be added instead when tallying the final score. For example, if the subject answered with 5, 1 would be added to the score instead, if a subject answered with 4, 2 would be added. In addition to summing the answers, the time taken to analyze each situation and answer each section in the "situational security" section was also summed and used as a time total in the analysis.

Fifteen of 22 questions from the security survey were counted towards the final survey score due to restrictions of using some statistical analysis methods on Likert scale answers [14]. Due to these restrictions, only answers on a 5-point scale were counted; answers on a 2, 3, or 4-point scale were ignored in this analysis. This is a threat to validity is a limitation of the study. This will be discussed further in the Threats to Validity section.

3 Results

The survey was administered over one week and received 79 total responses. Figure 2 depicts the distribution of security scores, Fig. 3 depicts the distribution of time totals, and Fig. 4 depicts the distribution of the Big Five Personality Traits. Visually, the security scores, extraversion, and neuroticism follow relatively normal distributions, the security scores are positively skewed, and agreeableness, conscientiousness, and openness appear negatively skewed.

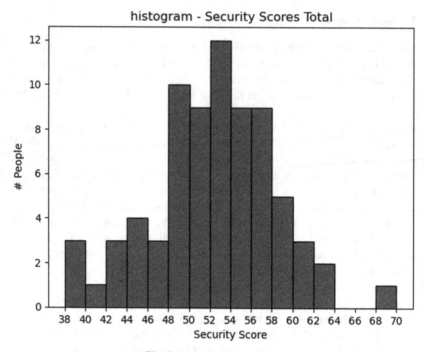

Fig. 2. Security Score Totals

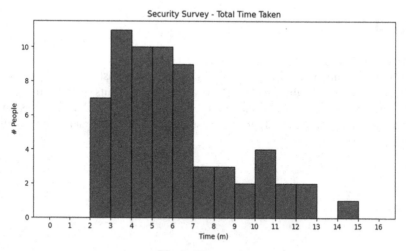

Fig. 3. Time totals

3.1 Analysis

The goal of this analysis was to determine whether a statistically significant relationship existed between security/time scores and individual personality scores. To achieve this, subjects were split into 4 groups corresponding to the 4 quartiles of individual personality

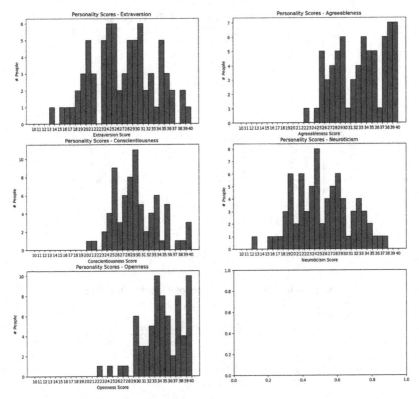

Fig. 4. Big Five Personality Scores

trait scores. Figure 5 illustrates these four group's security scores as they relate to the extraversion personality trait, and Fig. 6 shows the same group's time totals as they relate to the extraversion personality trait. Each personality trait was analyzed independently of each other; thus the subject group distributions vary depending on the personality trait. The following analysis will only show examples of the extraversion personality trait due to space constraints; however, the rest of the graphs for the other personality traits can be found in the replication package [5].

The security scores and time totals from quartiles 1 and 4 were then tested with the Mann-Whitney U Test and the Pearson Correlation Coefficient to determine whether a statistical difference existed between the two groups. The statistical test results of the two groups can be seen in Table 1 and Table 2. The results of the U-test and P-test show that there was no statistical difference and significance between security/time scores and each of the Big Five Personality Traits as all p scores were greater than 0.05.

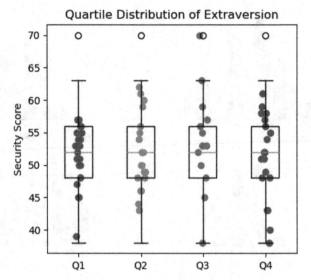

Fig. 5. Security Score vs. Extraversion Quartile Distribution

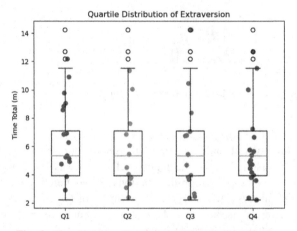

Fig. 6. Time Total vs. Extraversion Quartile Distribution

Table 1. Security Score Vs. Personality Score Tests

Test	Extraversion	Agreeableness	Openness	Conscientiousness	Neuroticism
Mann Whitney U	u=218	u=249.5	u=178.5	u=196	u=186
	p=0.824	p=0.607	p=0.301	p=0.724	p=0.724
Pearson Correlation	r=0.0167	r=0.00988	r=-0.0146	r=0.0355	r=-0.0208
	p=0.874	p=0.835	p=0.806	p=0.956	p=0.756

Table 2. Time Vs. Personality Score Tests

Test	Extraversion	Agreeableness	Openness	Conscientiousness	Neuroticism
Mann Whitney U	u=107	u=215.5	u=133	u=191.5	u=176
	p=0.0871	p=0.0936	p=0.375	p=0.543	p=0.232
Pearson Correlation	r=-0.0203	r=-0.0266	r=-0.0314	r=0.00697	r=-0.0396
	p=0.888	p=0.933	p=0.901	p=0.764	p=0.861

4 Discussion and Augmented Cognition Applications

The analysis of the survey results show that no statistical difference exists between the security scores and time totals for high and low scorers of individual personality traits ($p > .05$). However, the Mann-Whitney U test highlighted a $p < .1$ for Extraversion and Agreeableness when compared to time. The data is trending towards a significant relationship between time and these factors.

Although no statistically significant relationships were found for both RQ1 and RQ2, the trend towards time spent and personality test scores (Extraversion and Agreeableness) should be further explored. The general conclusion is in contradiction to prior research on this topic [2, 4, 13] that each found at least one of the Big Five Personality Traits to have a significant relationship to Social Engineering vulnerability.

4.1 Threats to Validity

The largest threat to the validity of this study is the self-created security survey. Two aspects of the survey that may have contributed to the "no statistically significant relationship" findings are general survey design and the choice to use a survey over other security vulnerability-measuring methods. Various aspects of the survey could have been designed for additional accuracy and precision. First, was the choice to create questions with non-Likert scale responses. Performing statistical analysis methods used in this study on Likert scale questions requires all questions to be on the same Likert scale [12]. This caused 7 of the 22 security questions to be discarded which may have affected the individual security scores of the subjects. Second, the method to measure elapsed time while taking the survey was variable. Times were self-reported and used a third-party tool instead of automation or time-stamp collection. This was generally a limitation of the survey medium–Google Forms–but nevertheless introduced non-precise time measurements. This was seen in the survey responses themselves as user-input error was available for some in the time fields. In the future, a different survey medium with automated time-stamp collection for individual question responses would decrease the error.

The choice to conduct a survey over a closed-lab experiment or a full immersion test may have also led to variations in level of Social Engineering vulnerability. As discussed in the Methods section, the self-reporting nature of surveys have different affordances and limitations compared to other mediums.

4.2 Future Work

There are many opportunities for future research including a deeper of analysis of additional personality traits and the refinement of instrumentation. Although the Big Five Personality Traits did not initially yield statistically significant results, there was a lead for Extraversion and Agreeableness when comparing time and personality traits. This research approach can be combined with additional personality factors such as locus of control (internal/external) to determine if these may further delineate differences between groups. It is surmised that additional factors such as these aligned with time, security score, and the interaction between time and security score may provide evidence of additional findings.

Many of the lessons learned and discussed in the Threats to Validity section can be implemented in future research on Social Engineering vulnerability. Implementing a closed-lab or full immersion study using more accurate measuring mediums would greatly improve the validity of the work and may help achieve the goal of improving our overall security posture. Overall, performing this study again would be beneficial. Other studies that focus on qualitative data rather than quantitative would also be intriguing as none of the qualitative data collected from this study was used in answering the research questions.

4.3 Conclusion

To help reduce the effectiveness of Social Engineering we must first ask what within ourselves makes us so vulnerable to it. One school of thought is that our cognition—more specifically the Big Five Personality Traits—can help measure one's vulnerability to Social Engineering attacks. However, this study highlighted the importance of exploring factors beyond the Big Five Personality Traits and such as locus on control and their interactions to attain fine-tuned results. The goal of this study was to determine whether our personality traits could be used in such a way, or not. Although this study showed that our personality traits were not significantly related to our Social Engineering vulnerability; it highlighted the potential for future research by expanding the factors and analysis methods. Future works in this field may take away the lessons learned from this study to illuminate new pathways for augmented cognition Social Engineering research.

Acknowledgements. This material is based upon work supported by the National Science Foundation (NSF) under Grant No. 1662487. Any opinions, findings, and conclusions or recommendations expressed in this material are those of the authors and do not necessarily reflect the views of the NSF.

References

1. Abraham, S., Chengalur-Smith, I.: An overview of social engineering malware: trends, tactics, and implications. Technol. Soc. **32**(3), 183–196 (2010). https://doi.org/10.1016/j.techsoc.2010.07.001

2. Albladi, S.M., Weir, G.R.S.: User characteristics that influence judgment of social engineering attacks in social networks. HCIS **8**(1), 1–24 (2018). https://doi.org/10.1186/s13673-018-0128-7

3. Kaouthar, C., et al.: Overview of social engineering attacks on social networks. Procedia Comput. Sci. **198**, 656–661 (2022). https://doi.org/10.1016/j.procs.2021.12.302

4. Brian, C., Kemi, K.: The impact of personality traits on user's susceptibility to social engineering attacks. In: Australian Information Security Management Conference (2018). https://doi.org/10.25958/5c528ffa66693

5. Imanaka, J.: Replication Package, https://github.com/jimanaka/personality-traits-as-predictors-for-social-engineering-vulnerability

6. John, O.P., Srivastava, S.: The big-five trait taxonomy: history, measurement, and theoretical perspectives. In: Pervin, L.A., John, O.P. (eds.) Handbook of personality: Theory and research, vol. 2, pp. 102–138. Guilford Press, New York (1999)

7. Halevi, T., Lewis, J., Memon, N.: Phishing, personality traits and Facebook. arXiv Prepr. arXiv1301.7643 (2013)

8. Alseadoon, I., Othman, M.F.I., Chan, T.: What is the influence of users' characteristics on their ability to detect phishing emails? In: Sulaiman, H.A., Othman, M.A., Othman, M.F.I., Rahim, Y.A., Pee, N.C. (eds.) Advanced Computer and Communication Engineering Technology. LNEE, vol. 315, pp. 949–962. Springer, Cham (2015). https://doi.org/10.1007/978-3-319-07674-4_89

9. Arif, K., Janabi, E.A.: Social engineering attacks. J. Multi. Eng. Sci. Technol. (JMEST) **4**(6) (2017)

10. Krombholz, K., Hobel, H., Huber, M., Weippl, E.: Advanced social engineering attacks. J. Inf. Sec. Appl. **22**, 113–122 (2015). https://doi.org/10.1016/j.jisa.2014.09.005

11. Finn, P., Jakobsson, M.: Designing ethical phishing experiments. IEEE Technol. Soc. Mag. **26**(1), 46–58 (2007). https://doi.org/10.1109/mtas.2007.335565

12. Gail, S.M., Artino, A.R.: Analyzing and Interpreting data from Likert-type scales. J. Grad. Med. Edu. **5**(4), 541–542 (2013). https://doi.org/10.4300/jgme-5-4-18

13. Sven, U., Quiel, S.: The social engineering personality framework. In: 2014 Workshop on Socio-Technical Aspects in Security and Trust (2014). https://doi.org/10.1109/stast.2014.12

14. Wang, Z., Zhu, H., Sun, L.: Social engineering in cybersecurity: effect mechanisms, human vulnerabilities and attack methods. IEEE Access **9**, 11895–11910 (2021). https://doi.org/10.1109/access.2021.3051633

Intelligent Wellness

Eric Miller[1] [iD], Robert Hanlon[2] [iD], Paul Lehrer[2] [iD], Kate Mitchell[1][✉] [iD], and Monte Hancock[2]

[1] Living Centerline Institute, Brisbane, QLD 4000, Australia
kateindymitchell@gmail.com
[2] Living Centerline Institute, Naples, FL 34113, USA

Abstract. The United States healthcare model has become increasingly reductive with components of a patient's health profile dissected between isolated specialized fields. A declining primary care sector has exacerbated this compartmentalization as knowledge within these specialties becomes siloed, forcing treatment to become reactionary and sequential in the absence of a holistic perspective. This can lead to overlooked component interactions such as conflicting treatment plans or compounding illness. However, recent advancements in digital technologies may provide a solution through the facilitation of open communication between specialties. Intelligent Wellness, for instance, refers to a simultaneous optimization model of patient care which identifies and responds to imbalances in a person's measurable stress through reference to their entire health profile. This model holistically examines three pillars of an individual's mental, physical, and financial wellbeing. Taking inspiration from naturally and mechanically occurring negative feedback loop systems, such Intelligent Wellness would collect comprehensive, real-time data on a participant's internal functioning state and their relevant environmental factors. Such data would then be analyzed and delivered back to the participant in the form of personalized behavioral recommendations for effectively improving baseline health. This collection, analysis, and delivery would occur through a digital twin medium that acts to accurately simulate and predict a participant's dynamic wellbeing.

Keywords: Psychophysiological Economics · Intelligent Wellness · Digital Twin

1 Glossary

Term	Definition
Allostasis	The process by which a state of internal, physiological equilibrium is maintained by an organism in response to actual or perceived environmental and psychological stressors

(continued)

D. D. Schmorrow and C. M. Fidopiastis (Eds.): HCII 2023, LNAI 14019, pp. 232–249, 2023.
https://doi.org/10.1007/978-3-031-35017-7_16

(*continued*)

Term	Definition
Allostatic Load	An imbalance of a person's internal physiological equilibrium that occurs through the cumulative burden of chronic stress, once the imbalance exceeds an individual's ability to cope allostatic load occurs
Burnout	A state of emotional, physical, and mental exhaustion caused by excessive and prolonged stress, often as a result from improperly managed chronic workplace stress
Digital Homeostasis	A dynamic state of equilibrium controlled through a system of feedback controls which stabilize an optimal state of wellness through the reduction of tension from external stressors
Digital Phenotyping	The study of inferred behavioral patterns as observed from digital data obtained through smart devices such as smartphones and wearable sensors
Digital Therapeutics	Software driven and clinically validated therapies that treat, manage, and prevent disease, delivered through various technologies such as mobile applications, virtual reality, and connected devices
Digital Twin	An accurate digital representation of its real-world counterpart created through comprehensive and real-time data collection and analysis
Financial Pathology	A branch of psychophysiology that researches the maladaptive patterns of financial beliefs and behaviors that lead to clinically significant distress or impairment due to financial strain or an inability to appropriately apply one's financial resources
Intelligent Wellness	The application of optimal outcomes derived through the combinatorial optimization of psychophysiological economic variables within one's digital twin in order to intervene in real time decision making within one's physical self for the full range of human experiences around wellbeing
Silo	Storage structures used metaphorically to describe a style of insular information management which fails to allow for exchanges of specialized knowledge across fields
Wellness Engineer	Licensed professionals in the fields of psychology, medicine, and financial planning, that incorporate objective scientific tools, technology, and techniques from their respective specializations, in conjunction with a supported AI-based algorithm, to provide adjusted recommendations to increase a participant's decision-making capabilities, self-awareness, and general health in the face of external stressors

2 Introduction

Rising levels of technological literacy and increased dependence on complex digital goods and services has resulted in the average American consumer possessing a greater knowledge of the functioning of their devices than the functioning of their personal health [39]. For instance, a car's engine alone may have up to 30 sensors to inform the driver of impediments to maintaining the vehicle's peak efficiency and reliability. Information from these various sensors is not only displayed via dashboard but relayed to an engine control unit (ECU) which moderates the engine's operational functions to best accommodate any imbalances. Therefore, even as the driver is made aware of their vehicle's current functional state – allowing them to pre-emptively minimize further damage through early intervention – the ECU has already adjusted in real-time to changes in the engine's capacity. This adaptation has occurred without a requirement for the driver to possess specialized mechanical knowledge, as this knowledge becomes accessible instead through the colloquial delivery of relevant information. In contrast, decisions made about an individual's personal health and wellness are reactive and commonly made by default. This is because medical knowledge is kept within its professional field and made inaccessible to the average person. This lack of information creates barriers to deciding upon and committing to long-term health and wellness goals. Commonly this means insubstantial health complications are left untreated until they have worsened or become observable.

Ordinarily, this problem is circumvented by regular interactions with general health services. However, resource and staffing shortages, alongside a declining focus on primary care and holistic services in health care, have diminished the consistency and effectiveness of these interactions. This issue has been further heightened by a growing and aging population alongside burdens caused by the ongoing COVID-19 pandemic – both of which have increased rates of hospitalization and further stressed an overworked healthcare system [12]. Therefore, basic informational access to an individual's personal health status must be approached from a different perspective – one that is adaptive to the changing technological landscape of modern living. This article argues for taking a quantitative and holistic approach to personal health wherein a person's life is modelled as a sequence of vectors which define a trajectory of health over time [19]. By giving numeric value to a person's wellness state and the factors contributing to it, data obtained from the individual can be processed and analyzed through a digital modelling algorithm. Adaptive digital twin technology can therefore be used to replicate, in real-time, the wellness state of an individual, and in doing so provide an early indication of stress imbalances that may cause more serious illness if left unattended. By taking advantage of mobile device developments and consumer engagement with digital technology, true Intelligent Wellness can assist individuals in maintaining the homeostatic functioning of their health without further burdening healthcare services.

3   Background

A key obstruction to an individual's ability to maintain their own wellness efficiently comes from limitations in access to information. This information comes in two parts: an awareness of the state of their current bodily functions, and the knowledge required to maximize the health of these functions. Ordinarily, this access is granted through the primary healthcare system which acts to measure and analyze the entirety of a person's health. However, access to these health systems can be restricted by financial, geographical, and healthcare resource barriers. The current healthcare industry's workforce crisis has, in particular, greatly diminished the accessibility of primary healthcare across the Western world. For instance, a gradual aging of the primary care workforce has resulted in imbalances between supply and demand – increasing wait-times, and subsequently increasing hospital admissions [13]. This aging is caused by a decline in medical graduate entries [13, 28] resulting in the average age of PCPs rising each year [13]. Without strong primary care, other health sectors become overburdened with patient influx and broader populational health declines [13, 45]. These imbalances were further exacerbated by the COVID-19 pandemic which saw rising hospitalizations [12], declining healthcare worker mental health [36], and an over-expenditure of allocated funding [26, 27]. These lead to high turnover rates within the healthcare industry, with turnovers in primary care resulting in approximately $979 million USD annually for excess healthcare expenditure in both the public and private sectors [43]. Of this $260 million USD can be attributed to burnout-related turnover [43].

3.1 Primary Care Burnout

Over the past decade it has been estimated that US physicians face a burnout rate of 50% or higher, with this percentage increasing among primary care physicians (PCP) [1]. In a study produced by Sumit Agarwal et al. [1], interviews conducted with PCP participants found six common influences for this high rate. Of these influences, participants expressed dissatisfaction with their workload being excessively heavy, subject to unreasonable expectations, and increasingly involving less clinical work in exchange for more administrative work [1]. Furthermore, participants had become demoralized and conflicted by their working conditions, feeling increasingly undervalued by local institutions, and found that the healthcare system's values appeared to contradict their own [1]. A core belief held by many participants of the study was that emphasis on patient satisfaction and patient expectations had come at the cost of PCP's being able to set professional boundaries [1].

The concerns raised within the Agarwal report were corroborated in a recent study by Tait Shanafelt et al. [42] which found that despite median working hours remaining consistently high across 2011 to 2021, levels of emotional exhaustion, depersonalization, and depression had all risen significantly while career satisfaction had dropped. With declining satisfaction with their work-life balance, burnout rates climbed to approximately 60% [42] (Figs. 1 and 2).

An important finding of this study, however, showed a modest increase in work-life balance satisfaction with an associated drop in physician burnout between 2017 and 2020. The paper indicated a relationship between this drop and corresponding changes made to the care delivery system leading up to the COVID-19 pandemic [42]. These changes included an increase in virtual care strategies, a decrease in documentation requirements which reduced administrative burdens, a reduction in the compartmentalization of expertise through the creation of interdisciplinary environments, and a normalization of team-based care [42]. While burdens created by the COVID-19 surge of 2020 and beyond would seemingly overwhelm the job satisfaction brought about by these changes, their impact on reducing burnout rates provides valuable insight for creating long-term workforce strategies. If burnout related turnover is to be mitigated, then these strategies must prioritize an unburdening of the healthcare industry. This means a reduction in

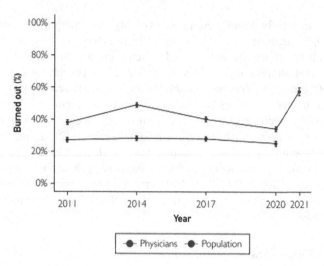

Fig. 1. Changing rates of burnout in physicians contrasted against a broader population control [42].

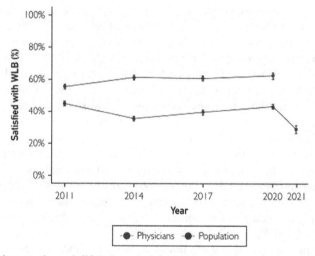

Fig. 2. Changing rates in work-life balance satisfaction in physicians contrasted against a broader population control [42].

patient demand and an enhancement of the efficiency of current health systems. The former is achieved by improving public health literacy and personal baseline health so as to reduce hospitalizations, while the latter relies on a greater integration of digital health services that facilitate cross-disciplinary communication.

4   Health and Digital Technology

Digital health is a moniker used to describe a full array of devices, applications, and software that support clinical diagnosis and treatment [14]. The use of these technologies has become essential for reducing inefficiencies and improving access to care for patients, with their use becoming further normalized by the COVID-19 pandemic. Telehealth, for example, facilitates the communication between patients and healthcare providers within a shared digital space, allowing for the remote delivery of clinical healthcare. Often this occurs when appointments with health professionals are completed over video or phone. This improves access to care, slows the spread of infection, and increases the convenience and efficiency of health services [33]. Understandably, the use of telehealth markedly increased throughout surges in the COVID-19 pandemic, with surveys showing a peak growth of 78 times pre-COVID telehealth usage in April 2020 [10]. This growth eventually stabilized in 2021 where surveys showed 37% of adults 18 and over had used telehealth services within a 12-month period [33] (Fig. 3).

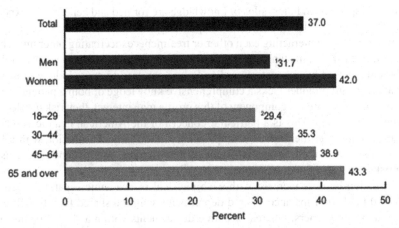

Fig. 3. Sourced from the National Center for Health Statistics. Percentage of adults aged 18 and over that participated in an appointment with a doctor, nurse, or other health professional over video or phone call within a 12 month period in 2021. Separated by age and sex [33].

Due to this rise in usage, public trust in digital health technologies and financial investment in virtual care platforms have increased substantially, creating a foundation for further innovation within the field [10].

Another essential digital health technology is the electronic health record (EHR) which digitizes a patient's health history to be accessed by any authorized person within a shared system. This portability enables the efficient transfer of patient information between health providers, supporting a holistic and systems-oriented approach to healthcare [35] and improving process-based performance measures [49]. However, portability is currently restricted to access via compatible systems, therefore incompatibilities restrict information exchange. In America, many of these systems are provided by competing software vendors [35] with the average health system being found to use 18 different EMR vendors across their various affiliated providers [46]. While interoperability is possible between different EHR systems, it cannot be guaranteed even between different systems shared by the same vendor [9]. This phenomenon exemplifies how reductive silos act as the main subtractor to an effective digital health, systems approach to medicine.

5 Reductionism in Health

Methodological reductionism can be broadly described as the explanation of a complex system through a deconstruction and examination of the system's individual components [22]. This approach assists in understanding larger, more complex issues expediently, however, it comes at the sacrifice of overlooking essential component interactions and how they affect their broader systems [3]. An emphasis on the importance of specialized knowledge in Western medicine has stunted holistic knowledge of health on a systematic scale, evidenced by a declining primary care workforce [28]. This decline corresponds to a growing specialized sector, with each field acting independently of one another. Within these specialized fields, silos of knowledge are formed and generalized expertise is lost. This increases the risk of, for example, negative medication interactions, such as treatment plans counteracting each other or treatments exacerbating other underlying health issues [44]. For instance, a diuretic therapy treatment regime used to relieve fluid buildup caused by congestive cardiac failure can lead to acute kidney injury [5]. When a healthcare provider lacks a comprehensive knowledge of both a patient's entire health profile and how each component of this profile may interact, they risk overlooking important risk factors. This is a particular concern of the American healthcare system as a patient may refer themselves to a specialist without any consultation with a PCP. Without this consultation, specialists may be left unaware of a patient's pre-existing health risks or ongoing treatment plans.

Information barriers increase with each physical or academic separation between specialized fields. For instance, shared departments within a shared facility will experience little to no barriers, whereas separate departments within a shared facility may experience minor barriers, and separate departments in separate facilities will experience greater barriers. These barriers increase substantially when information is exchanged across disciplines such as between physical health and mental health, meaning complex patient's often experience fragmented care that fails to address their full array of health requirements [23]. Managing these barriers necessitates effective and efficient communication between a patient's various healthcare and wellbeing providers [47].

6 Intelligent Wellness

An Intelligent Wellness model of patient care provides a systems approach to achieving optimized wellbeing. In contrast to traditional reductionist application, systems medicine examines the composite characteristics of a system, utilizing computational and mathematical tools to analyze the full array of internal complex component interactions [2, 3]. Therefore, rather than specializing in the maintenance of a specific area of health, Intelligent Wellness would holistically manage a patient's entire health ecosystem. This would encompass mental, physical, and financial wellbeing, as each of these components impact one another [32]. While the relationship between mental and physical health has been commonly studied [29], the inclusion of financial wellbeing as an essential element of Intelligent Wellness speaks to the growing field of financial pathology which recognizes that maladaptive patterns of financial behavior can directly influence a person's physical and mental wellbeing [32]. This primarily occurs through the development of stress-related illness as shown below (Fig. 4).

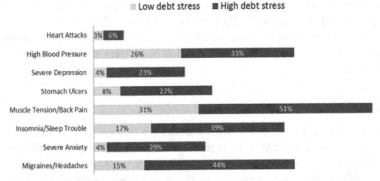

Fig. 4. Link between financial stress and the development of stress-related illness. Statistics taken from Associated Press. AOL Health Poll, Debt Stress: The toll owing money takes on the body (2008) [32].

Therefore, creation of an Intelligent Wellness system would require a connected network of patient information regarding each facet of a person's health identity. Ideally, such a model would act both as a platform to communicate information between specialists within these three wellness fields, and as a predictive analytical tool to provide personalized real-time targeted warnings and recommendations to the participant [32]. To achieve this, personal wellness within these categories must be quantifiable and exportable.

6.1 Psychophysiological Economics

Psychophysiological economics is an emerging field of study related to an evaluation of psychological and physiological responses as they pertain to economic behavior [16]. It relies on an assumption that behavioral, cognitive, and physiological mechanisms interrelate to shape wellness, and that therefore behavioral and cognitive processing cannot be separately examined but must be collaboratively approached in the creation of economic interventions [16]. In contrast to behavioral economics and behavioral finance, which study the observable cognitive reasoning behind an economic decision, psychophysiological economics measures the involuntary physiological activities and behaviors produced by the peripheral nervous system – specifically the autonomous nervous system which regulates body processes such as heart rate, respiration, digestion, and sweating [16]. Heart rate variability, in particular, provides accurate insights on the underlining health of a person's mental and physical systems as improper heart rate oscillation denotes systematic instability or deterioration [30]. It is this focus on measurable responses that allows for the quantitative study of an individual's reaction to environmental stressors, rather than their cognitively planned reaction [16]. Such measures may be taken through use of surface electromyography for muscle tension patterns, respiratory feedback for breathing patterns, and cardiovascular activity for heart rate variability [20] among other tools. Therefore, psychophysiological economics allows for the monitoring of stress levels to directly link external stressors with internal wellbeing – providing essential data for wellness engineers. To determine whether a level falls outside of normal ranges, and in doing so evaluate whether internal wellbeing has been impacted, a baseline health must be calculated. This baseline is unique to every person [20], pre-necessitating the use of personalized and adaptive technology that can evolve with real-time, comprehensive data in its development of effective health recommendations.

6.2 Digital Twin

The concept of a digit twin, or the virtual modelling of a physical object in its environment, has existed for decades. Perhaps the most famous prototype of this being the National Aeronautics and Space Administration's (NASA) "living model" of the Apollo 13 mission [4] – which was created in response to the explosion of an oxygen tank and subsequent collateral damage to the main engine. This "living model" encompassed the use of NASA training simulators which were adapted to reflect the conditions of the Apollo 13 spacecraft. These simulators were connected to a digital network of computers which provided the computational power necessary for simulating the explosion [15]. Telemetry data of Apollo 13's conditions were transferred through telecommunications technology and provided real-time information on the vessel's changing mass, center of gravity, and engine thrust [15]. This data paired the "living model" to its physical counterpart and allowed a backup crew to practice maneuvers to accurately assess both how the initial explosion occurred and what strategies could predictably provide the best outcomes.

Despite the use of digital data to adapt the simulators, the "living model" cannot be technically described as a digital twin due to the physical nature of the reproduction [17]. However, its reliance on real-time data identifies this example as an early predecessor of digital twin technology as discussed by Michael Grieves [18] in a 2002 conference. It was here that digital twin modelling was described as a means of Product Lifecycle Management, as the use of real-time comprehensive data allowed the model to evolve alongside the product's various lifestyle stages [18]. In contrast to standard simulation technologies – which also utilize digital models to replicate a system's various processes – digital twin modelling generates an entire virtual environment through continuously linked and accurate data. It could be said, therefore, that the difference between a digital twin and a simulation is largely a matter of scale [24]. While a simulation typically studies one particular process, the creation of a virtual environment enables the digital twin to run any number of useful simulations in order to study multiple processes [24].

The accuracy of this virtual environment is reliant upon the inclusion of a two-way flow of real-time information. Information is first exchanged when object sensors provide relative data to the system processor and are exchanged again when insights created from the processor are shared back with the original source object [24] (Fig. 5).

Digital Twin Model

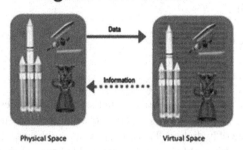

Fig. 5. Visual representation of the two-way information exchange between the physical and digital twin [18].

By relying on multi-sourced, real-time data, the digital twin is able to simultaneously study multiple processes from multiple vantage points, forming a holistic analysis of a complete system [24]. This gives greater potential for improving healthcare and precision medicine through the adaptation of digital twin modelling to human wellness systems [21].

Digital Twin Modelling in Healthcare. Increased data variety and complexity stands as the main distinguisher between a product digital twin and a human digital twin [21]. This complexity comes from the unique health profile of each participant, and the requisite specialized knowledge required to both understand and enhance said profile [21]. Furthermore, in order to algorithmically evaluate the complete functioning of an individual, data must be made quantifiable. While objective physiological data can be obtained through wearable sensors that monitor the functions of the autonomous nervous system, this fails to capture the full range of measurable health signifiers. Digital phenotyping assists in filling in gaps by compiling a profile of behavior through the inclusion of data collected from smart devices. This data includes all interactions across online social networks which act to identify and characterize a participant. Browsing history, online communications, prescribed mailing lists, and geolocation data among other interactions can – once collected, organized, and processed – typify an individual's behavior, lifestyle, and biomarkers. This can assist in the early identification of health issues, such as the occurrence of relapses or the development of mental or financial disorders.

To capture both data sources, the digital twin would create an Intelligent Wellness ecosystem through a network connection of devices including:

- Wearable biosensors;
- Peripheral smart pill dispensers;
- Smart inhalers;
- Ingestible smart pills;
- Implantable devices;
- Smart injectors;
- Smartphone applications;
- AI assistants; and
- Smart speakers.

The bio behavioral readings emanating from these varied sources and sensors would be rendered back to the participant, reflecting everything from their ongoing blood pressure to their degree of hydration. This rendered data, with supporting content, would drive personalized and actionable health choices and behavioral changes.

7 Conceptual Design of a Mobile Health Service

The use of mobile applications as a form of personal management has become normalized in recent decades. Mobile health (mHealth) services in particular have seen a meteoric rise in use, with a 2015 study finding that 58% of smartphones had downloaded some form of health-related application [32]. This has cemented mHealth as an integral part of the cost-effective, secure, and remote delivery of healthcare services worldwide [48]. According to the World Health Organization (WHO), mHealth and related digital technologies have the "potential to revolutionize how populations interact with national health services" [48]. This has been evidenced by innovative services such as the AI-powered triage tool launched by Babylon which, as of December 2021, managed over 2.5 million patients and completed over 4,000 consultations daily [8]. The accessibility of this tool has reshaped healthcare delivery, allowing for immediate access to PCP's and prescriptions regardless of patient location [7]. However, the number and hyper-specificity of many of these applications can lead to users gaining a fragmented understanding of their personal wellbeing [32] as well as creating further silos of information due to a lack of communication between separate mHealth services. Ideally, mHealth would provide a platform for the exchange of specialized knowledge, allowing for a holistic engagement with every facet of a participant's wellbeing.

Furthermore, by managing the three pillars of wellness – mental, physical, and financial wellbeing – mHealth can maintain a self-stabilizing wellness ecosystem. The inspiration for such a system comes from the naturally occurring process of homeostasis, which describes the negative feedback loop by which an organism maintains internal stability by adjusting to external stimulus [11]. In simple terms this requires a three-part response, wherein (1) the external stimulus is first identified through a sensor, (2) the stimulus is compared to a baseline level of functioning to evaluate whether a change has occurred, and (3) the organism responds in a way to bring internal measures back to this baseline. We may regard this final process as allostasis – or the active regulation required to maintain or re-establish homeostasis [38]. Through the application of digital twin technology, these natural processes can be augmented by the mHealth service to provide actionable recommendations to improve a participant's general wellness – maintaining a homeostatic state in the face of aggregating external stressors. The digital twin must therefore replicate an organism's three-part response through phases of data collection, analysis, and delivery.

7.1 Data Collection

Comprehensive and real-time data is an essential element for ensuring a digital twin model is accurate and adaptable. An element of this comprehensiveness is the inclusion of both normal state data easily obtained from the real conditions of the physical twin and "low-probability data" which includes extreme and unpredictable environmental stressors [50]. Low probability data cannot be reliably measured directly from the physical twin as it requires the occurrence of rare, and often catastrophic, events [50]. For example, the participant developing a chronic and terminal condition. Therefore, the inclusion of this data pre-necessitates the use of virtual models that can develop simulation data that adequately reflects the internal mechanisms and rules of the physical twin [50]. To assist in this, specialized knowledge – otherwise known as domain knowledge – is collected from a variety of sources such as field appropriate experts, populational surveys, and historical accounts [50]. This information, in combination with normal state data obtained by the physical twin, assists the virtual model in developing simulated data on low-probability scenarios [50].

The co-ordination of these data sources occurs through a real-time feedback loop of information transference that enables the virtual model to adapt its parameters to reflect the current physical twin's specifications [50]. Such co-ordination requires the synthetic integration of diversities between data [50]. This integration is known as data fusion and is a necessary process for making the underlying relations between multi-sourced data complementary through the merging of results – thus allowing for data to be verified, corrected, and supplemented [50]. The virtual model will then communicate its impacted real-time simulation data to the mHealth service provider for fine tuning and reassessment in compliance with the service provider's intended method of data extraction and analysis [50], such as an incorporation of digital therapeutic guidelines. At this point service-related data and domain knowledge are applied to the virtual model which is then communicated back to the physical twin in the form of prognosis and recommendations [50] (Fig. 6).

Our approach to data modelling is formalistic wherein each user is represented as an ordered list of numeric values in a finite-dimension vector space [92]. Inspired by Martin Seligman's [40] five measurable elements of wellbeing – positive emotion, engagement, relationships, meaning, and accomplishment (PERMA) – these vectors would act as quantifiable expressions of otherwise subjective wellbeing [41]. Through the inclusion of physical measurements and personal financial information, all of which is sourced both from the participant and relevant third parties, a person's functioning wellbeing can be represented analytically.

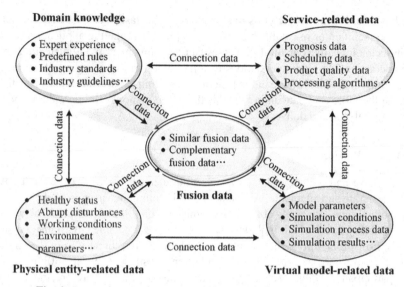

Fig. 6. Interactions between data within the digital twin modelling [50].

As an example of how these vectors could be identified, 25 components [20] have been labelled as follows (Fig. 7):

Psychological	Physical	Financial
Positivity	Weight	Spending less than income
Engagement	Blood Pressure	Bills paid on time
Relationships	Sugar	Sufficient liquid savings
Meaning		Sufficient long-term savings
Accomplishment	Age	Manageable debt load
Emotional Stability	Sleep	Prime credit score
Optimism	Diet	Appropriate insurance
Resilience	Heart Rate	Expenditure planning
Self Esteem		
Vitality		

Fig. 7. 25 components of wellness divided amongst the categories of mental, physical, and financial wellbeing.

These components cohabitate a shared homeostatic environment and as such when one component reaches its allostatic load and becomes incapable of self-regulation it can run on to negatively impact the other components. For instance, insufficient expenditure planning which has led to reckless financial decisions may cause increased stress and anxiety to a participant [32]. The corresponding impact of this psychological response to heart rate and blood pressure can imbalance a range of accompanying physical regulatory responses [31] leading to reduced health in a variety of functions. By quantifying wellness, each component can be algorithmically analyzed against a baseline target value to ensure wellbeing is improved and negative health spirals are proactively prevented [20]. It is at this stage that data analysis becomes essential.

7.2 Data Analysis

Once data has been collected or inferred from participant provided information, it must be compared to a baseline performance so that deviations may be identified [20]. This baseline is created through a coupled closed loop system that evolves with continued data input from the participant. This is to account for natural variations between individual health baselines. However, until sufficient and sustained personalized data has been collected, broader populational data must be relied upon to account for information gaps. This means that analysis will become more accurate over time at the cost of early generalizations. Consequently, the learning curve created by this evolvement may detrimentally impact initial participant engagement.

Deviations from this baseline must be similarly analyzed, as each deviation is quantified and weighted according to their corresponding wellness vector [20]. At this stage domain knowledge is essential for quantifying how a vector interacts with and impacts other wellness factors. The analysis of these multi-component interactions, however, requires an unconventional approach to machine intelligence as ordinarily a single algorithmic program will be created using a single set of data, which is insufficient for balancing multiple complex processes and their interactions. An ensemble method of approach assists with this through the deployment of multiple programs, each calibrated to analyze a specific aspect of the imputed data. This allows some programs to be good at extrapolating indicators of physical strain from the data, while other programs focus on mental or financial indicators. Knowledge of the disparate strengths and weaknesses of each program is essential and allows for the accurate evaluation of each programs results. The collaboration of these various programs and results occurs through an adjudicator system which determines the final systems-level solution by weighing each produced result in reference to how the associated program was evaluated in it's specific context.

This ability to weigh and compromise between conflicting program enables the ensemble method to create comprehensive recommendations that limit negative component interactions. However, before these recommendations can become actionable, the system must be able to predict the current capabilities of the participant so as to not alienate or frustrate them into non-compliance. Part of this actionability can be maintained through the thoughtful delivery of data.

7.3 Data Delivery

Daniel Kahneman's [25] cognitive theory on system 1 and system 2 thinking divides decision making into the automatic and the effortfully conscious. While system 2 may provide logically reasoned decisions, it is the quick and intuitive responses of system 1 that encompass the majority of default decision making [25]. Often, it is only when a problem in system 1 thinking is detected that system 2 will fully activate, allowing for active decision making to occur [25]. Therefore, to encourage a participant in achieving their sustained health goals, it is important that each system is engaged, both at the conscious and unconscious level.

Despite their prevalence, research indicates that mHealth services as a whole experience lower rates of compliance and quicker attrition rates in user engagement than in-person alternatives [6]. Evidence also suggests that the effectiveness of mHealth declines with duration and complexity. This occurs when a service exceeds three-months or when a service is multi-targeted [37], such as the case for our Intelligent Wellness service. The greatest barriers to retention, however, are a lack of support features and technical difficulties within the app design [6]. Engagement can therefore be increased in longer running and complex programs through the use of intuitive and well-developed programming that encourages a user's intrinsic motivation through management of their system 1 processing.

Self-determination theory is a framework for studying intrinsic motivation and has found that such motivation occurs through the satisfaction of three inherit psychological needs [34]. These needs include *autonomy* – the ability to maintain causal agency in decision-making; *competence* – the satisfaction of overcoming a challenge; and *relatedness* – a meaningful interconnection with others [34]. It is essential that these needs are maintained throughout the lifecycle of a mHealth service as studies showed steep declines in compliance at the termination of individual goals [34]. Providing regular check-ins can act to prolong user satisfaction after the completion of a milestone, which is important for sustaining engagement with long-term therapies that provide unobservable accomplishments.

Research shows the potential for gamification as a motivating factor for sustained and voluntary engagement. This process involves the application of game design elements (GDE) in non-game contexts as a means of addressing a participant's psychological needs [34]. For instance, the inclusion of immersive and interactive decision-making can visually communicate user choices, satisfying their autonomous requirements [34]. Meanwhile, the use of reward elements such as tokens or achievements acts to stimulate the cognitive processes which evaluate personal accomplishment and competency [34]. As these rewards are controlled by the mHealth service they can act to visualize otherwise unobservable health milestones, retaining a sense of overcoming challenge in the face of long-term goals. Finally, while relatedness can be supported through connective social interaction, such as the creation of online social networks, single-player experiences can simulate these social functions through supported narrative elements [34] that create a relationship between the participant and the mHealth service provider.

By gamifying user interactions, data delivery can become an essential motivator for continued compliance with directions and recommendations. As a participant's ability to comply with these recommendations will vary dependent on internal capabilities and external pressures, it is essential that these GDEs are attuned to the specific "difficulty level" required by each individual [20]. The digital twin, therefore, acts to support the personalization of mHealth gamification, with real-time data acting to modify the user experience in order to maintain engagement. When the recommendations are adopted and participant behavior is modified, the mHealth system will become notified of these changes and adapt to the changing state of user wellness thus closing the negative feedback loop.

8   Conclusion

COVID-19 had an inarguable impact on the delivery of health services worldwide. Strains caused by increased hospitalizations acted to exacerbate underlying systematic issues within the healthcare industry, which has led to unprecedented rates of physician burnout. A pre-existing decline in graduate entry PCPs has resulted in the primary care sector experiences the brunt of this burden. In absence of a strong primary care sector, information between the various health specialties has become lost in silos leading to a fragmented healthcare model. However, surges within the pandemic have also resulted in innovations across digital health – increasing public and industrial confidence in various digital health technologies. This confidence has created a corresponding increase in mHealth service usage, allowing for the accessible distribution of healthcare. These services, however, are vulnerable to the same reductive silos that have impacted traditional health services, as mHealth providers tend to limit the scope of their applications to meet specific health needs. Through application of digital twin technology, mHealth can revolutionize diagnosis and treatment through the creation of a holistic health profile. Drawing from a patient's physical, mental, and financial information, this digital twin can act as an accurate representation of the participant within their impacting environment – providing pre-emptive warnings and recommendations that allow individuals to understand and take control of their personal wellbeing. Adaptive digital health technology is the way forward for addressing healthcare barriers and increasing health literacy amongst average consumers. This is essential for managing the healthcare workforce crisis post-COVID and is the logical next step for digital health.

References

1. Agarwal, S., Pabo, E., Rozenblum, R., Sherritt, K.: Professional dissonance and burnout in primary care. JAMA Int. Med. **180**(3), 395–401 (2020)
2. Ahn, A., Tewari, M., Poon, C., Phillips, R.: The clinical applications of a systems approach. PLoS Med. **3**(7), 956–960 (2006). https://doi.org/10.1371/journal.pmed.0030209
3. Ahn, A., Tewari, M., Poon, C., Phillips, R.: The limits of reductionism in medicine: could systems biology offer an alternative? PLoS Med. **3**(6), 709–713 (2006). https://doi.org/10.1371/journal.pmed.0030208
4. Allen, B.: Digital Twins and Living Models at NASA. NTRS (2021). https://ntrs.nasa.gov/citations/20210023699
5. Al-Naher, A., Wright, D., Devonald, M., Pirmohamed, M.: Renal function monitoring in heart failure – what is the optimal frequency? A narrative review. BJCP **84**(1), 5–17 (2017). https://doi.org/10.1111/bcp.13434
6. Amagai, S., Pila, S., Kaat, A., Nowinski, C., Gershon, R.: Challenges in participant engagement and retention using mobile health apps: literature review. JMIR **24**(4) (2022). https://doi.org/10.2196/35120
7. Babyl homepage. https://www.babyl.rw/
8. Babylon. Babylon launches AI in Rwanda in next step towards digitising healthcare in Rwanda. https://www.babylonhealth.com/press/babylon-launches-ai-in-rwanda
9. Bernstam, E., et al.: Quantitating and assessing interoperability between electronic health records. JAMIA **29**(5), 753–760 (2022)

10. Bestsennyy, O., Gilbert, G., Harris, A., Rost, J.: Telehealth: a quarter-trillion-dollar post-COVID-19 reality? McKinsey & Company (2021). https://www.mckinsey.com/industries/healthcare/our-insights/telehealth-a-quarter-trillion-dollar-post-covid-19-reality

11. Billman, G.: Homeostasis: the underappreciated and far too often ignored central organizing principle of physiology. Front. Physiol. **11** (2020). https://doi.org/10.3389/fphys.2020.00200

12. CDC. Laboratory-Confirmed COVID-19-Associated Hospitalizations. https://gis.cdc.gov/grasp/covidnet/covid19_5.html

13. Deloitte Access Economics.: General Practitioner Workforce Report 2022. Deloitte Access Economics, Melbourne (2022)

14. FDA. What is Digital Health. Accessed 09 Feb 2023

15. Ferguson, S.: Was Apollo 13 The First Digital Twin?

16. Grable, J.: Psychophysiological economics: introducing an emerging field of study. J. Financ. Serv. Prof. **67**(5), 16–18 (2013)

17. Grieves, M.: Physical Twins, Digital Twins, and the Apollo Myth. https://www.linkedin.com/pulse/physical-twins-digital-apollo-myth-michael-grieves/

18. Grieves, M.: Virtually intelligent product systems: digital and physical twins. In: Flumerfelt, S. Schwartz, K. Mavris, D. Briceno, S. (eds.) Complex Systems Engineering: Theory and Practice, American Institute of Aeronautics and Astronautics, vol. 256, pp. 175–200 (2019). https://doi.org/10.2514/5.9781624105654.0175.0200

19. Hancock, M., Bowles, B., Hanlon, R., Wiser, J.: Repurposing the quality adjusted life year: inferring and navigating wellness cliques from high sample rate multi-factor QALY. In: Schmorrow, D.D., Fidopiastis, C.M. (eds.) HCII 2021. LNCS (LNAI), vol. 12776, pp. 158–177. Springer, Cham (2021). https://doi.org/10.1007/978-3-030-78114-9_12

20. Hanlon, B., et al.: Feedback control for optimizing human wellness. In: Schmorrow, D.D., Fidopiastis, C.M. (eds.) HCII 2020. LNCS (LNAI), vol. 12197, pp. 171–190. Springer, Cham (2020). https://doi.org/10.1007/978-3-030-50439-7_12

21. Hassani, H., Huang, X., MacFeely, S.: Impactful digital twin in the healthcare revolution. MDPI **6**(3), 83–99 (2022). https://doi.org/10.3390/bdcc6030083

22. Honderich, T.: The Oxford Companion to Philosophy, 2nd edn. Oxford University Press, Oxford (2005)

23. Horvitz-Lennon, M., Kilbourne, A., Pincus, H.: From silos to bridges: meeting the general health care needs of adults with severe mental illnesses. Health Aff. **25**(3), 659–669 (2006)

24. IBM. What is a digital twin? https://www.ibm.com/au-en/topics/what-is-a-digital-twin

25. Kahneman, D.: Thinking Fast and Slow. Penguin Books, London (2011)

26. KaufmanHall.: Financial Effects of COVID-19: Hospital Outlook for the Remainder of 2021. American Hospital Association (2021). https://www.aha.org/guidesreports/2021-09-21-financial-effects-covid-19-hospital-outlook-remainder-2021

27. Khullar, D., Bond, A., Schpero, W.: COVID-19 and the financial health of US hospitals. JAMA **323**(21), 2127–2128 (2020). https://doi.org/10.1001/jama.2020.6269

28. Knight, V.: American Medical Students Less Likely To Choose To Become Primary Care Doctors. KHN (2019). https://khn.org/news/american-medical-students-less-likely-to-choose-to-become-primary-care-doctors/

29. Lehrer, P.: Anger, stress, dysregulation produces wear and tear on the lung. Thorax **61**, 833–834 (2006). https://doi.org/10.1136/thx.2006.057182

30. Lehrer, P., Eddie, D.: Dynamic processes in regulation and some implications for biofeedback and biobehavioral interventions. Appl. Psychophysiol. Biofeedback **38**(2), 143–155 (2013). https://doi.org/10.1007/s10484-013-9217-6

31. Lehrer, P., et al.: Heart rate variability biofeedback improves emotional and physical health and performance: a systematic review and meta analysis. Appl. Psychophysiol. Biofeedback **45**(3), 109–129 (2020). https://doi.org/10.1007/s10484-020-09466-z

32. Living Centerline. Mind, Body, Balance Sheet White Paper. https://www.livingcenterlinein stitute.com/post/2020/09/01/mind-body-balance-sheet-white-paper

33. Lucas, J., Villarroel, M.: Telemedicine use among adults: United States, 2021. In: NCHS Data Brief no. 445. National Center for Health Statistics, USA (2022). https://doi.org/10.15620/cdc:121435

34. Mitchell, R., Schuster, L., Jin, H.: Playing alone: can game design elements satisfy user needs in gamified mHealth services? Health Promot. Int. **37**(2) (2022). https://doi.org/10.1093/heapro/daab168

35. Pew. More Universal Use of Electronic Health Records is Improving Patient Care. https://www.pewtrusts.org/en/research-and-analysis/articles/2022/11/16/more-universal-use-of-electronic-health-records-is-improving-patient-care

36. Ricci-Cabello, I., et al.: Impact of viral epidemic outbreaks on mental health of healthcare workers: a rapid systematic review. medRxiv (2020). https://doi.org/10.1101/2020.04.02.20048892

37. Romeo, A., et al.: Can smartphone apps increase physical activity? Systematic review and meta-analysis. JMIR **21**(3) (2019). https://doi.org/10.2196/12053

38. Romero, M., Dickens, M., Cyr, N.: The reactive scope model - a new model integrating homeostasis, allostasis, and stress. Horm. Behav. **55**(3), 375–389 (2009). https://doi.org/10.1016/j.yhbeh.2008.12.009

39. Schwartz, S., Wildenhaus, K., Bucher, A., Byrd, B.: Digital twins and the emerging science of self: implications for digital health experience design and "small" data. Front. Comput. Sci. **2**(31), 1–16 (2020)

40. Seligman, M.: Flourish: Positive Psychology and Positive Interventions. Penguin Books, London (2011)

41. Seligman, M.: PERMA and the building blocks of well-being. J. Posit. Psychol. **13**(4), 333–335 (2018). https://doi.org/10.1080/17439760.2018.1437466

42. Shanafelt, T., et al.: Changes in burnout and satisfaction with work-life integration in physicians during the first 2 years of the COVID-19 pandemic. Mayo Clin. Proc. **97**(12), 2248–2258 (2022)

43. Sinsky, C., Shanafelt, T., Dyrbye, L., Sabety, A., Carlasare, L., West, C.: Health care expenditures attributable to primary care physician overall and burnout-related turnover: a cross-sectional analysis. Mayo Clin. Proc. **97**(4), 693–702 (2022)

44. Sperling, L.: Silos in healthcare are bad for us. Here's the cure. World Economic Forum (2020). https://www.weforum.org/agenda/2020/11/healthcare-silos-are-bad-for-us-heres-the-cure/

45. Starfield, B., Shi, L., Macinko, J.: Contribution of primary care to health systems and health. Milbank Q. **83**(3), 457–502 (2005). https://doi.org/10.1111/j.1468-0009.2005.00409.x

46. Sullivan, T.: Why EHR data interoperability is such a mess in 3 charts. Healthcare IT News (2018)

47. Vermeir, P., et al.: Communication in healthcare: a narrative review of the literature and practical recommendations. IJCP **69**(11), 1257–1267 (2015). https://doi.org/10.1111/ijcp.12686

48. WHO.: mHealth: Use of appropriate digital technologies for public health report. https://apps.who.int/gb/ebwha/pdf_files/WHA71/A71_20-en.pdf

49. Yuan, N., Dudley, R., Boscardin, J., Lin, G.: Electronic health records systems and hospital clinical performance: a study of nationwide hospital data. JAMIA **26**(10), 999–1009 (2019)

50. Zhang, M., et al.: Digital twin data: methods and key technologies [version 2]. Digital Twin (2022). https://doi.org/10.12688/digitaltwin.17467.2

Augmented Cognition Instructional Design for Studio-Based Learning

Branden Ogata[✉] and Michael-Brian Ogawa

Department of Information and Computer Sciences, University of Hawai'i at Mānoa,
1680 East-West Road, Honolulu, Hawaii 96822, USA
{bsogata,ogawam}@hawaii.edu

Abstract. Learning by Teaching is a pedagogical method in which students instruct others, gaining a deeper understanding of the material than they would from merely learning the content for themselves. Studio-Based Learning is a practice within Learning by Teaching that has pupils present their work to their peers and provide feedback on those artifacts shown. Although prior research has established that Studio-Based Learning produces many benefits for students, few studies have demonstrated consistent improvements in terms of student learning. This study examines how the modality of a course and the quality of participation in studio activities influence the effects of Studio-Based Learning on student academic outcomes, which inform best practices for future implementations of Studio-Based Learning. We also propose augmented cognition approaches for examining the efficacy of Studio-Based Learning.

Keywords: Learning by teaching · Studio-based learning · Peer review

1 Introduction

In traditional instructional models, students passively receive data that their teachers transfer to them; *learning by teaching* inverts this, assigning students a more active role in assisting their classmates [1]. More specifically, *studio-based learning* involves the iterative development of student solutions following the same processes that their instructors would in addressing a problem [2]. This process entails proposing a solution, critiquing that artifact in conjunction with peers, and using feedback to iteratively improve the work [3]. Many applications of studio-based learning in computer science education have focused on the *critique* phase of this process, having students present their individual work for review from peers [4,5].

Studio-based learning produces several benefits for students such as improved communication and collaboration skills [6–8] along with increased motivation and interest in the field [9,10]. Kumar, Silva, and Prelath also identified *mastery learning* [11] as another advantage of studio-based learning. While perceptions of self-efficacy decrease in both traditional and studio-based courses, that negative change is only significant for traditional instruction [12], perhaps because giving

© The Author(s), under exclusive license to Springer Nature Switzerland AG 2023
D. D. Schmorrow and C. M. Fidopiastis (Eds.): HCII 2023, LNAI 14019, pp. 250–268, 2023.
https://doi.org/10.1007/978-3-031-35017-7_17

and receiving feedback in the studio system enables students to better evaluate their progress through the course.

These improvements in soft skills are useful for retention in Computer Science programs [13]. However, studio-based learning has not resulted in consistent quantitative improvements in student achievement. Some studies of studio-based learning suggest that the technique produces superior performance on homework assignments and examinations relative to traditional lectures [14,15], and Collision et al. in particular found that students who participated in studio activities outperformed those in traditional labs in a long-term retention quiz eight weeks after treatment. In contrast, other studies [4,6,12] found no significant difference in student achievement between traditional and studio-based instruction.

Course modality - whether instruction is in person, online, or some hybrid of the two - may influence these student achievement outcomes. For example, Ho found that 85% of students preferred face-to-face discussions over online chat because in-person interactions afforded greater expressivity and immediacy [16]. Hundhausen et al. found that 82% of students in face-to-face studios believed that the process was beneficial compared to 31% of students in online studios, though the authors noted that implementation details may have limited the efficacy of their online studio sessions [6]. However, online studio-based learning can still produce student achievement comparable to traditional instruction [17], and after some initial technical struggles students in online studio-based courses express positive sentiments toward the course [18]. Later, Polo et al. showed that participants in online studios must utilize collaboration and critical thinking skills just as they would in an in-person studio [8]. Although students should therefore have opportunities to develop and practice those soft skills regardless of modality, the in-person or online implementations of studio sessions may affect the extent to which students learn those skills.

Quality of participation is another factor in the effectiveness of studio-based learning. Peer reviews directly provide students with suggestions on how to improve what they have done thus far, and such feedback can certainly help students [19]; indeed, pupils may perceive this to be the primary advantage of participating in peer reviews. However, participants in studio-based activities also benefit from providing feedback to others [20]. Indeed, Althauser and Darnall found that students who provided high-quality feedback during peer reviews earned better grades on their own revised work [21]. This capacity to achieve superior results through helping others aligns with the theoretical foundation of learning by teaching mentioned above.

This study specifically seeks to answer the following questions:

1. What impacts do the modality of a course (in-person, online, hybrid) and the quality of participation in peer review have on student achievement?
2. How do the subject matter of a project and the timing of the project in the semester impact student achievement on peer-reviewed projects?
3. How do the answers to the above question inform instructional design from the perspective of augmented cognition?

2   Methodology

ICS 101 is a course offered at the University of Hawai'i at Mānoa that covers fundamental computing concepts and productivity software usage. The course includes both in-person and online lectures to cover theory along with lab sessions for training in practical software skills. Over the past few years, ICS 101 has transitioned from a mostly in-person course to an online variant and is presently a hybrid course with a mixture of in-person and online lectures and lab sessions. This study examines the in-person Fall 2019 ($n = 184$), online Fall 2021 ($n = 194$), and hybrid Fall 2022 ($n = 243$) semesters.

The ICS 101 curriculum includes peer reviews on four key projects, covering Microsoft Word, Microsoft PowerPoint, Microsoft Excel, and Websites (using HTML and CSS). For the most part, the ICS 101 course schedule remained consistent across the three semesters examined in this study; in particular, the aforementioned units were covered in the same order and at roughly the same time during the semester, removing a potential confounding variable. In order to participate in these peer reviews, students must first complete a draft of the project. During peer review days, teaching assistants divide students into groups; participating students then provide feedback on the drafts of their group members. Each peer review session is scheduled to last for an hour and fifteen minutes, though teaching assistants may spend some of that time familiarizing students with peer review procedures and on course maintenance. At the end of each peer review session, participating students submit a document detailing the discussions within their groups. After completing the peer review, students further refine their projects before submitting their finalized artifacts; this *in-flow peer review* [22] aligns with recommendations to require that students improve and resubmit their work after receiving feedback [5, 6].

The in-person and hybrid peer reviews were performed within computer labs where students had access to hardware on which they could present their drafts to others. For the purposes of this study, "hybrid" refers to the instructional modality, not the peer review mechanisms. The online peer reviews were conducted on a conferencing tool that allowed students to remotely share their screens and communicate through audio, video, and text; users connected to this tool through their personal devices. Upon completing the peer review, students submitted a worksheet summarizing the discussions within their peer review groups.

ICS 101 teaching assistants assigned grades to both peer reviews and projects. Specifically, teaching assistants deducted points from peer reviews if the draft from the author of the review was incomplete or late, or if the feedback was incomplete, of inadequate quality, or missing entirely. This study examines the de-identified student grades on peer reviews and projects: all student identifiers were removed, and the names of the teaching assistants who graded student work were converted to a single letter.

The grading criteria for projects focus primarily on whether certain skills are utilized correctly and applied in a manner consistent with the purpose of the document. For analysis in this study, peer review scores are treated as full, partial, or no credit while project scores are converted to percentages. Although separately coding the different reasons for deductions on the peer review is feasible in and of itself, doing subsequent analyses on such coded data is not possible due to the limited number of cases where certain deductions were applied. For example, the data gathered for this study only includes one online peer review where the student submitted an incomplete draft and provided inadequate feedback to others in the peer review group. This data also includes students who did not submit peer reviews or their completed projects for the purpose of tracking students who do not participate in these activities; the analysis of results below will also consider a subset of this data where students who dd not participate in peer reviews or submit projects for a unit are omitted.

This study uses analysis of variance (ANOVA) to identify significant differences in project scores resulting from modality (in-person, online, hybrid), quality of participation in peer review activities (full, partial, none), and interactions between those two factors. The same analyses are then applied to the subset of data for each individual project. Because variance between teaching assistants who grade the peer reviews and projects may be a confounding variable, this paper also focuses on two pairs of teaching assistants who worked across multiple semesters; since we expect teaching assistants to remain consistent in their grading, changes in the grades that those teaching assistants give to their students may be attributed to the differences in modality.

3   Results

3.1   Overall Analyses

ANOVA (Table 1) shows significant main effects for both modality ($F(2, 2475) = 17.922$, $p < 0.001$, $\eta^2 = 0.010$) and quality of participation ($F(2, 2475) = 564.368$, $p < 0.001$, $\eta^2 = 0.310$). However, the interaction between these two factors is not significant.

Table 1. Project Scores for Course Modalities and Participation Qualities

Modality				
		In-Person	*Online*	*Hybrid*
Participation	*Full*	M = 0.787	M = 0.874	M = 0.833
		SD = 0.252	SD = 0.212	SD = 0.250
	Partial	M = 0.669	M = 0.758	M = 0.738
		SD = 0.325	SD = 0.263	SD = 0.300
	None	M = 0.266	M = 0.377	M = 0.390
		SD = 0.350	SD = 0.416	SD = 0.415

A Scheffé post hoc test indicates that statistically significant differences exist between the *In-Person* and *Online* modalities along with the *In-Person* and *Hybrid* modalities; the *Online* and *Hybrid* modalities do not differ significantly.

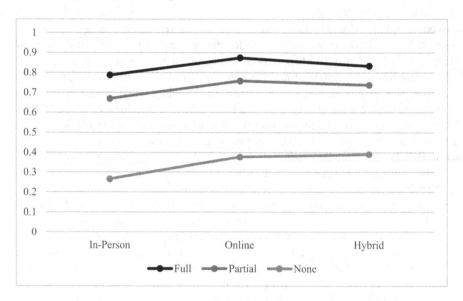

Fig. 1. Project Scores for Course Modalities and Participation Qualities

The scores for the *In-Person* semester were thus significantly lower than those in the *Online* and *Hybrid* semesters (Fig. 1).

Another Scheffé post hoc test found significant differences between all three levels for quality of participation in peer review. Students who participated adequately in their peer review activities tended to have higher project scores than those whose participation in peer reviews was insufficient, and in turn even marginal participation in peer reviews resulted in better performance than those who were not present for peer review at all.

While the overall interaction between modality and quality of participation in peer review did not significantly impact project scores, a Scheffé post hoc test also found some significant differences between individual combinations of the factors shown in Table 1. In particular, while *Full* and *Partial* participation in peer review are significantly different as noted above, *In-Person Full* and *In-Person Partial* are not, though the mean project score for *In-Person Full* (0.787) is still larger than the mean project score for *In-Person Partial* (0.669). None of the *Partial* participation cases differ significantly from each other across modalities. *In-Person Full* (0.787) is significantly lower than *Online Full* (0.874), while *In-Person None* (0.266) is significantly lower than *Hybrid None* (0.390).

The results when omitting those students who did not participate in peer review or submit projects for a particular unit are mostly similar to those in the full data set (Table 2). However, while *Full* participation quality remains significantly different from *Partial* participation quality, the difference between *Partial* and *None* is no longer significant with this reduced data set. In fact, while the difference between *Hybrid Full* (0.833) and *Hybrid Partial* (0.738) remains significant, there is no significant difference between the *Hybrid Full* (0.833) and

Hybrid None (0.758) cases according to a Scheffé post hoc test: the mean for *Hybrid None* is higher than that for *Hybrid Partial* (Fig. 2).

Table 2. Project Scores for Course Modalities and Participation Qualities - Omitting Non-Participating Students

Modality				
		In-Person	*Online*	*Hybrid*
Participation	*Full*	M = 0.787	M = 0.874	M = 0.833
		SD = 0.252	SD = 0.212	SD = 0.250
	Partial	M = 0.669	M = 0.758	M = 0.738
		SD = 0.325	SD = 0.263	SD = 0.300
	None	M = 0.598	M = 0.747	M = 0.758
		SD = 0.278	SD = 0.257	SD = 0.236

3.2 Analyses of Individual Projects

The results of ANOVA on individual projects are generally similar to those for the overall data. However, some meaningful differences did exist. Specifically, modality was not a significant factor on the Word project, though quality of participation remained significant (F(2, 612) = 2.554, $p < 0.001$, $\eta^2 = 0.253$) as indicated in Table 3.

Table 3. Word Project Scores for Course Modalities and Participation Qualities

Modality				
		In-Person	*Online*	*Hybrid*
Participation	*Full*	M = 0.756	M = 0.842	M = 0.802
		SD = 0.254	SD = 0.245	SD = 0.266
	Partial	M = 0.631	M = 0.646	M = 0.698
		SD = 0.343	SD = 0.347	SD = 0.336
	None	M = 0.275	M = 0.406	M = 0.358
		SD = 0.341	SD = 0.401	SD = 0.402

The Website project also deviated from the overall analysis results. While ANOVA still found significant differences in modality (F(2, 612) = 4.194, $p = 0.016$, $\eta^2 = 0.008$) and the final project scores for the in-person condition were still lower than the online and hybrid modalities (Table 4), only the difference between in-person and hybrid cases was significant according to a Scheffé post

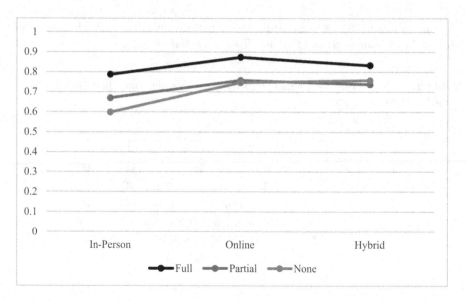

Fig. 2. Project Scores for Course Modalities and Participation Qualities - Omitting Non-Participating Students

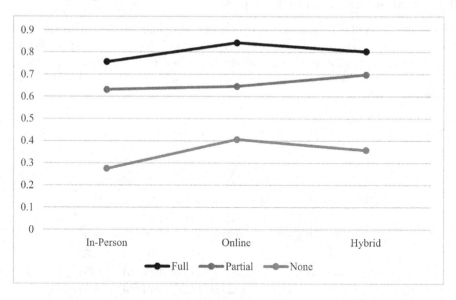

Fig. 3. Word Project Scores for Course Modalities and Participation Qualities

hoc test whereas the in-person modality differed significantly from both the online and hybrid modalities in the complete data set. Furthermore, the overall results showed significant differences between all participation quality levels; the Website project also identified participation as a significant factor (F(2, 612)

$= 38.032$, $p < 0.001$, $\eta^2 = 0.370$), but a subsequent Scheffé post hoc test only found significant differences between the *Full* and *None* levels and the *Partial* and *None* levels (Fig. 3).

Table 4. Website Project Scores for Course Modalities and Participation Qualities

Modality		In-Person	Online	Hybrid
Participation	*Full*	M = 0.809	M = 0.868	M = 0.879
		SD = 0.286	SD = 0.255	SD = 0.255
	Partial	M = 0.761	M = 0.817	M = 0.840
		SD = 0.288	SD = 0.263	SD = 0.268
	None	M = 0.229	M = 0.336	M = 0.379
		SD = 0.358	SD = 0.435	SD = 0.441

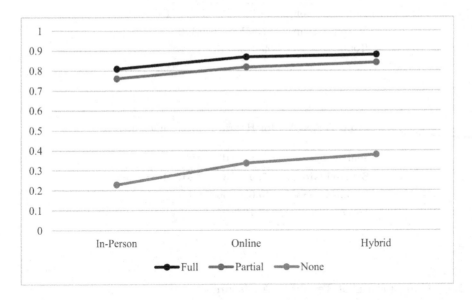

Fig. 4. Website Project Scores for Course Modalities and Participation Qualities

Performing ANOVA on the results separated by modality only found significant differences for the PowerPoint project. PowerPoint project scores were significantly higher than those for all other projects in the *In-Person* (F(3, 732) = 8.390, $p < 0.001$, $\eta^2 = 0.033$) and *Online* (F(3, 772) = 6.985, $p < 0.001$,

$\eta^2 = 0.026$) semesters (Tables 5 and 6). For the *Hybrid* semester (Table 7), PowerPoint project scores were significantly higher than those for the Word and Excel projects, but not the Website project ($F(3, 968) = 4.282$, $p = 0.005$, $\eta^2 = 0.013$) (Fig. 4).

Table 5. ANOVA for In-Person Project Differences

Source	SS	df	MS	
Between Groups	3.314	3	1.105	F = 8.390
Within Groups	96.368	732	0.132	
Total	99.682	735		

Table 6. ANOVA for Online Project Differences

Source	SS	df	MS	
Between Groups	2.642	3	0.881	F = 6.985
Within Groups	97.331	772	0.126	
Total	99.973	775		

Table 7. ANOVA for Hybrid Project Differences

Source	SS	df	MS	
Between Groups	1.535	3	0.512	F = 4.282
Within Groups	115.632	968	0.119	
Total	117.167	971		

3.3   Comparison of Teaching Assistants

The above results appear to indicate that in-person teaching led to inferior performance on projects. However, because the teaching assistants for the course were different for each modality, it is possible that these teaching assistants were the actual cause of these differences in performance even though they all graded according to the same rubric. Another ANOVA (Table 8) found a significant difference between how teaching assistants graded projects ($F(15, 2468) = 6.290$, $p < 0.001$, $\eta^2 = 0.037$), with a Scheffé post hoc test finding that most

Table 8. ANOVA for Comparing Teaching Assistant Project Grading

Source	SS	df	MS	
Between Groups	11.813	15	0.899	F = 6.290
Within Groups	309.002	2468	0.125203	
Total	320.814	2483		

of these differences involved teaching assistant L, with another significant difference between teaching assistants J and K. The average grades from teaching assistant L were the lowest of all the teaching assistants examined in this study, with teaching assistant J giving out the second-lowest grades.

A two-factor ANOVA examining modalities and teaching assistants is not possible because the teaching assistants working with ICS 101 changed during the three semesters under examination. However, it is possible to examine two teaching assistants who worked during both the in-person and online semesters. When examining the project scores for the teaching assistants labeled G and L (Table 9): the teaching assistant was a significant factor ($F(1, 416) = 3.894$, $p = 0.049$, $\eta^2 = 0.009$) while modality was not. A similar ANOVA comparing two teaching assistants across the online and hybrid semesters (Table 10) did not find significant main effects for modalities or teaching assistants; however, there was a significant interaction between those two factors ($F(1, 416) = 3.894$, $p = 0.049$, $\eta^2 = 0.009$), specifically when considering the decrease in project scores that teaching assistant I gave from the online semester (0.802) to the hybrid semester (0.682) (Figs. 5 and 6).

Table 9. Course Modality (In-Person, Online) and Teaching Assistant Impacts on Project Grades

Modality			In-Person	Online
Teaching Assistant	G		M = 0.643	M = 0.632
			SD = 0.375	SD = 0.413
	L		M = 0.549	M = 0.579
			SD = 0.370	SD = 0.368

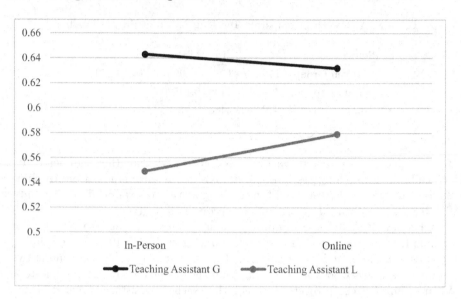

Fig. 5. Course Modality (In-Person, Online) and Teaching Assistant Impacts on Project Grades

Table 10. Course Modality (Online, Hybrid) and Teaching Assistant Impacts on Project Grades

Modality			
		Online	Hybrid
Teaching Assistant	A	M = 0.745	M = 0.758
		SD = 0.362	SD = 0.334
	I	M = 0.802	M = 0.682
		SD = 0.236	SD = 0.348

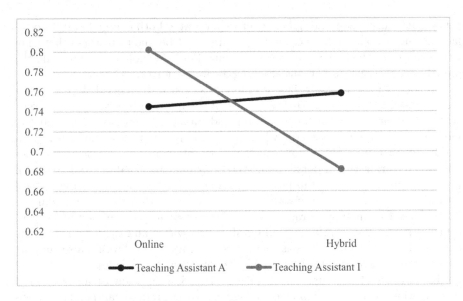

Fig. 6. Course Modality (Online, Hybrid) and Teaching Assistant Impacts on Project Grades

4 Discussion

4.1 Research Question 1: What Impacts do the Modality of a Course (In-Person, Online, Hybrid) and the Quality of Participation in Peer Review Have on Student Achievement?

The overall results from the ANOVA seem to associate in-person peer reviews with inferior project scores. The average student in the *In-Person Full* category received higher project scores than those in the *In-Person Partial* and *In-Person None* groups. However, the difference between *In-Person Full* and *In-Person Partial* was not significant.

Although the difference between *In-Person Full* and *Online Full* is significant, the difference between *In-Person Full* and *Hybrid Full* is not significant. This suggests that adequate participation in online peer reviews tends to result on achievement levels superior to those from adequate participation in in-person peer reviews while satisfactory participation on in-person and hybrid peer reviews leads to comparable performances on projects.

No significant difference exists between the *In-Person Partial*, *Online Partial*, and *Hybrid Partial* outcomes. This indicates that students who participate but do not adequately contribute in peer reviews perform similarly on projects regardless of modality.

At the same time, the average *In-Person None* score is significantly lower than that of the *Hybrid None* group, indicating that the negative impact of not participating in peer reviews is greater for in-person courses than it is for hybrid courses. The in-person and hybrid peer reviews were both conducted in face-to-face settings, so any differences in the results must be due to factors other than the location in which the peer reviews occur. Possible explanations include the modality of instruction and the teaching assistants for the students.

As noted in Sect. 3.2, significant differences exist in the checklist grades that teaching assistants gave to their students. A comparison of two teaching assistants who worked across the in-person and online semesters did not identify modality as a significant factor while the teaching assistants did differ significantly. Furthermore, the three teaching assistants who gave the lowest grades all worked during the in-person semester. This indicates that the differences in project scores between the in-person semester and other modalities might have been due to the teaching assistants for those terms rather than the modalities themselves. To remove the grading of teaching assistants as a confounding factor, a future study may involve regrading all peer reviews and projects across the three semesters examined to ensure consistent grading. This would also support a deeper analysis of the feedback that students gave and received.

The quality of participation in peer reviews is significant at all levels: full participation resulted in significantly higher project grades than partial participation, and in turn partial participation produced higher project grades than no participation. An exception to this becomes apparent when examining interactions between modality and participation quality: the project scores for full and partial participation were not significantly different for the in-person semester. This suggests that the disadvantages of substandard participation in peer reviews are less meaningful for primarily in-person instruction.

No significant differences exist between partial and no participation after filtering out students who received grades of 0 for both the peer review and project for a given unit. This indicates that poor participation in peer review is no better than not participating at all in terms of student achievement. In fact, students who did not participate in peer reviews during the hybrid semester outperformed those whose participation in peer reviews was inadequate.

4.2   Research Question 2: How do the Subject Matter of a Project and the Timing of the Project in the Semester Impact Student Achievement on Peer-Reviewed Projects?

Results of the overall analysis indicate that in-person peer-reviewed checklists had significantly lower grades than the scores for online and hybrid peer-reviewed checklists. In addition, all levels of participation differed significantly from each other. This serves as a baseline for the examination of individual projects.

Course modality was not significant for the Word project. A possible explanation for this involves the timing of the project: because the Word project is the first major project of the semester and is the first unit with a peer review, students are likely to be equally unfamiliar with the expectations for projects regardless of modality. In addition to the direct impact this has on checklist scores, the novelty of the peer review process would also affect the quality of peer feedback. To address this, it may be worthwhile for instructors to have their students practice performing peer reviews at least once before assigning a peer review on a major project.

Although the overall data set contained significant differences between the in-person and hybrid semesters along with the in-person and online semesters, the only significant difference in modality for the Website project is between the in-person and hybrid semesters. Specifically, the Website project scores were significantly higher in the hybrid condition than in the in-person case. The Website project also differed from the overall results in that there was no significant difference between full and partial participation in the peer review.

These results for the Website project suggest that substandard participation in peer review activities does not have a significant negative impact on students for the Website project, especially with hybrid instruction. This may have been due to the specifications for this project: students were required to upload their website files to a University-managed server to receive full credit for the peer review activity. Some students may have had a website draft that met or nearly met all requirements for the final project but received partial credit for the peer review because their websites were not available online at the time of the peer review. These students fit into the *Partial* level of participation but likely received higher scores on the project itself, which would explain the lack of a significant difference between *Full* and *Partial* participation for this project. A confounding variable in this analysis is that the time available for students to complete the Website project varied across the semesters under observation: students in the in-person semester had just over a day after their Website peer reviews to complete their projects whereas there was over a week between the Website peer reviews and deadlines for the Website projects in the online and hybrid variants of the course. Furthermore, the in-person semester ended with a final examination that students may have prioritized over the Website project; the online and hybrid semesters had no such examinations and so the Website project was the last major assessment of those semesters. Teaching assistants may have also graded more leniently during the hybrid semester.

The general trends for project scores (Fig. 7) are similar for all three modalities: the average scores increase from Word to PowerPoint, decrease for Excel, and increase slightly for the Website project. However, the only significant difference between projects is for the PowerPoint project; during the in-person and online semesters the PowerPoint project scores differed significantly from all other project scores, while in the hybrid semester the PowerPoint project scores differed significantly from the Word and Excel project scores but not the Website project score. One interpretation of this is that the difficulty of the PowerPoint project is lower than the other projects for this course. Alternatively, the grades that students received on the Word peer review project may have motivated greater exertions on the corresponding work for the subsequent PowerPoint unit.

Figures 8, 9, and 10 show general trends in full, partial, and no peer review participation for the three modalities involved in this study. Non-participation tended to increase throughout the online semester. In contrast, during the in-

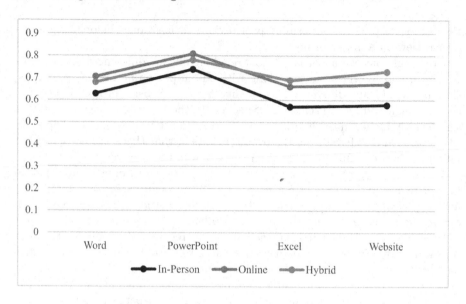

Fig. 7. Average Project Scores

person and hybrid semesters, non-participation decreased from the Word peer reviews to the PowerPoint peer reviews before increasing for subsequent peer reviews. This might suggest that students began to skip online peer reviews sooner than in other modalities, though confirming that assertion would require examining attendance records for the online courses to determine whether such students were absent during all lab sessions or just peer reviews.

This decreased rate of attendance did not have a discernible impact on project scores. For example, of the three semesters in this study, the online semester had the lowest percentage of students who received full credit and the highest percentage of students who received no credit on the peer review for the PowerPoint project. However, the online PowerPoint project scores were higher than those for the in-person and hybrid modalities.

4.3   Research Question 3: How do the Answers to the Above Questions Inform Instructional Design from the Perspective of Augmented Cognition?

Although the results of this study seem to suggest that the scores of in-person peer reviewed projects were inferior to those in other modalities, it is improbable that in-person peer reviews themselves lead to lower project grades since the peer reviews in the in-person and hybrid semesters were both face-to-face and the hybrid project scores were comparable to online project scores. The different teaching assistants involved in grading across these three semesters would also likely distort the results presented in this paper. Regrading the peer review materials and projects that students submitted across the three semesters would

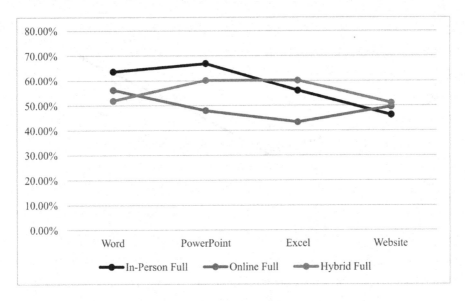

Fig. 8. Peer Review Participation Quality - Full

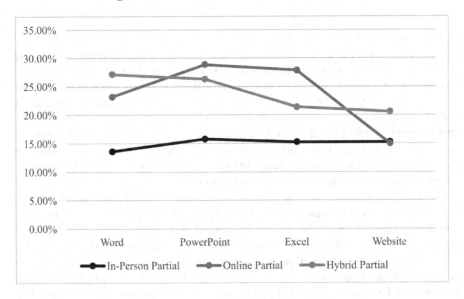

Fig. 9. Peer Review Participation Quality - Partial

remove the potential confounding factor that these multiple graders might have introduced.

The peer reviews that this study examined had students record the feedback mentioned within their groups; these recordings may not accurately reflect the discussions that took place, so the quality of feedback in the actual peer review

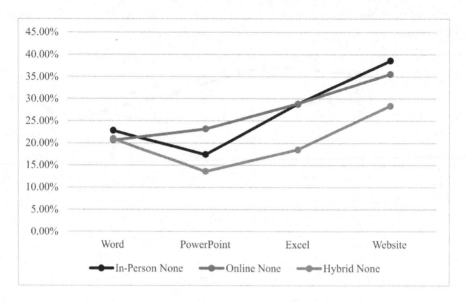

Fig. 10. Peer Review Participation Quality - None

may not match what is evident in the documents that students submitted. To address this concern, a future study might record what students say during peer review instead of depending upon participants to write or type what they discuss. Other studies have examined student discourse in studios [23] and peer tutoring [24], with Roscoe and Chi linking *knowledge-building* and *metacognitive* statements to positive learning outcomes. A closer examination of the feedback that students provide and receive in peer reviews might reveal differences in communication across in-person and online peer review settings. Such an analysis may also better identify connections between the quality of feedback in studio-based learning activities and student achievement.

In addition to peer review feedback, analyses of cognition-based metrics such as timing mechanisms could further support developments in instructional design. Many tools such as web-based shared documents can track feedback progress, measuring the time spent on certain tasks. Therefore, a deeper analysis of time spent converting feedback into actionable behaviors could yield suggestions for optimal implementations of studio-based learning. A feedback response section could be incorporated into live peer review sessions to assess student cognition pertaining to the modification of their artifacts under review based on feedback from group members. Identifying how this time-based component affects student performance will highlight the benefits of studio-based learning, help to optimize the design of studio-based instruction, and better support students in meeting learning objectives. Overall, many possibilities exist for aligning augmented cognition perspectives with instructional design considerations for studio-based learning approaches.

References

1. Duran, D.: Learning-by-teaching. Evidence and implications as a pedagogical mechanism. Innov. Educ. Teach. Int. **54**(5), 476–484 (2017). https://doi.org/10.1080/14703297.2016.1156011
2. Brandt, C.B., Cennamo, K., Douglas, S., Vernon, M., McGrath, M., Reimer, Y.: A theoretical framework for the studio as a learning environment. Int. J. Technol. Des. Educ. **23**(2), 329–348 (2013). https://doi.org/10.1007/s10798-011-9181-5
3. Brocato, K.: Studio based learning: proposing, critiquing, iterating our way to person-centeredness for better classroom management. Theory Pract. **48**(2), 138–146 (2009). https://doi.org/10.1080/00405840902776459
4. Hundhausen, C.D., Narayanan, N.H., Crosby, M.E.: Exploring studio-based instructional models for computing education. In: Proceedings of the 39th SIGCSE Technical Symposium on Computer Science Education, pp. 392–396 (SIGCSE 2008), Association for Computing Machinery, New York, NY, USA (2008). https://doi.org/10.1145/1352135.1352271
5. Simon, B., Hundhausen, C., McDowell, C., Werner, L., Hu, H., Kussmaul, C.: Students as teachers and communicators. In: Fincher, S., Robins, A. (eds.) The Cambridge Handbook of Computing Education Research, pp. 827–858. Cambridge University Press, Cambridge (2019)
6. Hundhausen, C.D., Agrawal, A., Agarwal, P.: Talking about code: integrating pedagogical code reviews into early computing courses. ACM Trans. Comput. Educ. **13**(3), 1–28 (2013). https://doi.org/10.1145/2499947.2499951
7. Kumar, J.A., Silva, P.A., Prelath, R.: Implementing studio-based learning for design education: a study on the perception and challenges of Malaysian undergraduates. Int. J. Technol. Des. Educ. **31**(3), 611–631 (2020). https://doi.org/10.1007/s10798-020-09566-1
8. Polo, B.J., Silva, P.A., Crosby, M.E.: Applying studio-based learning methodology in computer science education to improve 21st century skills. In: Zaphiris, P., Ioannou, A. (eds.) LCT 2018. LNCS, vol. 10925, pp. 361–375. Springer, Cham (2018). https://doi.org/10.1007/978-3-319-91152-6_28
9. Myneni, L., Ross, M., Hendrix, D., Narayanan, N.H.: Studio-based learning in CS2: an experience report. In: Proceedings of the 46th Annual Southeast Regional Conference, pp. 253–255. ACM-SE 46, Association for Computing Machinery, New York, NY, USA (2008). https://doi.org/10.1145/1593105.1593171
10. Reardon, S., Tangney, B.: Smartphones, studio-based learning, and scaffolding: helping novices learn to program. ACM Trans. Comput. Educ. **14**(4), 1–15 (2014). https://doi.org/10.1145/2677089
11. Yeager, D.S., Dweck, C.S.: Mindsets that promote resilience: when students believe that personal characteristics can be developed. Educ. Psychol. **47**(4), 302–314 (2012). https://doi.org/10.1080/00461520.2012.722805
12. Hundhausen, C., Agrawal, A., Fairbrother, D., Trevisan, M.: Does studio-based instruction work in CS 1? An empirical comparison with a traditional approach. In: Proceedings of the 41st ACM Technical Symposium on Computer Science Education, pp. 500–504 (SIGCSE 2010), Association for Computing Machinery, New York, NY, USA (2010). https://doi.org/10.1145/1734263.1734432
13. Lewis, T.L., Smith, W.J., Bélanger, F., Harrington, K.V.: Are technical and soft skills required? The use of structural equation modeling to examine factors leading to retention in the CS major. In: Proceedings of the Fourth International Workshop on Computing Education Research, pp. 91–100 (ICER 2008), ACM, New York, NY, USA (2008). https://doi.org/10.1145/1404520.1404530

14. Collison, C.G., Cody, J., Stanford, C.: An s_N1-s_N2 lesson in an organic chemistry lab using a studio-based approach. J. Chem. Educ. **89**(6), 750–754 (2012). https://doi.org/10.1021/ed101035d

15. Hendrix, D., Myneni, L., Narayanan, H., Ross, M.: Implementing studio-based learning in CS2. In: Proceedings of the 41st ACM Technical Symposium on Computer Science Education, pp. 505–509 (SIGCSE 2010), Association for Computing Machinery, New York, NY, USA (2010). https://doi.org/10.1145/1734263.1734433

16. Ho, M.C.: The effects of face-to-face and computer-mediated peer review on EFL writers' comments and revisions. Australas. J. Educ. Technol. **31**(1) (2015). https://doi.org/10.14742/ajet.495

17. Polo, B.J.: SBL-online: implementing studio-based learning techniques in an online introductory programming course to address common programming errors and misconceptions. Ph.D. thesis, University of Hawai'i at Mānoa (2013)

18. Koutsabasis, P., Vosinakis, S.: Rethinking HCI education for design: problem-based learning and virtual worlds at an HCI design studio. Int. J. Hum.-Comput. Interact. **28**(8), 485–499 (2012). https://doi.org/10.1080/10447318.2012.687664

19. Hattie, J., Timperley, H.: The power of feedback. Rev. Educ. Res. **77**(1), 81–112 (2007). https://doi.org/10.3102/003465430298487

20. Nicol, D., Thomson, A., Breslin, C.: Rethinking feedback practices in higher education: a peer review perspective. Assess. Eval. High. Educ. **39**(1), 102–122 (2014)

21. Althauser, R., Darnall, K.: Enhancing critical reading and writing through peer reviews: an exploration of assisted performance. Teach. Sociol. **29**(1), 23–35 (2001). https://www.jstor.org/stable/1318780

22. Clarke, D., et al.: In-flow peer review. In: Proceedings of the Working Group Reports of the 2014 on Innovation and Technology in Computer Science Education Conference, pp. 59–79 (ITiCSE-WGR 2014), Association for Computing Machinery, New York, NY, USA (2014). https://doi.org/10.1145/2713609.2713612

23. Fleming, D.: Design talk: constructing the object in studio conversations. Des. Issues **14**(2), 41 (1998). https://doi.org/10.2307/1511850

24. Roscoe, R.D., Chi, M.T.H.: Tutor learning: the role of explaining and responding to questions. Instr. Sci. **36**(4), 321–350 (2008). https://doi.org/10.1007/s11251-007-9034-5

Individual Deep Fake Recognition Skills are Affected by Viewer's Political Orientation, Agreement with Content and Device Used

Stefan Sütterlin[1,2,3(✉)] 🄳, Torvald F. Ask[3,4] 🄳, Sophia Mägerle[1], Sandra Glöckler[1], Leandra Wolf[1], Julian Schray[1], Alava Chandi[1], Teodora Bursac[1], Ali Khodabakhsh[4] 🄳, Benjamin J. Knox[4,5] 🄳, Matthew Canham[6], and Ricardo G. Lugo[3,4] 🄳

[1] Faculty of Computer Science, Albstadt-Sigmaringen University, Sigmaringen, Germany
stefan.suetterlin@hs-albsig.de
[2] Centre for Digital Forensics and Cyber Security, Tallin University of Technology, Tallinn, Estonia
[3] Faculty for Health, Welfare and Organization, Østfold University College, Halden, Norway
[4] Department of Information Security and Communication Technology, Norwegian University of Science and Technology, Gjøvik, Norway
[5] Norwegian Armed Forces Cyber Defense, Lillehammer, Norway
[6] Beyond Layer Seven, LLC, Oviedo, USA

Abstract. AI-generated "deep fakes" is increasingly used by cybercriminals conducting targeted and tailored social engineering attacks, and for influencing public opinion. To raise awareness and efficiently train individuals in recognizing deep fakes, understanding individual differences in the ability to recognize them is central. Previous research suggested a close relationship between political attitudes and top-down perceptual and cognitive processing styles. In this study, we investigate the impact of political attitudes and agreement with the political message content on individual deep fake recognition skills. 163 adults (72 females = 44.2%) judged a series of video clips with politicians' statements across the political spectrum regarding their authenticity and their agreement with the message content. Half of the presented videos were fabricated via lip-sync technology. In addition to agreement with each statement made, global political attitudes towards social and economic topics were assessed via the Social and Economic Conservatism Scale (SECS). There were robust negative associations between participants' general and social conservatism and their ability to recognize fabricated videos, especially when where there was agreement with the message content. Deep fakes watched on mobile phones and tablets were considerably less likely to be recognized compared to when watched on stationary computers. This is the first study to investigate and establish the association between political attitudes and interindividual differences in deep fake recognition. The study supports recently published research suggesting relationships between conservatism and perceived credibility of conspiracy theories and fake news in general. Implications for further research are discussed.

Keywords: Deep fake recognition · political orientation · social engineering

D. D. Schmorrow and C. M. Fidopiastis (Eds.): HCII 2023, LNAI 14019, pp. 269–284, 2023.
https://doi.org/10.1007/978-3-031-35017-7_18

1   Introduction

In the age of increasing cyber security threats, the technological arm's race between threat actors and cybersecurity specialists spiral into material battles, where ever more sophisticated zero-day exploits are required to overcome constantly developing network defence, and vice versa. The risks attached to purchases of attractive zero-day or half-day exploits on the gray or black market, the necessity of trust, and the need for trusted double-blind auction opportunities are in principle not very different from their physical equivalents. Particularly for Advanced Persistent Threats (APT) to successfully target high-profile actors, the technological efforts that are required, the necessary expertise and/or funding required to circumvent or compromise cyber security infrastructure are not affordable for or available to many of those intending to launch a cyber attack (Meakins, 2019). As a result, the exploitation of the human factor becomes more relevant (Wang, Sun & Zhu, 2020). The term social engineering has been described as "any act that influences a person to take an action that may or may not be in their best interest" ([www.social-engineer.com]; Hadnagy, 2018; Mouton et al., 2014). Social engineering relies on stable human traits such as for example trust, agreeableness, and conscientiousness (Uebelacker & Quiel, 2014). The methods used to take advantage of these evolutionary rooted weaknesses (exploits) are well known tactics of persuasion (Cialdini, 1993). Persuasion tactics are particularly successful where they meet unprepared, unaware, and inexperienced individuals who do not consider themselves relevant targets, do not recognize the attack situation, and do not apply any defence strategies. Social engineering-enabled cyberattacks are estimated to account for up to 98% of all cyberattacks in 2020 (Purplesec, 2021), with absolute numbers continuously rising (IBM Security, 2020; Verizon, 2021). While social engineering attacks remain rather unchanged in regard to the human characteristics and weaknesses they target, and the persuasion techniques or cognitive vulnerabilities they exploit, their modus operandi develops parallel to technological developments and societal trends. In more recent years, social engineering attacks benefited increasingly from technological advancement. Automatized or semi-automatized open-source personality assessment allows for resource-efficient individual profiling of susceptibilities (Azucar et al., 2018; Golbeck et al., 2011; Kosinski et al., 2013), providing the ground for tailored mass-spear phishing campaigns.

Deep Fakes have the potential to become a disruptive technology changing the way we think about security aspects of virtual human-human interaction. The associated cost of DF scams was estimated to exceed 250 million USD in 2020 (iProov, 2020). The Global Trends Unit of the European Parliament associated the rise of DF with increased risks of being impersonated as an individual resulting in increased online abuse, and on a societal level contributing to political disinformation and fostering social unrest (European Parliament, 2018). AI-generated DF are becoming increasingly sophisticated and are in some cases hardly distinguishable for human eyes from authentic products (Korshunov & Marcel, 2020; Rossler et al., 2019). While the market for software tools producing DF of acceptable quality keeps developing (Lyu, 2020), it provides individuals and cybercriminal gangs, as well as state actors with a constant supply to improve their arsenals. Human targets exposed to DF attacks are rendered relatively unaware, with most common cybersecurity awareness campaigns not yet preparing their customers for this attack vector. By applying DF, classic social engineering attack vectors exploiting human trust tendencies and other vulnerabilities are empowered by new technological means. The logic of social engineering, however, remains unchanged: the circumvention of technological safeguards by application of psychological means. Once a sufficient credibility of DF generation has been achieved, only little IT knowledge will be required to implement it for a specific purpose, such as impersonating a superior in a spear-phishing context. In this asymmetric context, forensic detection tools, cyber security experts with knowledge about DF risks, and comparable means of detection or mitigation are not in place due to where and how the attack can be camouflaged as unsuspicious conversation.

To date, many adversaries such as individual cybercriminals may not yet have the necessary resources, competencies or the required raw material featuring the target to produce perfect impersonifications. Available low-tech fakes bear, depending on their sophistication, familiarity with the impersonated individual, the situational context and the target person's personal vulnerabilities, an inter-individually varying risk of being detected as inauthentic. While there is a constantly progressing field of authentication tools and strategies available (e.g. Hu et al., 2021; Rossler et al., 2019), cybersecurity awareness and resilience training needs to take the individual risk factors into account in order to develop adaptive training scenarios to improve the vigilance, judgment and evaluation performance when encountering synthetic media. This training should be developed, implemented, and validated with the same care as is currently the case in phishing simulation campaigns. One precondition for efficient and effective training or awareness interventions is an understanding of the underlying human factors contributing to successful or unsuccessful differentiation between imperfect faked and authentic information. Both short-term cognitive factors such as stress, workload, and vigilance, and long-term cognitive factors related to personality and individual differences (e.g., gender, age, political orientation), expertise, and culture may affect situation awareness during a social engineering attack. This occurs by influencing the interaction between perception, working memory, decision-making, and action (Montañez et al., 2020). While recognition and judgment of faked audiovisual material without technological assistance is the major step every countermeasure against social engineering attack needs to take, there is very little knowledge about the individual differences that affect deep fake recognition. Previous social engineering attack frameworks (e.g., Uebelacker & Quiel, 2014) have for the most part not considered the differing cognitive requirements and cognitive-emotional processes involved in human DF recognition, and it is only recently that these influences have started to be addressed (Montañez et al., 2020).

DF can be classified into five types: (1) face-swap/identity-swap, (2) face-reenactment/puppet-mastery, (3) lip-syncing, (4) facial attribute manipulation, and (5) entire face synthesis (Masood et al., 2021) which can be separated into two main categories of facial manipulation methods (Zollhöfer et al., 2018): 1) facial expression manipulation and 2) facial identity manipulation. Glitches and minor errors in imperfect deep fakes such as asynchronous lip movements can reveal the inauthenticity. Eye-tracking studies revealed the interplay between attentional focus and imperfections of DF, resulting in an eye-tracking database provided by Gupta and colleagues (2020). The cognitive processes involved make DF recognition a perceptual task benefitting from experience and knowledge (top-down), but also determined by attentional control and shifts (bottom-up). It is therefore to be expected that marked and robust inter-individual differences in DF recognition performance exist.

To raise awareness and train individuals in recognizing the most widespread DF, the understanding of what may cause individual differences in the ability to recognize them is key for the development of educational content and methods suitable to enhance robust DF related cybersecurity awareness. While there is currently a lack of research on individual predictors of DF recognition performance, considerable knowledge exists regarding the relationships between visual perception and visual judgment, cognitive styles, and political orientation. Research on visual perception suggests powerful top-down influences on very early visual processing (Fig. 1). Findings on ambiguous pictures and binocular rivalry suggest that even very early attentional processes, such as precon-scious attentional resource allocation, is affected by higher-level cognitive evaluations of associated sets of stimuli. This suggests both bottom-up and knowledge-driven top-down processes from early attentional resource allocation to interpretation and evaluation of perceived patterns (e.g., Balcetis et al., 2012; Tong et al., 1998; Van Koningsbruggen et al., 2011). Even very openly laid out physical properties of the immediate physical environment one interacts with, such as distances or slopes, have been mentioned to be perceived differently depending on how much a person tries to avoid certain cognitions (Balcetis & Dunning, 2007). Regarding the later processes of higher cognitive judg-ments of perceived messages and the corresponding judgment regarding their authen-ticity, recent research suggests a causal relationship between trait-like conservatism and belief in untrue political statements (Garrett & Bond, 2021).

Our study aims to combine and apply the well-established work on early cognitive influences on visual perception, with more recent work on higher cognitive functioning and authenticity judgment, in the context of moderately difficult authentic or inauthentic video clips with political content. We investigated technically unaided human fake detec-tion performance featuring politicians making political statements, where a part of the presented videos has been faked via lip synchronization (facial expression manipulation).

To the best of our knowledge, this is the first study to investigate the relationship of visual perception in DF contexts and political orientation. We took into account that respondents may use smartphones, tablets or desktop/laptop devices when responding to the online survey. Remote social engineering techniques can be expected to be more successful, where situational awareness is reduced due to for example smaller screen size, or simultaneous parallel activities (multitasking) (Canham et al., 2022). In order to determine and quantify if and how much device choices impact the individual and momentary cybersecurity risk profile and may thus inform attackers choice of attack vectors and implementation of social engineering attacks, device choice effects need to be taken into account. We thus investigated the device choice effect on the rela-tionship between political attitude and specific statement agreement on DF recognition performance.

In sum, we hypothesized (Hypothesis H_1) trait conservatism to be negatively associ-ated with successful identification of videos as authentic or faked; we also expected to see that the subjectively perceived probability of authenticity was positively associated with trait conservatism (Hypothesis H_{2a}) and the agreement with the video's spoken message

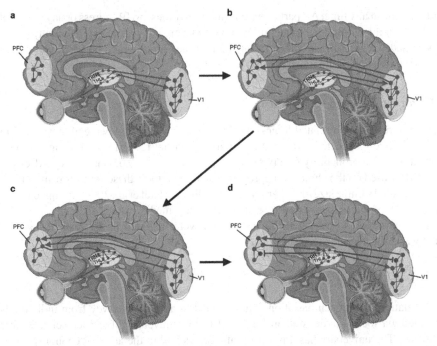

Fig. 1. Visual representation of top-down perceptual filtering. The PFC exerts top-down control on perception by changing the activity in TRN which serves as an inhibitory filter between preconscious and conscious perceptual processing (Nakajima et al., 2019; Philips et al., 2016; Pinault, 2004). **a** Visual stimuli enter the eye and are processed in the THL before being relayed through the TRN filter to enter conscious processing in V1. **b** Perceptual information is sent from visual cortices to the PFC where it is represented in working memory and processed according to perceptual goals. **c** The PFC combines perceptual information from V1 with task-related information to change how the TRN filters visual information from the THL to V1. **d** Input from V1 to PFC is altered according to top-down control. PFC = prefrontal cortex. THL = Thalamus. TRN = Thalamic reticular nucleus. V1 = Primary visual cortex. Blue dots = activated nodes. Blue arrows = Excitatory projections. Red dots = inhibited nodes. Red lines = inhibitory projections.

content (Hypothesis H_{2b}). Finally, we expected overall recognition performance to be lower on smartphones and tablets compared to laptops or desktop devices (Hypothesis H_3).

2 Methods

2.1 Ethics

The present study complies with the Declaration of Helsinki and is in line with the Recommendations for the Conduct, Reporting, Editing and Publication of Scholarly Work in Medical Journals. Participants gave their informed consent prior to the study and were debriefed about the study's purpose after completing the data collection. No deception was taking place. Participants were informed that they could withdraw from participation at any time. All participation was anonymous, no IP address or any personal information that could lead to identification of participants was registered at any point. It was made clear to all participants that some of the videos would be faked and do not represent the view of the impersonated public figure.

2.2 Participants and Recruitment

Literature research on related topics of knowledge-driven visual perception resulted in a conservatively expected estimated effect size of partial $f2 = .15$. Following common conventions, the probability of a type-I-error was set at $\alpha = 0.05$ and for type-II-errors $\beta = 0.20$. Based on the choice of appropriate analytical tools these settings resulted in a recommended sample size of 68 participants (G*Power; Faul et al., 2009). A convenience sample of 164 participants was recruited via social media, where 163 ($n_{female} = 72$; 44.2%) participants completed the survey and were included in the further analysis. Data was collected via Google Forms.

2.3 Design and Procedure

A correlational approach based on data obtained in an online-survey from individuals recruited via social media, students and staff from a university of applied sciences was followed. The university has a portfolio of courses within the areas of economy, technology and life sciences. Participants provided basic socio-demographic data and were presented with twelve video clips of 10 to 26 s duration. The clips were presented in randomized order and contained brief political statements by German politicians covering the breadth of the political spectrum following a consensus decision of the authors and categorization into left-wing, neutral and right-wing political orientations. Five videos were faked, seven were authentic. Participants were asked about the authenticity of the videos (10-point Likert-scale ranging from ("1 = certainly not authentic" to "10 = certainly authentic") and about the degree to which they agreed with the political statement that was made (4-point Likert-scale ranging from "agree not at all" to "fully agree"). General conservative traits were also assessed. Following the survey, participants were debriefed in more detail about the purpose of the study and had the opportunity to leave an email address to participate in a lottery for five prizes in the value of 20 EUR.

2.4 Equipment and Measures

The 12-Item Social and Economic Conservatism Scale (SECS; Everett, 2013) was used for measuring conservatism. The scale consists of 12 items that are rated on a 0–100 scale by asking "How positive or negative do you feel about each issue on the scale". The total score as well as two subscales, economic and social conservatism, can be computed. Sample items for the social conservatism subscale (7 items) include 'abortion, limited government, traditional marriage' and for the economic conservatism subscale (5 items) include 'tax, welfare benefits, fiscal responsibility'. The scale shows good overall reliability (Cronbach's $\alpha = .88$). For this study, the SECS was translated to German and showed acceptable reliability (Cronbach's $\alpha = .71$).

2.5 Videos

Lip-sync approaches take an arbitrary audio track as input and use it to derive a video of a target person with matching mouth region movements. The audio track can be an authentic recording, an audio-deepfake recording with a transformed identity (a.k.a. voice conversion) or be generated by text-to-speech synthesis. Deep Fakes were made using Wav2Lip by uploading one audio track (in.wav format) and one video track (in.mp4 format) per DF. Wav2Lip analyses the mouth area and adapts the mouth movement to the new fake sound, the old sound is replaced by the new one. First, videos of real politicians who talk slowly, move little, and do not open their mouths wide were collected. Then audio with similar voices or the voice of the same person with a different statement were collected. The correct percentage of identified fake videos and participant agreement with the content of the video were used as dependent variables. Deep Fake Identification (DFI) was computed as a binary variable and correct identification percentages were computed. Participant agreement with the video content was measured on a X-point Likert scale (do not agree- totally agree) and averages for both real and fake videos were computed. Reliability was acceptable for both the real videos (Cronbach's $\alpha = .79$) and the fake videos (Cronbach's $\alpha = .68$).

2.6 Pilot Study

A pilot study with 19 video clips was conducted and a community sample of 39 persons were recruited. Detection performance, means and distributions were analyzed in order to select five clips that showed medium difficulty and covered the whole range of the political spectrum (two left-wing, two right-wing, one neutral). This selection was included into the main study (see below).

2.7 Data Reduction and Analysis

Statistical analysis was done with JASP version 14.1 (Gross-Sampson, 2020). All variables were checked for normality. Where criterion was not met, non-parametric alternatives were chosen. Bivariate correlations were calculated, and all variables were entered in the calculation. For the regression analysis, the conservatism scale including its subscales (SECS) was entered as the independent variable and Deepfakes as the dependent variable. To test the influence of pc/mobile device on DF identification, non-parametric independent samples test was used (Mann-Whitney U).

3 Results

Descriptive statistics and correlations between conservatism, detection accuracy, and agreement with content can be found in Table 1.

3.1 H_1: Conservativism and Deep Fake Identification

To test if being more conservative (SECS scores) predicted less correct video clip categorization (i.e., recognizing the status as being an authentic or faked/synthetic video), a regression analysis was performed where the SECS sub scales were entered as the independent variables and the number of correct deep fake identifications was entered as the dependent variable.

The SECS score was associated with more correct identifications ($R^2 = .056$, $F = 7.22$, $p = .01$; Fig. 2). The association between conservatism and correct identifications was due to a significant correlation between the SECS social subscale (beta = $-.267$, $t = -3.08$, $p = .002$), while SECS subscale on economic conservatism remained insignificant (beta = $.129$, $t = 1.49$, $p = .139$).

Table 1. Descriptive statistics and correlations between conservativism, detection accuracy, and agreement with content ($N = 163$).

	Mean	SD	Min	Max	1	2	3	4	5	6	7
1. SECS total	5.10	1.08	2.92	8.00							
2. Social subscale	5.17	1.45	1.43	8.57	.947***						
3. Economic subscale	5.01	0.94	2.80	8.40	.685***	.449***					
4. Correct identification	7.73	2.29	0.00	12.00	−.203**	−.241**	−.010				
5. Authenticity rating of authentic videos	3.49	0.45	2.00	4.00	−.053	−.136	.175*	.609***			
6. Agreement with content in real videos	1.75	0.31	1.00	3.00	−.299***	−.305***	−.185*	.286***	.264***		
7. Authenticity rating of faked videos	2.42	0.90	1.00	4.00	.193**	.147	.184*	−.576***	.000	−.111	
8. Agreement with content in fake videos	1.66	0.31	1.00	3.00	.123	.100	−.148	−.150	.134	.128	.355***

Notes. Non-parametric correlations (Spearman's rho). SECS = Social and Economic Conservativism Scale.
* p < .050. ** p < .010. *** p < .001.

To test if being more conservative (SECS) was associated with the authenticity ratings and agreement of spoken content, regression analyses were performed where the SECS sub scales were entered as the independent variables and video ratings and agreement with the statements made in the videos for both the real (H_{2a}) and fake (H_{2b}) videos were entered as the dependent variables.

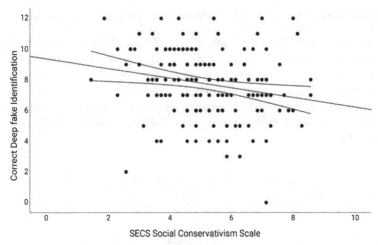

Fig. 2. Scatterplot with linear regression line showing correlation between social conservativism and number of correctly classified video clips. Confidence intervals to the mean.

In line with previous research, age showed positive trends of being associated with conservatism (rho $= .141, p = .073$). When controlled for age (beta $= -.063, t = -.808$, $p = .420$), the effect of conservatism on deep fake recognition persisted ($R^2 = .060, F = 3.37, p = .020$), suggesting that age-typical media consumption habits or age-affected IT-literacy did not explain the effect.

3.2 H$_{2a}$: Effect of Conservativism on Judgment of Videos' Degree of Authenticity

For authentic videos, trait conservatism measured as SECS total score predicted perceived authenticity ($R^2 = .067, F = 5.75, p = .004$), where both the social (beta $= -.214, p = .014$) and the economic subscales (beta $= .275, p = .002$) were significant predictors.

For faked videos, trait conservatism predicted higher authenticity ratings ($R^2 = .042$, $F = 3.49, p = .033$). While both scales were not significant predictors when analysed separately (SECS social: beta $= .076, t = .868, p = .387$), the economic conservatism (beta $= .158, t = 1.81, p = .072$) did show some weak tendencies of being associated with higher authenticity ratings of faked videos for fake video ratings.

3.3 H$_{2b}$: Effect of Agreement with Message Content on Judgment of Video's Degree of Authenticity

Participants who agreed more with the message content of authentic videos, judged them to be more authentic ($r = .264, p < .001$; Table 1). Participants who agreed more with the message content of faked videos, rated them also as more likely to be authentic ($r = .355, p < .001$; Table 1).

3.4 H₃: Influence of Device Used on Authenticity Judgment Accuracy

Figure 3 shows the result from the Mann-Whitney U tests. People identified more deep fakes correctly ($U = 1821.50, Z = 2.42, p = .016$) when using a laptop or desktop device ($N = 110; M_{rank} = 82.94$) over a mobile phone or tablet ($N = 44; M_{rank} = 63.90$). Using a laptop or desktop ($M_{rank} = 81.96$) led to higher levels of perceived authenticity ratings ($U = 1929.00, Z = 1.98, p = .047$) than using phones or tablets ($M_{rank} = 66.34$). More female participants used mobile phones or tablets (66%) compared to males ($\chi^2 = 6.09$, $df = 1, p = .019$).

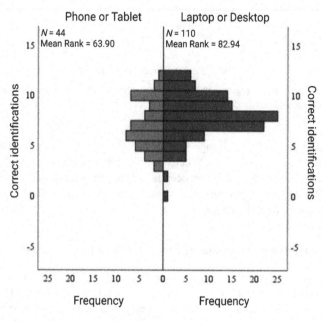

Fig. 3. Comparisons of deep fake recognition accuracy between phones/tablets and laptop/desktop devices.

4 Discussion

This research investigated how general political orientation on the conservatism domain is associated with detection accuracy of deep faked videos. Due to the novelty of the topic of individual differences in DF recognition, we consider this a first pilot study into a new thematic topic area which is likely to trigger more research activity in the future.

Previous research indicated a positive relationship between trait conservatism and the perceived credibility of conspiracy theories (Garret & Bond, 2021). Our study aimed to test this hypothesis in the more specific field of deep fake recognition, which is currently an increasingly relevant element of political dis-/misinformation as well as the spread of conspiracy theories. Our results suggest a moderate, but statistically significant relationship between conservatism and deep fake recognition. According to these initial results, more socially (but not economically) conservative political views were associated with more susceptibility to believing that video clips to be authentic. This association between trait conservatism and deep fake recognition performance seemed to be carried by the individual's extent of agreement with the political statement that is transported in the video. There was a positive linear relationship between agreeing with the spoken message content and the degree to which the message transporting video was considered authentic. While this association was found for both authentic and faked videos, the association was slightly (but not significantly) stronger for the category of faked videos.

This research also showed that using a mobile phone increased DF susceptibility. Using a mobile phone led to higher failure rates in detecting DF, thus supporting the hypothesis. This may in part be explained by the fact that humans tend to perform worse when detecting DF in videos with smaller screen size or due to artifacts from the faked videos with low resolution being masked by the quality compression (Rossler et al., 2019). Research on susceptibility to remote online social engineering (ROSE) attacks suggest a higher vulnerability when portable devices, in particular smartphones, are used (Powell & Canham, 2021). This was confirmed to be also true for DF recognition in this study. It was beyond the scope of this study to investigate causal pathways and disentangle them, but we consider it plausible to assume that both factors, the reduced situational awareness resulting from (1) smaller screens and (2) multitasking/distraction may have contributed. Since smaller screens are partially compensated by the closer distance to the eye and thus a similar visual field angle, perhaps (2) is more likely to be true and should be considered in future studies to inform human-centered security-relevant design.

While gender effects were not part of the initial research question, preliminary analyses indicate that female participants reported significantly more mobile phone use than males (66%). Taken with the findings from the first hypothesis that conservatism would be associated with DF identification, this could explain why females performed worse than males on DF detection, but differences are not significant or have small effect sizes and are thus not included here in detail. These findings add to the previous research that gender might not influence DF detection (Montañez et al., 2020). Gender effects have not been reported before in DF recognition. Previous research suggested women might be more susceptible to social engineering (e.g., Halevi et al., 2015; Lin et al., 2019; Sheng et al., 2010) but previous studies mainly focused on personality traits and susceptibility to phishing emails.

The effects from this study are in line with very recent findings on the inaccuracy in regards to the judgment of political statements' truth and conservatism in a US-American sample (Garrett & Bond, 2021). It also gives support to recent literature on top-down processes of visual perception (Aitken et al., 2020a, 2020b; Panichello & Turk-Browne, 2021). The participants were clearly instructed to judge the authenticity and can be assumed to have searched for technical glitches, inconsistencies, spectral artifacts, and aberrations. These perceptions have to be compared with internal cognitive representations of what a hypothetical "normal" (authentic) standard model could be.

4.1 Limitations

This study has several limitations that could have influenced the results. The participants were recruited through convenience sampling and from a specific region in Germany and are thus not necessarily representative on a national or international level. Also, affinity for information technology (IT) was not assessed in the sample. People more accustomed to using or being exposed to IT media might have a better understanding of social media influence and social engineering. However, previous research on other deceptive means applied in cybercrimes, such as phishing simulations, suggest that IT-affinity may be related to overconfidence and is not per se a relevant protective factor (Pattinson et al., 2012). The variable of age, which is commonly related to IT-affinity, did not have any statistically significant impact on the overall findings.

While there were significant findings both at group levels and at the gender levels, effect sizes were small. The sample size met the power analysis requirements, but the small yet significant findings could be due to the relationship of the variables is not as strong as hypothesized, the fact that larger sample sizes produce smaller (and more accurate) effects, or that the sample was homogenous in their location, resulting in a restriction-of-range effect.

4.2 Future Research

The present findings have to be replicated in other countries, with larger samples, and preferably with an equal distribution of pads, laptops, and mobile phones between genders in order to make conclusions about gender effects. The nature of this survey and the informed consent required for data collection and processing prepares the participants for the challenge and induces a critical evaluation from their side. In real life conditions, targets of DF-related social engineering attacks are unlikely to be prepared and may have a certain level of personal knowledge and trust in relation to the individual shown. Thus, the findings of this study may have stronger relevance for the area of political disinformation than individual social engineering as it is carried out in for example spear-phishing attacks.

To investigate perceptual processes underlying individual differences in DF recognition closer, eye- tracking may be a useful tool to assess whether areas in the videos that contain synthetic artifacts are visually scanned equally between individuals that perform well, compared to individuals that do not perform well on the DF detection task. It may also be necessary to pair eye-tracking data with EEG recordings to see if there is a difference in DF artifact-detection associated responses (event related potentials) between participants who are visually scanning the same areas of the DF. This will be important to determine if top-down knowledge (e.g. expectations influenced by conservativism) affects perceptual processes at the attention allocation- or encoding-level of DF stimuli processing. Dissociating the effects of attention and expectation on early sensory processing is not straightforward (Rungratsameetaweemana & Serences, 2019) and should be properly addressed in future research. Comparing the differences in DF detection between DF facial identity manipulation techniques and facial expression manipulation techniques may go further in demonstrating the extent to which top-down processes influence perceptions. Facial identity manipulation DF may have less of the expressive characteristics of the impersonated individual, or a timing of expressive behaviors that are a little off from the impersonated individual, thus providing additional clues that may give away the DF. To pick up on these characteristics will, however, require that participants are somewhat familiar with the impersonated individual and pose new methodological challenges for future research designs. Lastly, very recent research suggests that the relationship between conservatism and belief in conspiracy theories is partially explained by the personality trait of conscientiousness (Lawson & Kakkar, 2021). Despite the conceptual differences between the concept of beliefs into conspiracy theories on one hand, and the very perceptual task of recognizing technical artifacts in deep fakes, future studies should consider these findings and the effects personality traits such as conscientiousness have on cognitive processing.

It was beyond the scope of this study to investigate cognitive-perceptual pathways on an intraindividual level, as this would have required techniques such as gaze-tracking and time-sensitive stimulus presentation. Future research might thus target more on these covert processes and their interaction with political attitudes. Since the present study used the DF technique of facial expression manipulation (lip syncing). Not being familiar with the politician impersonated in a DF will reduce the likelihood of detecting micro expressions that are incongruent with that politician's usual facial-expressive behaviors. Conversely, not being familiar with the politicians in the videos could perhaps go further in isolating the effects of the interaction between participant's political attitudes and the political message in a DF video on perceptual processing. Nevertheless, we believe that the effects related to being familiar with the politician in the DF compared to not being familiar with the politician in the DF should be addressed sufficiently by using a mix of known and unknown politicians.

The presented results regarding political attitudes and agreement with message content may inform future research on individual perception and recognition processes. It was beyond the scope of this online survey to investigate cognitive processes during video presentation, as this would require standardized laboratory conditions and a higher degree of repetition. Nevertheless, the identified variables my play a role in the future identification of individual cognitive processing styles. Tahir et al. (2021) used gaze-tracking and self-report to understand the detection perceptual process on DF data. They discovered that humans tend to focus on the major regions of the face such as eyes, hair, and nose, and report eyes, nose, forehead, lips, cheeks, and expression as the visual cues they used for detection. In a similar study on face-swap data by Wohler et al. (2021), the participants fixated on mouth and nose and reported blur artifacts, contour artifacts, and unnatural expressions or eye movements. Participants in another study by Thaw et al. (2020) self-reported artifacts such as lack of expressions, lack of emotions, and unnatural behavior as well as flickering, blurred faces, rendering artifacts, and abnormal mouth movements as justification for their decision. Findings from political psychology suggest characteristic stimulus processing, priorisation, risk proneness and sensitivity to threatening stimuli in conservative persons compared to those with more liberal attitudes (Schreiber et al., 2013). Future research my proceed with combining perceptual psychology and research on political attitudes with deep fake recognition skills in order to explain political phenomena related to disinformation and conspiracy believes, and thus inform the recent efforts into the development of countermeasures (see e.g., Compton et al., 2021).

5   Conclusion

The study suggests a statistically significant association between conservatism and the ability to recognize deep fakes. A driving factor for this effect appears to be the level of agreement with the political message transported by the synthetic media. Portable devices such as phones have a deteriorating effect on deep fake recognition skills. The study is in line with recent research on conservatism and perceived credibility of political disinformation and conspiracy theories. While effect sizes being small to moderate, this study may inform future research to investigate relevant and novel psychological aspects in order to provide a more comprehensive overview over influencing factors that could explain social engineering processes and vulnerabilities targeted by synthetic media.

Acknowledgements. This study was supported by the Norwegian Research Council (project number 302941). A preprint of this article is available at PsyArXiv (Sütterlin et al., 2021).

References

Aitken, F., Menelaou, G., Warrington, O., Koolschijn, R.S., Corbin, N., et al.: Prior expectations evoke stimulus-specific activity in the deep layers of the primary visual cortex. PLoS Biol. **18**(12), e3001023 (2020a)

Aitken, F., Turner, G., Kok, P.: Prior expectations of motion direction modulate early sensory processing. J. Neurosci. **40**(33), 6389–6397 (2020b)

Azucar, D., Marengo, D., Settanni, M.: Predicting the big 5 personality traits from digital footprints on social media: a meta-analysis. Pers. Individ. Differ. **124**, 150–159 (2018)

Balcetis, E., Dunning, D.: Cognitive dissonance and the perception of natural environments. Psychol. Sci. **18**(10), 917–921 (2007)

Balcetis, E., Dunning, D., Granot, Y.: Subjective value determines initial dominance in binocular rivalry. J. Exp. Soc. Psychol. **48**(1), 122–129 (2012)

Canham, M., Posey, C., Constantino, M.: Phish derby: shoring the human shield through gamified phishing attacks. In: Frontiers in Higher Education. Advance Online Publication (2022)

Cialdini, R.B.: The Psychology of Persuasion. New York (1993)

Compton, J., van der Linden, S., Cook, J., Basol, M.: Inoculation theory in the post-truth era: extant findings and new frontiers for contested science, misinformation, and conspiracy theories. Soc. Pers. Psychol. Compass **15**(6), e12602 (2021)

European Parliament Global Trendometer. Essays on medium- and long-term global trends. ISSN 2529-6345 (2018)

Everett, J.A.: The 12 item social and economic conservatism scale (SECS). PLoS ONE **8**(12), e82131 (2013)

Garrett, R.K., Bond, R.M.: Conservatives' susceptibility to political misperceptions. Sci. Adv. **7**(23), eabf1234 (2021)

Golbeck, J., Robles, C., Turner, K.: Predicting personality with social media. In: CHI 2011 Extended Abstracts on Human Factors in Computing Systems, pp. 253–262 (2011)

Goss-Sampson, M.A.: Statistical analysis in JASP 0.14: a guide for students (2020)

Gupta, P., Chugh, K., Dhall, A., Subramanian, R.: The eyes know it: Fakeet-an eye-tracking database to understand deepfake perception. In: Proceedings of the 2020 International Conference on Multimodal Interaction, pp. 519–527 (2020)

Hadnagy, C.: Social Engineering: The Science of Human Hacking. Wiley, Hoboken (2018)

Halevi, T., Memon, N., Nov, O.: Spear-phishing in the wild: a real-word study of personality, phishing self-efficacy and vulnerability to spear-phishing attacks. Soc. Sci. Res. Netw. (2015)

Hu, S., Li, Y., Lyu, S.: Exposing GAN-generated faces using inconsistent corneal specular highlights. In: ICASSP 2021 - 2021 IEEE International Conference on Acoustics, Speech and Signal Processing (ICASSP) (2021)

IBM Security: Cost of a data breach report 2020 (2020). https://www.capita.com/sites/g/files/ngi nej291/files/2020-08/Ponemon-Global-Cost-of-Data-Breach-Study-2020.pdf

iProov: The Threat of Deepfakes. The consumer view of deepfakes and the role of biometric authentication in protecting against their misuse (2020). https://www.iproov.com/wp-content/ uploads/2021/05/iProov-Deepfakes-Report.pdf

JASP Team (2020). JASP (Version 0.14.1)

Korshunov, P., Marcel, S.: Deepfake detection: humans vs. machines. arXiv preprint arXiv:2009. 03155 (2020)

Kosinski, M., Stillwell, D., Graepel, T.: Private traits and attributes are predictable from digital records of human behavior. Proc. Natl. Acad. Sci. **110**(15), 5802–5805 (2013)

Lawson, M.A., Kakkar, H.: Of pandemics, politics, and personality: the role of conscientiousness and political ideology in the sharing of fake news. J. Exp. Psychol.: Gener. **151**, 1154 (2021)

Lin, T., et al.: Susceptibility to spear-phishing emails: effects of internet user demographics and email content. ACM Trans. Comput.-Hum. Interact. **26**(5), 32 (2019). https://doi.org/10.1145/ 3336141

Lyu, S.: Deepfake detection: current challenges and next steps. In: 2020 IEEE International Conference on Multimedia & Expo Workshops (ICMEW), pp. 1–6. IEEE (2020)

Masood, M., Nawaz, M., Malik, K.M., Javed, A., Irtaza, A.: Deepfakes generation and detection: state-of-the-art, open challenges, countermeasures, and way forward. arXiv preprint arXiv: 2103.00484 (2021)

Meakins, J.: A zero-sum game: the zero-day market in 2018. J. Cyber Policy **4**(1), 60–71 (2019)

Montañez, R., Golob, E., Xu, S.: Human cognition through the lens of social engineering cyberattacks. Front. Psychol. **11**, 1755 (2020)

Mouton, F., Leenen, L., Malan, M.M., Venter, H.S.: Towards an ontological model defining the social engineering domain. In: Kimppa, K., Whitehouse, D., Kuusela, T., Phahlamohlaka, J. (eds.) HCC 2014. IAICT, vol. 431, pp. 266–279. Springer, Heidelberg (2014). https://doi.org/ 10.1007/978-3-662-44208-1_22

Nakajima, M., Schmitt, L.I., Halassa, M.M.: Prefrontal cortex regulates sensory filtering through a basal ganglia-to-thalamus pathway. Neuron **103**(3), 445–458 (2019)

Panichello, M.F., Turk-Browne, N.B.: Behavioral and neural fusion of expectation with sensation. J. Cogn. Neurosci. **33**(5), 814–825 (2021)

Pattinson, M., Jerram, C., Parsons, K., McCormac, A., Butavicius, M.: Why do some people manage phishing e-mails better than others? Inf. Manag. Comput. Secur. **20**(1), 18–28 (2012)

Phillips, J.M., Kambi, N.A., Saalmann, Y.B.: A subcortical pathway for rapid, goal-driven, attentional filtering. Trends Neurosci. **39**(2), 49–51 (2016)

Pinault, D.: The thalamic reticular nucleus: structure, function and concept. Brain Res. Rev. **46**(1), 1–31 (2004)

Powell, K., Canham, M.: User be aware: is your smart phone or TV putting you at risk? In: Proceedings of the 65th Annual Meeting of the Human Factors and Ergonomics Society. Human Factors and Ergonomics Society, Santa Monica (2021)

Purplesec: 2021 Cyber Security Statistics. The Ultimate List Of Stats, Data & Trends (2021). https://purplesec.us/resources/cyber-security-statistics/

Rossler, A., Cozzolino, D., Verdoliva, L., Riess, C., Thies, J., Niessner, M.: FaceForensics++: learning to detect manipulated facial images. In: 2019 IEEE/CVF International Conference on Computer Vision (ICCV) (2019)

Rungratsameetaweemana, N., Serences, J.T.: Dissociating the impact of attention and expectation on early sensory processing. Curr. Opin. Psychol. **29**, 181–186 (2019)

Schreiber, D., et al.: Red brain, blue brain: evaluative processes differ in Democrats and Republicans. PLoS ONE **8**(2), e52970 (2013)

Sheng, S., Holbrook, M., Kumaraguru, P., Cranor, L., Downs, J.: Who falls for phish? A demographic analysis of phishing susceptibility and effectiveness of interventions. In: 28th ACM Conference on Human Factors in Computing Systems, pp. 373–382 (2010)

Sütterlin, S., et al.: Individual deep fake recognition skills are affected by viewers' political orientation, agreement with content and device used. PsyArXiv (2021). https://doi.org/10.31234/osf.io/hwujb

Tahir, R., et al.: Seeing is believing: exploring perceptual differences in DeepFake videos. In: Proceedings of the 2021 CHI Conference on Human Factors in Computing Systems, pp. 1–16 (2021)

Thaw, N.N., July, T., Wai, A.N., Goh, D.H.L., Chua, A.Y.: Is it real? A study on detecting deepfake videos. Proc. Assoc. Inf. Sci. Technol. **57**(1), e366 (2020)

Tong, F., Nakayama, K., Vaughan, J.T., Kanwisher, N.: Binocular rivalry and visual awareness in human extrastriate cortex. Neuron **21**(4), 753–759 (1998)

Uebelacker, S., Quiel, S.: The social engineering personality framework. In: 2014 Workshop on Socio-Technical Aspects in Security and Trust, pp. 24–30. IEEE (2014)

Van Koningsbruggen, G.M., Stroebe, W., Aarts, H.: Through the eyes of dieters: biased size perception of food following tempting food primes. J. Exp. Soc. Psychol. **47**(2), 293–299 (2011)

Verizon: DBIR 2021 Data breach investigations report (2021). https://www.verizon.com/business/en-gb/resources/reports/dbir/

Wang, Z., Sun, L., Zhu, H.: Defining social engineering in cybersecurity. IEEE Access **8**, 85094–85115 (2020)

Wöhler, L., Zembaty, M., Castillo, S., Magnor, M.: Towards understanding perceptual differences between genuine and face-swapped videos. In: Proceedings of the 2021 CHI Conference on Human Factors in Computing Systems, pp. 1–13 (2021)

Zollhöfer, M., et al.: State of the art on monocular 3D face reconstruction, tracking, and applications. Comput. Graph. Forum **37**(2), 523–550 (2018)

The Augmented Cognition of Religion and Spirituality in Media

Suraj Sood[✉]

Autism Behavior Consultants, Torrance, USA
surajsoodx@gmail.com

Abstract. Human-computer interaction (HCI) leads to augmented cognition (AC). Cognitive augmentation can be visualized as a pyramid with four layers: from bottom to top, these are data, information, knowledge, and wisdom. The data-information-knowledge hierarchy is well-known in data science; however, wisdom has often been left out. Wisdom is the ideal end of any practice that aims to augment user cognition.

In this chapter, the cultural phenomenon of spirituality and the societal organizations of religion are implicated in HCI as important tools for wisdom-granting AC. The phenomenon and organizations in question are taken up in a landscape of digital HCI applications including video gaming and streamed visual and auditory content. It is shown that these media take up spirituality and religion in unique and novel ways, lending to interesting experiences for users.

This chapter examines specific examples of the manifestation of spirituality and religion in contemporary digital culture. Such examples have been diffused across platforms like Twitch, YouTube, Discord, Amazon Prime Video and Netflix, Facebook, and Spotify. Attention is also paid to the global multimedia franchises *Pokémon*, *Yu-Gi-Oh!*, and *Digimon*, all of which take up god and the power of gods in reimagined ways. Role-playing games like *Guild Wars* and *RuneScape* are also discussed in this context.

Through online dating, people are finding their soulmates virtually more than before, further implicating religion and spirituality in the computational realm. This chapter explores fake religion and playful mythology as a function of excited gaming communities and franchises. The "Godhead" phenomenon [1] is treated as the ultimate in augmented cognition that is not entirely or necessarily—yet is potentially—a function of human-machine symbiosis.

Global possibilities for diverse activities, religious interaction, and learning about religion, spirituality, and mythology exist given HCI. There is potential for religious practice to augment cognition to the highest level in humanity, up to the soul and spirit levels of reality (both manifest and absolute reality, in Hindu metaphysics). With a strong cognitive foundation, augmented cognition can proceed for any given person. Augmented cognition can reach toward the highest levels of Wilberian holarchy and Blavatsky's sevenfold constitution of man.

Keywords: religion · spirituality · digital media · wisdom · data science

© The Author(s), under exclusive license to Springer Nature Switzerland AG 2023
D. D. Schmorrow and C. M. Fidopiastis (Eds.): HCII 2023, LNAI 14019, pp. 285–313, 2023.
https://doi.org/10.1007/978-3-031-35017-7_19

1 Introduction

After March 1st, 2014, cries on the world wide web such as, "Praise [Lord] Helix!" abounded. The origin—the event "Twitch Plays *Pokémon Red Version*" [51]—was the first phenomenal Twitch stream in terms of the social media streaming platform's cultural effect. Various other imaginings and re-imaginings of gods and goddesses in contemporary anime and video games have surfaced this century, including the Alpha Pokémon Arceus and *Yu-Gi-Oh!* Duel Monsters Slifer the Sky Dragon (Sky Dragon of Osiris from the original Japanese), Obelisk the Tormentor, and The Winged Dragon of Ra. A common message of two filmographic efforts portraying these monster gods, *Pokémon: The Arceus Chronicles* and *Yu-Gi-Oh! The Dark Side of Dimensions* (respectively), is that beings with godly power can help save humanity; however, after such beings do so, humans must learn to live for themselves. Arceus serves as the creator of the Pokémon universe, functionally serving as its god. In 2022, this Pokémon received its own much-anticipated game, *Pokémon Legends: Arceus*. Through depictions of gods like Arceus, Slifer, Obelisk, and The Winged Dragon of Ra, human viewers and gamers can augment their understandings of god. Franchises like *Yu-Gi-Oh!* in particular also deal heavily with the notion of soul. The eye is commonly referred to as a window to a person's soul, reflecting "folk wisdom that intimately marries eye and soul" ([48], p. 66).

Human users of computers can engage in a number of activities toward better-understanding God. In addition to those just discussed in watching certain anime and playing certain video games, one can measure their level of "philosophical health". Such an online quiz determines if one has any logical inconsistencies in their philosophical framework. The augmentative promise of reading one's results from this quiz is philosophical tension-reduction, a clear candidate for augmenting a person's belief structure (Fig. 1).

[38] discusses the evolution of expertise on a computationally expansive level:

"…a community of experts—hunter, healer, tailor, and so on—whose combined computational capacities far surpass a community where every brain is the same…. For computational expansion this community-of-experts design is brilliant…"

"[This] design requires additional innate behaviors to dissipate psychological tensions and preserve social cohesion. Such behaviors might collectively be termed *sacred practices*, where 'sacred' means 'reverence for the ineffable'—what casual speech cannot be expressed."

"Sacred practice includes sex, music, dance, drama, and a multitude of unifying ceremonies surrounding birth, puberty, marriage, and death. It includes stories, jokes, and prayer. Such practices elicit intense emotions such as awe, joy, grief, and laughter—which somehow relieve intrapsychic and interpersonal tensions" (p. 102).

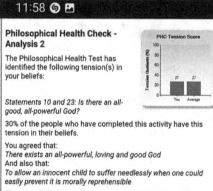

Fig. 1. Examples of philosophical tension revealed after completing an online quiz.

In the above quotation, the humanities and lived human experience are linked to the sacred as the author equates *Homo sapiens'* modern level of economic advancement with its computational ability. Sacred practices as listed here serve as tension-reducers for potentially overloading levels of stress that modern living can cause (Fig. 2).

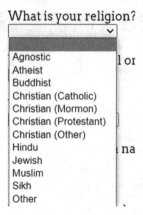

Fig. 2. Religious identification dropdown following completion of an online "temperaments" quiz.

In taking up the notion of god, one should eschew the "God trick of seeing everything from nowhere" ([37], p. 581). This could be considered an epistemic-theological fallacy of ignoring blind spots inherent to being human (even with AC through computational interaction). This aside, there are a large number of HCI activities one could partake in toward the end of theosophical or religious AC. One example is taking theological notes at events like Philosophy in the Park (hosted by the nonprofit group, New Acropolis) on a tablet such as Amazon's Kindle Fire. A related question is: could Godhead [1] be treated as an ultimate form of AC? Repeated exclamations of "oh, my god" in Pokémon video game streams (as in, e.g., [17]); screaming "oh, my God" along with suited music (e.g., the song "Westbound & Down" by American metalcore band Of Mice & Men) played from one's (e.g., Android) smartphone while driving; and comedic phrasings such as "God up" [18] as a challenge to the universe's perceived "unintelligent design" (i.e., containing existential design flaws) are examples of using god's name in vain during HCI. Such examples serve entertainment purposes at least, but could be viewed as forms of augmented affect if they lift the human user's mood. It is worth inquiring what such exclamations mean.

[35] concluded with a hopeful proposal of postphenomenological HCI and the more general loving ecology (or, ecology of love). [36] approaches the latter with its intersectional focus on ecotheology and love. Ecotheology is taken up on social media platforms like Instagram: e.g., in the form of story-posts praising and detailing the crematory technique "aquamation" (alkaline hydrolysis), including information about its use and chemistry. Postphenomenology can also be conducted on more general uses of the personal computer (PC), e.g. users' lock screen images. A religious example of a lock screen image depicts the Hindu Goddess Rati and her mythological mate, Kama. Unlocking such a PC could feel *like entering into a place of love*.

Using technology as a medium for and enabler of religious learning and practice is done, e.g., as [10] (available in Amazon Audible audiobook format) undertakes comparative mythology and multi-religious global history. Religion and religious deities appear in various forms of digital media. More recent manifestations of such subject matter include video games, romantic comedy, and anime. In these forms of media, gods are invented anew, discussed ironically, or recharacterized. God and religion in computer-enabled media are represented in terms of either activities (e.g., holiday participation) or content such as images and readings (e.g., [31, 32])[1]. One could also update religious reading progress and desires on Amazon's Goodreads website and app (Figs. 3, 4 and 5).

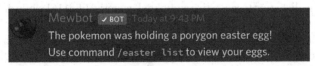

Fig. 3. The term *easter egg* is expressed by a bot in the group chat app Discord. This term, derived from the Christian holiday Easter and its frequent cultural use of eggs, refers to a special item found in a digital game.

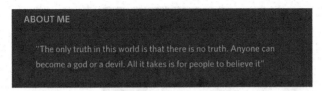

Fig. 4. A Discord user's "About Me" section, including a quoted view on truth and belief in polar theological terms.

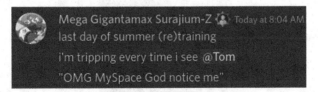

Fig. 5. Discord messages sent in an academic psychology Discord server. One of the server's admins, using MySpace founder Tom's iconic profile picture and name, is ironically referred to as "MySpace God" by a staff member.

Religious discourse regarding Islam and Hinduism lecture-viewing via screen share on distinct Discord servers is an example of religious e-learning. More generally, one could reach religious truth and discover value in virtues (e.g., equanimity) in the process of exchanging emails comprised of psycho-theosophical discourse. Examples of religion or spirituality taken up in the Discord chat platform include telling Buddhist-inspired jokes, sharing Tarot results showcasing *Yu-Gi-Oh!* Trading Card Game Egyptian God Decks through Facebook Messenger, and looking at *Yu-Gi-Oh!* card art depicting the Sacred Beast monsters while at a summer work training conference.

---

[1] William James' theosophy and W.E.B. DuBois' analysis of African-American religion can be read in the Portable Document Format (PDF) and as a Kindle electronic book (e-book), respectively.

2 Greco-Christianity

Transcendent HCI (e.g., as studied in [53]) can be a multireligious and pan-spiritual endeavor. Missionaries in the Church of Jesus Christ of Latter-day Saints tradition utilize the Bible study app *The Book of Mormon*. Clinical psychologist Jordan B. Peterson made his Bible lecture series publicly available on the video-streaming platform YouTube. An individual could report on their personal phenomenology of religious awakening experiences: e.g., listening to evocative audiobook material like [16] while driving toward a sunset and subsequently discussing one's discovery of God in a blog hosted on a virtual community of practice (VCoP). More generally, one could post and share on a felt sense of being "spirit-mates" via blogging sites like WordPress. *The Alchemist* by Paulo Coelho, a novel that can be read on a tablet like Amazon's Kindle, discusses the soul and language of the world as its main character discovers them for himself (Figs. 6 and 7).

Fig. 6. Screenshot of a Trainer's Vaporeon about to be fed a Nanab Berry at the Temple of Poseidon *Pokémon GO* Gym in Greece.[2]

> 🔒 paypal.com/webapps/hermes?flow=1-P&ulReturn=true8

Fig. 7. The Greek deity Hermes' name appears in a PayPal URL.

---

[2] Capitalizations of "Trainer" and "Gym" used are consistent with their use in [13].

3 Indic Religions

Old webpages containing religious wisdom can be accessed via the free-to-use Wayback Machine service. An example includes wisdom on non-attachment, a virtue commonly preached in Buddhist theosophy:

"[With] Aparigraha (non-grasping, attachment).... We begin to question why we are hanging on to this idea of the perfect relationship. It's caused us to 'unfriend' people [on social media websites like Facebook] and disengage from others who seem to care for us. We wonder why we are so attached to having some need met, why we keep grasping for some great prize. It's making us tired and depressed. We decide to give it a name. We call out its name when we see it working its way into our thoughts...." [39] (Fig. 8).

Fig. 8. *Pokémon GO* gift from a PokéStop of a Buddha statue.

Buddhist practitioner and leader Mingyur Rinpoche noted that chasing cognitions leads to deleterious identification with them, diminishing the quality of subsequent behavior [3]. In his view, humanity has in common wanting to be happy and not to suffer.

Excerpts from religious founders like the Buddha can also be found online, including: "Holding on to anger is like grasping a hot coal with the intent of throwing it at someone else; you are the one who gets burned" [2]. There is much content online pertaining to the Dalai Lama, including an interview (posted on YouTube in 2011) hosting him on The 7pm Project [4]. In this interview, the Dalai Lama said, "[The] very purpose of our life...is joyful life. Our life—our existence—very much lives with our hope. So, hope means something good...nobody say[s] hope [is] something bad. No. So, therefore— the very purpose of our life is happiness" (1:08–1:30). Buddhist meditation can also be done in virtual groups like the Dharma Stream (which takes place in-person in Georgia, United States).

Regarding Hinduism, Google's Maps app can be used to learn about, locate, and travel to Hindu temples. One can listen to music via their smartphone, achieving ecstasy and a feeling of transcendence at a temple and mosque respectively. Online, one can learn about Hinduism, including the roles of Gods Shiva, Vishnu, and Brahma. Amidst this process, romantic inspiration could even be derived from Shiva's love story (Fig. 9).

Fig. 9. Webpage for podcast episode "Sikhism with Dilpreet Jammu" (viewed from a user's shared Discord screen).

4   Humanism: Education/Scholarship and Paganism/Scandinavian Religion

Continental philosophy that can be learned about through YouTube podcasting and electronically-accessible translations takes up both spirit and soul. In the Hegelian master-servant dialectic, the hypothetical servant puts their spirit into the field of their creative work, leading to their independence and personal transformation [44]. Regarding his conception of "alētheia", Heidegger stated and inquired as follows:

> "We are questioning concerning technology, and we have arrived now at *alētheia*, at revealing. What has the essence of technology to do with revealing? The answer: everything. For every bringing-forth is grounded in revealing. Bringing-forth, indeed, gathers within itself the four modes of occasioning-causality-and rules them throughout. Within its domain belong end and means, belongs instrumentality... *Instrumentality is considered to be the fundamental characteristic of technology* [emphasis added]. If we inquire, step by step, into what technology, represented as means, actually is, then we shall arrive at revealing. The possibility of all productive manufacturing lies in revealing...

"Technology is a way of revealing. If we give heed to this, then another whole realm for the essence of technology will open itself up to us. It is the realm of revealing, i.e., of truth [emphasis added]" ([46], p. 12).

Of spirit, Deleuze asserted that "in a society of control, the corporation has replaced the factory, and the corporation is a spirit, a gas" ([40], p. 2). Of soul, Deleuze philosophized: "Marketing has become the center or the 'soul' of the corporation. We are taught that corporations have a soul, which is the most terrifying news in the world" ([40], p. 3).

In theosophy (i.e., theological philosophy), arguments concerning the existence of God abound. These can also be learned about via electronic resources like YouTube podcast videos. In the "Continental Philosophy lectures" series of the Overthink Podcast, such an argument is provoked via presentation of Sartre's existential atheism [41]. In the "necessary being" argument, God exists as a necessary being who prevents an infinite regress from rendering the existence of the known universe logically impossible.

4.1 Nordic Religion

Nordic religion includes Nornir Goddesses that are portrayed in digital media. In *Yu-Gi-Oh! Duel Monsters*, Zigfried's dueling cards Urd, Verdande, and Skuld [5] are such examples. In Marvel's popular The Avengers franchise, Thor—god of lightning; Loki—Thor's brother, and god of mischief; and Odin, father of the Aesir are also portrayed as such cards in the *Yu-Gi-Oh! 5D's* anime series.

4.2 Education/Scholarship and Social Settings

AC can take place in various educational and scholarly settings. Scheduling and coordinating Rakhi via a shared virtual calendar is one example of using HCI to augment cognition of religious observation. Religious holidays on a virtual calendar—such as in the special educational classroom context—include, in the month of April alone: Ramadan, Easter, and Passover. AC can also take place in the university setting via activities like writing a term paper (for, e.g., an anime course) that focuses at least in part on religion (e.g., Hinduism).

Learning about Quetzalcoatl can be done via webpage [52] open on (e.g.) a Samsung tablet. Regarding spirituality, Wilber's "all quadrants, all levels" (AQAL) [1] evolutionary epistemology and metaphysics is analogous to Blavatsky's sevenfold constitution of the human [25]. Both philosophies include hierarchical ontogenesis, with evolution emerging from the body to the mind, and from mind to spirit or soul. Literary "waxing" can be gleaned from YouTube videos mentioning or about god, such as the line "our hidden gods in the language of life, itself" [26].

5 (Video) Games

In *Call of Duty*'s "zombies" mode, wormholes can be thought of as a metaphorical gateway leading to one's soulmate, a meaningful postphenomenology experience in the digital media video-gaming context.

5.1 Nintendo

Pokémon—especially their Mythical and Legendary variants—can have godlike powers. Ho-Oh is a Pokémon that, according to in-series legend, revived three perished Pokémon from death, granting its creations powers over nature (wind, water, volcanic activity, and thunder). Celebi is a Mythical Pokémon with the power to travel through time. Some—such as the mythological creator of the universe (and of space, time, and antimatter deities) Arceus; the respective deities of space and time, Palkia and Dialga; and Rayquaza, which is revered by the fictional Draconid people—are deified. Others, such as the fan-termed "Kami trio"—Tornadus, Thundurus, and Landorus—represent gods that were worshipped in the real world. Tornadus and Thundurus of the Kami trio were inspired by the mythological Japanese gods of wind and thunder respectively, Fujin and Raijin (Fig. 10).

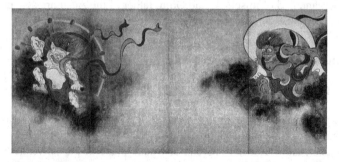

Fig. 10. Thunder god Raijin (left) and wind god Fujin (right) [15].

Raijin & Fujin (Japanese lightning and wind Gods, respectively) were recreated as Thundurus and Tornadus in the core series video games *Pokémon Black* and *White*. The Pokémon Celebi references historic, spirit-based Japanese religion ([14], 14:04), possibly Shintoism. Of Shintoism, "ichirei shikon—one spirit, four souls—is an idea of Japanese Shintoism in which the mind consists of a spirit called 'naohi' that is connected with the heaven and four souls" [29].

What can be learned from "indie" competitive Pokémon battling rules? Communities such as Smogon define a small set of their own rules for what becomes known as a metagame, consisting of standard Pokémon and sets that are used in competitive teams. The Pokémon Mega Rayquaza was suspected and tested to be more powerful than Arceus (the primary Pokémon god) [54]. Regardless of this, Arceus could be expected to defeat Mega Rayquaza one-on-one. The official Pokemon games for the Nintendo Switch console—*Brilliant Diamond* and *Shining Pearl*—respectively focus on the deities of time, Dialga, and space, Palkia. In the region these games take place, Sinnoh (based on northern Japan), the creator of the universe referred to mythologically as "Original One" is Arceus.

Pokémon video games are not the only Nintendo-owned games that could be argued to involve godlike forces. *In The Legend of Zelda: Oracle of Seasons* and *Oracle of Ages*, the player has the ability to control the flow and passage of time. In the Pokemon movie *Arceus and the Jewel of Life*, Arceus represents the biblical Old Testament god in its vengeance. The Nintendo Switch title *Pokémon Legends: Arceus*, acronymized recently by the game's fandom as *PLA*, the player is rewarded for doing what Arceus commands them to.[3] A *PLA* player wins by carrying out Arceus' will, i.e., to meet all Pokémon in the game. In this same game, the phrase "Almighty Sinnoh" is used to refer to the deities Palkia and Dialga, worshiped respectively by the game's Pearl Clan and Diamond Clan (Fig. 11).

Fig. 11. From left to right: the Pokémon Giratina (Origin Forme), Dialga (Origin Forme), Arceus, and Palkia (Origin Forme) in Game Freak's 2022 Nintendo Switch title *Pokémon Legends: Arceus* [19]. Giratina, Dialga, and Palkia collectively make up what the Pokémon fandom refers to as the "creation trio". Arceus created the creation trio in Pokémon's mythology, and explicitly through an in-game event in *Pokémon: Heart Gold* and *Soul Silver* versions for the Nintendo DS handheld gaming system.

After executing Arceus' will in *PLA*, the player is allowed to battle the Original One. Arceus' battle theme sounds anxious, conveying the urgency of creation. The player began the game with the "Arc Phone", which acts as the player's map and sends them messages periodically from Arceus [55]. Arceus was also made encounterable, battle-able, and catchable in *Brilliant Diamond* and *Shining Pearl* (via special in-game item distribution). Grit is demonstrated by some players (e.g., in [56]) who reset their games hundreds or thousands of times to find a "Shiny", i.e. alternate-colored, version of the Pokémon. Arceus is ironically worshipped within the Pokémon community, as in the Facebook Page "Arceism" naming a fictional religion centered around it [6].

---

[3] A degree of separation could be felt between one's self-avatar ("selfitar") and a light, "luminous" deity.

(Importantly, religion is real for devoted peoples the world over.) One can mentally invoke other deities, e.g. Neptune—as in the cognition *thank Neptune*, directed at having "Net Balls" with which the attempt to capture Dynamax Carracosta in *Pokémon Sword* was made—while gaming.[4] PLA holds the possibility of battling and capturing God; another role-playing game (RPG), specifically the *Guild Wars 2* expansion *Path of Fire*, features the storyline of resisting a fallen god (Fig. 12).

Fig. 12. Gift stickers in *Pokémon GO* can be collected at in-game Stops corresponding to real-world religious sites: e.g., "Church of God" and "Providence Church" (above).

"RNJesus" serves as a playful portmanteau of "RNG" and "Jesus" among players of indeterministic, chance-based games. The *PLA* player is given a part of Arceus after demonstrating their worthiness to it (by defeating it in battle after carrying out its will). Notably, Arceus' signature battle Move is Judgment, which changes Type—e.g., Fire or Water—based on Arceus' own (it can be any Type the player chooses). Arceus as a God is powerful, gracious, rewarding, and can take many forms (Fig. 13).

---

[4] A similar cognition could be *praise Grimmsnarl*, where Grimmsnarl—like Carracosta—is a capturable Pokémon. Dynamax Raids in *Pokémon Sword* and *Shield* may be enjoyed given they are highly cinematic for Pokémon video games. Postphenomenologically, the question arises: can one faithfully interpret one's own experiential account (of the technological)?.

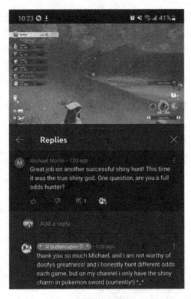

Fig. 13. Initial YouTube comment here jokingly refers to "the true shiny god".

5.2 Massively Multiplayer Online Role-Playing Games (MMORPGs)

RuneScape and Digimon. The MMORPG *RuneScape* includes three gods in its fictional lore: Saradomin, Zamorak, and Guthix [7] High-end armor for each can be obtained, traded, and worn by players. The video game *Digimon Survive* features a polytheistic "Beast God" faith, Kemonogami [34]. The desirable ending of this game provokes the question of whether tears can be sufficient atonement for wrongdoing ([42], 37:38). This ending also features humans and "Digimon"—Digital Monsters—in front of a Shinto shrine ([42], 45:06–47:51) (Fig. 14).

Fig. 14. Spiritual takeover in *Digimon Survive*.

Guild Wars and Guild Wars 2. In *Guild Wars 2*, "Karma" can be acquired and spent on in-game goods by players. In the traditional *Guild Wars* lore, there are six deities that are either goddesses (two, which becomes three later in the storyline) or gods (four, which becomes three later) (Table 1).

Table 1. All information placed on table from [8]

	Type of God or Goddess	Domain	Worshiping or following professions
Kormir	Goddess	Order, Spirit, Knowledge and Truth	
Dwayna	High Goddess	Healing, Air, Warmth and Life	Healing Prayers Monks, Leadership and Motivation Paragons, Air Elementalists, and Wind Prayers Dervishes
Lyssa	Twin Goddess (along with twin, Ilya)	Beauty, Water, Energy and Illusion	Assassins, Energy Storage Elementalists, Mysticism Dervishes, and Mesmers
Balthazar	Heroic God	War, Fire, Strength and Challenge	Warriors, Fire Elementalists, Command Paragons, and Smiting Monks
Grenth	Arbiter God	Darkness, Ice, Death and Judgment	Necromancers, Ritualists, Water Elementalists, and Assassins
Melandru	Mother Goddess	Nature, Earth, Protection and Growth	Rangers and Earth Elementalists and Dervishes

Chokocooka is a "Grawl" (beast) goddess for whom the player can build a "beautiful shrine" as part of the *Guild Wars 2: Living World Season 3* storyline. In "Facing the Truth", part of the *Path of Fire* expansion, one's character must "seek an audience with the gods" [12]. The non-playable character (NPC) Palawa Joko refers to himself as "God-king". Skills the player can use include the aforementioned gods' and goddess' names, including "Avatar of Melandru" (there is an "Avatar of" skill for each God and Goddess). The "Sunspear" group is found to have "eight virtues: valor, humility, honor, **honesty** [emphasis added], justice, compassion, sacrifice, and loyalty" [57] For Maslow [33], honesty is a Being-value or B-value. The *Guild* Wars games include an afterlife-like area known in the lore as "The Mists".

5.3 Other (Video) Games

The Yu-Gi-Oh! video game titled *The Sacred Cards* was released for the Game Boy Advance handheld console. In the computer game *NieR: Automata*, droids chant, "Be as Gods" as they battle with the player and willingly sacrifice themselves. The possibility of becoming greater than human or more expansive is touched on in *NieR: Automata* and in the transhumanism discussed in [9]. The transhuman idea of God existing in machines is also present in the anime film, *Ghost in the Shell*. An example of a video gaming activity involving religious content is naming one's character—e.g., in *Maple Story*—"Siddhartha", after the first name of the original Buddha. According to Julia Martin, "An Overgod, also called an over-power, was a type of deity that existed [in the *Dungeons & Dragons* 'Forgotten Realms' campaign setting] beyond the normal ranking of the gods and of concepts such as alignment. Such beings existed beyond the bounds of the normal cosmology" [58]. Conceptually, this Overgod is similar to the necessary being who created the universe per the philosophical cosmological argument. Being defeated by a player in the Pokémon Online battle simulator who discussed their religious activities outside of the server is another example of religion existing in the digital gaming context.

6 Anime/Film/(Social) Media

Discord servers with separate channels and emojis for major religions exist. The Discord server Awakening from the Meaning Crisis features channels for these religions (including the recent channel made for discussion of Hinduism); the server 5D+ Ascended Platform Of LightWarriors features several emojis depicting religious imagery, e.g. the Jewish menorah (Fig. 15).

Filipinos after they're cured: Alleluia God saved my life!
Doctors:

Fig. 15. Discourse via Discord about people from the Philippines, "Alleluia God", and medical doctors.

Learning about Islam and customary utterances—e.g., "mashallah habibi", Arabic for, "bless you, my love"—and playing god with another's username (e.g., referring to a user colloquially referred to as "Mu" as "godmu") are activities one can undertake in a Discord server. Also in a Discord server, one can acquire religious (e.g., Christian) wisdom, such as its warning against divorce; one can also gain such wisdom via audiobook-listening, such as author Jordan B. Peterson's question of whether one is on good terms with their brother. In the British royalty drama series *The Crown* (available for watching on one's computer, e.g. in DVD format), monarchy is referred to as a calling from God. Also in this series, a sacred promise is defined as commitment that cannot be broken. This series also involves sacred ceremony. One can attend religious events, such as the Hindu festival of lights known as Diwali, remotely through video chat services like Messenger if one is unable to attend in-person (Figs. 16 and 17).

Fig. 16. A collective family prayer via WhatsApp.

Fig. 17. A birthday wish and accompanying blessing posted onto a user's Facebook profile.

One can attain religious wisdom from the posts of Facebook friends, e.g. the wisdom to deny oneself. The Godly Dating 101 page has insight that is curated primarily for a Christian following (e.g., [59]), but can be applicable for members of other religions. On Instagram, one can post religious or spiritual content, such as videos of prayer to gods (whether traditional or fictional) for life success. VCoP's can be used to discuss, theorize on, and clarify the nature of gods or goddesses. For instance, the "Religion & Mythology" subforum of "The World and Beyond" forum on INTJforum—a VCoP designed primarily for the INTJ Myers-Briggs personality type—affords religious discourse among members, moderators, and administration. One thread may involve salient religious themes; members may write about finding religion's value increasingly in their lives. One can also self-disclose identification with, e.g., the Protestant work ethic via VCoP journaling. Also via such journaling, members may playfully refer to a user as "god" or "God". Members may share perceptions of one another in specified threads, for example deeming a user enlightened. Other playful uses of "God" can be found in digital music, e.g. in the song "She's a God" by pop-punk rock band Neck Deep (which can be streamed on Spotify). The podcasts of spiritual leaders can also be listened to digitally (again, e.g., on Spotify": the popular speaker Eckhart Tolle, in one podcast episode, distinguishes between conventional language and what he terms the "real [deep] truth" [50]. Returning again to digital music, the pronouncement "I am a God" is made at the beginning of Machine Gun Kelly's track, "emo girl". Machine Gun Kelly's pop-punk album *mainstream sellout* includes references to God and soul, viz. in the track titled "god save me" and lyrics "…you sold your/Soul…" in the album's title track. One may conduct an AC experiment on encoding the message of meaningful lyrics by sharing them on a VCoP. Artist KennyHoopla sings: "You are not…Jesus, he hates LA" in his song cowritten with drummer Travis Barker, "hollywood sucks//", provoking the listener into a critical reflection on Hollywood culture [43].

Tet in the anime *No Game No Life* is considered its One True God, who plays games but does not battle in war. The main character and his sister aim to challenge Tet. In *Yu-Gi-Oh! 5D's*, protagonist Yusei Fudo's "sign of the Crimson Dragon" could be analogized to the Godhead. In *Yu-Gi-Oh! GX*, protagonist Judai Yuki's duel with Osiris/Slifer the Sky Dragon represents a clash with this Egyptian God from the original *Yu-Gi-Oh!* series, *Duel Monsters*; in *5D's*, the three main characters must duel against the series' reimagining of the Nordic Gods Odin, Thor, and Loki. In *Duel Monsters*, protagonist Yugi Muto collects the powerful Egyptian God Cards from three of his adversaries in the Battle City Tournament. Spiritual cohabitation is seen in the *Yu-Gi-Oh!* series *Duel Monsters*, *GX* and *ZEXAL*. Specifically, these series involve ancient or past life souls in present-day vessels' respective bodies, evil alter egos (e.g., *GX*'s Light of Destruction), duel spirits (*Duel Monsters* and especially *GX*), and the character Astral (*ZEXAL*). *GX* Episode 159 includes mention of the "sacred will of the Supreme King" (13:08–13:17). Also in *GX*, Fubuki Tenjoin—under the influence of "Nightshroud" [11]—states: "My soul will not fall so easily to Darkness!" He then activates his Trap Card "Red-Eyes Spirit" to resurrect a "Red-Eyes" monster. In one of the *GX*'s series last episodes, Judai summons "God Neos" to defeat Season 4's primary antagonist (Darkness). While watching such anime, one may view humorous Crunchyroll ads for media in some way dealing with god, e.g. the anime *Konosuba – God's Blessing on this Wonderful World!* Yugi and Pharaoh Atem's battle with Zorc in *Duel Monsters*, Season 5 offers the interesting notion that gods (in this case, Slifer, Obelisk, and Ra) need to be fused in order to defeat evil. The language of Nightshroud (interchangeable with Darkness) near the end of *GX*, Season 4–as translated from the original Japanese into English—closely resembles Arceus' in the English playthrough of *PLA* (using words like "thou"). In *Digimon Adventure: Last Evolution Kizuna*, Eosmon's final "DigiVolution" is based on the Greek/Roman goddess of dawn, Eos/Aurora. In *Digimon Adventure*, a quest of the main group of characters (referred to as the "DigiDestined") is to find Holy Digimon; such an anime is viewable via the Google Chromecast. The Digimon Garudamon is based on a Hindu bird demigod[5] (Fig. 18).

In the film *Shrek 2* (at 20:48), the "Fairy Godmother Song" is sung including the lyric, "your soul will cleanse". Religious confusion exists in films like *A Very Harold & Kumar Christmas* (2011), used to comedic (as well as provocative) effect. In this movie (at 47:03), the protagonists' friend Goldstein—a Jewish man converted to Christianity—states that he has "an appointment to get uncircumcised". At such cinematic moments, comedic context is important for the viewer interested in the AC of religion to keep in mind, as being potentially offensive to some yet lighthearted to others. Another example of such a case is this same movie's depiction of Jesus Christ in heaven: actor Neil Patrick Harris (acting as himself) refers to Jesus here as a "dirty hippie" while recounting his experience to protagonists Harold and Kumar. In superhero franchise DC's Netflix series *The Flash*, the "Speed Force" exists as a science-fictional god realm from which protagonist Barry Allen (also superhero The Flash) derives his supernatural bodily speed. In this show series, Godspeed (also the name of an American heavy metal band) serves

---

[5] In *Digimon Adventure* (Season 1, Episode 45), Digital Monster Gabumon verbalized to Machmon: "I heard the cries of your *soul* [emphasis added] in your racing" (9:06).

Fig. 18. Lyric from Bonnie Tyler's song, "Holding Out for a Hero".

as a later-series antagonist. This show provokes the question of whether soul or consciousness (these are experienced by a viewer as having been conflated by the episode in question) is not requisite for "personality", specifically in the case of character Caitlin Snow's superpowered alter-ego "Frost". In another superhero Netflix series, *Daredevil* (a Marvel franchise), God and the Catholic Christian tradition exist as recurring themes, especially in Season 3. At one point, Matthew Murdock (whose vigilante alter-ego is known as Daredevil) is referred to as "God's soldier". In the film *The Imitation Game* (2014), lead character Alan Turing—based on the historical and now-famous mathematician credited for inventing the Turing test—asks: "Was I God? No. Because God didn't win [World War II]. We did", referring to his cryptographic team's efforts to aid the Allied Forces against Axis Germany [24]. In another Netflix show series, *Never Have I Ever*, main character Devi prays to multiple Hindu gods (in Season 1, Episode 1); she also engages in Ganesh Puja (Episode 4 of the same season). In this series, Devi is told of the story of a child who was on the receiving end of a car crash having God tell him to go to Yale (Episode 4, 13:10–13:17). In Season 1, Episode 5 of this show, Devi's friend Fabiola fakes saying grace (3:06). One of Devi's teachers says at one point in this episode: "God, whoever she is, is smiling on us today" (6:40–41). The narrator of Season 1, Episode 10 speaks of the soulful gaze of the band Doobie Brothers. In Season 2, Episode 2, the "Sherman Oaks God" is referred to (11:21) (Figs. 19 and 20).

Fig. 19. One of Devi's teachers utters a Muslim greeting meaning, "Peace be unto you" [23].

Fig. 20. Friend Aneesa exasperatedly recounts to Devi the former's mother reacting to Aneesa's sacrilegious Twitter post.

Also in *Never have I* Ever, the ironic and desperate possibility of a "just and merciful God" is expressed (In Season 3, Episode 6). Also approached is the notion of setting oneself free, in some way, through setting another free, per character Ben's father. A friend of Devi's mother Dr. Vishwakumar reacts, "Oh, *God*…" upon learning of Devi's leg paralysis (Season 3, Episode 7). This points back to the different ways people say "oh(, my) God" (most relevantly in this chapter's context, digitally). In the movie *Yes, God, Yes*, the body is said to be a gift from God that must be honored.

Fig. 21. In Netflix film *To All the Boys I've Loved Before*, Lara-Jean Covey's younger sister "Kitty" responds tongue-in-cheek to her father on the topic of menstruation.

In the *To All the Boys* romantic comedy film trilogy, the word "God" is used in various ways. Like in *Shrek 2*, it is used as part of a song lyric (Fig. 22). It is also used to express self-exasperation (Fig. 21) and mortification (Fig. 22). The word is even used to comedic effect (Fig. 23).

In DC's *Legends of Tomorrow*, character Gwyn Davies frequently invokes God, uttering "God almighty". In the show series *The Boys* (Season 1, Episode 2), character Madelyn Stillwell says: "Gods need to be pure and perfect, and they need to stay that way".

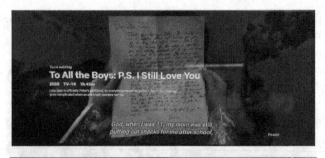

Fig. 22. In Netflix film *To All the Boys: P.S. I Still Love You*, Lara-Jean Covey is shocked at the contents of a love letter she wrote.

Fig. 23. Lyric from Ashe's song, "Moral of the Story".

The anime *Bleach* features "Soul Society (尸魂界, literally 'Dead Spirit World')", "the afterlife for those who live in the World of the Living in Japan. It is meant to correspond to Heaven or Nirvana in Human belief systems. It is the place where most departed souls and the Shinigami dwell" [60]. The theme of sacrifice is in both *Pokémon: The First Movie* and *Harry Potter and the Deathly Hallows: Part 2*, with the main character in each (Ash Ketchum and Harry, respectively) voluntarily confronting a situation that temporarily incapacitates them in deathlike manners (Fig. 24).

Fig. 24. In Netflix film *To All the Boys: Always and Forever*, Lara-Jean Covey's father jokes about Kitty becoming interested in the opposite gender.

7   Conclusion

Importantly, in four of the media discussed—*Guild Wars 2*, *Pokémon Legends: Arceus*, *Pokémon Brilliant Diamond* and *Shining Pearl*, and *Yu-Gi-Oh! Duel Monsters*—battles with the gods are climaxes, not definitive ends, of their respective stories. In a more "real world", casual setting, one could remind another human agent—for instance, a former tutee—of their bond by sharing with them an instance of a phrase they previously shared (e.g., "God wink" as it appears on a license plate). One could also engage in remote tutoring concerning the philosophical "problem of evil" and proof of God's existence as an ultimate, omnipotent, and omniscient being. Theological notions of soul [61] and prayer [62] are even invoked in Twitter posts about valued TV series, such as CW's *Batwoman*. "Spirit" and "soul" are used interchangeably in popular media (such as in *Yu-Gi-Oh! Duel Monsters*), but they have been distinguished elsewhere. Neo-Jungian James Hillman considers the spirit masculine (active) and soul feminine (passive). *Yu-Gi-Oh!* series *Duel Monsters*, *GX*, and *ZEXAL* each involve the stealing of souls from duelists who have lost important card duels. In this series' fifth iteration, *Arc-V*, character Gong states that a dueling card deck is comparable to a duelist's soul. Soul is also evoked in the lyrics of ZEXAL's theme song, "Halfway to Forever", with the lyric: "The bonds of our souls can't be replaced" [63]. Don Thousand—"Barian" deity in *Yu-Gi-Oh! ZEXAL*—is another God who, after being defeated by the protagonist, falls (similar to Balthazar in *Guild Wars 2: Path of Fire*) (Fig. 25).

In *The Crown*, an episode is titled "Act of God"; the phrase "act of God" appears as a legal phrase in *Suits* (Season 7). In the episode of *The Crown* mentioned, Prince Phillip knelt before Queen Elizabeth, in so doing showing his submission to her monarchy and God. It is said in this show that God gives monarchs people to rule. Elizabeth's anointment is referred to as a holy, sacred moment. In Season 7 of *Suits*, character Sheila refers to Louis as having come across like a "Viking God". A Yu-Gi-Oh! Monster Card recently printed in the Trading Card Game (TCG) is called "God of Archery", appearing variously online (e.g.: [27], 19:21). In [28], "The Yugi-gods" are humorously invoked (Fig. 26).

Fig. 25. *Yu-Gi-Oh!* Monster Card of a fictional venomous snake deity.

Fig. 26. Renditions of Raijin and Fujin also appear together in the *Yu-Gi-Oh! Arc V* anime series (Season 1, Episodes 42–43).

"Crushing" souls is taken up in *Yu-Gi-Oh! The Dark Side of Dimensions*. The Winged Dragon of Ra and Arceus are each depicted as wrathful gods (the former in *Duel Monsters'* Battle City arc, and the latter in *Pokémon: Arceus and the Jewel of Life*. Gender identity is related to "some form of earth deity" [22] (Fig. 27).

"Spirit Break" is taken up in Pokémon (the *Ultimate Journeys* anime and *Sword* and *Shield* games) as one of two signature moves of the Pokémon Grimmsnarl. Spirit break is also taken up in the movie *Space Jam: A New Legacy* (Fig. 28).

In [21], a nonserious allusion to is made to "rabbit gods". One limitation for this chapter's analysis is its near-total reliance on the English language for its articulation. (Specifically, any hegemonic language's utility as an abstract unifier of culturally, historically, etc. distinct religious notions is inherently limited.) Also, it is an open question whether transhumanism is a passing intellectual fad with application attempts that should

Fig. 27. Purportedly unused game content from *Pokémon Black* and *White* [20].

Fig. 28. Shiny Togepi hatched in a livestream recording of *Pokémon Sword* or *Shield* gameplay. Here, the second-to-bottommost user comment reads: "I hope arceus blesses you with baby".

be distinguished from theosophy.[6] Blavatsky's presentation of the sevenfold constitution of humanity includes a linear developmental hierarchy leading from physiology, to mind (specifically intellect), and finally *atama* or will. There is a similar hierarchy implicit in the *Pokémon* anime, where a trio of legendary Pokémon—Mesprit, Uxie, and Azelf—is matched respectively with protagonists Dawn (Hikari in Japanese), Brock, and Ash Ketchum. Azelf is referred to as the Willpower Pokémon in its video game "Pokédex" entry, reinforcing the will's dominance over intellect—represented by Uxie, the Knowledge Pokémon—and emotion (where Mesprit is the emotion Pokémon). The main point of this chapter is that everyday media consumption can be instructive on

---

[6] An appreciably deep treatment of the interdependence between technology and mysticism can be found in [47].

the most meaningful aspects of life, viz. religion and God. Knowing God is more than justified true belief (barring philosophical Gettier cases), but wisdom leads human users to divinity. Important religious messages findable via electronic or digital media include the wisdom to love one's enemies (per theosopher Matthieu Ricard) and the defining of love style agape as "spiritual love" (per an e-textbook dealing with relationships). God is omnipresent and omnipotent, and has been shown in this chapter to be taken up differently across a wide array of digital media (Fig. 29).

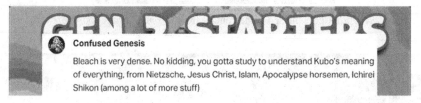

Fig. 29. Multi-religiosity in a YouTube comment [30].

Via YouTube, the human user can learn of God arguments and watch videos about fictional gods like Arceus (viz., gameplay footage of Arceus). Quora is a platform on which users can ask and answer theosophical questions and bridge understandings between distinct traditions. For instance, the holy trinities that are part of Christianity and Hinduism can be linked in such a fashion (Fig. 30).

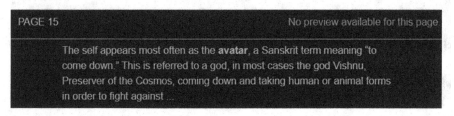

Fig. 30. Hindu theology from a Google Books preview [45].

Sherry Turkle, in her book chapter "The Human Spirit in a Computer Culture" [49], wrote of "hackers find soul in the machine", losing themselves in process of merging minds with a "universal system" (p. 307). She also inquired, "if mind is machine, who is the actor? Where is responsibility, spirit, soul?" (p. 308). "We cede", she wrote, "to the computer the power of reason, but at the same time, in defense, our sense of identity becomes increasingly focused on the soul and the spirit in the human machine" (pp. 312–13). The spirit of AC or its committed working group, "AugCog" covers activities like learning about "do-it-yourself" ("DIY") brain-computer interface (BCI), which has been taken up on a psychology Discord server. More playfully, one can learn of another's "spirit animal", also via a Discord psychology server. The Immersive King Tut—"an epic journey of pharaohs and gods", and a cultural HCI event experienceable in Los Angeles—includes mythological information about the Egyptian Gods Ra (sun God) and Osiris (God of death). (Obelisks were also included in the visual portion of the four-wall audiovisual presentation.) Examples of religious and spiritual AC through HCI at their best stimulate humans to cultivate a better relation with God, a worship-worthy figure like the Buddha, and others.

References

1. Wilber, K.: Sex, Ecology, Spirituality: The Spirit of Evolution, 2nd edn. Shambhala, Boston (2000)
2. https://openmindplatform.org/wp-content/uploads/2018/02/Excerpts-from-Buddha%E2%80%99s-The-Dhammapada.pdf. Accessed 22 Jan 2022
3. Mingyur Rinpoche, Y., Swanson, E.: The Joy of Living: Unlocking the Secret and Science of Happiness. Random House, New York (2007). [Audible version]
4. https://www.youtube.com/watch?v=CFKUbjRjaIo. Accessed 22 Jan 2022
5. https://www.yugioh.com/yu-gi-oh/down-in-flames-part-2/67. Accessed 22 Jan 2022
6. https://www.facebook.com/BookOfArceism/. Accessed 22 Jan 2022
7. https://oldschoolrunescape.fandom.com/wiki/Gods. Accessed 22 Jan 2022
8. https://wiki.guildwars.com/wiki/Gods_of_Tyria. Accessed 22 Aug 2022
9. Kurzweil, R.: The Age of Spiritual Machines: When Computers Exceed Human Intelligence. Penguin Books, London (2000)
10. Peterson, J.: Maps of Meaning: The Architecture of Belief. Random House, New York (2002). [Audible version]
11. https://yugioh.fandom.com/wiki/Nightshroud. Accessed 1 Feb 2022
12. https://wiki.guildwars2.com/wiki/Facing_the_Truth#In_the_Mists. Accessed 5 Feb 2022
13. https://niantic.helpshift.com/hc/en/6-pokemon-go/faq/83-battling-at-gyms/#:~:text=Battle%20at%20Gyms,time%20it%20loses%20a%20battle. Accessed 8 Feb 2022
14. https://www.youtube.com/watch?v=04jwJ6k65Jc. Accessed 22 Mar 2022
15. https://nipponrama.com/raijin-and-fujin/. Accessed 22 Mar 2022
16. Osteen, J.: Your Best Life Now: 7 Steps to Living at Your Full Potential. Time Warner Audiobooks (2004). [Audible version]
17. https://www.youtube.com/watch?v=EItAf9ESXLs&list=PLOiTiVAUx4bivjSs5J9dIp9JMOmlhvVPz&index=3. Accessed 22 Mar 2022
18. https://www.youtube.com/watch?v=6FqWP4bc50A. Accessed 23 Mar 2022
19. https://gamingintel.com/wp-content/uploads/2022/01/Giratina-Dialga-Arceus-Palkia-Pokemon-Legends-1024x576.jpg. Accessed 26 Mar 2022
20. https://www.youtube.com/watch?v=GLGFHARHdbc. Accessed 11 Apr 2022
21. https://youtu.be/EvKue3LIKtI. Accessed 11 Apr 2022
22. https://pride-color-schemes.tumblr.com/post/148268817900/earthgender. Accessed 11 Apr 2022
23. https://ccnmtl.columbia.edu/projects/mmt/mxp/notes/5140.html. Accessed 11 Apr 2022
24. https://www.imdb.com/title/tt2084970/characters/nm1212722. Accessed 15 Apr 2022
25. Blavatsky, H. P.: Key to Theosophy. Global Grey (2013). [Kindle version]. (Original Work Published in 1889)
26. https://www.youtube.com/watch?v=_ykN6P0Cz0k. Accessed 22 May 2022
27. https://www.youtube.com/watch?v=SdHmv0RL8kM. Accessed 22 May 2022
28. https://youtu.be/T3fICod0jmc. Accessed 22 May 2022
29. https://www.japanese-wiki-corpus.org/Shinto/Ichirei%20shikon.html. Accessed 5 Jul 2022
30. https://www.youtube.com/watch?v=zJz6hJ4V2M0. Accessed 5 Jul 2022

31. James, W.: The varieties of religious experience: a study in human nature. eBooks@Adelaide (2009). https://csrs.nd.edu/assets/59930/williams_1902.pdf. Accessed 5 Jul 2022. (Original Work Published in 1902)
32. Du Bois, W. E. B.: The Souls of Black Folk. G&D Media (2019). [Kindle version]
33. Maslow, A.H.: Religions, Values, and Peak-Experiences. Penguin Compass, New York (1976)
34. https://www.youtube.com/watch?v=6buYrC_om6E. Accessed 4 Aug 2022
35. Sood, S.: Love as augmented cognition: passionate gaming in the era of virtual romance. In: Schmorrow, D.D., Fidopiastis, C.M. (eds.) HCII 2022. LNCS, vol. 13310, pp. 381–401. Springer, Cham (2022). https://doi.org/10.1007/978-3-031-05457-0_29
36. Davary, B.: Ecotheology and Love: The Converging Poetics of Sohrab Sepehri and James Baldwin. Lexington Books, Lanham (2022)
37. Haraway, D.: Situated knowledges: the science question in feminism and the privilege of partial perspective. Fem. Stud. **14**(3), 575–599 (1988)
38. Sterling, P.: What is Health? Allostasis and the Evolution of Human Design. The MIT Press, Cambridge (2020)
39. https://web.archive.org/web/20210730061947/. https://takemetotheriveryoga.com/wpsite/brahmacharya-conservation-of-life-force-energy/. Accessed 31 Oct 2022
40. Deleuze, G.: Postscript on the societies of control. http://home.lu.lv/~ruben/Deleuze%20-%20Postscript%20On%20The%20Societies%20Of%20Control.pdf. Accessed 20 Aug 2022
41. https://www.youtube.com/watch?v=-KNlVzAbadA&t=352s. Accessed 20 Aug 2022
42. https://www.youtube.com/watch?v=bEkE9pv1-wk. Accessed 21 Aug 2022
43. https://genius.com/Kennyhoopla-and-travis-barker-hollywood-sucks-lyrics. Accessed 20 Aug 2022
44. https://www.youtube.com/watch?v=bKz-HtOPvjE&t=207s. Accessed 20 Aug 2022
45. https://www.google.com/books/edition/The_Online_Self/bTzADAAAQBAJ?hl=en&gbpv=0. Accessed 22 Aug 2022
46. Heidegger, M.: The Question Concerning Technology and Other Essays. Garland Publishing, Inc., New York (1977). (W. Lovitt, Trans.)
47. Glenn, J.C.: Future Mind: Artificial Intelligence: The Merging of the Mystical and the Technological in the 21st Century. Acropolis Books Ltd., Washington D.C. (1989)
48. Kugelmann, R.: The Windows of Soul: Psychological Physiology of the Human Eye and Primary Glaucoma. Bucknell University Press, Lewisburg (1983)
49. Turkle, S.: The Second Self: Computers and the Human Spirit. Simon and Schuster, New York (1984)
50. https://open.spotify.com/track/4ZiTR1ixLXGW3OoejQ5PVR?si=OUG0yq_JQIKaLOc6Sc0YEA&utm_source=copy-link. Accessed 25 Sept 2022
51. https://twitchplayswiki.fandom.com/wiki/Lord_Helix. Accessed 27 Sept 2022
52. https://www.cs.mcgill.ca/~rwest/wikispeedia/wpcd/wp/q/Quetzalcoatl.htm#:~:text=Quetzalcoatl%20(%22feathered%20serpent%22%20or,all%20mesoamerican%20peoples%20claim%20descent. Accessed 29 Sept 2022
53. Laarni, J., Ravaja, N., Kallinen, K., Saari, T.: Transcendent experience in the use of computer-based media. https://dl.acm.org/doi/pdf/10.1145/1028014.1028082?casa_token=x7-esegN2OgAAAAA:_XOcDyU46aNGS2swMDb-2eIt5KA2Fyx8AbuR5Psk4oUuxbRXpm6kHBiZPW9mMACeYqIYNT0eLB0. Accessed 30 Sept 2022
54. https://www.smogon.com/smog/issue39/anything-goes. Accessed 8 Oct 2022
55. https://bulbapedia.bulbagarden.net/wiki/Arc_Phone#Functions. Accessed 10 Oct 2022
56. https://www.youtube.com/watch?v=sJ6YQFDkh4Q. Accessed 10 Oct 2022
57. https://wiki.guildwars2.com/wiki/The_Sunspear_Creed. Accessed 13 Oct 2022
58. https://forgottenrealms.fandom.com/wiki/Overgod. Accessed 14 Oct 2022

59. https://m.facebook.com/story.php?story_fbid=pfbid02qTmoq8yufsQt2XjMniu1suK5hEhJQ xtZKX7vsMVJL1EuCtiFw4bcLwBq65i5XNtBl&id=100044567793600&eav=Afb9w4Lgs 7arDpw_qE49sBn_37nBtA_qjkFHNSBa8AMqM82hWyGBx6tVZ2jzUC46mRg. Accessed 17 Oct 2022
60. https://bleachfanfiction.fandom.com/wiki/Soul_Society_(Seireitou). Accessed 24 Oct 2022
61. https://twitter.com/BatwomanWriters/status/1506710772813991938?t=HSBE4LFM-zi4 59AfFmv4zQ&s=19. Accessed 24 Oct 2022
62. https://twitter.com/BatwomanWriters/status/1506382544584859648?t=I-XufPGdSKky87 sZnLmiRw&s=19. Accessed 24 Oct 2022
63. https://yugioh.fandom.com/wiki/Halfway_to_Forever_(song). Accessed 24 Oct 2022

Augmented and Virtual Reality
for Augmented Cognition

Modulating Virtual Affective Elicitation by Human Body Odors: Advancing Research on Social Signal Processing in Virtual Reality

Sergio Cervera-Torres[1]([✉])[iD], Maria Eleonora Minissi[1][iD], Alberto Greco[2][iD], Alejandro Callara[2][iD], Saideh Ferdowsi[3][iD], Luca Citi[3][iD], Luna Maddalon[1][iD], Irene Alice Chicchi Giglioli[1][iD], and Mariano Alcañiz[1][iD]

[1] Human-Centred Technology Research Institute (HUMAN-Tech). Polytechnic University of Valencia, Valencia, Spain
scertor@i3b.upv.es
[2] Research Center "E. Piaggio", University of Pisa, Pisa, Italy
[3] School of Computer Science and Electronic Engineering, University of Essex, Colchester, UK

Abstract. Human sensory systems are capable of encoding emotion-related signals during social interactions (e.g., fearful or happy facial expressions). In this regard, many emotion elicitation procedures have been reported within the scope of social signal processing research. Most of these procedures rely on socially relevant stimuli, such as emotional face images, videos, and, more recently, virtual reality (VR) scenes. Unfortunately, procedures involving cross-modal interactions beyond visual and acoustic stimuli, such as olfaction, are still scarce. In this sense, neuroscience supports a close link between the olfactory and affective systems. Moreover, experimental research has reported faster appraisals of emotional face images when congruent valence-laden artificial scents were presented (e.g., positive scent-happy face; negative scent-fearful face). Interestingly, recent findings indicate that emotion-related human-body odors (HBOs) might also modulate affective appraisals during a neutral virtual reality experience. However, whether and how emotion-related HBOs modulate affective VR experiences requires further examination. Here, an approach to this research question is proposed from a Virtual Reality-based Behavioral Biomarker (VRBB) experimental framework. Concretely, in the first place, a novel affective elicitation procedure based on social-emotional VR is introduced, wherein electro-dermal activity (EDA), heart-rate variability (HRV), electroencephalography (EEG), and affective appraisals, will be accounted for. In a second step, the modulating role of HBOs will be investigated regarding those measures. This work presents the envisioned model, details of the devised VEs, and a research design to test concrete hypotheses.

Keywords: Human Body Odors (HBO) · Emotion · Virtual Environment · social signal processing

D. D. Schmorrow and C. M. Fidopiastis (Eds.): HCII 2023, LNAI 14019, pp. 317–327, 2023.
https://doi.org/10.1007/978-3-031-35017-7_20

1 Introduction

1.1 Social Signal Processing

Social cognition can be defined as "the study of mental processes involved in perceiving, attending to, remembering, thinking about, and making sense of the people in our social world [1]". A particular aspect of social cognition refers to social interactions, understood as complex dynamics between individuals, which involve emotions, verbal and nonverbal behavior, and varying contexts [2]. In this regard, social neuroscience has emerged as the interplay of different disciplines, including neuroscience, personality, cognitive and social psychology, to advance our understanding of the social interaction components as related to their bodily substrates [3]. To be more precise, this discipline investigates, among other questions, how multimodal behavioral cues correlate with emotional and cognitive processes linked to social interaction [4]. The expression *behavioral cue* describes a set of temporal changes in neuromuscular and physiological activity that last for short intervals (milliseconds to minutes). This goal is achieved through a broad range of methods, among which social signal processing is gaining momentum. This methodological approach includes the measurement of electrical brain activity, neuroimaging, psychophysiological measurements, and computational modeling. These methods are either used alone or together with more qualitative research tools, such as behavioral observation and self-reporting [5].

The case of emotions is very representative of social signal-processing research. Emotions, such as fear and happiness, can be characterized by a set of distinctive behavioral cues (e.g., micro-facial expressions or vocal utterances [6–8]). They also can be linked to psychophysiological measurements among which electrodermal activity (EDA) and heart rate variability (HRV) are two of the most important [9]. Notably, fear and happiness serve important communicative and social adaptive functions during social interactions (e.g., approach-avoidance behaviors). On the one hand, learning about potential threats either by experiencing fear directly or vicariously through social transmission, is critical for survival [10]. On the other hand, it is assumed that happiness and social behavior mutually enhance each other so that healthy social relationships promote happiness, and a happy mood fosters social interactions [11].

1.2 Olfactive Cues and Emotional Response Modulation

Many studies have designed emotion elicitation procedures by relying on socially relevant stimuli, such as emotional face images [12], videos [13], and, more recently, virtual reality (VR) scenes [14]. In these procedures, participants are typically exposed to the stimuli and then asked to self-report, for example, their experienced emotional valence (from very positive to very negative) and arousal (from very high to very low) according to a numerical scale. Unfortunately, research on social (and emotional) signal processing has only scarcely focused on cross-modal interactions beyond visual and acoustic, as with olfaction [15, 16]. The sense of olfaction is particularly connected to the amygdala and the orbitofrontal cortex, thus providing a close link with the limbic system, which is directly related to emotion processing [17]. In this line of reasoning, experimental research has shown that valence-laden artificial scents can modulate the processing of emotional faces. For example, modulation effects of pleasant (e.g., strawberry fragrance) and unpleasant (e.g., pyridine) artificial scents have been investigated regarding appraisals of happy and disgusted face images. In general, the findings seem to support faster appraisals regarding happy faces by the pleasant scent and an inhibition effect by the unpleasant scent [18]. Importantly, beyond artificial scents, the question of how human body chemosignals ("human body odors; HBOs") may modulate emotional processing is reaching great attention. Typically, HBOs are collected by axillary sweat of individuals who are exposed to an emotional elicitation procedure via, for example, videos eliciting happiness or fear [19]. The donors are usually asked to rate how their feelings according to concrete emotions (e.g., angry, fearful, sad, happy, disgusted, neutral, surprised, calm, and amused) and/or affective dimensions (valence and arousal) on a numerical Likert scale. Sweat pads are kept in separate vials and stored in a − 80 °C freezer. In this regard, it has been shown that fear-related HBO facilitated faster evaluations of fearful face images as compared to others depicting disgust or anger [20]. Moreover, happiness and fear-related HBO have been shown to increase neural responses to the processing of neutral faces as compared to neutral HBO [21]. Therefore, to date, modulation of HBO regarding responses to emotional face images has been demonstrated at both, behavioral and neural activation levels.

1.3 Olfactive Cues and Virtual Reality

It is worth noting that beyond responses to static emotional face images, methodological approaches capable of exploiting ecological validity by increasing the sense of immersion and presence, are needed to deepen how sensorial cues, particularly olfaction, relate to social interactions that resemble the complexity of real-life contexts. Virtual reality (VR)-based experimental settings entail such advantages [22]. For example, the validity of VR has been increasingly supported for emotion induction and psychotherapy [23]. Furthermore, VR settings can also provide major advantages in experimental control, reproducibility, and multimodal interaction. Therefore, methodologically speaking, VR settings move beyond laboratory-controlled contexts requiring participants to observe static stimuli, from which findings are more difficult to generalize to "real" contexts. Along with this reasoning, the investigation of olfaction within VR is reaching great attention [24]. Some findings indicate, for example, that unpleasant artificial scents induce a greater sense of presence than pleasant scents (e.g., [25]). In addition, other findings point out that cross-modal congruency between audiovisual and olfactory stimuli may also increase processing fluency and stimuli liking [26]. Furthermore, a recent study also pointed out that HBO, and more concretely, fear-related HBO increased the participants reported anxiety and, in turn, promoted negative impressions of a neutral character within a virtual reality environment representing a bar [27].

However, research involving HBO within VR settings is very scarce, thus, requiring a deeper examination. In this regard, the project here raises the question of whether, as for artificial scents, affective congruency effects might be expected from audiovisual and HBO stimuli. This question is approached from a VR-based Behavioral Biomarkers (VRBB) framework [28], a term coined to highlight the application of social signal processing techniques in VR (i.e., including psychophysiological and subjective emotional assessments). Specifically, as elaborated in the following sections, the project here will test in a first step, affective elicitation capabilities of novel virtual environments (VE) including social signals. The hypothetical rationale that emotional HBOs modulate the elicited affectivity of those social-emotional VE, will be tested in a second step, expecting that modulation effects will be more noticeable when affective HBO and VR are congruent (see Fig. 1).

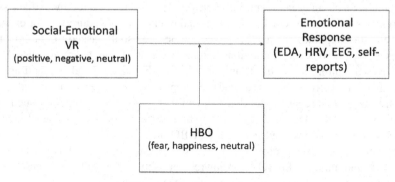

Fig. 1. Hypothesized model

2 Methods

2.1 Social-Emotional Virtual Environments

The social-emotional virtual environments (VE) in this project build upon prior research using "emotional" virtual parks to elicit positive, negative, or neutral affectivity (EMMA Project) [29]. In general, the park is partially surrounded by buildings and is square-shaped. There are street lamps, benches, and bins along the roads. Additionally, there is a fountain, a playground area, and a bandstand. The park is multimodal in the sense that includes visual and acoustic stimuli (see Fig. 2). The most relevant aspect is that some features of the park can be altered (e.g., light, colors, or sounds) in line with a to-be-elicited emotional valence (positive, negative, neutral; see Figs. 3–5 upper part).

However, this "emotional" park was not designed to explicitly convey social meaning. Accordingly, novel social-emotional VEs are designed to include social meaning by including virtual agents. Virtual agents are pre-programmed elements that can take human-shape forms. In this case, they are developed to convey positive, negative, or neutral affectivity depending on the scenario. Nonetheless, they are not designed to be responsive agents. Specifically, within each affective VE, two different situations with virtual agents will be displayed. Within the neutral VE, a woman shows up first, walking across the park. She looks at the clock on her mobile phone and she continues walking. Then, two young men appear and sit for a while on the stairs of the bandstand. One of them asks the other for the time (Fig. 3). Within the positive VE, a man and a woman show up running. The man is exhausted, and the woman motivates him; she says that if he reaches the stairs of the bandstand, he will have fulfilled his goal. When he arrives,

Fig. 2. The general structure of the "emotional" park for affective elicitation

they both celebrate his achievement with joy. Then, a father and his son appear playing in the park. They laugh a lot. The child approaches the screen and greets looking in the participant's direction. The father catches him, friendly, and they both leave the park (Fig. 4). Finally, within the negative VE, a woman appears scolding her son while crossing the park. The boy is crying because he doesn't want to go home. The mother tells him to stop crying and tries to explain that they cannot stay longer at the park because it's raining. Afterward, a man with a black hoodie appears abruptly and sits on a bench. He shows an unfriendly attitude. At some point, he turns in the participant's direction and says, "don't look at me".

Fig. 3. Non-social neutral park (upper part) and social neutral park (lower part). The weather is partly cloudy, and the leaves of the trees are green and reddish-brown. There are no flowers or butterflies. There are some birds, and the fountain shows a constant water flow.

Fig. 4. Non-social positive park (upper part) and social positive park (lower part). The weather is sunny and bright, the fountain shows constant changes in the water flow. Birds, butterflies, flowers, and a soft wind make the flowers and leaves move. The bandstand is surrounded by vegetation.

Fig. 5. Non-social negative park (upper part) and social negative park (lower part). The weather is stormy and dark. The wind is strong and makes the leaves move rapidly. The fountain is dry. The streetlights are on, but some of them are not working, another is flicking, and one of the grills of the park opens to close constantly because of the wind.

All the parks are modeled with Unity 3D and have the same layout with a constant number of non-virtual agents in the non-social emotional scenarios (i.e., park elements) and a constant number of virtual agents in the social-emotional scenarios (i.e., human avatars).

2.2 Apparatus

The VEs are VR scenarios designed for a semi-immersive CAVE system where three different video projectors are directed to three walls of a $4 \times 4 \times 3$ m room. Concretely, the Optoma HD35UST projectors (Optoma, Alicante, Spain) with an ultra-short-throw lens. The projectors will be connected to a personal computer (Intel Core i7-7700 CPU @3.6 GHZ with dual DVI output Nvidia Geforce GTX 1060 6 GB). A Logitech Z906 500W 5.1 THX (Logitech, Canton Vaud, Switzerland) will be used as the sound system.

In line with the VR-based Behavioral Biomarkers (VRBB) framework, psychophysiological measures in terms of EDA, HRV, and EEG will be recorded during the social-emotional and non-social VEs. The Shimmer3 GSR + and Shimmer3 ECG units (Shimmer Sensing, Dublin, Ireland) at will be used for EDA and HRV assessments at128 Hz y 0,001–100 μS. To do so, the device is placed on the participants' non-dominant wrist, while its electrodes are placed on the second phalanx of the ring and middle fingers of the same hand. The signal provided by the Shimmer3 sensor will be processed using Ledalab (v3.4.8.) of the Matlab software, to inspect and correct for further artifacts.

On the other hand, the LiveAmp 32 EEG channel (Brain Vision Inc.) will be used to record neural activity. Finally, the project will use a 3-channel olfactometer developed to deliver the HBO from pads at a slow flow rate (50 ml/min).

2.3 Design and Hypotheses

Study I
The potential of the above-described VE to elicit affectivity will be investigated, in the first place. The main hypotheses of this study are:

(a) The positive, negative, and neutral VE will elicit a distinctive pattern of affective responses, particularly in terms of emotional valence.
(b) The social VE will elicit stronger physiological responses than the non-social VE.

These hypotheses will be tested following a 3×2 experimental design with the factors *VE* (positive, negative, neutral), and *context* (social, non-social) manipulated within participants. Social and non-social contexts will be presented sequentially within each affective VE but the presentation order will be counterbalanced across participants. The order of the affective VE will also be counterbalanced.

Study II
Once the elicitation procedure by the virtual emotional parks is tested, they will be used to investigate the central research question of whether and how emotional HBO modulate such affective elicitation. Concretely, odor stimuli will consist of neutral, happiness, and fear-related HBO collected by armpit sweat (see details in the introduction).

The main derived hypotheses are:

(a) Emotional HBO (happiness and fear) will show stronger effects on the emotional responses than neutral HBO [cf. 27], particularly during social VE.

(b) HBO modulation effects will be stronger under congruent conditions (positive VE-happiness HBO; negative VE-fear HBO) than incongruent conditions [cf.]

These hypotheses will be tested following a 3x3x2 experimental design with the factors *affective VE* (positive, negative, neutral), *HBO* (fearful, happy, neutral), and *context* (social, non-social) manipulated within participants. As for Study I, social and non-social contexts will be displayed in sequential order within each affective VE but the order will be counterbalanced across participants.

2.4 Experimental Procedure

In both studies, participants will first sign an informed consent. Olfactive sensitivity will be screened via the Sniffin' Sticks test before the experimental testing [30]. Moreover, the Liebowitz Social Anxiety Scale (LSAS; [31]) and Beck Depression Inventory (BDI-II; [32]) will be also administered. Once in the lab, two experimenters will place first the shimmer EDA and HRV sensors on the participants. Then the EEG sensors will be set. To do so, participants will be asked to sit on a chair in the middle of the CAVE, two meters from the front wall. Electroencephalography (EEG) will be synchronized with EDA, HRV, and the olfactometer (with airflow distributed through nose-positioned vials). A psychophysiological baseline assessment will be taken before the experimental testing by asking participants to keep their eyes closed for 60 s and then to keep their eyes open for 60 more seconds in front of a black screen. Then, participants will rate their felt emotional valence and arousal level on a 9-point Likert scale. As above-mentioned, participants will experience the positive, negative, and neutral VEs, presented in counter-balanced order. Social and non-social VE versions will be blocked within each affective category and will last 30 s each. They will be presented sequentially with an interstimulus interval of one second with clean air. The happy, fear, or neutral-related HBO will be administered automatically during the VEs (one HBO each; see Fig. 3). To do so, triggers are programmed to send an on-off signal at the beginning and end of each VE.

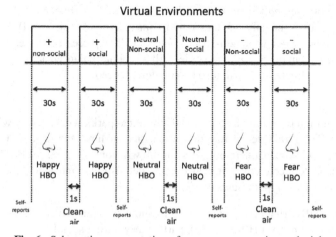

Fig. 6. Schematic representation of a congruent experimental trial.

Participants will rate the self-perceived emotional valence and arousal, after each VE category. The next environment will start after these ratings (Fig. 6).

It should be noted that the VE and HBO factors will not be fully crossed to avoid habituation effects. In this regard, a generalized linear mixed model approach (GLMM) will be used to model the data following a stimuli-within-condition design. In this design, the stimuli (HBO) are nested within conditions (VE) and participants respond to all conditions. In brief, to assess the affective elicitation, all subjects experienced the VEs, which were presented in a randomized order. Self-reports of emotional valence and arousal were measured on a 9-point Likert scale before and after each exposure.

Measures. Electro-dermal activity (EDA), heart rate variability (HRV), electroencephalography (EEG), and self-reports of affective valence and arousal.

3 Discussion

The work here proposes novel social-emotional VEs to investigate, first, how social (vs. non-social) virtual environments integrating human-shaped virtual agents, elicit positive and negative affective responses. This project builds upon prior research implementing emotion elicitation procedures in form of "emotional" parks [29]. In a second step, these VE will serve as a framework to investigate how emotion-related human body odors (HBO) modulate those affective responses. Specifically, HBO affective modulation will be investigated at physiological, cognitive, and behavioral levels. To do so, a VR-based Behavioral Biomarkers (VRBB) framework [28] highlighting the application of social signal processing techniques in VR, will be used (i.e., including psychophysiological and subjective assessments). Specifically, fear and happiness HBO will be investigated. Fear and happiness are two of the most fundamental basic emotions. On one hand, fear is an emotion that can occur in response to stimuli that are perceived as threatful. Moreover, fear can be characterized by elevated physiological arousal and fight-flight behavioral responses [33]. On the other hand, happiness is an emotion that can be defined by positive affectivity ranging from serenity to intense joy and can be linked to approach behaviors [11]. Learning about the potential of HBOs to modulate affective responses, will advance our knowledge regarding social signal processing, particularly within VR frameworks. Experimentally, VEs facilitate the investigation of crossmodal interactions within a more ecologically valid environment. On the other side, investigating HBOs might be of advantage for VR-based treatments, which mainly rely on visual and acoustic stimuli.

Acknowledgment. This project is funded by the European Union (EU) Horizon 2020 Project "POTION-Promoting Social Interaction through Emotional Body odors" (Grant Number: 824153).

References

1. Moskowitz, G.B.: Social Cognition: Understanding Self and Others. Guilford Press, New York (2005)

2. Argyle, M.: Social Interaction: Process and Products, 2 ed. Routledge, New York (2017). https://doi.org/10.4324/9781315129556
3. Redcay, E., Schilbach, L.: Using second-person neuroscience to elucidate the mechanisms of social interaction. Nat. Rev. Neurosci, **20**(8), 495–505 (2019). https://doi.org/10.1038/s41 583-019-0179-4
4. Vinciarelli, A., Pantic, M., Bourlard, H., Pentland, Y.A.: Social signal processing: state-of-the-art and future perspectives of an emerging domain. In: Proceedings of the 16th ACM International Conference on Multimedia, pp. 1061–1070. New York (2008). https://doi.org/10.1145/1459359.1459573
5. Burgoon, J.K., Magnenat-Thalmann, N., Pantic, M., Vinciarelli, Y.A.: Social Signal Processing. Cambridge University Press, Cambridge (2017)
6. Hamm, A.O.: Fear, anxiety, and their disorders from the perspective of psychophysiology. Psychophysiology, 57(2), e13474 (2020). https://doi.org/10.1111/psyp.13474
7. Scherer, K.R., Banse, R., Wallbott, Y.H.G.: Emotion inferences from vocal expression correlate across languages and cultures. J. Cross-Cult. Psychol. **32**(1), 76–92 (2001). https://doi.org/10.1177/0022022101032001009
8. Pietro, C., Silvia, S., Giuseppe, Y.R.: The pursuit of happiness measurement: a psychometric model based on psychophysiological correlates. Sci. World J. **2014**, e139128 (2014). https://doi.org/10.1155/2014/139128
9. Motogna, V., Lupu-Florian, G., Lupu, Y E.: Strategy for affective computing based on HRV and EDA. In: 2021 International Conference on e-Health and Bioengineering (EHB), pp. 1–4 (20210. https://doi.org/10.1109/EHB52898.2021.9657654
10. Debiec, J., Olsson, Y.A.: Social fear learning: from animal models to human function. Trends Cogn. Sci. **21**(7), 546–555 (2017). https://doi.org/10.1016/j.tics.2017.04.010
11. Quoidbach, J., Taquet, M., Desseilles, M., de Montjoye, Y.A., Gross, J.J.: Happiness and social behavior. Psychol. Sci. **30**(8), 1111–1122 (2019). https://doi.org/10.1177/095679761 9849666
12. Langner, O., Dotsch, R., Bijlstra, G., Wigboldus, D.H., Hawk, S.T., Van Knippenberg, A.D.: Presentation and validation of the radboud faces database. Cogn. Emotion **24**(8), 1377–1388 (2010). https://doi.org/10.1080/02699930903485076
13. Di Crosta, A., et al.: The chieti affective action videos database, a resource for the study of emotions in psychology. Sci. Data 7(1), 32 (2020). https://doi.org/10.1038/s41597-020-0366-1
14. Li, B.J., Bailenson, J.N., Pines, A., Greenleaf, W.J., Williams, L.M.: A public database of immersive VR videos with corresponding ratings of arousal, valence, and correlations between head movements and self report measures. Front. Psychol. **8**, 2116, Accedido: 17 de enero de 2023 (2017). https://www.frontiersin.org/articles/10.3389/fpsyg.2017.02116
15. Semin, G.R., de Groot, Y J.H.B.: The chemical bases of human sociality. Trends Cogn. Sci. **17**(9), 427–429 (2013). https://doi.org/10.1016/j.tics.2013.05.008
16. de Groot, J.H., Semin, G.R., Smeets, M.A.: On the communicative function of body odors: a theoretical integration and review. Perspect. Psychol. Sci. **12**(2), 306–324 (2017). https://doi.org/10.1177/1745691616676599
17. Hackländer, R.P.M., Janssen, S.M.J., Bermeitinger, C.: An in-depth review of the methods, findings, and theories associated with odor-evoked autobiographical memory. Psychon. Bull. Rev. 26(2), 401–429 (2018). https://doi.org/10.3758/s13423-018-1545-3
18. Leppänen, J.M., Hietanen, Y.J.K.: Affect and face perception: odors modulate the recognition advantage of happy faces. Emotion 3(4), 315–326 (2003). https://doi.org/10.1037/1528-3542.3.4.315
19. D'Aniello, B., Semin, G.R., Alterisio, A., Aria, M., Scandurra, A.: Interspecies transmission of emotional information via chemosignals: from humans to dogs (Canis lupus familiaris). Anim. Cogn. 21(1), 67–78 (2017). https://doi.org/10.1007/s10071-017-1139-x

20. Kamiloğlu, R.G., Smeets, M.A.M., de Groot, J.H.B., Semin, Y G.R.: Fear odor facilitates the detection of fear expressions over other negative expressions. Chem. Senses, **43**(6), 419–426 (2018). https://doi.org/10.1093/chemse/bjy029

21. Callara, A.L., et al.: Human body odors of happiness and fear modulate the late positive potential component during neutral face processing: a preliminary ERP study on healthy subjects. In: 2022 44th Annual International Conference of the IEEE Engineering in Medicine & Biology Society (EMBC), pp. 4093–4096 (2022). https://doi.org/10.1109/EMBC48229.2022.9871495

22. Parsons, T.D., Gaggioli, A., Riva, Y.G.: Virtual reality for research in social neuroscience. Brain Sci. **7**(4), 42 (2017). https://doi.org/10.3390/brainsci7040042

23. Diniz Bernardo, P., Bains, A., Westwood, S., Mograbi, D.C.: Mood induction using virtual reality: a systematic review of recent findings. J. Technol. Behav. Sci. **6**(1), 3–24 (2020). https://doi.org/10.1007/s41347-020-00152-9

24. Flavián, C., Ibáñez-Sánchez, S., Orús, Y.C.: The influence of scent on virtual reality experiences: the role of aroma-content congruence. J. Bus. Res. **123**, 289–301 (2021). https://doi.org/10.1016/j.jbusres.2020.09.036

25. Baus, O., Bouchard, S.: Exposure to an unpleasant odour increases the sense of Presence in virtual reality. Virtual Reality **21**(2), 59–74 (2016). https://doi.org/10.1007/s10055-016-0299-3

26. Liu, R., Hannum, M., Simons, Y.C.T.: Using immersive technologies to explore the effects of congruent and incongruent contextual cues on context recall, product evaluation time, and preference and liking during consumer hedonic testing. Food Res. Int. **117**, 19–29 (2019). https://doi.org/10.1016/j.foodres.2018.04.024

27. Quintana, P., Nolet, K., Baus, O., Bouchard, Y.S.: The effect of exposure to fear-related body odorants on anxiety and interpersonal trust toward a virtual character. Chem. Senses **44**(9), 683–692 (2019). https://doi.org/10.1093/chemse/bjz063

28. Alcañiz Raya, M., et al.: Application of supervised machine learning for behavioral biomarkers of autism spectrum disorder based on electrodermal activity and virtual reality. Front. Hum. Neurosci. **14**, 90 (2022). https://www.frontiersin.org/article/10.3389/fnhum.2020.00090

29. Baños, R.M., Liaño, V., Botella, C., Alcañiz, M., Guerrero, B., Rey, B.: Changing induced moods via virtual reality. In: IJsselsteijn, W.A., de Kort, Y.A.W., Midden, C., Eggen, B., van den Hoven, E. (eds.) PERSUASIVE 2006. LNCS, vol. 3962, pp. 7–15. Springer, Heidelberg (2006). https://doi.org/10.1007/11755494_3

30. Wolfensberger, M.: Sniffin'Sticks: a New Olfactory Test Battery», Acta Oto-Laryngologica, vol. 120, n.º 2, pp. 303–306, ene. 2000, doi: https://doi.org/10.1080/000164800750001134

31. Caballo, V.E., Salazar, I.C., Arias, V., Hofmann, S.G., Curtiss, Y J.: Psychometric properties of the Liebowitz Social Anxiety Scale in a large cross-cultural Spanish and Portuguese speaking sample. Braz. J. Psychiatry, **41**, 122–130 (2018). https://doi.org/10.1590/1516-4446-2018-0006

32. Magán, I., Sanz, J., García-Vera, Y.M.P.: Psychometric properties of a spanish version of the beck anxiety inventory (BAI) in general population. Span. J. Psychol. **11**(2), 626–640 (2008). https://doi.org/10.1017/S1138741600004637

33. Catterall, W.A.: Regulation of Cardiac Calcium Channels in the Fight-or-Flight Response. Current Mol. Pharmacol. **8**(1), 12–21 (2015)

Augmented Reality to Reduce Cognitive Load in Operational Decision-Making

Bethan Moncur[1,2]($\boxtimes$) , Maria J. Galvez Trigo[2] , and Letizia Mortara[1]

[1] Institute for Manufacturing, Department of Engineering,
University of Cambridge, Cambridge, UK
bam49@cam.ac.uk
[2] School of Computer Science, University of Lincoln, Lincoln, UK

Abstract. Augmented reality (AR) technologies can overlay digital information onto the real world. This makes them well suited for decision support by providing contextually-relevant information to decision-makers. However, processing large amounts of information simultaneously, particularly in time-pressured conditions, can result in poor decision-making due to excess cognitive load. This paper presents the results of an exploratory study investigating the effects of AR on cognitive load. A within-subjects experiment was conducted where participants were asked to complete a variable-sized bin packing task with and without the assistance of an augmented reality decision support system (AR DSS). Semi-structured interviews were conducted to elicit perceptions about the ease of the task with and without the AR DSS. This was supplemented by collecting quantitative data to investigate if any changes in perceived ease of the task translated into changes in task performance. The qualitative data suggests that the presence of the AR DSS made the task feel easier to participants; however, there was only a statistically insignificant increase in mean task performance. Analysing the data at the individual level does not provide evidence of a translation of increased perceived ease to increased task performance.

Keywords: Augmented Reality · Decision-Making · Decision Support System · Cognitive Load · Ease · Performance

1 Introduction

Decision-making occurs at all levels of an organisation, from long-term strategic decisions down to day-to-day operational decisions. Decision-makers can gain insights from information stored in their memory and surrounding environment to make effective decisions. However, processing large amounts of information simultaneously, particularly in time-pressured conditions, can result in poor decision-making due to cognitive load. The ever-increasing volume of information available with Industry 4.0, coupled with tough demands for rapid and accurate provision of services, place excess cognitive burdens on human operators [14]. Therefore, reducing the cognitive demands of workers is an important and timely goal for Human-Computer Interaction researchers to pursue.

D. D. Schmorrow and C. M. Fidopiastis (Eds.): HCII 2023, LNAI 14019, pp. 328–346, 2023.
https://doi.org/10.1007/978-3-031-35017-7_21

Cognitive Load Theory describes a model of human cognitive architecture centred on a permanent knowledge base in the long-term memory and a temporary conscious processor of information in the working memory [16]. The working memory has limited capacity and duration, so there is a limit to the amount of information that can be held and used in the execution of cognitive tasks [4]. Therefore, decision support systems (DSS) are being designed to alleviate cognitive load by externally providing relevant and appropriate information to decision-makers [29].

DSS can be characterised as "interactive computer-based systems which help decision-makers utilize data and models to solve unstructured problems" [31], although more recent work on DSS extends the definition to include "any computer-based system that aids the process of decision-making" [9]. For example, satellite guided navigation systems, such as GoogleMaps, are DSS that provide insights such as journey distances and traffic conditions to help users decide which route to take between two points.

Many DSS make use of visualisations to communicate complex information with clarity and speed [7,25,32]. Situated visualisations provide the benefit of overlaying insightful information onto the problem environment [18]. The information conveyed in situated visualisations could be based on the context, location, objects in view, or sensor data from the environment [15]. Literature suggests that the use of visualisations in this way can act as a substitute for keeping track of information in the working memory - in other words, the visualisations can be used as a form of "external memory" [23]. Situated visualisation can be achieved through traditional visualisation methods, such as placing physical signs and images into the real world. However, augmented reality (AR) provides an opportunity to situate digital information in the real world that can be interacted with and modified in real-time.

AR can be defined as a "human-machine interaction tool that overlays computer-generated information in the real-world environment" [19]. It is seen as the 'middle ground' of the mixed reality spectrum between telepresence (completely real) and virtual reality (VR, completely simulated) [20]. AR usually involves augmenting human vision with context-specific data; although, AR has the potential to be applied to other senses as well. The data overlaid on the real world allows the user to perceive information about objects that cannot be detected with their own senses [1].

A growing amount of literature has been published that investigates AR-based decision-making e.g., [13,21,27,28]. However, the research to date has tended to focus on evaluating the performance of users in a specified application rather than specifically investigating the effects of AR on cognitive load [14]. In addition, existing research tends to investigate the use of AR to provide step-by-step instructions for study participants to follow when completing a task (e.g., [8,35]) rather than to provide decision support. In these studies, the AR system essentially *substitutes* the cognitive processes of the decision-maker because they no longer have to reason about the solution to the problem. Few studies have investigated the use of AR to *augment* the cognitive reasoning of decision-makers without explicitly providing the solution to a task.

This paper aspires to contribute to the field of augmented cognition by investigating the effects of AR on cognitive load whilst decision-makers complete a task without the provision of step-by-step instructions. It is a widely held view that a more difficult task requires more complex mental operations, thus requiring more processing capacity, resulting in a greater cognitive load [22]. Therefore, the main research aim of this paper is to investigate whether the presence of an augmented reality decision support system (AR DSS) affects decision-makers' perceptions of the ease of completing a task. In addition, a review of the effects of AR systems on mental workload and task performance suggests that "when there are positive effects on mental workload, effects on task performance are most likely to be positive as well" [14]. Therefore, a secondary research aim is to investigate whether any changes in perceived ease of a task translate to changes in performance in the task.

An exploratory user study was conducted to investigate changes to perceived task ease and resulting changes to task performance. This involved recruiting participants to complete a bin packing task with and without the presence of an AR DSS. The research methodology, including the design of the AR DSS and bin packing task, is discussed in Sect. 2. The results and their implications are discussed in Sect. 3. Finally, the paper is concluded in Sect. 4 with a summary and suggestions for future work.

2   Method

The primary research question addressed in this paper investigates cognitive load as follows:

– Does the presence of an augmented reality decision support system (AR DSS) affect decision-makers' perceptions of the ease of completing a bin packing task?

The secondary research question asks:

– Do any changes in perceived ease of the task translate to changes in performance?

The research questions were investigated using a within-subjects experiment. Human participants were asked to complete a variable-sized bin packing task with and without the assistance of an AR DSS. A mixed methods approach was used: qualitative data was collected through semi-structured interviews to investigate the effect of the AR DSS on perceptions of the ease of the task, and quantitative data was collected to investigate the effects on the performance of decision-makers in the task.

2.1   Materials

To evaluate the effects of AR on cognitive load in operational decision-making, two experimental artefacts were designed: a bin packing task involving decision-making to solve a problem, and an augmented reality decision support system (AR DSS).

The Bin Packing Task. Many operational decisions in industry, such as minimising waste in stock-cutting and minimising makespan in machine scheduling, can be modelled using bin packing problems. Such problems consist of a set of items which need to be packed into bins whilst minimising an objective function, such as the number of bins, cost, or excess capacity of used bins. The variable-sized bin packing problem is a variation of the traditional one-dimensional bin packing problem. It consists of a set of items of different sizes (or weights) to be packed into a set of bins, where each bin has a given capacity and cost associated with it. The objective of the variable-sized bin packing problem is to minimise the total cost of packing all the items into the bins.

The problem is formally defined as follows [12]. There is a set J of bins with m different bin types. Each bin type $j, (j = 1, ..., m)$, has two properties: *capacity* b_j and *cost* c_j. A set I of n items must be packed into a minimum-cost set of bins, where each item $i, (1 \leq i \leq n)$, has a weight w_i. The binary variable x_{ij} is used to denote an item i packed into bin j and the binary variable y_j is used to indicate whether a bin j is used. Therefore, the objective function is to minimise the cost of the bins used for packing the items:

$$\min \left[\sum_{j \in J} c_j y_j \right] \tag{1}$$

with constraints that each item must be packed into one bin:

$$\sum_{j \in J} x_{ij} = 1, \ i \in I \tag{2}$$

and the total weight of all items loaded into a bin must not exceed the capacity of the bin:

$$\sum_{i \in I} w_i x_{ij} \leq b_j y_{ij}, \ j \in J \tag{3}$$

The bin packing task in this study consisted of a set of coloured blocks of different heights that needed to be packed into bins of various capacities and costs. The aim of the decision-maker was to pack all the items into bins for the minimum cost. To increase the cognitive demands placed on the decision-maker, the ratios of bin capacity to cost were non-monotonic so that both bin capacity and cost had to be considered. In addition, the smaller bins were designed to be too small to fit the larger items, thus further increasing the complexity of the problem.

The Augmented Reality Decision Support System (AR DSS). The aim of the AR DSS was *not* to provide the decision-makers with the solution to the bin packing problem; rather, it was to augment the scene with additional information that could be used by the decision-maker whilst completing the task. Therefore, the designs for the support mechanisms were based on the combination of two sources: optimisation-based online games, such as 'Fill the Fridge', and approaches for solving bin packing problems, such as the Best-Fit-Decreasing heuristic [12].

Figure 1 shows the AR DSS in action. There are two augmented images projected above the task area. The left-hand projection is of the items that still need to be packed, with the heights of the items augmented onto their centres. The right-hand projection shows the bins and the blocks that have already been packed, with augmentations showing the remaining capacity in each used bin in addition to the item heights. Above the right-hand augmentation, the projection shows the current cost of the packed solution and the arithmetic breakdown of that cost (the cost of each used bin, from left to right). In addition to the AR projections, decision-makers could also see information sheets displaying the height of each item, and the cost and capacity of each bin (not in view in Fig. 1).

Fig. 1. Annotated image of the augmented reality decision support system (AR DSS) in action. The left-hand projection shows the remaining blocks to be packed, and the right-hand projection shows the bins with the blocks already packed into them. The control condition (without the AR DSS) was identical except for the removal of the item heights and excess capacity information from the projections (however, the current cost and cost calculation were still shown).

The augmentations were created using OpenCV, an open source software library for computer vision applications. The blocks were detected using HSV-based colour thresholding and the positions of the bins were detected using ArUco markers.

2.2   Experiment Design

A within-subjects experiment was conducted with an experimental group of 14 participants to compare completion of the bin packing task in two conditions: the intervention condition involving the AR DSS (item heights and remaining capacity augmented onto the scene) and the control condition (no item heights or remaining capacity augmentations). Each participant completed a packing task twice, once with the control condition and once with the intervention condition.

The order that the participants experienced the control/intervention conditions was randomised, with an equal split in which condition they experienced first. Participants were counterbalanced because learning effects were expected to influence task performance. To mitigate the learning effects from completing the first task session, the participants packed a different set of items in each packing task (known as Task A and Task B, each consisting of 12 different blocks to pack). The order that the participants experienced Task A and Task B was also randomised. Therefore, there were four sub-groups of participants in the study according to the conditions during their first task session (Task A/B, control/intervention).

2.3   Data Collection

Qualitative data was collected through semi-structured interviews to investigate the effect of the AR DSS on perceptions of the ease of the task. Two methods of qualitative data collection were used for each participant: observations during the packing tasks, followed by a semi-structured interview. Observations included the apparent strategy that participants were using, the frequency at which individual blocks were removed and repacked into bins, and any statements made by the participant whilst they were completing the tasks. The semi-structured interview was designed to collect thoughts and attitudes of participants about the packing tasks and AR DSS. This approach was chosen over a questionnaire to provide depth to participant's answers and explore issues with the DSS design and requirements for future design iterations. Therefore, participants were asked to elaborate (where appropriate) on the following questions:

1. What is the highest level at which you have studied a maths-based subject?
2. Do you have any experience completing optimisation problems, such as playing games that involve optimisation, or solving decision problems like the knapsack problem or travelling salesperson problem?
3. Have you ever used a virtual or augmented reality headset?
4. Did you find the task challenging to complete?
5. Please describe your thought process or tactics for completing the task.
6. Did you find the augmented reality tips useful in completing the task?
7. How did the task with augmented reality compare to the task without augmented reality?
8. What (if anything) would you change about the task?
9. What (if anything) would you change about the augmented reality tips?

Quantitative data was collected to investigate the effect of the AR DSS on the performance of decision-makers in the task. Participant performance was measured by recording the cost of their packing solution after a 3-minute time limit. Two costs were recorded for each participant, one with the control condition and one with the AR DSS intervention. To enable comparison between task sessions, the recorded cost for each session was transformed into *excess cost* by normalising it against the optimum packing cost:

$$excess\ cost = \frac{recorded\ cost}{optimum\ cost} - 1 \tag{4}$$

Therefore, an excess cost of 0 occurred when the recorded packing solution for the participant had the same cost as the optimum solution. An excess cost of 0 represented optimum performance of the participant.

2.4   Data Analysis

Qualitative data analysis was performed on the responses to the semi-structured interview and observed remarks made by participants whilst they were completing the packing task. Corbin and Strauss' approach to content analysis was followed to analyse the data [3]. Open coding was performed to identify interesting phenomena in the data and assign them a code. In-vivo coding (coding categories generated from phrases in the data) ensured that concepts remained similar to participants' own words. Researcher-denoted concepts were used to describe instances in the data that could not be described directly by phrases in the data. Subsequently, codes that described similar contents were grouped together to form concepts. Relationships between the concepts were identified using axial coding to form categories. Finally, the connections between concepts and categories were used to create inferential and predictive statements about the phenomena emerging from the data.

Quantitative data analysis was performed in SPSS, a statistical software platform, to investigate the effect of the AR DSS on the performance of decision-makers in the task. The Wilcoxon signed-ranks test was performed to assess whether differences between the excess cost distributions with and without the AR DSS were statistically significant. This test was chosen because the data violated the assumption of normality (non-parametric) required for a within-samples t-test. In addition, descriptive analytics were used to compare how the performance of participants changed between task session 1 and task session 2 depending on the order in which participants experienced the intervention and control conditions.

2.5   Study Participants

Recruitment Method. Participants were recruited in a non-randomised way based on ease of access, known as a convenience sample. Resource constraints limited the data collection period to four days, so convenience was vital to recruiting participants within the time frame.

Recruitment Setting. 13 out of 14 participants were postgraduate students, 9 of which were in maths-based subjects. Therefore, the results of the study are unlikely to be generalisable to the wider population.

Inclusion and Exclusion Criteria. Participants had to be capable of giving informed consent, any gender, aged 18 or over, any ethnicity, and any socioeconomic group. Participants could not take part in the study if they were visually impaired.

Ethical Considerations. The project was granted favourable ethical opinion by a University Research Ethics Committee (Ethics reference UoL2022_9560) based on an application form and supporting documentation submitted through the Lincoln Ethics Application System (LEAS). Written consent was given by all research study participants after they had read the participant information form and been given the opportunity to have any questions answered.

Compensation. Participants did not receive an payments, reimbursements of expenses, or incentives for taking part in this research. The participants were in the research facility for 30 min in total.

Gender. Out of 14 participants, 9 identified as cisgender men and 5 identified as cisgender women.

2.6 Methodological Limitations

Materials. This study used projection-based AR, so the results may differ to other forms of AR, particularly those using head-mounted displays. In addition, some flickering of the augmentations occurred due to the influence of participants' positioning on lighting and camera-view. This raises interesting questions about the influence of trust in, and reliability of, augmentations in decision support systems. However, these questions are outside the scope of this study.

Experiment Design. The data for each participant in the study was collected at one point in time (cross-sectional). Collecting data at multiple points in time (longitudinal) could mitigate the learning effects from completing the first bin packing task session.

Data Collection. Cognitive load was not measured directly, but was inferred from participant interview responses. Future work could measure perceived cognitive load using the Paas mental effort scale [24], a self-assessed cognitive load scale, as used in [2]. Alternatively, objective measures of cognitive load could be explored, such as pupil dilation [11].

Data Analysis. Conceptualising the qualitative data was done systematically to mitigate influence from preconceived opinions. However, the codes and concepts were products of researcher interpretation, so may be susceptible to biases.

8 out of 14 participants experienced Task A in the first task session. During quantitative data analysis, variation between Task A and Task B was assumed to have minimal impact on participant performance. This assumption was verified by comparing mean excess cost across both task sessions for participants based on whether they experienced Task A or Task B in the first task session [Task A first: mean excess cost 0.1119, standard deviation 0.0557; Task B first: mean excess cost 0.0991, standard deviation 0.0556]. An alternative research method could involve using a separate control group to record baseline performances for each task.

Study Participants. The majority of the participants were postgraduate students with high maths ability, so the results of the study may not generalise to the wider population. Future studies would benefit from recruiting a larger number of participants from a wider pool.

3   Results and Discussion

3.1   The Effect of the AR DSS on Decision-Makers' Perceptions of Ease of the Task

The effect of the AR DSS on decision-makers' perceptions of ease of the task was investigated by performing content analysis on participant responses from semi-structured interviews and remarks that were observed whilst participants completed the packing task.

Results. Participant responses were separated into two broad categories based on taxonomies of human capabilities from the fields of psychology and Human-Computer Interaction [6,17]. The first category, *cognitive*, was used to group participants' responses relating to "reasoning, thinking and one's ability to solve problems in novel situations independent of acquired knowledge" [10]. The second category, *perceptual*, consisted of participant responses relating to their sensed environment through sensory organs, such as vision, hearing and touch [30]. The code structure that emerged from analysing the participant responses is shown in Fig. 2.

The main objective of collecting qualitative data was to investigate the effect of the AR DSS on how easy or difficult participants perceived the packing task to be. Under the 'Ease of Task' concept, 6 participants expressed that AR improved the ease of the task, 8 participants stated that the remaining bin capacity AR tips were useful, 3 participants described the AR block values overlaid onto the blocks as useful, and 1 participant highlighted that the values on the blocks were particularly useful in the unpacked items area. For example, one participant (ID 09) stated that AR made the task "easier to solve because [they] could

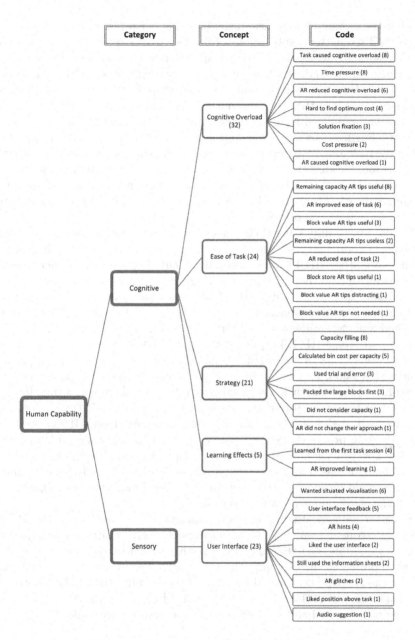

Fig. 2. An image showing the code structure that emerged during analysis of participants' responses to questions in a semi-structured interview and remarks made during the bin packing exercises. The numbers in brackets at the code level represent the number of participants that expressed a sentiment relating to the code. The numbers in brackets at the concept level are the totals of the brackets in the code category - some participants mentioned different aspects (codes) of the same concept, hence why the numbers are greater than the total number of participants (14).

see what the remaining capacity in the bins was much faster when they experimented and see better combinations of blocks when they were still in the block store". Another participant (ID 11) stated that the "packing was easier with AR because [they] could see how much [they] needed to pack without having to work it out". However, not all comments related to 'Ease of Task' were positive. 2 participants stated that they did not use the remaining capacity AR tips and 1 participant expressed that the block values overlaid onto the blocks were not necessary. Furthermore, 2 participants indicated that the AR DSS reduced the ease of the task and 1 participant stated that the AR block values were distracting. This was because the "AR values on the blocks drew attention away from the remaining capacity" (ID 08). Overall, there were more comments from participants indicating that the AR DSS made the task easier (18) than comments that were impartial (3) or negative (3).

In addition to discussing their perceptions about the ease of the task, some participants commented on their mental operations directly, with phrases such as "mental maths" (ID 13) and "mentally calculating" (ID 14). Others referred to the cognitive load they were experiencing, with phrases such as "mental load" (ID 02) and "mental capacity" (ID 12). 8 participants indicated that the task itself caused cognitive overload. For example, one participant (ID 10) stated that there was "a lot going on so there [was] too much to keep track of easily". Another participant (ID 12) expressed that they "didn't have the mental capacity to compute the costs [of the bins used]". This was in part due to the time pressure of the task session, as mentioned by 8 participants. One such participant (ID 11) explained that the task was "challenging because there was a time limit, so stress got in the way". 6 participants suggested that the AR DSS reduced the cognitive load of the task. For example, one such participant (ID 05) said that their "thought processes were quicker with AR because [they] didn't have to calculate how full the bins were". However, 1 participant (ID 08) explained that the AR DSS increased feelings of cognitive overload, saying "if I was a numbers person it would have been useful but for me, when I looked at the item size and saw all the other numbers, it was confusing".

Some participants also provided feedback on the user interface of the AR DSS. The most frequent comment (6 participants) concerned situated visualisation, whereby they indicated that the DSS may have been more effective if the AR tips were projected directly onto the real blocks. For example, one participant (ID 13) said that the DSS would be better if they "didn't have to look down and up". They elaborated that they were dissuaded from using the AR DSS because "looking between real and augmented took too much concentration".

Discussion. Content analysis indicates that the AR DSS had a positive effect on the decision-makers' perceptions of ease of the task. In total, there were 18 comments from participants indicating that the AR DSS made the task easier, 3 impartial comments and 3 negative. This aligns with previous studies reporting that AR improves perception and understanding of information in situations where decision-makers have to refer to external sources of information, such as monitor- or paper-based information [14].

A possible explanation for the improvement in perceived ease of the task with the AR DSS is that it reduced the cognitive load of participants. Cognitive Load Theory proposes three types of cognitive load: intrinsic (imposed by the task itself), extraneous (imposed by the presentation of task information), and germane (reflective of the effort required to generate mental schemas in the working memory and store them in the long-term memory) [33]. 8 participants indicated that intrinsic cognitive load was present through comments about the difficulty of the task. It has been suggested that presenting information in the context that it is required reduces extraneous load, enabling more cognitive resources to be focused on the generation of schemas, problem-solving, or task completion [14]. This aligns with the DSS literature, which suggests that AR could help to alleviate load on the working memory by acting as an "external memory" through provision of relevant and appropriate information to decision-makers [4,23,29]. Therefore, the use of AR to augment the task environment with information may have reduced extraneous cognitive load, thus resulting in increased perceptions of ease by participants.

It has been suggested that AR may reduce cognitive load because it "negates the need to switch between performing the task and searching for information to perform the task" [14]. 6 participants discussed situated visualisation and indicated that the AR DSS may have been more effective if the augmentations were projected directly onto the real blocks. This could further alleviate the need to cognitively map information from the projection to the real objects [26].

3.2   The Effect of the AR DSS on Task Performance

The performance of decision-makers was measured by the *excess cost* of their packing solution compared to the optimum, as given in Eq. 4. The lower the excess cost, the better the performance - an excess cost of 0 is the best achievable performance in the task.

Results. The performances of participants with and without the AR DSS are shown in the boxplots in Fig. 3, where a lower excess cost denotes a better performance. In the AR DSS condition, the participants' mean excess cost was 0.0969, the median was 0.0870, and the standard deviation was 0.06841. In the control condition, the participants had a higher excess cost mean of 0.1159, a higher median of 0.0882, and a higher standard deviation of 0.09498. The difference in means suggest that the performance of participants was better by 16.4% with the AR DSS compared to without, indicated by a decrease in excess cost above the optimum solution. In addition, the spread of the data is smaller, indicating that there was less variation in performance between participants when the AR DSS was present.

The distribution of data points for excess cost in the presence of the AR DSS departed significantly from normality (Shapiro-Wilk test for normality: $W(14) =$

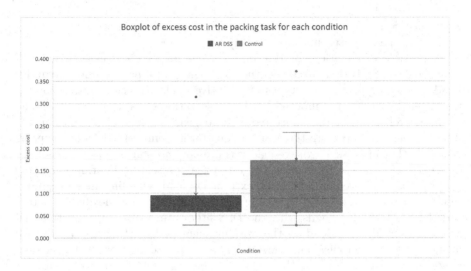

Fig. 3. An image showing boxplots of the excess cost of participants' bin packing solutions under each condition. A lower excess cost represents a better performance.

$0.666, p < 0.001$). Therefore, the non-parametric Wilcoxon signed-ranks test was used to measure the effect of the AR DSS on the performance of decision-makers. 5 participants had a higher excess cost (worse performance) in the AR DSS condition and 9 participants had a higher excess cost in the control condition. Therefore, more participants performed better with the AR DSS than without the AR DSS. Nevertheless, the Wilcoxon signed-ranks test showed that the AR DSS did not elicit a statistically significant change in performance, as measured by excess cost compared to the optimum ($Z = -0.628, p = 0.530$). Indeed, median excess cost was 0.0870 with the AR DSS compared to 0.0882 without the AR DSS. As a result, the null hypothesis that there was no significant difference between the excess cost with and without the AR DSS cannot be rejected.

The participants were counterbalanced to experience either the AR DSS or control condition first. However, analysing the data by task session in addition to intervention/control condition suggests that there is a relationship between them, as shown in Fig. 4. The participants that experienced the AR DSS condition in the first task session performed better in both conditions than those that experienced the control condition in the first task session. Mean participant performance improved between the first and second task session regardless of the order that conditions were experienced. However, performance improvement between the first and second task session was greater when the participant moved from the control condition in the first task session to the AR DSS condition in the second task session (compared to moving from the AR DSS condition to the control condition).

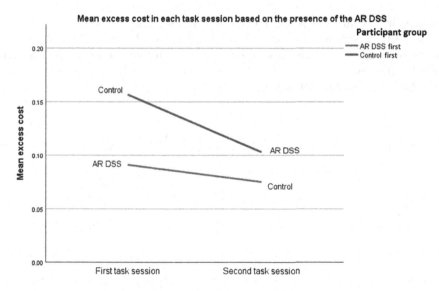

Fig. 4. The mean excess cost of participants in each task session separated based on whether the AR condition was experienced in the first or second task session. A lower excess cost indicates a better performance.

Discussion. The data indicates higher performance for participants when the AR DSS was present compared to when it was not; however, the difference in performance is not statistically significant. On average, participants that experienced the AR DSS in the first task session had a higher performance across both sessions. This finding implies that the use of AR could accelerate learning of approaches to solve novel problems. Furthermore, the amplified learning effects between the first and second task sessions when moving from the control condition to the AR condition suggest that the AR DSS improved learning above that of prior task experience alone. However, these findings were not anticipated, so the experiment was not designed to investigate learning effects specifically.

3.3 The Relationship Between Perception of Ease and Task Performance

Results. The aggregate data suggests that both perceived ease and task performance increase in the presence of the AR DSS; although, the increase in performance is not statistically significant. However, at the individual level, there is no correlation between change in perception of ease and change in performance. For each individual participant, Fig. 5 shows the perceived ease of the task with the AR DSS compared to without, plotted against the difference in performance between the task with the AR DSS and without. The x-axis represents the sentiments of each participant about the relative ease of the task under each condition. The three categories are researcher-denoted based on the interview content analysis, with each participant indicating either a positive, a negative or no change in perceived ease of the task. The y-axis displays the difference in task performance for each participant, calculated by subtracting the excess cost with the AR DSS from the excess cost without the AR DSS. The plot indicates that at the individual level there is no relationship between perceived ease of the task and performance in the task.

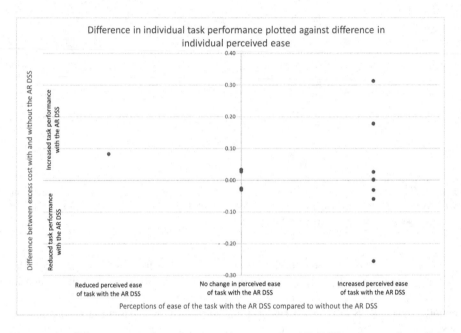

Fig. 5. The difference in task performance between the AR DSS and control condition plotted against the perceived ease of the task with the AR DSS compared to without.

Discussion. Previous findings suggest that improvements to task performance may result from AR freeing up mental resources such as the working memory, thus reducing cognitive load [14]. However, this study has been unable to demonstrate a relationship at the individual level between changes in perceived ease of the task and changes in task performance. A possible explanation for this is that participants' perceptions about the ease of the task do not correspond to their cognitive load. Alternatively, there may be factors other than cognitive load that affect perceptions about ease of the task and mean task performance. For example, studies investigating AR to provide instructions in assembly tasks suggest that AR could change the type of cognitive demands placed on the user [5], or introduce an additional source of attentional demand, resulting in attentional tunneling [34].

4   Conclusions

This paper aimed to contribute to the field of augmented cognition by conducting an exploratory study to investigate the effects of AR on cognitive load during operational decision-making.

An augmented reality decision support system (AR DSS) was developed to assist decision-making whilst participants completed a variable-sized bin packing task. The AR DSS used computer vision techniques to overlay information onto a projection of the scene. This included overlaying the size of the blocks onto their centres and displaying the remaining capacity over each bin in use. The overlaid information was designed to augment the decision-making process, not to provide instructions or solutions to the decision-maker.

The research study used a within-subjects experiment, collecting both qualitative and quantitative data. 14 participants completed two bin packing tasks, one with the AR DSS (intervention condition) and one without (control condition). The order that participants experienced the conditions was counterbalanced to account for learning effects between the task sessions. The primary research aim was to explore the effects of AR on the cognitive load of decision-makers. This was done by investigating the effects of the AR DSS on decision-makers' perceptions of the ease of completing a bin packing task. Participant perceptions were elicited by conducting semi-structured interviews. A secondary research aim was to investigate the link between changes in perceived ease of the task and changes in task performance. Participant performance was measured as a ratio of the cost of the participant's solution in the packing task compared to the optimum solution.

The qualitative data suggests that, more often than not, the presence of the AR DSS made the task feel easier to participants. This could be because it alleviated the load on the working memory by serving as an "external memory" [23], thus reducing extraneous cognitive load. The quantitative data does not indicate a statistically significant increase in task performance with the presence of the AR DSS. However, it does appear conducive to participants learning how to solve novel tasks. At the aggregate level, the collected data is insufficient to derive a relationship between perceived ease and task performance. Analysing the data at the individual level does not provide evidence of a translation of increased perceived ease to increased task performance. A possible explanation for this is that participants' perceptions about the ease of the task do not correspond to their cognitive load. Alternatively, there may be factors other than cognitive load that affect perceptions about ease of the task and mean task performance. For example, AR could change the type of cognitive demands placed on the user [5], or introduce an additional source of attentional demand, resulting in attentional tunneling [34].

4.1   Future Work

The findings from this study indicate that the presence of AR may impact the learning effects observed between task sessions 1 and 2. However, these findings were not anticipated. Future work could specifically investigate the learning effects of AR by asking participants to complete the first and second task sessions solely with either the AR DSS or control condition.

In addition, this project looked at projection-based augmented reality; however, 6 participants expressed that the DSS may have been more effective if the information were situated directly on the task. This could be explored in future work using an AR head-mounted display.

Suggestions for possible changes to research methodology in future work include:

- Increase the number of participants in the study to achieve statistically significant results.
- Use a wider participant pool to obtain results that are more applicable to the wider population.
- Perform a longitudinal study to minimise the learning effects of completing two bin packing task sessions.
- Obtain baseline performances for each task using a separate control group of participants.
- Use multiple coders for qualitative data analysis and check reliability of the coding using metrics such as Cohen's Kappa.

Acknowledgements. This work was supported by the Engineering and Physical Sciences Research Council [EP/S023917/1].

References

1. Azuma, R.T.: A survey of augmented reality. Presence: Teleoperators Virtual Environ. **6**, 355–385 (1997). http://www.cs.unc.edu/~azumaW
2. Baumeister, J., et al.: Cognitive cost of using augmented reality displays. IEEE Trans. Vis. Comput. Graph. **23**, 2378–2388 (2017). https://doi.org/10.1109/TVCG.2017.2735098
3. Corbin, J., Strauss, A.: Basics of Qualitative Research, 3rd edn. Techniques and Procedures for Developing Grounded Theory (2012). https://doi.org/10.4135/9781452230153
4. Cowan, N.: Working memory underpins cognitive development, learning, and education. Educ. Psychol. Rev. **26**(2), 197–223 (2013). https://doi.org/10.1007/s10648-013-9246-y
5. Deshpande, A., Kim, I.: The effects of augmented reality on improving spatial problem solving for object assembly. Adv. Eng. Inform. **38**, 760–775 (2018). https://doi.org/10.1016/j.aei.2018.10.004
6. Dommes, A., Cavallo, V.: The role of perceptual, cognitive, and motor abilities in street-crossing decisions of young and older pedestrians. Ophthalmic Physiol. Opt. **31**, 292–301 (2011). https://doi.org/10.1111/J.1475-1313.2011.00835.X
7. Eberhard, K.: The effects of visualization on judgment and decision-making: a systematic literature review. Manag. Rev. Q. (2021). https://doi.org/10.1007/s11301-021-00235-8

8. Elsayed, N., Thomas, B., Marriott, K., Piantadosi, J., Smith, R.: Situated analytics. Big Data Visual Analytics, BDVA 2015 (2015). https://doi.org/10.1109/BDVA. 2015.7314302

9. Finlay, P.N.: Introducing Decision Support Systems. NCC Blackwell (1994)

10. Fisher, G.G., Chacon, M., Chaffee, D.S.: Theories of cognitive aging and work. In: Work Across the Lifespan, pp. 17–45 (2019). https://doi.org/10.1016/B978-0-12-812756-8.00002-5

11. Gavas, R.D., Tripathy, S.R., Chatterjee, D., Sinha, A.: Cognitive load and metacognitive confidence extraction from pupillary response. Cogn. Syst. Res. **52**, 325–334 (2018). https://doi.org/10.1016/J.COGSYS.2018.07.021

12. Haouari, M., Serairi, M.: Heuristics for the variable sized bin-packing problem. Comput. Oper. Res. **36**, 2877–2884 (2009). https://doi.org/10.1016/j.cor.2008.12. 016. https://linkinghub.elsevier.com/retrieve/pii/S0305054808002748

13. Hilken, T., Keeling, D.I., de Ruyter, K., Mahr, D., Chylinski, M.: Seeing eye to eye: social augmented reality and shared decision making in the marketplace. J. Acad. Mark. Sci. **48**, 143–164 (2020). https://doi.org/10.1007/s11747-019-00688-0

14. Jeffri, N.F.S., Rambli, D.R.A.: A review of augmented reality systems and their effects on mental workload and task performance. Heliyon **7**, e06277 (2021). https://doi.org/10.1016/j.heliyon.2021.e06277

15. Kalkofen, D., Sandor, C., White, S., Schmalstieg, D.: Visualization techniques for augmented reality. In: Furht, B. (ed.) Handbook of Augmented Reality, pp. 65–98. Springer, New York (2011). https://doi.org/10.1007/978-1-4614-0064-6_3

16. Kalyuga, S.: Cognitive load theory: how many types of load does it really need? Educ. Psychol. Rev. **23**, 1–19 (2011). https://doi.org/10.1007/S10648-010-9150-7/METRICS

17. Lazar, J., Feng, J.H., Hochheiser, H.: Research Methods in Human-Computer Interaction, 2 edn. Morgan Kaufmann (2017). https://www.vlebooks.com/Product/Index/938873?page=0

18. Lenuik, T.A., Velazquez, L.E., Murley, S.R., Greiner, N., Willis, R.: Mixed reality: the new reality in DoD decision making. MODSIM World (2015)

19. Martins, N.C., et al.: Augmented reality situated visualization in decision-making. Multimed. Tools Appl. **1198** (2021). https://doi.org/10.1007/s11042-021-10971-4

20. Milgram, P., Kishino, F.: A taxonomy of mixed reality visual displays. IEICE Trans. Inf. Syst. (1994). http://vered.rose.utoronto.ca/people/paul_dir/IEICE94/ieice.html

21. Mirbabaie, M., Fromm, J.: Reducing the cognitive load of decision-makers in emergency management through augmented reality. In: Proceedings of the 27th European Conference on Information Systems (ECIS) (2019)

22. Mulder, G.: Mental load, mental effort and attention. In: Moray, N. (ed.) Mental Workload. NATO Conference Series, vol. 8, pp. 299–325. Springer, Boston (1979). https://doi.org/10.1007/978-1-4757-0884-4_18

23. Munzner, T.: Visualisation. Fundamentals of Computer Graphics (2018). https://learning.oreilly.com/library/view/fundamentals-of-computer/9781482229417/

24. Paas, F.G.W.C.: Training strategies for attaining transfer of problem-solving skill in statistics: a cognitive-load approach. J. Educ. Psychol. **84**, 429–434 (1992). https://doi.org/10.1037/0022-0663.84.4.429

25. Perdana, A., Robb, A., Rohde, F.: Interactive data and information visualization: unpacking its characteristics and influencing aspects on decision-making. Pac. Asia J. Assoc. Inf. Syst. 75–104 (2019). https://doi.org/10.17705/1pais.11404

26. Re, G.M., Oliver, J., Bordegoni, M.: Impact of monitor-based augmented reality for on-site industrial manual operations. Cogn. Technol. Work **18**(2), 379–392 (2016). https://doi.org/10.1007/s10111-016-0365-3

27. Rokhsaritalemi, S., Sadeghi-Niaraki, A., Kang, H.S., Lee, J.W., Choi, S.M.: Ubiquitous tourist system based on multicriteria decision making and augmented reality. Appl. Sci. **12**, 5241 (2022). https://doi.org/10.3390/app12105241

28. Sangiorgio, V., Martiradonna, S., Fatiguso, F., Lombillo, I.: Augmented reality based - decision making (AR-DM) to support multi-criteria analysis in constructions. Autom. Constr. **124**, 103567 (2021). https://doi.org/10.1016/j.autcon.2021.103567

29. Sauter, V.L.: Decision Support Systems for Business Intelligence, 2nd edn. Wiley, Hoboken (2010)

30. Shi, Z.: Introduction. In: Intelligence Science: Leading the Age of Intelligence, pp. 1–31 (2021). https://doi.org/10.1016/B978-0-323-85380-4.00001-4

31. Sprague, R.H.: A framework for the development of decision support systems. MIS Q.: Manag. Inf. Syst. **4**, 1–26 (1980). https://doi.org/10.2307/248957

32. Suwa, M., Tversky, B.: External representations contribute to the dynamic construction of ideas. In: Hegarty, M., Meyer, B., Narayanan, N.H. (eds.) Diagrams 2002. LNCS (LNAI), vol. 2317, pp. 341–343. Springer, Heidelberg (2002). https://doi.org/10.1007/3-540-46037-3_33

33. Sweller, J., van Merrienboer, J.J.G., Paas, F.G.W.C.: Cognitive architecture and instructional design. Educ. Psychol. Rev. **10**, 251–296 (1998). https://doi.org/10.1023/A:1022193728205

34. Tang, A., Owen, C., Biocca, F., Mou, W.: Comparative effectiveness of augmented reality in object assembly, pp. 73–80. ACM (2003). https://doi.org/10.1145/642611.642626

35. Techasarntikul, N., et al.: Guidance and visualization of optimized packing solutions. J. Inf. Process. **28**, 193–202 (2020). https://doi.org/10.2197/ipsjjip.28.193

The Effect of Metacognitive Judgments on Metacognitive Awareness in an Augmented Reality Environment

Sara Mostowfi[1], Jung Hyup Kim[1(✉)], Ching-Yun Yu[2], Kangwon Seo[1], Fang Wang[2], and Danielle Oprean[3]

[1] Industrial and System Engineering Department, University of Missouri, Columbia, MO, USA
Sm3yp@umsystem.edu, {kijung,seoka}@missouri.edu
[2] Information Technology Department, University of Missouri, Columbia, MO, USA
{cytbm,wangfan}@missouri.edu
[3] Info Science and Learning Technology Department, University of Missouri, Columbia, MO, USA
opreand@missouri.edu

Abstract. Being conscious of your thought processes is known as metacognition. It supports students in being more aware of their actions, motivations, and the potential applications of the skills [1]. This study investigates how different metacognitive judgment questions affect students' metacognitive awareness in an augmented reality (AR) environment. The outcomes of this study will help us to understand what metacognitive monitoring method is more effective in the AR learning environment. According to the literature, students with high knowledge about cognition have higher test performance, while students with low regulation have a challenge during planning, organizing, and elaborating strategies. The dependent variables of the study are student learning performance and metacognitive awareness inventory (MAI) score, and one independent variable is the metacognitive judgment question Retrospective Confidence Judgment (RCJ) and Judgment of Learning (JOL). We hypothesized that the students with high performance would have improved MAI scores in both groups. The experiment was done with two groups (RCJ and JOL). Both groups responded to the pre-post metacognitive awareness inventory questionnaire. During the experiment, the MAI questionnaire was asked two times. In round one, the MAI questionnaire was asked at the beginning of lecture one; however, in round two, the questionnaire was asked at the end of lecture two. Results indicated significant differences in RCJ low performers. In RCJ, the participants whose performance was significantly reduced in lecture 2 had a higher improvement on MAI both regulation and knowledge about cognition. Overall, the result of our study could advance our understanding of how to design an advanced instructional strategy in an AR environment.

Keywords: Metacognition · Augmented Reality · Retrospective Confidence Judgment · Judgment of Learning

© The Author(s), under exclusive license to Springer Nature Switzerland AG 2023
D. D. Schmorrow and C. M. Fidopiastis (Eds.): HCII 2023, LNAI 14019, pp. 347–358, 2023.
https://doi.org/10.1007/978-3-031-35017-7_22

1 Introduction

When using augmented reality (AR) as a learning tool, students tend to retain more information, be more motivated, and make more progress in their studies [2]. However, multiple pieces of information in the AR environment may cognitively overload students, and students may lack the knowledge to use the gadgets in the AR learning environment. Providing a highly engaging environment with a high level of presence and agency without significantly scaffolded lessons may cause learners to not effectively monitor or adjust their affective, cognitive, metacognitive, and motivational processes.

Different metacognitive strategies are used during the learning process such as planning, monitoring, and evaluating [3]. Students need to possess metacognitive knowledge to manage ongoing cognitive processes and choose the best learning tactics. Metacognitive monitoring traces the flow of cognitive information from the object-level to the meta-level. The monitoring can be via both prospective metrics, such as judgment of learning (JOL) by assessment of future recall or retrospective confidence judgment (RCJ) on past performances [4].

Both retroactive and prospective monitoring are essential for the self-regulated development of problem-solving skills. The method through which students analyze their performance on a problem they have just accomplished is known as retrospective monitoring, also referred to as self-assessment (SA). Furthermore, for students to achieve a strong performance on a task, they must equip an accurate metacognitive judgment of performance. Based on this viewpoint, students with low- performance are unskilled and need to be made aware of their lack of talent in the task. Furthermore, as metacognitive judgments guide study choices, low performers need to improve their monitoring precision to identify better when they have acquired the content [5]. Students can also identify where their knowledge is lacking and map out possible actions to fill such gaps. The difference between performance and confidence is expected to be brought to the student's attention. With a comprehension of the instructional materials, this method helps students calibrate their RCJs [6]. Prospective monitoring is how students predict how well they would perform on a (similar) problem in a future test.

Judgments-of-Learning (JOL) is another monitoring tool that one can use to determine how likely it is that a recently or currently learned material will be remembered in the future [7]. In this study, regarding JOL, the students' knowledge the JOL students' knowledge will be assessed based on the question: "Roughly what % of the information from scene #1 do you think you would be able to recall? and then write it here ____%." participants were asked for a percentage (i.e., 0–100) response to indicate their judgment of learning.

On the other hand, in the RCJ group, students were asked the question "How confident are you about your response to the question you recently answered?" Retrospective confidence assessments typically reveal either overconfidence or underconfidence [8, 9]. If the student's performance is higher than their confidence level, they are underconfident. If the confidence level is higher than performance, they are over-confident. For students to achieve strong performance on a task, they should equip an accurate metacognitive judgment of performance. Based on this viewpoint, students with low-performance will deal with more pressure since they are not only unskilled but also unaware of their lack of talent in the task.

1.1 Metacognitive Assessment Inventory (MAI)

Different researchers have studied metacognition and its connections to academic achievement. Some researchers employ self-report inventories to evaluate metacognitive abilities and link them to accomplishment measures [10, 11]. Other researchers look at monitoring accuracy on various tasks to gauge metacognitive regulation. The calibration of performance is used to determine how accurately the monitoring works. The average difference between each test question's actual response and the students' assessment of how well they responded is used to calculate local monitoring accuracy. Global assessments are done following the conclusion of the entire test. The gap between the final test result and how well the students believe they performed on the test is defined as global monitoring accuracy. Global monitoring accuracy is thought to represent cumulative metacognitive control, whereas local monitoring accuracy is a measure of ongoing metacognitive control during testing [12].

Two metacognitive variables are measured by the MAI: regulation of cognition (17 items) and knowledge of cognition (17 items). Planning, information management techniques, comprehension monitoring, debugging tactics, and evaluation subcategories constitute cognition regulation. In the discussion of earlier research, Schraw and Dennison [10] point out that learners with higher metacognitive awareness are more strategic in their learning processes, are better problem solvers, and do better than learners with lower metacognitive awareness. The findings also indicated that the MAI is a highly valid and reliable method for evaluating learners' metacognitive awareness and offers insightful predictions about learners' future cognitive performance [13].

This study investigated how different metacognitive judgment questions affect students' metacognitive awareness in an AR environment. The outcomes of this study will help us to understand what metacognitive monitoring method is more effective in the AR learning environment. We hypothesized that the students with high performance have high MAI scores. The experiment was done with two groups. Both groups responded to the pre-post metacognitive awareness inventory questionnaire.

2 Method

2.1 Apparatus

The study was conducted in the ergonomics lab at the University of Missouri. Engineering students learned a topic in biomechanics in an augmented reality learning environment using Microsoft HoloLens and Near Field Electromagnetic Range (NFER) system. Overall, two lectures have been included in two rounds. During each learning lecture, students should move on specific sign numbers while moving a table equipped with a NEFR tag and place it on a cross mark area. Participants are also allowed to watch each scene more than once by returning to that specific number and moving the table. All learning contents were developed in Unity 2022 software and assigned to a particular location marked by the number from 1–7 (lecture one) and 1–8 (lecture two). The system consists of four parts that can cover the entire learning area: (a) two locators, (b) NFER sensors (tags worn by participants), (c) a laptop with the tracking software, and (d) a router (to provide a data link) [14]. Each tag has a unique frequency that can categorize various themes. For HoloLens to find participants and show them the appropriate AR modules, HoloLens merged the data exported from the NFER database (Fig. 1).

Fig. 1. The overall system architecture, including devices [15]

2.2 Participant

A total of 31 students (mean age at baseline ±SD, 21.75 ±4.27) were recruited from the University of Missouri. Sixteen participants were tested with RCJ metacognitive monitoring feedback tool. Other fifteen students with JOL metacognitive monitoring feedback tool.

2.3 Learning Content

One of the core topics in ergonomics courses, biomechanics was chosen as the major engineering education resource in this project. The lectures were divided into seven modules (lecture one) and eight modules (lecture 2). In each scene, five three-dimensional arrays of gray boxes are arranged at various angles in front of their eyes and radially arranged around them at a constant distance of 200 cm. During the learning process, an instructor (male or female) guides students through a different part of the scene based on the voice. To completely scan the learning area, participants had to swivel their head, and torso both left and right based on the voice and the instructor's movement (see Fig. 2).

Scene arrangement

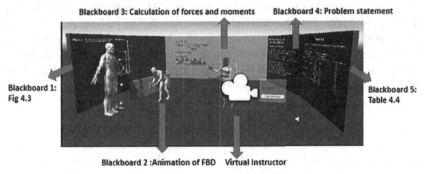

Fig. 2. The arrangement of items in the AR environment

2.4 Experiment Procedure

The experiment was done in two groups. Both groups responded to the pre-post metacognitive awareness inventory questionnaire. In group A (RCJ group), participants' confidence and performance were calculated by answering "how well do you think you have performed in question #?" After a question about the scene content. On the other hand, in group B (JOL group), the JOL rating was used to predict how much of the learned material they would be able to recall in the future before answering a question about the scene content. For each group, there are two lectures of learning within 48 h. For RCJ (group A) and JOL (group B), in lecture one, the metacognitive awareness inventory questionnaire will be asked at the beginning of lecture one, whereas at the end of lecture 2.

Before the experiment, participants were given a demographic questionnaire in which they answered questions related to their computer experience level, major, and whether they had previous experience in an AR or VR environment. Then participants were trained via PowerPoint file to learn how to do the learning process, answer questions and interact with the systems. Then based on the participant group (A = RCJ) and Group (B = JOL) and lecture, the MAI questionnaire was given to them before (Lecture 1) or after (Lecture 2). After the training session, participants were equipped with HoloLens and an NFER tag. During the experiment, as mentioned before, participants must move their table, place it on the crossed mark, and look straight at the number on the wall to see the AR content. Participants can also move freely while watching each module content, but they should move the table while watching the AR content.

3 Result

Thirty-one students completed the AR learning process in two groups (RCJ and JOL) and completed the MAI questionnaire whether before (lecture 1) or after (lecture 2). The collected data were from students' performance, MAI questionnaire, and metacognitive awareness monitoring. The focus of this study was only on performance and MAI data;

for that we separated both low performers' and high performers' MAI data. Then, we narrowed down our focus on students' responses to the MAI questionnaire, which changed from 0 (No) to 1 (yes) between lecture 1 and lecture 2. The performance comparison indicated no significant difference between lecture 1 and lecture 2 for high performers in the JOL group (see Table 1). Furthermore, in terms of cognition comparison and knowledge of cognition, there is no significant difference between lecture 1 and lecture 2 for high performers (see Tables 2 and 3).

Table 1. Performance Comparison for high performers in JOL

Lecture	Mean	SD	F	p-value
1 (Easy)	85.714	16.496	0.300	0.5939
2 (Hard)	89.796	10.799		

Table 2. Regulation of Cognition Comparison for high performers in JOL

Lecture	Mean	SD	F	p-value
1 (Easy)	0.76	0.15	0.0416	0.8417
2 (Hard)	0.74	0.10		

Table 3. Knowledge of Cognition Comparison for high performers in JOL

Lecture	Mean	SD	F	p-value
1 (Easy)	0.75	0.16	0.0175	0.897
2 (Hard)	0.74	0.11		

The comparison of performance indicated that there is a significant difference between lecture 1 and lecture 2 for low performers in the JOL group (p-value = <.005) (Table 4). Furthermore, in terms of the MAI score subcategory (cognition comparison and knowledge of cognition there is no significant difference between lecture 1 and lecture 2 for high performers (see Tables 5 and 6).

Table 4. Performance Comparison for low performers in JOL

Lecture	Mean	SD	F	p-value
1 (Easy)	90.48	7.38	6.4286	**0.0296**
2 (Hard)	76.19	11.66		

Table 5. Regulation of Cognition Comparison for low performers in JOL

Lecture	Mean	SD	F	p-value
1 (Easy)	0.77	0.20	0.035	0.8554
2 (Hard)	0.75	0.15		

Table 6. Knowledge about Cognition Comparison for low performers in JOL

Lecture	Mean	SD	F	p-value
1 (Easy)	0.75	0.21	0.0395	0.8465
2 (Hard)	0.73	0.17		

The performance comparison indicated that there isn't any significant difference between lecture 1 and lecture 2 for high performers in the JOL group (see Table 7). Furthermore, regarding cognition comparison and knowledge of cognition, there is no significant difference between lecture 1 and lecture 2 for high performers (see Tables 8 and 9).

Table 7. Performance Comparison for high performers in RCJ

Lecture	Mean	SD	F	p-value
1 (Easy)	92.85	7.82	0.2981	0.5995
2 (Hard)	95.23	7.38		

Table 8. Regulation of Cognition Comparison for high performers in RCJ

Lecture	Mean	SD	F	p-value
1 (Easy)	0.86	0.12	0.0422	0.8414
2 (Hard)	0.87	0.11		

Table 9. Knowledge about Cognition Comparison for high performers in RCJ

Lecture	Mean	SD	F	p-value
1 (Easy)	0.89	0.09	0.0238	0.8804
2 (Hard)	0.89	0.07		

According to Table 10, the performance comparison indicated a significant difference between lecture 1 and lecture 2 for low performance in the RCJ group. Furthermore, in terms of MAI score subcategory cognition comparison (p-value = 0.0541) and knowledge of cognition (p-value = 0.0332) there are significant differences between both lecture 1 and lecture 2 for low performers (see Tables 11 and 12).

Table 10. Performance Comparison for low performers in RCJ

Lecture	Mean	SD	F	p-value
1 (Easy)	100.00	0	63.4390	**<0.001**
2 (Hard)	75.71	9.64		

Table 11. Regulation of Cognition Comparison for low performers in RCJ

Lecture	Mean	SD	F	p-value
1 (Easy)	0.68	0.13	4.2440	0.0541
2 (Hard)	0.79	0.11		

Table 12. Knowledge about Cognition Comparison for low performers in RCJ

Lecture	Mean	SD	F	p-value
1 (Easy)	0.65	0.10	5.3182	**0.0332**
2 (Hard)	0.76	0.11		

4   Discussion

There is evidence from various studies that success in learning outcomes and metacognitive capacity are strongly correlated [16]. Furthermore, several investigations have demonstrated that metacognitive inventory (such as MAI) is a trustworthy method for forecasting metacognitive abilities [10, 17]. In this study, we planned to understand which metacognitive monitoring probe improves student metacognitive awareness in the AR learning environment. The outcomes of the current research will help us understand which metacognition monitoring method is better in terms of strengthening metacognitive awareness during the learning process. Based on the literature, we hypothesized that the students with high performance in AR would have high MAI scores in both groups (RCJ and JOL). However, the results indicated only improvement in MAI score for students with low performance in the RCJ group. In addition, there is no improvement in the MAI score for both low and high performers in the JOL group.

First, we tried to find why the change in metacognitive awareness was more evident in the RCJ group than in JOL. In the RCJ group, the metacognitive confidence question asked learners to make confidence judgments about their performance by percentage. Such a question inherently invokes and measures self-monitoring [18]. Furthermore, Kauffman, Ge [18] observed that confidence judgment is not only a good predictor of self-monitoring, but also self-monitoring is positively related to metacognitive knowledge. Kim [19] results showed that exposure to retrospective confident judgment regarding self-evaluation of a given task and actual task performance could improve the correct decision-making process and situational awareness in a dynamic environment. In our experiment, even though lecture 2 and lecture 1 were different in terms of difficulty, people's metacognitive awareness did not change between the two lectures for both performers (low and high) in JOL. To judge their future performance in a task, people use general knowledge about their memory functioning and their previous experience with a given type of content [20]. Although task difficulty might affect both the decision and metacognitive judgment, Siedlecka, Paulewicz [21] found no differences in metacognitive accuracy between the two prospective conditions. To sum up, confidence judgments are more accurate when they refer to the response that is already given than when they are about a future response. Furthermore, retrospective judgments are highly influenced by the speed and accuracy of immediately making decisions. In the RCJ group, the confidence level of students about their response was measured right after their answer to the question. Students may feel underconfident or overconfident based on their metacognitive awareness level. A phenomenon known as the hard-easy effect may also have happened: feeling overconfident in difficult tasks and underconfidence in easier tasks [22]. In addition, we found more changes in both low and high performers MAI scores in RCJ because of greater accuracy and calibration of retrospective judgments (RCJ) compared to prospective judgments (JOL). This increase in the accuracy of retrospective judgment can be explained through other access to the internal state of evidence supporting a particular choice rather than only the aggregate likelihood of success [23].

Considering the experiment provided students rewatching the learning modules again, students who were overconfident about their performance did not rewatch the learning content since they felt they had learned the learning material very well. However, compared to RCJ and JOL, the students who experienced the RCJs were often selected to restudy some AR modules based on their confidence level. They were more likely to redo the modules when their retrospective confidence level was low, which helped them improve their understanding. It means RCJ is a better method for monitoring student's metacognitive awareness.

The comparison between students' metacognitive awareness in both groups for two types of performers (high performers, and low performers) also showed no significant difference between student metacognitive awareness in terms of both knowledges of cognition and regulation of cognition in the JOL group. However, there is a significant difference in the RCJ group for low performers in terms of regulation of cognition and knowledge about cognition. In the RCJ group, the participants whose performance was significantly reduced in lecture 2 had a higher improvement on MAI both regulation and knowledge about cognition. In this group, students could predict their performance better by answering how confident they were about their answers after responding to a question. However, for the high performers, the MAI score was not improved due to the illusion of knowing phenomena which is an overestimation of performance. It means that their abilities to be self-regulated learners still need to be enhanced by recognizing their academic weaknesses. On the other hand, the low performers' MAI score was improved even though their performance was significantly decreased in lecture 2. In our experiment, the difficulty level of lecture 2 was higher than that of lecture 1. In the literature, it has been suggested that the attributes of the learning material could influence metacognitive awareness [24]. Hence, the higher level of learning material in lecture 2 might trigger them to look back on their weakness.

5 Conclusion

AR can provide a fertile ground for the practice of subliminal training techniques, assuring a high-quality experience. AR will also provide a new guideline for developing more effective learning content for students to observe their learning and be aware of their learning process. Understanding which metacognitive monitoring method is effective in student metacognitive awareness is important to improve students' academic performance and calibration. The results of the pre-test and post-test MAI questionnaire via two groups, RCJ and JOL, showed an increase in metacognitive awareness of low performers in the RCJ group. It means RCJ is a more effective monitoring method for improving metacognitive awareness for low performers in AR. The reason behind metacognitive awareness improvement can be explained through the difficulty level of the lectures, that the concepts in lecture 2 are challenging to understand compared to lecture 1. However, further analysis will be needed to understand this phenomenon. Comparing both groups revealed that the metacognitive awareness with different performances might be more recognizable in RCJ than in JOL. Retrospective confidence judgments could help students realize their metacognitive status to improve their learning rate. Therefore, metacognitive monitoring feedback may change student learning behavior to improve performance. In addition, it could improve learners' performance and adaptability to a particular problem, making them self-directed and independent, and helping them develop logical thinking and judgment [25]. Overall, successfully identifying which metacognitive monitoring is appropriate in helping students with different levels of performance may be crucial in ensuring that students have the support and materials they require to succeed. It also allows instructors to apply the best approach to detect these students early in the learning process in the AR environment.

Acknowledgments. This study was funded by the National Science Foundation (NSF).

References

1. Jaleel, S.: A Study on the metacognitive awareness of secondary school students. Univ. J. Educ. Res. 4(1), 165–172 (2016)
2. Radu, I.: Why should my students use AR? A comparative review of the educational impacts of augmented-reality. In: 2012 IEEE International Symposium on Mixed and Augmented Reality (ISMAR). IEEE (2012)

3. Schraw, G.: Promoting general metacognitive awareness. Instr. Sci. **26**(1–2), 113–125 (1998)
4. Le Berre, A.-P., et al.: Differential compromise of prospective and retrospective metamemory monitoring and their dissociable structural brain correlates. Cortex **81**, 192–202 (2016)
5. Morphew, J.W.: Changes in metacognitive monitoring accuracy in an introductory physics course. Metacogn. Learn. **16**(1), 89–111 (2020). https://doi.org/10.1007/s11409-020-09239-3
6. Huff, J.D., Nietfeld, J.L.: Using strategy instruction and confidence judgments to improve metacognitive monitoring. Metacogn. Learn. **4**, 161–176 (2009)
7. Jameson, K.A., et al.: The influence of near-threshold priming on metamemory and recall. Acta Physiol. (Oxf) **73**(1), 55–68 (1990)
8. Hacker, D.J., et al.: Test prediction and performance in a classroom context. J. Educ. Psychol. **92**(1), 160 (2000)
9. Kim, J.H.: The effect of metacognitive monitoring feedback on performance in a computer-based training simulation. Appl. Ergon. **67**, 193–202 (2018)
10. Schraw, G., Dennison, R.S.: Assessing metacognitive awareness. Contemp. Educ. Psychol. **19**(4), 460–475 (1994)
11. Sperling, R.A., et al.: Metacognition and self-regulated learning constructs. Educ. Res. Eval. **10**(2), 117–139 (2004)
12. Nietfeld, J.L., Cao, L., Osborne, J.W.: Metacognitive monitoring accuracy and student performance in the postsecondary classroom. J. Exp. Educ. 7–28 (2005)
13. Koriat, A., Shitzer-Reichert, R.: Metacognitive judgments and their accuracy: insights from the processes underlying judgments of learning in children. In: Chambres, P., Izaute, M., Marescaux, P.J. (eds.) Metacognition. Springer, Boston (2002). https://doi.org/10.1007/978-1-4615-1099-4_1
14. Guo, W., Kim, J.H.: Using metacognitive monitoring feedback to improve student learning performance in a real-time location-based augmented reality environment. In: Proceedings of the IIE Annual Conference. Institute of Industrial and Systems Engineers (IISE) (2020)
15. Guo, W., Kim, J.H.: Designing augmented reality learning systems with real-time tracking sensors. In: Ayaz, H., Asgher, U., Paletta, L. (eds.) AHFE 2021. LNNS, vol. 259, pp. 269–276. Springer, Cham (2021). https://doi.org/10.1007/978-3-030-80285-1_32
16. Callender, A.A., Franco-Watkins, A.M., Roberts, A.S.: Improving metacognition in the classroom through instruction, training, and feedback. Metacogn. Learn. **11**(2), 215–235 (2015). https://doi.org/10.1007/s11409-015-9142-6
17. Pedone, R., et al.: Development of a self-report measure of metacognition: the metacognition self-assessment scale (MSAS). Instrument description and factor structure. Clin. Neuropsychiatry **14**(3), 185–194 (2017)
18. Kauffman, D.F., et al.: Prompting in web-based environments: Supporting self-monitoring and problem solving skills in college students. J. Educ. Comput. Res. **38**(2), 115–137 (2008)
19. Kim, J.H.: Simulation training in self-regulated learning: investigating the effects of dual feedback on dynamic decision-making tasks. In: Zaphiris, P., Ioannou, A. (eds.) LCT 2014, Part I. LNCS, vol. 8523, pp. 419–428. Springer, Cham (2014). https://doi.org/10.1007/978-3-319-07482-5_40
20. Koriat, A., Levy-Sadot, R.: Conscious and unconscious metacognition: a rejoinder, pp. 193–202. Academic Press (2000)
21. Siedlecka, M., Paulewicz, B., Wierzchoń, M.: But I was so sure! Metacognitive judgments are less accurate given prospectively than retrospectively. Front. Psychol. **7**, 218 (2016)
22. Gigerenzer, G., Hoffrage, U., Kleinbölting, H.: Probabilistic mental models: a Brunswikian theory of confidence. Psychol. Rev. **98**(4), 506 (1991)
23. Pouget, A., Drugowitsch, J., Kepecs, A.: Confidence and certainty: distinct probabilistic quantities for different goals. Nat. Neurosci. **19**(3), 366–374 (2016)

24. Novia, H., et al.: The development of metacognitive awareness related to the implementation of metacognitive-based learning. In: Journal of Physics: Conference Series. IOP Publishing (2019)
25. Rum, S.N.M., Ismail, M.A.: Metocognitive support accelerates computer assisted learning for novice programmers. J. Educ. Technol. Soc. **20**(3), 170–181 (2017)

Cognitive Load Quantified via Functional Near Infrared Spectroscopy During Immersive Training with VR Based Basic Life Support Learning Modules in Hostile Environment

Mert Deniz Polat[1] , Kurtulus Izzetoglu[1]([✉]) , Mehmet Emin Aksoy[2,5] , Dilek Kitapcioglu[3] , Tuba Usseli[4] , and Serhat Ilgaz Yoner[5]

[1] School of Biomedical Engineering, Science and Health Systems, Drexel University, Philadelphia, PA 19104, USA
ki25@drexel.edu

[2] Center of Advanced Simulation and Education, Acıbadem Mehmet Ali Aydınlar University, Istanbul, Turkey

[3] Department Medical Education, Medical Faculty, Acıbadem Mehmet Ali Aydınlar University, Istanbul, Turkey

[4] Department of Anesthesia, Vocational School of Health Services, Acıbadem Mehmet Ali Aydınlar University, Istanbul, Turkey

[5] Department of Biomedical Device Technology, Acıbadem Mehmet Ali Aydınlar University, Istanbul, Turkey

Abstract. This study investigates the use of functional near infrared spectroscopy (fNIRS) as a tool for assessing cognitive workload in virtual reality (VR) based medical education. Specifically, the study explores the effect of simulator immersion and distraction on cognitive workload during a Basic Life Support (BLS) training course delivered by a VR-based serious gaming module. Nineteen participants with no prior knowledge of BLS guidelines completed a VR-based serious gaming BLS training module and were randomly assigned to two groups for the BLS examination; the first group had experienced medium distraction while the second group had a high level of distraction. All participants then took a hands-on BLS exam at the end of the study protocol. The results show significant decrease in cognitive workload measured by fNIRS during the training sessions. The oxygenation levels at the prefrontal cortex were significantly higher for the participants who had taken the high distraction VR-exam, suggesting a higher neural involvement compared to the group who had taken the medium distraction VR-exam. However, unlike hands-on exam, no significant difference between two groups was determined for the VR-based exam. The results demonstrate that fNIRS can be used to measure cognitive workload in VR-based medical training and provide further insights for optimizing serious game-based learning tools.

Keywords: Human performance · medical training · learning · virtual reality · cognitive workload · fNIRS · functional brain imaging

D. D. Schmorrow and C. M. Fidopiastis (Eds.): HCII 2023, LNAI 14019, pp. 359–372, 2023.
https://doi.org/10.1007/978-3-031-35017-7_23

1 Introduction

1.1 Background

The advancement in technology introduced a new set of learning tools. Serious gaming is one of these emerging tools which has been increasingly adopted into the medical training domain [1]. The benefits of interactive learning such as serious games have been demonstrated and reported in previous studies [2, 3]. These benefits include increased motivation, diligence and better subject understanding [4]. Further, virtual reality (VR) systems enable these learning modules with high immersion, controllable parameters and dynamic conditions, hence making it more engaging and attentive for the users [5, 6]. However, further studies for evaluating the efficacy of these modules and a more in-depth analysis of user performance, such as user's cognitive workload are required. Assessment of the cognitive workload will not only quantitatively assess the efficacy of these new learning tools, but also provide additional performance metrics to enhance and optimize serious game-based learning tools.

The relation between cognitive processes, sensory and motor skills with task specific activation in the prefrontal cortex (PFC), has been shown in several studies utilizing functional brain imaging techniques such as functional magnetic resonance imaging (fMRI), or functional near infrared spectroscopy (fNIRS) [7–9]. fMRI studies helped mapping of brain activity changes in response to the cognitive tasks, yet its mobility and field operation appears as a limiting factor [10]. On the other hand, fNIRS is a is a safe, non-invasive, real-time, and field deployable optical modality. The fNIRS studies have been able to quantify the cognitive workload during learning in association with the changes in cerebral hemodynamics for the last two decades [11–13]. This cerebral hemodynamics can be measured by the fNIRS as follows: with increased neuronal activity, regional metabolic demand increases which leads to additional supply of oxygenated hemoglobin (HbO) and deposit of deoxygenated hemoglobin (HbR). HbO and HbR have distinct optical characteristics which presents different absorption characteristics to emitted near infrared light. Collected photons from the cortical region can be processed with the modified Beer-Lambert Law to acquire relative HbO and HbR concentrations (Jöbsis, 1977; Villringer, 1997; K. Izzetoglu et al., 2004).

fNIRS measures as a cognitive performance assessment tool has been employed in medical education studies. The medical training tasks investigated by utilizing fNIRS systems include surgical operations (laparoscopic, dental, robot assisted surgery) as well as medical profession training, such as a Basic Life Support (BLS) training [13, 16–18]. As an exemplary case, Aksoy et al. (2019) studied a VR-based serious gaming BLS training for individuals who underwent training sessions during a seven-day course. The study reported increase in the behavioral performance results determined from serious gaming scores and decrease in cerebral oxygenation in the left PFC region of subjects as quantified by the fNIRS. As a follow-up to this BLS training study, we have explored how varying levels of simulator immersion affects learners' cognitive workload in this new study. Hence, in this article we investigate if there is any significant difference in oxygenated or deoxygenated hemoglobin concentration due to changing PFC activation between groups engaged in low and high distraction levels during BLS exam.

2 Methodology

2.1 Participants

19 subjects (15 Female, 4 Male, Age: 20.42 ± 0.96) with no prior knowledge about adult Basic Life Support guidelines volunteered for this study. All participants took a preliminary test that assesses their initial knowledge about adult BLS guidelines [19].

This study has been approved by the Ethical Committee of Acıbadem Mehmet Ali Aydınlar University where this study was conducted. All participants gave written informed consent in accordance with the Declaration of Helsinki [20].

2.2 Experimental Protocol

Basic Life Support (BLS), a healthcare training course where a medical professional delivers an adequate response to an individual amid cardiac or respiratory arrest is selected for this research study [19]. The BLS training and exam protocol utilizes VR based serious gaming module (3DMedsim® GmbH, Bochum, Germany) compatible with ERC 2021 BLS guidelines as the simulation environment [2, 19]. As for the VR instrument, participants wore a high resolution and rate VR headset (HTC Vive Pro 2®, Tauyan City, Taiwan), minimize the risk of dizziness. Figure 1 (left) shows the participants wearing the VR headset and fNIRS probe.

Fig. 1. Participants complete the BLS training protocol at the experiment site. Participants wear a virtual reality headset and fNIRS probe during the training and examination tasks (left). Serious game training module occurs in low distraction (seaside scenario) condition (top middle). Serious game examination module occurs in medium distraction (subway station scenario, bottom middle) and high distraction (warzone scenario) conditions (top right). All subjects participate in a hands-on exam at the end of the protocol (bottom right).

Following a baseline fNIRS recording of 20 s, all participants completed two sessions of training modules under low level distraction (sea-side environment scenario) considered as the acquisition phase. Upon completing the training modules, participants were randomly assigned into two groups, VR1 and VR2. VR1 group (n = 10) participated in the BLS examination module with a medium level of distraction (subway station

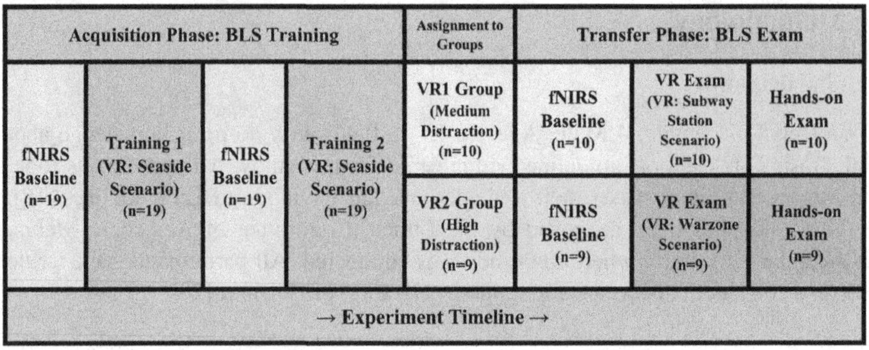

Acquisition Phase: BLS Training				Assignment to Groups	Transfer Phase: BLS Exam		
fNIRS Baseline (n=19)	Training 1 (VR: Seaside Scenario) (n=19)	fNIRS Baseline (n=19)	Training 2 (VR: Seaside Scenario) (n=19)	VR1 Group (Medium Distraction) (n=10)	fNIRS Baseline (n=10)	VR Exam (VR: Subway Station Scenario) (n=10)	Hands-on Exam (n=10)
				VR2 Group (High Distraction) (n=9)	fNIRS Baseline (n=9)	VR Exam (VR: Warzone Scenario) (n=9)	Hands-on Exam (n=9)
→ Experiment Timeline →							

Fig. 2. Experiment protocol workflow. Participants were split into two groups upon receiving training under low distraction conditions. The two groups participated in examinations under varying levels of distraction prior to entering a hands-on exam.

scenario) whereas VR2 group (n = 9) participated in the BLS examination session under a high level of distraction (simulated war-zone scenario). All subjects participated in a hands-on exam that concluded the transfer phase. Figure 2 displays the protocol execution for both groups. During the exam sessions, performance measures of the participants were collected via the built-in score reporting of the serious gaming modules. Table 1 presents the scoring system reported by the module.

Table 1. The rubric for the scoring of BLS serious gaming module

Criteria	Serious Gaming Module Score	Criteria	Serious Gaming Module Score
Check Safety	5	4th CPR30	4
Check Consciousness	9	4th Ventilation	2
Head Tilt	5	5th CPR30	4
Check Breathing	6	5th Ventilation	2
Call for Help	5	2nd Carotid Pulse	0
Get AED[a]	5	AED Use Pad	5
Check Carotid Pulse	0	AED On Off	5
1st CPR30[b]	4	Stand Clear	5
1st Ventilation	2	AED Shock	5
2nd CPR30	4	Final CPR	15
2nd Ventilation	2	Check Rhythm	0
3rd CPR30	4	Total score	100
3rd Ventilation	2		

[a] AED: automated external defibrillator
[b] CPR: cardiopulmonary resuscitation

2.3 Functional Near Infrared Spectroscopy

To monitor the hemodynamic response of the participants from the prefrontal cortex (PFC), a continuous wave fNIRS device (fNIR Devices, LLC, Potomac, MD) was employed for this study. The fNIRS probe provided the data acquisition from 16 distinct optodes from the PFC region. The probe houses 4 LED sources with 730 and 850 nm wavelengths, 10 photodetectors, and the readout circuitry that operates at 2 Hz sampling rate. The layout of the probe is shown at Fig. 3.

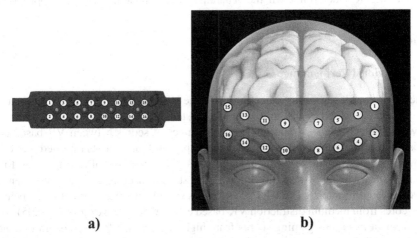

a)   b)

Fig. 3. This study utilizes a Functional near infrared spectroscopy (fNIRS) system. (a) The fNIRS probe contains 4 sources and 10 detectors. (b) The 16 measurement channels are overlayed on the prefrontal cortex

It is known that the instrument noise, motion artifacts and physiological confounders can interfere with fNIRS signals [8, 21]. Hence, the fNIRS data was preprocessed by applying a wavelet-based motion artifact removal and a low-pass FIR filter with 0.1 Hz cutoff frequency to reject confounding signals, such as cardiac and respiratory oscillations [21–23]. The filtered light intensity data was then processed with Modified Beer-Lambert Law to obtain the relative oxygenated hemoglobin (HbO) and relative de-oxygenated hemoglobin (HbR) concentration measures [12]. In this study, the left hemisphere and right hemisphere of the prefrontal cortex are the regions of the interest: (ROI) as they are associated with brain activities during learning and training [13, 24–26]. In this paper, the changes in the corresponding ROIs, i.e., left and right hemispheres of the PFC, were calculated by averaging the fNIRS readings from channels 1–8 and 9–16 respectively (see Fig. 3).

To further our understanding in the trainee's performance, we calculated the following indices: Relative Neural Efficiency (RNE) and Relative Neural Involvement (RNI) indices are computed using the standardized performance scores and hemodynamic measures (HbO, HbR, OXY) following an existing two-dimensional model [27–29]. Equations 1 and 2 show the calculation for RNE and RNI where P represents the standardized performance score (serious gaming LMS score) and M represent standardized mental effort (HbO or HbR).

$$RNE = (P - M)/\sqrt{2} \qquad (1)$$

$$RNI = (P + M)/\sqrt{2} \qquad (2)$$

Due to a limited sample size, the choice of adequate statistical method requires analyzing the distribution of the dataset. Therefore, Shaphiro-Wilk test was conducted for each variable to determine whether a parametric or nonparametric test is appropriate.

3   Results

3.1   Behavioral Performance

Basic Life Support performance scores during the VR-based and hands-on examination modules were reported by the built in scoring system of the serious-gaming modules as shown in Table 1. Figure 4 and depicts the changes of scores between VR-based and hands-on examination modules for the two groups. All four datasets returned p > 0.05 following Shaphiro-Wilk test which suggests parametric statistical testing. Therefore, parametric tests, paired t-test and Student's t-test were used to compare the changes between groups (Table 2). The VR1 group shows significant improvement in the behavioral scores from medium distraction VR-based exam to hands on exam (p < 0.05). The improvement in serious gaming scores from high distraction VR-based exam to hands on exam in VR2 group was also statistically significant (p < 0.01). The scores of VR1 and VR2 groups during the VR-based and hands-on examination modules on the other hand were significantly different (p > 0.05).

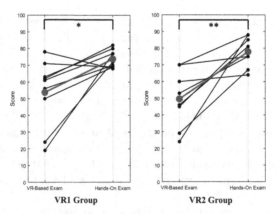

Fig. 4. Serious game exam scores between VR-based and hands-on examination modules. Red line shows the means across subjects at each module. Significant results are annotated on graphs as: *: p < 0.05, **: p < 0.01. (Color figure online)

Table 2. Descriptive statistics and comparisons (paired t-test) for serious game exam scores (*: $p < 0.05$, **: $p < 0.01$).

	n	VR-Based Exam		Hands-On Exam		df	t
		Mean	SD	Mean	SD		
VR1 Group	9	53.778	20.011	73.778	5.286	8	−2.800*
VR2 Group	8	49.6250	17.179	77.8750	9.203	7	−3.974**

3.2 Functional Near-Infrared Spectroscopy Results

Mean HbO and HbR values from each task per subject is included in the analysis. Figure 5 shows the changes in HbO and HbR measures during the acquisition phase. HbO and HbR data at all regions return $p > 0.05$ following Shaphiro-Wilk test which suggests parametric statistical testing. Paired t-tests were conducted for both HbO and

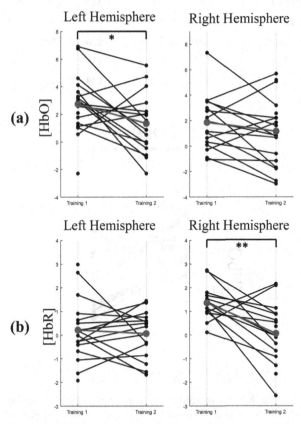

Fig. 5. Averaged HbO and HbR measures during the acquisition phase. Red line shows the means across subjects at each module. Significant results are annotated on graphs (*: $p < 0.05$, **: $p < 0.01$). (Color figure online)

HbR (see Table 3). The changes in HbO on the left hemisphere showed significant change in response training (p < 0.05). On the other hand, no significant change was determined on the left hemisphere for the HbR. However, HbR on the right hemisphere indicated significant change (p < 0.01) between two training modules (Fig. 5b). Further preliminary analysis was performed on each quadrant, namely, left dorsolateral prefrontal cortex (LDLPFC), right dorsolateral prefrontal cortex (RDLPFC), left anterior medial prefrontal cortex (LAMPFC), and right anterior medial prefrontal cortex (RAMPFC) and statistically significant change was only observed on the LDPFC (p < 0.05) (see Fig. 6 and Table 3).

Table 3. Descriptive statistics and comparisons (paired t-test) for VR-based training modules (*: p < 0.05, **: p < 0.01).

	n	Training 1		Training 2		df	t
		Mean	SD	Mean	SD		
Left Hemisphere HbO	16	3.103	1.856	1.332	2.206	15	2.698*
Left Hemisphere HbR	15	0.175	1.0540	0.035	1.007	14	0.435
Right Hemisphere HbO	16	1.805	2.155	0.820	2.566	15	1.737
Right Hemisphere HbR	14	1.358	0.729	0.175	1.298	13	3.068**
LDLPFC HbO	15	3.123	1.903	1.134	2.229	14	2.749*

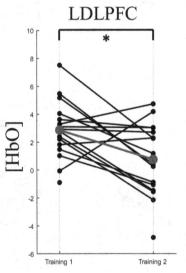

Fig. 6. HbO measures at left dorsolateral prefrontal cortex (LDLPFC) during the acquisition phase. Red line shows the means across subjects at each module. Statistical significance is annotated on graph (*: p < 0.05). (Color figure online)

In this paper, the transfer phase is defined as the VR-based BLS exam and hands-on BLS exam. The HbO and HbR results from this transfer phase are shown in Fig. 7. The left hemisphere HbO from the hands-on BLS exam module is shown to significantly deviate ($p < 0.05$) from normal distribution following the Shaphiro-Wilk test which suggest nonparametric statistical testing. All other fNIRS data collected during the transfer phase return $p > 0.05$ following Shaphiro-Wilk test. Left hemisphere HbO (Wilcoxon Rank Sum test, $p < 0.01$) shows significant differences between VR1 and VR2 groups during the hands-on BLS exam (Table 4). There were no significant changes between the two groups on the other regions during the hands-on BLS exam as well as during VR-based exam ($p > 0.05$).

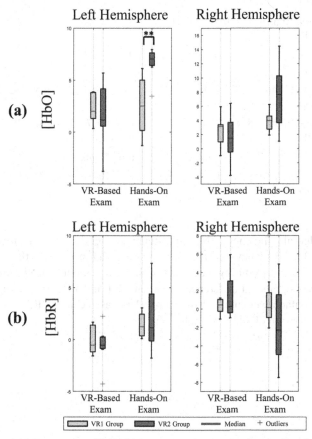

Fig. 7. HbO and HbR measures during the transfer phase. Boxplot median is shown as red horizontal line. Significant results are annotated on graphs (**: $p < 0.01$)

Table 4. Descriptive statistics and comparisons ([a]Student's t-test, [b]Wilcoxon Rank Sum test) for examination modules (**: $p < 0.01$).

	VR1 Group			VR2 Group			df	t
	n	Mean	SD	n	Mean	SD		
[a]VR-based Exam: Left Hemisphere HbO	8	2.312	1.390	9	1.854	2.947	15	0.401
[a]VR-based Exam: Left Hemisphere HbR	8	−0.0780	1.345	7	−0.549	1.956	13	0.551
[a]VR-based Exam: Right Hemisphere HbO	9	2.368	2.034	9	1.352	3.012	16	0.838
[a]VR-based Exam: Right Hemisphere HbR	7	0.317	0.855	8	1.344	2.445	13	−1.052
[a]Hands-on Exam: Left Hemisphere HbR	8	1.406	1.139	9	1.927	2.966	15	−0.466
[a]Hands-on Exam: Right Hemisphere HbO	7	3.881	1.437	9	7.089	4.335	14	−1.867
[a]Hands-on Exam: Right Hemisphere HbR	8	0.340	1.772	8	−1.769	4.184	15	1.320
	n	Σrank	U	n	Σrank	U	W	p
[b]Hands-on Exam: Left Hemisphere HbO	8	40	52	7	80	4	80	**0.00373

Relative Neural Efficiency (RNE) and Relative Neural Involvement (RNI) metrics were calculated for the hands-on BLS exam module. Figure 7 shows the RNE and RNI metrics of the two groups during the hands-on BLS exam module. RNI (Student's t-test, $p < 0.05$) shows significant differences between VR1 and VR2 groups suggesting that the trainees who underwent the high distraction VR-based exam (VR2), highly involved during hands-on exam (Table 5) (Fig. 8).

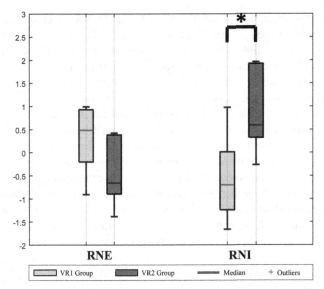

Fig. 8. Relative Neural Efficiency (RNE) and Relative Neural Involvement (RNI) metrics during the hands-on BLS exam. Boxplot median is shown as red horizontal line. Significant results are annotated on graphs (*: $p < 0.05$). (Color figure online)

Table 5. Descriptive statistics and comparisons (paired t-test) for Relative Neural Efficiency (RNE) and Relative Neural Involvement (RNI) metrics during the hands-on BLS exam (*: $p < 0.05$).

	Training 1			Training 2			df	t
	n	Mean	SD	n	Mean	SD		
RNE	8	0.315	0.722	5	−0.395	0.778	11	1.677
RNI	8	−0.568	0.910	5	0.945	0.967	11	*−2.850

4 Discussion

The VR-based serious gaming Basic Life Support (BLS) training modules were studied here. Previously, we reported an increase in the behavioral results (serious gaming scores) and decrease in cerebral oxygenation in the left prefrontal cortex (PFC) region of subjects [16]. The results were in agreement with other functional brain imaging studies that had also focused on training and its association with brain activity changes in the PFC region. This new study also demonstrated the similar trend while a trainee becomes proficient on a given task, i.e., while the behavioral performance improves, HbO changes in the PFC decrease (Figs. 4 and 5a).

Furthermore, we explored how varying levels of simulator immersion affects learners' cognitive workload. The simulator immersion was graded by changing levels of distraction during BLS training and examination. The cognitive workload was assessed by investigating performance scores as well as by the fNIRS which did not reveal significant difference between groups under varying levels of distraction during VR-exam. However, the group with higher distraction, i.e., VR2 group who had taken the VR-based exam under simulated warzone setting displayed significantly higher HbO levels than VR1 group who had taken the exam under simulated subway station setting. The former setting, i.e., warzone distraction, is assumed to induce higher distraction compared to the latter setting, in which the training environment was simulated and conducted at a subway station. To better understand the relation between the behavioral (via serious-gaming score) and cognitive workload (via fNIRS measures), Relative Neural Efficiency (RNE) and Relative Neural Involvement (RNI) metrics were computed. During the hands-on BLS exam which is also assumed to be a transfer phase of the training in this paper, VR2 group shows significantly higher neural involvement than VR1 group. This is a critical finding as it suggests that the effect of the distraction on training could be significant and calls for further studies. Increasing the subject pool and adding more distraction levels will address this study's limitations and will provide further details on learning in hostile environments.

References

1. Olszewski, A.E., Wolbrink, T.A.: Serious gaming in medical education: a proposed structured framework for game development. Simul. Healthc. **12**(4), 240 (2017). https://doi.org/10.1097/SIH.0000000000000212
2. Aksoy, E.: Comparing the effects on learning outcomes of tablet-based and virtual reality-based serious gaming modules for basic life support training: randomized trial. JMIR Serious Games **7**(2), e13442 (2019). https://doi.org/10.2196/13442
3. Jayakumar, N., Brunckhorst, O., Dasgupta, P., Khan, M.S., Ahmed, K.: e-learning in surgical education: a systematic review. J. Surg. Educ. **72**(6), 1145–1157 (2015). https://doi.org/10.1016/j.jsurg.2015.05.008
4. Pellas, N., Fotaris, P., Kazanidis, I., Wells, D.: Augmenting the learning experience in primary and secondary school education: a systematic review of recent trends in augmented reality game-based learning. Virtual Reality **23**(4), 329–346 (2018). https://doi.org/10.1007/s10055-018-0347-2
5. Hanson, K., Shelton, B.E.: Design and development of virtual reality: analysis of challenges faced by educators. J. Educ. Technol. Soc. **11**(1), 118–131 (2008)
6. Soliman, M., Pesyridis, A., Dalaymani-Zad, D., Gronfula, M., Kourmpetis, M.: The application of virtual reality in engineering education. Appl. Sci. **11**(6), 2879 (2021). https://doi.org/10.3390/app11062879
7. Izzetoglu, K., Bunce, S., Onaral, B., Pourrezaei, K., Chance, B.: Functional optical brain imaging using near-infrared during cognitive tasks. Int. J. Hum.-Comput. Interact. **17**(2), 211–227 (2004). https://doi.org/10.1207/s15327590ijhc1702_6
8. Izzetoglu, M., et al.: Functional near-infrared neuroimaging. IEEE Trans. Neural Syst. Rehabil. Eng. **13**(2), 153–159 (2005). https://doi.org/10.1109/TNSRE.2005.847377
9. Logothetis, N.K., Wandell, B.A.: Interpreting the BOLD signal. Annu. Rev. Physiol. **66**(1), 735–769 (2004). https://doi.org/10.1146/annurev.physiol.66.082602.092845
10. Parasuraman, R., Wilson, G.F.: Putting the brain to work: neuroergonomics past, present, and future. Hum. Factors J. Hum. Factors Ergon. Soc. **50**(3), 468–474 (2008). https://doi.org/10.1518/001872008X288349

11. Curtin, A., Ayaz, H.: The age of neuroergonomics: towards ubiquitous and continuous measurement of brain function with fNIRS: the age of neuroergonomics and fNIRS. Jpn. Psychol. Res. **60**(4), 374–386 (2018). https://doi.org/10.1111/jpr.12227

12. Izzetoglu, K., et al.: The evolution of field deployable fnir spectroscopy from bench to clinical settings. J. Innov. Opt. Health Sci. **04**(03), 239–250 (2011). https://doi.org/10.1142/S17935 45811001587

13. Shewokis, P.A., Shariff, F.U., Liu, Y., Ayaz, H., Castellanos, A., Lind, D.S.: Acquisition, retention and transfer of simulated laparoscopic tasks using fNIR and a contextual interference paradigm. Am. J. Surg. **213**(2), 336–345 (2017). https://doi.org/10.1016/j.amjsurg.2016. 11.043

14. Jöbsis, F.F.: Noninvasive, infrared monitoring of cerebral and myocardial oxygen sufficiency and circulatory parameters. Science **198**(4323), 1264–1267 (1977). https://doi.org/10.1126/ science.929199

15. Villringer, A.: Functional neuroimaging. In: Villringer, A., Dirnagl, U. (eds.) Optical Imaging of Brain Function and Metabolism 2. Advances in Experimental Medicine and Biology, vol. 413, pp. 1–18. Springer, Boston (1997). https://doi.org/10.1007/978-1-4899-0056-2_1

16. Aksoy, E., Izzetoglu, K., Baysoy, E., Agrali, A., Kitapcioglu, D., Onaral, B.: Performance monitoring via functional near infrared spectroscopy for virtual reality based basic life support training. Front. Neurosci. **13** (2019). https://www.frontiersin.org/articles/10.3389/fnins.2019. 01336. Accessed 24 Jan 2023

17. Izzetoglu, K., Aksoy, M.E., Agrali, A., Kitapcioglu, D., Gungor, M., Simsek, A.: Studying brain activation during skill acquisition via robot-assisted surgery training. Brain Sci. **11**(7), Art. no. 7 (2021). https://doi.org/10.3390/brainsci11070937

18. Perry, S., et al.: Getting to the root of fine motor skill performance in dentistry: brain activity during dental tasks in a virtual reality haptic simulation. J. Med. Internet Res. **19**(12), e371 (2017). https://doi.org/10.2196/jmir.8046

19. Olasveengen, T.M., et al.: European resuscitation council guidelines 2021: basic life support. Resuscitation **161**, 98–114 (2021). https://doi.org/10.1016/j.resuscitation.2021.02.009

20. World Medical Association: World medical association declaration of Helsinki: ethical principles for medical research involving human subjects. JAMA **310**(20), 2191–2194 (2013). https://doi.org/10.1001/jama.2013.281053

21. Reddy, P., Izzetoglu, M., Shewokis, P.A., Sangobowale, M., Diaz-Arrastia, R., Izzetoglu, K.: Evaluation of fNIRS signal components elicited by cognitive and hypercapnic stimuli. Sci. Rep. **11**(1), 23457 (2021). https://doi.org/10.1038/s41598-021-02076-7

22. Izzetoglu, M., Bunce, S.C., Izzetoglu, K., Onaral, B., Pourrezaei, K.: Functional brain imaging using near-infrared technology. IEEE Eng. Med. Biol. Mag. **26**(4), 38–46 (2007). https://doi. org/10.1109/MEMB.2007.384094

23. Molavi, B., Dumont, G.A.: Wavelet-based motion artifact removal for functional near-infrared spectroscopy. Physiol. Meas. **33**(2), 259 (2012). https://doi.org/10.1088/0967-3334/33/2/259

24. Ayaz, H., Shewokis, P.A., Bunce, S., Izzetoglu, K., Willems, B., Onaral, B.: Optical brain monitoring for operator training and mental workload assessment. Neuroimage **59**(1), 36–47 (2012). https://doi.org/10.1016/j.neuroimage.2011.06.023

25. Kelly, A.M.C., Garavan, H.: Human functional neuroimaging of brain changes associated with practice. Cereb. Cortex **15**(8), 1089–1102 (2005). https://doi.org/10.1093/cercor/bhi005

26. Leff, D.R., et al.: Functional prefrontal reorganization accompanies learning-associated refinements in surgery: a manifold embedding approach. Comput. Aided Surg. **13**(6), 325–339 (2008). https://doi.org/10.3109/10929080802531482

27. Paas, F., Tuovinen, J.E., Tabbers, H., Van Gerven, P.W.M.: Cognitive load measurement as a means to advance cognitive load theory. Educ. Psychol. **38**(1), 63–71 (2003). https://doi.org/ 10.1207/S15326985EP3801_8

28. Reddy, P., Shewokis, P.A., Izzetoglu, K.: Individual differences in skill acquisition and transfer assessed by dual task training performance and brain activity. Brain Inform. **9**(1), 1–17 (2022). https://doi.org/10.1186/s40708-022-00157-5

29. Shewokis, P.A., et al.: Brain-in-the-loop learning using fNIR and simulated virtual reality surgical tasks: hemodynamic and behavioral effects. In: Schmorrow, D.D., Fidopiastis, C.M. (eds.) AC 2015. LNCS (LNAI), vol. 9183, pp. 324–335. Springer, Cham (2015). https://doi.org/10.1007/978-3-319-20816-9_31

Method of Loci in VR Web Search: Memory Retention Support by Organizing Search Results in a VR Room

Yumiho Takeuchi[✉], Yoshiyuki Shoji[ORCID], and Martin J. Dürst[ORCID]

Aoyama Gakuin University, Sagamihara, Kanagawa 252-5258, Japan
takeuchi@sw.it.aoyama.ac.jp, {shoji,duerst}@it.aoyama.ac.jp

Abstract. This paper investigates whether the *Method of Loci* is also effective for Web search in a VR environment. The *Method of Loci* (often called Mind Palace) is one of the most famous Mnemonic; when memorizing things, placing them in a building reproduced in the brain makes them easier to recall. We implemented a browser that is movable within the VR space, and VR rooms to verify whether such a Mnemonic could be used for Web searches in VR. The subject experiment compared four types of rooms: a Sequential-alignment room, a White room, a 4-colored wall room, and a Realistic room with furniture. In each VR room, users can freely create Web browser windows, and they can place, scale, tilt, and manage the windows anywhere in the room. Six participants searched for many things, compared them, and decided on their opinions in the VR room. The result shows that participants who searched in realistic rooms remembered more details of their searches a week later.

Keywords: Virtual Reality · Web Search · Information Retrieval · Method of Loci

1 Introduction

With the rapid spread of VR (Virtual Reality) devices in recent years, opportunities for work to be performed in the VR space have increased. In addition to its original use for general game purposes, in an increasing number of cases, it is being used for practical software projects, such as construction use, events, and experience-based training. VR has the ability to work even if the object itself is not in that location, can return it to its original state immediately in case of failure, and checks the results in a three-dimensional way. The use of VR is progressing in a wide range of fields, such as education and training VR, since it can also be used for training where there would otherwise be the risk of physical danger.

Yumiho Takeuchi researched at Aoyama Gakuin University until 2021 but now works at a company.

Despite the VR space being so convenient and experience-based, unlike work performed on a conventional computer screen, it has the disadvantage that it is challenging to search while working. For example, when searching during VR work, it is sometimes necessary to remove one's head-mounted display and search using a separate computer or smartphone. Moreover, even if the search takes place without removing the headset, it is necessary to close the software the worker was using and launch a search browser. Even if the search function is embedded within the VR space, it is necessary to input text and search in the VR space, where it is difficult to carry out the input process. Although, in reality, it is possible to search on the spot using a smartphone or PC, current VR technology has not yet developed to a state where it is possible to search with any level of comfort.

Several measures of resolution have been considered for resolving these kinds of issues relating to the difficulty of searching within the VR space. If we focus on complex issues surrounding the input of text, innovation regarding the following is required:

- Reducing the effort of input,
- Reducing the frequency of text input, and
- Reducing the number of searches itself.

We can broadly categorize these into two approaches: reducing the effort required for input and making repeat searches unnecessary. Many studies have focused on the approach of reducing the effort for input in the VR space and making text input a more comfortable process [1,4,11]. These include, for example, keyboards that make use of hand tracking [6]. With a software keyboard that uses the pinch input format, a circle is made using the thumb and other fingers, and this corresponds to the keyboard layout. With this format, as the software displays vocabulary after judging the context, this enables text entry at a low cost but has the feel of predictive text conversion. Methods have also been conceived that can reduce the frequency of text input by using information search technology, such as query recommendations. This kind of technology is not limited to the VR space, and is commonly used for search engines in mobile devices with complex text input.

On the other hand, however easy it is to enter text and however much the effort of inputting text is alleviated, it does not change the fact that it is necessary to suspend work to search while experiencing VR. The approach taken in this study is to reduce the number of searches. The objective of conventional methods has been to make input more comfortable when searching. On the other hand, if the number of searches themselves can be reduced, this could provide an indirect solution to the complexity of searching in a VR environment. It has been said that in Web searches carried out until now, most search queries are repeat searches of information that has already been searched before. According to a survey by Teevan [12], 40% of queries are repeat search queries. If we can eliminate repeat searches, there will be an opportunity to perform complicated procedures may be reduced by up to 40%, even if the text input and search procedures are complicated in a VR environment.

In this study, therefore, we propose a method in which, by allowing the search results to stay longer in the memory, we can eliminate the need to perform repeat searches on content that has already been searched. When investigating multiple items of information, the researched content does not easily become entrenched in human memory.

This study focuses on a famous method, the *Method of Loci* (also called "Mind Palace" or "Memory Journey"), as a method of allowing the retrieved contents to remain in memory for a more extended period of time. The *Method of Loci* is a method of retaining people and objects in one's mind by associating them. For example, consider the case that a person wants to memorize the ingredients for dinner for shopping. When using the Method of Loci, they first imagine their house in their mind. After that, they place the ingredients for appetizers in the entryway, the ones for the main dish in the living room, and the ones for dessert in their bedroom. Walk around that house and try to visualize what they need to buy in each order. In this way, they are not just memorizing words; people can also use their brain area for grasping space, making things easier to memorize and recall [7,9]. The aim, therefore, is to create an environment in which users can freely place search result Web pages in the VR space and organize them by freely moving them around. Therefore, by linking the search results in the VR space to places and organizing them in this way, there are expectations that the Method of Loci can be used to remember the results more effectively and reduce the number of searches during VR work.

The proposed method uses a Web browser that can search in the VR space, and make bookmark-like saves in the VR space. Figure 1 shows the actual screenshot of our system named the "Special bookmark"; a system that allows users to freely arrange browsers on the space and organize search results. The following VR rooms were created in order to verify what kind of space promotes memory retention based on the Method of Loci (see Fig. 2):

- **Sequential** Allainment room is a space that is just ordered like traditional bookmarks,
- **White** room is the user can freely allocate a browser in a spatial sense, but the direction in which the user is facing is unclear,
- **Four-colered** wall room is that the user can freely arrange the browser in a spatial sense, with painted walls on all four sides, and
- **Realistic** room with furniture in which a variety of objects are placed, as in a real room.

We conducted an experiment in which participants were asked actually to perform a retrieval task in each room. It makes it possible to verify what factors aid in memory retention and the effectiveness of this method.

2   Related Work

In this study, we proposed a method enabling better memory retention of search results for a more practical method of searching in VR environments. Therefore,

Fig. 1. A sample of a VR space where search result windows can be freely positioned. A browser window can be placed anywhere in the room, at any angle, and scaled down to any size.

this study is positioned in terms of an introduction to related research on Web browsing support in VR and the retention of accessed information in memory.

2.1 Web Browsing Support in VR

Web browsing support exists as a measure to counteract the difficulties presented when searching in a VR space. Among these difficulties, most studies have looked at methods of reducing the effort required to input text in VR. Speicher *et al.* [11] performed a comparative survey on six input methods. The results of the investigation revealed that the input performance of the method of crucial selection by pointing using VR controller ray casting is the optimal method.

Boletsis *et al.* [1] proposed a method in which text could be input by using a controller as a drumstick and mapping the motion of a drum beating to the key input. In this study, we aim to assist in accessing information in the VR space at a different level from the comfort of text input and browsing. These are interface improvements within the VR space so they can be used together without modification.

2.2 Retention of Information in Memory

Many studies have looked at methods of retaining information in memory. In studies by Bui *et al.*, [3] and Einstein *et al.* [5], it was noted that powers of memory are improved by notetaking. Gordon *et al.* [2] elucidated the possibility of strengthening memory related to one's own concepts or episodes.

Sequential Alignment

The browser windows opened by the user are automatically aligned. They have only an order, not a position, which is the same as a conventional list-type bookmark.

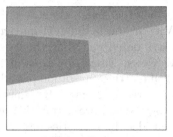

White Room

The user can place their browser windows in a plain white room, but they can not know the direction.

4-colored Wall Room

Users are free to put their browser windows in the room as they wish. The walls are painted in different colors for east, west, north, and south, so they can understand the direction in which they have put their window.

Realistic Room

Users are free to put their browser window in the room where their furniture is placed. Furniture is concrete and easy to call by name.

Fig. 2. Four different interior rooms. Each has a different level of abstraction. Users can put their search results windows in these rooms and organize them.

There have also been studies linking VR space and memory. Krokos *et al.* [10] asked participants to perform memory-related tasks in a visually immersive VR space, and verified that memory methods based on the Method of Loci could be effective in the VR space. Through this experiment, it was noted that both vestibular perception and cerebral reception help to retain things in memory. In this study, the Method of Loci is applied more specifically in the VR space to research on a Web page to determine what kind of space is adequate.

On the other hand, Hine *et al.* [8] noted that in experiments using memory with VR, this has a different impact on memory than in reality. In other words, a gap was noted regarding the ease of retaining memory, based on active and passive views. Elsewhere, Unsworth *et al.* [13] studied the influence of visual fidelity and active navigation provided in a virtual environment. This study also targets retrieval during VR games and works as a future application of this technology. When promoting this research in the future, it will be necessary to fully consider the memories and impressions that are unique to the VR space.

In a study strongly related to ours, Yang *et al.* examine the effectiveness of memory palace methods in general tasks that can be placed within a VR space [14]. Unlike their study, our research is a more localized, Web search-focused analysis. For this reason, we compared four different rooms rather than a large-scale comparison of effects.

3   "Spacial Bookmark" Approach

This section describes the method proposed in this study. In this study, we propose a method of memory retention based on the Method of Loci. Memory retention is achieved by placing things to remember in space, and based on the Method of Loci, the browser can be placed in the space freely reproduced in VR and saved like a bookmark. We named it the "Spacial Bookmark" approach.

The search results can then be organized on the place in a VR space. At this time, if the space in which the browser is placed in a white space without walls or ceilings, it will be unclear where it has been placed, given that it will not be possible to ascertain the eastern, western, northern, and southern directions. Therefore, the browser was placed in a room with four colored walls. However, even with color within the space, it was very abstract and difficult to ascertain the location. Therefore, the hypothesis was postulated that placing furniture and the like within the space would create a location that could more easily be expressed in words. To verify this hypothesis, we created three spaces based on the proposed method and one space that reproduced the conventional bookmarks within the VR space. Furthermore, when performing searches using these spaces, we added a memory function to enable an analysis of the search behavior of the users.

3.1   Overview of the Spatial Bookmark

In this study, we could organize the space by placing a screenshot of a Web page within the space. Whereas bookmarks on a typical computer are represented as a list or a tree divided into folders, bookmarks here are stored as coordinates within the space. The advantage of handling these kinds of bookmarks spatially in this way is that, based on the Method of Loci, it would be easier for the search results to be retained in memory, and it would be possible to reduce the effort required for repeat searches.

The Method of Loci is the method of memorization passed down since Ancient Roman times, and made famous by being summarized in the book "The Art of Memory" in 1966 by Yates [15]. This method is also commonly referred to as the memory palace method, the memory palace, or the journey method. In this method, when memorizing items, a person imagine an arbitrary place, and link the item they want to remember by placing the item in that place. At this time, the place they imagine can be an actual place like their home, an imaginary place, or even one of their body parts. It is thought that, as their memorize a place and the item to remember as a pair in this way, there are more cues when recalling, and this makes it easier to recall things.

3.2   Creating Browser Placable in Space

We generated multiple browser windows within the space, and created an environment in which they could be placed freely. The user is able to move freely within the environment and use the VR tracking device to generate a single tabbed browser window at any location. The generated browser can then be left at that location. In this way, it would appear as though the screenshot of the website seen at that location is placed there as is, and after touching the browser again, it would be possible to browse using that browser again.

The browser itself would have the same capabilities as conventional browsers, but there would be certain restrictions for using multiple browsers within the VR space. First, the "Back" button is allocated to one button on the controller, and all other navigation functions (*i.e.*, Forward, Update, etc.) are excluded. The concept is such that the user should access pages with individual information from the search results page when actually searching, return to the search result page if there is no information to be retained, and if there is information to be retained, place the entire window in the VR space and start a new window. The Close button is excluded for the same reason. This is because we want the user to overwrite and reuse windows other than those left as bookmarks within the VR space. Further, as, on this occasion, the information search is being carried out as the main task, we have yet to make it impossible to enter URLs directly. Finally, when a link is clicked, a new tab is opened, so the function to open a new window has been excluded. In this experiment, all browsers operate on a single tab. This is because multiple windows are placed within the VR space instead of opening multiple tabs within a single window.

When operating the browser on an actual VR device, the user wears VR goggles by changing the direction of his/her face up, down, left, or right, and is able to walk around within the space to the extent allowed by the cable. The browser operations are mainly operated with VR controls performed with both hands. In addition to its position detection ability, in terms of the direction the controller is facing, the controller has three physical buttons enabled on the controller: a trigger that can be pulled with the index finger, a side button that detects the user's grip, and a touchpad button that can be operated using the thumb. When the trigger is pressed, this has the role of the left click within the browser. This is also used when generating a new window or making active a window that has already been generated. If the user presses the side button, the user can grasp the browser window. The user can move the window in the grasped state, and by releasing this grasp, place the window in the location of their choice. As the controller is held in both hands at this time, they can grasp the window with both hands, and stretch and shrink it, in order to expand or contract the size of the window. By using this function, they can enlarge the window state when searching within the browser window and reduce it to a small state when simply placed within the space. The touchpad in a thumb-press position was used as a physical button for detecting presses, rather than as a touchpad. If they press the touchpad while operating the browser, they can move one step back in the browser history.

3.3   Creating a VR Space to Spatial Bookmarks

Several spaces have been prepared to actually allocate windows for browsers where it is possible to place windows as bookmarks within the created space. The aim of this study is to determine the space that can best facilitate the memorization of retrieved content based on the Method of Loci. In the original book on the Method of Loci by Yates, the space in which the object to be remembered is placed can be anywhere, such as a museum or a palace. However, within the VR space, as there are restrictions on physical movements as well as mechanical restrictions, it is possible that the optimal space will change. For example, a space where the user walks along a long route and places a memory in each room would be difficult to reproduce with VR.

For this reason, in this study, we prepared the following three VR rooms in phases:

- Most abstract space where the user can not know the direction,
- Slightly less abstract space painted in four colors,
- Space in which the place of allocation is expressed specifically in words,

and were able to organize the searches and results within the respective spaces. We set the spaces to the same size to prevent any disparity between spaces.

Abstract Rooms. We created two VR rooms in which users are able to simply search and move the search browser within the VR space. These are the most primitive spaces for organizing information. In these spaces, the test participant generated windows and searched in spaces that were nothing in particular and were able to allocate the windows they liked to their favorite places within the space.

The first abstract space is completely indistinguishable from front to back and left to right and is surrounded on all sides by pure white walls. The image of the actual space is shown in the upper right of Fig. 2. It is possible to search within this space, and place the search browser in the desired location, but as the user does not know in which direction they are facing, the mutual placement of browsers is all relative. For this reason, even if they can remember something by saying "placed to the left on the previous page," they cannot say "placed in the western direction."

The second space is a room like the first space, but with the concept of direction added. An image of the actual room is shown in the bottom left of Fig. 2. In this room, the four walls are color-coded in four colors; red, blue, yellow, and green. As a result, the browser is not simply relative, and also has meaning as an absolute position. In this space, the user can organize related pages together by considering the direction, such as "Let us place pages related to this topic in the direction of the red wall and pages related to different topics in the direction of the blue wall," which allows users to organize the information based on direction.

Specific Room. In addition to the two abstract spaces, a specific space based on the motif of an actual room was prepared. An image of the actual space is shown in the bottom right of Fig. 2. In this space, we can see a simple arrangement of furniture, with a bookshelf, bed, desk, and chair. In this space, the coordinates, in addition to having a relative position, have an absolute position as the azimuth, and also have fine-grained absolute positions, such as "placed near this furniture."

The types of furniture placed in this space are limited to furniture where the name easily comes to mind for whoever is looking at it. Other objects with more difficult-to-recall names were not placed in said space. This is because the name of the furniture is thought to become a hint for people to more easily recall where they placed things later.

In this space, it is possible to organize information in terms of where things were placed, by linking to objects, in the form of "This perspective on this topic is placed on the top-left of the TV" or "a perspective on a separate topic is placed on the bed."

Space only Has Order. The bookmarks in conventional browsers only have order and a hierarchical structure, and do not possess spatial coordinates. For the purpose of comparative experiments, we created a space that reproduced bookmarks with only order in the VR space. An image of the actual space is shown in the top left of Fig. 2.

In this space, by pressing the Favorites button in a place where the user wants to leave a bookmark, a new window opens next to the user. The user is able to continue searching by using this window. In this space, the user is not able to freely move the browser. For this reason, it can only remember in terms of order within a series, in that a certain page is "bookmarked before that page" or "was bookmarked first."

3.4   Collecting Behavior Logs for Analysis

Operational logs remain for each search browser in the space. The time, movement coordinates, and investigated URLs are recorded in the log. Elements recorded as time include the time that the Web browser was generated and the time it was in the active state. When a browser is moved for the purpose of the organization, it records from where it was moved from and to and when. Finally, the URL actually accessed is recorded as the behavior within the browser.

Additionally, the screen actually seen by the user in the VR space can be captured as video. By combining these three logs and screen captures, the user can learn the browser's behavior within the space, such as what kind of web pages are opened and how they move.

4   Evaluation Experiment

We implemented the proposed method and evaluated each space through subject experiments to confirm in which space the search contents are most easily remembered.

4.1   Implementation

We implemented the system using Unity to enable the browser to be placed within the proposed VR space. The implementation used OpenVR and SteamVR. In this experiment, we used HTC Vive and HTC Vive Cosmos, respectively, for the experimental head mount displays. When implemented, room-scale tracking was enabled, and this allowed the user to use the controller to actually physically walk and place the browser within the room without moving. For the browser implementation, we used an *Embedded Browser*, generally sold as a Unity asset. With the Embedded Browser, the Chromium browser for Desktop use can be used within the VR space. For the experiment, we restricted some functions; the user cannot open multiple tabs in a single window, and cannot open menus.

The four spaces, including comparative methods, were reproduced in the respective VR spaces, and the following were implemented:

- **White** Room is a space where the user can not know what direction they are facing,
- **4-colored** wall room is a space separated into Four colors
- **Realistic** room with furniture is a space in which the location can be easily expressed in words, and
- **Sequential** alignment is a space in which the browser is automatically placed in the horizontal direction.

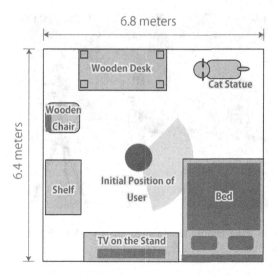

Fig. 3. Layout view of the Realistic room. Objects that are easy to describe in words are arranged around the user's initial position.

The first **White** room is a space that is six meters long and two meters high. It is square and surrounded by white walls, so the user cannot know what direction they are facing. The **4 wall color** space was also 6 m long and 2 m high, in the same way. The structure of the space itself is the same as in **White**, but the walls surrounding the four sides are painted red, blue, yellow, and green, respectively. The space with furniture has a variety of furniture placed within a room that is six meters long. As shown in Fig. 3, objects such as a TV, bed, shelf, desk, and cat are placed inside the room.

The experiment with the participant was carried out in a specialist lab with a dedicated 6.4×8.6 m VR experiment space. An image of the experiment is shown in Fig. 4. In terms of the setup for the actual experiment, HTC Vive tracking sensors were placed three meters apart, and participants were free to walk between them in order to search the Web and organize the results.

4.2 Experiment Settings and Procedure

We evaluated the extent to which information could be retained over the long term when linked to information when searching in the VR space. For this purpose, we requested that the six participants perform a search task in VR, collect logs, and then go back to them one week later to check the extent of their recall regarding the search content. The time required for the search task was two hours per person.

The search task imposed on the test participants was to collect and organize a wide range of information and, finally, provide a conclusion. The test participants finally performed decision-making based on the collected information and created

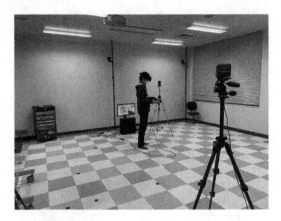

Fig. 4. Experiments were conducted in a room-scale VR environment of 6.8 × 6.4 m using HTC VIVE.

one ranking. Specifically, we first created a list of candidate Ferris wheels, such as "the most suitable Ferris wheel for a date in Japan," and then examined the location and facilities of each the candidate Ferris wheels, and finally sorted them in order of their suitability.

This kind of search task mimics typical search behavior in everyday life. For example, let us suppose we buy a new smartphone. At that time, we always choose which smartphone is best based on certain information we gather, such as image quality and performance. In this way, natural search behavior is gathering information when searching, examining, and selecting the information we want.

The actual experimental procedure is as follows: First, the test participant answers a questionnaire in advance regarding their method of performing searches and whether he/she has used VR. Next, the test participant operates the proposed system for 30 min in order to become familiar with the VR operations, and freely perform Web browsing. Then, after a 30-minute break, he/she performs search tasks in the four spaces over the course of one hour. After completing the search tasks, the test participants ranked their own search results based on what they searched for and selected the top three results. Then, one week later, they answered regarding what extent they remembered the top three rankings of the search results.

4.3   Experimental Task

In terms of a search task in which participants examine a large quantity of information, discard certain information, and make decisions, a search task is set in which they choose their top three, respectively from

- **Ferris wheel**: Finding the best Ferris wheel considered to be appropriate for dating in Japan, and

Table 1. Combination of a given experimental task and a VR room for each participant. Considering order effects, each participant experiences the realistic room and one other room.

Participant ID	Fisrt Task	Second Task	First Room	Second Room
1	Ferrs Wheel	Migration	Realistic	4-colored
2	Ferrs Wheel	Migration	Realistic	White
3	Ferrs Wheel	Migration	Realistic	Sequential
4	Ferrs Wheel	Migration	4-colored	Realistic
5	Ferrs Wheel	Migration	White	Realistic
6	Ferrs Wheel	Migration	Sequential	Realistic
7	Migration	Ferrs Wheel	Realistic	4-colored
8	Migration	Ferrs Wheel	Realistic	White
9	Migration	Ferrs Wheel	Realistic	Sequential
10	Migration	Ferrs Wheel	4-colored	Realistic
11	Migration	Ferrs Wheel	White	Realistic
12	Migration	Ferrs Wheel	Sequential	Realistic

- **Migration prefecture**: Finding a prefecture in Kyushu (an area in Japan) suitable for working and raising children if you move there when you are 30 years old.

It is not possible to create a ranking for these two tasks unless multiple searches are performed. In the Ferris wheel task, participants were given an abstract search goal of finding the "most appropriate one for a date" and were required to go to multiple Ferris wheel-related Web sites in turn to find information on what they themselves considered appropriate for a date. In the migration point task, based on the search goal of finding a place "appropriate for working and raising children," as part of this task, participants were asked to examine the suitability of each of the Kyushu prefectures from various perspectives in terms of working and raising children. By comparing and examining information, they finally create a ranking of the top three. The test participants were prohibited from creating rankings by browsing only summary or ranking sites. This was to ensure that they made their own decisions.

4.4   Experimental Participants

A combination of the four spaces was created, taking the order effect into consideration. Given that the superiority or inferiority of each method could not be discussed without a minimum of twelve participants, we were only able to verify the combinations represented in Table 1. When performing these tasks, an equal number of test participants performed the proposed method first as the number performing it later. Additionally, as there were two types of tasks and four types of spaces, the 12 participants performed the tasks in an interchangeable order, that is to say, before and after the space and before and after the task.

4.5   Questionnaire on the Day and One Week Later

participants were asked to respond to the top three rankings in the search task they performed for that day's evaluation. In the evaluation, after one week had passed, the test participants responded in regard to how much they recalled.

In addition to the ranking items, they answered in regard to whether they could remember what information was placed where. They were also requested to respond with how they were able to recall the information. In this way, it is possible to judge the recall and reaffirmation. To confirm recall, they were asked whether they recalled the rankings themselves. To confirm reaffirmation, they were asked whether they remembered what was placed where.

4.6   Results of the Experiment

In this experiment, to measure to what extent it was entrenched in memory, it was judged whether the rankings in the search task on the day in question and one week later matched. In the experiment conducted on this occasion, the degree of memory retention of the participants could not be assessed by ranking the retrieval tasks, and there were differences in the quality of how much information they could recall. In regard to the i-th ranking element created in task t by test participant u, the matching $co(u, t, i)$ between the answer a_{morrow} immediately after the task and the answer one week later of a_{later} is defined as

$$\begin{cases} 1: & a_{\mathrm{morrow}} = a_{later}, \\ 0: & \text{otherwise.} \end{cases} \tag{1}$$

At this time, the extent to which the search results of task t are entrenched in the memory of test participant u is expressed as the mean matching level:

$$f_{task}(t, u) = \sum_{i=1}^{\mathrm{ranknum}} \frac{co(u, t, i)}{\mathrm{ranknum}}. \tag{2}$$

Here, this is set as ranknum = 3. If this value is summarized for each space and the set of tasks carried out in this space r is expressed as $T(r)$, this becomes:

$$\sum_{t \in T(r)} \frac{f_{task}(t, u_t)}{|T(r)|}. \tag{3}$$

At this time, the executor of the tasks carried out in this room is expressed as u_t.

As shown in Table 2, a space with **Realistic** room is able to support memory retention better than a **White** space, but not as good as a room with **4-colored** walls.

The number of people who remembered the place in which the information was placed and the number of people who remember the information itself for each space is shown in Table 3. The space in which the highest percentage

Table 2. Memory retention rate after one week for each VR room. Because participants examined several candidates and answered the top three, it shows the correct answer rate for each of their top three answers.

Room Type	1st	2nd	3rd	Average
Realistic	0.91	0.83	0.91	0.89
4-colored	1.00	1.00	0.75	0.91
White	0.50	0.50	0.75	0.58
Sequential	0.75	0.75	0.75	0.75

Table 3. Details of what participants remembered after one week from the survey evaluation

Room Type	Location where they put browser		What they searched for	
	Remembered	Forgotten	Remembered	Forgatten
Realistic	11	1	11	1
4-colored	2	2	2	2
White	2	2	1	3
Sequential	–	–	1	3

of participants who remembered all the information was found was the space **Realistic** room with furniture, Furthermore, the **Realistic** room also had the highest percentage of people who remembered what kind of information was investigated.

5 Discussion

In this section, we focus on the four stages based on the experiment results, of support for the retention of information in each space, VR familiarity, sequential effects, and memory, and discuss whether the proposed method supports memory retention. In general, there was a high degree of memorization of search results one week later for all rooms. In regard to the memory task in the **Realistic** room, although there was no particular trend toward higher memory retention when taking the average of all test participants, there were differences in how much detail of the retrieved results could be remembered.

First, we shall discuss the results of each method. In addition to having the second highest retention rate among all spaces, the space with **Realistic** room had the highest percentage of participants who remembered the location in which the information had been placed. When comparing **Realistic** room against the existing method, the test participants moved more during the search. It is considered possible, therefore, that the physical movement of the participant's body, as well as the difference in the space, may have impacted memory retention.

The following should be noted: Some test participants who experimented with this combination used a unique memorization method of linking the information and words together. Specifically, in the **Realistic** room, they used word association to memorize the information and the furniture placement locations. This is kind of a pun; such as "Kagoshima (the name of a prefecture) is in a cage." When using this method of memorization, whereas all the information researched in the **Realistic** room was remembered, some of the information in the **Sequential** a space was forgotten. Having the user associate the VR space with things that can be easily expressed using words is thought to enable effective memory retention when the user associates the VR space with existing memory methods such as word association.

The room with **4-colored** wall had the highest memory retention among all the spaces, but when asked whether they could remember the place where the information was placed and what information was searched, half of the respondents answered that they could not. Compared to the **Realistic** room, many made mistakes when recalling the placement location. Specifically, the test participants remembered where they had placed the information on the Ferris wheel that was supposed to be in second place, and where they had placed the information on the Ferris wheel that was in third place, but in reverse order.

Compared to all other spaces, the level of memory retention was lowest in the **White** space. This may be because, compared to the **Realistic** room and the **4-colored** wall room, it was hard to summarize what had been placed and where. Specifically, one test participant placed a summary of all Ferris wheels to his/her own right in the **White** space, but answered that he/she had put the information for each Ferris wheel on his/her left side. They made a mistake with the placement of information on the left and right, and this content was not remembered in detail.

In the **Sequential** alignment space, in the majority of cases, the test participant did not remember the search results. This is thought to be because actions could not be summarized without moving the browser, as in the **Realistic** room. Specifically, if we focus on one test participant, in the migration point task, they researched locations in terms of the three items of ease of working, the convenience of transportation, and positive effect on child-rearing. However, one week later, they could not remember what kind of information they had researched. On the other hand, if we focus on memory retention, the level of memory retention is not as high as the **White** space. This may have been because the act of active summarization in the **White** space was more burdensome from a work perspective, they focused more on the operation, and the result of this was that it was easier to focus on the information in the less intensive **Sequential** alignment, making it easier to retain the information.

In terms of VR familiarity, all test participants responded that it was easier to perform the later task than the first task because they were familiar with the operation. Given the effect of VR familiarity, it is possible that the later results may be more easily retained in memory due to the effects of familiarity. The majority of test participants had a higher level of memory retention for the search task performed first than for the search task performed later. Some participants remembered information in more detail in the first search task than in the later search task. As one of the test participants did not remember the results of either task, if we consider that this participant should be excluded as an outlier, the later search task did not produce abnormally high results. Based on this, we can consider that the impact of VR familiarity is low.

It is also possible that the order effect may have impacted memory retention. As many of the test participants were experiencing VR for the first time, the search results for the first task carried out may have remained particularly strong in memory. In this experiment, the memory retention of the latter space of test participants who experienced the **Realistic** room first was relatively low. It is thought that the search task conducted first had a greater freshness, and this may have made a significant difference in the rankings. In addition, the test participants who performed the **Realistic** room task later had greater memory retention from the later search task than the earlier search task. For this reason, it is considered that, though the order effect has an impact on the results, even when considering the order effect, the **Realistic** room is thought to be able to support memory retention.

The aim of this study is to support memory retention. For this purpose, we confirmed recall and reaffirmation in four stages. Recall was confirmed based on whether the test participants could remember the ranking. However, in this experiment, there was no significant difference in memory accuracy among the test participants in any of the spaces. This is thought to possibly be due to the search task being simple on this occasion. As the top three items were the top three items in the simple search task, there was no significant difference. This was also more memorable due to the VR experience, which is something that is not usually experienced. For this reason, it was not possible to determine whether improved recall occurred with the present method in the **Realistic** room. For reaffirmation, on the other hand, differences appeared between the **Realistic** room and the other spaces in terms of remembering the places information was placed and what information was searched. The places information was placed were remembered more in the **Realistic** room than the other spaces, and the searched information was remembered in more detail. More reaffirmation is thought to have occurred in the **Realistic** room than in the other rooms.

Based on this, it may be suggested that, although there was no significant difference in the number of search results that could be recalled when considering the possibility of memory support based on the Method of Loci, it may have had an effect on the amount of content remembered.

6   Conclusion

This study proposed a *Method of Loci*-based method named "spatial bookmark" for facilitating the recall of search results. It allows placing the search browser that performs the search in the VR space by itself. Four rooms were created within the VR space: a realistic room that could be easily expressed in words, a space color-coded with four colors, a pure white space, and the Sequential space like traditional bookmarks. An experiment was conducted in which participants collected information from the Web and made a ranking. One week after the experiment, a survey was conducted regarding how much of the search content was remembered, using a questionnaire. Based on the experiment results, it was impossible to accurately measure the same day and next day evaluation of the rankings due to the simplicity of the search task. However, the quality of memory retention differed between the spaces. Information was recalled the most when searching in a room with **4-colored** walls. The content of the information researched in the **Realistic** room was remembered in detail, and the location of placement was also remembered accurately. Finally, our study showed the possibility of making users remember their searches by organizing the search results in a non-abstract room.

Acknowledgements. This work was supported by JSPS KAKENHI Grants Number 21H03775, 21H03774, and 22H03905. The research was also supported by ROIS NII Open Collaborative Research 2023 (Grant Number 22S1001).

References

1. Boletsis, C., Kongsvik, S.: Text input in virtual reality: a preliminary evaluation of the drum-like VR keyboard. MDPI Technol. **7**(2), 31 (2019)
2. Bower, G.H., Gilligan, S.G.: Remembering information related to one's self. J. Res. Pers. **13**(4), 420–432 (1979)
3. Bui, D.C., Myerson, J., Hale, S.: Note-taking with computers: exploring alternative strategies for improved recall. J. Educ. Psychol. **105**(2), 299 (2013)
4. Carter, L., Potter, L.E.: Spatial virtual keyboard for wand based virtual reality. In: Proceedings of the 5th Symposium on Spatial User Interaction, p. 161 (2017)
5. Einstein, G.O., Morris, J., Smith, S.: Note-taking, individual differences, and memory for lecture information. J. Educ. Psychol. **77**(5), 522 (1985)
6. Fashimpaur, J., Kin, K., Longest, M.: Pinchtype: text entry for virtual and augmented reality using comfortable thumb to fingertip pinches. In: Extended Abstracts of the 2020 CHI Conference on Human Factors in Computing Systems, pp. 1–7 (2020)
7. Hartley, T., Lever, C., Burgess, N., O'Keefe, J.: Space in the brain: how the hippocampal formation supports spatial cognition. Philos. Trans. R. Soc. B Biol. Sci. **369**(1635) (2014)
8. Hine, K., Tasaki, H.: Active view and passive view in virtual reality have different impacts on memory and impression. Front. Psychol. **10** (2019)
9. Hok, V., Save, E., Lenck-Santini, P.P., Poucet, B.: Coding for spatial goals in the prelimbic/infralimbic area of the rat frontal cortex. Proc. Natl. Acad. Sci. **102**(12), 4602–4607 (2005)
10. Krokos, E., Plaisant, C., Varshney, A.: Virtual memory palaces: immersion aids recall. Virtual Real. **23**(1), 1–15 (2019)
11. Speicher, M., Feit, A.M., Ziegler, P., Krüger, A.: Selection-based text entry in virtual reality. In: Proceedings of the 2018 CHI Conference on Human Factors in Computing Systems, pp. 1–13 (2018)
12. Teevan, J., Adar, E., Jones, R., Potts, M.A.: Information re-retrieval: repeat queries in yahoo's logs. In: Proceedings of the 30th Annual International ACM SIGIR Conference on Research and Development in Information Retrieval, pp. 151–158 (2007)

13. Unsworth, N., Engle, R.W.: The nature of individual differences in working memory capacity: active maintenance in primary memory and controlled search from secondary memory. Psychol. Rev. **114**(1), 104 (2007)
14. Yang, F., Qian, J., Novotny, J., Badre, D., Jackson, C.D., Laidlaw, D.H.: A virtual reality memory palace variant aids knowledge retrieval from scholarly articles. IEEE Trans. Vis. Comput. Graph. **27**(12), 4359–4373 (2021)
15. Yates, F.A.: The Art of Memory, vol. 64. Random House, New York (1992)

Understanding Human Cognition and Performance in IT Security

Cognitive Security: An Architecture Informed Approach from Cognitive Science

Gareth Doherty[✉]

Department of National Defence, Ottawa, ON K1K 4M7, Canada
GARETH.DOHERTY@forces.gc.ca

Abstract. The study of *cognitive warfare* is an emerging multi-disciplinary area of research that aims to understand the individual, social, and technological dimensions of malicious efforts to influence and otherwise degrade the cognitive capacities of military and non-military targets for competitive advantage. By extension, research on *cognitive security* aims to understand how defence and civilian organizations can defend against threats in the cognitive domain. This paper aims to contribute to ongoing discussions on the human factors dimensions of cognitive warfare by outlining an approach that looks at cognitive vulnerabilities as a function of information processing features of architectural accounts of cognitive processes. Dual process theories/models of cognition are used as a representative example of the general approach. I argue that dual process theories (a) can provide a valuable model for how we ought to conceptualize cognitive vulnerabilities as features of well understood cognitive processes and (b) that viewing cognitive vulnerabilities this way enables answers to key practical questions in the cognitive security domain.

Keywords: cognitive security · cognitive bias · dual-process models

1 Introduction

All warfare is based on deception. Hence, when able to attack, we must seem unable; when using our forces, we must seem inactive; when we are near, we must make the enemy believe we are far away; when far away, we must make him believe we are near. (Sun Tzu, The Art of War)

The idea that the manipulation of the minds of adversaries is a central feature of conflict is by no means novel and is likely as old as organized warfare itself. In that regard, cognitive warfare has always been a part of conflict in some manner. However, societal changes, and advances in technology, among countless other factors, has led to a hyper-connected world where communications and influence campaigns can operate at a scale and with sophistication never before imagined. Corresponding changes in military doctrine by adversaries that license below-threshold or hybrid conflict as a means to achieve national objectives, mean that social media and cyberspace more generally have been legitimized as targets for influence campaigns requiring new ways of thinking about defence and security issues related to human agents. The 'changing of hearts and

D. D. Schmorrow and C. M. Fidopiastis (Eds.): HCII 2023, LNAI 14019, pp. 395–415, 2023.
https://doi.org/10.1007/978-3-031-35017-7_25

minds' through coordinated disinformation campaigns that exploit cognitive, social, and technological factors is a growing threat to liberal democracies globally. Research on cognitive security looks to identify potential weaknesses in the cognitive domain both for defensive as well as offensive purposes. In this context, the exploitation of cognitive biases is an often-cited source of concern for researchers and practitioners in cognitive security. This paper aims to contribute to ongoing discussions of the threat posed by cognitive biases for cognitive security, arguing for the benefits of a 'cognitive architecture' informed approach to practical questions related to mitigating cognitive vulnerabilities.

2 Cognitive Biases as Cognitive Security Vulnerabilities

Cognitive warfare can be understood in general terms as a broad domain of activities that aim to exploit facets of human cognition for the purpose of changing the way people think and act in a manner that aligns with an adversary's objectives. This includes efforts to manipulate individuals or groups that include military and non-military actors up to and including large segments of a civil society. *Cognitive security,* by extension, can be understood as efforts aimed at strengthening the defence of individuals – military or otherwise – and social groups against threats and/or vulnerabilities to cognitive warfare tactics and strategies of adversaries.

As nations begin to invest research and development activities to enhance cognitive security, understanding critical cognitive vulnerabilities and, derivatively, exploring the means to reduce exposure to those vulnerabilities, is a central task facing researchers and strategists alike. The oft-cited extant research on cognitive biases and bias mitigation represents an important area of inquiry with the potential to inform questions aimed at identifying individual level vulnerabilities and assessing the prospects of building capabilities to enhance *cognitive fitness* and *cognitive resilience*. The current thesis is that understanding cognitive biases as information processing vulnerabilities that are simply natural consequences of processing features our cognitive architecture, provides us with a useful framework to inform discussions in the cognitive security domain.

As a general phenomenon, the exploitation of cognitive biases as a means to influence judgment, decision-making, and behaviour is a pervasive practice. Socially sanctioned applications are spreading in organizations across public and private sectors alike, with the formation of behavioural science units whose primary purpose is to design programs that 'nudge' people towards behavioural outcomes that support the organization's goals, such as public policy changes in the case of government. A classic example in this vein is the use of 'choice architecture' to frame decisions regarding organ donation (Thaler and Sunstein 2008). Countries that implement 'opt out' organ donation policies enjoy much higher participation rates in those programs than countries with 'opt in' policies. This is explained by default processing features of cognition aimed at the minimization of cognitive effort ('cognitive miserliness'), which dictate that most people will take the path of least resistance, thereby favouring policies that benefit from people's inertia. The legitimacy of nudge-based programs rests on the concept of 'libertarian paternalism', which allows for the free choice of individuals (the 'libertarian' part) but structures choices in a way that leads to desired outcomes ('paternalism'). Further examples abound in industry, where marketing and advertising firms invest millions annually to better understand and exploit human psychology with the goal of shaping beliefs about and attitudes towards the products and services their firms represent. These are widely accepted practices that constitute 'fair game' in the market, presenting a challenging nuance for governments concerned with cognitive security in relation to adversaries: How and where do we draw the moral boundaries in influence campaigns for friend and foe alike?

Though there is much to be learned from socially sanctioned uses of cognitive factors, for the remainder of this paper we will restrict our focus on examples more directly related to cognitive warfare. In these cases, facets of human cognition, specifically cognitive biases as they are understood in the psychological literature, represent potential vulnerabilities in the context of activities such as social engineering, including online influence campaigns, where human cognition is manipulated for nefarious goals. As an illustrative example, consider the rather banal role of *confirmation bias* in political polarization online through social media. *Confirmation bias* is the cognitive disposition to seek out, favour, and recall information that is partial to an individual's pre-existing beliefs and values, regardless of the information's veracity (Nickerson 1998). Already, platform algorithms (e.g., those of Twitter, Facebook, Instagram, TikTok) are designed, for marketing and advertising purposes, principally to push content towards users that will increase time spent on the platform by presenting content the algorithm determines users will 'like', thereby ensuring recipients receive a steady stream of content that is already aligned with the person's antecedent interests. In combination with confirmation bias, whereby users self-select information that confirms their existing beliefs, there is thus a reinforcing effect further entrenching existing beliefs and attitudes contributing to polarization across a wide array of social and political affinities on these platforms.

Numerous other examples are readily available that make clear that cognitive biases can be exploited for both good and nefarious ends, such as the use of *anchoring effects* in negotiations, the role of the *Dunning-Kruger effect* (Kruger and Dunning 1999) in online overconfidence of people's own perceived expertise on subjects when they are an actual novice (e.g. sharing of vaccine disinformation), or the leveraging of the *availability heuristic* (Tversky and Kahneman 1973) by deploying swarms of bots sharing disinformation on a critical topic to create the impression of a widely held and therefore socially sanctioned belief on a topic, especially where none exists, with the explicit goal of swaying public opinion towards a minority opinion. For the purposes of the present paper, I will take for granted that cognitive biases can and are being used both individually and in combination for tactical and strategic purposes that don't always align with the interests of the individuals/groups that are the target of these activities. Research on categorizing the types of cognitive attacks that are currently in use and analyses of the mechanisms by which they work, will be an important point of intersection with the approach offered here.

It should also be noted that cognitive biases represent only a subgroup of cognitive effects that adversaries might leverage to advance their aims. For example, 'change blindness' in visual processing is a lower-level perceptual cognitive blind spot that results in the failure to detect a change in a visual stimulus (Levin and Simons 1997). This is different from yet another form of blindness, 'inattentional blindness' which affects attention processing when a subject is given a distracting task the prevents them from noticing stimuli in their visual field. A more holistic view of cognitive vulnerabilities across all domains of cognitive processing (i.e., perception, attention, memory, retrieval/recall, and thinking, emotions etc.) would be an important extension of the approach taken here, whereby a taxonomy of cognitive processes and sub-processes could be used to systematically review biases and related cognitive effects for their potential for exploitation. Such a taxonomy could then be used to inform mitigation strategies.

3 Towards an Architectural Approach to Cognitive Security

A core feature of the approach in this paper is that the examination of cognitive biases as cognitive security vulnerabilities can benefit from 'architectural approaches' to the study of human cognition. The advantage of this approach is that it can be used as an organizing framework for research in the sense of enabling a taxonomy of cognitive vulnerabilities. Secondly, by tying cognitive vulnerabilities to processes/mechanisms underlying cognition we can, in some cases, better understand how and why these biases emerge in the first place, due to the causal nature of cognitive process models. Finally, an understanding of the mechanisms at play can support research on the identification and design of interventions for mitigating unwanted effects of cognitive biases.

Standard approaches to cognitive psychology, and the interdisciplinary field of cognitive science more generally, look at human cognition from an *information processing perspective*: inputs into cognitive processes are fundamentally informational in nature and the processes that operate over that information can be described functionally, as information processing mechanisms (Pylyshyn 1986). A common way of capturing the processing domains and sub-domains in cognitive psychology frames cognitive processes as stages of processing of inputs/stimuli from the environment. These models differ in terms of the complexity/fidelity of cognitive processes they represent (e.g., 4 box vs 7 box diagrams etc.) but ultimately share the goal of communicating the primary cognitive processes underlying human thinking and how they work together. A highly simplified model is shared below in Fig. 1.

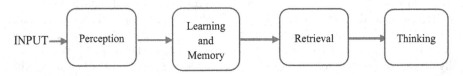

Fig. 1. Stages of Cognitive Processing (Taken from Groome et al. 2014)

This diagram depicts cognition as consisting of four primary processing domains, whereby inputs (distal stimuli) from the environment are processed by perceptual mechanisms (proximal stimuli), the outputs of which form the basis of learning and are stored in various layers of memory (e.g., short term memory, long term memory, working memory etc.) to be retrieved and used by downstream processes central to thinking. More complex models exist that add to this basic taxonomy of processes with other processing domains, including attention, language, emotional processing, motor control (action), social cognition, and executive function/metacognition. Within some of these stages, even further subdivision of component domains has been performed, such as for the various perceptual modalities in perception. For example, David Marr's (1982) model of visual processing – one of the seminal accounts of an information-based approach to visual perception – offered both a novel computational approach and detailed theory of the stages of visual processing.

For research on cognitive security, there are a number of advantages of process models of cognition. Since the causal relationships between processing stages are well enough understood, it is possible to model and explain downstream effects to enable a causal view of interventions focused on any preceding processing stage. Further, processing models are naturally aligned with frameworks that that look at the command-and-control dimensions in military decision making, such as Boyd's OODA loop. As Fig. 2 shows below, this highly simplified version of Boyd's OODA Loop consists of four main processing stages that can be mapped to the stages of cognitive processing.

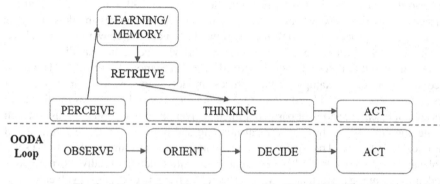

Fig. 2. Mapping Cognitive Processes to Simplified OODA Loop

This mapping follows from the fact that Boyd's OODA loop is fundamentally a description of information processing activities, though not necessarily *cognitive* activities, depending on whether we are representing a system view (e.g., Command and Control process for targeting) or an individual decision maker's view. By linking human cognitive processes with more formal representations of decision/action feedback loops, we can much more accurately represent how a targeted effect on a cognitive process might interfere with our own or adversaries' OODA loop cycles.

4   Dual-Process Models of Cognition as a Framework for Cognitive Security

Dual process models of cognition represent a sub-domain of research on thinking (the last box in our simplified process model above). These theories/models emerged from the 'heuristics and biases' research program that began to emerge in the 1970s and 1980s in the work of Daniel Kahneman, Paul Slovic and Amos Tversky among others (see, e.g., Kahneman, Slovic, and Tversky 1982). Some of the earliest work in this area, Daniel Kahneman's *prospect theory*, showed that human cognizers did not handle financial losses and gains (*loss aversion*) according to central assumptions in economic theory, namely, that humans are maximizers of expected utility in their economic decision making (Kahneman and Tversky 1979). The general pattern of research on human rationality has since followed this model, identifying numerous ways in which human reasoning is sub-optimal relative to some normative model of reasoning, judgment, or decision-making. For example, studies have shown that people violate the axioms of probability theory in their reasoning, fail to test hypotheses, display confirmation bias in their judgments, and show overconfidence in situations that do not warrant it. It is this body of literature that is the source of research on cognitive biases more generally (for a representative summary, see Piattelli-Palmarini 1994).

Dual process models of higher order reasoning emerged in response to research on cognitive biases with the goal of helping to understand how and why deviations from normative models of reasoning occur. However parallel insights were developed in a variety of other disparate research domains beyond applications in the psychology of higher-order reasoning, including learning theory (Reber 1993) and social cognition (Epstein 1994). In this paper, the focus is exclusively on dual process models of higher order cognitive processes, though it is worthwhile to note the convergence in related disciplines towards the same mechanisms is further evidence of their validity.

A generic dual process theory developed by Keith Stanovich (1999, 2004) will be used as our principal example of dual process models below, as it is paradigmatic of this class, offers a consolidated view of the main processes and properties implicated in this area of research, and is of particular interest given its intersection with his research on the cognitive foundations of critical thinking and his work on the theoretical and empirical foundations of rationality. Further, Stanovich's generic theory also offers useful explanatory resources through an account of cognitive deficits relative to normative models of reasoning performance, which is useful for framing of cognitive vulnerabilities related to cognitive security discussions. It also provides an account of some types of interventions that support cognitive security through improved reasoning. Finally, Stanovich's work has led to an assessment tool, the Comprehensive Assessment of Rationality (CART), that identifies thinking dispositions that are predictive of normative performance in relation to cognitive biases.

Dual process models of cognition share the core idea that there are two main types of thinking: (i) *Type 1* processes, that are automatic, unconscious, fast, heuristic, and associative and (ii) *Type 2* processes, that are deliberate, conscious, slow, and analytical. These two categories of thinking have also been referred to as System 1 and System 2 (e.g., Kahneman 2011; Stanovich 1999, 2004) as well as 'intuitive thinking' and 'reflective thinking', respectively.[1] Type 1 (or System 1) is widely understood to operate on the basis of the principles of associative processing and, as such, are attuned to statistical properties of stimuli in the environment, including *similarity* (e.g., shared features between objects – what 'dogs' have in common) and *temporal structure* (e.g., temporal correlation of objects – such as thunder and lightning). According to Sloman (1996), "associative systems are able to divide perceptions into reasonable clusters on the basis of statistical (or at least quasi-statistical) regularities" (Sloman 1996, p. 4). They are also "largely unconscious, and relatively undemanding of computational capacity…[conjoining] properties of automaticity and heuristic processing as these constructs have been variously discussed in the literature (Stanovich 1999, p. 144).

Central to the present discussion is the idea that Type 1 processes are our primary, or 'default,' mode of reasoning due to their role in enabling us to respond quickly and effectively to changes in our environment, without requiring our attention. As a result, the majority of the tasks that occupy our mental lives are handled by Type 1 processes.[2] Lastly, *task construal* (how information processing tasks are framed), is highly contextual for Type 1 processes, which is to say that they automatically retrieve information stored in memory to contextualize (make sense of) stimuli for further action using information from previous exposure/experience that operate heuristically (Stanovich 2004, p. 36). In response to criticisms that Type 1 processes are not an ontologically distinct "system", but rather a system of systems, Stanovich refers to these processes elsewhere as the Autonomous Set of Systems (or TASS) (Stanovich 2004). This set of processes includes dedicated modular processes, reflexes, and learned processes that have become automatic through overlearning. It is also an evolutionarily older system that operates well when activated in benign (or friendly) environments, namely those (natural environments) that shaped its development. In contrast, the limits of Type 1 processes are evident when they are deployed in more hostile environments, such as those presented by modern life.

A benign environment means one that contains useful (that is, diagnostic) cues that can be exploited by various heuristics (for example, affect-triggering cues, vivid and salient stimulus components, convenient and accurate anchors). Additionally, for an environment to be classified as benign, it must also contain no other individuals who will adjust their behavior to exploit those relying only on Type 1 processing. In contrast, a hostile environment for heuristics is one in which there are few cues that are usable by autonomous processes or there are misleading cues (Kahneman and Klein 2009).

---

[1] For a variety of reasons explained by Evans and Stanovich (2013), they have reverted to the Type1/Type2 distinction to avoid mislaid criticisms implied by the terms "System 1/System 2", namely that the terms suggest two ontologically distinct systems rather than collections of processes with shared processing attributes (i.e., Types). Nothing of importance hangs on this for the following discussion. For ease of exposition, I will use System1/System2 and Type 1/Type 2 interchangeably, while noting my endorsement of Evans and Stanovich's reversion to the Type-Type 2 distinction for additional clarity.

[2] In more recent publications, Stanovich (2004) argues that System 1 is not in reality a single system but refers to a rather large set of systems, which he now refers to as TASS (The Autonomous Set of Systems). Accordingly, System 1 ought to be considered a system of systems which contains modular mechanisms, heuristic processes, and learned processes that have become automatic (Stanovich 2004, p. 36). However, nothing of importance hangs on this refinement and, for the ease of exposition, the terms System 1 and System 2 will be preserved.

Another way that an environment can turn hostile for a user of Type 1 processing occurs when other agents discern the simple cues that are being used and arrange them for their own advantage (for example, advertisements, or the strategic design of supermarket floor space in order to maximize revenue) (Stanovich et al. 2020, p. 1112).

The contextualizing tendency of System 1 is one of the primary reasons overzealous System 1 processing leads to the emergence of cognitive biases, thereby limiting its range of validity/applicability. This phenomenon has been referred to by Stanovich (2003) as the "fundamental computational bias." The *fundamental computational bias* (FCB) is "the tendency to automatically bring prior knowledge to bear when solving problems" (Stanovich 2003, p. 4. At its core, the FCB emerges from the tendency of Type 1 processes to process task information in interactional or social terms. Although the social cognitive dimensions of Type 1 cognition also have interesting consequences for how we look at human cognition in the cognitive security domain, it will not be discussed further in this paper.[3] One of the component biases, *belief bias*, provides a powerful demonstration of this processing feature. *Belief bias* is the propensity to contextualize problems using one's pre-existing beliefs to understand (contextualize) and ultimately solve a problem. Consider the following example (Stanovich 2003, p. 2):

P1. All living things need water
P2. Roses need water.
C. Therefore, roses are living things.

Is this a logically valid argument? By definition, a logically valid argument is one where, if the premises are true, the conclusion cannot be false. Validity refers to the logical structure of the argument, specifically the logical relationship between the premises and the conclusion. Most subjects will judge this to be a valid argument. The reason is that people know antecedently that roses are living things. That belief obscures the fact that you cannot conclude, or logically derive, this from the premises as stated. Although its true that all living things need water, this is different from the claim that all things that need water are living – which is what you need to draw the conclusion that 'roses are living things', from the premise that 'they need water.' The faulty reasoning in the argument can be made clear by substituting the terms in the same logical structure as follows, where we don't have a believable conclusion (Ibid.)

P1: All insects need oxygen
P2: Mice need oxygen
C: Therefore, Mice are insects.

---

[3] For further a deeper discussion on the social dimensions of dual process models of cognition, see Doherty (2012) or Stanovich (2003).

It should be clear in this case how the believability (belief bias) of the rose syllogism distorts our thinking in this case. Belief bias is simply one of the many cognitive biases that issue from default processing features of System 1.

Type 2 processes by comparison deploy serial processing, governed by formal rules, are computationally expensive (effortful), and involves conscious deliberate attention. As Stanovich (1999) describes it, System 2 (Type 2 processes) brings together the various characteristics that have been viewed as typifying controlled processing. System 2 encompasses the processes of *analytic intelligence* that have traditionally been studied by information processing theorists trying to uncover the computational components of intelligence (Stanovich 1999, p. 144).

The core features of System 2, understood as an analytic processor, follow from the view that it uses rules to operate over abstract symbolic representations of problems and is often language based. The symbolic nature of System 2 processing also underlies explanations of how it can perform as an override function of System 1 processes. As such, task construal for System 2 is also typically decontextualized (abstract), depersonalized, and asocial. A more comprehensive summary of the features of both systems is captured below in Table 1. A principal function of Type 2/System 2 processes is to provide an override function to Type 1 generated outputs that are inappropriate overgeneralizations deployed in task domains that require System 2 processes instead. This overgeneralization is main explanation for how Type 1 and Type 2 processes come into the various kinds of conflict exhibited in the heuristics and biases literature – where Type 1 processes endeavour to solve tasks demanding Type 2 solutions. Finally, System 2 processes are also responsible for inhibiting the impulses (e.g., emotional regulation) of System 1. This role is consistent with research regarding the role of executive function in inhibitory control of System 1 impulses.

It is also worth mentioning that Type 2 processes are not without their own challenges. One of the gifts of Type 2 processes – their ability to narrowly and intensely focus on certain features of stimuli for analytic processing – can itself lead to unwanted effects. One of the most radical demonstrations comes from research on *inattentional blindness*. Simons and Charbris in their book *The Invisible Gorilla* summarize a series of experiments where individuals watch a video of teams passing a basketball in different coloured shirts (black and white), and the subjects are required to count the number of passes between players wearing white shirts, while ignoring the black shirts (Simons and Chabris 1999). What the subjects don't notice while performing the task, is that a person in a gorilla suit walks into the middle of the passing circle! The reason is that System 2 processes have been engaged to manage the counting task, absorbing attentional focus, leading to blindness towards other information readily available in their visual field. Without that task, everyone notices the gorilla.

Table 1. Properties of System 1 and System 2.

	Type 1 Processes (System 1)	Type 2 Processes (System 2)
Properties	Associative Holistic Parallel Automatic Relatively undemanding of cognitive capacity Relatively fast Acquisition by biology, exposure, and personal experience Associative explanations/relations	Rule-based Analytic Serial Controlled Demanding of cognitive capacity Relatively slow Acquisition by cultural and formal tuition Causal-logical explanations
Task Construal	Highly contextualized Personalized Conversational and socialized	Decontextualized Depersonalized Asocial
Type of Intelligence	Interactional (e.g. pragmatic processing)	Analytic (e.g. psychometric IQ)

5 Interaction of Type 1 and Type 2 Processes and the Emergence of Cognitive Biases

Type 1 processes, as our default mode of processing, are the processes first triggered in response to stimuli, a response that is automatic and autonomous in its functioning. Cognitive biases, more often than not, are features of these default processing mechanisms that emerge in task environments that instead require the kind of thinking that is characterized by Type 2 processes. Put differently, cognitive biases are thought to emerge when Type 1 processes are used to solve tasks/problems that require Type 2 processes, thereby generating 'irrational' responses when judged by the normative standards of Type 2 processing contexts. Daniel Kahneman (2011) has described the experimental literature and associated tasks that pit Type 1 and Type 2 processes against one another, capturing this natural conflict between the two. The default processing nature of Type 1 processes is one of the primary accounts of how many cognitive biases emerge.

As previously mentioned, in relation to Type 1 processes, one of the important functions of Type 2 processes is to exert inhibitory control, overriding Type 1 processes responses. The ability of Type 2 processes to perform this function stems from their ability to represent problems symbolically and therefore decouple problems from contextual constraints, allowing analytic processes to operate over the symbolic representations instead. Because of the domain general nature of symbolic processing, it allows for a more flexible repertoire of responses (i.e., alternative choices) than available via automatic implicit responses. But, as Stanovich et al. (2008) put it, "the ability to suppress Type 1 processing gets the job only half done. Suppressing one's response is not helpful unless a better response is available as to substitute for it" (p. 255). The generation of alternative courses of action is a secondary role of System 2 processes, as a function their ability to represent other states of affairs and thereby provide cognitive and behavioural flexibility. The cognitive resources required to perform this duty include, hypothetical and consequential reasoning, as well cognitive simulation, which are features of Type 2 processes (Ibid.).[4]

Type 1 processes have also been described as "what you see is all there is" (WYSIATI) type mechanisms: that is, they are set up to process information that is explicitly captured from the available information in the stimulus. To be sure, this information is often also enriched with existing information (knowledge/beliefs) stored in memory, but even this information is itself a product of personal experiences (Tetlock and Gardner 2015). As a consequence, Type 1 processes are unable to represent, for example, negative (or false) states of affairs, or alternative states of affairs. Johnson-Laird (1999) has referred to a similar phenomenon in his work on mental models, called the *principle of truth*, whereby only facts as they are presented to/by Type 1 processes can be represented in problem solving and false states of affairs fail to be represented. As a result, Type 1 processes are unable to solve problems whose solution requires representing alternative or negative states of affairs. Consider the following example from Stanovich (2008, p. 256):

> Jack is looking at Anne but Anne is looking at George. Jack is married but George is not. Is a married person looking at an unmarried person?
>
> (A) Yes (B) No (C) Cannot be determined

As they point out, a vast majority of people answer (C), which is incorrect. To fully work out the problem, you need consider two possibilities that are not contained explicitly in the problem statement: (i) Anne is married and (ii) Anne is not married. This requires *fully disjunctive reasoning* that considers all possible states of the world related to this problem. In scenario one, we know that Jack is married, so if Anne is not married then the response must be (A). In scenario two, if Anne *is* married, then *she* looking at an unmarried person, namely George. So, either way, someone is looking at an unmarried person. The reason people opt for C is that the problem does not explicitly tell us what Anne's status is in the problem description, creating the superficial appearance that the solution is uncertain, unless you work out the possibilities, which is a System 2 type task. In order to trigger fully disjunctive reasoning, a System 2 ability, one must override the System 1 response in this case, 'cannot be determined', in order to deploy System 2 resources.

Drawing on the above examples, we see that there are at least four principal mechanisms that can be implicated in the biased processing. First, the foundation of most cognitive biases is the default nature of Type 1 processing, which itself typically stems from the default to efficient processing, or cognitive miserliness. There is a further subset of biases related to cognitive efficiency that includes a Type 2 form of 'miserly' processing that defaults to *serial associative cognition* with a focal bias. According to Stanovich et al. (2010), "[s]erial associative cognition is not rapid and parallel, such as Type 1 processes, but is nonetheless rather inflexibly locked into an associative mode that takes as its starting point a model of the world that is given to the subject" (p. 205). This is consistent with the view presented by Evans (2006), whereby System 1 processes

---

[4] For an extended discussion of decoupling mechanisms, see Leslie (1987).

are responsible for generating the inputs to System 2 processes, which results in the most easily constructed model being focused on first.

In the case of the default to Type 1 processing for most tasks, a second failure mechanism related to the override function by Type 2 processes, correspond to a subset of cognitive biases which depend on the successful detection and execution of Type 2 process overrides. Further, many Type 2 tasks require sustained decoupling in order to enable processes like hypothetical reasoning and simulation to take place, as in the fully disjunctive reasoning task above, which requires both override and sustained decoupling to think through the hypothetical scenarios in which Anne is married vs not.

A third source of cognitive errors is related to *mindware*: "the rules, knowledge, procedures, and strategies that a person can retrieve from memory in order to aid decision making and problem solving" (Stanovich and Stanovich 2010). *Mindware gaps* are present in problems that represent a "comprehension error" where, for example, the lack of knowledge in a certain domain is directly responsible for processing errors where that knowledge is crucially implicated. For example, violations of the conjunction rule in probability theory, as in the Linda Task (Tversky and Kahneman, 1983), are attributable to lacking the requisite knowledge of probability theory (mindware gap), namely the conjunction axiom, rather than a function of the processing features of System 1 and System 2.

Fourth, *contaminated mindware* can explain deviations from normative performance on reasoning and judgment tasks, in those situations where the relevant mindware is operating as it should but contains knowledge, rules, or procedures that distort processing. The egocentric processing that is emblematic of myside bias, represents an evolutionarily adaptive response that, in the wrong context, results in processing errors. Myside bias is present whenever "people evaluate evidence, generate evidence, and test hypotheses in a manner biased toward their own prior opinions and attitudes" (Stanovich et al. 2013, p. 259). It has a close relationship with belief bias and confirmation bias, which are themselves egocentric processing tendencies. In any task that requires objective or impartial judgment, such as the evaluation of scientific evidence, or judicial decision making, etc., myside bias creates a distorting effect.

Table 2 below, adapted from Stanovich (2008), provides a simple taxonomy of cognitive biases tied to the failed cognitive mechanisms that explain how they emerge in the associated experimental research.

Table 2. Taxonomy of Cognitive Biases/Effects Tied to Types of Cognitive Failures.

Type of Cognitive Failure – leading to bias	Explanatory Mechanism	Sample Tasks, effects and processing styles implicated in this failure
Cognitive Efficiency-Miserliness	Default to Type 1 Processing	Vividness effects Attribute substitution Impulsivity Availability heuristic

(continued)

Table 2. (*continued*)

Type of Cognitive Failure – leading to bias	Explanatory Mechanism	Sample Tasks, effects and processing styles implicated in this failure
	Serial Associative Cognition with a Focal Bias	Framing Effects Myside processing Confirmation bias Failure to perform fully disjunctive reasoning
Override Failure	Failure of Sustained Decoupling	Denominator neglect Belief Bias
Mindware Gap	Missing Probability Knowledge	Conjunction errors Non-causal Baserates
	Ignoring alternative Hypotheses	Confirmation bias 4 Card Selection Task
Contaminated Mindware	Evaluation disabling strategies	Confirmation bias Conspiratorial thinking
	Self-egocentric processing	Myside bias

6   Applying Dual-Process Models to Cognitive Security

Linking the preceding discussion back to cognitive security, we can now see how the dual process model framework can be used to understand and respond to cognitive vulnerabilities in a more applied context. Consider, for example, how the use of bot accounts in social media to sway public opinion works by exploiting default Type 1 processing, such as the availability heuristic. Since these are automatic processes, they are relatively easy to exploit. In the simplest of cases, the targeted use of bots on social media aims to influence public opinion by reinforcing a desired narrative by creating the false impression that a particular belief is widely held within the social networks where bots are active. For those already sympathetic to the narrative, the bots can create a reinforcing effect by creating the appearance, through a high frequency of messages (availability bias), that suggest one's pre-existing beliefs (confirmation bias and/or belief bias) are widely shared beyond one's own social network.[5] Advertising and marketing algorithms create an amplifying effect by reinforcing and pushing content in a way that further reinforces individual cognitive biases and social cognition effects.

Having identified categories of cognitive failure and the associated mechanisms involved moves us closer understanding how we might intervene. A literal reading of the

---

[5] These types of attacks are not limited to these mechanisms, as they can also be used in conjunction aspects of social cognition, such as the *bandwagon effect* or *groupthink*, where we believe things simply because other members of our perceived ingroup share similar beliefs (see, e.g., Schmitt-Beck 1996). The *social* nature of social media, unlike traditional media platforms, adds an additional layer of complexity, by exploiting the effect that social networks have on our thinking.

above categories of cognitive failure, implies a fairly straightforward list of intervention types that target individual challenges for overcoming cognitive vulnerabilities:

1. Cognitive miserliness → Learn to use Type 2 process override
2. Override failure → Improve override detection and execution ability
3. Mindware Gap → Acquire Mindware
4. Contaminated Mindware → Correct Mindware

Figure 3 below, taken from Stanovich and West (2008, p. 687) captures a logical process flow that maps on to solution types that are tied to the cognitive factor implicated in resolving an instance of biased processing:

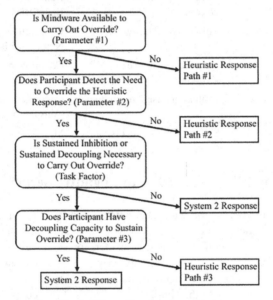

Fig. 3. Bias mitigation flow chart.

We can derive from this process flow the cognitive requirements outlined above for mitigating cognitive biases and similarly represent the consequences of a failure to address them, in terms of processing. As the diagram makes clear, there is a default to heuristic responses that can only be overcome with the successful ability to (i) detect the need to override; (ii) to sustain inhibition and decouple for alternative processing; and (iii) having the requisite mindware in situations where it is required to achieve the normative response.

Having identified aspects of cognition that would need to be targeted to address the corresponding biases, practical questions remain regarding what individual level interventions would be needed to support the appropriate cognitive changes to mitigate these effects. In all of these cases, cognitive change would depend on some form of education and training. To be clear, this does not preclude other kinds of environmental interventions, like "prebunking," which enriches mindware with information and thinking strategies that prepare a person in advance of a disinformation attack, or warning labels on sources of disinformation, which cue subjects' metacognitive abilities to detect bias and bring onboard Type 2 processes to evaluate content. An important extension of this work would be to document how various cognitive augmentation techniques might support individual level vulnerabilities. However, in the remainder of this paper, the focus will be on the factors that enable learning better cognitive habits to mitigate vulnerabilities overall.

7 Rationality, Intelligence, and Bias Mitigation

The ability of Type 2 processes to provide an override function to the processing defaults of Type 1 heuristic processes, represents an important area of research that can contribute to discussions of cognitive security. This represents one of the primary internal (or psychological) mechanisms available to individual cognizers to address cognitive biases.[6] To the extent that Type 2 resources can be brought to bear in situations where cognitive biases are at play, they operate by enabling individuals to inhibit (Type 1) responses that are not fit for the (Type 2) task. This is achieved by reflecting on and validating their thinking, which in turn enables more alternative responses to flexibly respond to situations.

The feasibility of using Type 2 processes as a corrective mechanism to the vulnerabilities that cognitive biases represent depends on the extent to which we can expect (a) individuals to either have, and be able to execute, this ability and/or (b) whether or not these abilities are ultimately learnable or trainable. Central to this discussion are questions regarding individual differences in cognitive ability and the degree to which these differences are implicated in the necessary mechanisms for inhibition of Type 1 responses, in order to execute other Type 2 cognitive processes, like reflective thinking, hypothetical reasoning, and simulation.

To clearly understand the role of individual differences, it is necessary to enrich the simplified Type 1/Type 2 model we have been discussing thus far. Stanovich (Stanovich 2004; Stanovich et al. 2008, 2020; Stanovich and West 2008) now presents what he calls a tripartite model that refines the stages of processing related to Type 2 process overrides of Type 1 processes. Figure 4 below provides a schematic overview of the structure, including references to where individual differences have an impact.

The 'algorithmic mind' is a new addition to the structure and is an additional level of processing in Type 2 processes. The distinction between algorithmic and reflective processes is by no means as clear a distinction between autonomous processes (System 1) and System 2. The reason is that "the algorithmic and reflective mind will both

---

[6] External supports where some of the cognitive burden of correcting biases is offloaded to the world are also an incredibly important solution domain. For example, to address Covid-19 misinformation, major platforms such as Facebook began to tag content that contained discussions of Covid-19 related material to alert readers that they may be consuming content from non-reputable source. In this way, tags cued System 2 type processes to enable individuals to reflect on whether the content they were about to read is trustworthy. The value of these approaches cannot be understated, given the ease with which they can be implemented at scale, in comparison to interventions focused on cognition. These external supports, though a highly important area for investigation, will not be considered in detail here.

share properties (capacity-limited serial processing for instance) that differentiate them from the autonomous mind" (Stanovich 2009, p. 58). According to Stanovich (2009), "[t]he difference between the reflective mind and the algorithmic mind is captured operationally in the distinction that psychologists make between tests of intelligence and tests of critical thinking" (Ibid., p. 60). More specifically, it is a distinction that maps on to the systematic ways in which cognition breaks down in the experimental literature (Ibid.). Algorithmic level disruptions typically reflect "general impairments in intellectual ability" (Ibid.). As such, performance on algorithmic processing tasks are correlated with measures of fluid intelligence and represent an important area of individual differences captured as differences in cognitive ability. In contrast, breakdowns in reflective thinking are attributable instead to individual variance in thinking dispositions (also referred to as "cognitive styles" in that literature) that are predictors of *rational* thought. These predictors are explained in more detail below.

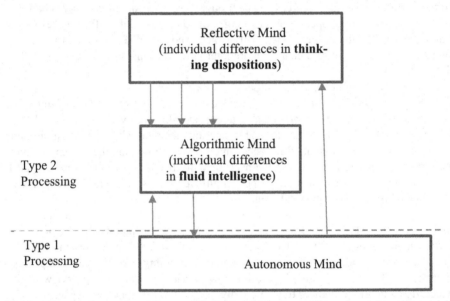

Fig. 4. Tripartite Structure and Locus of Individual Differences. (Reproduced from (Stanovich and Stanovich 2010))

In the context of discussions of individual differences in abilities to overcome cognitive biases, and the prospects for the teachability of the relevant skills, there are two main observations: (i) that presence of cognitive biases in people's thinking are not strongly correlated with cognitive ability (e.g. SAT scores), meaning that even high performers on cognitive ability tests commit these errors, but; (ii) the ability to avoid some cognitive biases is underpinned by cognitive ability as described in measures of fluid intelligence. However, when fluid intelligence is controlled for, the residual variance in these tasks is attributable to differences in thinking dispositions that are central to rational thinking, where rational thinking is distinct from cognitive ability. In sum, "individual differences in rational thought and action can arise because of individual differences in fluid intelligence (the algorithmic mind) or because of individual differences in thinking dispositions (the reflective mind) or from a combination of both" (Stanovich et al. 2020, p. 1117).

These differences are most notable in the execution of cognitive decoupling for the purposes of overriding Type 1 processes in situations where we have conflicting responses required by Type 1 and Type 2: As Stanovich and West (2008) remark,

Resolving the conflict in favor of the analytic response may require cognitive capacity, especially if cognitive decoupling must take place for a considerable period of time while the analytic response is computed. Cognitive decoupling is involved in inhibiting the heuristic response and also in simulating alternative responses. Recent work on inhibition and executive functioning has indicated that such cognitive decoupling is very capacity demanding and that it is strongly related to individual differences in fluid intelligence...(p. 687).

Stanovich et al. (2008, 2020) provide a richer account of the details regarding the mechanisms involved in explaining individual differences related to overcoming cognitive biases and their relation algorithmic and reflective processing. There are two main takeaways for discussions related to interventions aimed at improving cognitive security vulnerabilities that issue from exploitation of cognitive biases. First, individual differences in measures of fluid intelligence will be a limiting factor across individuals with respect to the ability to decouple from System 1 processes, especially situations that require sustained inhibition or sustained decoupling to carry out the override function. This is because fluid intelligence is essentially unchangeable through intervention. In these situations, interventions aimed at addressing risks related to cognitive biases will likely require external (non-individual level) interventions (e.g., formal processes filtering information before it reaches the individual) to augment the individual level deficits.

Secondly, intelligence on its own is insufficient to predict performance on overcoming cognitive biases. The separability of rational thinking dispositions as predictors of normative performance underscores the need to support training and education that inculcates these thinking dispositions. As we will see in the next section, regardless of cognitive ability, there is independent justification for more widely applied interventions aimed at enhancing the critical thinking skills that underpin the kind of rationality that is essential to overriding System 1 responses and enabling alternative courses of action.

8 The Rationality Quotient and Predictors of Cognitive Performance

If having an adequate IQ, as measured by tests of fluid intelligence, does not insulate one from thinking biases, what's missing? Individual differences, after controlling for cognitive ability, must be a function of other factors that are essential for normative performance on these tasks. These differences can be explained, in many cases, as differences in thinking dispositions that are representative of rational thinking. The phenomenon of people behaving irrationally in spite of having the relevant cognitive abilities to do otherwise, is referred to by Stanovich (2004) as *dysrationalia*: "an inability to think and behave rationally despite adequate intelligence" (p. 163).

According to Stanovich et al. (2020), to be rational, "a person must have well-calibrated beliefs and must act appropriately on those beliefs to achieve goals – both of these depend on the thinking dispositions of the reflective mind" (p. 1116). They further distinguish two types of rationality to clarify this notion, (a) *epistemic rationality* and (b) *instrumental rationality*. *Epistemic rationality* corresponds to the lay notion 'good judgment,' and measures of it look at (i) the extent to which a person's beliefs correspond with the world (i.e., how true or accurate they are) and (ii) the tendency for a person to follow thought-processes that will lead them to accurate/true beliefs.

Instrumental rationality is a more practical assessment of people's reasoning that looks at whether their thinking helps them to achieve their goals and maps on to common sense notions of 'good decision making.' It is related to epistemic rationality in that getting what you want by making good decisions often depends on understanding how the world works and having thought processes that, more often than not, will lead you to believe things that are actually true. Of note, neither of these skills – of good judgement and decision-making – is measured in intelligence tests but they are an important part of what we believe constitutes *rational* behaviour. Most importantly, rationality is malleable (i.e., teachable) in ways that intelligence is not. Thus, interventions aimed at ameliorating faulty cognitive processes when it comes to truth seeking, ought to target those factors that underpin rationality, as opposed to those that underpin (unchangeable) fluid intelligence.

In their book *The Rationality Quotient*, Stanovich, West and Toplak (2016) lay out the empirical foundation for a comprehensive test of rational thinking that tracks the above forms of rationality. The main stated goals of designing the Comprehensive Assessment of Rational Thinking (CART) tool are both to create a measurement instrument that defines predictors of normative (rational) performance in thinking tasks as well as drawing "more attention to the skills of rational thought by measuring them systematically" (Ibid., p.xiii). Given the fact that rationality is not grounded in intelligence, it represents an important domain of research for informing research on critical thinking more generally, but also bias mitigation specifically.

The CART consists of wide variety of subtests, that measure individual attributes that either contribute to or are constitutive of rationality. For example, it looks for the presence of rational thinking abilities and the quality of reasoning skills: this includes abilities like collecting enough information before deciding; seeking other viewpoints; thinking extensively about a problem before making up one's mind; and thinking about the consequences of decisions. Reasoning in this way tends to result in more accurate judgments and more correct decisions. The instrument also looks for the presence or absence of mental habits that support good thinking, including measures of the tendency to be actively open minded ("actively open-minded thinking"), the tendency to want to think deliberately/explicitly about an issue ("need for cognition"), and the propensity to consider the future in decisions. They test for dispositions to think reflectively about problems and to validate one's own thinking (Type 2 processes). These habits increase the likelihood that one will deploy the reasoning abilities tested in the first criterion. Finally, the CART tests whether individuals have the relevant knowledge that supports rational thinking in important areas, such as mathematical and financial literacy, as well as economic knowledge and knowledge of science (basic scientific facts about the world of biology, physics, etc.), and other relevant domains of knowledge.

In total, the basic framework consists of 4 domains of subtests that roughly map on to the taxonomy of cognitive failures above that are not correlated with intelligence tests that can be summarized as follows (Ibid., p. 65):

1. Tasks saturated with processing requirements (detection, sustained override, hypothetical thinking);
2. Rational thinking tasks saturated with knowledge (mindware gaps);
3. Avoidance of contaminated mindware;
4. Thinking dispositions that foster thorough and prudent thought, unbiased thought and knowledge acquisition.

What the CART measures is a rationality quotient (RQ) that parallels IQ but instead defines the factors underlying rationality. In the context of cognitive security discussions, it provides an assessment tool that enables the identification of areas of deficiency that can, theoretically, be addressed through training and learning interventions. Irrationality caused by mindware gaps is the most easily remediable, as it is entirely due to missing strategies and declarative knowledge that can be taught. Overriding the tendencies of Type 1 processes is most often done with learned mindware, and sometimes the override function fails because of inadequately instantiated mindware. In such a case, inadequately learned mindware is the source of the problem (p. 222) and fixing it is the solution. Further, teaching people to be more open-minded, to seek other viewpoints, to put more effort into thinking tasks before making conclusions, to reflect on one's own thinking to validate it, all support a kind of epistemic regulation that ensures we get accurate and constructive answers more often than not. These dispositions play an important role in insulating us from a default to Type 1 processing, as they are deliberately focused on Type 2 processes that are the hallmark of reflective thinking.

Beyond identifying factors that can be addressed through training, the CART is a psychometric measurement tool that may also be useful to discussions in cognitive security scientific research focused on the measurement of cognitive resilience, whereby the concept of rationality itself and CART subtests might inform notions of cognitive resilience. Further, this instrument can also be applied in organizational settings to inform efforts to baseline cognitive abilities and identify areas for improvement. Finally, the tool might also prove useful in research on recruitment or talent management for military occupations where having a high RQ and the associated critical thinking skills it implies could be correlated with better on the job performance for individuals working in information based roles like cyber operations, intelligence, and related roles.

9   Conclusion

Reducing the complexity of any problem space is an important step towards finding workable solutions. The modest goal of this paper was to provide an example of an approach to developing a framework for capturing cognitive vulnerabilities in a manner that provides some meaningful improvement on the status quo. Mapping cognitive biases or other cognitive effects on to models of cognitive processes has the potential to ground thinking about cognitive vulnerabilities and efforts to improve cognitive security in more robust explanatory/causal frameworks. There are no doubt limitations to this approach, nor should it be considered a panacea for a notoriously complex problem space. For example, its' success depends in part on the level of precision of models of cognition themselves, which are still works in progress, including the dual-process model discussed here. As these models improve, architectural approaches to cognitive security will also be more fruitful. However, the view outlined in this paper adds value to current discussions by providing a template of sorts to inform a more integrated view of cognitive biases and the associated cognitive processes for research on cognitive security.

References

Boyd, J.R.: The essence of Winning and Losing. https://www.coljohnboyd.com/static/docume nts/2018-03_Boyd_John_R_edited_Hammond_Grant_T_A_Discourse_on_Winning_and_ Losing.pdf

Doherty, G.: The social origins of cross-cultural differences in cognition: a dual process approach. In: Payette, N., Hardy-Vallee, B. (eds.) Connected Minds: Cognition and Interaction in the Social World, pp. 188–211. Cambridge Scholars Publishing, Cambridge (2012)

Epstein, S.: Integration of the cognitive and the psychodynamic unconscious. Am. Psychol. **49**(8), 709–724 (1994)

Evans, J.S.B.T.: The heuristic-analytic theory of reasoning: extension and evaluation. Psychon. Bull. Rev. **13**(3), 378 (2006)

Evans, J.S.B.T., Stanovich, K.E.: Dual-process theories of higher cognition: Advancing the debate. Perspect. Psychol. Sci. **8**, 223–241 (2013)

Groome, D., et al.: An Introduction to Cognitive Psychology: Processes and Disorders, 3rd edn. Psychology Press (2014)

Johnson-Laird, P.: Deductive reasoning. Annu. Rev. Psychol. **50**, 109 (1999)

Kahneman, D., Tversky, A.: Prospect theory: an analysis of decision under risk. Econometrica Econometric Soc. **47**(2), 263–291 (1979)

Kahneman, D., Slovic, P., Tversky, A.: Judgment Under Uncertainty: Heuristics and Biases. Cambridge University Press (1982)

Tversky, A., Kahneman, D.: Extension versus intuitive reasoning: the conjunction fallacy in probability judgment. Psychol. Rev. **90**(4), 293 (1983)

Kahneman, D., Klein, G.: Conditions for intuitive expertise: a failure to disagree. Am. Psychol. **64**(6), 515–526 (2009)

Kahneman, D.: Thinking, Fast and Slow. Farrar, Straus and Giroux, New York (2011)

Kruger, J.M., Dunning, D.: Unskilled and unaware of it: how difficulties in recognizing one's own incompetence lead to inflated self-assessments. J. Pers. Soc. Psychol. **77**(12), 1121–1134 (1999)

Leslie, A.M.: Pretense and representation: the origins of "theory of mind." Psychol. Rev. **94**(4), 412–426 (1987)

Levin, D.T., Simons, D.J.: Failure to detect changes to attended objects in motion pictures. Psychon. Bull. Rev. **4**, 501–506 (1997)

Marr, D.: Vision: A Computational Investigation into the Human Representation and Processing of Visual Information. W.H. Freeman, San Francisco (1982)

Nickerson, R.: Confirmation bias: a ubiquitous phenomenon in many guises. Rev. Gen. Psychol. **2**(2), 175–220 (1998)

Piattelli-Palmarini, M.: Inevitable Illusions: How Mistakes of Reason Rule Our Minds. Wiley (1994)

Pylyshyn, Z.: Computation and Cognition: Toward a Foundation for Cognitive Science. MIT Press, Boston (1986)

Reber, A.S.: Implicit Learning and Tacit Knowledge: An Essay on the Cognitive Unconscious. Oxford University Press (1993)

Sloman, S.A.: The empirical case for two systems of reasoning. Psychol. Bull. **119**, 3 (1996)

Schmitt-Beck, R.: Mass media, the electorate, and the bandwagon: a study of communication effects on vote choice in Germany. Int. J. Public Opin. Res. **8**, 266–291 (1996)

Simons, D.J., Chabris, C.F.: Gorillas in our midst: Sustained inattentional blindness for dynamic events. Perception **28**(9), 1059–1074 (1999)

Stanovich, K.E.: Who is Rational? Studies of Individual Differences in Reasoning. Laurence Erlbaum Associates, Mahwah (1999)

Stanovich, K.E.: The fundamental computational biases of human cognition: heuristics that (sometimes) impair decision making and problem solving. In: Davidson, J.E., Sternberg, R.J. (eds.) The Psychology of Problem Solving, pp. 291–342. Cambridge University Press, New York (2003)

Stanovich, K.: The Robots Rebellion: Finding Meaning in the Age of Darwin. The University of Chicago Press, Chicago (2004)

Stanovich, K.E., Toplak, M.E., West, R.F.: The development of rational thought: a taxonomy of heuristics and biases. Adv. Child Dev. Behav. **36**, 251–285 (2008)

Stanovich, K.E., West, R.F.: On the relative independence of thinking biases and cognitive ability. J. Pers. Soc. Psychol. **94**, 672–695 (2008)

Stanovich, K.E.: Distinguishing the reflective, algorithmic, and autonomous minds: Is it time for a tri-process theory? In: Evans, J., Frankish, K. (eds.) In Two Minds: Dual Processes and Beyond, pp. 55–88. Oxford University Press, Oxford (2009)

Stanovich, K.E., Stanovich, P.J.: A framework for critical thinking, rational thinking, and intelligence. In: Preiss, D., Sternberg, R.J. (eds.) Innovations in Educational Psychology: Perspectives on Learning, Teaching and Human Development, pp. 195–237. Springer, New York (2010)

Stanovich, K.E., West, R.F., Toplak, M.E.: Myside bias, rational thinking, and intelligence. Curr. Dir. Psychol. Sci. **22**, 259–264 (2013)

Stanovich, K.E., West, R.F., Toplak, M.E.: The Rationality Quotient - Toward a Test of Rational Thinking. MIT Press, Cambridge (2016)

Stanovich, K.E., Toplak, M.E., West, R.F.: Intelligence and rationality. In: Stererg, R.J. (ed.) Cambridge Handbook of Intelligence, 2nd edn., pp. 1106–1139. Cambridge University Press, New York (2020)

Tetlock, P.E., Gardner, D.: Superforecasting: The Art and Science of Prediction. Crown Publishers/Random House (2015)

Thaler, R.H., Sunstein, C.R.: Nudge: Improving Decisions About Health, Wealth, and Happiness. Yale University Press (2008)

Tversky, A., Kahneman, D.: Availability: a heuristic for judging frequency and probability. Cogn. Psychol. **5**(2), 207–232 (1973)

Changing Hearts and Minds: The Role of Cybersecurity Champion Programs in Cybersecurity Culture

Victoria Granova$^{(\boxtimes)}$ [iD], Atefeh Mashatan [iD], and Ozgur Turetken [iD]

Toronto Metropolitan University, Toronto, ON, Canada
{vgranova,amashatan,turetken}@torontomu.ca

Abstract. Humans have often been written off as the weakest link in the cybersecurity industry. This paper looks at the human factor from a different perspective, seeking ways to leverage the human element to improve cybersecurity. The human element and its importance in cybersecurity defense and security incidents have been widely studied. The relationship between organizational cybersecurity culture and cybersecurity posture has also been examined in the literature. What is lacking is the examination of how an organization could improve its cybersecurity culture. Accordingly, we explore the possibility of cybersecurity champions to impact organizational cybersecurity culture, thereby improving the organization's cybersecurity posture. The option of leveraging cybersecurity champions to impact culture is proposed, and existing theoretical bases of Champion Theory and Promotor Theory in innovation management are explored to support the implementation of cybersecurity champions. These theories are then applied to existing cybersecurity culture research. Innovation champions exhibit transformational leadership characteristics to inspire innovation; four types of promotors (expert promotors, power promotors, process promotors and relationship promotors) use their various sources of power to remove barriers to innovation. Eight hypotheses are developed about the possible effect of the presence of cybersecurity innovation champions and cybersecurity promotors on four factors which have been found to have significant impact on information security culture in previous research (Tejay & Mohammed, 2022): group cohesiveness or alignment, professional codes (codes of ethics or conduct), informal work practices, and cybersecurity awareness.

Keywords: Cybersecurity · Cybersecurity Culture · Cybersecurity Champions · Culture Change · Innovation

1 Introduction

The enterprise cybersecurity landscape is growing increasingly in scope, scale and complexity [1]. Attacks are becoming increasingly prevalent and costly. Average data breach costs have increased year over year globally, from 3.5 million USD in 2014, to 4.35 million USD in 2022 [2] (IBM, 2022). The largest breaches in terms of data record exposed were Cam4 in 2020 with 10.8 billion records, and Yahoo 2013 breach with 3 billion

D. D. Schmorrow and C. M. Fidopiastis (Eds.): HCII 2023, LNAI 14019, pp. 416–428, 2023.
https://doi.org/10.1007/978-3-031-35017-7_26

records [3]. The global cybersecurity insurance market has also doubled from 2.5 billion USD in 2015, to 5 billion USD in 2019 [4]. The top 10 breaches in 2020 alone exposed over 30 billion records [5]. According to industry research, cybersecurity breaches are inevitable, and organizations need to prepare by building a culture of cyber-resiliency [5]. Cyber resiliency is the ability to adapt and recover from attacks or stresses on cybersecurity resources [6]. Per Gartner, building a cybersecurity culture and tailored awareness and training programs is a key component of maturing an organization's cybersecurity program and building resiliency, alongside technical controls such as critical incident response tools and capabilities [7]. People are also a key part of the definition of organizational security posture, which is the security status of an organization's information systems which include people, hardware, software, and policies [8]. To have a more holistic view of cyber resiliency, one needs to consider the combination of technology, processes and people in place to help an organization withstand and recover from cybersecurity threats and attacks.

In the past seven years, enterprises have increased their investment in technology, with a positive spend increase year-over-year since 2016, with 2022 being the only year with a 0.2% decline. Gartner forecasts IT spending worldwide to increase by 2.4% in 2023 within the categories of data center systems, software, devices, IT Services, and communications services [9]. Despite this significant investment in technology, the highly impactful security breaches discussed above demonstrate that technology alone cannot sufficiently address cybersecurity threats: human factors must be a key consideration.

1.1 Tracing the Human Element in Enterprise Cybersecurity

When tracking both IT and cybersecurity spending, human security spending as a category is conspicuously absent. For example, Canalys breaks down cybersecurity spending into identity access management, vulnerability and security analytics, data security, web and email security, network security, and endpoint security [10]. Statista considers categories such as application, cloud, data, and network security, as well as consumer and enterprise spend [11]. The absence of human security from these categorizations implies that efforts and spend to secure the human factor are either not tracked or do not exist. This absence exists despite industry researchers such as Verizon pointing out the year-over-year increase in the human involvement in incidents [12], and Gartner calling for C-level executives to increase their focus on the human element [13].

Gartner predicted that organizations and cybersecurity will begin to use a human-centric approach to cybersecurity [13]. The report also acknowledges that the human element is continuing to be an effective threat vector for attacks [13]. Gartner [13] also determined that the cybersecurity industry needs to do more to reduce friction and barriers to cybersecurity compliance for users. Poor implementation of strategic cybersecurity initiatives such as Zero Trust also hinders companies from developing a positive cybersecurity culture [13]. Gartner's number one recommendation is to make cybersecurity culture the first priority; this can be achieved through collaboration (co-design) and role-modeling risk-based decision making [13]. Another recommendation from the report is to evaluate the human factors that stop cybersecurity controls from being effective; human factors must be taken into account when designing and implementing cybersecurity controls [13]. Cybersecurity principles must also be integrated into the organizational culture to avoid adversarial relationships between cybersecurity and business [13].

While labor and human resources costs can vary drastically by industry, a recurring average in industry reports is 30%, and can increase if the organization is in the service industry [14]. For example, in 2021, Canadian statistics reported that wages and labor and commissions constituted 40% of revenue for engineering and computer services [15]. As human capital is one of the highest expenses (if not the highest expense) for a business, it is important to leverage humans as a critical part of the cybersecurity defense strategy – humans are, after all, a critical pillar of the information technology People, Process, Technology framework [16]. Additional complexity arising from organizational trends such as borderless workforces, is an additional argument for focusing research on the human element in cybersecurity [17].

Individual analyses of high-profile breaches have demonstrated that the human element plays a large role in the success of attacks resulting in significant financial consequences. For example, in 2014, Yahoo suffered from a large-scale breach that resulted in a data compromise of all its 3 billion customers [18]. This breach began as a spear phishing attack, where specific employees were sent targeted emails to trick them into clicking a link and granting the attacker access to Yahoo's systems [19]. In 2016, Verizon was undertaking an acquisition of Yahoo and the news of this data breach decreased the buy-out price by $350 million – from $4.8 billion to $4.48 billion [20]. A class-action lawsuit was also filed against Yahoo, which resulted in a $117.5 million settlement [21].

Target was the victim of another high-profile breach. Although Target had invested in cybersecurity infrastructure, this successful attack was the result of a phishing email sent to one of Target's trusted vendors, which then allowed the attackers to gain access to Target's network [20]. The attackers were then able to install memory-scraping malware on Target's point-of-sale terminals, accessing the personal information, including debit and credit cards of 40 million Target customers [20]. As a result, Target suffered high costs, a total of $252 million, and its profits declined by 46% reportedly due to the decline in customer trust [20].

More recently in 2022, Twilio suffered a data breach that resulted in unauthorized access to "hundreds" of Twilio customers' data [22]. Using a tactic known as "smishing", attackers targeted a small number of current and former Twilio employees through mobile text messages [22]. The attackers would send fake password reset links in text messages; once clicked, the links led the victims to fake Twilio login pages, where the employees were convinced to enter (and thus reveal) their credentials [22]. The attackers then used the harvested credentials to access internal Twilio tools and applications and were able to access customer data [22].

These types of human or social attacks are examples of social engineering, where psychological manipulation is used to achieve an attacker's objectives [23]. According to industry research, social engineering is a frequent first step in the attack chain, often followed by leveraging stolen credentials or delivering and executing malware as a second step to further the attack [12]. Phishing remains the top threat action in breaches, and financially-motivated social engineering continually increases year-over-year [24].

The human element continues to be a driver for breaches, with humans being involved in 82% of breaches [12]. This involvement ranges from phishing and errors to stolen credentials and misuse [12].

While it is difficult to effectively measure the value of human capital, management research emphasizes the importance of humans as the biggest asset of an organization [25]. Despite the difficulty of determining the exact value or return on the investment in the human element, it is an important area of consideration [5]. Addressing or strengthening the human element against social engineering attacks may help mitigate such attacks [26]. While considered the weakest link in cybersecurity [27], the human element has potential to become one of cybersecurity's strongest layers of defense. It is critical to view the human element as an important asset instead of discounting it as an inevitable weak link in the cybersecurity chain. This paper focuses on a conceptual exploration of how the presence of a cybersecurity champion program would impact cybersecurity culture change in organizations.

1.2 Cultural Factors in Cybersecurity

Organizational culture is comprised of employee values and beliefs, assumptions, and visible artifacts, such as behavior or language [28, 29]. Information security culture can be defined as the perception of the organization's shared values and beliefs that are leveraged in an individual's interaction with the organization's systems and processes [23, 30]. Da Veiga et al. conducted research to determine a complete definition of information security culture, demonstrating that it is contextualized to employee behavior regarding the protection of information, and is informed by awareness, training, and communication [29]. Over time, the behavior becomes automatic, driven by employee assumptions, values, knowledge, attitude, and perceptions of information protection [29]. The culture would then yield information protection (protecting the confidentiality, integrity and availability of data) and leads to internal and external trust and integrity [29].

At the beginning of the century, researchers such as Eloff & Von Solms [31] noticed that organizations' approach to cybersecurity requires a more holistic approach than solely focusing on certification, and would need to expand into the procedural and process domains. Von Solms [32] introduced the idea of a third wave of information security where cybersecurity needed to be approached broadly – through a lens of both certification and a comprehensive information security culture. Ruighaver et al. [33] argued that supporting a security culture would *often* mean that security policies and technical controls need to be redesigned. More recently, studies such as Tejay & Mohammed [34] demonstrated the connection between culture and the success of an organization's information security programs.

1.3 Influencing Cybersecurity Culture

Information security culture must be created in an organization by incorporating cybersecurity in everyday work performance, or risk exposure to cybersecurity threats [32]. It is important to incorporate cybersecurity into culture as a key function to be considered alongside technology improvements [35]. Industry researchers continue to stress the importance of cybersecurity culture as part of a cyber defense strategy [13]. Cybersecurity culture needs to be considered as a basic building block of an organization's cybersecurity defense framework. It is also important to strengthen organizational cybersecurity posture sustainably and holistically by changing beliefs and attitudes, instead of short-term cybersecurity behavior change that is achieved through training and information [26]. However, there is a gap in academic literature regarding actionable methods in improving the factors that can influence cybersecurity culture.

Tejay & Mohammed found that four factors have a significant impact on information security culture: group cohesiveness or alignment, professional codes (codes of ethics or conduct), informal work practices, and cybersecurity awareness [34]. Group cohesiveness refers to the inclination for team members to work toward a common goal [34]. Professional codes are the common rules that are followed by the members of a profession. These professional codes may be codes of ethics or conduct which individuals feel a moral obligation to observe [34]. Survey questions related to professional codes would cover adherence to standards of professional conduct and participating in continuing professional development [34]. Informal work practices are normatively driven, rather than rule-based, work practices [34]. The fourth category that influences information security culture, per Tejay & Mohammed, is information security awareness [34].

Tejay & Mohammed found that security culture positively impacts employees' perception of information security success [34]. They argue that perceptions, in turn, influence security behavior and would lead to security efforts being more successful [34]. The current paper proposes implementing cybersecurity champions as a method of influencing cybersecurity culture via the above mentioned four factors of group cohesiveness, professional codes, informal work, and information security awareness.

1.4 Cybersecurity Champions

Literature provides inconsistent definitions of the term "cybersecurity champion". Haney & Lutters [37] defines the term as security professionals who promote cybersecure behaviors as a major part of their job role. Alhsaikh defines champions as a role performed by employees who do not necessarily occupy security job roles [38]. Alshaikh & Adamson further define the cybersecurity champion role as supporting the security team's awareness messaging and supporting other teams to be security-compliant [26].

This paper posits that changing the components of cybersecurity culture can be viewed as a type of change or innovation. Innovation is defined as an organization adopting a new idea or behavior and is a means of change for an organization [39]. This change can arise in response to external factors or may be made to preemptively change the internal environment [39]. Therefore, we extend theory from the innovation field, such as Innovation Champions and Promotors [36], to drive innovation in the form of organizational cybersecurity culture change. We propose that cybersecurity champions in the form of Innovation Champions and Promotors [36] can help organizations capitalize on their human capital by positively impacting cybersecurity culture in organizations.

2   Theoretical Background

Cybersecurity champions can be seen as a type of innovation agent to drive forward innovation – in this case, innovation through changing cybersecurity culture of an organization. As seen in Alshaikh & Adamson's research, implementing a cybersecurity champions program can result in employees internalizing cybersecure behaviors and compliance with policies leading to culture change [26]. While, to our knowledge, there has not been any research on cybersecurity champions through the lens of innovation agents, there is extensive research in business innovation research.

Leveraging theory from the organizational innovation field, one can view cybersecurity champions as innovation agents like an innovation champion or promotor. Two theories from the innovation field support the concept of *cybersecurity champion* and its effectiveness in influencing cybersecurity culture: Champion Theory and Promoter Theory. Champions are individuals who progress a change through inspiration or motivation [36]. Promoters are individuals who have power to overcome barriers [36]. Research has shown that individuals in various levels of the organization can participate in this role to drive organizational change and acceptance of new ideas [36].

Prior to determining whether cybersecurity champions would be able to impact cybersecurity culture, it is important to determine the characteristics of an effective champion. Howell & Higgins's 1990 study [40] investigated the behaviors, personality characteristics and influence tactics of champions. The researchers determined that champions showed higher innovativeness, risk taking, influence attempts, and used a greater variety of influence tactics. They could also clearly communicate the innovation with enthusiasm, commitment and involving others in the innovation. Champions espouse characteristics of transformational leadership such as the ability to inspire, exhibiting passion for innovation and motivation to process it, a propensity for taking risks, and a tendency for persistence in implementing the innovation in the implementation stage [36]. Other research [23] demonstrated a strong association of transformational leadership with perceived information security culture. Considering cybersecurity champions are a type of an innovation agent or champion, they must have strong communication skills, be skilled at influence tactics, be more prone to take risk, and exhibit enthusiasm and a skill in involving others in a common goal or innovation [36].

Promotor theory looks at how multiple players can work together to remove barriers to innovation [36, 41, 42]. These promotors could be *power* promotors, *expert* or *knowledge* promotors, *process* promotors, and *network* or *relationship* promotors [36, 43]. Power promotors leverage the power brought on by their role or position in the organizational hierarchy to overcome barriers to change [42]. Power promoters are best suited to overcome barriers such as ignorance, opposition from other teams or people leaders, and lack of resources [42]. Power promoters can use their control over resources and hierarchical potential to ease these barriers [42]. Power promoters use social and political influence to sponsor innovation or change, and can use their gatekeeping power roles to prioritize project or programs that are connected to the desired innovation or change [42].

Expert or knowledge promotors use their expertise and technical knowledge in the relevant subjects to overcome the barrier to change posed by lack of knowledge or understanding of the change or innovation [42]. The expert promotor can effectively advocate for the change by sharing their knowledge, and leverage expert power to persuade others [42].

Process promotors use their understanding of the organizational structure, processes, and communication skills to overcome bureaucracy and administrative barriers to innovation [42]. Process promotors are uniquely positioned to translate technical terminology or language associated with the innovation into business-specific terminology, promoting understanding and easing the challenges of achieving buy-in [42]. Process promotors can also be leveraged for their skills to transform the innovation vision into actionable steps and program plans [42].

Lastly, relationship or network promotors leverage their relationship building skills to bridge gaps between organizational departments and achieve buy-in by forging strong relationships with key contacts [42]. Thus, relationship promotors help overcome the barriers due to lack of cooperation [42]. Relationship promotors can also leverage their existing vast network and relationships to share knowledge about the innovation and persuade others [42].

Research in the public sector found that it is important to have both promotors and champions in an organization to support innovation [36]. Therefore, it can be argued that cybersecurity champions should likewise be varied in type, comprising of champions as well as different types of promotors. A well-rounded cybersecurity champions program should therefore, be proportionately comprised of individuals who are champions as defined in the innovation field, as well as power promotors, expert promotors, process promotors, and relationship promotors.

Alsaikh & Adamson discuss the usefulness of internal influence, such as those from cybersecurity champions, in enabling cyber influence strategies by aligning employees' values with those of the security team [26]. Tejay & Mohammed [34] determined several categories that impact security culture: group cohesiveness, professional code, informal work practices, and information security awareness in their mixed methods research. Existing literature shows that cybersecurity champion programs can improve the human element in cybersecurity through influence [26]. However, there is very little academic literature about the effect of cybersecurity champions on organizations.

Employees experience various challenges or barriers to behaving in a cybersecure manner, such as competing demands and time pressure [44]. A Cybersecurity Champions Program comprised of both innovation champions and promotors with a mandate to improve the cybersecurity culture may impact the influential factors of an organization's cybersecurity culture. In turn, a change to factors that influence culture could have an effect on the various barriers that employees experience to behaving cyber-securely.

3 Hypotheses Development

Drawing from the work of Tejay & Mohammed as well as Champions Theory and Promotor Theory, we develop several hypotheses [34]. These hypotheses could be tested in future work by using a survey instrument modeled after the Tejay & Mohammed study [34].

Per Tejay & Mohammed's 2022 study, group cohesiveness is the willingness to work together toward a common goal, and it significantly impacts cybersecurity culture [34]. Innovation champions exhibit traits of transformational leadership that inspires others to work toward an innovation. Cybersecurity champions who have innovation champion characteristics and can encourage others to rally around a common objective may have a similar impact to group cohesiveness. We propose:

H1. The presence of cybersecurity champions in an organization is positively related to group cohesiveness.

Per Tejay & Mohammed (2022), professional codes have an influence on cybersecurity culture. Tejay & Mohammed's survey questions related to professional codes would cover adherence to standards of professional conduct and participating in continuing professional development [34]. Expert promotors leverage their knowledge and expert power to gain trust with others and would model standards of professional conduct. Process promotors would leverage their knowledge to influence organizational structure and procedure to align with professional codes of conduct. Expert promotors and process promotors can also be leveraged to influence adherence to professional codes by removing barriers to knowledge acquisition. Therefore:

H2: The presence of cybersecurity expert promotors is positively related to professional codes.
H3: The presence of cybersecurity process promotors is positively related to professional codes.

Normatively driven work practices also have a significant impact on organizational cybersecurity culture [34]. Relationship or network promotors act in a bridging role to overcome barriers such as resistance to change [42]. Relationship promotors conduct activities such as identifying key contacts in other departments or organizations and building relationships with those contacts [42]. Relationship promotors can leverage their network to model and influence normative work practices to align more closely with the desired official work practices, that would be in line with cyber-secure behavior. Hence:

H4: The presence of cybersecurity relationship promotors is negatively related to informal work practice.

The fourth factor that influences information security culture, per Tejay & Mohammed, is information security awareness [34]. Innovation champions can promote security in informal settings and conversations, and inspire others to care and learn more about cybersecurity threats and defense practices. Following this we propose:

H5: The presence of cybersecurity champions is positively related to information security awareness.

Process promoters can remove procedural and systematic barriers to spreading knowledge and increasing the organizational level of information security awareness [42] hence we suggest:

H6: The presence of cybersecurity process promotors is positively related to information security awareness.

The knowledge specialty of expert promoters can be leveraged for credibility and translated into formal training sessions. Accordingly:

H7: The presence of cybersecurity expert promotors is positively related to information security awareness.

Power promoters can influence cybersecurity awareness by leveraging their hierarchical power to mandate awareness training or by prioritizing budgets on projects that involve cybersecurity awareness training [42]. From this:

H8: The presence of cybersecurity power promotors is positively related to information security awareness.

A model illustrating these hypothesized relationships can be seen in Fig. 1. Based on the above hypothesized relationships, we propose that Cybersecurity Champions Programs must be composed of both innovation champions and the four types of innovation promoters. Through leveraging the champions' variety of knowledge bases, one can influence the four factors of group cohesiveness, professional codes, informal work practices and cybersecurity awareness, which have been demonstrated to significantly influence information security culture.

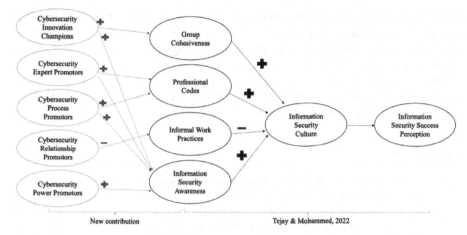

Fig. 1. The Research Model

4   Next Steps and Expected Contributions of the Research

We leverage Champions and Promotor theory from the innovation field of management to develop a set of hypotheses about the effect of cybersecurity champions on the four factors that influence information security culture as determined by Tejay & Mohammed [34]. The inspirational and leadership characteristics of champions, combined with identified expert, power, process and relationship promotors would produce a program of volunteers that are well-positioned to drive cybersecurity change throughout an organization.

This paper posits that the different types of innovation drivers such as champions and promotors could influence the different categories of information security culture [34]. Eight hypotheses are then proposed to empirically test the general theoretical framework.

The next stage for this research would be to empirically test the hypotheses. Data for empirical testing can be collected through web-based surveys. Following in the footsteps of the Tejay & Mohammed [34] study, the measurement model would first be assessed through Exploratory Factor Analysis and Confirmatory Factor Analysis, and then the hypotheses would be tested through the structural model testing in Partial Least Squares - Structural Equation Modeling.

The contribution of this research would yield practical implications in the field of cybersecurity management and provide direction on how to structure the cybersecurity program. This paper argues that including cybersecurity innovation champions and promotors will be a useful tool in influencing cybersecurity culture, ultimately leading to a stronger cybersecurity posture and higher cybersecurity resilience.

As the enterprise cybersecurity landscape grows in scope, scale and complexity, it is important to approach cybersecurity holistically from a people, process, and technology perspective [1]. Organizations which move from a centralized approach to decentralizing the cybersecurity function and leadership into business lines are reaping benefits in the form of a stronger cybersecurity posture [1]. Technology leaders often do not have access to tools or knowledge about change management and cultural change [16]. We hope that this paper inspires discussion and offers some actionable insights for the cybersecurity industry. Cybersecurity champions and promotors would be embedded in the business lines and are well-suited as a mechanism for distributing cybersecurity knowledge into decentralized model of cybersecurity control.

Future research can extend what is proposed in this paper by studying the concept of cybersecurity champions in the context of change management frameworks such as Kotter's Change Management framework or ESCAPE [16].

References

1. Firstbrook, P., et al.: Top trends in cybersecurity 2022. https://www.gartner.com/document/4011688?. Accessed 09 Feb 2022
2. Average cost of a data breach worldwide from 2014 to 2022 (in million U.S. dollars). https://www.statista.com/statistics/987474/global-average-cost-data-breach/. Accessed 06 Feb 2022
3. Number of compromised data records in selected data breaches as of August 2022 (in millions). https://www.statista.com/statistics/290525/cyber-crime-biggest-online-data-breaches-worldwide/. Accessed 06 Feb 2022
4. Marsh & Microsoft 2019 Global Cyber Risk Perception Survey. https://www.microsoft.com/en-us/security/blog/wp-content/uploads/2019/09/Marsh-Microsoft-2019-Global-Cyber-Risk-Perception-Survey.pdf. Accessed 12 Feb 2022
5. Maverick* Research: You Will Be Hacked, So Embrace the Breach. https://www.gartner.com/document/4003861?ref=ki-15959. Accessed 09 Feb 2022
6. NIST Glossary – Cyber Resiliency. https://csrc.nist.gov/glossary/term/cyber_resiliency. Accessed 12 Feb 2022
7. The Gartner IT Roadmap for Cybersecurity. https://www.gartner.com/en/information-technology/trends/the-it-roadmap-for-cybersecurity. Accessed 09 Feb 2022
8. NIST Glossary – Security Posture. https://csrc.nist.gov/glossary/term/security_posture. Accessed 12 Feb 2022
9. Information technology (IT) spending year-over-year growth worldwide from 2016 to 2023, by segment. https://www.statista.com/statistics/268940/percent-growth-in-it-spending-worldwide-by-segment/. Accessed 05 Feb 2022
10. Major cybersecurity agenda revealed for Canalys Forums 2022. https://www.canalys.com/newsroom/canalys-forums-2022-cybersecurity. Accessed 12 Feb 2022
11. Statista Technology Market Outlook: Cybersecurity – Market data Analysis & Forecasts. https://www.statista.com/study/124902/cybersecurity-report/. Accessed 12 Feb 2022
12. Verizon's 2022 Data Breach Investigations Report. https://www.verizon.com/business/resources/reports/dbir/. Accessed 05 Feb 2022
13. Gartner Predicts 2023: Cybersecurity Industry Focuses on the Human Deal. https://www.gartner.com/document/4023308?ref=solrAll&refval=353988961. Accessed 05 Feb 2022
14. Indeed: What You Need to Know About Labor Cost Percentages. https://www.indeed.com/hire/c/info/labor-cost-percentages. Accessed 05 Feb 2023
15. Government of Canada, 2021 Report for: NAICS 541330 - Engineering services - Financial Performance Data. https://ised-isde.canada.ca/app/ixb/fpd-dpf/report. Accessed 12 Feb 2023
16. Adnams, S.: CIOs need to address culture, people and process change in dynamic environments. https://www.gartner.com/document/3994914?ref=solrAll&refval=354255144. Accessed 05 Feb 2023
17. Vogel, G., Sanchez Reina, D., Mok, L.: Define your borderless entry strategy to attract scarce technical talent and address skills shortages. https://www.gartner.com/document/4022568?ref=solrAll&refval=354218115. Accessed 05 Feb 2023

18. Data breaches: Deloitte suffers serious hit while more details emerge about Equifax and Yahoo. Computer Fraud & Security, vol. 2017, no. 10 (2017)
19. Williams, M.: Inside the Russian hack of Yahoo: How they did it. https://www.csoonline.com/article/3180762/inside-the-russian-hack-of-yahoo-how-they-did-it.html. Accessed 12 Feb 2023
20. Shankar, N., Mohammed, Z.: Surviving data breaches: a multiple case study analysis. J. Comparat. Int. Manage. **23**(1), 35+ (2020)
21. CNBC: If you got an email about the $117.5 million Yahoo data breach settlement, here are your options. https://www.cnbc.com/2020/02/06/what-to-do-if-you-got-email-from-yahoo-about-a-data-breach-settlement.html. Accessed 05 Feb 2023
22. Twilio Incident Report: Employee and Customer Account Compromise. https://www.twilio.com/blog/august-2022-social-engineering-attack. Accessed 05 Feb 2023
23. Rocha Flores, W., Ekstedt, M.: Shaping intention to resist social engineering through transformational leadership, information security culture and awareness. North-Holland (2016)
24. Verizon's 2020 Data Breach Investigations Report. https://enterprise.verizon.com/resources/reports/2020/2020-data-breach-investigations-report.pdf. Accessed 05 Feb 2022
25. Fulmer, I.S., Ployhart, R.E.: "Our most important asset": a multidisciplinary/multilevel review of human capital valuation for research and practice. J. Manag. **40**(1), 161–192 (2014)
26. Alshaikh, M., Adamson, B.: From awareness to influence: toward a model for improving employees' security behavior. Pers. Ubiquit. Comput. **25**(5), 829–841 (2021). https://doi.org/10.1007/s00779-021-01551-2
27. Arachchilage, N.A.G., Love, S.: Security Awareness of Computer Users: A Phishing Threat Avoidance Perspective. Elsevier Ltd. (2014)
28. Schein, E.H.: Organizational Culture and Leadership. 4th edn. Wiley, USA (2010)
29. da Veiga, A., Astakhova, L.V., Botha, A., Herselman, M.: Defining organisational information security culture—perspectives from academia and industry. North-Holland (2020)
30. da Veiga, A., Eloff, J.H.P.: A framework and assessment instrument for information security culture. Comput. Secur. **29**(2), 196–207 (2010)
31. Eloff, M.M., Von Solms, S.H.: Information security management: an approach to combine process certification and product evaluation. Comput. Secur. **19**, 698–709 (2000)
32. von Solms, B.: Information security—the third wave? North-Holland (2000)
33. Ruighaver, A.B., Maynard, S.B., Chang, S.: Organisational security culture: extending the end-user perspective. North-Holland (2007)
34. Tejay, G.P.S., Mohammed, Z.A.: Cultivating security culture for information security success: A mixed-methods study based on anthropological perspective. North-Holland Pub. Co. (2022)
35. Govender, S.G., Kritzinger, E., Loock, M.: A framework and tool for the assessment of information security risk, the reduction of information security cost and the sustainability of information security culture (2021)
36. Bankins, S., Denness, B., Kriz, A., Molloy, C.: Innovation agents in the public sector: applying champion and promotor theory to explore innovation in the Australian public service. Aust. J. Public Adm. **76**, 122–137 (2017)
37. Haney, J.M., Lutters, W.G.: Cybersecurity advocates: discovering the characteristics and skills of an emergent role Emerald (2021)
38. Alshaikh, M.: Developing cybersecurity culture to influence employee behavior: a practice perspective. North-Holland (2020)
39. Damanpour, F.: Organizational complexity and innovation: developing and testing multiple contingency models. Manage. Sci. **42**(5), 693–716 (1996)
40. Howell, J.M., Higgins, C.A.: Champions of technological innovation. Adm. Sci. Q. **35**(2), 317–341 (1990)

41. Rost, K., Hölzle, K., Gemünden, H.-G.: Promotors or champions? Pros and cons of role specialisation for economic process. Schmalenbach Bus. Rev. **8**(4), 340–363 (2007). https://doi.org/10.1007/BF03396754

42. Witte, E.: Power and innovation: a two-center theory. Int. Stud. Manag. Organ. **7**, 47–70 (1977)

43. Klerkx, L., Aarts, N.: The interaction of multiple champions in orchestrating innovation networks: Conflicts and complementarities. Technovation **33**(6–7), 193–210 (2013)

44. Collins, E.I.M., Hinds, J.: Exploring workers' subjective experiences of habit formation in cybersecurity: a qualitative survey. Cyberpsychol. Behav. Soc. Netw. **24**, 599–604 (2021)

Privacy and Security Perceptions in Augmented Cognition Applications

Michael-Brian Ogawa[1]([⊠]), Brent Auernheimer[2], Barbara Endicott-Popovsky[3], Ran Hinrichs[3], and Martha E. Crosby[1]

[1] University of Hawai'i at Mānoa, Honolulu, HI 96822, USA
{ogawam,crosby}@hawaii.edu
[2] Computer Science Department, California State University, Fresno, CA 93740, USA
brent@csufresno.edu
[3] Portland State University, Portland, OR 97201, USA
{endic,hinrichs}@pdx.edu

Abstract. Perceptions of security and privacy influence users' behavior with security mechanisms such as passwords and multifactor authentication. Users tend to practice insecure behaviors based on their perception of security and convenience. This paper highlights the alignment between privacy and security perceptions and the possibilities for augmented cognition in HCI and instructional design to improve security-related behaviors for access control.

Keywords: Security education · privacy · augmented cognition · access control · perceptions of privacy and security

1 Introduction

The subtitle of Derek Thompson's [16] essay of how science advancements are implemented (or ignored) is "invention alone can't change the world; what matters is what happens next". That is, the implementation of an idea changes the world, not simply the invention itself. When it comes to online applications and data, one of the "next things" is security and privacy.

Privacy and security are the nexus of, among other things, applied research in UI/UX, regulations and politics, reward and punishment, cognition, and technology. Perhaps less obvious, access control is a social activity and evokes emotion. If you are wronged, or private information compromised, or worse, you are endangered, past feelings can influence the use of security technology. We suggest that applied research is augmenting the users' cognition with the practices of privacy and security.

Solutions to security and privacy risks involving human behavior assume we consistently act rationally and make deliberate decisions. The preponderance of research from psychology suggests that deliberate thinking is not common. Norman [13] refers to levels of processing: visceral, behavioral, and reflective working together. He states that reflective memories are often more important than reality when judging an experience because they may weigh positive interactions strongly enough to overlook severe drawbacks.

D. D. Schmorrow and C. M. Fidopiastis (Eds.): HCII 2023, LNAI 14019, pp. 429–440, 2023.
https://doi.org/10.1007/978-3-031-35017-7_27

1.1 Cognitive Processes

Cognitive processes fall under categories labeled either conscious (rational or reflective) or automatic (visceral or behavioral) cognition. According to Kahneman, [7], much of human behavior is controlled by nonconscious automatic cognition. The deliberate rational cognition upon which most security models are based is triggered when automatic cognition detects something that is not normal. Rational cognition is influenced by the automatic cognition that preceded it. Automatic cognition is a process of pattern-matching a stimulus to a person's existing heuristic mental model [15]. These heuristics are influenced by an individual's personality and experiences and are tied to individuals and specific security situations.

Cognition is a necessary part of human functioning that is involved in completing digital tasks [8]. During a digital task, conscious cognition is mainly dedicated to the task while automatic cognition attends to a broader scope of elements of human functioning including the task processing, evaluation of its presentation features and assessment of other components of the general environment. Automatic cognition is fast but not necessarily accurate. It works by matching stimuli in the current context to readily accessible heuristics that are instinctive or learned from past-experience. It may include appraisal activities such as fetching or forming various heuristics and making of non-conscious judgements [7, 9, 15].

1.2 Security Education and Training

Traditional approaches to security education and training assume rational cognition. A different education intervention is needed to improve security compliance as people operate in the automatic cognition mode [7]. In this case, attempts should be made to change an individual's heuristics or apply interventions that trigger rational or reflective cognition. Sometimes the results of the automatic system trigger the use of rational or reflective cognition. Initial empirical evidence suggests that most people's automatic cognition can detect the need for rational or reflective cognition, but there are large individual differences in choosing whether to override the automatic cognition mode and engage in processes that require considerably more effort [7].

1.3 Typical Access Controls

A typical access control implementation is multifactor authentication. Typically, two factors are used for authentication (2FA) as a combination of user characteristics (such as fingerprints), knowledge (e.g., passwords), and property (mobile phones, or physical tokens such as "security keys" available to consumers [12]. Marky et al. [10] call this inherence, knowledge, and something that is owned. Each of the three factors present risks: passwords can be shared, weak or forgotten; property (mobile phones, tokens) can be lost or compromised; and physical characteristics can be immutable, although research addressing this risk is underway [5].

Marky et al. [10] call this inherence, knowledge, and something that is owned. Although the use of multiple factors may seem obvious to technical staff, users can be frustrated if they don't understand the value of multifactor authentication. Marky et al.

note "users are generally willing to follow a longer authentication process in exchange for more security", but the benefit must be "evident".

Passwords have been the most common single factor (knowledge). However, challenges exist between the usability and memorability of passwords. Unlike symmetric keys that are controlled by the verifier, memorized passwords are constructed by the user and are expected to be successfully recalled. Therefore, similar passwords may be composed and used in other logins. In many cases, memorable passwords that rarely change and are used for multiple logins avoid insecure habits such as writing down passwords [1]. The current password environment has design inconsistencies. A study by Choong et al. [3] found that more than 80% of 4573 participants preferred to create memorable passwords and devised ways to write down passwords to remember unrealistic amounts of information. As a result, "getting locked out is perceived as the biggest waste of time" [3]. Moreover, results from a large-scale study of more than 7700 accounts report user frustration of changing passwords. Although users replace passwords, algorithms can predict the new password resulting in a security vulnerability [17]. Furthermore, results from a 109-participant survey found that complex passwords do not aid memorability [6]. This perspective disputes the view that users are the primary source of password insecurities and scrutinize ineffective policy commanding excessive mandates on cognition [3]. Furthermore, the password lifecycle weights memory load and login experiences by impacting password choice regeneration [3]. Although memorable passwords are preferred, usability and security represent different goals [2].

Students in our work authenticate using a combination of passwords, and "pushes" to a mobile phone app (or to a physical token). Although it is practiced in many universities, its requirement varies across campuses. Colnago et al. [4] studied adoption of 2FA at Carnegie Mellon University (CMU) and found students said "it's not really that horrible". Both Marky and Colnago collected qualitative and quantitative data from university students, which highlighted the possibility of more complex authentication approaches with increased security.

With access controls such as passwords and MFA being prominent security concerns for individuals, the goals of the study focused on security behaviors of novice users based on their security background. The research targeted users' perceptions and experiences to guide the inquiry. The following questions were used as a guide for the study:

1. How are students' perceptions of personal computer security impacted by learning about security risks?
2. What type of learning has the greatest impact on participants' security practices?
3. What factors influence password sharing practices?

2 Exploratory Study

2.1 Participants

The initial study was conducted with students enrolled in an introductory computer science course for non-majors. Approximately 200–300 students enroll in the course each semester, which focuses on technology applications and introductory programming concepts. Participants came from over 30 different majors with a majority focusing their studies on Business Administration. The course is taught in a hybrid format and includes a lecture and laboratory component. Both lecture and laboratory portions of the course meet in-person once a week and have an on-line asynchronous session. The lecture focuses on the context and principles of computer science, while the laboratory targets the implementation of application and programming skills. Approximately 75% into the semester, the course includes a week-long unit on computer security, which includes general security concepts and its application using permissions in online environments.

2.2 Polls and Surveys

In-class polls during the security lecture captured live data while students were learning security concepts. These poll questions were implemented using the Poll Everywhere software, where participants submitted their polls via a Web interface. Poll questions highlighted the affordances and drawbacks of active and passive learning opportunities as various pedagogical approaches were utilized to promote learning.

In addition to the live lecture poll, a survey to collect students' insights after the completion of the security unit (both in-class and on-line asynchronous sessions) was implemented. The survey focused on underlying reasons students took actions regarding their security practices and their overall security knowledge development.

2.3 Analysis

A mix of quantitative and qualitative methods were used to analyze data for the guiding questions. The first question utilized a histogram of responses and a t-test to determine if there was as significant change in security perceptions, while the second and third questions included qualitative data that were coded using and open- and axial-coding strategy to determine themes for security actions and practices reported by students.

3 Results

3.1 How Are Students' Perceptions of Personal Computer Security Impacted by Learning About Security Risks?

Prior to learning about computer security, the researchers polled the students to determine their perceived knowledge about computer security (Fig. 1). Overall, 56% of students felt that they did not know a lot about computer security, 11% believed that they had a strong background in the field, and 33% were neutral. Although students felt that they did not have a strong background in computer security, many were quite comfortable with the general security of their device usage (Fig. 2). Approximately 85% of students felt "okay" or better about their computer security prior to learning about security issues. Without learning about security, many participants did not have a strong background in the field and were quite comfortable with the security of their devices. After polling students, the instructor shared vignettes about security issues over the last decade including Heartbleed, Spectre, Meltdown, and various data breaches. After learning about these security issues, students were much more concerned about their security, with approximately 60% feeling vulnerable or not safe when asked about their feelings when using their devices. The paired t-test highlighted a significant change in means comparing the before and after responses by students ($p < .01$), with a before average of 2.60 and an after average of 2.07. These findings illustrate that those without knowledge of security issues were more comfortable with their security and that a short lecture (~10 min) about security risks can make a significant differences in perceptions of one's own security and its importance. It is vital to determine how the increase in knowledge-base can impact security practices of the participants to expand on Marky and Colnago's work.

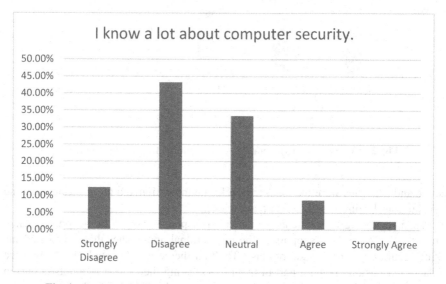

Fig. 1. Student initial perceptions about computer security prior to learning.

3.2 What Type of Learning Has the Greatest Impact on Participants' Security Practices?

The in-class lecture included a range of activities such as passive learning approaches (lecture) and active learning opportunities (activities completed by students). To supplement the passive lecture components, the instructor included poll questions to assess learning, guide content, and engage the students. The asynchronous lecture also utilized passive learning strategies (video lecture) and active learning approaches (working on activities and responding to questions on a quiz). Approximately 96% of the participants checked their email address at haveibeenpwned.com. Although 96% is a compelling number of participants, it is likely due to the check serving as one of the in-class activities. Therefore, the researchers measured the reported actions taken outside of class based on the in-class and asynchronous lectures (Fig. 3). Sixty-one percent of the students took a security action outside of class with 43% changing a password and 30% informing others about security risks. Thirty-nine percent did not take any actions to change their security practices. Of those that took action, 94% reported that the in-class

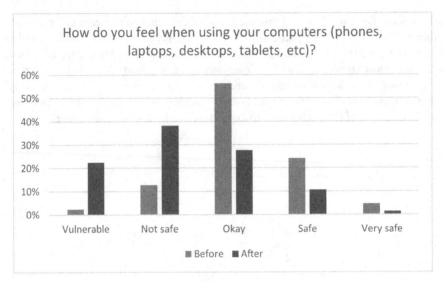

Fig. 2. Comparison of vulnerability levels before/after security vignettes.

lecture and activities were the main reason for taking action and 6% indicated that the asynchronous lecture was the underlying reason.

When reviewing the students' open-ended responses for taking action, we came across two major themes supporting the instructional approaches that led to students taking security actions outside of class. The first theme was the students' knowledge of data breaches and being a part of them by checking their email accounts at haveib eenpwned.com. Many found the in-class activity to check their email accounts to be engaging and quite surprising when they were a part of a data breach that included different types of sensitive information such as usernames, passwords, phone number, etc.

When they found that they were a part of a data breach, they changed their passwords on breached sites. A student highlighted concerns with breaches, "My bank account got hacked less than a week after the lecture bc of a PayPal data breach." While another discussed their password changing habits due to the issue, "[I] Changed password due to data breach." The second theme that emerged was the use of the same or similar passwords across on-line platforms. Many students cited their newly learned concern about credential stuffing, using known credentials on other Web sites. A student that changed their passwords indicated, "I found that I use similar passwords and email on numerous sites." The instructional approaches supporting both of these themes included a short lecture component (a few minutes) and an in-class activity to highlight the issues and were demonstrative of the issue. Therefore, embedding active learning strategies with passive lectures yielded more action from the students than any single approach.

Fig. 3. Actions participants took as a result of instruction

3.3 What Factors Influence Password Sharing Practices?

To address password sharing practices, we surveyed students to determine if they share their passwords along with the different types of accounts they use. Passwords were categorized as either school credentials (official use) or service credentials/sub account (such as streaming video services using another site's email address as a username). Interestingly, 30% of respondents shared their school credentials, while 79% shared their service credentials (Fig. 4). Students' feedback highlighted the varied perspectives on the services and why they shared their passwords or not. For their official school account, they noted that it was tied to many different services including their coursework, registration, records, financials, and campus services. They found these services to be essential and were concerned about sharing this content with others. Students who shared their credentials noted that they shared it with their parents to help account for services such as tuition payments. Participants also noted that multifactor authentication was a feature of their school account, so sharing passwords was less useful since the secondary authentication was needed. Respondents viewed service credentials as a specific usage compared to their school account. Many believed that they were paying for a service that could be utilized by multiple users such as streaming media. Therefore, they felt that they were getting "more bang for their buck" as others could use the service when they were not using it. In these cases, many reported sharing their credentials with those outside their immediate family, which is the opposite of school credentials that were shared with immediate family. They also found the lack or minimal use of multifactor authentication to be supportive of sharing their passwords. When comparing the two types of accounts, it is evident that convenience was a critical factor in sharing credentials with others.

The sharing of passwords was concerning to the researchers. They further studied credential sharing by asking if students planned to stop sharing their credentials after learning about its issues in the security unit. Of the respondents that shared passwords,

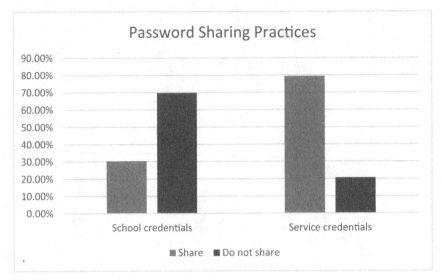

Fig. 4. Password sharing practices

59% indicated that they intended to stop sharing credentials, while 41% stated that they would continue with their prior practices. We find these numbers to be promising and believe that using different instructional design strategies informed by augmented cognition has the potential for increased impact on behaviors.

4 Emergent Study

4.1 Participants

Additional research emerged from the results of the initial study. It was conducted with 25 undergraduate computer science students enrolled in a Human-Computer Interaction (HCI) course. HCI covers concepts and methodologies from human factors, psychology and software engineering that address ergonomic, cognitive, and social factors in the design and evaluation of human-computer systems. The course meets synchronously online once a week for class discussions and on-line asynchronous sessions to work on group projects. Each week students submit answers for the weekly discussions prior to each class meeting. During the class, they actively participate in class discussions on the posted questions and after class they submit their reflections on the class discussion by the end of the day.

4.2 Questions and Reflections

Previous results suggested that participants valued convenience and that it was an important factor contributing to their actual behavior for the following topics: remembering their passwords, credential stuffing (reusing their credentials), sharing their credentials, and multifactor authentication. The researchers examined how these topics naturally emerged during the posts prior to the class discussion, during the discussion itself and in their reflective posts at the end of the class day. During the fourth week of the semester, readings from Norman, D. [13] were assigned. They read chapter 3, "Knowledge in the Head and in the World." This chapter includes, among other things, general ideas and several examples concerning computer security. The assigned question that they were required to answer was: Explain what Norman means when he stated, "Make something too secure, and it becomes less secure." The class discussion was related to implementation issues concerning privacy and security.

4.3 Results

Using their rational or reflective cognition, the students were aware of recommended safe password protection and multifactor authentication practices. However, the posted answers to the discussion questions, the class discussion and the reflection comments indicated that their behavior depended more on convenience than on their rational implementation of safe cybersecurity practices. The initial posts for 24 of the 25 students posted something about passwords and how best practices were not routinely followed (Fig. 5).

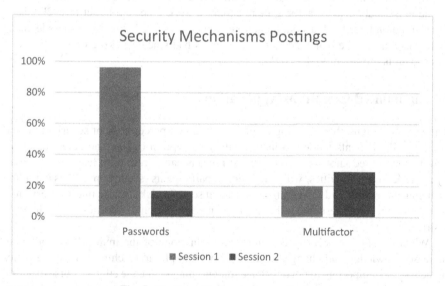

Fig. 5. Postings about security mechanisms

For example one student posted the following comment:

We value convenience more than anything. This is the reason why we create the same password for every website, so that we don't have to write them down everywhere, or remember a handful of passwords. This leads to a less secure person because if one account is compromised, then all accounts could be compromised. [sic]

Another student said:

The internet is a mess of credentials all of which are supposed to be unique (but almost never are in practice.) In my job, every time there is a large data breach, we will search through all the exposed accounts for any campus email addresses and disable any that used the same password for their university account as the exposed website. This usually is not more than 100 or so accounts for each data breach, but almost all accounts used the same password for both the exposed site and their university account. In 2019 when Chegg had a data breach, we disabled thousands of university users' accounts. It is clear in practice almost no one follows internet password security recommendations.

Password issues were only mentioned by 4 of the 24 students in their final posting, a dramatic decrease from the almost unanimous initial posting.

In the initial posting, only 5 of the 25 students discussed multifactor authentication, however, it was mentioned during the class discussion and mentioned by 7 of the 24 students in the final posting at the end of the class day. One of these students posted: After discussing what Norman says, the one comment that I found interesting the most is about two-factor authentication or 2FA. One said about how 2FA is required on their bank account and how tedious it can be. This tediousness leads to checking on the bank account less which is bad since checking on your bank account is important to do. [sic]

5 Augmented Cognition Applications

These studies highlighted the impact of instruction on perceptions of security risk and practices. Participants tended to increase their perception of risk and actual practices based on increased knowledge. The largest impacts came from mini lectures supported by active learning activities, which influenced participants' security practices including changing passwords and informing others about security risks. These findings serve as a foundation for future research utilizing augmented cognition to inform security-focused instruction.

When developing security education programs, one of the major challenges is to increase knowledge and change behaviors. For example, in teaching computing ethics in security, it is important to not only have students understand the ethical course of action but to make the ethical decision when the issue comes up in the "real world." Therefore, highlighting the mix of lecture and active learning opportunities may be critical to influence real-world decisions. Therefore, we propose augmented cognition approaches in future studies to better understand these factors and improve behaviors aligned with security-oriented education. Using time-based data aligned with on-line activities can help researchers to identify additional challenge and thought-process factors when refining learning opportunities for students. These time-based mechanisms can be used with a range of activities including tests, simulation assignments, and practical activities.

Human Computer Interaction (HCI) is a field that analyzes how users interact with information. Changes in psychophysiological signals of the human body are highly revealing of cognitive and emotional responses to stimuli, capturing even subtle and transient events. Psychophysiological tools, such as heart rate and skin conductance, can be very helpful in the characterization of emotional responses during human information interaction. Cognitive functioning activates various body systems such as the brain, facial brow muscles, heart and electrodermal systems. Various relationships between cognition and psycho-physiological signal change have been studied and documented. For example, some signals have been found to reflect such cognitive experiences as variation in mental workload [11], shift in attentive focus, and experiences of emotional affect such as disgust [14] Future research plans are to explore various psychophysiological correlates of cognitive interaction with cybersecurity events.

Acknowledgements. This material is based upon work supported by the National Science Foundation (NSF) under Grant No. 1662487. Any opinions, findings, and conclusions or recommendations expressed in this material are those of the authors and do not necessarily reflect the views of the NSF.

References

1. Adams, A., Sasse, M.A.: Users are not the enemy. Commun. ACM **42**(12), 40–46 (1999)
2. Andriotis, P., Tryfonas, T., Oikonomou, G.: Complexity metrics and user strength perceptions of the pattern-lock graphical authentication method. In: Tryfonas, T., Askoxylakis, I. (eds.) HAS 2014. LNCS, vol. 8533, pp. 115–126. Springer, Cham (2014). https://doi.org/10.1007/978-3-319-07620-1_11
3. Choong, Y.-Y.: A cognitive-behavioral framework of user password management lifecycle. In: Tryfonas, T., Askoxylakis, I. (eds.) HAS 2014. LNCS, vol. 8533, pp. 127–137. Springer, Cham (2014). https://doi.org/10.1007/978-3-319-07620-1_12
4. Colnago, J., et al.: "It's not actually that horrible": exploring adoption of two-factor authentication at a university. In: Proceedings of the 2018 CHI Conference on Human Factors in Computing Systems, pp. 1–11 (2018). https://doi.org/10.1145/3173574.3174030
5. Feng, L., Cho, K.L., Song, C., Xu, C., Jin, X.: Brain password: a secure and truly cancelable brain biometrics for smart headwear. In: The 16th Annual International Conference, MobiSys 2018 (2018)
6. Gao, X., Yang, Y., Liu, C., Mitropoulos, C., Lindqvist, J., Oulasvirta, A.: Forgetting of passwords: ecological theory and data. In: 27th USENIX Security Symposium (USENIX Security 2018), pp. 221–238 (2018)
7. Kahneman, D.: Thinking, Fast and Slow. Macmillan (2011)
8. Karray, F., Alemzadeh, M., Saleh, J.A., Arab, M.N.: Human-computer interaction: overview on state of the art. Int. J. Smart Sens. Intell. Syst. **1**(1), 137–159 (2008). https://doi.org/10.21307/ijssis-2017-283
9. Loos, L.A., Ogawa, M.-B., Crosby, M.E.: Cognitive variability factors and passphrase selection. In: Schmorrow, D.D., Fidopiastis, C.M. (eds.) HCII 2020. LNCS (LNAI), vol. 12197, pp. 383–394. Springer, Cham (2020). https://doi.org/10.1007/978-3-030-50439-7_26
10. Marky, K., et al.: "Nah, it's just annoying!" a deep dive into user perceptions of two-factor authentication. ACM Trans. Comput.-Hum. Interact. **29**(5), 32, Article no. 43 (2022). https://doi.org/10.1145/3503514
11. Mogire, N., Minas, R.K., Crosby, M.E.: Probing for psycho-physiological correlates of cognitive interaction with cybersecurity events. In: Schmorrow, D.D., Fidopiastis, C.M. (eds.) HCII 2020. LNCS (LNAI), vol. 12197, pp. 405–415. Springer, Cham (2020). https://doi.org/10.1007/978-3-030-50439-7_28

12. Nield, D.: How to Unlock Your iPhone With a Security Key. Wired (2023). https://www.wired.com/story/how-to-unlock-iphone-physical-security-key/
13. Norman, D.: The Design of Everyday Things. Revised and Expanded Edition. Basic Books (2013)
14. Picard, R.: Automating the recognition of stress and emotion: from lab to real-world impact. Multimed. IEEE. **23**, 3–7 (2016). https://doi.org/10.1109/MMUL.2016.38
15. Posner, M.I., Snyder, C.R.R.: Attention and cognitive control. In: Solso, R.L. (ed.) Information Processing and Cognition: The Loyola Symposium, pp. 55–85. Lawrence Erlbaum Associates, Hillsdale (1975)
16. Thompson, D.: Why the Age of American Progress Ended: Invention Alone Can't Change the World; What Matters is What Happens Next. The Atlantic (2023)
17. Zhang, Y., Monrose, F., Reiter, M.K.: The security of modern password expiration: an algorithmic framework and empirical analysis. In: Proceedings of the 17th ACM Conference on Computer and Communications Security, pp. 176–186. ACM (2010)

CyberEscape Approach to Advancing Hard and Soft Skills in Cybersecurity Education

Rūta Pirta-Dreimane[1]([✉])[iD], Agnė Brilingaitė[2][iD], Evita Roponena[1][iD],
Karen Parish[3][iD], Janis Grabis[1][iD], Ricardo Gregorio Lugo[4][iD],
and Martiņš Bonders[1][iD]

[1] Institute of Information Technology, Riga Technical University, Riga, Latvia
{Ruta.Pirta-Dreimane,Evita.Roponena,Grabis,Martins.Bonders}@rtu.lv
[2] Institute of Computer Science, Vilnius University, Vilnius, Lithuania
Agne.Brilingaite@mif.vu.lt
[3] Department of Information Security and Communication Technology,
Norwegian University of Science and Technology, Gjøvik, Norway
Karen.Parish@ntnu.no
[4] Faculty of Health, Welfare and Organisation, Østfold University College,
Halden, Norway
Ricardo.G.Lugo@hiof.no

Abstract. Incorporating gamification elements and innovative approaches in training and educational programs are promising for addressing cybersecurity knowledge gaps. Cybersecurity training should consider a combination of hard and soft skills to deal with the diversity of cyber incidents. Therefore, this research aims to investigate if soft skills such as communication and collaboration enhances students' performance in practical task execution and if the CyberEscape approach promotes students engagement and self-efficacy.

This paper presents a cybersecurity game CyberEscape based on the intervention mapping methodology previously defined in the research. A virtualised infrastructure simulating the business environment works as a hybrid escape room. Physical resources and prepared information materials complement the game to support the scenario and ensure student engagement. The work employs a multiple-methods research approach. Participants filled out questionnaires in the pre-event and post-execution phases. Additionally, the participants were involved in small group semi-structured interviews. Results of the pilot study show a positive impact on student competence improvement and increased interest in cybersecurity.

Keywords: Cybersecurity education · Incident response · Incident management training · Crisis communication and collaboration · Gamification · Escape room design

© The Author(s) 2023
D. D. Schmorrow and C. M. Fidopiastis (Eds.): HCII 2023, LNAI 14019, pp. 441–459, 2023.
https://doi.org/10.1007/978-3-031-35017-7_28

1   Introduction

Cyber crises require deep technical knowledge, but in addition general skills and behavioural traits are essential to ensure good team collaboration, responsibility distribution, and efficient work in problem-solving during incident management processes. Escape rooms have recently become popular in higher education as they provide an engaging way to develop students' competences [21]. Escape rooms have been used in group exercises to build critical thinking and problem-solving skills and to enhance students' communication and collaboration [12, 26]. Incident management is a vital capability of companies, as it helps to ensure company readiness to respond to cyberthreats and minimise their negative impact effectively. Incident management processes might involve several roles, such as incident commander, incident responders, forensics investigators, communication leads and legal counsels. Technical expertise, communication, analytical, problem-solving, and collaboration skills are also essential in incident response. Behavioural aspects also play a significant role in incident management as the nature of incident response duties can be stressful and emotionally challenging [3]. Self-regulation and the ability to stay calm and focused can enhance the performance of cybersecurity specialists. Cybersecurity education programs must therefore consider the above dimensions to ensure specialists are prepared to handle incidents during cyber-attacks and ensure the continued operations of ICT systems.

This paper presents the CyberEscape approach to advancing hard and soft skills in cybersecurity education. The CyberEscape approach combines student-centred education methods, such as gamification [33], problem-based learning [19] and flipped classroom principles [14]. This pilot study applies the CyberEscape approach for IT bachelor level students. It considers crisis communication and crisis collaboration along with technical competences in incident management scenarios. In planning the education program, the design science problem-solving method [18] is used which enables multi-perspective examination of the problem and solution design. The pilot study is designed using the ADVANCES methodology [29] applying the competence model, course design process, and learning & training environment design. A wide range of on-site and online tools are used in the pilot study. The virtual laboratory and incident management tools promote students' hard skills. The collaboration tools support teamwork. The on-site environment is enriched with different game elements, such as Lego figures and posters, to promote student engagement.

The main objectives of the study are: (1) to investigate if communication, collaboration and team dynamics enhances students' performance in practical task execution and (2) to evaluate if the CyberEscape approach promotes students engagement and self-efficacy.

The paper is structured as follows. Section 2 reviews related work as a research background, and Sect. 3 presents the research methodology. The CyberEscape design, including competences, scenario, and setup environment, are presented in Sect. 4, and pilot study results are covered in Sect. 5. Section 6 provides conclusions and future research directions.

2   Background

In recent years, several studies using gamification methods for cybersecurity education and training have grown as these methods show positive outcomes. Cybersecurity-related tasks are adaptable for gamification that helps to engage students, develop interest in cybersecurity, and motivate them to solve tasks [27].

Various gamified educational tools are available online for cybersecurity training, for example, Cyber Threat Defender, CyberCIEGE, Cyber Protect, and Network Defense Training Game (NDTG). In the digitalized table-top card game Cyber Threat Defender, players can defend their assets and attack their opponents within the time limit [4]. CyberCIEGE [34] is another game-based training tool, but it is a 3D simulation of an office space where a player can interact with virtual employees while implementing security policies. The game provides different scenarios with multiple solutions and functionality to monitor the players' progress. Cyber Protect [11] encourages players to purchase and deploy tools for network protection against attackers. The NDTG [1] cybersecurity training platform includes cybersecurity scenarios in which players must defend the network. Most of these tools require technical knowledge to play. We drew inspiration from these different tools to develop our own approach.

Malone et al. [23] presented the framework Riposte, a browser-based game applicable to cybersecurity education. The framework enables the development of tasks with progressive difficulty and uses two styles of play: player versus player (PvP) and player versus environment (PvE). However, it is executed in the online environment with no possibility of observing team dynamics or improving students' soft skills. The study also highlighted that students interested in gamification before the case study achieved better learning outcomes.

Cybersecurity training often includes Capture the Flag (CTF) exercises. However, due to the informal nature of the CTF, it is challenging to map the competences defined by security experts [35]. In the jeopardy CTFs, the most common format, the player chooses the challenges with different point values from provided categories. The CyberEscape integrates a similar approach. Švábenský et al. [35] concluded that CTFs games mainly improve data and network security knowledge. However, technical competences are not enough for the player in real life cybersecurity challenges, where team collaboration and a calm mind during stressful situations are as important as technical knowledge.

The escape room game format has been introduced previously for educational gamification. The escapeED framework [7] provides a development methodology and highlights six core elements of an educational escape room: participants, objectives, theme, puzzles, equipment, and evaluation. The participant-centred escape room has objectives, defined as expected outcomes, within some theme as a context. Participants complete puzzles associated with the theme, and the equipment creates the room environment. The evaluation explains how the participants performed the puzzle-related tasks according to the objectives. These six core elements were also used to create the CyberEscape game setup.

Debello et al. [9] describe how they transformed their usual Cybersecurity study courses into gamified exercises proposing them as Escape the Classroom tasks. The task setup was changed compared to the traditional approach used in their university, as they proposed a strategy allowing students to compete with each other within the given time limit.

Virtual escape rooms are a popular approach for cybersecurity education. The CySecEscape 2.0. [22] virtual escape room created based on a physical escape room has gained mainly positive feedback from the participants. It includes puzzles addressing different topics, e.g., password hygiene, source code security, phishing, and identity theft. The ARI 3D [10] virtual escape room consists of a tutorial and three game levels including different tasks designed as mini-games, e.g., bad practices, password security, Internet fraud, and network security. The focus of both escape rooms is on improving cybersecurity awareness and not mimicking a real-life cybersecurity environment. These virtual and individually played games do not allow tracking the change in soft skill development.

The escape rooms can also improve information privacy competences. For example, Papaioannou et al. [28] developed an exciting scenario where the guardian angel helps the player with tasks. However, it has a dark end (the suicide of the main character) and this could be psychologically harmful to some players.

Beguin et al. [2] designed two on-site escape rooms—for the defense scenario (participants try to mitigate the vulnerabilities found in the room) and the attack scenario(participants play the hacker role and try to steal information). The students accepted this approach positively and stated that it improved their knowledge more than the same-length lecture could. However, there needs to be evidence of how useful the approach is for cybersecurity education. Another study [25] focuses on the deciphering and cybersecurity-unrelated tasks in the on-site escape room game. However, the researchers could not conclude whether the game engaged the participants' interests in cybersecurity.

The reviewed studies highlighted the importance of defining game objectives, understanding participant needs, and designing evaluation strategies in educational game development. The game should consider the time required to solve the tasks, needed tools, and background information.

Most reviewed studies on gamification applications in cybersecurity training described the design of virtual games played individually or in a team. The main advantage of this approach is that players can be in a different room, in the same room, or a specific place while participating in the game. However, this feature leads to the main disadvantage of virtual educational games—it is complicated to evaluate the player's soft skills essential for competent cybersecurity specialists.

All reviewed studies mainly focus on cyberthreat detection or mitigation. We contribute to the development of the field by adding additional incident management steps. In addition, we focus not only on the technical skill development, but also soft skills and collaboration. In this way we provide scenario training by mimicking a simplified cybersecurity work environment where the participant identifies the possible incidents in the fictional company and also learns how to classify and report them correctly.

3   Methodology

In planning the CyberEscape game, the work used the design science problem-solving method [18]. It is a systematic approach, connecting practical problems with domain-specific solutions by conducting multiple studies. The investigated challenge is integrating multi-dimensional areas in the education programs for better human performance in cyberspace [30].

Design science research seeks to enhance human knowledge by creating innovative artifacts: construct (chooses language for problem and solution definition and communication), model (uses constructs to represent a real-world problem and its solution), method (defines processes and provides guidance on how to solve problems), and instantiation (shows how the construct, models or methods can be implemented in a working system) [18].

The design science research process consists of three cycles to create one or many of the previously listed artifact types: relevance cycle, design cycle, and rigor cycle [17]. The relevance cycle usually starts with the design science research using the environment context. It provides research requirements to improve the knowledge base and solve the research problem. The design cycle includes artifact development and evaluation.

As part of the evaluation process we employ a social science research methodology with a multiple-methods approach that includes both post-positivistic and social constructionist constructs in the research design [20]. This approach to research design has the purpose of expanding the scope of the study as both quantitative and qualitative methods are used to explore the research objectives [15]. The first and second research objectives were addressed using a quantitative approach to measuring the students' performance, communication, collaboration, group dynamics self-efficacy and motivation. The participants completed the questionnaires during the pre-work and post-work phases of the teaching session.

In addition, to address the second objective, the research team adopted a qualitative approach using semi-structured group interviews to focus on the following: the student experiences of engagement during the practical CyberEscape, the student's perceptions of how the pre-exercise training (flipped learning approach) enhanced their self-efficacy. The design science framework was adapted from [18] to conduct the study (see Fig. 1). This study is the first design cycle of planned research aiming to evaluate the overall approach and find the improvements for the next design cycle. The intention is to determine if there is a need to repeat the relevance cycle. The rigor cycle supports the research with prior knowledge and ensures that the solution is innovative. Each cycle can be repeated several times if it is needed to achieve the best results.

Interviews with participants were conducted according to the established Code of Ethics for students, academic and administrative personnel of Riga Technical university (RTU) and the Code of Ethics of scientists published by the Charter of Latvian Academy of Sciences. All ethical principles were assured, and students' consent was collected as part of the registration form. The signs of ongoing photography were posted in the event area. All participants had the possibility to leave the game and stop the interviews at any time.

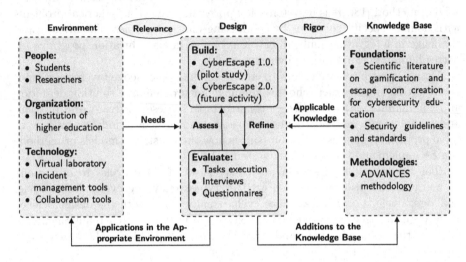

Fig. 1. Design science approach for CyberEscape (adapted from [18])

Figure 1 presents the environment, design and knowledge base of the CyberEscape approach. The knowledge base used to create the CyberEscape game are formed from the related literature on applications of the gamification for the cybersecurity education (see Sect. 2), security guidelines, standards [6,13], and ADVANCES methodology [29] guidelines. ADVANCES methodology is the foundation of the game design. It suggests to integrate different dimensions of cybersecurity competences into the education programs, considering the needs of study program participants, the context of real live cybersecurity scenarios, the associated work roles and tasks.

4   CyberEscape Design

In the game scenario design, the ADVANCES methodology [29] is applied as guidelines for the competence model, course design process, and learning and training environment design.

4.1   Competence Model

The core of the competence model is the work role *Cyber Incident Responder* defined by the European Union Agency for Cybersecurity (ENISA). Cyber Incident Responder [13] has duties to "monitor the organisation's cybersecurity state, handle incidents during cyber-attacks and assure the continued operations of ICT systems". The role has several tasks, such as: (1) Identify, analyse, mitigate and communicate cybersecurity incidents, (2) Assess and manage technical vulnerabilities, (3) Document incident results analysis and incident handling actions, (4) Cooperate with Secure Operation Centres (SOCs) and Computer Security Incident Response Teams (CSIRTs), and (5) Cooperate with key personnel for reporting of security incidents according to applicable legal framework. A wide set of competences are required for effective defined tasks execution (see Fig. 2).

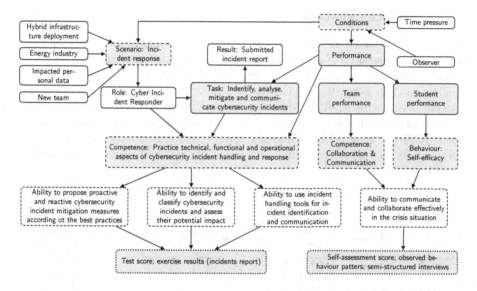

Fig. 2. CyberEscape competence model (a fragment)

The competence model of the learning scenario is prepared following the recommendations of the ADVANCES methodology [29], integrating hard and soft skills and expected behavior.

The ENISA defines main technical and operational competences, such as: (1) Technical, functional and operational aspects of cybersecurity incident handling and response; (2) Work on operating systems, servers, clouds and relevant infrastructures; (3) Incident handling communication procedures; (4) Computing networks and operating systems security, and (4) Incident handling recommendations and best practices.

Psychology experts and related industry and research studies [5,32] distinguish vital soft competences to promote specialist performance in the incident response: (1) Teamwork (collaboration); (2) Communication, presentation and reporting and (3) Working under pressure. Incident management can elicit a wide range of emotions, and cognitive and behavioral changes, such as increased stress levels and difficulty concentrating. Thus, not only individual competences, but also behavioral aspects play a significant role in effective task execution.

Self-regulation, confidence and adaptability may raise individual performance in crisis situations.

The hard and soft skills and expected behavior are the basis for learning outcomes of the scenario: (1) Ability to identify and classify cybersecurity incidents and assess their potential impact; (2) Ability to proactively and reactively mitigate cybersecurity incidents; (3) Ability to communicate confidently; (4) Ability to use incident handling tools for incidents identification, analysis, mitigation and communication; (5) Ability to collaborate effectively in a critical situation.

4.2   Game Scenario Overview

The learning scenario reflects the lifecycle of the information security incident management based on National Institute of Standards and Technology (NIST) incident handling recommendations [6]. The NIST suggests four interconnected incident management stages: (1) preparation for an incident, (2) detection and analysis of an incident, (3) incident discovery and recovery, and (4) post-incident analysis. The students take the role of Computer Security Incident Response Team (CSIRT) in a fictional mid-size energy sector company, and they must perform specific tasks across information security incident management lifestyle (see Fig. 3).

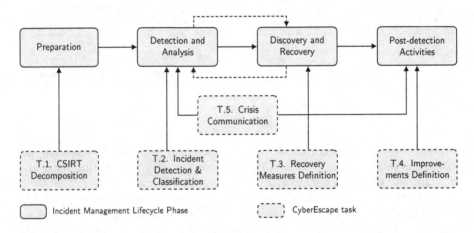

Fig. 3. CyberEscape tasks

Preparation for the incident requires creating an incident management policy, incident handling procedures, communication plan, team structure and acquiring the necessary resources and tools. The first task of the students (T.1.) is to formalize their roles and responsibilities to ensure the CSIRT function in the fictional company. The hybrid exercise incorporates both table-top exercises and virtual exercises that require definition of roles and responsibilities, taking into consideration the team size.

According to NIST [6], incident detection and analysis include 1) the definition of possible attack vectors, 2) incident detection using various sources, such as security software alerts, people, and logs, 3) incident analysis and validation, 4) incident documentation, 5) incident prioritisation, and 6) incident notification. Based on NIST the second task of the students (T.2.) is therefore to identify three incidents placed in a room: logical incident, physical incident, and organizational incident, and to classify them by specifying the incident name, short description, type (logical, physical, or organizational), category (incident subtype) and its impact (low, medium, high, or critical). The students used video materials to learn how to correctly fill out the provided incident classification table.

The third incident management stage is incident discovery and recovery. The phase includes incident containment, evidence gathering and recovery, and post-activities to gather incident knowledge and data to prevent those threats in the future. The third task of the students (T.3.) is to define the vulnerabilities that lead to the incident and to describe the immediate incident prevention actions. The fourth task (T.4.) is to describe actions to minimize identified vulnerability in the future, and it is associated with the last phase of the incident management life-cycle, i.e., post detection activities.

Crisis communication is an essential part of incident management, and it is integrated in several incident management life-cycle phases. The incident communication plan and communication channels (e.g., email, website, phone call, in person) are defined in the incident preparation phase to help CSIRT report the incidents to the appropriate roles such as CIO, head of information security, system owner, and others. The actual crisis communication is ongoing through incident detection and analysis, discovery and recovery and post-incident phases. The last task for the students (T.5.) is to create an incident report, choose appropriate communication channel, and report recipients.

4.3 Physical and Digital Environment

The game was executed in physical rooms and participants used a computer to access the virtual laboratory and office tools (e-mail, online collaboration tools). Students were asked to watch 5 learning videos before the practical tasks execution. Also, supplementary training materials were placed on the E-learning system. Printed instructions and a Lego corner (see Fig. 4) also provide the necessary game puzzle parts. Each group of students was located in a separate room in one geographical location and monitored by an observer.

The students were presented with a fictional company *Jurpils HES* (Jurpils Hydroelectric Power Plant) that contained a hydropower plant, a customer service shop, and a website. The fictional company maintains its ICCT services and is not relying on third-parties. The students received tasks and clues in the form of notes or emails from different employees in the company, e.g., the IT department manager, HR, communication department manager, and IT support. The main goal for each students team was to find hidden clues and use their knowledge to solve all tasks. Each team had an email address created for

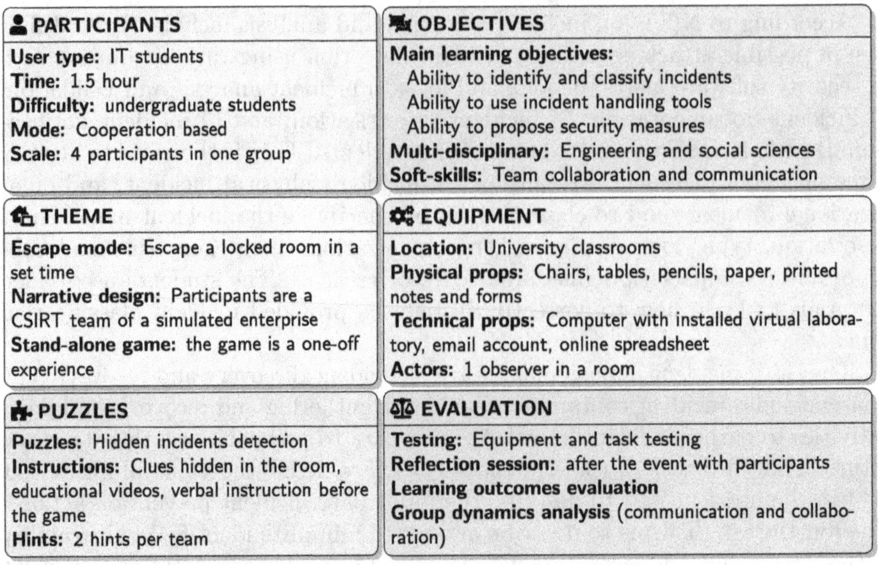

🧑 PARTICIPANTS	🎯 OBJECTIVES

User type: IT students
Time: 1.5 hour
Difficulty: undergraduate students
Mode: Cooperation based
Scale: 4 participants in one group
	Main learning objectives:
	    Ability to identify and classify incidents
	    Ability to use incident handling tools
	    Ability to propose security measures
	Multi-disciplinary: Engineering and social sciences
	Soft-skills: Team collaboration and communication

🪴 THEME	⚙️ EQUIPMENT
Escape mode: Escape a locked room in a set time **Narrative design:** Participants are a CSIRT team of a simulated enterprise **Stand-alone game:** the game is a one-off experience	**Location:** University classrooms **Physical props:** Chairs, tables, pencils, paper, printed notes and forms **Technical props:** Computer with installed virtual laboratory, email account, online spreadsheet **Actors:** 1 observer in a room
🧩 PUZZLES	⚖️ EVALUATION
Puzzles: Hidden incidents detection **Instructions:** Clues hidden in the room, educational videos, verbal instruction before the game **Hints:** 2 hints per team	**Testing:** Equipment and task testing **Reflection session:** after the event with participants **Learning outcomes evaluation** **Group dynamics analysis** (communication and collaboration)

Fig. 4. CyberEscape game setup (adapted from [7])

event purposes and was used to send additional information. Table 1 contains a brief description of the hidden incidents of the CyberEscape.

Table 1. Description of the hidden incidents

Incident name	Incident type	Identification source
Denial of service attack	Logical	Network log file analysis, situation description
Data loss (natural disaster)	Physical	Physical company model, situation description
Phishing	Organizational	Spam email, situation description

The provided notes contain the situation description but are insufficient to identify the incidents listed in Table 1. Therefore, participants needed additional sources to validate if the incident is an actual incident. They had to reconstruct the physical company model using Lego pieces hidden in the room to determine that the company data storage and server room are in a flooded river area.

The spam email contained a form asking the receiver to fill in the sensitive data and was sent to each team. The organizers intended to see if anyone filled it out and planed to use it to initiate the scenario of the phishing campaign.

The students were offered the opportunity to use the Wireshark tool for network log analysis of the *Jurpils HES* website in the virtual laboratory to identify a Denial-of-Service (DoS) attack. This incident required performing an additional task to decrypt a password using a hidden key for the virtual machine.

The virtual laboratory was a central component of the CyberEscape game. Virtualization technologies enabled the development of a controlled environment to simulate DoS attacks safely. Moreover, this environment could be easily scaled according to the number of students. The CyberEscape utilized bare metal virtualization and nested virtualization technologies (see Fig 5). Bare metal virtualization uses the open-source Proxmox Virtual Environment (Proxmox VE) as a hypervisor based on the KVM hypervisor and Linux containers (LXC). Proxmox VE supports all the infrastructure necessary for DoS simulation, e.g. virtual machines, containers, virtual networks, network rate limit, and centralized management of DoS scripts. The DoS attack was performed against the fictional company environment developed using nested virtualization. Each student group had an Ubuntu Desktop 22.04 virtual machine with the Apache web server deployed in a dedicated nested Proxmox VE hypervisor. Any remote communication with the virtual machine was lost during a DoS attack, and services like VNC, SSH were unavailable. Therefore, nested virtualization enabled direct connection to the virtual machine from the Proxmox VE hypervisor console.

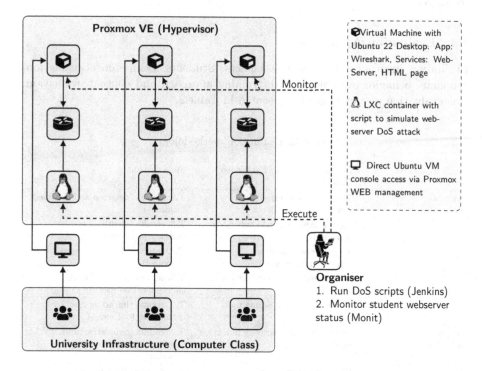

Fig. 5. Virtual laboratory architecture

CyberEscape participants were able to trace and analyze this DoS attack using the network protocol analyzer Wireshark. They were expected to block the attack using a virtual machine hypervisor firewall that simulates the company's main firewall in real life. DoS scripts were executed from specially created LXC containers. Each LXC container attacked the specified hypervisor and the Ubuntu Apache Web server.

The organizers managed the DoS attack from a separate virtual machine with the open-source automation server Jenkins installed. Using Jenkins, for each student group, it was possible to configure individual automatically executed scripts to perform different scenarios and set attack parameters, e.g. at specific and predefined time intervals.

The Hping3 network tool was used to simulate web server SYN Flood Attack—the most common and effective way to attack a Web server and make its services unavailable. The attack also made the entire virtual machine network adapter and all protocols unavailable. The open-source process supervision tool Monit enabled monitoring of the progress of the attack and the effectiveness of blocking.

The architecture is a completely isolated environment and could not harm the external infrastructure of the university. Users could access it from any place via the Internet, and the attack automatization enabled implementation of dynamic scenarios.

4.4 Evaluation Approach

Evaluation incorporates three key aspects: Students' competence evaluation, Students' behavior evaluation, and Training approach and content evaluation. The evaluation methodology is presented in Table 2.

Table 2. Evaluation methodology

Evaluation Goal	Learning Outcome/Evaluation Criteria	Measurement
Students competence	To identify and classify cybersecurity incidents	T.2. results (detected and classified incidents)
	To reactively mitigate cybersecurity incidents	T.3. results (identified incident reaction measures)
	To proactively mitigate cybersecurity incidents	T.4. results (identified improvement measures)
	To communicate confidently in a crisis situation	T.5. results (prepared crisis communication message)
	To use incident handling tools	T.2. results (infrastructure monitoring tool usage)
Students behavior	To collaborate effectively in a crisis situation	T.1. results (team structure), TWLQ results & Group interaction observation
Training approach	Engagement increase	Students feedback results
	Competence increase	Students feedback results

Students' competences are evaluated by considering execution results of the practical tasks and self-assessment before and after the CyberEscape game. Students' behavior is evaluated by team assessment that help to identify factors that may influence communication and performance both at the individual and team level. The Team Workload Questionnaire (TWLQ) [31] was used to measure workload demands in the teams. The TWLQ Items are scored on an 11-point Likert scale (range: very low - very high) with higher scores indicating higher levels of subjective workload. The TWLQ has two dimensions, the Teamwork component (communication, coordination, team performance monitoring) and Task-Team component (time-share, team emotion, team support). The TWLQ shows good reliability on all subscales (Cronbach's a ¿.70) and also for this research (Teamwork Cronbach's $a = .673$; Task-team Cronbach's $a = .626$). Statistical analysis was done with JASP version .16.1. All variables were not normally distributed, therefore non-parametric analyses are used. Alpha levels for hypothesis testing were set at the 0.05 level. A multiple linear regression was computed with the TWLQ entered as predictors and the score of the teams as the dependent variable. For the training approach and content evaluation students feedback results were captured (questionnaire, interviews).

5   CyberEscape Delivery Results

The CyberEscape game event was organized for bachelor students from different study levels (1st-3rd year). They were invited to participate and compete in the CyberEscape. Five groups of students applied with four students in each.

The study included a quantitative and qualitative assessment according to the evaluation methodology presented in Table 2.

5.1   Objective 1: Communication, Collaboration and Group Dynamics

In the interviews, CyberEscape participants reflected that team collaboration is a critical success factor in the incident reaction and overall the game have increased relevant competences. Meanwhile, the longer team cooperation experience is required to work effectively as a team.

Students demonstrated the ability to solve practical tasks. The average tasks completion score was 60%, the best result was 80% of total 100%. The result is perceived as good, given the students' low competences level in IT incident management prior to the assignment, as well as the limited time of the task execution (1.5 h for all five tasks).

Students self-assessment showed improvement in all competences included in the learning scenario (see Fig. 6). Meanwhile, the competence level still is improvable, as the CyberEscape was a "stand-alone" game and the students' previous knowledge level in cybersecurity was low.

CyberEscape was most helpful in improving the following knowledge: (1) Incident reaction roles and (2) Incident handling tools. Incident reaction roles

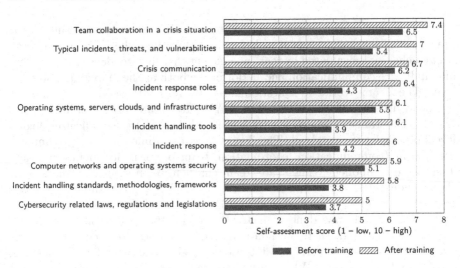

Fig. 6. Student competences self-assessment

were presented in the learning video, supplemented by the NIST Incident management guide [6], that recommended the structure of the team. The incident management team setup was integrated also in the practical task (T.1). Incident handling tools were used in the practical tasks as part of the virtual laboratory (T.2, T.3).

CyberEscape was less helpful in improving the following knowledge: (1) Crisis communication and (2) Operating systems, servers, clouds and infrastructures. Crisis communication recommendations were included in the learning video, supplemented by the A Guide to Effective Incident Management Communications [24]. Crisis communication was integrated also in the practical task (T.5). However, it is important to note that students rated their ability to communicate effectively in a crisis situation relatively highly before the training, although they admitted in interviews that they had not put these skills into practice. The slight increase in competence may therefore be due to an overly high initial assessment. Operating systems, servers, clouds and infrastructures was assumed as prerequisite of the training, no additional learning materials were provided. In order to complete the tasks, coordinated collaboration within the team is required. Each team nominated a leader, mostly servant-leadership style was observed what is one of the suggested leadership styles in the cybersecurity [8]. Still the observations showed that the coordination of the tasks can be improved for effective tasks execution. Teams with previous experience of working together demonstrated more efficient execution of tasks what is a common pattern in teams collaboration. This indicates the importance of teamwork requiring exercises in the cybersecurity education.

The TWLQ results showed that participants rated their team collaboration as good (8.6 of 10 points). Also the communication effectiveness was rated as good (8 points). However the teams have faced some difficulties, such as time share demand, e.g., share and manage time between task-work (work done individually) and team-work (work done as a team). Descriptive statistics and correlations (ρ) for the outcome score and workload items can be found in Table 3.

Table 3. Descriptive statistics and correlations (ρ)

Score	Mean	SD	1	2	3	4	5	6	7
Communication Demand	31.98	21.15	–						
Coordination Demand	8.00	1.92	.125	–					
Team Performance	6.32	2.50	.527*	.519*	–				
Monitoring Demand	4.11	2.58	.274	.311	.480*				
Time Share Demand	5.79	3.14	.581*	.033	.520*	.450	–		
Team Support	4.37	3.22	.147	−.170	.096	.300	.519*	–	
Team Emotion Demand	3.05	2.97	.366	.423	.346	.330	.605**	.253	–

$^*p < .05, ^{**}p < .01, ^{***}p < 0.001$

To see the influence of team workloads on performance, hierarchical multiple regressions were performed where Team Workloads were entered in the first step and Task-team workloads entered in the second step. Team workloads (Communication $\beta = -.096$, Cooperation $\beta = .480$, Team Performance Monitoring $\beta = .445$) could positively predict team performance in the exercise ($R^2 = .487$, $F = 4.11$, $p = .030$) but task-team workloads factors (team support $\beta = .241$, team emotional demand $\beta = -.291$, timeshare demands $\beta = .311$) were not significant in influencing performance ($\Delta R^2 = .172$, $F = 1.69$, $p = .233$).

5.2   Objective 2: Engagement and Self-efficacy

When evaluating if the CyberEscape approach promotes student engagement and self-efficacy, the results from the questionnaires reveal that student engagement in the CyberEscape was high. Nearly 90% of students stated that the CyberEscape game had increased their interest in cybersecurity. This result is supported by the interview data where students stated that they were interested in similar games in the future and enquired about further education possibilities to study cybersecurity. All student groups admitted that the game was interesting and had a good atmosphere. In addition, students reported increased self-efficacy and rated the CyberEscape higher than the theoretical videos. 88.8% of students agreed that the CyberEscape had increased their knowledge of IT incident management. Meanwhile, the importance of the videos was acknowledged by 61.3% of students to be helpful. In the interviews, students suggested that the videos should include more technical tutorials, as currently the main focus was on operational, leadership and general competences [16] related knowledge units. However, the flipped learning approach was evaluated positively. Students suggested that the including subtitles and English terms in the videos would increase their perception. Students also mentioned that they found the phishing incident distracting from other tasks because of the spam email. However, it was one of their tasks and was included to show possible situations of real life. Moreover, one group stated that they preferred traditional task presentation over the more active CyberEscape game approach. They may prefer to have a more passive approach, however, further investigation is needed to explore why.

6   Conclusions and Future Work

The main objectives of the study were: (1) to investigate if communication, collaboration and team dynamics enhances students' performance in practical task execution; (2) to evaluate if the CyberEscape approach promotes students engagement and self-efficacy. Using an escape room approach to gamification in cybersecurity education promotes field-specific competence development, integrating hard and soft skills. The approach stimulates creative and critical thinking and requires efficient communication and collaboration in solving complex cyber puzzles and tasks. An Escape room is a fun activity keeping high student engagement. Meantime, the approach has several limitations and challenges. The escape room setup is time-consuming and requires human and specific technical resources. More importantly, the gamification scenario might unbalance the distribution of hard and soft skills within a small participant group. Therefore, it cannot ensure comparable personal development in all cybersecurity knowledge areas compared to traditional learning methods.

In the future, we plan to develop an upgrade for the game, CyberEscape 2.0. The lessons learned and knowledge acquired from the CyberEscape 1.0 delivery will be used as a basis for further development. A new version could include the following key improvements: extensive technical tutorials about computer and operating system protection, enhanced video material for training, and learning analytics components powered by computer vision and data science.

The long-term vision is to create an internationally reusable program for running an educational escape room game. It will enhance cybersecurity capabilities and attract young specialists as the world experiences increasing cybersecurity threats and a vast demand for cybersecurity professionals.

We also have identified the need for further investigation as to the students perceptions of active learning approaches such as CyberEscape.

Acknowledgements. The "Advancing Human Performance in Cybersecurity", ADVANCES, benefits from nearly €1 million grant from Iceland, Liechtenstein and Norway through the EEA Grants. The aim of the project is to advance the performance of cybersecurity specialists by personalizing the competence development path and risk assessment. Project contract with the Research Council of Lithuania (LMTLT) No is S-BMT-21-6 (LT08-2-LMT-K-01-051).

References

1. Ashley, T.D., Kwon, R., Gourisetti, S.N.G., Katsis, C., Bonebrake, C.A., Boyd, P.A.: Gamification of cybersecurity for workforce development in critical infras-

tructure. IEEE Access **10**, 112487–112501 (2022). https://doi.org/10.1109/access.2022.3216711

2. Beguin, E., et al.: Computer security oriented escape room. IEEE Secur. Priv. **17**(4), 78–83 (2019). https://doi.org/10.1109/MSEC.2019.2912700

3. Budimir, S., Fontaine, J., Huijts, N., Haans, A., Loukas, G., Roesch, E.: Emotional reactions to cybersecurity breach situations: a scenario-based survey study. J. Med. Internet Res. **23**, e24879 (2020). https://doi.org/10.2196/24879

4. Center for Infrastructure Assurance & Security: Cyber Threat Defender - The UTSA CIAS. University of Texas at San Antonio. https://cias.utsa.edu/ctd/. Accessed 1 Feb 2023

5. Chen, T.R., Shore, D.B., Zaccaro, S.J., Dalal, R.S., Tetrick, L.E., Gorab, A.K.: An organizational psychology perspective to examining computer security incident response teams. IEEE Secur. Priv. **12**(5), 61–67 (2014). https://doi.org/10.1109/MSP.2014.85

6. Cichonski, P., Millar, T., Grance, T., Scarfone, K.: Computer security incident handling guide. NIST Spec. Publ. **800**(61) (2012). https://doi.org/10.6028/NIST.SP.800-61r2. Revision, National Institute of Standards and Technology

7. Clarke, S.J., Peel, D.J., Arnab, S., Morini, L., Keegan, H., Wood, O.: EscapED: a framework for creating educational escape rooms and interactive games to for higher/further education. Int. J. Serious Games **4**(3) (2017). https://doi.org/10.17083/ijsg.v4i3.180

8. Cleveland, S., Cleveland, M.: Toward cybersecurity leadership framework. In: The Thirteenth Midwest Association for Information Systems Conference Proceedings, MWAIS, p. 49 (2018). https://aisel.aisnet.org/mwais2018/49

9. Debello, J.E., Schmeelk, S., Dragos, D.M., Troja, E., Truong, L.M.: Teaching effective cybersecurity through escape the classroom paradigm. In: IEEE Global Engineering Education Conference, EDUCON, pp. 17–23. IEEE (2022). https://doi.org/10.1109/EDUCON52537.2022.9766684

10. Decusatis, C., et al.: A cybersecurity awareness escape room using gamification design principles. In: 12th IEEE Annual Computing and Communication Workshop and Conference, CCWC, pp. 765–770. IEEE (2022). https://doi.org/10.1109/CCWC54503.2022.9720748

11. Department of Defense: Cyber Protect - DoD Cyber Exchange. https://public.cyber.mil/training/cyber-protect/. Accessed 1 Feb 2023

12. Duncan, K.J.: Examining the effects of immersive game-based learning on student engagement and the development of collaboration, communication, creativity and critical thinking. TechTrends **64**(3), 514–524 (2020). https://doi.org/10.1007/s11528-020-00500-9

13. European Union Agency for Cybersecurity: European cybersecurity skills framework (ECSF). ENISA reports (2022). https://www.enisa.europa.eu/publications/european-cybersecurity-skills-framework-role-profiles

14. Gilboy, M.B., Heinerichs, S., Pazzaglia, G.: Enhancing student engagement using the flipped classroom. J. Nutr. Educ. Behav. **47**(1), 109–114 (2015). https://doi.org/10.1016/j.jneb.2014.08.008

15. Greene, J.C.: Engaging critical issues in social inquiry by mixing methods. Am. Behav. Sci. **56**(6), 755–773 (2012). https://doi.org/10.1177/0002764211433794

16. Hajny, J., Ricci, S., Piesarskas, E., Levillain, O., Galletta, L., De Nicola, R.: Framework, tools and good practices for cybersecurity curricula. IEEE Access **9**, 94723–94747 (2021). https://doi.org/10.1109/ACCESS.2021.3093952

17. Hevner, A.: A three cycle view of design science research. Scand. J. Inf. Syst. **19**(2), 87–92 (2007)

18. Hevner, A.R., March, S.T., Park, J., Ram, S.: Design science in information systems research. MIS Q. **28**(1), 75–105 (2004)
19. Hmelo-Silver, C.: Problem-based learning: what and how do students learn? Educ. Psychol. Rev. **16**, 235–266 (2004). https://doi.org/10.1023/B:EDPR.0000034022.16470.f3
20. Kuckartz, U.: Qualitative Text Analysis: A Guide to Methods, Practice & Using Software. SAGE Publications Ltd., Thousand Oaks (2014). https://doi.org/10.4135/9781446288719
21. López-Belmonte, J., Segura-Robles, A., Fuentes-Cabrera, A., Parra-González, M.E.: Evaluating activation and absence of negative effect: gamification and escape rooms for learning. Int. J. Environ. Res. Publ. Health **17**(7) (2020). https://doi.org/10.3390/ijerph17072224
22. Löffler, E., Schneider, B., Asprion, P.M., Zanwar, T.: CySecEscape 2.0–a virtual escape room to raise cybersecurity awareness. Int. J. Serious Games **8**, 59–70 (2021). https://doi.org/10.17083/ijsg.v8i1.413
23. Malone, M., Wang, Y., James, K., Anderegg, M., Werner, J., Monrose, F.: To Gamify or not? On leaderboard effects, student engagement and learning outcomes in a cybersecurity intervention. In: Proceedings of the 52nd ACM Technical Symposium on Computer Science Education, SIGCSE, pp. 1135–1141. ACM (2021). https://doi.org/10.1145/3408877.3432544
24. Manley, B., McIntire, D.: A guide to effective incident management communications. Software Engineering Institute, Cargenie Melon University, February 2021. https://resources.sei.cmu.edu/library/asset-view.cfm?assetid=651816
25. Mello-Stark, S., VanValkenburg, M.A., Hao, E.: Thinking outside the box: using escape room games to increase interest in cyber security. In: Daimi, K., Francia III, G. (eds.) Innovations in Cybersecurity Education, pp. 39–53. Springer, Cham (2020). https://doi.org/10.1007/978-3-030-50244-7_3
26. Murphree, C., Vafa, S.: Use of escape rooms in education. In: Proceedings of Society for Information Technology & Teacher Education International Conference, pp. 1837–1842. Association for the Advancement of Computing in Education (AACE) (2020). https://www.learntechlib.org/p/215961
27. Nieto-Escamez, F.A., Roldán-Tapia, M.D.: Gamification as online teaching strategy during COVID-19: a mini-review. Front. Psychol. **12** (2021). https://doi.org/10.3389/fpsyg.2021.648552
28. Papaioannou, T., Tsohou, A., Bounias, G., Karagiannis, S.: A constructive approach for raising information privacy competences: the case of escape room games. In: Katsikas, S., Furnell, S. (eds.) Trust, Privacy and Security in Digital Business (TrustBus), vol. 13582, pp. 33–49. Springer, Cham (2022). https://doi.org/10.1007/978-3-031-17926-6_3
29. Pirta-Dreimane, R., et al.: Application of intervention mapping in cybersecurity education design. In: Frontiers in Education, vol. 7 (2022). https://doi.org/10.3389/feduc.2022.998335
30. Pirta-Dreimane, R., Brilingaitė, A., Roponena, E., Parish, K.: Multi-dimensional cybersecurity education design: a case study. In: IEEE International Conference on Dependable, Autonomic and secure Computing, International Conference on Pervasive Intelligence and Computing, International Conference on Cloud and Big Data Computing, International Conference on Cyber Science and Technology Congress, DASC/PiCom/CBDCom/CyberSciTech, pp. 1–8. IEEE (2022). https://doi.org/10.1109/DASC/PiCom/CBDCom/Cy55231.2022.9927931

31. Sellers, J., Helton, W.S., Näswall, K., Funke, G.J., Knott, B.A.: Development of the team workload questionnaire (TWLQ). In: Proceedings of the Human Factors and Ergonomics Society 58th Annual Meeting, vol. 58, no. 1, pp. 989–993 (2014). https://doi.org/10.1177/1541931214581207
32. Steinke, J., et al.: Improving cybersecurity incident response team effectiveness using teams-based research. IEEE Secur. Priv. **13**(4), 20–29 (2015). https://doi.org/10.1109/MSP.2015.71
33. Subhash, S., Cudney, E.A.: Gamified learning in higher education: a systematic review of the literature. Comput. Hum. Behav. **87**, 192–206 (2018). https://doi.org/10.1016/j.chb.2018.05.028
34. Thompson, M.F., Irvine, C.E.: CyberCIEGE: a video game for constructive cyber security education. Call Signs **6**(2), 4–8 (2015)
35. Švábenský, V., Čeleda, P., Vykopal, J., Brišáková, S.: Cybersecurity knowledge and skills taught in capture the flag challenges. Comput. Secur. **102**, 102154 (2021)

Measuring Behavioural Cybersecurity: An Overview of Options

Tommy van Steen[✉] [ID]

Institute of Security and Global Affairs, Leiden University, Turfmarkt 99, 2511DP The Hague, The Netherlands
t.van.steen@fgga.leidenuniv.nl

Abstract. As the field of cybersecurity is maturing, there is more attention to the behaviour of end-users in securing data and systems. Awareness campaigns are gaining popularity and behavioural change initiatives are deployed. However, many organisations do not know where to start when attempting to effectively measure the maturity of the behavioural component in their cybersecurity strategy. While some measures, such as knowledge, attitudes and skills are assessed, (objective) measurements of behaviour, and the interplay between these factors are less commonly measured. This paper discusses the importance of measuring behavioural cybersecurity and presents an overview of possible measurements and relevant factors. First, the paper outlines why measuring behavioural cybersecurity is vital in understanding behaviour related problems and coming up with evidence-based solutions. Then, the various measurement levels and current practices are discussed before turning to options regarding these levels. These include both self-reported as well as objective behavioural measurements in addition to attitudes, knowledge and skills. Lastly, some issues surrounding these measurements are discussed including spill-over effects and ethical considerations.

Keywords: Behavioural cybersecurity · Organisational cybersecurity · Measures · Behavioural models · Behavioural factors

1 Introduction

The behaviour of end-users is a vital component in keeping organisations secure. To achieve this, many organisations are using awareness campaigns to improve cybersecurity behaviours. In addition to awareness campaigns, there is a growing field that focuses on developing training methods for end-users [see for instance 1, 2] and broader behavioural change interventions for cybersecurity [3]. This field can be described as 'behavioural cybersecurity', which is defined as "[the study of] how the behaviour of end-users can be changed to better support the cybersecurity of individuals, organisations, and the wider society." [4].

As the field is maturing, more scientific research is conducted on the topic of behavioural change interventions for cybersecurity behaviour. In these interventions, the goal is often to change a measurable outcome such as the click rate of phishing emails,

D. D. Schmorrow and C. M. Fidopiastis (Eds.): HCII 2023, LNAI 14019, pp. 460–471, 2023.
https://doi.org/10.1007/978-3-031-35017-7_29

or the strength of a newly created password. One of the differences between behavioural change interventions and awareness campaigns is that the latter can, implicitly, assume a certain level of rationality present in the end-user. Where awareness campaigns often simply provide information about risks and solutions [5], behavioural change interventions usually acknowledge the irrationality of people when making decisions, and taking those processes into account when attempting to influence behaviour. However, for many organisations, it is unclear how to measure behavioural cybersecurity factors to assess the current situation and any problems arising. Furthermore, there is a need to understand why these problems occur and how to measure the effectiveness of any solution organisations implement to improve cybersecurity behaviour. This paper outlines the importance of thoroughly measuring cybersecurity behaviour, discusses which factors can and should be measured, and outlines some current options that are available to measure a range of factors either in the setting of a scientific study, or as part of an ongoing behavioural change effort in organisations.

2   The Importance of Measuring Cybersecurity Behaviour

There are various reasons why measuring cybersecurity behaviours and related factors is relevant. These reasons can be categorised into 1) identifying potential problems, 2) understanding the current situation, and 3) evaluate the effectiveness of proposed solutions.

Measuring behaviours and related factors deepens the understanding of the current situation, as behavioural insights are often skewed due to personal biases of the security experts within organisations. Where an expert might consider certain behaviours to be problematic and highly risky, it is unlikely that the expert has an objective view of the situation. It is possible that they overestimate the number of employees who perform the risky behaviour, or how often they do so. At the same time, there is also the possibility that due to a confirmation bias, or the availability heuristic [6], experts overestimate risks as they more easily recall instances where people showed the unwanted behaviour, compared to the correct behaviour. An example of this can be the locking of computer screens when end-users leave their desk. A cybersecurity expert who takes a look at the various workstations in a department during lunchtime is more likely to spot, and later remember, all the screens that were not locked, than the screens that were. By measuring these factors objectively, (e.g., record per workstation whether the screen is locked, unlocked, or the machine is completely switched off) the security expert has a clearer understanding of the size of the problem they are dealing with.

When measuring the number of workstations that are not locked while the end-user is away, the expert gains insights in the size of the problem. However, it does not indicate why this problem is occurring. Is it merely an oversight of the employees, who are simply not aware of, or do not agree with, the importance of locking a screen? Is the issue that the employees do not know how to lock their screens? Or perhaps they simply assume that there is a high level of social control, so that if they do leave their screens unlocked, their co-workers will make sure no other people will use their workstation while they are away. By measuring not just the number of unlocked workstations left unattended, but also measuring factors such as knowledge of the risks, capability to lock the screen, and employees' awareness of potential consequences of co-workers or strangers accessing your workstation, the security expert gains a better understanding of how to deal with this problem moving forward.

Once the security expert has verified that the problem exists and has a better understanding of why the problem occurs, the final benefit of measuring behaviours and associated factors is gaining understanding of whether a proposed solution worked in practice. Again, the goal is not to merely measure the behaviour of end-users by checking how many workstations have been left unlocked. Additional measurements about knowledge and skills can help understand whether the various factors associated with the behaviour have improved as well. This is especially important if the proposed solution did not work as well as hoped. In that case, understanding better where the influence attempt failed can inform future iterations of the proposed solution.

3   Which Measurement Levels Exist?

To measure cybersecurity behaviour related factors, it is important to realise what factors predict behaviour and potential changes in behaviour. Depending on the specific behaviour that is addressed, a behavioural model might be chosen that best fits the type of behaviour on the outset. Once a model is chosen, factors specific to the behaviour at hand might be added to improve the model and thereby the understanding of the mechanisms that lead to people performing the secure behaviour. Some frequently used models include the theory of planned behaviour [7] and the COM-B model [8] while other models such as protection motivation theory [9] and the technology acceptance model [10] are also used. While these models all have a unique view of what factors cause behaviour to occur, some high-level similarities are present. In general, there tends to be a focus on both individual factors including attitudes and required skills, as well as situational factors such as social support for, and barriers to, the performance of certain behaviours. Furthermore, most behavioural models incorporate a distinction between the intention to perform a behaviour and actual behaviour. For the purpose of measuring cybersecurity behaviour and understanding why people are behaving in a risky manner, there are five different aspects that are worth measuring: attitudes, knowledge, skills, intentions, and behaviour. Below, these aspects are discussed in greater detail.

3.1   Attitudes

Attitudes generally refer to the beliefs and opinions people hold regarding a topic or behaviour. In cybersecurity, this can include asking people questions about whether they believe cybersecurity to be of general importance, and whether they feel responsible for ensuring that any (sensitive) data they work with is stored safely and securely. Additionally, it can cover beliefs surrounding the relative importance of cybersecurity compared with, for example, productivity or the role cybersecurity should play in people's lives outside of work. Measuring attitudes is often relatively easy as surveys can be designed to include a range of topics on which people can offer their thoughts and views.

3.2 Knowledge

In addition to attitudes, many organisations are also interested in measuring the level of knowledge that end-users have about cybersecurity. Do they know the risks of sharing passwords or using private email accounts for work related messages and file sharing? Measuring knowledge adds to an attitude measurement by splitting knowing what to do and being supportive of those behaviours into two distinct categories. Some employees might strongly support cybersecurity when asked, but are not knowledgeable on what they can do to work more securely. The opposite outcome is perhaps more common: people know perfectly well which steps to take to improve their cybersecurity behaviour, but do not support these steps as they do not see cybersecurity as a significant issue, or might choose productivity over working securely.

3.3 Skills

People might have sufficient knowledge about what is required to improve cybersecurity, for instance knowing that a strong password helps securing an email account. However, knowing that a strong password is beneficial is not equal to having the skills to create and remember a strong password. As a result, recording only attitudes and knowledge is not sufficient when attempting to measure whether people are ready to behave securely. Measuring whether people have the skills to perform the behaviour is a necessary addition, especially as knowledge and attitude are often assessed via closed survey questions, which can be more prone to socially desirable responding. Assessing the skillset of employees is less prone to this bias, as it often includes demonstrating the skill itself. For instance, in addition to asking people whether they see the importance of protecting (work) accounts and data, and whether they know the benefits of a strong password, end-users can be asked to create a strong password to test whether they know what would be considered a strong or weak password. This password can then be assessed on its strength [11].

3.4 Intentions

In most instances, we would expect people who hold not only a positive attitude towards a behaviour, but who also have sufficient knowledge, and have the necessary skillset to perform the behaviour to automatically behave in a secure fashion. However, it is possible that important behaviour specific predictors have been missed, and that self-reported or objective outcome measures are not possible. Measuring intentions can be a solution in all those instances, as intentions are usually measured using a set of survey questions and can be distributed during both a regular behavioural cybersecurity measurement, as well as directly after an intervention or awareness program has been completed. While the intention-behaviour gap [12] suggests that merely relying on intentions does not always lead to correct inferences about behaviour, it can provide initial insights in the current level of cybersecurity behaviour.

3.5 Behaviour

Measuring behaviour using either self-reported behavioural measurements or objective measurements is often the most insightful, while at the same time the most difficult to achieve. Measuring behaviour through self-reports is relatively easy, but might suffer from socially desirable responding, whereas objective measurements are not always possible or are considered unethical depending on the situation. However, as the goal of behavioural change is to change behaviour, and not merely to change an attitude or increase knowledge, measuring behavioural outcomes is often the most direct and the most important measurement of intervention success.

4 Current Practices in the Field

There is a discrepancy between the types of behavioural outcomes that can be measured theoretically and what is often used in the field to determine the effectiveness of behavioural cybersecurity initiatives. Where scientists might use a test battery consisting of most if not all categories as described above, the reality of measuring cybersecurity behaviour in real-world settings is often more limited. For instance, a study investigating the contents and methods of assessing the effectiveness of governmental awareness campaigns showed that most campaigns do not test the effectiveness of their efforts [5]. The few campaigns that did report data only recorded engagement with online materials such as how many social media users were presented with their awareness messages, or the number of visits to the campaign website in the time the campaign was active. While this provides some initial insights into the reach of these campaigns, it does not prove insightful in assessing whether the campaign changed attitudes, knowledge, skills intentions and/or behaviour. As a result, it is unclear what the specific goal is of these campaigns and whether this goal has been achieved by designing and running awareness campaigns [5].

In commercially available awareness campaigns, effectivity tests are often limited. In some cases, organisations offering these campaigns design a generic set of materials that can be adjusted to some extent in collaboration with the organisation that requires their service. These generic campaigns might have been pre-tested in a specific organisation, or by having communication experts assessing the materials. However, the effectiveness is often not tested in the organisation that the adjusted campaign is used for.

Even if the client asks for proof regarding the effectiveness of the awareness campaign, this proof could be considered limited from a scientific point of view. For example, the organisation that offers awareness campaigns as a service might run basic surveys to measure factors such as employees' interest in cybersecurity, how much fun they had while taking part in the awareness campaign or they might incorporate short quizzes to test cybersecurity knowledge levels pre and post the running of the awareness campaign. If the scores are high enough, these are interpreted as having had a positive impact on people's cybersecurity awareness, with the assumption that increased awareness leads to improved cybersecurity behaviours. This, however, is not automatically the case. As a result, organisations spend the limited resources they have allocated to awareness campaigns on initiatives that are not proven to be effective, and where the long-term effects of these campaigns are completely unknown. While we cannot expect organisations to have an interest in gathering data on their campaigns' effectiveness to the same extent as scientists would like to see, the current practice of merely measuring awareness or knowledge is insufficient to draw conclusions about the practical usefulness of the campaigns that are rolled out across departments and organisations [13].

5 Self-reported Measurements

Measuring behavioural cybersecurity factors can be achieved in a wide range of methods. One important distinction is that of measuring factors through self-reports or objective measurements. Self-reports are usually easier to obtain, as they often entail sending out surveys, while objective measures on the other hand can involve more elaborate set-ups which require more time and effort to achieve. In this section various options to measure behavioural cybersecurity factors through surveys are covered before discussing potential objective measures in the next section.

To measure attitudes, knowledge and skills as well as intentions and behaviours, scientists and practitioners turn to two different methods of survey design. On the one hand, there are surveys and measurements that are designed on a case-by-case basis for the specific situation that is assessed. For example, some studies designed questionnaires based on theory of planned behaviour factors to assess the effectiveness of gamification [3], or created tailor made scales to assess people's views on cybersecurity [14]. The advantage of using tailor made questionnaires and scales is that they are created to test the specific outcomes that the researchers and practitioners are interested in. Additionally, it can be insightful to ask questions about the specific set-up or system that is in place at a particular department or include questions about a specific campaign that has been launched. However, the clear downsides include the lack of validation of the scales, and the difficulty in comparing the findings from one study with other studies or comparing one organisation to other organisations in the same sector. As a result, it can be difficult to assess whether the level of knowledge, attitudes, skills, and intentions of own employees falls short -or widely exceeds- expectations across organisations.

The other method is to develop or adopt more general scales and measurements that have shown to have a high validity and reliability. Several of such scales exist, often addressing a set of factors covering multiple measurement levels. For instance, one of them is the Human Aspects of Information Security Questionnaire (HAIS-Q) [15]. This questionnaire addresses three aspects of behavioural cybersecurity: knowledge, attitudes and behaviour. By combining these three factors, the HAIS-Q not only focuses on the self-reported behaviour of end-users, but also can shine light on some predictive factors that might explain why people report a low or high level of security behaviour. The HAIS-Q has been developed for the Australian context and the authors suggest that a level of socially desirable responding to the items in this questionnaire might be due to the Australian culture [16]. However, socially desirable responding might be an issue in other scales and surveys as well, so it remains unknown whether this criticism of the HAIS-Q is unique to that specific questionnaire, or whether this is a wider problem with measurements using self-reports to investigate behavioural cybersecurity constructs.

Aside from the HAIS-Q, many other scales have been designed to capture behavioural cybersecurity factors. For instance, Egelman and Peer designed the Security Behaviour

Intentions Scale (SeBIS) [17]. This scale consists of 16 items covering various aspects of cybersecurity. The items contain statements about what people say they will do in certain situations, such as installing software updates when they are available, differentiating passwords for different accounts and locking your computer when leaving it unattended. A third measure of importance was designed by Hadlington [18], who combined four scales that were designed based on other scales to measure a range of cybersecurity related factors. The four proposed scales were the abbreviated impulsiveness scale (ABIS), the online cognition scale (OCS), the risky cybersecurity behaviours scale (RScB) which was to a degree based on the SeBIS scale discussed earlier, and the attitudes towards cybersecurity and cybercrime in business (ACT-IB). Combining various measurement levels into a single questionnaire can help improve understanding of the underlying mechanisms of cybersecurity behaviour. An additional advantage is that more knowledge on how the various scales relate to each other, the easier it becomes to use shorter scales or only subscales of the measurements for predictive purposes. This can be advantageous when there is no possibility of an in-depth measurement of cybersecurity behaviour and related factors within an organisation or department.

In addition to broad questionnaires covering all types of cybersecurity behaviours, there are also initiatives to develop measurements for specific areas of cybersecurity or even single cybersecurity behaviours. For example, Ifinedo [19] investigated the problem of noncompliance with cybersecurity policies by developing a measure for people's willingness to comply with these policies. For this study, Ifinedo combined a set of existing scales to create a measurement that can be used to gauge someone's general tendency to comply with cybersecurity policies.

On the level of specific cybersecurity behaviours, Williams and Joinson designed a scale to measure factors related to people's interest in searching for information to protect themselves against phishing. [20]. Their measurement is based on the protection motivation theory, with items designed to specifically address protection motivation theory factors in relation to responses to potential phishing attacks.

6   Objective Behavioural Measurements

While surveys are informative in measuring predictive factors of cybersecurity behaviour, measuring behaviour through surveys can suffer from self-reporting biases. Therefore, objective measures of behaviour are of greater importance when trying to understand the size of the problem at hand, or the effectiveness of a behavioural change intervention or policy solution. These objective measures often cost more time and money to conduct, and might require technical changes to the systems that are used by the end-users. One distinction that can be made is that of measuring behaviour in real-world situations and the use of scientific set-ups where end-users are presented with specific situations that can be controlled by the researchers, such as is the case in lab studies or (online) mock-ups of platforms. In this latter environment, it is often relatively easy to measure behaviour objectively. For example, studies can ask end-users to create a strong password and the strength of the password can be calculated using a formula [21]. Furthermore, the memorisation of a strong password could be tested by asking participants to create a strong password, and then ask them to later fill in the same password.

Other tests can include showing people a set of emails where they need to decide which of these emails is in fact a phishing email, and where they indicate which aspects of the message seem malicious. In the nudging literature on cybersecurity, scientists often incorporate a mock-up of a platform to establish whether people make different choices under certain nudging conditions, such as deciding which privacy settings to choose [e.g., 22, 23].

Whereas implementing objective measures is relatively easy in controlled environments, this is often more complex in real-world settings. There, the environment cannot always be controlled as easily. Complicating factors can for example include the presence of colleagues who might interfere with an objective assessment of employees' individual behaviours, or technical issues in updating systems to change monitoring procedures. In real-world settings, objective behavioural measures for cybersecurity behaviours could take the form of two options: observations and technical measurements.

6.1 Observations

Depending on the type of focal behaviour, observations might be possible. For instance, as outlined earlier, if the question is whether people lock their screens when leaving their desk for lunch or bathroom breaks, an observer can simply go into the offices of a department and register which workstations have been left unattended. Similar methods can be explored when measuring the adherence to policies regarding the use of personal devices in workspaces, the use of personal USB accessories, or the use of privacy screens on laptops to prevent shoulder surfing. While observations have their advantages in terms of seeing actual behaviour and can be an objective method to measure the size of some behavioural cybersecurity threats, the use of observations is relatively limited. Not only can it be costly to have personnel go into every office to collect the required data, there is also the risk of people warning each other that another observation round is taking place, urging colleagues to lock their screen, ditch their USB accessories or put their privacy screens back in place before the observer reaches their workstation. Furthermore, the use of observers might make employees feel uneasy and being watched as they go about their daily work activities. However, using observations in tandem with self-reported measures might help attenuate the most pressing downsides of both measurement methods for cybersecurity behaviours that cannot be measured directly with the use of technical solutions.

6.2 Technical Measurements

As most cybersecurity behaviours take place in interaction with a system, there are various options to measure the behaviour of end-users through this system. The most well-known example is how responses to phishing messages are recorded and analysed. Organisations that want to know how well their employees can spot a phishing email often resort to sending out a fake phishing email to their employees and measure how many employees clicked on the hyperlink in the email [24]. Often, the people who click on the phishing link are then directed to a webpage explaining that this was a phishing email intended to test their phishing awareness level and offering them additional training to be better able to spot these types of emails in the future. This type of metric offers an objective measurement of the number of people who have clicked on the hyperlink as a percentage of the number of people receiving the test email. Building on this, technical measurements can be used to expand on the insights of these phishing tests. For example, it is possible to measure not only whether people clicked on the hyperlink, but also whether people opened the email to begin with, and, if they ended up clicking, whether they provided personal details (e.g., login credentials, social service numbers, (home) address and date of birth) on the webpage that they were redirected to. This way, security experts can not only measure the number of people who click, but also the number of people who provide information that might be used in a subsequent attack. In addition to metrics regarding the clicking behaviour, similar metrics can be used in the reporting of phishing emails. Not only can organisations measure how many people report the email to the relevant department, but also how quickly they do so after receiving the email. If an intervention to improve how employees deal with phishing emails has been successful, it can have reduced the number of people opening the email, clicking on the hyperlink and providing personal information, but also have increased the number of people reporting the email, and reduced the time it took them to do so.

Technical measurements that can be used to measure other cybersecurity behaviours can include tools to log the number of times people use the keyboard shortcuts for locking their screen, the number of times the workstation automatically locks due to inactivity, or the time people take to update any applications they are responsible for on an individual level. Incorporating these technical measurements often requires a strong collaboration with the IT department and can take some time to set up effectively.

7 Problems to Solve

This paper discussed a range of measurements that can be used to assess the current situation regarding behavioural cybersecurity, methods to measure the underlying mechanisms of issues that arise, and measurements that can be used to test the effectiveness of behavioural cybersecurity solutions. However, some outstanding problems still need to be solved. For instance, we need to carefully assess the ethical ramifications of decisions regarding which measurements to include in any behavioural cybersecurity programme. Is it ethically justifiable to monitor employees' behaviour through system logs, the use of keyloggers to measure how many people press Windows + L to lock their screen and using a range of other technical measurements? And is it ethical for an organisation to send fake phishing emails to their own employees to test their phishing awareness? One example from the UK shows the backlash this can create. During the COVID-19 pandemic, employees from a train company were sent a phishing test that showed a message of a financial bonus being awarded to all employees who had worked on trains during the COVID-19 pandemic. As employees were already unhappy with their situation as they felt they were on the front line, taking risks regarding their own health to keep the trains running, they were shocked when the promised bonus was in fact a phishing test [25]. While some discomfort might be unavoidable when distributing phishing tests, companies should be mindful of the ethical issues surrounding their behavioural cybersecurity measurements.

A second outstanding problem is that of spill over effects. All the measurements in this paper focus on measuring aspects of cybersecurity that have the attention of security experts and are the focus of awareness campaigns and behavioural change interventions. It is not yet clear however, to what extent the campaigns might have unintended side effects and influence other cybersecurity behaviours. For example, we can look at a behavioural change intervention that makes people more likely to set up two factor authentication for their personal accounts. While being successful in this manner, people might at the same time opt for less complex passwords as they feel that two factor authentication is an alternative rather than an addition to strong passwords. Other problematic spill-over effects could be found when looking into the so-called compliance budget [26], which suggests that people have a limit in terms of the number of policies and rules and regulations they feel they can comply with, and once the maximum is reached, they start ignoring new policy on those topics. So, while a behavioural change campaign can show a positive effect on a specific target behaviour, it is important to develop measures for a broader understanding of the effects the campaign has had on other types of cybersecurity behaviour as well to see whether the overall cybersecurity level of the organisation has in fact improved.

In addition to unwanted side effects on behavioural outcomes, another aspect that is often ignored, or considered difficult to measure, is the impact of the changed behaviour on overall productivity. Generally, cybersecurity is seen as a hinderance and any additional step that needs to be taken to perform a task in a secure fashion, is likely to lead to decreased productivity. This can include getting less work done, or missing tight deadlines, but can also mean that the work flow of employees is interrupted on a daily basis, causing distress and disgruntlement. Current measures do not account for this drop in productivity, which makes it often challenging to assess whether the improved cybersecurity behaviour is worth the effort in a cost-benefit analysis. Finding the balance between working securely while also maintaining a decent level of productivity is an important challenge that must be overcome in order to decide which awareness campaigns and behavioural change initiatives can and should be deployed.

As a final point, the adage that 'when the measure becomes the goal it stops being a useful measure' certainly applies to measuring cybersecurity behaviour. When employees are aware that their performance is measured through a specific observation, they can game the system by ensuring they score high on the measurements without changing their factual behaviour. For instance, in some organisations people might be aware that fake phishing emails will be distributed during a specific month or event. Managers who want to prove that their team is behaviour securely might be on the lookout for the fake phishing email, so that they can quickly spot it and let their team know they should not open the email. This artificially inflates their score on some cybersecurity measures, while emails sent on other days or during other times of the year might still be go unnoticed.

8 Conclusion

There are many different ways to investigate the current state of behavioural cybersecurity and the effectiveness of behavioural change initiatives. Ideally, a combination of survey data and objective behavioural measurements is employed to fully understand not only the cybersecurity behaviour end-users display, but also to better understand the mechanisms behind these behaviours. This helps in deepening our understanding of why it is that some people follow policies and guidelines while others decide to ignore cybersecurity advice and behave in a risky manner. The goal of measuring cybersecurity behaviour is not only to still the appetite of researchers for more knowledge and scientific insights, but also to critically assess whether the effort in both time and financial resources has paid off to improve cybersecurity behaviour in organisations. Only by critically assessing what works and what does not, can we improve the awareness campaigns, behavioural change initiatives and cybersecurity trainings that are offered to end-users and ensure that they are delivered in the most effective and efficient way possible.

References

1. Chowdhury, A., Maiti, S.K., Bhattacharyya, S.: How to communicate climate change 'impact and solutions' to vulnerable population of Indian Sundarbans? From theory to practice. Springerplus 5(1), 1–17 (2016). https://doi.org/10.1186/s40064-016-2816-y
2. Albrechtsen, E., Hovden, J.: Improving information security awareness and behaviour through dialogue, participation and collective reflection an intervention study. Comput. Secur. 29, 432–445 (2010)
3. van Steen, T., Deeleman, J.R.A.: Successful gamification of cybersecurity training. Cyberpsychol. Behav. Soc. Netw. 1–6 (2021). https://doi.org/10.1089/cyber.2020.0526
4. van Steen, T.: When choice is (not) an option: nudging and techno-regulation approaches to behavioural cybersecurity. In: In: Schmorrow, D.D., Fidopiastis, C.M. (eds.) Augmented Cognition. HCII 2022. Lecture Notes in Computer Science(), vol. 13310. pp. 120–130. Springer, Cham (2022). https://doi.org/10.1007/978-3-031-05457-0
5. van Steen, T., Norris, E., Atha, K., Joinson, A.: What (if any) behaviour change techniques do government-led cybersecurity awareness campaigns use? J. Cybersecur. 6, 1–8 (2020). https://doi.org/10.1093/cybsec/tyaa019
6. Tversky, A., Kahneman, D.: Judgment Under Uncertainty: Heuristics and Biases. Science, vol. 80, no. 185, pp. 1124–1131 (1974)
7. Ajzen, I.: The theory of planned behavior. Organ. Behav. Hum. Decis. Process. 50, 179–211 (1991). https://doi.org/10.1016/0749-5978(91)90020-T
8. Michie, S., van Stralen, M.M., West, R.: The behaviour change wheel: a new method for characterising and designing behaviour change interventions. Implement. Sci. 6, 42 (2011). https://doi.org/10.1186/1748-5908-6-42
9. Rogers, R.: A protection motivation theory of fear appeals and attitude change (1975). http://search.ebscohost.com/login.aspx?direct=true&db=psyh&AN=1976-04488-001&site=ehost-live%5Cnpapers2://publication/uuid/8D45EFD8-4F1C-431B-8819-E2210FF3D68E. https://doi.org/10.1080/00223980.1975.9915803
10. Venkatesh, V., Bala, H.: Technology acceptance model 3 and a research agenda on interventions. Decis. Sci. (2008). https://doi.org/10.1111/j.1540-5915.2008.00192.x
11. Peer, E., Egelman, S., Harbach, M., Malkin, N., Mathur, A., Frik, A.: Nudge me right: Personalizing online security nudges to people's decision-making styles. Comput. Human Behav. 109, 106347 (2020)
12. Moghavvemi, S., Salleh, N.A.M., Sulaiman, A., Abessi, M.: Effect of external factors on intention–behaviour gap. Behav. Inf. Technol. 34, 1171–1185 (2015)
13. Bada, M., Sasse, M.A., Nurse, J.R.C.: Cyber security awareness campaigns: why do they fail to change behaviour? In: Proceedings of International Conference Cybersecurity Sustainable Society 118–131 (2015)

14. Fabisiak, L., Hyla, T.: Measuring cyber security awareness within groups of medical professionals in Poland. In: Proceedings of the Annual Hawaii International Conference on System Sciences 2020, pp. 3871–3880, January 2020. https://doi.org/10.24251/hicss.2020.473

15. Parsons, K., McCormac, A., Butavicius, M., Pattinson, M., Jerram, C.: Determining employee awareness using the human aspects of information security questionnaire (HAIS-Q). Comput. Secur. **42**, 165–176 (2014)

16. Parsons, K., Calic, D., Pattinson, M., Butavicius, M., McCormac, A., Zwaans, T.: The human aspects of information security questionnaire (HAIS-Q): two further validation studies. Comput. Secur. **66**, 40–51 (2017)

17. Egelman, S., Peer, E.: Scaling the security wall: developing a security behavior intentions scale (SeBIS). In: Proceedings of the 33rd Annual ACM Conference on Human Factors in Computing Systems, pp. 2873–2882 (2015)

18. Hadlington, L.: Human factors in cybersecurity; examining the link between Internet addiction, impulsivity, attitudes towards cybersecurity, and risky cybersecurity behaviours. Heliyon. **3**, e00346 (2017). https://doi.org/10.1016/j.heliyon.2017.e00346

19. Ifinedo, P.: Understanding information systems security policy compliance: an integration of the theory of planned behavior and the protection motivation theory. Comput. Secur. **31**, 83–95 (2012)

20. Williams, E.J., Joinson, A.N.: Developing a measure of information seeking about phishing. J. Cybersecur. **6**, 1–16 (2020). https://doi.org/10.1093/cybsec/tyaa001

21. Hartwig, K., Reuter, C.: Nudging users towards better security decisions in password creation using whitebox-based multidimensional visualisations. Behav. Inf. Technol., 1–24 (2021). https://doi.org/10.1080/0144929X.2021.1876167

22. Wang, N., Wisniewski, P., Xu, H., Grossklags, J.: Designing the default privacy settings for facebook applications. In: Proceedings of the Companion Publication of the 17th ACM Conference on Computer Supported Cooperative Work & Social Computing, pp. 249–252 (2014)

23. Cho, H., Roh, S., Park, B.: Of promoting networking and protecting privacy: effects of defaults and regulatory focus on social media users' preference settings. Comput. Human Behav. **101**, 1–13 (2019)

24. Steves, M., Greene, K., Theofanos, M.: Categorizing human phishing difficulty: a phish scale. J. Cybersecur. **6**, tyaa009 (2020)

25. Topham, G.: Train firm's 'worker bonus' email is actually cybersecurity test (2021)

26. Beautement, A., Sasse, M.A., Wonham, M.: The compliance budget: managing security behaviour in organisations. In: Proceedings of the 2008 New Security Paradigms Workshop, pp. 47–58 (2008). https://doi.org/10.1145/1595676.1595684

Raising Cybersecurity Awareness Through Electronic Word of Mouth: A Data-Driven Assessment

Dane Vanderkooi⬤, Mohamad Sadegh Sangari⬤, and Atefeh Mashatan(✉)⬤

Cybersecurity Research Lab (CRL), Ted Rogers School of Management, Toronto Metropolitan University, Toronto, ON M5B 2K3, Canada

{dvanderkooi,mssangari,amashatan}@torontomu.ca

Abstract. Awareness of the many cybersecurity threats, vulnerabilities, and solutions to mitigate these threats/vulnerabilities is instrumental in improving basic cybersecurity behaviours. A healthy body of knowledge has been devoted to exploring how to better increase awareness, in any given topic, among members of the general public which have explored the role of word of mouth (WOM) and electronic word of mouth (eWOM) in spreading awareness. In recent years, the rise of social media platforms as an alternative communication channel has created efforts to promote cybersecurity awareness online regarding the numerous cybersecurity threats. However, little research attention has been devoted to exploring eWOM communication on social media surrounding cybersecurity awareness. Moreover, no research to date has considered the impact of the COVID-19 pandemic on these eWOM discussions related to cybersecurity awareness. To address these literature gaps, this research collected 227, 270 relevant tweets surrounding cybersecurity awareness from 2018 to 2022 conducting an exploratory analysis of the corpus using social network analyses, topic modelling and semantic similarity analysis. The results found topics rose in prominence and then dissipated as newer topics emerged while information was found to spread incredibly far despite a high degree of community forming, suggesting the online discourse is very open and evolving over time. These findings illustrate the potential of social media as an effective tool for raising cybersecurity awareness. The impact of COVID-19 observed an increase in the reach of information in addition to new specific topics emerging in the discourse, but the effects appear to be temporary.

Keywords: Cybersecurity Awareness · Electronic Word of Mouth (eWOM) · Social Media · Data-Driven Analysis

1 Introduction

Cybersecurity awareness or cyber awareness has become a necessity in an era of unprecedented levels of cybersecurity threats [1, 2]. It refers to an approach to educating online users to be cognizant of various cyber threats and the vulnerabilities of modern computing systems, in addition to understanding responsibilities and how to mitigate cyber

D. D. Schmorrow and C. M. Fidopiastis (Eds.): HCII 2023, LNAI 14019, pp. 472–490, 2023.
https://doi.org/10.1007/978-3-031-35017-7_30

threats [3]. Research on the subject has found that the more aware individuals are of cybersecurity threats, the more likely they are to engage in good cybersecurity practices, such as compliance with organizational cybersecurity policies [4]. One increasingly popular method of raising public cybersecurity awareness is through online promotion, using social media platforms, such as Twitter, to spread awareness regarding cybersecurity threats and vulnerabilities as well as effective cyber protection practices [5]. The advantage of such an approach is that social media platforms can spread information via electronic word of mouth (eWOM) [6] and social ties [7], allowing for information diffusion to occur faster and reach greater distances than more traditional communication methods. Today, many organizations, governments, and not-for-profits are taking advantage of social media platforms to raise cybersecurity awareness [5]. Additionally, it should be noted that a majority of efforts to raise cybersecurity awareness occur within organizations, particularly larger organizations rather than efforts to target the public [8]. Modern organizations stand to lose their reputation in addition to the impact to their bottom line, hence they invest in efforts to raise cybersecurity awareness of their employees. However, there is a gap in training and awareness of the general public, a challenge typically met by government and non-for-profit led initiatives [9]. This present study does not focus on the enterprise setting, but rather is interested in how to leverage eWOM on social media to raise awareness. Given the low cost of usage (often free even), mass adoption rates of social media platforms and their ability to rapidly spread information across large distances, these platforms could prove to be quite useful to government/non-for-profit efforts to raise awareness without exhausting financial resources. In this vein, small to medium sized businesses could also benefit given their often more intensive resources constraints. Even large organizations with abundant resources could potentially benefit from social media use and employ this technology to cut costs on their internal awareness campaigns.

While eWOM on social media has been shown to influence real-life behaviours in a variety of different contexts (e.g., marketing), little research has explored eWOM in the cybersecurity behaviour context. Analyzing the eWOM regarding cybersecurity can provide a unique understanding of how crowds discuss and engage in cybersecurity matters and the gaps that may exist in cybersecurity in human-computer interactions. However, to date, no research has explored eWOM surrounding cybersecurity awareness. Interestingly, in recent years, the COVID-19 pandemic has impacted eWOM in a variety of ways, bringing new opportunities to be leveraged by stakeholders [10]. The pandemic came with new forms of cyber threats and caused new trends, such as the transition to working from home, creating new cybersecurity vulnerabilities for public users. This motivates investigating how the COVID-19 pandemic has impacted the eWOM discussions of cybersecurity awareness. Moreover, these expected changes may manifest over time. Understanding how both changes in information diffusion and changes in thematic topic structure occur over time could help understand how awareness is raised on social media. For instance, is information simply spreading far or is the information being retained, creating awareness? Understanding how cybersecurity awareness activities come in alignment with such impacts is necessary to further raise awareness among the public, considering current cyber risks and vulnerabilities. As such, this study is guided by the following research questions:

RQ1: What are the major themes of cybersecurity awareness activities on social media and how have the thematic structure of the related content evolved over time?

RQ2: How does the diffusion of cybersecurity awareness content occur on social media?

RQ3: How has the COVID-19 pandemic impacted eWOM discussions surrounding cybersecurity awareness?

To answer the research questions, this research applied a data-driven approach to analyze eWOM discussions regarding cybersecurity awareness. Applying such an approach allows for the wisdom of the crowd (i.e., the collective opinion of a group of individuals) to be leveraged to create insights for making better-informed decisions [11] while reducing the probability of typical analysis and interpretation biases [12]. Popular approaches to analyzing social media data may include text analytics methods, such as topic modelling, to identify key topics within the discourse [13], and computational network analysis methods, to assess network properties, such as social network analysis (SNA) [14]. This study applies SNA and topic modelling to analyze large volumes of tweets related to cybersecurity awareness. Topic modelling was conducted in a comparative study of the popular algorithms of latent Dirichlet allocation (LDA) [15] and non-negative matrix factorization (NMF) [16]. The evolution of the topics over time and the changes for the periods before and after the pandemic were investigated using semantic similarity analysis. The results from the data-driven analysis identify the main foci of eWOM discussions around cybersecurity awareness and how they have evolved in response to changes in the cybersecurity landscape, particularly due to the COVID-19 pandemic. The rest of this paper is organized as follows, literature review is in Sect. 2, followed by the methods in Sect. 3 and results in Sect. 4. Next there is the discussion in Sect. 5 and then a conclusion, limitations and future work in Sect. 6.

2   Literature Review

This section provides a brief overview of the related works on the importance of raising cybersecurity awareness and then reviews how eWOM on social media can be used to raise cybersecurity awareness.

2.1   The Importance of Raising Cybersecurity Awareness

Cybersecurity awareness comprises of two elements. The first refers to an approach to educating online users to be cognizant of various cyber threats and vulnerabilities of modern computing systems [3]. The second refers to understanding how to mitigate and protect against these threats [3]. There have been some variants of this concept, such as "information security awareness," "internet security awareness "security awareness" or sometimes lumped in with other factors to include a broader variable of security education training and awareness (SETA) [4] but in general, these refer to similar ideas surrounding a level of insight regarding potential cybersecurity threats and vulnerabilities in computing systems as well as corresponding mitigating solutions. Literature has shown that increasing one's awareness of cybersecurity threats and protection strategies can improve cybersecurity hygiene such as organizational policy compliance [4]. This relationship has been demonstrated in both individual studies [17, 18] and broader meta-analytical research [4]. A healthy body of knowledge surrounding the idea of cybersecurity awareness has been devoted to exploring factors that influence awareness levels [9], how cybersecurity awareness impacts various behaviours [18] and how to assess an individual's level of cybersecurity awareness accurately and objectively [3]. For instance, the work of de [9] explored how the specific framing of cybersecurity vulnerabilities and threats can influence efforts to raise awareness. The work of Zwilling [18] found that higher rates of awareness were associated with using protective tools and technology. Finally, Rahim et al., conducted a systematic literature review identifying all current approaches to objectively assessing an individual's cybersecurity awareness level [3].

Our research falls into the category of research dedicated to exploring strategies that can improve an individual's level of awareness. Cybersecurity awareness determinants are typically organized into two categories individual and organizational factors [19]. Organizational factors can include variables such as the quality and fairness of information security policy and individual factors include variables such as self-efficacy and awareness of technology security [19]. In light of efforts to identify variables that can increase one's awareness, various governments, corporations, and nonprofits have devoted extensive resources to promotional efforts and campaigns to raise cybersecurity awareness among members of the general public [8]. One prominent example is the creation of an annual cybersecurity awareness month, which occurs in October for Americans and other western nations such as Canada and is dedicated to promoting efforts to raise awareness among members of the general public [8]. Other efforts are sometimes focused on raising awareness among specific demographic groups who might be more vulnerable to cybersecurity threats, such as children's specific educational efforts [20] or undergraduate students [21].

2.2 eWOM as a Method of Raising Cybersecurity Awareness

Many institutions may spread information surrounding cybersecurity awareness campaigns. They often use either formal, physical word-of-mouth (WOM) communication, such as presentations or posters, or electronic word-of-mouth (eWOM) digital communication, such as emails or mobile texting. Increasingly, some efforts have been placed into using social media platforms to raise awareness. Even in the earlier days of social media, some cybersecurity researchers posited using social media platforms as methods for raising awareness [22]. Despite early calls to use social media platforms, a surprising absence of attention has persisted with extraordinarily little focus being placed on leveraging these platforms. Even as late as 2019, researchers continue to emphasize social media platforms as a viable, effective method of raising cybersecurity awareness [23].

Pro-social media cybersecurity awareness advocates often highlight certain advantages of social media communication over more traditional communication methods, including even digital methods such as emailing or videoconferencing. One commonly referenced advantage of using social media is the notion that people want to communicate with mediums they are conformable with, and use daily, which for the case of many people in today's generation, happens to be social media platforms [23]. This ubiquity of modern social media itself may prove to be a good enough reason to consider using it as the *de facto* communication strategy to raise awareness, but there are many other benefits to using social media for awareness purposes. For instance, another key advantage of social media is the ability to send information across large distances, transcending organizational and national boundaries, to communicate at a global level [24]. Social media platforms allow any individual or organization to create an account and share information at no financial cost whereby they can freely share information with others, through posts (i.e., tweets). Moreover, this information transmission can enable information to go 'viral' whereby it will spread rapidly and be viewed by potentially many millions of other users [25]. Other users can also respond and/or further spread/share this information with their own opinions, commenting, mentioning, replying, liking/favoriting others' posts etc., creating social ties between users.

Another key benefit of social media communication is the ability to relatively easily empirically analyze and quantify the information being spread, which would be much more challenging and limited in comparison with traditional communication methods. Analyzing large volumes of eWOM communication obtained from social media can then be used to leverage the 'wisdom of the crowd', which can lead to powerful, data-driven insights to better inform decision-making. The wisdom of the crowd phenomena refers to the idea that aggregating large volumes of individual opinions on a particular issue can lead to better insight when compared to the opinions of a single or group of experts [11]. There are many ways of analyzing social media data, ranging from content analyses like text mining, sentiment analysis and topic modelling, to network analyses all of which can provide value depending on the specific objectives of the analyses. For instance, sentiment analyses could be used to identify crowd polarity while network analyses could be used to identify influencers or assess the reach of information within a given online discussion. There are many opportunities for social media data to be leveraged to better promote cybersecurity awareness. However, social media as a communication platform to raise awareness regarding cybersecurity is not without caveats that must be mentioned. In this specific context, the major drawback of using social media is the potential for the spreading of misinformation and disinformation [26]. In general, misinformation refers to false information that is deliberately spread whereas disinformation refers to false information that is spread unintentionally. Formal academic research has found that false information can spread faster than actual real accurate information [27]. In a cybersecurity awareness setting, misinformation can create additional threats and vulnerabilities via ignorance. However, given that the bulk of social media campaign efforts to raise cybersecurity awareness stem from official government agencies or established non-for-profits, it can be expected that they are promoting accurate and up to date information.

Contrasting the pros and cons of social media with traditional communication methods (including digital methods such as email or television) social media offers a cost-effective approach to spreading information that could potentially be viewed by millions. As mentioned, despite the potential of social media, no research to the best of the authors' knowledge has explored cybersecurity-related eWOM on any given social media platform, creating a large area of neglect within the literature, worthy of exploration. More precisely, to date, no work has explored eWOM communications pertaining to cybersecurity awareness, on social media, including any analyses of relevant social media data. Addressing this area of neglect could greatly help with future efforts to raise cybersecurity awareness. For instance, exploring eWOM discourse surrounding cybersecurity awareness from the perspective of SNA would enable the assessment of how far information is spreading, how centralized the flow of information is or how segmented actors within the network are (e.g., echo chamber). Alternatively, we can consider another perspective such as topic modelling, and examine how certain cybersecurity awareness-related topics change year over year. Such data-driven insights could foster better future endeavors to raise awareness depending on how the present WOM discussions are taking place. Considering the following hypothetical situation, a network analysis determines that the eWOM discussion surrounding cybersecurity awareness has very low reciprocity (suggesting people are not engaging with each other). This insight could help the manager of a cybersecurity organization better tailor future information postings on social media to encourage reciprocal discussion, using a tactic like gamification to better improve user engagement with the information.

A final consideration for this research is the potential impact of the COVID-19 pandemic on eWOM discussions surrounding cybersecurity awareness. With many individuals across the globe being forced to continue their working occupation from home as a result of the lockdowns, this has created numerous cybersecurity vulnerabilities and opportunities for cybercriminals. The normalization of work-from-home environments creates additional attack vectors [28]. For example, many companies have their employees use their home networks and personal devices which often lack standard organizational security protections as they work from home. In lieu of this, it comes as no surprise that recent research revealed that the number of reported cyber attacks has become significantly more frequent since the beginning of the pandemic [29]. In parallel, social media researchers observed that social media became the most popular form of communication during the pandemic, as many users increased their use of social media as a communication medium in response to the lockdowns imposed by many countries across the globe [30]. Based on these observations, it can be reasonably expected that the COVID-19 pandemic impacted the eWOM of social media users discussing cybersecurity awareness. Despite the increase in attention to growing cybersecurity threats fostered by the pandemic in combination with increased social media usage rates, no research has explored eWOM communications on social media pertaining to cybersecurity awareness either broadly or more specifically to assess the impact of COVID-19. Given the establishment of how important raising cybersecurity awareness is to improving cybersecurity hygiene, this research aims to address this gap in the literature.

3 Methods

To address the research questions, we relied on a data-driven methodology. Twitter was selected as the social media platform for data collection due to its popularity as a microblogging social media platform where people express their opinions on a variety of matters including politics, society, culture and other trending topics [31]. It has been widely used to collect and analyze eWOM in various domains (e.g., [32, 33], making it quite suitable for exploring eWOM surrounding discussion pertaining to cybersecurity awareness. We collected five sets of tweets, totaling 227, 270 tweets using a custom-built Python script that connects to the Twitter API to permit the retrieval of historical Twitter data. The five sets of data pertained to each year collected, starting from 2018 to 2022. The start date for each year was January 1st while the end date was December 31st. This range was selected to assess the potential impact of the COVID-19 pandemic and given each nation responded to the pandemic at different periods we used the cutoff between 2019 and 2020 as the point of inflection for assessing the impact of COVID, with 2020 being a transition year. We collected tweets posted with the hashtags #cyberawareness, #cybersecurityawareness, and #cyberaware. The SNA was conducted using Netlytic, an established service that is widely applied for various social network analyses [14]. The extracted data from Python was organized in comma separated values (CSV) files that were automatically preprocessed by Netlytic to check for duplicate tweets. The groups of tweets were analyzed through SNA and network visualization. More specifically, we examined name networks which include tweet mentions (i.e., someone mentions someone else), looking at the total network degree to get a broad sense of the whole network and ensuing eWOM discourse. Additionally, we focus on assessing both micro (e.g., centrality which reflects how controlled the discourse is) and macro (e.g., diameter which reflects how far the information diffuses) network properties for each year. The networks were visualized using the deep reinforcement learning (DrL) algorithm due to its effectiveness in visualizing larger networks [34]. The collected data was further preprocessed for topic modelling to remove undesirable content such as links, media attachments, such as emojis, that potentially affect the accuracy of the topic modelling.

The topic modelling is conducted in a comparative study of the popular algorithms of latent Dirichlet allocation (LDA) [15] and non-negative matrix factorization (NMF) [16]. To compare the accuracy of each algorithm and assess their relative performance, the coherence score value was utilized as a metric of accuracy [35]. To examine how topics, compare between years, semantic analysis was conducted using the soft cosine similarity function [36]. This comparison examines each pair of topics according to their top keywords (regardless of the size of the dataset). The similarity score ranges from 0 to 1, with values closer to 1 reflecting a higher degree of topic similarity. The soft cosine similarity provides more meaning and performs better when compared to a standard cosine as it assumes that the similarity between topics is already known, such as the case with language synonyms. The word embedding model, fastText, which was created from a large collection of Wikipedia articles, was utilized [37]. Specifically, the MALLET (machine learning for language toolkit) [38] was implemented to enable more effective implementation of the Gibbs sampling to estimate the LDA parameters. This approach improves the quality of the LDA results and fosters the creation of much more accurate topic models. This has been demonstrated in prior research, including textual data in a cybersecurity context [39]. The Gensim Python library was employed in order to implement the LDA MALLET model for each year's respective dataset. To compare the impact of the pandemic, topics from 2018 and 2019 were aggregated and compared against the aggregated topics of 2021 and 2022.

4   Results

The results of the SNA name network (Twitter mentions) visualizations for each year is displayed in Figs. 1, 2, 3, 4 and 5. Illustrated in Fig. 1 is the 2018 Name Network. Each node represents an individual tweet that contained one of the relevant cybersecurity awareness hashtags. The clusters reflect a sub-community that formed, and is mention each other in discussion. The links between nodes identify the social ties, which in a name network, are created whenever one Twitter user mentions another user. In particular, it can be observed in 2018 that the there is several clusters outside of the center area have no interaction with each other, which is reflected by the low diameter or reach of the information within the network.

Fig. 1. 2018 Name Network

Figure 2 illustrates the 2019 Name Network where some notable changes can be obverted in comparison to 2018. In particular, more community forming can be viewed via the emergence of many sub-clusters. Moreover, many social ties in this figure are much longer and spreading between clusters, suggesting that information is penetrating the smaller communities.

In contrast to 2018 and 2019, the 2020 Name Network, illustrated in Fig. 3, shows a continual increase in community forming as even more sub-clusters form. Information continues to diffuse great lengths across the network as illustrated by the longer social ties.

The 2021 Name Network, however, shows different characteristics. As illustrated in Fig. 4, the visual appearance bears much more resemblance to the network visualization

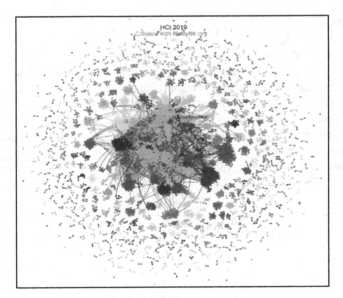

Fig. 2. 2019 Name Network

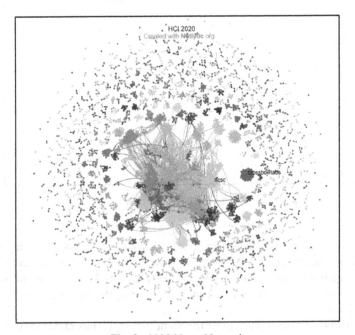

Fig. 3. 2020 Name Network

in 2018, there are still distinct communities but much less, and no long social ties, suggesting a large decrease in information diffusion.

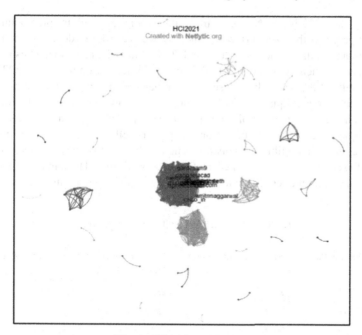

Fig. 4. 2021 Name Network

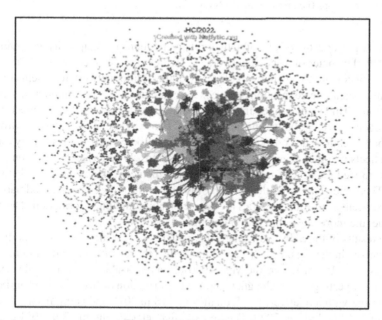

Fig. 5. 2022 Name Network

Finally, the 2022 Name Network, illustrated in Fig. 5, exhibits some bounce back when compared to the previous year, whereby we see a large degree of community forming, more similar to the years 2019 and 2020. Similarly, large social ties reemerge, and represent an increase in the reach (diffusion) of information relative to 2021.

The results of the network analyses are summarized in Table 1 and Table 2, respectively. In Table 1 the unique tweet volume, number of unique posters, number of posters with social ties and the number of social ties. The unique tweet volume reflects the number of unique tweets. The number of unique posters reflects the number of individual Twitter account users within the network. The number of posters with ties reflects the number of users who have mentioned another user on Twitter. The number of social ties reflects to the total number of social ties within the network, including self-looping ties.

Table 1. Initial SNA Results - Name Network

Year	Unique Tweet Volume	No. of Unique Posters	No. of Posters with Ties	No. of Social Ties[*]
2018	65771	7910	232	2066
2019	42448	6768	5583	47243
2020	32012	6026	4513	36444
2021	37689	7114	218	9477
2022	49350	10800	6709	57219

[*] Including self-loops (i.e., retweeting one's own tweet)

Table 2 presents the results of network diameter, density, reciprocity, centrality and modularity. Diameter of a social network on Twitter signifies the distance of the information diffusion within the network. Density of the Twitter network represents the ratio of potential social tie connections between users against the actual amount of social tie connections. This value ranges from 0 to 1 whereby values closer to 1 reflect greater network density. Reciprocity reflects the ratio of two-way social ties, whereby two users would both mention each other. This value and ranges between 0 and 1 whereby a higher value reflects a higher degree of two-way interactions. Whereas, centralization reflects how centralized the flow of information is within the network and has value between 0 and 1. The more centralized the network, the higher the value. Finally, modularity is a value between 0 and 1 that signifies the degree of sub-community formation. The higher the value, the more clustering of sub-community occurs.

The results of the SNA show interesting patterns for certain network properties that are visualized in the Figs. 1, 2, 3, 4 and 5 and reflect the network properties summarized in Tables 1, 2. In particular, the year 2020 observed a massive increase in network diameter, suggesting that the length in terms of information diffusion peaked during that year, starting with a relatively small diameter of 18 in 2018 and going from a diameter of 145 in 2019 to 1343 in 2020. The network diameter shrunk to 53 in 2021 and then went back up to 261 in 2022. A similar pattern can be observed for network modularity, which reflects the degree of community forming within a given network. In 2019 the

Table 2. Network Properties - Name Network

Year	Diameter	Density	Reciprocity	Centralization	Modularity
2018	18	0.01083	0.03288	0.1031	0.5783
2019	145	0.000409	0.1178	0.03866	0.7782
2020	1343	0.000456	0.08801	0.02047	0.8692
2021	53	0.04775	0.0352	0.2639	0.5131
2022	261	0.000306	0.09999	0.029	0.8623

network modularity was 0.5783, rising to 0.7782 in 2021 and peaking at 0.8692 in 2020 before dipping down in 2021 to 0.5131 and rising back up to 0.8623.

For the topic modelling analyses, the results for both LDA and NMF algorithms identified 300 topics from 2018 to 2019. When comparing the accuracy of found that LDA outperformed NMF for most topics across all years apart from 6 topics, based on their coherence score values. As such, this research proceeded to focus on only the LDA topics. The results of these analyses including the topic, the top keywords associated with the topic and the relative percentage of the topic versus the total corpus may be found in Table 3.

Table 3. LDA Topics From 2018 to 2022

ID	Top 5 Topic Keywords	Corpus Proportion
T0 (2018)	security, cybersecurity, business, risk, threat	19.50%
T1	privacy, information, share, kid, app	7.13%
T2	password, account, authentication, make, protect	4.17%
T3	card, credit, make, scam, information	5.96%
T4	device, security, software, update, network	7.09%
T5	infrastructure, month, cybersecurity, work, week	4.14%
T6	cybersecurity, career, security, learn, student	9.39%
T7	web, attack, hacker, hack, user	10.05%
T8	email, phishe, scam, link, click	6.42%
T9	attack, breach, business, cybersecurity, datum	11.36%
T10	month, cybersecurity, tip, awareness, stay	14.79%
T0 (2019)	security, user, device, update, system	8.76%
T1	password, account, authentication, make, multifactor	4.32%
T2	security, tool, hardware, protection, trust	2.17%
T3	security, business, cybersecurity, threat, risk	21.30%

(*continued*)

484   D. Vanderkooi et al.

Table 3. (*continued*)

ID	Top 5 Topic Keywords	Corpus Proportion
T4	email, phishe, scam, attack, link	7.73%
T5	attack, breach, datum, report, year	10.88%
T6	cybersecurity, security, awareness, join, today	7.18%
T7	device, app, datum, make, information	6.48%
T8	cybersecurity, security, read, job, article	7.85%
T9	payment, fraud, company, card, service	5.58%
T10	medium, information, share, protect, avoid	5.13%
T11	month, cybersecurity, awareness, tip, stay	12.62%
T0 (2020)	stay, tip, make, protect, time	13.29%
T1	payment, card, today, business, service	7.03%
T2	attack, target, report, phishe, cyberattack	15.30%
T3	security, cybersecurity, business, risk, threat	26.24%
T4	email, scam, phishe, link, report	10.39%
T5	cybersecurity, security, awareness, join, today	11.35%
T6	password, account, make, authentication, find	4.56%
T7	security, device, datum, update, user	11.84%
T0 (2021)	cybersecurity, month, tip, security, awareness	11.09%
T1	vulnerability, attack, target, user, security	7.19%
T2	device, security, datum, software, protect	7.26%
T3	cybersecurity, security, risk, business, read	14.71%
T4	cybersecurity, security, training, awareness, employee	8.78%
T5	scam, fraud, stay, information, call	6.39%
T6	threat, attack, security, cybersecurity, cyberattack	6.66%
T7	expert, network, attack, infosecurity, datum	3.98%
T8	password, account, make, hack, hacker	4.38%
T9	attack, breach, datum, business, ransomware	8.89%
T10	business, security, protect, visit, datum	8.45%
T11	email, phishe, link, scam, click	5.74%
T12	cybersecurity, join, today, event, register	6.48%
T0 (2022)	cybersecurity, security, join, today, event	7.57%
T1	attack, cyberattack, target, threat, business	8.46%
T2	datum, breach, information, access, protect	6.04%

(*continued*)

Table 3. (*continued*)

ID	Top 5 Topic Keywords	Corpus Proportion
T3	cybersecurity, security, threat, read, trend	6.78%
T4	fraud, scam, crime, victim, beware	5.22%
T5	tip, month, cybersecurity, security, stay	9.10%
T6	email, phishe, link, attack, scam	6.13%
T7	vulnerability, security, update, device, software	4.52%
T8	password, account, authentication, sheet, credit	4.97%
T9	computer, web, tool, user, file	5.85%
T10	cybersecurity, security, awareness, training, employee	6.70%
T11	security, business, cybersecurity, threat, protect	14.41%
T12	security, read, service, cybersecurity, solution	8.41%
T13	share, watch, video, follow, time	5.84%

The similarity analyses results, visualized as a heat map, are in Fig. 6. The results of the topic modelling produced rich topics including both more specific and broader themes that relate to cybersecurity. For instance, broader themes such as 'business security risk' emerged across all years as well as more specific themes such as information privacy, credential/password management, hacking and cyberattack etc. The most prominent and consistently occurring theme across all years in terms of a relative percentage of the total corpus was focused on the generic theme of business security risks. This theme took up 19.5% of the total corpus in 2018, and 21.3% in 2019, peaking at 26.24% in 2020 and

		2018											2019											
		T0	T1	T2	T3	T4	T5	T6	T7	T8	T9	T10	T0	T1	T2	T3	T4	T5	T6	T7	T8	T9	T10	T11
2021	T0	0.33	0.58	0.3	0.28	0.24	0.45	0.52	0.13	0.29	0.27	0.74	0.33	0.58	0.3	0.28	0.24	0.45	0.52	0.13	0.29	0.27	0.74	0.14
	T1	0.39	0.18	0.33	0.14	0.48	0.28	0.14	0.76	0.24	0.33	0.19	0.39	0.18	0.33	0.14	0.48	0.28	0.14	0.76	0.24	0.33	0.19	0.81
	T2	0.38	0.45	0.61	0.37	0.73	0.36	0.23	0.44	0.32	0.32	0.39	0.38	0.45	0.61	0.37	0.73	0.36	0.23	0.44	0.32	0.32	0.39	0.5
	T3	0.76	0.2	0.24	0.11	0.28	0.43	0.27	0.32	0.17	0.44	0.3	0.76	0.2	0.24	0.11	0.28	0.43	0.27	0.32	0.17	0.44	0.3	0.32
	T4	0.72	0.31	0.37	0.24	0.25	0.51	0.52	0.26	0.23	0.43	0.47	0.72	0.31	0.37	0.24	0.25	0.51	0.52	0.26	0.23	0.43	0.47	0.22
	T5	0.18	0.3	0.25	0.75	0.22	0.17	0.16	0.23	0.52	0.29	0.22	0.18	0.3	0.25	0.75	0.22	0.17	0.16	0.23	0.52	0.29	0.22	0.2
	T6	0.6	0.18	0.25	0.14	0.34	0.41	0.28	0.33	0.3	0.64	0.34	0.6	0.18	0.25	0.14	0.34	0.41	0.28	0.33	0.3	0.64	0.34	0.35
	T7	0.35	0.27	0.23	0.09	0.4	0.26	0.14	0.26	0.12	0.21	0.21	0.35	0.27	0.23	0.09	0.4	0.26	0.14	0.26	0.12	0.21	0.21	0.28
	T8	0.3	0.34	0.57	0.28	0.23	0.26	0.4	0.3	0.32	0.29	0.48	0.3	0.34	0.57	0.28	0.23	0.26	0.4	0.3	0.32	0.29	0.48	0.22
	T9	0.4	0.11	0.23	0.23	0.22	0.29	0.21	0.47	0.3	0.7	0.22	0.4	0.11	0.23	0.23	0.22	0.29	0.21	0.47	0.3	0.7	0.22	0.33
	T10	0.65	0.38	0.38	0.38	0.39	0.46	0.41	0.36	0.47	0.62	0.55	0.65	0.38	0.38	0.38	0.39	0.46	0.41	0.36	0.47	0.62	0.55	0.36
	T11	0.24	0.26	0.26	0.4	0.21	0.16	0.26	0.28	0.8	0.28	0.33	0.24	0.26	0.26	0.4	0.21	0.16	0.26	0.28	0.8	0.28	0.33	0.24
	T12	0.26	0.27	0.17	0.14	0.09	0.32	0.65	0.11	0.15	0.21	0.51	0.26	0.27	0.17	0.14	0.09	0.32	0.65	0.11	0.15	0.21	0.51	0.1
2022	T0	0.33	0.58	0.3	0.28	0.24	0.45	0.52	0.13	0.29	0.27	0.74	0.33	0.58	0.3	0.28	0.24	0.45	0.52	0.13	0.29	0.27	0.74	0.14
	T1	0.39	0.18	0.33	0.14	0.48	0.28	0.14	0.76	0.24	0.33	0.19	0.39	0.18	0.33	0.14	0.48	0.28	0.14	0.76	0.24	0.33	0.19	0.81
	T2	0.38	0.45	0.61	0.37	0.73	0.36	0.23	0.44	0.32	0.32	0.39	0.38	0.45	0.61	0.37	0.73	0.36	0.23	0.44	0.32	0.32	0.39	0.5
	T3	0.76	0.2	0.24	0.11	0.28	0.43	0.27	0.32	0.17	0.44	0.3	0.76	0.2	0.24	0.11	0.28	0.43	0.27	0.32	0.17	0.44	0.3	0.32
	T4	0.72	0.31	0.37	0.24	0.25	0.51	0.52	0.26	0.23	0.43	0.47	0.72	0.31	0.37	0.24	0.25	0.51	0.52	0.26	0.23	0.43	0.47	0.22
	T5	0.18	0.3	0.25	0.75	0.22	0.17	0.16	0.23	0.52	0.29	0.22	0.18	0.3	0.25	0.75	0.22	0.17	0.16	0.23	0.52	0.29	0.22	0.2
	T6	0.6	0.18	0.25	0.14	0.34	0.41	0.28	0.33	0.3	0.64	0.34	0.6	0.18	0.25	0.14	0.34	0.41	0.28	0.33	0.3	0.64	0.34	0.35
	T7	0.35	0.27	0.23	0.09	0.4	0.26	0.14	0.26	0.12	0.21	0.21	0.35	0.27	0.23	0.09	0.4	0.26	0.14	0.26	0.12	0.21	0.21	0.28
	T8	0.3	0.34	0.57	0.28	0.23	0.26	0.4	0.3	0.32	0.29	0.48	0.3	0.34	0.57	0.28	0.23	0.26	0.4	0.3	0.32	0.29	0.48	0.22
	T9	0.4	0.11	0.23	0.23	0.22	0.29	0.21	0.47	0.3	0.7	0.22	0.4	0.11	0.23	0.23	0.22	0.29	0.21	0.47	0.3	0.7	0.22	0.33
	T10	0.65	0.38	0.38	0.38	0.39	0.46	0.41	0.36	0.47	0.62	0.55	0.65	0.38	0.38	0.38	0.39	0.46	0.41	0.36	0.47	0.62	0.55	0.36
	T11	0.24	0.26	0.26	0.4	0.21	0.16	0.26	0.28	0.8	0.28	0.33	0.24	0.26	0.26	0.4	0.21	0.16	0.26	0.28	0.8	0.28	0.33	0.24
	T12	0.26	0.27	0.17	0.14	0.09	0.32	0.65	0.11	0.15	0.21	0.51	0.26	0.27	0.17	0.14	0.09	0.32	0.65	0.11	0.15	0.21	0.51	0.1
	T13	0.36	0.36	0.22	0.25	0.12	0.4	0.79	0.13	0.23	0.31	0.59	0.36	0.36	0.22	0.25	0.12	0.4	0.79	0.13	0.23	0.31	0.59	0.12

Fig. 6. LDA Topics Similarity Between 2018–2019 and 2021–2022

then going back down to 14.71% in 2021 and 14.41% in 2022. Conversely, other themes only manifested in one or two years, taking up a portion of the corpus discourse before dissipating. The similarity heatmap helps illustrates the variance in similarity before and after the start of the COIVID-19 pandemic. It is evident that certain topics stayed very similar in nature following the pandemic start while others are much more distinct and unique, suggesting a notable change between the pre-pandemic and post-pandemic thematic structure of the corpus.

5 Discussion

The major themes of cybersecurity awareness activities on social media and how the thematic structure of the related content evolved over time was examined to answer RQ1. The key topics surrounding eWOM discussions of cybersecurity awareness focus on specific and broader dimensions of cybersecurity. Certain topics grew in popularity and then diminished over time. In particular, certain topics actually peaked during the pandemic transition year (2020). This peak in 2020 in all likelihood reflects the transition from work to home, as new cybersecurity vulnerabilities emerged [29], suggesting that the focus on general security risks to businesses was maintained throughout the duration of the pandemic. In line with the SNA findings regarding network diameter, the rise and decline in the relative dominance of this topic within the corpus following 2020 suggest that awareness was raised regarding this topic as it diminished in 2021 and 2022, rather than just spreading the information across the network. Together the results of both SNA and topic modelling suggest the corpus changes its foci to new topics that emerged. For instance, a topic theme related to registering for a cybersecurity awareness event emerged only in 2021 and did not emerge in any other years. These changes in topics reflect the dynamic nature of the online discourse surrounding conversations of cybersecurity awareness. Certain topics may trend and gain popularity, while others may only emerge briefly before dissipating. Over time, the discourse evolves and moves onto new subjects which continue diffuse across the network.

The social network properties of cybersecurity awareness activities on social media were examined to answer RQ2, the information diffusion surrounding Twitter eWOM discussions pertaining to cybersecurity awareness varies considerably. Given that this research focuses on raising awareness, arguably the most important network metric would be network diameter, which reflects how far information diffuses [14]. This long distance of information diffusion occurs despite 2020 being the smallest in terms of overall tweet volume. This finding likely reflects the change in working dynamics as many individuals began transitioning from work to home, becoming more active on social media. In 2021, many people began to slowly transition back to working at the office, this change is likely reflected by the decrease in network diameter. A similar pattern was observed with respect to network modularity. This pattern also likely reflects the transitions to work from home and later back towards the office as people began to use more social media while working from home, the degree of community forming increased and then decreased as people moved back to the office. Interestingly, sub-communities have begun reforming following the return to the office suggesting that individuals are still discussing cybersecurity awareness online. This observation is further supported by the number of unique posters which peaked in 2022. Interestingly, in the years 2020 and 2022 where modularity was highest, network diameter was also very high, suggesting that despite a high degree of community forming, information still spread and penetrated these groups, suggesting a much more open forum of eWOM cybersecurity awareness discussions.

Lastly, the impact of the pandemic on eWOM discussions from the perspective of topic modelling and SNA were examined to answer RQ3. This research has confirmed that the pandemic impacted the eWOM discussions surrounding cybersecurity awareness on Twitter. In terms of the network properties, the reach of information (diameter) and the degree of community forming (modularity) were most impacted by the COVID-19 pandemic. From the perspective of topic modelling, the pandemic influenced the dominance of certain topics whereby some rose in prominence and then dropped following the beginning of the pandemic. As the topic similarity heatmap illustrates, some topics remained very similar before and after the start of the pandemic, while others became much more distinct, further reflecting changes in thematic structure of the discourse. In addition, following the beginning of the pandemic, new topics emerged within the discourse. However, based on the data observed in 2021 and 2022, it appears that the majority of the impact elicited by the pandemic was short-term, with the bulk of the impact being observed in 2020, the transition year. Many topics and network properties that experienced a large change during the transition year, observed less variance in the following years. Based on these observations we can reasonably concluded that the pandemic is unlikely to have any long-lasting impact on the online discourse as the world continues to transition back to pre-pandemic norms.

5.1 Research Implications

In terms of implications for practice, we have two main recommendations. Despite the disruption caused by the pandemic, information diffused the farthest during the transition year of 2020. This occurred despite a high degree of community forming (modularity) which often impedes the flow of information between actors in the network. A similarly high degree of diffusion and modularity was observed in 2022 following the transition back to the office as the responses to the pandemic wavered. Based on this information, it can be maintained that social media platforms like Twitter are incredibly useful in raising cybersecurity awareness. In line with prior works [22, 23], we strongly encourage cybersecurity awareness advocates/champions to continue to use social media platforms as a communication tool to raise awareness. Any organization that aims to raise cybersecurity awareness but is not using social media should strongly consider leveraging these platforms. Based on the observed success, mass adoption, ease of use and low cost, we can encourage more resources to be dedicated to using social media as the de facto platform to spread awareness over conventional tools such as emails, presentations or posters/flyers.

The results of the topic modelling analyses found that certain cybersecurity topics trend more frequently in certain years over others. These trends can be leveraged by relevant stakeholders. Building on the first recommendation, we encourage efforts to raise awareness on social media to focus on specific themes of cybersecurity as a second recommendation. A more tailored and focused discussion would likely amplify its reach, help the information spread further and potentially reach a great number of users. Moreover, a more specific focus may also help with information retention and increase awareness among audience members. In addition, given the rapidly evolving field of cybersecurity, new threats and vulnerabilities emerge constantly. In response to newly emerged threats, specific campaigns on social media could be tailored to focus on raising awareness of newer threats as a responsive tactic. The rapid dissemination potential of social media may be especially useful in trying to raise awareness for as many people are possible to mitigate the potential threats and vulnerabilities before major attacks occur.

6   Conclusion, Limitations and Future Work

In sum, this research has collected over 200,000 tweets pertaining to eWOM cybersecurity awareness discussions between 2018 and 2022. This data was analyzed using SNA and topic modelling which highlight social media's great potential as an effective communication channel to raise awareness regarding cybersecurity threats, vulnerabilities and mitigation strategies. In particular both general and specific topic themes emerged and changed over time, while information diffusion was shown to be quite strong despite a high degree of community forming within the network. Moreover, the pandemic was shown to have a significant impact on the eWOM discussion, with certain topics changing to more distinct themes that emerged after the start of the pandemic. Additionally, the pandemic also played a role in the information diffusion across the network and notably impacted network diameter and modularity however, the overall impact of the pandemic on the eWOM discussions appears to be temporary. This research is relying on the data to which this study has been confined to. Social media data, while valuable in its often-large volume of data, cannot always be generalizable. The results of this research have opened up several avenues for future research directions, for instance, this research focused on applying SNA and topic modelling analyses to the Twitter data but there are numerous other approaches to analyzing social media data. Future studies of this nature should consider incorporating other forms of analysis, such as sentiment analyses, time series analyses, influencer (top poster) analyses, or machine learning to draw further insights from the eWOM surrounding cybersecurity awareness. Moreover, future studies should also consider exploring other topics pertaining to cybersecurity, such as more specific topics like 'phishing' or 'credential management' to see if similar trends manifest. A final suggestion for future work is to focus on how users engage with different topics, such as identifying prominent accounts and disseminating surveys to identify their attitudes and beliefs regarding their use of social media as a method of raising cybersecurity awareness.

References

1. Choo, K.K.R.: The cyber threat landscape: Challenges and future research directions. Comput. Secur. **30**, 719–731 (2011). https://doi.org/10.1016/j.cose.2011.08.004
2. Blackwood-Brown, C., Levy, Y., D'Arcy, J.: Cybersecurity awareness and skills of senior citizens: a motivation perspective. J. Comput. Inf. Syst. **61**, 195–206 (2021). https://doi.org/10.1080/08874417.2019.1579076

3. Rahim, N.H.A., Hamid, S., Kiah, L.M., Shamshirband, S., Furnell, S.: A systematic review of approaches to assessing cybersecurity awareness. Kybernetes **44**, 606–622 (2015). https://doi.org/10.1108/K-12-2014-0283

4. Cram, A.W., D'Arcy, J., Proudfoot, J.G.: Seeing the forest and the trees: a meta-analysis of the antecedents to information security policy compliance. MIS Q. Manag. Inf. Syst. **43**, 525–554 (2019). https://doi.org/10.25300/MISQ/2019/15117

5. Bahl, A., Sharma, A., Asghar, M.R.: Vulnerability disclosure and cybersecurity awareness campaigns on twitter during COVID -19. Secur. Priv. **4**, 1–14 (2021). https://doi.org/10.1002/spy2.180

6. Verma, S., Yadav, N.: Past, present, and future of electronic word of mouth (EWOM). J. Interact. Mark. **53**, 111–128 (2021). https://doi.org/10.1016/j.intmar.2020.07.001

7. Shiue, Y.C., Chiu, C.M., Chang, C.C.: Exploring and mitigating social loafing in online communities. Comput. Human Behav. **26**, 768–777 (2010). https://doi.org/10.1016/j.chb.2010.01.014

8. Nurse, J.R.C.: Cybersecurity awareness. Encycl. Cryptogr. Secur. Priv., 1–4 (2021). https://doi.org/10.1007/978-3-642-27739-9_1596-1

9. de Bruijn, H., Janssen, M.: Building cybersecurity awareness: the need for evidence-based framing strategies. Gov. Inf. Q. **34**, 1–7 (2017). https://doi.org/10.1016/j.giq.2017.02.007

10. Rani, A., Shivaprasad, H.N.: Revisiting the antecedent of electronic word-of-mouth (eWOM) during COVID-19 pandemic. Decision **48**(4), 419–432 (2021). https://doi.org/10.1007/s40622-021-00298-2

11. Yi, S.K.M., Steyvers, M., Lee, M.D., Dry, M.J.: The wisdom of the crowd in combinatorial problems. Cogn. Sci. **36**, 452–470 (2012). https://doi.org/10.1111/j.1551-6709.2011.01223.x

12. Maass, W., Parsons, J., Purao, S., Storey, V.C., Woo, C.: Data-driven meets theory-driven research in the era of big data: opportunities and challenges for information systems research. J. Assoc. Inf. Syst. **19**, 1253–1273 (2018). https://doi.org/10.17705/1jais.00526

13. Mustak, M., Salminen, J., Plé, L., Wirtz, J.: Artificial intelligence in marketing: topic modeling, scientometric analysis, and research agenda. J. Bus. Res. **124**, 389–404 (2021). https://doi.org/10.1016/j.jbusres.2020.10.044

14. Gruzd, A., Paulin, D., Haythornthwaite, C.: Analyzing social media and learning through content and social network analysis: a faceted methodological approach. J. Learn. Anal. **3**, 46–71 (2016). https://doi.org/10.18608/jla.2016.33.4

15. Blei, D.M., Ng, A.Y., Jordan, M.I.: Latent Dirichlet allocation. J. Mach. Learn. Res. **3**, 993–1022 (2003)

16. D Lee, Seung, H.: Learning the parts of objects by nonnegative matrix factorization. Nature **401**(6755). (1999)

17. Bulgurcu, B., Cavusoglu, H., Benbast, I.: Information security policy compliance: an empirical study of rationality-based beliefs and information security awareness. MIS Q. **34**, 523–548 (2010)

18. Zwilling, M., Klien, G., Lesjak, D., Wiechetek, Ł, Cetin, F., Basim, H.N.: Cyber security awareness, knowledge and behavior: a comparative study. J. Comput. Inf. Syst. **62**, 82–97 (2022). https://doi.org/10.1080/08874417.2020.1712269

19. Alshboul, Y., Streff, K.: Beyond cybersecurity awareness: antecedents and satisfaction. In: ACM International Conference Proceeding Series, pp. 85–91 (2017). https://doi.org/10.1145/3178212.3178218

20. Quayyum, F., Cruzes, D.S., Jaccheri, L.: Cybersecurity awareness for children: a systematic literature review. Int. J. Child-Comput. Interact. **30**, 100343 (2021). https://doi.org/10.1016/j.ijcci.2021.100343

21. Hong, W.C.H., Chi, C.Y., Liu, J., Zhang, Y.F., Lei, V.N.L., Xu, X.S.: The influence of social education level on cybersecurity awareness and behaviour: a comparative study of university

students and working graduates. Springer, US (2022). https://doi.org/10.1007/s10639-022-11121-5

22. Aloul, F.A.: The need for effective information security awareness. J. Adv. Inf. Technol. **3**, 176–183 (2012). https://doi.org/10.4304/jait.3.3.176-183

23. Potgieter, P.: The awareness behaviour of students on cyber security awareness by using social media platforms: a case study at central university of technology, vol. 12, pp. 272–280 (2019). https://doi.org/10.29007/gprf

24. Trusov, M., Bucklin, R.E., Pauwels, K., Trusov, M., Bucklin, R.E., Pauwels, K.: Effects of word-of-mouth versus traditional marketing : findings from an internet social networking site. **73**, 90–102 (2009)

25. Wadbring, I., Ödmark, S.: Going viral: news sharing and shared news in social media. Observatorio (OBS*) **10**(4) (2016). https://doi.org/10.15847/obsOBS1042016936

26. Allcott, H., Gentzkow, M.: Social media and fake news in the 2016 election. J. Econ. Perspect. **31**, 211–236 (2017). https://doi.org/10.1257/jep.31.2.211

27. Vosoughi, S., Roy, D., Aral, S.: The spread of true and false news online. Science **359**, 1146–1151 (2018)

28. Pranggono, B.: COVID-19 pandemic cybersecurity issues. Internet Technol. Lett. **4**, 4–9 (2021). https://doi.org/10.1002/itl2.247

29. Alawida, M., Esther, A., Isaac, O., Al-rajab, M.: A deeper look into cybersecurity issues in the wake of COVID-19 : a survey. J. King Saud Univ. - Comput. Inf. Sci. **34**, 8176–8206 (2022). https://doi.org/10.1016/j.jksuci.2022.08.003

30. Kaya, T.: Technology in society the changes in the effects of social media use of Cypriots due to COVID-19 pandemic. Technol. Soc. **63**, 101380 (2020). https://doi.org/10.1016/j.techsoc.2020.101380

31. Abul-Fottouh, D.: Brokerage roles and strategic positions in twitter networks of the 2011 Egyptian revolution. Policy Internet **10**, 218–240 (2018). https://doi.org/10.1002/poi3.169

32. Hopke, J.E., Hestres, L.E.: Visualizing the paris climate talks on Twitter: media and climate stakeholder visual social media during COP21. Soc. Media + Soc. **4** (2018). https://doi.org/10.1177/2056305118782687

33. Jacobson, J., Mascaro, C.: Movember : Twitter conversations of a hairy social movement. Soc. Media + Soc. **2** (2016). https://doi.org/10.1177/2056305116637103

34. Martin, S., Brown, W.M., Wylie, B.N.: DRL: distributed recursive (graph) layout. Sandia National Lab (2007)

35. Lau, J.H., Newman, D., Baldwin, T.: Machine reading tea leaves: automatically evaluating topic coherence and topic model quality. In: 14th Conference of the European Chapter of the Association for Computational Linguistics, EACL 2014, pp. 530–539 (2014). https://doi.org/10.3115/v1/e14-1056

36. Blair, S.J., Bi, Y., Mulvenna, M.D.: Aggregated topic models for increasing social media topic coherence. Appl. Intell. **50**(1), 138–156 (2019). https://doi.org/10.1007/s10489-019-01438-z

37. Sangari, M.S., Mashatan, A.: A data-driven, comparative review of the academic literature and news media on blockchain-enabled supply chain management: Trends, gaps, and research needs. Comput. Ind. **143**, 103769 (2022). https://doi.org/10.1016/j.compind.2022.103769

38. McCallum, A.K.: Mallet: a machine learning for language toolkit (2002). http://mallet.cs.umass.edu

39. Alagheband, M.R., Mashatan, A., Zihayat, M.: Time-based gap analysis of cybersecurity trends in academic and digital media. ACM Trans. Manag. Inf. Syst. **11** (2020). https://doi.org/10.1145/3389684

Author Index

D. D. Schmorrow and C. M. Fidopiastis (Eds.): HCII 2023, LNAI 14019, pp. 491–492, 2023.
https://doi.org/10.1007/978-3-031-35017-7